ECONOMICS
DICTIONARY

ECONOMICS DICTIONARY

Second Edition

DONALD W. MOFFAT

ELSEVIER

New York • Amsterdam • Oxford

Elsevier Science Publishing Co., Inc.
52 Vanderbilt Avenue, New York, NY 10017

Distributors outside the United States and Canada:

Elsevier Science Publishers B. V.
P. O. Box 211, 1000 AE Amsterdam, The Netherlands

First edition published in 1976
© 1983 by Elsevier Science Publishing Company, Inc.

Library of Congress Cataloging in Publication Data

Moffat, Donald W., 1925–
    Economics dictionary.

    Includes index.
    1. Economics—Dictionaries. I. Title.
HB61.M54   1983   330′.03′21   83-9001
ISBN 0–444–00798–9

Manufactured in the United States of America

To Ken
with love
Dad

PREFACE

This *Economics Dictionary* is intended as a companion for all who listen to the news, read newspapers or trade journals, or study economics or related business subjects. With increasing frequency economics is in the news, television specials are devoted to economics, and well-known economists appear as guests on programs ranging from news reviews to midnight talk shows. As a result, special attention was given in this dictionary to including words and expressions (even colloquialisms) that are seen and heard in everyday life.

Extensive cross-referencing (by capital letters) is used because it was impossible to predict whether you, the reader, would think first *Finance, functional* or *Functional finance*. No fixed rule was used, because your time is more important than a rule. Instead, each such entry was considered carefully. Sometimes a full definition is included with the form of entry under which it was felt most readers will look; the other form is included with a cross-reference. In many cases the full definition is included with both (or several) forms of entry.

It is well known that efficiency involves a trade-off. To maximize "economy" (minimize the price of the book), we could have repeated nothing, and used a maximum amount of cross-references. To minimize the reader's time, we could have repeated full definitions with every form an entry could take. Since neither extreme seemed right for all entries, my general guideline was to repeat short definitions whenever it seemed that readers might look up one version of a term as often as another.

A dictionary limits itself to short definitions; an encyclopedia gives thorough explanations. Although this is a dictionary, it was clear that a firm policy dictating how terse all entries should be would not best serve you, the reader. This time I turned to my students for advice, students who ranged from freshmen to those for whom I was thesis adviser, from economics majors to those fulfilling a general education requirement. Surprisingly, almost all of them wanted the same depth of explanation:

For expressions found in the popular and trade press but not in textbooks, the students asked for a full explanation in tutorial language.

For expressions involved in controversy, they wanted a summary of the pros and cons.

They believed that ordinary economics expressions, even though found in text-books, should be included, but with only a brief explanation.

They wanted a list of abbreviations.

Few people seemed inclined to compromise on mathematics; those who did not want rigorous mathematics wanted none at all. I decided to include a minimum of formulas with the entries and to present a sampling of the next level of mathematics in the appendix.

These suggestions were greatly appreciated. Combined with comments on the first edition, they formed guidelines for determining the depth of explanation of each entry.

The most important decision, repeated thousands of times while writing this book, was whether or not to include an item. In most cases, the choice was not difficult, because nearly every entry in this dictionary results from a question raised in some of the correspondence I enjoy or from a question asked by one of my students. During classes I made notes of their questions, some of which were prompted by reading assignments in the text, some by outside reading assignments, some by outside reading not assigned.

Appreciation must be expressed for the large number of Federal Reserve System publications made available and for the cooperation received when questions were directed to various Federal Reserve districts. Special thanks are also due to Ameritrust for the detailed chart that is used in the entry ECONOMIC FLUCTUATIONS. Many thanks also to the AFL-CIO for their prompt response to my request for information and for the glossary they allowed me to use.

ABBREVIATIONS

AAA	Agricultural Adjustment Act (see FARM RELIEF AND INFLATION ACT)
ACH	AUTOMATED CLEARINGHOUSE
ACRS	ACCELERATED COST RECOVERY SYSTEM
AFC	AVERAGE FIXED COSTS
AFDC	AID TO FAMILIES WITH DEPENDENT CHILDREN
AFL	AMERICAN FEDERATION OF LABOR
AFL-CIO	AMERICAN FEDERATION OF LABOR–CONGRESS OF INDUSTRIAL ORGANIZATIONS
AID	AGENCY FOR INTERNATIONAL DEVELOPMENT
AMEX	AMERICAN STOCK EXCHANGE
ANOVA	ANALYSIS OF VARIATION
APC	AVERAGE PROPENSITY TO CONSUME
APR	ANNUAL PERCENTAGE RATE
APS	AVERAGE PROPENSITY TO SAVE
ARM	ADJUSTABLE RATE MORTGAGE
ASE	AMERICAN STOCK EXCHANGE
ATC	AVERAGE TOTAL COST
ATM	AUTOMATED TELLER MACHINE
ATS	AUTOMATIC TRANSFER SERVICE
AVC	AVERAGE VARIABLE COSTS
BEQB	*Bank of England Quarterly Bulletin*
BIP	BALANCE OF INTERNATIONAL PAYMENTS
BIS	BANK FOR INTERNATIONAL SETTLEMENTS
BL, B/L	BILL OF LADING
BLS	Bureau of Labor Statistics
CBD	CASH BEFORE DELIVERY
CBI	CONFEDERATION OF BRITISH INDUSTRY

CBO	CONGRESSIONAL BUDGET OFFICE
CCA	CAPITAL CONSUMPTION ALLOWANCES
CD	CERTIFICATE OF DEPOSIT
CEA	COMMODITY EXCHANGE AUTHORITY
CEA	COUNCIL OF ECONOMIC ADVISORS
CIA	CASH IN ADVANCE
CIO	CONGRESS OF INDUSTRIAL ORGANIZATIONS
CIPC	CASH ITEMS IN PROCESS OF COLLECTION
CL	CARLOAD
COD	CASH ON DELIVERY
C OF C	CHAMBER OF COMMERCE
COLA	Cost of Living Allowance (see ESCALATOR CLAUSE)
COPE	Currency Overprinting and Processing Equipment (see CURRENCY MANUFACTURE)
CPFF	Cost Plus Fixed Fee (see COST-PLUS PRICING)
CPI	CONSUMER PRICE INDEX
CPIF	Cost Plus Incentive Fee (see COST-PLUS PRICING)
CPS	CURRENT POPULATION SURVEY
CWO	CASH WITH ORDER
DC	DIRECT COSTS
DD	Day of Deposit (see INTEREST DATES)
DI	DISPOSABLE INCOME
DIME	DENVER INCOME MAINTENANCE EXPERIMENT
ED	Census Enumeration District (see CURRENT POPULATION SURVEY)
EDP	ELECTRONIC DATA PROCESSING
EFT	ELECTRONIC FUNDS TRANSFER
EMA	EUROPEAN MONETARY AGREEMENT
EMF	EUROPEAN MONETARY FUND
EOM	END OF MONTH
EPU	EUROPEAN PAYMENTS UNION
ERP	EUROPEAN RECOVERY PROGRAM
EURO CD	EURODOLLAR CERTIFICATE OF DEPOSIT
FC	FIXED COSTS
FCA	FARM CREDIT ADMINISTRATION
FCIC	FEDERAL CROP INSURANCE CORPORATION
FDIC	FEDERAL DEPOSIT INSURANCE CORPORATION
FEUR	FULL EMPLOYMENT UNEMPLOYMENT RATE
FHLBB	FEDERAL HOME LOAN BANK BOARD
FIFO	FIRST IN, FIRST OUT
FIRST AAA	FIRST AGRICULTURAL ADJUSTMENT ACT
FMCS	FEDERAL MEDIATION AND CONCILIATION SERVICE

FNMA	FEDERAL NATIONAL MORTGAGE ASSOCIATION
FOMC	FEDERAL OPEN MARKET COMMITTEE
FRB	Federal Reserve Board (see BOARD OF GOVERNORS OF THE FEDERAL RESERVE SYSTEM)
FRCS	FEDERAL RESERVE COMMUNICATIONS SYSTEM
FSLIC	FEDERAL SAVINGS AND LOAN INSURANCE CORPORATION
FTC	FEDERAL TRADE COMMISSION
FUTA	FEDERAL UNEMPLOYMENT TAX ACT
FY	FISCAL YEAR
GATT	GENERAL AGREEMENT ON TARIFFS AND TRADE
GAW	GUARANTEED ANNUAL WAGE
GNMA	GOVERNMENT NATIONAL MORTGAGE ASSOCIATION
GNP	GROSS NATIONAL PRODUCT
GNPIPD	GNP IMPLICIT PRICE DEFLATOR
HMO	HEALTH MAINTENANCE ORGANIZATION
HQW	HIGHEST QUARTERLY WAGE
HUD	HOUSING AND URBAN DEVELOPMENT
IBRD	INTERNATIONAL BANK FOR RECONSTRUCTION AND DEVELOPMENT
IMF	INTERNATIONAL MONETARY FUND
IRA	INDIVIDUAL RETIREMENT ACCOUNT
IRS	INTERNAL REVENUE SERVICE
LCL	LESS THAN CARLOAD
LDC	LESS DEVELOPED COUNTRY
LFPR	LABOR FORCE PARTICIPATION RATE
LRA	LAGGED RESERVE ACCOUNTING
LTL	LESS THAN TRUCKLOAD
MC	MARGINAL COST
MCD	MONTHS FOR CYCLICAL DOMINANCE
MDTA	MANPOWER DEVELOPMENT AND TRAINING ACT
MEC	MARGINAL EFFICIENCY OF CAPITAL
MEW	MEASURE OF ECONOMIC WELFARE
MFN	Most Favored Nation (see GENERAL AGREEMENT ON TARIFFS AND TRADE)
MICR	MAGNETIC INK CHARACTER RECOGNITION
MP	MARGINAL PRODUCT
MPC	MARGINAL PROPENSITY TO CONSUME
MPP	MARGINAL PHYSICAL PRODUCT
MPS	MARGINAL PROPENSITY TO SAVE
MR	MARGINAL REVENUE
MRA	MARGINAL RESERVE ACCOUNTING
MRP	MARGINAL REVENUE PRODUCT

MRS	MARGINAL RATE OF SUBSTITUTION
MRT	MARGINAL RATE OF TRANSFORMATION
MRTS	MARGINAL RATE OF TECHNICAL SUBSTITUTION
NAAQS	NATIONAL AMBIENT AIR QUALITY STANDARDS
NASD	NATIONAL ASSOCIATION OF SECURITIES DEALERS
NCUA	NATIONAL CREDIT UNION ADMINISTRATION
NEP	NEW ECONOMIC POLICY
NGPA	NATURAL GAS POLICY ACT
NHS	NATIONAL HEALTH SERVICE
NI	NATIONAL INCOME
NIA	NATIONAL INCOME AND PRODUCT ACCOUNTS
NIRA	NATIONAL INDUSTRIAL RECOVERY ACT
NLRB	National Labor Relations Board (see NATIONAL LABOR RELATIONS ACT)
NNP	Net National Product (see GROSS NATIONAL PRODUCT)
NOW	NEGOTIABLE ORDER OF WITHDRAWAL
NRA	NATIONAL RECOVERY ADMINISTRATION
NRR	NET REPRODUCTION RATE
NSA	Not Seasonally Adjusted (see SEASONALLY ADJUSTED)
NYSE	NEW YORK STOCK EXCHANGE
OBL	ORDER BILL OF LADING
OECD	ORGANIZATION FOR ECONOMIC COOPERATION AND DEVELOPMENT
OEEC	ORGANIZATION FOR EUROPEAN ECONOMIC COOPERATION
OEO	OFFICE OF ECONOMIC OPPORTUNITY
OJT	ON THE JOB TRAINING
OMB	OFFICE OF MANAGEMENT AND BUDGET
OR	OPERATIONS RESEARCH
OSHA	OCCUPATIONAL SAFETY AND HEALTH ADMINISTRATION
OTC	OVER THE COUNTER
P&L	PROFIT AND LOSS
PC	PERSONAL CONSUMPTION EXPENDITURES
PERT	PROGRAM EVALUATION AND REVIEW TECHNIQUE (sometimes called Program Evaluation Research Task)
POE	PORT OF ENTRY
POS	POINT OF SALE
PPI	PRODUCER PRICE INDEX
PR	PUBLIC RELATIONS
PSU	Primary Sampling Unit (see CURRENT POPULATION SURVEY)
PWA	PUBLIC WORKS ADMINISTRATION
QCD	Quarters for Cyclical Dominance (see MONTHS FOR CYCLICAL DOMINANCE)

RCPC	REGIONAL CHECK PROCESSING CENTER
REA	RURAL ELECTRIFICATION ADMINISTRATION
RFC	RECONSTRUCTION FINANCE CORPORATION
RIA	REGULATORY IMPACT ANALYSIS
RP	REPURCHASE AGREEMENT
RPD	RESERVES AVAILABLE FOR PRIVATE NONBANK DEPOSITS
SA	SEASONALLY ADJUSTED
SBL	STRAIGHT BILL OF LADING
S&L	SAVINGS AND LOAN ASSOCIATION
SDRs	SPECIAL DRAWING RIGHTs
SEC	SECURITIES AND EXCHANGE COMMISSION
SIC	Standard Industry Classification
SIME	SEATTLE INCOME MAINTENANCE EXPERIMENT
SMSA	STANDARD METROPOLITAN STATISTICAL AREA
SUA	SPECIAL UNEMPLOYMENT ASSISTANCE
TAB	TAX ANTICIPATION BILL
T&E	TRAVEL AND ENTERTAINMENT CARD
T&L	THRIFT AND LOAN ASSOCIATION
TC	TOTAL COSTS
TFC	TOTAL FIXED COSTS
TUC	TRADES UNION CONGRESS
TVA	Tax on Value Added (see VALUE ADDED TAX); TENNESSEE VALLEY AUTHORITY
TVC	TOTAL VARIABLE COSTS
UCC	UNIFORM COMMERCIAL CODE
UDC	UNDERDEVELOPED COUNTRY
UI	Unemployment Insurance (see UNEMPLOYMENT COMPENSATION AMENDMENTS)
UIB	UNEMPLOYMENT INSURANCE BENEFITS
ULPA	Uniform Limited Partnership Act (see FORMS OF BUSINESS ORGANIZATION)
UPC	UNIFORM PRICING CODE
VAT	VALUE ADDED TAX
VC	VARIABLE COSTS
VFCR	VOLUNTARY FOREIGN CREDIT RESTRAINT
WBA	WEEKLY BENEFIT AMOUNT
WPA	WORKS PROJECTS ADMINISTRATION
WPI	WHOLESALE PRICE INDEX
XIMF	Expanded International Monetary Fund (see BANCOR)
ZEG	ZERO ECONOMIC GROWTH
ZPG	Zero Population Growth (see NET REPRODUCTION RATE)

.

ECONOMICS
DICTIONARY

A

ABILITY-TO-PAY PRINCIPLE. A doctrine which holds that the equity function of government requires that, in determining tax liability, a major criterion should be who can afford to pay, rather than who will receive the benefits. In fact, there is often an inverse relationship between who pays and who receives benefits; public parks financed by taxes from persons with higher incomes are more likely to be used by those with lower incomes, while the higher income individuals use private clubs and parks. See also BENEFIT-RECEIVED PRINCIPLE.

ABRASION. Wearing away of a coin during use and circulation. Abrasion is a significant factor in an economy which uses full bodied coins (see NEUTRAL MONEY) because coins of the same denomination can then have different values depending on the amount of abrasion each has sustained.

ABSOLUTE ADVANTAGE. See COMPARATIVE ADVANTAGE.

ABSOLUTE COST ADVANTAGE. When a producer, because of efficiency, location, or other factors, is able to produce a good or service at a lower cost than other producers of the same product, that producer is said to have an absolute cost advantage.

ABSTINENCE THEORY OF INTEREST. If the cost of borrowed money (i.e., the interest paid) were zero, the demand for money would far exceed the supply because most people would rather have their goods and services *now*. Therefore, for some to be able to borrow money, others must make money available by abstaining from current spending; the interest they earn is inducement for this abstinence. Also called *Agio theory of interest*.

ACCELERATED COST RECOVERY SYSTEM (ACRS). A provision of the ECONOMIC RECOVERY TAX ACT of 1981, the ACRS shortens the period over which an asset can be fully depreciated and allows firms to claim more of the depreciation earlier in the tax life of the asset. Equipment that had previously been permitted to depreciate in 8.6 years can have an ACRS life of 5 years; the depreciation of industrial plants that previously averaged 23.8 years can be completed in 15 years. The purpose of ACRS is to encourage business investment as a step toward having the private sector lead the economic recovery.

ACCELERATED DEPRECIATION. A tax law provision which allows business firms to write off the cost of all or certain CAPITAL GOODS expenditures at a rate faster than is usually allowed. The purpose is to provide incentives for increased investment spending, with the ultimate objective of expanding the economy. The ACCELERATED COST RECOVERY SYSTEM is a specific recent example of accelerated depreciation.

ACCELERATIONIST THEORY. Holds that the PHILLIPS CURVE applies only to the short run and that in the long run FISCAL POLICY is not controlling because unemployment has a natural rate which is determined by nonfinancial factors such as IMPERFECT COMPETITION in labor and product markets.

ACCELERATION PRINCIPLE. When a change in demand for the nation's output of goods and services causes a change in INDUCED INVESTMENT, a coefficient (sometimes called the *accelerator*) can be established:

> Coefficient of Acceleration =
> (Change in Investment)
> ÷ (Change in Demand)

In its simplest application, this coefficient can be assumed to be a constant. However, it soon becomes apparent that without the usual qualification, OTHER THINGS BEING EQUAL, the coefficient will be a function of MANUFACTURING CAPACITY, general economic conditions, interest rates, general intensiveness (whether LABOR INTENSIVE or CAPITAL INTENSIVE), and many other factors.

The acceleration principle is often given as one of the factors which cause ECONOMIC FLUCTUATIONS. Assume that the economy is steady (either holding constant or changing at a constant rate) and that then there is an increase in total demand followed shortly by a return to the previous steady condition. That increase in demand will be followed by an increase in investment spending (CAPITAL ACCUMULATION); then, when demand returns to its long-run trend level, investment will also return to its long-run trend level. But several years later that larger stock of capital will begin wearing out and need replacement, which will then

put expansionary pressures on the economy. This principle is credited to John Maurice Clark.

ACCELERATOR. See ACCELERATION PRINCIPLE.

ACCEPTANCE BILL. A financial instrument in which a *drawer* orders a *drawee* to pay a sum of money to a *payee*. This method of making payment is standard in international commerce. Also known as a *bill of exchange*, or *draft*.

ACCEPTANCES. With regard to the CONSOLIDATED STATEMENT OF CONDITION OF ALL FEDERAL RESERVE BANKS, acceptances are recognized in two categories: (1) Bought Outright—Prime bankers' acceptances bought outright by the Federal Reserve Bank of New York for its own account. (2) Held Under REPURCHASE AGREEMENTs—Prime banker's acceptances bought by the same Federal Reserve bank for its own account under agreements with nonbank dealers.

Bankers' acceptances are drafts or bills of exchange that banks have "accepted" as their own liabilities, in effect substituting their credit for that of their customers. Acceptances of the largest and best-known banks are considered prime-quality money-market instruments. In 1955, the FEDERAL OPEN MARKET COMMITTEE authorized the Federal Reserve Bank of New York to deal in prime bankers' acceptances for its own account.

The New York Reserve Bank conducts open market operations for the Federal Reserve System, with about 25 primary dealers in government securities and bankers' acceptances. The MANAGER OF THE SYSTEM OPEN MARKET ACCOUNT is senior vice president in charge of the New York Reserve Bank's securities department and is appointed annually by the FEDERAL OPEN MARKET COMMITTEE to carry out its policy directives.

Ownership of the System open market account portfolio is allocated among all the Reserve banks, except for acceptances and securities held under REPURCHASE AGREEMENTs, which are carried on the books of the New York Reserve Bank. On the combined statement of condition, net purchases or sales of securities are reflected in proportional increases or reductions in the security holdings of each Reserve bank and in its holdings of gold certificates.

In a *prime banker's acceptance*, the dealer agrees to buy the acceptance back on a specified date (usually within 15 days) or earlier, at the dealer's option. The Reserve bank also has the right to require repurchase any time before maturity of the agreement, but this right is rarely exercised.

These dealers receive, in effect, short-term loans. Bank dealers are excluded from repurchase agreements with the New York Reserve Bank because they have access to direct, short-term borrowing from the Federal Reserve at the DISCOUNT RATE.

ACCESSION. In labor economics, an addition to the payroll, regardless of whether the person is being rehired or has never worked for the employer before.

ACCOMMODATION SIGNATURE. In financial economics, the signature of a party who is not the primary DEBTOR but who is, either primarily or secondarily, accepting some responsibility for repayment of the debt. This practice is usually followed when the lender does not feel that the interest rate and other conditions are consistent with the risk when only the primary debtor is involved.

ACCOUNT MANAGER. Usually refers to the MANAGER OF THE SYSTEM OPEN MARKET ACCOUNT.

ACCOUNTS PAYABLE. Liability accounts which record amounts to be paid to others, often for purchases of goods or services.

ACCOUNTS RECEIVABLE. Asset accounts which record amounts to be received from others, often from sales of goods or services.

ACCRUAL BASIS. In economics, *accrual basis* has the same meaning as in accounting; revenues and expenditures are recognized when the transaction takes place. This method contrasts with *cash basis*, in which revenues and expenditures are recognized when payment is made.

ACCRUED INTEREST. Interest which has been earned but not yet credited or paid. The expression is often used in connection with BONDs because bond holders are paid at stated times, usually twice a year. When a person sells a bond, the usual practice is for the new owner to pay to the previous owner the amount of earnings to the date of the sale (accrued interest); the new owner will receive payment for the full amount of earnings at the end of the period.

ACCUMULATED DIVIDEND. The dividend in arrears on cumulative preferred stock which must be paid before dividends can be paid to common stockholders. Also called *cumulative dividend*. See CAPITAL STOCK.

ACREAGE ALLOTMENT. Part of the continuing stream of legislation known in the U.S. as the *farm program*. It includes giving farmers an allotment or limit to the amount of their land that they may use to grow designated crops.

ACROSS-THE-BOARD INCREASE. A wage increase given to all employees at the same time, as opposed to a merit increase or other increase which is determined on an individual basis. The across-the-board (or general) increase may be a fixed amount, a fixed percentage, or some more complex arrangement, but the main point is that the formula applies to all employees and individual productivity is not recognized. The claim is often made that if an area is dominated by a large employer, then a general wage increase by that employer will be followed by general price increases in the area.

ACT FOR INTERNATIONAL DEVELOPMENT OF 1950. U.S. program for making scientific developments and industrial techniques available for the improvement of the economies and potentials of LESS DEVELOPED COUNTRIES. It is often called the *Point Four Program* because it grew out of the fourth point of President Truman's inaugural address in 1949.

ACTIVE STOCK. An issue of CAPITAL STOCK that can be expected to be bought and sold in significant quantities every business day.

ACT TO REGULATE COMMERCE. Legislation enacted February 4, 1887, for the purpose of regulating carriers, especially on waterways. Also known as the Cullom Act, it created the Interstate Commerce Commission. Since its original enactment, the act has had numerous amendments and supplements; today, the result is known collectively as the Interstate Commerce Act.

ACTUAL INVESTMENT. The sum of FIXED INVESTMENT and CHANGE IN BUSINESS INVENTORIES. The word *actual* emphasizes that the result of both PLANNED INVESTMENT and UNPLANNED INVESTMENT is being considered. Also called *realized investment.* See also GROSS PRIVATE DOMESTIC INVESTMENT.

ACTUAL RESERVES. See BANK RESERVES.

ACTUARY. A person who uses statistics to calculate insurance rates so that expenses (a large part of which are claims payments) will equal income (mainly inflow from premiums). See NORMAL PROFIT.

ADJUSTABLE RATE MORTGAGE (ARM). A mortgage that includes a provision to renegotiate the interest rate periodically. This provision is a benefit to the borrower if interest rates fall after the mortgage contract is signed, and a benefit to the lender if interest rates rise.

ADJUSTED BALANCE METHOD. A method of calculating the FINANCE CHARGE on consumer loans. With this method, the creditor adds the finance charges after subtracting payments made during the billing period. See also PREVIOUS BALANCE METHOD and AVERAGE DAILY BALANCE METHOD.

ADJUSTER. In insurance, the person who analyzes and evaluates claims and reaches a settlement with claimants.

ADJUSTMENT BOND. An industrial BOND which is sold with the specific intention of using the proceeds to readjust the capitalization of the business. Also called a *reorganization bond.*

ADJUSTMENT CREDIT. Borrowing by member banks from a Federal Reserve bank for a short period (usually no more than a few days) for the purpose of making temporary adjustments in their reserves. See BANK RESERVES. Reasons for such borrowing generally include unexpected increases in load demand, sudden deposit losses, or temporary and unexpected difficulties in obtaining funds through the facilities of the money market.

ADMINISTERED PRICE. A price which results from other than the interplay of forces in PURE COMPETITION; for example, when the government establishes a price. When the administered price is due to MONOPOLY or OLIGOPOLY conditions, there is seldom a sharp distinction between a competitive price and the administered price; the forces are usually so subtle that not even the parties to the transaction know exactly how the price was determined.

ADMINISTRATOR. A person authorized by a court to oversee the execution of a will in which the deceased did not name an *executor.* The collective expression for a person who is both executor and administrator is *personal representative.*

AD VALOREM DUTY. A customs duty which uses the value of entering goods, rather than size, weight, category, or other criteria, as a basis. See also CLASSIFIED TAX; CUSTOMS DUTY; SPECIFIC DUTY.

ADVANCE. Payment of all or part of a bill before payment is due. Sometimes an advance is paid for no more than the amount that has been earned at the time. For example, a contract may specify that full payment is to be made upon completion of all work, but the buyer actually pays one-fourth of the amount each time one-fourth of the work is completed.

ADVANCE BILL. A BILL OF EXCHANGE prepared prior to shipment of goods. This arrangement might be used in a situation where the buyer's credit rating is such that the seller is not willing to make shipment before being assured of payment.

ADVANCE, PRELIMINARY, AND FINAL ESTIMATE. Sequence in which the U.S. Census Bureau releases figures, as shown by the following example using monthly estimates of sales by retail stores. The first actual SEASONALLY ADJUSTED monthly estimate is the *advance estimate*, published about ten days after the close of the month. This estimate is derived from weekly figures collected from a subsample. Approximately a month later, a *preliminary estimate* is published, based on data from the Census Bureau's full reporting sample of retail stores. This estimate is then subject to further revision—usually slight—and, after additional checking and correction, a *final estimate* becomes available about two months after the release of the advance estimate.

ADVANTAGES OF SCALE. The result of ECONOMIES OF SCALE. It occurs when an increase in quantity produced allows—because of such factors as SPECIALIZATION and quantity discounts on materials used—a reduction in unit costs.

ADVERSE BALANCE. In international economics, describes a nation's balance sheet when the amount of money flowing out of the nation during a given period (usually a year) exceeded the amount flowing in. See BALANCE OF INTERNATIONAL PAYMENTS and MERCHANDISE ACCOUNT.

ADVERSE CLEARING. Describes the point of view of a bank whose reserve account is reduced during CHECK CLEARING.

ADVERSE SELECTION. This phrase is best explained by quoting an example from the 1982 ECONOMIC REPORT OF THE PRESIDENT.

> Assume that some insurance company offered actuarily fair insurance against this risk [having a low income] and charged all persons the same premium. (That is, the amount of the premium equals the expected cost of having a low income.) Since most persons are averse to risk, they might buy this insurance even though the premium would be somewhat greater than the expected cost because of the expense of writing the insurance. Some persons would be better risks than average, and new insurance companies would compete with the first company for these better risks. This would leave the original company insuring only the bad risks, which the company would then find financially intolerable. Ultimately, one class of persons would be unable to obtain any insurance.

ADVISORY AGENT. A TRUST arrangement in which the trustee reviews the portfolio and gives investment advice but does not have full discretionary powers. Such advice is usually accepted by clients, and although approval in writing is proper, it is often carried out after telephoned approval, with written consent being provided later for the records.

AFL-CIO. See AMERICAN FEDERATION OF LABOR-CONGRESS OF INDUSTRIAL ORGANIZATIONS.

AGE DISTRIBUTION. A summary of the percentage or numbers of people who are in each of various age brackets. This information is important to economists because total amount and type of demand, as well as UTILITY values, are functions of age classification. It also shows the ratio of the productive segment of the population to the nonproductive segment and provides information used in making a prediction of the same ratio at a time in the future. Age distribution is also used by school systems in making plans for student needs, teacher availability, and other variables.

AGENCY FOR INTERNATIONAL DE-VELOPMENT (AID). U.S agency created for the purpose of administering economic aid in the form of grants and loans to less developed nations.

AGENCY SHOP. In labor economics, a place of employment which has a union contract requiring all employees to pay dues to the union, although none of the employees is technically required to join the union.

AGENT. A party who is given the legal power to commit its PRINCIPAL to a legally binding contract. One function of the FEDERAL RESERVE SYSTEM is to act as agent for the U.S. government; thus a contract signed by an authority of the System is, legally, a contract signed by the U.S. government.

AGGREGATE. In economics, as a verb, *aggregate* means to collect statistics for more than one item and present the combined statistics. For example, GNP is an aggregation of figures for consumption, government, investment, and net exports. As an adjective it means total or overall, such as when aggregate figures are shown.

AGGREGATE DEMAND. Total spending for goods and services.

AGGREGATIVE ECONOMICS. See MACROECONOMICS.

AGIO THEORY OF INTEREST. See ABSTINENCE THEORY OF INTER-EST.

AGRIBUSINESS. A word used to emphasize that agriculture is no longer the pastoral life which allowed farmers to avoid the pressures of urban living and industrial employment. Thus, much farming in the U.S. is done on large commercial farms, with four percent of its farms producing about 47 percent of its agricultural output.

AGRICULTURAL ADJUSTMENT ACT (AAA). During the GREAT DEPRES-SION, two AAAs were passed to bring about price inflation by controling and limiting farm production. The first AAA, enacted in 1933, was declared unconsti-tutional in 1936 because of the taxing method it used to obtain funds (see FARM RELIEF AND INFLATION ACT). The second AAA was passed in 1938.

AGRICULTURAL BANK (Yugo.: Ju-goslovenska Poljpriverendna Banka). One of the specialized banks within the commercial banking system of Yugo-slavia. As its name implies, the bank provides funds for the financing of ag-ricultural capital expenditures. Its short-term crop loans are negligible.

AGRICULTURAL CREDIT ACT. Legislation of 1923 which created the Federal Intermediate Credit Banks. These banks sell debt instruments to the public and use the proceeds to make short-term agricultural loans.

AGRICULTURAL MORTGAGE COR-PORATION (U.K.). An organization that makes loans to farmers who use their land for security. Most of the loans are provided through, or in conjunction with, commercial banks.

AGRICULTURAL PARITY. The price level of farm commodities which bears a relationship between overall price levels and specific farm prices, related to a given period. For example, if selling a certain number of bushels of corn enabled a farmer to buy a specific market basket (see CON-SUMER PRICE INDEX) in a base year, then parity today would mean that the same number of bushels of corn would buy the same market basket.

AGRICULTURAL REVOLUTION. The transition from traditional methods to the extensive use of machinery in farming, and to human control of soil chemistry and animal breeding. It is generally con-sidered that the agricultural revolution took place in the mid- to late 1800s, al-though some identify the changes of the

1700s, especially in Europe, as its beginning.

AGRICULTURE. This SECTOR receives special emphasis in economics because (1) it provides the basic materials for feeding, clothing, and housing the world's population; (2) one of the statistics often used to measure economic development is the percentage of productive effort which goes to the agriculture sector (see LESS DEVELOPED COUNTRY); (3) agriculture was the main issue in the physiocratic school of economic thought (see PHYSIOCRACY); (4) it employs labor resources ranging from the least skilled to those with graduate degrees; and (5) it has always been a vital element of national growth and survival.

AID TO FAMILIES WITH DEPENDENT CHILDREN (AFDC). Part of the U.S. welfare program which makes payments to families that have insufficient income to support the children for whom they are responsible. Usually means payments to mothers when there is no father in the home.

AIRLINE DEREGULATION ACT OF 1978. A major piece of legislation which established a timetable for giving the airlines more freedom to operate and compete. As a result, on December 31, 1981, the Civil Aeronautics Board (CAB) lost its power to determine the routes of individual airlines. Complete deregulation will be reached when the CAB is terminated on January 1, 1985.

ALDRICH-VREELAND ACT. U.S. legislation that created the NATIONAL MONETARY COMMISSION to conduct a thorough study of the nation's monetary and banking system. The commission's report, called the *Aldrich Plan*, was published in 1911. It included several recommendations that became part of the FEDERAL RESERVE SYSTEM, which was created in 1913.

ALLOCATIONS FAMILIALES (Fr.). See FAMILY ALLOWANCES.

ALLOCATIVE EFFECTS. A change in the way an item of limited quantity is distributed, usually due to an outside influence in the economy. For example, if a government program put more money into the economy and the result was simply an increase of spending on goods and services in the same proportion as previously, there would be no allocative effect; if the result was a proportionately greater spending for certain items, there would be an allocative effect. If the new allocation brought more aggregate UTILITY, then the allocative effects would be considered desirable.

ALLONGE. In financial and legal economics, a piece of paper added to a negotiable instrument for the purpose of providing room for endorsement signatures. The allonge legally becomes a part of the instrument.

ALLOWED TIME. (1) In quota and bonus systems, *allowed time* is the amount of time alloted for completion of a certain task. Sometimes incentive pay is earned by employees who complete the task is less than the allowed time. (2) When referring to indirect expenses of production, *allowed time* includes rest periods, time to change into special clothing, and other times which are necessary but not directly productive.

ALL-SAVERS CERTIFICATE. A provision of the ECONOMIC RECOVERY TAX ACT of 1981 that authorized thrift institutions and commercial banks to issue all-savers certificates which had tax-exempt status. The purpose was to encourage saving in those institutions, which were in need of additional funds.

ALTERNATIVE COST. See OPPORTUNITY COST.

AMERICAN FEDERATION OF LABOR (AFL). Because many believed that unions should be organized by craft, the AFL was created in 1886 with Samuel Gompers as its president. The Knights of Labor, which previously provided the main unification for labor unions was organized by industry. In 1955 the AFL merged with the CIO to create the AFL-CIO.

AMERICAN FEDERATION OF LABOR-CONGRESS OF INDUSTRIAL ORGANIZATIONS (AFL-CIO). Formed in 1955 by merger of the AFL and the CIO (which had been formed in 1938), this organization represents the vast majority of U.S. labor unions. Its functions include coordinating organized labor as well as undertaking political actions such as lobbying for legislation favorable to labor.

AMERICAN STOCK EXCHANGE (AMEX, ASE). Located in New York City, the AMEX provides the nation's second largest marketplace for buying and selling stocks, bonds, and other securities. Because it grew rather spontaneously from informal gatherings of traders in the street, it was once known as the Curb Exchange. See also NEW YORK STOCK EXCHANGE.

AMORTIZATION. Making payments which reduce the PRINCIPAL amount of a debt.

ANALOG COMPUTER. Any device which uses one measurable quantity to stand for another and, on the basis of this analog, computes values for the latter quantity. Today, an analog computer is usually understood to be an electronic computer in which voltages and currents are used as the analogs of items in the physical world, such as pressure, frequency, velocity, etc. Unlike a DIGITAL COMPUTER, the analog computer does not work in discrete values and therefore is not used for accounting and financial work. Since the late 1950s, rapid improvements in versatility, speed, and size of digital computers have diminished the use of analog computers to the point where most people think of a computer and a digital computer as one and the same.

ANALOGY. Analogies are used in ECONOMETRICS whenever a MODEL is constructed. For example, the change of numbers in an econometric equation is the analog of the change which it represents in the actual economy. When the model is worked by a computer, then the variable being considered is the analog of its counterpart in the economy.

ANALYSIS OF VARIATION (ANOVA). A systematic mathematical analysis for the purpose of identifying and categorizing the differences between sets of data or between a function and a set of data. ANOVA usually includes total error, error about the mean, residual error, and others, usually in a squared-error form. See Mathematical Regression in the appendix.

ANNOUNCEMENT EFFECT. The change in market price, or other economic condition, that occurs upon the mere knowledge of something later that will cause the change. For example, if an organization is going to purchase land for a shopping center, land prices will rise as soon as these intentions are known.

ANNUALLY BALANCED BUDGET. The situation in which expenditures equal income. Usually refers to the federal government, but can also refer to other levels of government or to any budget. It is especially important for the federal government because the condition of the nation's budget greatly affects the overall economy.

A policy requiring that the budget be balanced annually would prevent fiscal authorities from using the budget to expand the economy when they desired, or from cooling the economy when it is too expansionary. On the other hand, proponents of the annually balanced budget point out that the federal budget is in DEFICIT almost every year. The conclusion is that fiscal authorities use this powerful control only for its expansionary powers; almost never for control when the economy is too expansionary. Therefore the problems caused by the resultant NATIONAL DEBT are not balanced by the benefits derived from freedom to manipulate the budget.

ANNUAL PERCENTAGE RATE (APR). The annual rate of interest which, when used in the simple interest-rate formula, equals the amount of interest payable in other methods of calculating. Sometimes called the *effective annual rate*.

ANNUAL RATE. When statistics are given for periods of other than a year, they are often adjusted so that if the prevailing conditions were present for the entire year, the change for the entire year would be at the annual rate which is given. For example, if the CONSUMER PRICE INDEX increased 1 percent during one QUARTER, it could be said that the index was increasing at an annual rate of 4 percent. Actually, more sophisticated statistics would be used to weight the figures before extending them to a full year, because the statistical environments of all quarters are not identical.

Care must be exercised when extending short-run figures because they can fluctuate widely. Moreover, presenting the figures for a month, converted to an annual rate, may not represent what is actually expected for the year. For example, the table shows deviations in the MONEY SUPPLY for 1970 through mid-1973. Each figure is an annual rate, obtained by projecting the rate from a shorter period. Note that the shorter the period from which data was taken, the larger the annual projection becomes. The same result is found whether average deviation or maximum deviation is being examined.

	Form of data	
	Average deviation	Maximum deviation
Monthly	3.8	8.8
Quarterly	2.4	5.5
Semi-annually	1.8	4.1

ANNUAL REPORT OF THE FEDERAL RESERVE SYSTEM. The Board of Governors of the FRS is required to submit an annual report to the U.S. Congress. A significant portion of the report consists of a record of policy actions taken by the FEDERAL OPEN MARKET COMMITTEE. The Board also submits an *Annual Report to Congress on Truth in Lending*, which contains information on the Board's administrative role under TRUTH IN LENDING, an assessment of the extent to which compliance is being achieved, and suggestions for changes in the regulation.

ANNUITANT. Person to whom payments of an ANNUITY are made.

ANNUITY. A financial arrangement whereby one party (often an insurance company) pays another party (i.e., the annuitant) a specified amount periodically, either for a specified length of time or for the life of the annuitant.

ANTAGONISTIC COOPERATION. Situation in which each person involved acts in a way that is mutually beneficial for the system, even though such action may not be best from his or her point of view. Because the individuals realize that selfishness would destroy the entire system, they seek to maintain it by not optimizing their individual positions.

ANTIBANK MOVEMENT. By the middle of the nineteenth century, the U.S. had twice established an official national bank, but each time the charter had been allowed to expire. The deficiencies of a banking system without central control in this *wildcat banking period* caused public opinion to demand and obtain legislation that tightened down on banking conditions, even going so far as to put an end to banking in several states. Although many of the inadequacies of the arrangement were addressed by the NATIONAL BANKING ACT of 1864, others remained until the FEDERAL RESERVE SYSTEM was created in 1913.

ANTI-CORN-LAW LEAGUE (U.K.). An amalgamation of individuals who felt that the CORN LAWS were making agricultural imports too expensive and those who felt that international trade in general was hampered by restrictive laws in all nations. The league fought for repeal of the Corn Laws.

ANTIDUMPING DUTY. An import tariff which is imposed for the purpose of raising the domestic price of a product exported by another nation at an unjustifiably low price. See DUMPING.

ANTIGROWTH MOVEMENT. A movement whose proponents feel that continued economic growth should be terminated, either completely or selectively. They contend that more goods and services per capita can be achieved only at the expense of the quality of life, such as by polluting the air and water, and moving in on forests and other natural areas.

ANTI-INJUNCTION ACT. This legislation of 1932 very significantly strengthened the position of labor unions. One of the act's most important provisions greatly restricted the conditions under which an employer could obtain an injunction to terminate a strike.

Another important provision outlawed *yellow dog contracts*, in which workers would not be considered for employment unless they agreed in writing not to take part in union activities. Also known as the *Norris-La Guardia Act*.

ANTI-RACKETEERING ACT. Legislation of 1934 which gave jurisdiction to federal law enforcement authorities in situations in which a crime, such as a robbery, interfered with the movement of goods in interstate commerce.

ANTI-STRIKEBREAKING ACT. Legislation of 1936 which prohibits interstate transportation of people for the purpose of using force or threats against lawful striking and picketing. Also known as the Byrnes Act.

ANTITRUST. See CLAYTON ANTITRUST ACT; SHERMAN ANTITRUST ACT.

A POSTERIORI. Describes the type of data, information, knowledge, statistics, etc. that are available after examination or analysis. The cause-effect relationship

thus established is empirical and is sometimes said to derive generalizations out of specifics. See A PRIORI.

APPLIED ECONOMICS. Economics of financial or economic decisions, as opposed to economics limited to the academic world. The main difference is in the MODELs used; since applied economics involves translating principles and theories into working policies and actions, it must include third-, fourth-, and higher-order effects in its models. On the other hand, models for nonapplied economics range from those used in introductory economics courses to models more complicated than those used in applied economics (perhaps to provide information with which the models of applied economics can be upgraded).

APPORTIONED TAX. A tax which is collected from one or more tax districts and then redistributed over a larger number of districts which may or may not include the districts which were the source of the tax.

APPRECIATION. Increase in the value of an item. With regard to money and international exchange, one nation's money appreciates in terms of another nation's money when more of the latter is needed to exchange for a given amount of the former. In this situation, the money of one nation appreciates and the money of the other nation *depreciates*.

APPRENTICE. An individual who is learning an art, trade, or calling under the supervision of skilled journeymen. Apprentices receive pay for their work during the on-the-job phase of an apprenticeship program. This compensation, which is usually figured as a percentage of the journeyman rate, is paid by the employer. Labor unions often take an active role in establishing apprenticeship programs and in overseeing the training of apprentices.

APPROPRIATIONS. When used in connection with the federal budget, the amounts of money which are authorized for various government programs. When the money is actually spent it is referred to as *expenditures*. The distinction between appropriations and expenditures is important to economists because of the effect of each on the economy. However, economists sometimes disagree about the the significance of an "anticipation effect" whereby the mere announcement of an increase in government appropriations triggers an increase in business and consumer spending.

A PRIORI. Describes data, information, knowledge, and so on that is known beforehand, rather than as a result of experiments or tests. In coin-tossing experiments, the fact that the coin will land tails-up about half the time is *a priori*, as is the shape of the DEMAND SCHEDULE in economics. See A POSTERIORI.

ARBITRAGE. Simultaneously buying something in one market and selling it in another. In economics, arbitrage usually refers to buying and selling the currencies of two or more countries in different markets.

ARBITRATION. A method of settling disputes, misunderstandings, etc. by inclusion of a third party, called the *arbitrator*, who makes a decision based on the merits and facts of the situation. It is common in labor disputes to use an arbitrator both for the settling of negotiations leading to a contract and for the interpretation of parts of existing contracts which may have resulted in grievances. Depending on agreement between the principal parties, arbitration can be compulsory or non-compulsory, and the findings of the arbitrator can be binding or merely taken as recommendations.

ARBITRATION OF EXCHANGE. Settlement of a debt involving the money systems of at least three nations. The debtor is in nation A, the creditor is in nation B, and payment is made with a BILL OF EXCHANGE written in nation C. The purpose of such an arrangement is to take advantage of variations and inconsistencies in INTERNATIONAL EXCHANGE rates.

ARBITRATOR. Person appointed to act as a judge or referee in a dispute—usually a labor dispute.

AREA-WIDE BARGAINING. Labor negotiations which cover all the members of a union and all the employers of the union members in a specific geographical or industrial setting.

ARITHMETIC MEAN. See AVERAGE.

ARITHMETIC PROGRESSION. A sequence of numbers, each of which is obtained by adding a constant to the preceding number. For an example in economics, see THOMAS MALTHUS. See also GEOMETRIC PROGRESSION.

ARROW'S PARADOX. A situation described by Kenneth Arrow in *Social Choice and Individual Values* (New York: Wiley, 1951) in which a certain set of conditions could lead to a vote being won by a minority of voters. The analysis of this paradox is not simple, and several papers have been devoted to its examination.

ARTICLES OF INCORPORATION. Document that formally indicates approval of authorities for creation of a corporation. Also called *certificate of incorporation*. See also FORMS OF BUSINESS ORGANIZATION.

ARTIFICIAL CAPITAL. Certain economists define the economic resource, *capital*, as artificial capital, and the natural resource *land* as NATURAL CAPITAL. See ECONOMIC RESOURCES.

ARTISAN. In labor economics, a worker who employs a skill. Applies to art in the conventional sense as well as to trades.

ASKED. See SPREAD.

ASKI TRADING SYSTEM (Ger.). An arrangement of the 1930s which was designed to promote international trade on a mutual basis. Currency of a special issue was used to pay for imported goods and services; that same currency would be accepted back as payment for exported goods and services.

ASSESSMENT. The determination that a certain payment is or will be required. In the government sector, an assessment is the valuation of property as the basis for property tax. In the private sector, it refers to charges, such as the charge each company member of an INDUSTRIAL ASSOCIATION is assessed to cover the cost of an advertising campaign.

ASSET. An item of value. A completely liquid asset is money, because it can be spent and converted easily into another form of asset. An example of a nonliquid asset is an art treasure because there are relatively few potential buyers and converting it to another form of asset would involve considerable effort and maybe a loss. In financial economics, asset accounts represent the sum of what an organization owns, plus what it has in connection with debt (liabilities).

ASSET COMPOSITION. As used in the banking industry, the relative amount of loans, compared to investments, in its portfolio.

ASSIGNAT (Fr.). A paper currency used after the French Revolution. It was officially removed from circulation in 1796.

ASSIGNEE. A person to whom rights in a contract are transferred but who was not originally a party to the contract. See ASSIGNMENT.

ASSIGNMENT. In business economics and contract law, the transfer of rights in a contract to a person who was not originally a party to the contract. For example, A owes some money to B; C does some work for B; as payment, B gives C the right to collect the money that is owed by A. B is the assignor, and C is the assignee.

ASSIGNOR. A person who transfers a contract right to another who was not originally a party to the contract. See ASSIGNMENT.

ASSIMILATION. In financial economics, the working of a new issue of securities into the market. When the securities are first sold by the issuing enterprise, the price is established by deliberate decision; after assimilation, the price is determined by SUPPLY-AND-DEMAND forces of the financial MARKETPLACE.

ASSOCIATION AGREEMENT. In labor economics, an agreement reached by confederations of unions and employers.

ASSUMED BOND. A bond which is issued by one corporation but for which payment of principal, interest, or both is guaranteed by a different corporation. Also known as a *guaranteed bond* or an *indorsed bond.*

ASTRONOMICAL THEORY OF BUSINESS CYCLES. A theory which holds that sunspots affect agricultural output, which in turn affects the world's economy. This theory was developed in the attempt to find some regularity in ECONOMIC FLUCTUATIONS and to relate that regularity to a predictable criterion.

ATOMISTIC ECONOMY. An economy characterized by small production units acting independently. The phrase had more application prior to the industrial revolution.

AT THE MARKET. An expression used in financial economics to indicate that a transaction is to take place at the most favorable price the financial MARKETPLACE will yield at the time, rather than wait until a specified price can be reached.

AUSTERITY PROGRAM. A deliberate economic policy of reduction in the standard of living. It is always meant to be a temporary measure, designed to provide a one-time solution to an economic problem such as balance of the government budget. In addition, it might be implemented to make more FACTORS OF PRODUCTION available for manufacturing CAPITAL GOODS (by using less productive effort in making consumer goods) so that the economy will be stronger in the future.

AUSTRIAN SCHOOL. A branch of economic thinking which shows that MARGINAL UTILITY analysis can answer many questions that previously defied explanation.

AUTARCHY. The condition of economic units not being dependent or interactive with other economic units, as with an isolated nation.

AUTHORIZED STOCK. The amount of CAPITAL STOCK which a corporation is authorized to sell. The portion it actually sells is *issued stock*; the portion it holds for possible future issuance is *authorized but unissued*, or *potential*, *stock*.

AUTOMATED CLEARINGHOUSE (ACH). An arrangement of the FEDERAL RESERVE SYSTEM for electronic transfer of funds. A central computer accepts and executes the electronic messages (generally provided from computer tape) that are necessary for a "paperless" transfer of funds. At present, the Federal Reserve System provides the only nationwide ACH network, clearing nearly all ACH transfers outside of New York City. The Federal Reserve System has actively promoted ACHs hoping to increase the efficiency of the payments mechanism by reducing its reliance on the traditional paper check. However, over 80 percent of ACH transfers continue to be government-related.

AUTOMATED TELLER MACHINE (ATM). A computer-controlled terminal, usually located on the premises of a financial institution, through which customers can make deposits and withdrawals, and conduct other transactions that once could be done only with the assistance of a teller.

AUTOMATIC CHECKOFF. In labor economics, an arrangement for paying dues and other ASSESSMENTs to a labor union; the employer automatically deducts the amounts from the employee's pay, and gives those amounts directly to the union. Also called *compulsory check-off*.

AUTOMATIC STABILIZER. A device that, by its very nature, tends to expand the economy when it is slowing down and contract the economy when its growth is too rapid for long-run stability. See BUILT-IN STABILIZER.

AUTOMATIC TRANSFER SERVICE (ATS). Provides for the automatic transfer of appropriate amounts from savings to checking to cover checks written or to meet minimum balance requirements.

AUTOMATIC WAGE ADJUSTMENT. A plan by which wages are raised (or possibly lowered) upon the occurrence of a particular event such as a change in the CONSUMER PRICE INDEX or the receipt of a college degree. See also ESCALATOR CLAUSE.

AUTOMATION. Use of sophisticated CAPITAL equipment to perform functions which previously only humans were capable of performing. Opponents of automation point to a soft-drink bottling plant that produces 100,000 bottles a day with 20 employees and claim that without automation the plant would employ 50 people. According to the proponents, without the price savings of automation, customers wouldn't buy 100,000 bottles a day, and fewer than 20 people would be employed to produce the quantity the market wanted.

Throughout history, the human race has been replacing its labor with devices. Although there is no precise definition of just where the line to automation is crossed, most people agree that the difference between automation and mere machinery is that the former takes over some of the "thinking" functions of humans.

AUTONOMOUS INVESTMENT. Purchases of capital equipment which are triggered by internal pressures rather than because increased demand made them necessary. For example, a piece of machinery may be replaced merely because a new one is more efficient. In practice, very few investments are purely autonomous. Generally, new capital equipment is purchased to meet the requirements of demand; if the new equipment costs more because it is superior to the old, some part of the purchase price can be considered autonomous investment by an economist doing an analysis. See INDUCED INVESTMENT.

AUTONOMOUS TARIFF SYSTEM. Unilateral establishment of tariff rates and policies, with no reliance on treaties or other international considerations.

AUTONOMOUS VARIABLE. In ECONOMETRICS, a variable whose value is a function of items not controllable by economists, such as psychological factors or weather. See also ENDOGENOUS; EXOGENOUS.

AVAIL. The net return of a transaction, after subtracting costs from gross return.

AVERAGE. In popular usage, the sum of values divided by the number of values summed. If an individual earned $200, $210, and $214 in each of three weeks, his or her average weekly earnings would be $624 divided by 3, or $208. To be technically correct, this calculation gives only one of several types of average, the *arithmetic mean*. Other averages are the *geometric mean*, *median*, and *mode*. Deliberate selection of a certain average is one means by which individuals use or misuse statistics.

Arithmetic mean. This average is proper to use when the size of individual differences is significant to the entire group. For example, suppose the price of a certain commodity changes every day and we desire a single number to indicate the price over a period of a month. The arithmetic mean should be used because, if the price on one day was far different from the other days, it is right for the price on that day to influence the average.

Geometric mean. This average is found by *multiplying* all n values and then taking the nth root of the final product. It is appropriate to use when the values are subject to a percentage change from one to the next—for example, when a firm's profits increase a certain percentage each

year. The geometric mean forms the basis for the COMPOUND INTEREST formula.

Median. When the data field is arranged in increasing or decreasing order, this measure is the point which has just as many data points above it as below it. For example, suppose hourly wages in a certain plant are as follows:

Employee A—$15.00
Employee B—$16.00
Employee C—$17.00
Employee D—$18.00
Employee E—$75.00

The median would be $17.00 per hour, and employee E's large wage does not affect the median; the median would be $17.00 even if employee E earned $17.01 per hour. The choice, then, depends on why the average is being calculated. The median is a good choice if the purpose is to estimate what a new employee might earn; however if the marketing department wants a figure to use in pricing, the arithmetic mean is more informative.

Mode. The mode is the value which occurs most often. If a store manager is offered a special price on a carload of shirts of one size, his or her main concern will be what size shirt has sold in the largest quantity; the manager will not be interested in the arithmetic mean of the shirt sizes sold. A *bimodal distribution* is one in which there are two peaks of equal size.

Weighted average. When all the data points are not equally significant, *weights* can be attached to them selectively so that the result will be more meaningful. Consider, for example, the CONSUMER PRICE INDEX. A change in the price of milk has a greater effect on the household budget than does an equal change in the price of paprika, and therefore these items are figured in with weights reflecting the differences in the effects.

AVERAGE DAILY BALANCE METHOD. A method of calculating the FINANCE CHARGE for consumer credit.

With this method, the creditor adds the debtor's balances for each day in the billing period and then divides that sum by the number of days in the billing period.

AVERAGE FIXED COSTS (AFC). The sum of FIXED COSTS (those costs that are independent of the number of units produced) divided by the number of units produced. The larger the number of units which can be produced at a given level of fixed costs, the smaller the AFC will be. AFC can be thought of as the portion of fixed costs which should be allocated to each unit produced. For a listing of the various types of costs, see COSTS.

AVERAGE PROPENSITY TO CONSUME (APC). The ratio of consumption expenditures to DISPOSABLE PERSONAL INCOME. Considering that the only possibilities for disposable income are spending (consuming) or saving leads to the relationship APC + APS = 1, where APS is the *average propensity to save*. See also MARGINAL PROPENSITY TO CONSUME.

AVERAGE PROPENSITY TO SAVE (APS). See AVERAGE PROPENSITY TO CONSUME.

AVERAGE REVENUE PRODUCT. In MICROECONOMICS, the total revenue which will be realized by using a given quantity of FACTORS OF PRODUCTION.

AVERAGE TOTAL COST (ATC). The sum of AVERAGE FIXED COSTS and AVERAGE VARIABLE COSTS. ATC is usually found by dividing overall total cost by the number of units which were produced for that cost. For a listing of the various types of costs, see COST.

AVERAGE VARIABLE COSTS (AVC). The sum of VARIABLE COSTS (those costs that depend on the number of units produced) divided by the number of units produced. AVC can be thought of as the amount of variable costs that should be allocated to the total cost of each unit produced. For a listing of the various types of costs, see COST.

AWARD. The ruling of an ARBITRATOR.

B

BABY BOOM GENERATION. Because marriages were delayed during World War II and families were scattered for years, plans to have children were fulfilled at an unusually high rate for several years after the war. The accompanying table shows how the youngest segment of he population, as a percentage of the total population, changed after the war.

Year	Percent of population under 5	Year	Percent of population under 5
1940	8.01	1960	11.26
1941	8.13	1961	11.17
1942	8.38	1962	10.97
1943	8.79	1963	10.75
1944	9.05	1964	10.51
1945	9.28	1965	10.20
1946	9.37	1966	9.77
1947	10.00	1967	9.34
1948	10.17	1968	8.92
1949	10.46	1969	8.57
1950	10.78	1970	8.37
1951	11.19	1971	8.30
1952	10.99	1972	8.14
1953	11.01	1973	7.93
1954	11.08	1974	7.69
1955	11.19	1975	7.44
1956	11.25	1976	7.13
1957	11.33	1977	7.03
1958	11.37	1978	7.03
1959	11.35	1979	7.09

The baby boom generation is very important in economics because it affects the composition of goods and services demanded for many generations. At first there was a relative increase in the demand for baby clothes, baby food, toys, etc. As the "bulge" in AGE DISTRIBUTION moved to other years, it has continued to affect the demand for consumer items, as well as the number of workers available and the years of experience they offer. In the future, the same bulge will move out of the work force and into retirement.

BACKING. When something of little or no inherent value represents something of value, the latter is the backing. A check you write has no value in itself but the money in your checking account backs it and gives it some value. The term is usually used with regard to a monetary system; when nations had stores of gold equal to the amount of money issued, it was said that their money was backed by gold or that they were on a gold standard.

BACK PAY. Wages paid to an employee for wage liabilities incurred in the past. Reasons for back pay might include unlawful discharge, a change in rules, or a negotiated increase made retroactive (if a labor contract expires and workers agree to continue working during negotiations, there is usually a tentative agreement that any settlement will be made retroactive).

BACKTRACK. A process in which an employee terminated due to lack of work obtains another position within the company which had been filled by a worker with less seniority. He or she replaces that worker, who then replaces someone in another position, and so on; ultimately it is the person with the least seniority who is actually terminated. Backtrack occurs when a labor contract specifies that layoffs due to insufficient work must be in strict order of seniority, although many nonunion employers also give considerable emphasis to seniority when making layoffs.

Backtrack is also called *bumping*. Those who favor it point out that it prevents the employer from using low workload as an excuse to get rid of individuals merely because of personality conflict, and employers often welcome it because it relieves them of the undesirable decision of who will receive notice.

Opponents point out that (1) since an employee who has been given notice can choose whether or not to bump someone else, hard feelings often result when the privilege is exercised; (2) labor costs are made unnecessarily high because of frequent retraining; (3) productivity is low because only time on the job, not efficiency, is recognized.

BACKWARD BENDING SUPPLY CURVE. Normally, a SUPPLY SCHEDULE shows a direct relationship between price and quantity supplied; the higher the price that can be obtained, the more suppliers are willing to provide. However, with certain situations, such as the supplying of labor by individuals for a price (i.e., wage), there is evidence that when an income goal is reached, further increases in the wage rate result in *less* labor being supplied. Thus there is an inverse relationship between price and quantity supplied.

BAD MONEY. See GRESHAM'S LAW.

BAILEE. In a BAILMENT, the party who has possession of goods belonging to the bailor.

BAILMENT. Legal situation in which one party (the bailee) has possession of property belonging to another (the bailor). A bailment can arise either when the goods are transferred (as when they are stored in a warehouse) or when title is transferred (as when the bailor buys goods but leaves them in possession of the seller—who then becomes the bailee—to be picked up later).

BAILOR. In a BAILMENT, the party who has title to goods which are in possession of the bailee.

BALANCED BUDGET. A budget in which expenditures are equal to revenues and neither a SURPLUS nor a DEFICIT occurs. Usually used in connection with a government budget. See ANNUALLY BALANCED BUDGET.

BALANCED BUDGET MULTIPLIER. A change in GROSS NATIONAL PRODUCT which results from government taxing and spending by equal amounts. This concept is based on the fact that a portion of the money not taken from the public in taxes will be saved and therefore withdrawn from the CIRCULAR FLOW OF MONEY.

BALANCE OF INTERNATIONAL PAYMENTS (BIP). (The following description was adapted from *Dictionary of Economic and Statistical Terms*, published by the U.S. Department of Commerce.) The BIP account is a record of economic transactions between the U.S. (and its residents) and the rest of the world. The measurement, which is in dollars, covers a fixed time period during which the transactions take place. The transactions involve:

Merchandise. Movable goods such as wheat, machines, books, and automobiles

Services. Intangible output that is regarded as being transferred at the instant of performance, such as transportation, insurance, and, by convention, the yields on international investments, which are considered as fees for the use of capital

Private and governmental capital. For example, financial claims and ownership of property

Monetary gold. Although a physical commodity, monetary gold is treated in the same manner as a financial asset.

An international transaction may involve the exchange of one asset (commodity, service, or capital) for another, or it may involve a gift of an asset. By recording the offsetting figures of exchange and creating a special category of unilateral transfers as the offset for gifts, the balance of payments is presented as a double-entry record, similar in many ways to ordinary business accounts.

Credit items represent the transfer to nonresidents of real or financial assets or services; debit items represent the acquisition from nonresidents of the same types of assets or services. Examples of this classification in practice are as follows:

1. A U.S. export of merchandise is a credit item, and a U.S. import of merchandise is a debit item.
2. A service performed by U.S. residents for foreigners (such as the sale of services to foreign travelers in the U.S.) is a credit item, and a service performed by foreigners for U.S. residents (such as those traveling abroad) is a debit item.
3. An increase in U.S. investments abroad is a debit item, because it involves the acquisition of a claim on a foreign person, company, bank, or government.
4. A U.S. unilateral transfer to a foreigner is likewise a debit item matching the credit item of the physical asset or service given.
5. An increase in foreign investments in the U.S. is, by contrast, a credit item.
6. Repayment of debt is treated as the reacquisition of the debt instrument. Therefore, repayment of debt by a foreigner is a credit item, whereas

U.S repayment of debt to a foreigner is a debit item.

The process of settlement varies from case to case. For example, a U.S. commodity export is a credit. Simultaneously, a debit is created—the U.S claim on on foreigners. The means of settling the claim will vary. Possibilities include:

1. An increase in U.S. holdings of financial assets—liabilities or promises to pay of foreigners to U.S. residents. This is the same as an increase in U.S. investment abroad.
2. A decrease in foreign holdings of assets in the U.S. (for example, payment out of a foreign deposit in a U.S. bank). Since these assets are liabilities of U.S. residents, the decrease is a decrease in foreign investment in the U.S.

Double-entry bookkeeping means that total debits must always equal total credits. In this sense, the balance of payments must always balance. However, the actual collection of statistical data is from a wide variety of sources, and so it is necessary to make estimates of some figures. Consequently, debit and credit entries are not exactly offsetting, and a balancing item, errors and omissions, is required.

Credits are counted as positive, and debits as negative. If the balancing item required to make the algebraic sum of credits and debits equal to zero is positive, it indicates that total credits have been underestimated, total debits have been overestimated, or some combination of these effects has occurred.

Relation of BIP and national income and product accounts. The classifications of U.S. BIP accounts have been made in a way that makes it possible to integrate their results with the NATIONAL INCOME AND PRODUCT ACCOUNTS. In these accounts, the four major transacting groups are households, business, government, and the rest of the world.

The BIP records transactions with the rest of the world.

The sum of purchases of these four groups must equal the national output of goods and services plus imports of goods and services.

If there were no unilateral transfers and no errors and omissions, net sales of goods and services to the rest of the world (i.e., exports minus imports) would be numerically equal to net foreign investment, since the algebraic sum of credits and debits is zero.

In the national accounts of the U.S., gifts to foreigners are treated as if they were purchases of goods and services from foreigners by U.S. households or the U.S. government. Unilateral transfers in kind are completely eliminated from the external sector of the national accounts. Hence, the "net balance on goods and services and unilateral transfers" is equal to the net foreign investment in the GROSS NATIONAL PRODUCT. It measures the excess of goods, services, and cash transferred to foreigners (except for gifts in kind) over goods, services, and cash acquired from foreigners.

The meaning of net foreign investment. Net foreign investment is as a significant measure of the change in international financial asset ownership that has occurred over a period of time. Since net foreign investment is measured by the balance on goods, services, and unilateral transfers, any errors and omissions in the estimates of these transactions are also implicitly reflected in the size of net foreign investment. Thus, positive net foreign investment—an increase in U.S. claims on the rest of the world—must be associated with a positive net export of goods and services, allowing for the fact that gifts are claims foregone.

Overall balance on official reserve transactions basis. By combining official reserve transactions, an overall measurement can be constructed of official settlements in the U.S. balance of payments over a period of time. These transactions consist of movements of gold, changes in the U.S. government's holdings of convertible foreign currencies, changes in the U.S. gold position in the IMF, and changes in foreign official holdings of dollar assets.

An overall surplus on the official reserve transactions basis indicates a net increase in the U.S. international reserve position; an overall deficit indicates a net decrease. It should be noted that an increase in foreign official dollar holdings constitutes an increase in monetary reserves of this type—in the absence of an increase in U.S. holdings of monetary gold or convertible currencies, an increase in world monetary reserves is achieved only through a deficit on the official reserve transactions basis in the U.S. balance of payments.

Overall balance on liquidity basis. U.S. dollar assets are also held by foreign individuals, companies, and banks. They are, of course, liabilities of the government, corporations, commercial banks, and U.S. residents to foreigners. Part of these private holdings is fixed investments, and part is monetary assets. Since money is liquid, it is necessary to establish a dividing line between assets that are liquid—money and near money—and assets that are not.

The statistical measure is conditioned by available reports. A foreign asset is considered liquid if it serves as money directly or is freely convertible into money with a minimum risk of changes in market values. By convention, short-term liabilities to foreigners reported by U.S. banks (including short-term investments held in custody accounts for foreigners) and foreign holdings of all U.S. government marketable securities are regarded as liquid.

The measure of overall balance on liquidity basis includes transfers affecting U.S. official reserve assets (gold, convertible currencies, and IMF position) and liquid liabilities to all foreigners. A surplus on liquidity basis involves an increase in U.S. official reserve assets, a decrease

Balance of International Payments. In lines 1–12, quarterly data are seasonally adjusted.

Item of credits or debits	1976	1977
1 Balance on current account	4,605	−14,092
2 Not seasonally adjusted	—	—
3 Merchandise trade balance[a]	−9,306	−30,873
4 Merchandise exports	114,745	120,816
5 Merchandise imports	−124,051	−151,689
6 Military transactions, net	674	1,679
7 Investment income, net[e]	15,975	17,989
8 Other service transactions, net	2,260	1,783
9 Memo: Balance on goods and services[b,c]	9,603	−9,423
10 Remittances, pensions, and other transfers	−1,851	−1,895
11 U.S. government grants (excluding military)	−3,146	−2,775
12 Change in U.S. government assets, other than official reserve assets, net (increase, −)	−4,214	−3,693
13 Change in U.S. official reserve assets (increase, −)	−2,558	−375
14 Gold	0	−118
15 Special drawing rights (SDRs)	−78	−121
16 Reserve position in International Monetary Fund	−2,212	−294
17 Foreign currencies	−268	158
18 Change in U.S. private assets abroad (increase, −)[b]	−44,498	−31,725
19 Bank-reported claims	−21,368	−11,427
20 Nonbank-reported claims	−2,296	−1,940
21 U.S. purchase of foreign securities, net	−8,885	−5,460
22 U.S. direct investments abroad, net[b]	−11,949	−12,898
23 Change in foreign official assets in the U.S. (increase, +)	17,573	36,656
24 U.S. Treasury securities	9,319	30,230
25 Other U.S. government obligations	573	2,308
26 Other U.S. government liabilities[d]	4,507	1,240
27 Other U.S. liabilities reported by U.S. banks	969	773
28 Other foreign official assets[e]	2,205	2,105
29 Change in foreign private assets in the U.S. (increase, +)[b]	18,826	14,167
30 U.S. bank-reported liabilities	10,990	6,719
31 U.S. nonbank-reported liabilities	−578	473
32 Foreign private purchases of U.S. Treasury securities, net	2,783	534
33 Foreign purchases of other U.S. securities, net	1,284	2,713
34 Foreign direct investments in the U.S., net[b]	4,347	3,728
35 Allocation of SDRs	0	0
36 Discrepancy	10,265	−937
37 Owing to seasonal adjustments	—	—
38 Statistical discrepancy in recorded data before seasonal adjustment	10,265	−937
Memo: Changes in official assets		
39 U.S. official reserve assets (increase, −)	−2,558	−375
40 Foreign official assets in the U.S. (increase, +)	13,066	35,416
41 Change in Organization of Petroleum Exporting Countries official assets in the U.S. (part of line 25 above)	9,581	6,351
42 Transfers under military grant programs (excluded from lines 4, 6, and 11 above)	373	204

Data are from Bureau of Economic Analysis, Survey of Current Business (U.S. Department of Commerce).

[a]Data are on an international accounts (IA) basis. Differs from the census basis primarily in including imports into the U.S. Virgin Islands and excluding military exports, which are part of line 6.

[b]Includes reinvested earnings of incorporated affiliates.

[c]Differs from the definition of "net exports of goods and services" in the national income and product (GNP) account. The GNP definition makes various adjustments to merchandise trade and service transactions.

Figures are in millions of U.S. dollars.

1978	1978		1979		
	Q3	Q4	Q1	Q2	Q3
− 13,478	− 3,164	85	415	− 1,056	762
—	− 5,892	1,120	1,731	− 182	− 3,080
− 33,770	− 7,949	− 5,971	− 6,115	− 7,716	− 7,282
142,052	36,532	39,412	41,348	42,792	47,337
− 175,822	− 44,481	− 45,383	− 47,463	− 50,508	− 54,619
492	247	− 239	34	− 217	− 384
21,645	4,952	6,599	6,864	7,465	8,794
3,241	819	1,010	954	775	1,008
− 8,392	− 1,931	1,399	1,737	307	2,136
− 1,934	− 463	− 524	− 517	− 466	− 504
− 3,152	− 770	− 790	− 805	− 897	− 870
− 4,656	− 1,390	− 994	− 1,094	− 1,001	− 756
732	115	182	− 3,585	343	2,779
− 65	0	− 65	0	0	0
1,249	− 43	1,412	− 1,142	6	0
4,231	195	3,275	− 86	− 78	− 52
− 4,683	− 37	− 4,440	− 2,357	415	2,831
− 57,033	− 8,774	− 29,442	− 2,958	− 15,507	− 25,348
− 33,023	− 5,488	− 21,980	6,572	− 8,266	− 15,956
− 3,853	− 29	− 1,898	− 2,719	668	n.a.
− 3,487	− 475	− 918	− 1,056	− 629	− 2,111
− 16,670	− 2,782	− 4,646	− 5,755	− 7,280	− 7,281
33,758	4,641	18,764	− 9,391	− 10,043	5,562
23,542	3,029	13,422	− 8,872	− 12,859	5,030
656	443	− 115	− 5	94	335
2,754	122	2,045	− 164	257	191
5,411	963	3,156	− 563	2,321	− 100
1,395	84	256	213	145	106
29,956	10,717	10,475	10,868	16,100	17,497
16,975	7,958	7,556	7,157	12,067	13,009
1,640	1,004	− 177	− 651	1,086	n.a.
2,180	− 1,053	1,549	2,583	− 239	1,579
2,867	528	540	790	1,161	591
6,294	2,280	1,008	989	2,025	2,317
0	0	0	1,139	0	0
10,722	− 2,145	930	4,606	11,163	− 495
—	− 2,716	1,301	985	737	− 3,756
10,722	571	− 371	3,621	10,426	3,261
732	115	182	− 3,585	343	2,779
31,004	4,519	16,719	− 9,227	− 10,299	5,371
− 727	− 1,794	1,803	− 1,916	151	1,488
259	69	63	31	48	85

[d]Primarily associated with military sales contracts and other transactions arranged with or through foreign official agencies.

[e]Consists of investments in U.S. corporate stocks and in debt securities of private corporations and state and local governments.

in liquid liabilities to foreigners, or some combination thereof. On the other hand, a deficit entails a decrease in assets, an increase in liabilities, or both.

U.S. liquid liabilities denominated in dollars and owned by foreigners—"foreign dollar balances"—are not only part of other countries' official and private reserves but also the means of commercial settlement. An increase in their supply is achievable only through a deficit in the overall liquidity balance of the U.S. The meaning of any figure for the liquidity balance has to be interpreted with this in mind. To an unassessable degree, the change in dollar balances held by both official and private foreign residents is deliberate and desired, as long as the U.S. reserve position is sufficient to facilitate the exchange of dollars into foreign currencies without restrictions and at stable exchange rates. The accompanying table, taken from Federal Reserve Bulletin (January 1980), gives some statistics for a few representative years.

An informative article on balance of payments is "Balance of Payments Deficits: Measurement and Interpretation," by John Pippenger, in the November 1973 issue of *Federal Reserve Bank of St. Louis Review*.

BALANCE OF PAYMENTS. See BALANCE OF INTERNATIONAL PAYMENTS.

BALANCE OF TRADE. See MERCHANDISE ACCOUNT.

BALANCE ON GOODS AND SERVICES. See BALANCE OF INTERNATIONAL PAYMENTS.

BALANCING MARGINS. A theoretical concept that explains the actions of a rational consumer. Such a person should spend his or her next dollar (see MARGINAL) on the item which will bring the most satisfaction (see UTILITY UNITS); margins are balanced when the last of each kind of item the consumer bought results in the same amount of utility. Any other arrangement would bring less total utility to the consumer.

BALLOON PAYMENT. See PICKUP PAYMENT.

BANCO DE MEXICO (Mex). The CENTRAL BANK of Mexico. It performs the traditional duties of a central bank, such as issuing currency, supervising the nation's banking system, and advising the government on MONETARY POLICY and credit. In addition, it has assumed the nontraditional function of redirecting the flow of credit to specific SECTORs. Some activities, such as agriculture, have received this preferential treatment because their role in fulfilling the government's goal of development is regarded as essential.

However, the most important reallocation of credit is a result of the central bank's position in financing government deficits. Through the mechanism of legal reserve requirements, the central bank allocates government domestic debt in the banking system. The funds placed on deposit at the central bank for meeting reserve requirements are used to purchase high-yield government bonds. The procedure is not limited to commercial banks, but is also extended to reserves of investment banks. As a result, funds available to the government through reserve requirements represent about 25 to 30 percent of the total liabilities of the financial system.

Allocation and availability of credit are obviously the primary concerns of Banco de Mexixo. Unlike monetary policy in the U.S., the cost of credit is not given a great deal of attention in Mexico. As a result, the level of interest rates in Mexico is not a very reliable indicator of central bank activity.

See MEXICAN BANKING SYSTEM. [Adapted from *Federal Reserve Bank of St. Louis Review* (June 1973), page 21.]

BANCOR. This was to be the name of an international monetary unit under the Keynes Clearing Arrangement, proposed at the BRETTON WOODS conference in 1944. In effect, a world CENTRAL BANK was to be established, which would operate with central banks of other nations to make loans, buy government securities and in general, provide international LIQUIDITY. The proposal was first presented by JOHN MAYNARD KEYNES, and was later modified by Robert Triffin. It is also known as the Triffin Plan. One of the main reasons the plan was not accepted was that it required a substantial transfer of authority from individual central banks to the world central bank, plus establishment of the Expanded International Monetary Fund (XIMF).

BANKABLE BILL. A BILL OF EXCHANGE that, because of the low risk associated with the parties involved, can be readily negotiated for value prior to its due date.

BANK CALL. A communication which requires that a bank supply authorities with a financial statement. A STATE BANK receives calls from the agency responsible in state government; a NATIONAL BANK receives calls from the COMPTROLLER OF THE CURRENCY.

BANK CLEARINGS. The settling and payment of net amounts due from payment instruments, such as checks that have been received. Also called *clearings*.

BANK CREDIT. Loans adjusted plus investments.

BANK DISCOUNT. See DISCOUNT.

BANKERS' ACCEPTANCES. See ACCEPTANCES.

BANK EXAMINER. Banking institutions are subject to planned as well as unannounced visits from state authorities, federal authorities, and the FEDERAL RESERVE SYSTEM. Together, the individuals and the agencies they represent are known as bank examiners.

BANK FOR COOPERATIVES. One of the NEW DEAL provisions designed to alleviate the GREAT DEPRESSION. This legislation of 1933 made loan money available specifically for farm cooperatives.

BANK FOR INTERNATIONAL SETTLEMENTS (BIS). An international banking organization created in 1930, in Basel, Switzerland, for the purpose of handling claims remaining from World War I, including German reparation payments. After that function was removed by the Lucerne Conference in 1932, the BIS assumed a position of liaison among the CENTRAL BANKS of most nations, a function that was of overall benefit during World War II. The liaison function, which continues today, is one of the reasons that the BIS has survived several attempts to terminate it. Its place in the international financial world was considerably reduced in 1944 at the BRETTON WOODS conference.

At present, the BIS has 29 members, 28 of which are central banks. The Federal Reserve is represented at BIS meetings, but is not a member. The BIS is the only international financial institution in which most Eastern European countries—excluding the Soviet Union, East Germany, and Albania—are members.

BANKHEAD-JONES FARM TENANT ACT. Legislation of 1937 designed to spread the ownership of farms to smaller units. It made money available over a long term (40 years) to nonowners, such as tenant farmers, to purchase small farms.

BANK HOLDING COMPANY. Defined by the BANK HOLDING COMPANY ACT as a company that: (1) directly or indirectly owns, controls, or has power to vote 25 percent or more of the voting shares of a bank; (2) controls in any manner the election of a majority of the directors or trustees of a bank; or (3) exercises a controlling influence over the management or policies of a bank. Any company that qualifies as a bank holding company must register with the FEDERAL RESERVE SYSTEM and file reports with it. Also, a bank holding company must obtain the approval of the Board of Governors (of the Federal Reserve System) before acquiring more than 5 percent of the shares of either additional banks or permissible nonbanking companies.

BANK HOLDING COMPANY ACT. An act passed by the U.S. Congress in 1956 and amended in 1966 and 1970, it was designed to achieve two basic objectives; (1) to control BANK HOLDING COMPANY expansion in order to avoid the creation of monopoly or restraint of trade in banking; and (2) to allow bank holding companies to expand into nonbanking activities that are related to banking while maintaining a separation between banking and commerce.

BANK HOLIDAY. In general, any day in which banks do not open for business. Also refers to a period in early 1933 when U.S. banks were closed by government decree in order to let a panic subside. Because of the insolvencies and illiquid positions of a growing number of banks at that time, public confidence was lost to the point that withdrawals threatened to terminate the entire banking system. On February 14, 1933, the governor of Michigan declared banks in that state closed for eight days. By the time Franklin D. Roosevelt was sworn in as president, on March 4, bank holidays had been declared in every state, and cash withdrawals of deposits could no longer be made. On March 6, Roosevelt declared a four-day nationwide bank holiday, during which time the condition of individual banks was appraised. Confidence was regained, and almost immediately upon reopening, the banks began receiving deposits of cash that had been withdrawn. The bank holiday officially ended with passage of the EMERGENCY BANKING RELIEF ACT on March 9, 1933.

BANKING ACT. Legislation of 1933 designed to remove from the banking system certain weaknesses that were believed to be factors in the GREAT DEPRESSION. Significent provisions of the act (1) separated commercial banking from investment banking and (2) created the FEDERAL DEPOSIT INSURANCE CORPORATION.

BANKING DAY. Any day during which a bank is open to the public.

BANKING POLICY. Early in its existence the BOARD OF GOVERNORS of the FEDERAL RESERVE SYSTEM recognized that each of its activities should be directed toward banking policy or credit policy. Its *banking policy* is the influence the board exerts over loans and investments of individual member banks; the objective is to promote a sound banking industry. Its *credit policy* is impersonal and directed toward influencing the total volume and cost of credit without consideration of specific economic entities.

BANK MERGER ACT. Legislation designed to maintain competitive conditions in the banking industry and to allow for orderly growth. The act required, for the first time, prior approval by federal bank regulatory authorities for bank mergers. It also set forth criteria to be followed by the authorities in ruling on bank merger proposals.

BANK NOTE. Paper currency issued by NATIONAL BANKs, carrying a promise to pay, usually in gold, upon demand of the bearer. The practice was terminated by legislation in 1935, when Treasury money and later FEDERAL RESERVE NOTES became the circulating paper money and LEGAL TENDER.

BANK OF ENGLAND (U.K.). The CENTRAL BANK of the U.K., founded under private ownership in 1694 and nationalized in February 1946, when stockholders were paid with funds raised through a government bond issue. One of the bank's functions is to loan money to underwriters who deal with treasury bills. As part of MONETARY POLICY, the bank establishes a *bank rate*, in effect a rediscount rate used when purchasing bills from discount houses. Because of its central position, the bank influences other interest rates by controlling the bank rate. As another tool of monetary policy, OPEN MARKET OPERATIONS are conducted in a manner similar to that of the FEDERAL OPEN MARKET COMMITTEE in the United States.

BANK - OF - FIRST - DEPOSIT AP-PROACH. An approach that has been considered in the constant search for ways to handle the mushrooming use of personal checks. It proposes that all checks be stopped, read, processed, and retained by the bank to which they are presented for payment; only the *information* they contain would be transmitted beyond that point. The traditional system returns all checks to their writers in order to provide proof of payment in case of denial by the payee—a situation that occurs with an extremely small number of checks. If only contested checks were retrieved from the files of the bank where they were first presented for payment, there would be a net saving of time and expense. More on this subject can be found in *Electronic Money and the Payments Mechanism* (Federal Reserve Bank of Boston, pp. 27ff).

BANK OF FRANCE (Fr.). The CENTRAL BANK of France. It was privately owned from its establishment by Napoleon Bonaparte in 1800 until it was nationalized in 1946. Its MONETARY POLICY is effected through the control of minimum LIQUIDITY RATIOs which must be maintained by commercial banks, and by rediscounting short- and medium-term paper from commercial and public sources.

BANK OF ISSUE. The bank in each nation which is responsible for issuing and regulating currency. When referring to a BANK NOTE, *bank of issue* indicates the bank that issued and promised to pay the note.

BANK OF JAPAN. The CENTRAL BANK of Japan. Created under private ownership in 1882, it is now required by law to have at least 55 percent public ownership. Its operations are similar to those of other central banks, although the Bank of Japan exerts economic control by placing more emphasis on discount policy (see DISCOUNT RATE) than others do.

BANK OF NORTH DAKOTA. Only COMMERCIAL BANK in the U.S. which is owned by a state. It functions in the same way as privately owned banks but it makes very few loans to the private sector; most of its loans are to state agencies.

BANK OF SWEDEN (Sveriges Riksbank). The CENTRAL BANK of Sweden. Unlike several other central banks, it has been government owned since its creation in 1668. It is also the world's oldest central bank. It performs most of the functions of other central banks, but it does not hold reserve accounts of commercial banks and is not considered a bankers' bank. Funds for INVESTMENT RESERVE are held.

BANK OF THE UNITED STATES. An early attempt at a CENTRAL BANK. The bank, which was chartered twice (neither charter was renewed), was given some of the responsibilities now assigned to the FEDERAL RESERVE SYSTEM. See FIRST BANK OF THE UNITED STATES, SECOND BANK OF THE UNITED STATES.

BANK PREMISES. The land, buildings, and equipment of the FEDERAL RESERVE BANKs and their branches, less an allowance for depreciation on buildings and equipment. This item appears on the *Consolidated Statement of Condition of All Federal Reserve Banks.* [Adapted from *Glossary: Weekly Federal Reserve Statements,* by the Federal Reserve Bank of New York.]

BANK RATE (U.K.). Discount rate imposed by the BANK OF ENGLAND.

BANK RESERVE EQUATION. A calculation of the FEDERAL RESERVE SYSTEM which combines numerous forces in the country's economic life that affect the activities of the banking system. Over the longer run, the major factors affecting member bank reserves are Federal Reserve credit, holdings of international monetary reserves, and currency in circulation. Other factors, which do not change greatly over the longer run, include Treasury currency outstanding, Treasury deposits, and foreign and other nonmember bank deposits at the Reserve banks.

BANK RESERVES. Funds set aside by depository institutions to meet reserve requirements. For MEMBER BANKs, reserve requirements are satisfied with holdings of VAULT CASH and balances at the Federal Reserve banks. Depository institutions that are not members of the Federal Reserve System may hold their reserves in the same manner, or they may pass the reserve balances through a correspondent institution to the Federal Reserve banks. There are three types of reserves:

1. *Required reserves.* The minimum amount which a bank must have as reserves, according to the formula:

Required reserves =
Reserve ratio × Deposits

Therefore, the *reserve ratio* is a number which tells banks what percentage of their deposits must be kept as reserves. This number becomes a tool of MONETARY POLICY; expansionary tendencies are created by lowering the reserve ratio, and contractionary tendencies are created by raising it. This policy tool works in two ways: lowering it will immediately convert some existing required reserves into excess reserves (thereby allowing banks to loan more money); at the same time, the multiplier by which the entire banking system can expand the MONEY SUPPLY is increased. See also MONEY; MONEY SUPPLY EXPANSION MULTIPLIER. The reserve ratio is set by the Board of Governers of the Federal Reserve System, within limits set by Congress. See RESERVE REQUIREMENTS.

2. *Actual reserves.* The amount a bank has as its reserves
3. *Excess reserves.* Actual reserves minus required reserves. Excess reserves are the basis for expansion of the nation's money supply. See

also PRIMARY RESERVES; SECONDARY RESERVES.

BANKRUPTCY. A court ruling which gives a bankrupt party a chance to start over either by declaring most of its debts canceled, or providing for a workable repayment schedule. It is important to distinguish between *bankruptcy* (a condition declared by a court) and *insolvency* (mere inability to pay current debts).

BANKRUPTCY ACTS. Congressional legislation which was designed to coordinate the entire bankruptcy field. Thus bankruptcy is now declared by federal courts. Most of the acts deal with corporate, rather than personal, bankruptcy.

BANKRUPTCY BILL OF 1934. See FRAZIER-LEMKE BANKRUPTCY BILL.

BANKWIRE. An electronic communication network owned by an association of banks and used to transfer messages between subscribing banks.

BANQUE NATIONALE POUR LE COMMERCE ET L'INDUSTRIE (Fr.). One of the largest commercial banks in France, nationalized in 1945.

BAR CHART. Graph in which the values of a variable (quantity, frequency, etc.) are represented by the lengths of a series of bars. A bar chart could be used to show the amount of wheat shipped in each of a series of years.

BARGAINING AGENT. A union or other association of workers recognized by a government agency or management as the representative of a group of workers in collective bargaining.

BARGAINING RIGHT. The right of workers to negotiate, through chosen representatives, the terms and conditions of employment. Also the right of a union designated by a majority of workers to represent those workers in collective bargaining.

BARGAINING UNIT. A group of workers or employers determined by federal or state labor relations boards as appropriate for collective bargaining.

BAROMETER. A statistical measure that reflects the general state of economic or business activity or conditions. It is usually a single number formed by combining selected weighted statistics, and is often a LEADING INDICATOR.

BARTER. Trade that is conducted in goods and services, without MONEY. Trade and commerce are slow to grow under under a barter system, for several reasons:

1. To fully evaluate a good or service, it would be necessary to know its exchange rate in terms of every other good and service in the world. Money solves this impediment by serving as a *standard of value*.
2. There must be a coincidence of wants; each party wanting to trade must have exactly what the other wants, at a time when it is wanted. Money solves this impediment by serving as a *medium of exchange*.
3. Wealth in a barter system consists of commodities, some of which are perishable. Money solves this problem reasonably well by serving as a *store of value*.

BASE PAY. An individual's rate of pay for a normal work period. Actual pay may include overtime pay, bonus, and other premiums.

BASE PERIOD. When economic statistics are referred to a certain period of time, that time is called the *base period*. See CONSUMER PRICE INDEX.

In the field of unemployment insurance, *base period* refers to a period of time during which the claimant's earnings in covered employment determine both the weekly benefit and the total amount of benefits that can be received during the benefit year.

BASE RATE OF PAY. When an employee's compensation is figured on an incentive plan plus a minimum amount, that amount is often referred to as the *base rate*. Like other *rates*, it is assumed

to be per unit of time, such as dollars per hour or per week.

BASE YEAR. A specific year used as a BASE PERIOD.

BASIC CROPS. Collective term used to identify the crops which are controlled by price supports.

BASING-POINT SYSTEM. A practice in which all suppliers of a product quote shipping charges as if shipping were from one single location, even though they may actually ship from plants in various parts of the nation. This system is not acceptable in the U.S. because (1) it is prima facie evidence of collusive pricing arrangements and (2) it gives large suppliers an advantage over small local suppliers.

BEAR. In financial economics, an individual who makes investment decisions consistent with a feeling that the securities market will generally decline.

BEARER. In financial economics, the person in possession of a check or other instrument. If the instrument is considered to belong to the person who possesses it, it is known as *bearer paper*. Negotiable instruments which are *payable to bearer* do not provide any more protection than currency because anyone who finds or otherwise obtains them can convert them to cash.

BEGGAR-THY-NEIGHBOR POLICY. PROTECTIONISM, usually with the intention of improving domestic employment, but without concern that any such gain in employment in one nation must cause an opposite change in employment in the trading partner. When one nation adopts this policy, others often retaliate, maybe even going a step further. These steps can escalate to a trade war, with the result that world trade and worldwide employment are reduced.

BELL-SHAPED CURVE. The graph of a frequency distribution which looks like the silhouette of a bell. See NORMAL DISTRIBUTION.

BENEFIT-COST ANALYSIS. A technique used, especially by government, to determine if a large project should be undertaken. An attempt is made to project all benefits and all costs over the life of the project, if feasible, or for a long period of time. Opponents of benefit-cost analysis say that it is a time-consuming exercise with little value, because many numbers, such as the life of a large concrete dam, are pure guesses. In addition, they say that some figures, such as dollars, are easy to quantify, but others, such as convenience and pleasure, are subjective.

BENEFIT-RECEIVED PRINCIPLE. Principle holding that the burden of taxation and other costs of government should be borne by those who will receive the benefit of the resultant government spending. Programs which give government money to people who have no money would be obvious exceptions. According to this principle, pet license fees should be used just for animal regulation, gasoline taxes should only be used for highways and other expenditures for motorists, and facilities such as public parks should charge user fees which cover their costs. Opponents argue that the government's function of maximizing utility units requires the use of the ABILITY-TO-PAY PRINCIPLE. Also called *cost of service principle*.

BENEFIT YEAR. In the field of unemployment insurance, a one-year period following a claim filed by a worker indicating that a new period of unemployment is starting.

BENEFITS IN KIND. Welfare payments made by the government in a form other than cash, such as public housing, food stamps, and medical care.

BEST FIT. A graph line which, by estimation or by mathematical means, represents the closest approximation to a series of data points. See LEAST SQUARES; Mathematical Regression in the appendix.

BID. See SPREAD.

BIDDING. A procedure provided for in labor contracts under which an employer must notify employees of new job openings or vacancies that are available in the plant or industry. It further specifies that selection for each available job will be based upon seniority among the applicants qualified to perform it. The person selected is usually given time to learn the job.

BILATERAL MONOPOLY. An economic situation in which a single supplier (monopoly) and a single buyer (monopsony) are trading or negotiating.

BILL. An amount which is due to be paid. Also, a shortened expression for various instruments, such as BILL OF EXCHANGE and BILL OF LADING. Several entries in this dictionary give the meaning of specific types of bills which have come into popular use in commerce and economics. Often used synonomously with *invoice*.

BILL OF CREDIT. Paper currency which is printed without backing or security. Sometimes called *greenbacks* or *fiat money*.

BILL OF EXCHANGE. A financial instrument in which a *drawer* orders a *drawee* to pay a sum of money to a *payee*. This method of paying is generally used in international commerce. Also known as a *draft* or *acceptance*.

BILL OF LADING (BL or B/L). Document that forms a contract between shipper and carrier, as well as a receipt for the goods and claim document at destination.

BILL OF SALE. Document which records the fact that a sale took place, as well as such facts as the names of the parties, identification of goods, price, method of payment, and conditions for transfer of title.

BIMETAL STANDARD. A money system in which either or both of two precious metals (usually gold and silver) are kept as reserves to back the money supply. Authorities always specify the ratio at which the metals are used as *backing*. However, if the ratio of prices in another country differs by even a slight amount, international investors will draw all of one metal out of circulation.

BINDER. An agreement, usually documented, that makes a contract effective while a more formal agreement is being finalized or processed. Binders are commonly used in insurance contracts to provide immediate coverage.

BLACKLIST. A list of individuals or firms with whom circulators of the list are to refuse to do business. It may be a list of companies that hire nonunion labor. At one time workers who supported union activities were blacklisted so that employers could refuse to hire them.

BLACK MARKET. Illegal sale of a product. A black market can develop because a product (such as certain drugs) cannot be sold legally to the public. In addition, if the government sets a ceiling price which is below the EQUILIBRIUM PRICE, a shortage will develop and a black market often follows.

BLACK THURSDAY. October 24, 1929, generally accepted as the beginning of a long period of declining stock market prices. See STOCK MARKET CRASH.

BLANK BILL. A BILL OF EXCHANGE with the name of the seller temporarily left blank.

BLANK ENDORSEMENT. An endorsement on a negotiable instrument, consisting of only the signature of the transferor; opposed to a *restrictive endorsement*, which includes instructions (such as "for deposit only") or the name of the transferee. See also CONDITIONAL ENDORSEMENT; QUALIFIED ENDORSEMENT; RESTRICTIVE ENDORSEMENT; SPECIAL ENDORSEMENT.

BLANKET BILLS. Until 1929, U.S. paper currency measured 8.42 by 3.13 inches, now described as the "old, large size," or *blanket*, bills. In July 1929, the dimensions were changed to 6.14 by 2.61 inches.

BLOC. Cooperative influence among individuals who are concerned with legislation in a certain category. The term is sometimes used to identify legislators (such as congressional representatives) who vote in unison according to a bloc's self-interests. See FARM BLOC.

BLOCK GRANT. A nonspecific, or unconditional, grant, particularly a grant from the federal government. One issue in the *Economic Report of the President, 1982* is the consolidation of a number of categorical grant programs into block grant programs as the first in a series of steps toward revising the role of the central government in the Federal system.

BLUE EAGLE AGREEMENT. See NATIONAL RECOVERY ADMINISTRATION. *Blue Eagle Agreement* was the name used because of the emblem (featuring a dark blue eagle) issued to companies that participated in the program.

BLUE SKY LAWS. A series of state statutes which were passed to prevent fraudulent and misrepresented sales of securities to the uninformed public.

BOARD OF DIRECTORS. In the corporate form of business enterprise a board of directors is elected by the owners (stockholders) to serve as the top level in the corporate structure (see FORMS OF BUSINESS ORGANIZATION). The board sets major policy and appoints officers of the company, but usually takes no part in day-to-day management.

BOARD OF GOVERNORS (OF THE FEDERAL RESERVE SYSTEM). The apex of the FEDERAL RESERVE SYSTEM's organization is the Board of Governors in Washington, D.C., whose prime function involves the formulation of MONETARY POLICY. In addition, the Board has broad supervisory and regulatory responsibilities over the activities of commercial banks and the operations of FEDERAL RESERVE BANKS.

Members of the Board constitute a majority of the FEDERAL OPEN MARKET COMMITTEE, which is the most important monetary-policy-making body. In addition to functioning as part of the Open Market Committee, the Board establishes reserve requirements for member banks, reviews and approves DISCOUNT RATE actions of the Federal Reserve banks, issues regulations governing the administration of the discount window at those banks, establishes ceiling rates of interest that member banks may pay on deposits, and sets margin requirements for credit purchases in the stock market.

The Board's responsibilities include the foreign activities of member banks, and the operations of the Federal Reserve banks. It also administers the law that regulates activities of bank holding companies.

The Board is an agency of the federal government. It consists of seven members appointed by the president of the U.S. and confirmed by the Senate. Board members are appointed for terms of 14 years, and their terms are arranged so that one expires every 2 years. A member may not be reappointed after serving a full term. The president names the chairman and vice chairman of the Board from among the Board members. They serve 4-year terms and may be redesignated.

BOARD OF INQUIRY. A group appointed by the president under authority granted in the TAFT-HARTLEY ACT to study labor disputes that pose a threat of national emergency and to make recommendations.

BOLSHEVIKS (U.S.S.R). Revolutionaries who wanted to overthrow the Soviet government through DICTATORSHIP OF THE PROLETARIAT, as opposed to the *Mensheviks,* who advocated first a government of the BOURGEOISIE, expecting it to be replaced in a revolution of the PROLETARIAN CLASS.

BOND. An instrument of debt, sold by organizations in both the industrial and government SECTORs. There are many varieties of bonds, but most are sold in units of $1000, have stated maturity dates, and earn stated amounts of interest. See *Concise Desk Book of Business Finance* (Englewood Cliffs, N.J.: Prentice-Hall, 1984) for a description of types of bonds.

BOND MARKET. See MONEY MARKET.

BOND RATINGS. An assessment of bonds that is based on the likelihood that the issuer will be able to pay both interest as due, and principal upon maturity. Two organizations, Moody's Investors Service, Inc. and Standard & Poor's Corporation, provide the majority of ratings. They are given in alphabetical codes as shown in the accompanying table. See also RISK.

	Moody's		Standard & Poor's
Aaa	Highest grade	AAA	Highest grade
Aa	High grade	AA	High grade
A	Higher medium grade	A	Upper medium grade
Baa	Lower medium grade	BBB	Medium grade
Ba	Somewhat speculative	BB	Lower medium grade
B	Speculative	B	Speculative
Caa	Very speculative	CCC	Outright speculative
Ca	Highly speculative	CC	Outright speculative
C	Income bond; not paying interest	C	Income bond; not paying interest
Daa	In default; some salvage value	DDD	In default; some salvage value
Da	In default	DD	In default
D	In default; minimal salvage value	D	In default; minimal salvage value

BONUS. A payment in addition to that which is expected; often applied to wages. It may be a one-time bonus—for example, when an employer announces that, because the previous year's profits were good, all employees (or certain ones—

labor contracts often prohibit the employer from any action that is not negotiated through the union) will receive a bonus. A bonus may be built in, as when a sales representative receives a new car every year in which his or her sales exceed a certain amount. Finally, pay for dangerous work, night work, travel, or other special assignment is also called a bonus.

BONUS INTEREST. Describes interest that savings institutions pay from the 1st of the month for money deposited by the 10th of the month. The practice was very popular in the 1970s. A less frequent practice is the paying of interest on money that has been withdrawn during the last three days of a business quarter.

BONUS STOCK. Stock which is given free. A common example is a purchase agreement which states that a buyer of a certain number of shares of *common stock* (see CAPITAL STOCK) will receive free one share of *preferred stock*. Stock given in return for services rendered, such as helping organize the corporation and obtaining its charter, is also called bonus stock.

BOOK-ENTRY SYSTEM. Serious problems may be encountered in the physical transfer of securities between banks and dealers, between dealers and other investors, or in the storage of securities. To help resolve such problems, the Federal Reserve banks and the U.S. Treasury have instituted a computerized book-entry system. In this system, ownership of U.S. Treasury and certain federal agency securities is recorded on the books of the Federal Reserve banks, and transfers may be effected without the necessity of transporting the securities. Use of the Federal Reserve's communications system in combination with the book-entry system provides an efficient and secure method of transferring ownership of government and agency securities and for making interest payments.

BOOK VALUE. The value of a business asset as shown on the accounts—usually purchase price minus accumulated depreciation. Book value is not necessarily the same as *market value*—the amount the firm would receive if it sold the asset. Book value is sometimes used as an approximation for market value, especially if the asset is not regularly traded and there is no way of knowing what the market value is until it is sold.

BOOM. A rapid (and usually unstable) expansion of the economy in general or a particular part of it. A boom usually involves rising incomes, a plentiful supply of jobs, and inflation, and it is frequently followed by a *bust*

BOOTLEG WAGES. Generally, wages higher than labor contract requirements, paid by an employer to secure critical skills when unemployment is low and it is difficult to fill vacancies.

BORROWED RESERVES. The amount of reserves which originated, not from banks, but by borrowing from the FEDERAL RESERVE SYSTEM (see BANK RESERVES; RESERVE BALANCE; DISCOUNT RATE). When borrowed reserves are subtracted from excess reserves, the result is *free reserves*. If the result is a negative number, they are *net borrowed reserves*.

BOTTLENECK INFLATION. An inflation which results from a shortage in a particular SECTOR of the economy. If the output of that sector cannot be bypassed, the shortage will cause price increases. These increases, which are then passed on to buyers, cause other shortages or price increases or both until a general inflation results. Also called *sectoral inflation*.

BOTTOMRY BOND. A BOND whose indenture agreement provides security for its owners in the form of a mortgage on a ship.

BOURGEOISIE. The class of people identified in Marxist doctrine as living off the labors of the PROLETARIAN CLASS, meaning that the latter does not receive the full benefits it is entitled to for selling the only ECONOMIC RESOURCE it has—its labor.

BOURSE (Fr.). A stock market or securities marketplace.

BOYCOTT. Planned refusal to deal with a party in order to force certain concessions—usually economic concessions. It can involve a nation's refusing, by law or popular action, the goods and services of another (see also EMBARGO). It can also be as localized as the tenants of an apartment refusing to buy at a certain store.

In labor economics, there are a variety of boycotts, all related to a general refusal to deal with an employer:

1. *Consumer boycott.* Refusal to purchase the goods of an employer
2. *Primary boycott.* Boycott by employees of their employer
3. *Product boycott.* Refusal by employees to handle or work with goods owned or manufactured by someone other than their own employer, in order to place indirect pressure on the owner or manufacturer
4. *Secondary boycott.* Refusal to deal with a neutral party; usually accompanied by a demand that the neutral party bring pressure upon an employer to accede to its union's demands.

BRACKET CREEP. The situation in which incomes rise due to inflation, and that rise puts taxpayers in higher income tax brackets so that a larger percentage of their income is automatically paid to governments. The result, even without deficit spending, is that the relative size of the government sector increases. INDEXING of tax brackets is a means of decreasing this problem.

BRANCH BANK. A banking location separate from the home location. When figures are given on the number of banks in the nation, branches are not counted, even though they may be significant in number. Reserve requirements (see BANK RESERVES) are applied collectively to a banking firm and all its branches. State laws vary greatly, ranging from *unit banking laws* which prohibit branch banking to laws that allow the practice without limit.

BRANDT COMMISSION REPORT. The result of one of the investigations into problems of the LESS DEVELOPED COUNTRIES.

BRASSAGE. The cost of making coins out of bullion. See also MINTAGE.

BREADBASKET. Generally, a nation or an area that others depend on for supplying food.

BREAK-EVEN POINT. The quantity of production at which all costs allocated to a product are equal to all revenues from its sale. At quantities smaller than the break-even point, there is a net loss; at larger quantities, there is a profit, assuming the usual condition of total revenue increasing faster than total costs.

BRETTON WOODS. A milestone conference attended by 44 nations at Bretton Woods, New Hampshire, in June 1944 to prepare for the reconstructions which would be needed after World War II. The INTERNATIONAL MONETARY FUND and the INTERNATIONAL BANK FOR RECONSTRUCTION AND DEVELOPMENT were established at this meeting. See also BANCOR.

BRICK. See CURRENCY MANUFACTURE.

BROAD MARKET. A day on the stock exchange when large numbers of securities are bought and sold but cannot be identified with particular industries.

BUBBLE. A speculative venture on an unsound basis, with a high probability of yielding nothing.

BUDGET. Generally, a plan by which monetary expenditures for a selected time in the future are organized to show what inflows will be available to meet the outflows. A *capital budget* shows the planned expenditures and sources of funds for purchases of *capital goods*. The word also has nonmonetary applications; a *manpower budget*, for example, shows how needs and availabilities will be matched. See also BALANCED BUDGET.

BUDGET AND ACCOUNTING ACT. Legislation of 1921 which set forth requirements for the preparation of a federal budget and established a Bureau of the Budget in the executive branch to administer the budget. The bureau's name was later changed to Office of Management and Budget (OMB). See also CONGRESSIONAL BUDGET AND IMPOUNDMENT CONTROL ACT.

BUDGET LINE. See EXCHANGE OPPORTUNITIES LINE.

BUDGET OFFICE. The Congressional Budget Office. It is an organization which provides to the legislative branch information pertaining to the budget, appropriations bills, or tax expenditures, as well as receipts, revenue estimates, and changing revenue conditions. See CONGRESSIONAL BUDGET AND IMPOUNDMENT CONTROL ACT.

BUFFER STOCK PLAN. A plan which is suggested repeatedly, with variations, as a means of smoothing out peaks and valleys in ECONOMIC FLUCTUATIONS. It calls for building inventories during recessionary periods (in order to create additional employment) and drawing down inventories in inflationary periods.

BUILDING AND LOAN ASSOCIATION. A name previously used for SAVINGS AND LOAN ASSOCIATION.

BUILT-IN STABILIZER. An economic force which tends to dampen fluctuations of the economy about its long-run growth path through COUNTERCYCLICAL effects. For example, a PROGRESSIVE TAX reduces the spending power of consumers in amounts which change faster than incomes, resulting in contractionary tendencies during expansionary periods, and vice versa.

BULL. In financial economics, an individual who makes investment decisions consistent with the belief that the securities market will generally rise.

BULLION. An ingot or bar of precious metal, such as gold or silver, in a very pure form.

BUMPING. In labor economics, the practice of exercising seniority rights during periods of layoff. If management must lay off employees as a result of loss of business, labor contracts usually specify that the worker last hired must be the first laid off. When the person with the least seniority in a department is given notice, he or she can bump someone with less seniority in a department in which he or she is qualified to work. It is also possible to use seniority to transfer from one work shift to another. See also BACKTRACK.

BURDEN. Gross cost of government, measured in terms of goods and services *not* produced by the private sector because ECONOMIC RESOURCES are limited. See also EXCESS BURDEN.

BUREAU OF ENGRAVING AND PRINTING. The world's largest securities manufacturing establishment, in Washington, D.C. The bureau employs 3,000 people and operates 24 hours a day. It designs, engraves, and prints U.S. paper currency; Treasury bonds, bills, notes, and certificates of indebtedness; U.S. postage and revenue stamps; and miscellaneous engraved items for approximately 75 departments and independent agencies of the federal government and its insular possessions. White House invitations, certificates, identification cards, and liquor strip stamps are some of the approximately 800 miscellaneous products printed by the bureau.

BUREAU OF THE BUDGET. Former name for OFFICE OF MANAGEMENT AND BUDGET. See also CONGRESSIONAL BUDGET AND IMPOUNDMENT CONTROL ACT.

BUREAU OF THE MINT. A division of the Treasury Department, with main offices in Washington, D.C., the bureau is responsible for producing coins. The Philadelphia Mint has been in continuous operation since it was authorized by the Coinage Act of 1792. It moved into a modern and highly efficient plant in 1969. Also known simply as "the mint."

BUSINESS AGENT. In labor economics, the person who represents the workers in negotiations with management. This individual is usually responsible for enforcing the resultant contract.

BUSINESS CYCLES. Variations above and below the trend line of an economy. Economies are constantly varying; depending upon the size and direction of an excursion, it may be defined as a RECESSION, DEPRESSION, INFLATION, or some other label. Because *cycle* suggests regularity and repeatability, and because reference is being made to the entire economy rather than just to the business sector, many economists prefer the expression ECONOMIC FLUCTUATIONS.

BUSINESS SECTOR. Economists divide the economy into three main sectors: consumer, business (also called industrial sector), and government. While it is recognized that economic units in all three sectors have much in common (all buy and sell; have inputs, outputs, and budgets; consume goods and services), grouping according to goals and motivations is highly significant because of the effect on economic decisions.

Most of the business sector is motivated by profit, and its long-run goal is survival and profit maximization. A subdivision of the business sector is the nonprofit organizations, and although their goals vary, they are usually centered about the function (medical research, private school, help the needy, etc.) they have to perform. See SECTOR.

BUSINESS TRANSFER PAYMENTS. In NATIONAL INCOME AND PRODUCT ACCOUNTS, money paid by the

BUSINESS SECTOR to persons for whom no goods or services are received at the time. Typical items included are corporate gifts to nonprofit institutions, consumer bad debts, and personal injury payments by businesses to persons other than employees. Estimates of unrecovered thefts of cash and capital assets, cash prizes, and similar items are included.

BUYERS' INFLATION. See DEMAND-PULL INFLATION.

BUYERS' MARKET. A period of time when the economy is characterized by excess supply. Can be applied to a single product or to an entire industry or economy. Because of the excess supply, competition among sellers will be intense; prices will be low or sellers will include additional services or both.

Strictly speaking, buyers are in command during a buyers' market. Therefore, the mere fact of a surplus that does not sell does not qualify the period as a buyers' market if the surplus is due to a slow economy or the buyers' inability to buy.

BUYERS' STRIKE. An organized refusal to buy certain products or to buy from a certain seller. In its usual form, a buyers' strike occurs when consumers, behind some leadership, forego all, or a significant part, of their regular purchases with the intention of forcing retailers to reduce prices.

BUYER'S SURPLUS. When an individual obtains a product at a price lower than the maximum he or she is willing to pay, the difference is the *buyer's surplus*. A DEMAND SCHEDULE (see also SUPPLY AND DEMAND) shows that at every point there is a buyer's surplus for some individual.

BYRNES ACT. Legislation of 1936 that prohibits interstate transportation of individuals for the purpose of using force or threats against lawful striking and picketing. Also known as the Anti-Strikebreaking Act.

C

CAISSE DES DEPOTS ET CONSIG-NATIONS (Fr.). The largest organization in France for generating liquidity. Most of its funds are loaned, through local and specialized lending organizations, for financing housing for low income families. In addition, it loans to different levels of government, it provides financing for specific projects at the local level, and it provides general financing through treasury bills and government bonds.

CALL. A right exercised, for example, when authorities require a financial statement from a bank (see BANK CALL), when additional payment is demanded on a partly paid stock subscription, or when a corporation "calls in an issue" (i.e., retires a securities issue). In the securities markets, *call* describes the option which gives an investor the privilege of buying up to a specified quantity of a security at a specified price; this type of call expires if not exercised within a specified time period. See also PUT; TAX AND LOAN ACCOUNT.

CALLABLE BOND. A BOND whose issuer has retained the right to retire all or part of the issue prior to maturity. In effect, the debtor has the right to pay off the loan early. The indenture specifies conditions under which the bonds may be called, time limitations, and prices.

CALLABLE PREFERRED STOCK. Preferred stock (see CAPITAL STOCK) which gives the issuing corporation the right to retire all or part of the outstanding shares by paying the stockholders according to a prearranged schedule.

CALL-IN PAY. The minimum which an employer promises to pay an employee who is asked to report to work. For example, if, because of a special meeting, a guard is asked to come from home to unlock a gate, it would not be fair to pay the guard for just the 30 seconds the task takes, so a minimum reporting pay is established. Also called *reporting pay*.

CALL LOAN. A loan which is in principle for one day but is often extended on a day-to-day basis at the same interest rate. In effect, then, it becomes a short-term loan for which repayment can be demanded on 24 hours' notice. Also called a *demand loan*.

CAMBRIDGE SCHOOL. A school of economic thought that began in the latter part of the 19th century. It is characterized by a re-evaluation of the ideas of the CLASSICAL SCHOOL and an updating of technical methods of analysis. One of its main deviations from the classical school is a decreasing dependence on LAISSEZ-FAIRE, or leaving control of an economy to natural forces. ALFRED MARSHALL (1842-1924), a professor of economics at Cambridge University, and his book *Prin-*

ciples of Economics (1890) are associated with this area of economic thought. Also called *neoclassical school*.

CANCUN SUMMIT. One of a series of international meetings attended by leaders of many nations, the Cancun summit was held in Mexico in October 1981. At the conference, President Reagan put forth the following principles for policy development, as listed in the *1982 Economic Report of the President*:

1. stimulating international trade by opening up markets
2. tailoring particular development strategies to specific needs and regions
3. guiding assistance toward the development of self-sustaining productive capacities
4. improving the climate in many developing countries for private investment and technology transfer
5. creating a political climate in which practical solutions can move forward rather than founder on the reef of government policies that interfere unnecessarily with the marketplace.

CAPACITY. See MANUFACTURING CAPACITY.

CAPILLARITY, LAW OF. The proposition that individuals will hold down family size in order to raise their own standard of living. This law credits people with rational thinking, but just the opposite has been evident throughout man's existence on earth. Today there is some evidence of a decreasing rate of population growth, but the reasons are more environmental than economic.

The practice actually seen is the IRON LAW OF WAGES, which holds that REAL INCOME has little hope of rising because people tend to increase family size rather than take advantage of impending increases in real income.

CAPITAL. Also known as *capital goods*. See ECONOMIC RESOURCES; CAPITAL FUNDS.

CAPITAL ACCOUNT. In accounting for BALANCE OF INTERNATIONAL PAYMENTS, the U.S. keeps a *capital account* which records the import and export of assets such as bonds and common stocks. More precisely, if the import or export of anything represents a change in claims, then its value is entered in the capital account.

Unlike other accounts, this traditionally concentrates on the flow of payment rather than on the asset. For example, when a bond is sold (exported) to another nation, the payment, called *capital inflow*, is entered as a credit in the capital account. Importing a bond would result in a *capital outflow*.

CAPITAL ACCUMULATION. A statistic maintained for each sector of the economy, it is the value of CAPITAL GOODS added. This item is watched by analysts because it forms the basis for productivity increases and economic growth. Also called *capital formation*.

CAPITAL ASSETS. Property that has value and is expected to last for a relatively long period of time. In the consumer SECTOR this expression can refer to major appliances, and in the business sector it generally refers to CAPITAL GOODS. In some writings, *capital asset* refers to the subject of an infrequent transaction, as opposed to an *ordinary asset*, in which an individual deals regularly.

CAPITAL BUDGET. A BUDGET which is limited to showing planned expenditures and sources of funds for purchases of CAPITAL GOODS.

CAPITAL CONSUMPTION ALLOWANCES (CCA). Sometimes defined simply as depreciation, a more complete definition is accounting charges which reflect estimates of wear and tear, obsolescence, destruction, and accidental losses of physical capital. The three components which make up the capital consumption allowances figure in NATIONAL INCOME AND PRODUCT ACCOUNTS are business depreciation charges, depreciation of owner-occupied dwellings, and accidental damage to fixed business capital. Allowances for depletion of natural resources are not included. See also GROSS NATIONAL PRODUCT; DEPLETION ALLOWANCE.

CAPITAL CONTROLS PROGRAM. A series of measures taken in the early 1970s to strengthen the U.S. dollar in world markets. The program had three main controls: (1) the Interest Equalization Tax (imposed on U.S. purchases of foreign securities), (2) limitations on overseas lending by U.S. banks, and (3) controls on overseas investments by U.S. corporations. The entire program was terminated in 1974.

CAPITAL DEEPENING. A change toward becoming more CAPITAL INTENSIVE, with the result that a larger percentage of total costs will be capital costs, while land, labor, or both will be a decreasing percentage of total costs. Sometimes the expression refers specifically to labor, meaning that each worker, on the average, works with more capital equipment.

Other expressions are similar but have subtle differences. *Capital quickening* refers to increasing sophistication of capital equipment, usually with regard to automation, and *capital widening* refers to an increase in capital goods that is keeping pace with an increasing number of workers.

CAPITAL EXPENDITURE. A monetary outflow for the purpose of obtaining industrial DURABLE GOODS.

CAPITAL FORMATION. See CAPITAL ACCUMULATION.

CAPITAL FUNDS. Liquid, or spendable, assets of a business (see LIQUIDITY). In popular use *capital* often has this same meaning, but to economists the latter refers to that ECONOMIC RESOURCE which is manufactured to assist production.

CAPITAL GAINS. Income which results from the sale of a capital asset for a higher price than was paid for it. One reason for distinguishing between this type of income and wages and salaries is that the types of income are charged different rates for income taxes.

CAPITAL GOODS. Items, such as machines, buildings, and roads, manufactured to assist production. As an ECONOMIC RESOURCE, *capital* is synonymous with capital goods.

CAPITAL INFLOW. See CAPITAL ACCOUNT.

CAPITAL INTENSIVE. Indicates that a relatively large percentage of total costs are capital; for example, the steel industry is capital intensive. Other industries or products might be described as *labor intensive* or *land intensive*.

CAPITALISM. An economic system characterized by the following:

1. There is private ownership of the means of production.
2. There is private ownership of property.
3. Questions, such as what will be produced and who will receive the output, are answered in the MARKETPLACE.
4. The main function of the government is to see that fair and free competition continues.

Pure capitalism, which has never existed, assumes these characteristics in pure form; *mixed capitalism*, the practical form found in today's capitalist nations, adapts compromises in the characteristics. For example, under pure capitalism, SOCIAL GOODS would be provided by private enterprise and would be found only where there is a market for them such that suppliers earn at least NORMAL PROFIT on their investment.

CAPITALIZATION BANKS (Mex.). See MEXICAN BANKING SYSTEM.

CAPITAL LEVY. A noncash tax. When imposed today, it is usually because the taxpayer has assets but not in the form of cash. In America the first tax (imposed by the House of Burgesses in Virginia, chartered by the London Company) consisted of 10 pounds of tobacco, to be paid by every male.

CAPITAL LIABILITY. A liability which arises from the financing of CAPITAL GOODS.

CAPITAL MOVEMENT. Using the proceeds from liquidating capital goods to obtain different capital goods or to obtain capital goods in a different place. Usually applies to international trade.

CAPITAL OUTFLOW. See CAPITAL ACCOUNT.

CAPITAL-OUTPUT RATIO. Ratio of the change in capital investment (net of gross investment minus CAPITAL CONSUMPTION ALLOWANCES) to the change in output. If a certain industry adds $2.5 million net to its capital equipment and its yearly output increases by $1 million, that industry has a capital-output ratio of 2.5:1. Because this ratio deals with changes only, it is often called *incremental capital-output ratio*.

CAPITAL PAID IN. With regard to the CONSOLIDATED STATEMENT OF CONDITION OF ALL FEDERAL RESERVE BANKS, the amount paid for Federal Reserve bank capital stock. All member banks are shareholders by law (Federal Reserve Act, Section 5) and must subscribe to shares of the Reserve bank of their district in an amount equal to 6 percent of their own paid-up capital stock and surplus. Of this amount, one-half must be paid in, and the other half remains subject to CALL by the Board of Governors. When a member bank changes its own capital or surplus, its ownership of Reserve Bank stock must be altered accordingly. [Adapted from *Glossary: Weekly Federal Reserve Statements*, by the Federal Reserve Bank of New York.]

CAPITAL QUICKENING. See CAPITAL DEEPENING.

CAPITAL RENT. Payment made by the user of a CAPITAL GOOD to the owner. See RENT.

CAPITAL SAVING. A lowering of CAPITAL's percentage in total costs of a product, usually because of the introduction of more efficient equipment. See also CAPITAL DEEPENING; CAPITAL INTENSIVE; LABOR SAVING.

CAPITAL STOCK. Ownership shares of a corporation. There are two general classifications of capital stock: (1) *common stock*, which carries voting privileges but does not include any promise regarding payment of DIVIDENDS and (2) *preferred stock* (also called *preference* or *prior* stock), which generally reverses these benefits. Since a corporation cannot know that it will make a profit with which to pay a dividend, preferred stock is further divided into *cumulative preferred* and *noncumulative preferred*; if the corporation misses paying a dividend to holders of the former, such a dividend must be paid before any payments can be made to common stockholders.

CAPITAL WIDENING. See CAPITAL DEEPENING.

CAPITATION TAX. A tax levied in a fixed amount on every person (sometimes every male), with certain exceptions, such as indigent persons. Collections are sometimes facilitated by combining them with a common function such as voting. Also called a *head tax* or a *poll tax*.

CAPTIVE MARKET. A situation stronger than a monopoly in that not only is there only one seller of the product, but there is a reason why the buyer cannot refuse to buy.

CAPTIVE PRODUCER. A producing company that is owned by a company that uses all or most of its output. See VERTICAL COMBINATION.

CARIBBEAN COMMISSION. Comprising France, the Netherlands, the U.K., and the U.S., a commission formed 1942 to improve trade and other relations among nations of the Caribbean Sea.

CARLOAD (CL). A shipment of goods that occupies an entire railroad car. See also LESS THAN CARLOAD.

CAR LOADINGS. The number of freight cars which were loaded during a reporting period (often 1 month). This statistic is often used, either by itself or as a component of a more inclusive measure, to evaluate economic activity.

CARRY. When an interest-bearing asset is pledged as collateral for a loan, the borrower is entitled to the interest earned, even while the security is in possession of the lender. When the debtor is able to keep borrowing costs below the interest received on the securities, it is said that the debtor "earns a return on the carry," or has a "positive carry." This term is especially applicable to nonbank dealers in government securities with COMMERCIAL BANKs and the FEDERAL OPEN MARKET COMMITTEE.

CARRY BACK. To apply losses from one year to a previous year's accounting for the purpose of calculating income taxes.

CARRY-OVER. Amounts to be spent on projects which are committed and already under way. Certain industries typically can be expected to have larger carry-overs than others—for example, public utilities—because so much of the capital equipment they purchase is special and has long lead times.

When applied to taxes, carry-over refers to applying losses from one year to the accounts of one or more future years.

CARTEL. A formal association of business firms that would otherwise be competitors. Cartels are illegal in the U.S. and the U.K. because they are effectively monopolies; their legality varies in other nations. Where they are allowed, their agreements on selling prices, output quotas, territories, and other items are legally enforceable.

CASCADE TAX. A tax levied at several stages of the manufacturing process. The word *cascade* is used because the tax at each stage becomes part of the base for figuring the tax at the next stage. Better known as a TURNOVER TAX.

CASH. With regard to the CONSOLIDATED STATEMENT OF CONDITION OF ALL FEDERAL RESERVE BANKS, coin and currency on hand in the FEDERAL RESERVE BANKS and branches, except gold certificates and FEDERAL RESERVE NOTES. Nearly all cash is coin; however, it also includes a very small amount of U.S. notes, which are still issued by the Treasury, and paper currencies, such as silver certificates, which are being retired.

The Consolidated Statement excludes all Federal Reserve notes issued by one Reserve bank and held by another from this item and from the liability account "Federal Reserve notes." The amount excluded appears in parentheses to the left of the figures on the cash line and on the Federal Reserve notes line.

[Adapted from *Glossary: Weekly Federal Reserve Statements*. Federal Reserve Bank of New York.]

CASH BASIS. This expression has the same meaning in economics as it does in accounting; revenues and expenditures are recognized when payment is made for a transaction. This method contrasts with *accrual basis*, in which revenues and expenditures are recognized when the transaction takes place.

CASH BEFORE DELIVERY (CBD). If used in a sales contract, CBD means that the seller is required to prepare the goods as specified and the seller's obligation continues to the point of delivery to the buyer; the seller then has the right to receive full payment before tendering the goods to the buyer.

CASH CIRCUIT. The circular flow of currency from the original bank of issue, usually through a disburser, and retailer, back to the bank. The term is most significant in Eastern European economies, where currency normally returns to a CENTRAL BANK after one trip directly through the circuit and the intermingling of monies in the cash and the NONCASH CIRCUITs is less likely. Also called *currency circuit*. [See George Garvey, *Money, Banking, and Credit in Eastern Europe* (New York: Federal Reserve Bank of New York, 1966).]

CASH DELIVERY. In the buying and selling of government securities as part of open market operations (see FEDERAL OPEN MARKET COMMITTEE), transactions that call for *cash delivery* require payment and delivery the same day; transactions for *regular delivery* involve payment and delivery on the following business day.

CASH DRAIN. See LEAKAGES; MONEY SUPPLY EXPANSION MULTIPLIER.

CASHIER'S CHECK. A check for which a financial institution is both DRAWEE and DRAWER. A person who does not have a checking account but needs a check can take cash into the institution and, usually for a charge, have a cashier's check prepared. Even those who have checking accounts often obtain a cashier's check; cash is specifically set aside for each one, and a PAYEE is likely to accept a cashier's check as readily as cash.

CASH IN ADVANCE (CIA). When included as part of a sales contract, CIA means that the seller has no obligations until the buyer pays the entire contract price.

CASH ITEMS IN PROCESS OF COLLECTION (CIPC). Checks and other cash items (for example, U.S. postal money orders and food stamp coupons) that have been deposited with the Federal Reserve banks as of the date of a statement for collection by the banks on behalf of either member or nonmember commercial banks. These items always exceed in amount their counterpart—*deferred availability cash items*—on the liability side of the accounting statement. That is because many

checks presented by Reserve banks are not collected by the time their reserve accounts are credited—Reserve banks must, by current regulation, credit member banks within 2 days. The difference between the two acounts is a measure of a type of Federal Reserve credit called *float*, which the Reserve banks generate in rendering collection services to member banks. [Adapted from *The Federal Reserve System Purposes and Functions*.]

CASHLESS/CHECKLESS SOCIETY. The ultimate arrangement as envisioned by some planners; all monetary assets would be recorded by computer, and all transfers (payments) would be electronic, without any physical possession or movement of money. See POINT OF SALE; ELECTRONIC MONEY. In recent years, several study programs and pilot projects have shown that practical limitations prevent society from ever being completely cashless/checkless; for some the goal is now called the *less-cash/less-check* society.

CASH ON DELIVERY (COD). A shipping arrangement which gives the shipper the right to withhold goods from the buyer until the latter pays for them. It is not considered to be a credit transaction, and seldom involves a credit check.

CASH WITH ORDER (CWO). Sometimes incorporated in a sales contract, CWO requires that the buyer pay the full contract amount before the seller will undertake any part of his obligation by preparing the material for delivery.

CASUAL WORKER. One who is on call to work when a regular worker is unable to report or when the work load temporarily requires more than the regular staff. A casual worker is usually paid only for time worked, although some arrangements provide a retainer just for being available, a minimum per month, or both. See also CALL-IN PAY.

CATEGORICAL GRANT. A grant, usually from the federal government to a state or local government, with restrictions as to its use. See also BLOCK GRANT.

CAVEAT EMPTOR (Lat.). "Let the buyer beware." This doctrine has little application to modern transactions because it places all responsibility on the buyer for discovering any defects, variations, or unacceptable parts of the merchandise or of the transaction itself. Once the sale is agreed upon, the buyer has no recourse.

CAVEAT VENDITOR (Lat.). "Let the seller beware." This doctrine places all responsibility on the seller for discovering anything unsatisfactory about the transaction or the merchandise involved.

CEDULAS HIPOTECARIAS (Mex.). See MEXICAN BANKING SYSTEM.

CEILING PRICE. A maximum price which may be charged, regardless of what price would be reached through the natural forces of SUPPLY AND DEMAND. Ceiling prices are usually ordered by government authorities, and result in shortages. See BLACK MARKET.

CELLER-KEFAUVER ACT. See CLAYTON ANTITRUST ACT.

CENTRAL BANK. A bank that coordinates the money and banking functions of a nation. Originally the primary responsibility for central banks was the handling of the nation's international reserves, but today they are responsible for nearly all functions considered part of MONETARY POLICY. The U.S. central bank is the FEDERAL RESERVE SYSTEM.

CENTRAL INSTITUTION. A form of monetary authority in several countries which exercises supervisory power over specialized credit institutions and/or provides certain services to them, such as lending and rediscounting. Transactions between central institutions and their members are frequent and sizable, and the members tend to hold the bulk of their redundant funds with the institutions. In some instances, such as in Italy and Sweden, the affiliated credit institutions (such as credit cooperatives) may keep all or part of the required reserves with their respective central institutions.

CENTRALIZATION. In management economics, a gathering of operations and decision-making authority in one place. For example, the expression "purchasing is centralized," means that all purchase orders are issued by one purchasing department and that all divisions or subsidiaries will obtain their purchased items through that department.

CENTRALLY PLANNED ECONOMY. An economy in which questions basic to all economics (such as what items will be produced, in what quantities, and at what prices) are answered deliberately by central authorities. In a way, a centrally planned economy is the direct opposite of pure CAPITALISM, where the questions are answered in the MARKETPLACE. Advocates of capitalism point to the efficiency of having these questions answered by the INVISIBLE HAND of the marketplace: the resulting goods and services will be more satisfying (see UTILITY UNITS) because they are in response to consumer demand, and every act of intervention into the natural forces of SUPPLY AND DEMAND sets off the need for a series of other actions to correct the distortions thus created. In addition, they point out that massive shortages do not occur, nor is there waste through overproduction of unwanted items, except for situations which can be explained as departures from marketplace decisions. Advocates of central planning (typically COMMUNISM) claim that decision-making and allocation are inefficient when made by consumers who are more concerned with self interest than with overall economic growth. They point out that, by shifting the nation's productive effort toward CAPITAL GOODS for a period of time, the sacrifices made by consumers will be repaid manyfold in later years because the capital intensive economy so created will be able to produce more consumer goods.

CENTRAL ORGANIZATION OF SAL-ARIED EMPLOYEES (Swed.). A confederation of labor unions, mostly of non-production workers such as supervisors and office staffs. Its members are employed in private as well as government jobs.

CENTRAL RESERVE CITY BANK. See DESIGNATION OF BANKS.

CENTRAL STATISTICAL ADMINIS-TRATION (U.S.S.R.). An agency which collects and analyzes economic data. One of the main users of these data is GOS-PLAN.

CERTIFICADOS FINANCIEROS (Mex.). See MEXICAN BANKING SYSTEM.

CERTIFICATE OF DEPOSIT (CD). A time deposit which cannot be withdrawn prior to the date specified without a monetary penalty. Such deposits are available from both thrift institutions and banks and can be purchased by individuals as well as in large amounts by corporations. See also MONEY.

CERTIFICATE OF INCORPORA-TION. Document that formally indicates the approval of state corporation authorities for the creation of a corporation. See also FORMS OF BUSINESS ORGA-NIZATION.

CERTIFICATE OF INDEBTEDNESS. A government document issued when short-term funds are borrowed.

CERTIFICATE OF NECESSITY. Document used by the federal government during the Korean War to grant an individual corporation's fast tax write-offs for the purchase of capital equipment considered crucial to meet the emergency.

CERTIFICATE OF ORIGIN. A customs document which formally records the country where a shipment of goods originated.

CERTIFICATION. In labor economics, the official designation of a union as the bargaining representative for employees in a particular bargaining unit.

CERTIFIED CHECK. A check which the DRAWER takes to the financial institution that has his or her account so that the institution can set aside from this account the amount of the check. Even if the account is then overdrawn, that amount is kept for paying that particular check; thus it will be more readily accepted by the PAYEE.

CERTIFIED UNION. In labor economics, a union which has been designated by federal or state labor relations boards as the exclusive bargaining agent for a group of employees.

CETERIS PARIBUS (Lat.). Other things being equal. This phrase is important in economics because there are always innumerable forces affecting every aspect of the economy, and no amount of detail could make an investigation truly represent the economy.

CHAIN BANKING. The actual control of a group of ostensibly independent banks by an organization which may or may not be another bank. Also called *group banking*. See also BANK HOLDING COMPANY.

CHAIN STORE. One of a group of retail outlets which belong to the same organization. The stores may or may not all have the same name, although most chains known to the public do. Some writers also refer to FRANCHISE operations as chain stores.

CHAMBER OF COMMERCE (C of C). An organization made up of local businesses (and sometimes local government) to promote and improve the quality of business relations within an area and with other areas. Most cities in the U.S. have a chamber of commerce; many of them concentrate on commercial interfacing with the rest of the world, by promoting tourism and exports and by getting involved with businesses moving into the area.

CHAMBER OF COMMERCE AND IN-DUSTRY (Jap.: NISHO). A large business organization to which Japanese companies and other associations belong. Its main purposes include correlation of business activities and influence of economic policies.

CHANGE IN BUSINESS INVENTO-RIES. A component of *gross private domestic investment,* which is used in NATIONAL INCOME AND PRODUCT ACCOUNTS, this statistic represents the value of the increase or decrease in the physical stock of goods held by businesses. Included are raw materials, semifinished goods, and finished goods ready for sale or shipment. An inventory increase is regarded as a positive investment because it represents production not matched by current consumption; an inventory decrease is regarded as a negative investment because it reflects consumption in excess of current production. Because changes in inventories are counted as investment, they are sometimes called *unplanned investment.*

Change in business inventories is important in economics because, for example, a high level of employment is not likely to continue if inventories are building up at the same time; it is likely that employment in the near future will decrease as inventories are consumed. See also BUFFER STOCK PLAN.

CHANGE IN DEMAND (SUPPLY). See SUPPLY AND DEMAND.

CHANGE IN QUANTITY DEMANDED (SUPPLIED). This expression is considerably different from CHANGE IN DEMAND (SUPPLY); see SUPPLY AND DEMAND.

CHARTIST. A follower of the securities markets whose decisions are based mostly on past and present movements of prices, quantities, and other statistics. This type of analysis contrasts with *fundamental analysis,* which holds that the price of a security is mostly a function of the strength, earning power, and similar characteristics of the issuing company.

CHEAP MONEY. Characteristic of a time period in which a unit of money loses its value. If prices increase after a person borrows money, it is said that he or she borrowed *good money* and is repaying with *cheap money,* because the lender will not be able to buy as much with the money after it is repaid as he or she could have at the time it was lent.

CHECK CLEARING. The check-clearing process is similar in most countries in that commercial banks (or other check-issuing financial institutions) and CENTRAL BANKs are involved. In the U.S. system, which is described here, the number of commercial banks (over 14,000) and the number of checks (well over 50 million) processed every day require the use of a highly developed system.

Local clearing. If the drawee (bank where the check writer has his account) and the payee's bank are in the same local area, the check clears through a *clearinghouse.* A location is selected (usually one of the area banks), and representatives of each bank meet there with the checks which have been presented to their respective banks. Credits are computed in both directions, and the net amount due each bank is paid.

Correspondent banks. When larger distances are involved, banks which do not clear through the FEDERAL RESERVE SYSTEM (either because they are not members or because they choose not to use the system) clear their checks through correspondent banks. A bank that uses this system will have established a correspondent relationship with several other banks which are available for this service in various parts of the nation. When the bank pays an out-of-town check, it sends it to the correspondent bank that covers the area where the drawee is located. The correspondent bank arranges for interbank payment.

Federal Reserve System. An example will be used to demonstrate the method.

Suppose that a person with an account in Bank D (the drawee bank) pays for a purchase with a check, and that the seller deposits the check in an account at bank S. Assume that the two banks are within the same Federal Reserve district but not in the same local clearinghouse area. From that point, the check will be cleared in the following sequence: (1) Bank S adds the amount of the check to the seller's account and then sends the check to the Federal Reserve district bank. (2) The Federal Reserve bank adds the amount of the check to the reserve account (see BANK RESERVES) of Bank S and subtracts the amount from the reserve account of Bank D. (3) The check is sent to Bank D, which then subtracts the amount of the check from the buyer's account.

If Bank S and Bank D are in different Federal Reserve districts, then after the first part of step 2 is finished, the check is sent to the Federal Reserve bank of the district that Bank D is in, and the second part of step 2 is finished.

Other variations can include a RE-GIONAL CHECK PROCESSING CEN-TER or an AUTOMATED CLEARING-HOUSE.

CHECK CREDIT. A loan which is made by a bank's adding to a borrower's checking account, rather than by handing over cash or a cashier's check.

CHECKING ACCOUNT. See DE-MAND DEPOSIT.

CHECKOFF. In labor economics, a system whereby union dues and assessments are deducted from the employees' paychecks by the employer and remitted to the union. With a voluntary checkoff, each worker authorizes the deduction; for an automatic (or compulsory) checkoff individual authorizations are not required.

CHRONIC DEFICIT. The occurrence of a negative BALANCE OF PAYMENTS for several years in a row, with no correction in the foreseeable future. If this condition remains too long, the nation will lose all its reserves and be unable to participate in world trade, so authorities have to take steps to reverse the payments flow. One solution is to provide import barriers such as quotas and duties (see MERCHANDISE ACCOUNT), but international trading partners are likely to retaliate with similar measures, leaving the *balance of trade* in the same or a worse position. Another measure is to devalue the currency, making exports more attractive to other nations and imports less attractive to citizens of the nation with the chronic deficit.

CHURITSU ROREN (Jap.). Federation of Independent Unions, a confederation of Japanese labor unions about one-fourth the size of the largest confederation.

CIRCULAR FLOW OF MONEY. In order for households to be customers of businesses, they must have a constantly replenished flow of income; in order for businesses to produce goods and services, they must have the same. Therefore, these two SECTORs of the economy are mutually dependent. The accompanying figure shows a product market (referring to

Circular flow. Simplified model shows that each sector must have spending power in order to be able to spend.

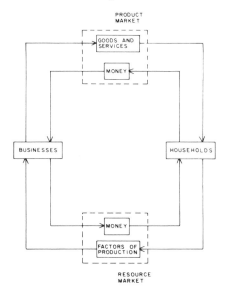

all consumer purchases) and a resource market (referring to business purchases of labor and other factors of production), with money flowing in one direction and purchases in the other direction.

CIRCULATING CAPITAL GOOD. A type of good so used in industry that it is consumed as it serves its purpose. Many fuels used directly in the manufacturing process are considered circulating capital. In one sense the fuels might be considered inventory because their single use means that, in effect, they become part of the finished product; in another sense, they are CAPITAL GOODS because they assist with the production process.

CIRCULATING MEDIUM. A *medium of exchange* (see BARTER) which circulates freely without endorsement, such as the recognized units of money.

CITY. In studies of economic history, it has been found that the city was the center of economic activity from the 1700s until communication technology made an economic unit of an entire nation. See also MANOR.

CIVILIAN LABOR FORCE. Exact definitions vary among nations; following is the definition used in the U.S. Generally, *civilian labor force* includes all who are either working or looking for work. Specifically, it is composed of all civilians over 16 years of age who are either employed or unemployed, except:

1. persons engaged in housework in their home
2. persons in school
3. persons with a new job not scheduled to begin for more than 30 days
4. persons unable to work because of long-term physical or mental illness
5. persons temporarily unable to work
6. retired persons
7. persons too old to work
8. persons doing less than 15 hours weekly of unpaid family work

9. seasonal workers surveyed in the off-season and not looking for work
10. inmates of institutions
11. persons not looking for work because they say no jobs are available
12. voluntarily idle persons

Since the labor force includes both employed and unemployed, the *unemployment rate* is the ratio of unemployed in this category to the total number of individuals in this category. For example, if 4 million persons in a civilian labor force of 100 million are unemployed, the unemployment rate is 4 percent. [Adapted from Herbert Runyon, "Counting the Jobless," *Federal Reserve Bank of San Francisco Monthly Review* (September 1972).]

The total labor force includes the military forces as well as the civilian labor force. A person cannot be counted as being in the military unless he or she is employed; because there is no military counterpart of unemployment, when a person is unemployed, he or she is a civilian unemployed.

CIVIL RIGHTS ACT OF 1964. Legislation aimed at stopping segregation in all places, public and private, that served the public, if they were in any way subject to federal or interstate regulation. Although there had been several civil rights acts prior to this one, their goals were mostly voting or education rights. See also EQUAL EMPLOYMENT OPPORTUNITY COMMISSION.

CLAD COINS. Dimes, quarters, half-dollars, and dollar coins, formerly "silver" (actually, the coins were only partially silver, even before coins were clad), are now made from *planchets*, which are punches from sheets of metal that have a copper core and permanently bonded layers of 75 percent copper and 25 percent nickel on each side. Clad coins were authorized by the Coinage Act of 1965, and all bore the date 1965 until August 1, 1966, at which time the practice of dating coins with the year of their manufacture was resumed. Clad coins duplicate the electrical properties of the "silver" coins and, therefore, although they are 9.3 percent lighter, they can be used interchangeably in coin-operated machines.

CLASS A, B, C DIRECTORS. Toplevel officers of FEDERAL RESERVE BANKs.

CLASSICAL SCHOOL. School of economic thought lasting from the mid-1700s to the 1800s, and characterized by LAISSEZ-FAIRE and the belief in a natural order. This school was directly opposed to the MERCANTILIST school, which measured wealth by hoards of gold and favored the use of government for privilege and protection. One of the classical economists was Adam Smith (1723-1790), who is famous for the book AN INQUIRY INTO THE NATURE AND CAUSES OF THE WEALTH OF NATIONS, published in England in 1776.

CLASSIFICATION OF BANKS. See DESIGNATION OF BANKS.

CLASSIFIED STOCK. CAPITAL STOCK that is grouped into various classes for the purpose of separating the rights that are included with ownership in each class.

CLASSIFIED TAX. A system of collecting government revenues by placing every taxable item within one of several classes. The rate of tax and/or other characteristics of the tax varies with each class. See also AD VALOREM DUTY.

CLASS PRICE. A price that results from a lack of PURE COMPETITION; one buyer or class of buyer pays a price higher than the general market price, usually because one of the requirements of pure competition, free flow of information, is missing.

CLASS STRUGGLE. One of the inevitable stages predicted by KARL MARX in replacing CAPITALISM with SOCIALISM. In this stage, workers exploited by the propertied class would overthrow the system and seize ownership.

CLAYTON ANTITRUST ACT. Largely the work of Henry Clayton, this act was passed by Congress on October 15, 1914, for the purpose of preventing undesirable monopolistic practices for which the SHERMAN ANTITRUST ACT had merely provided punishments. Prohibitions of the Clayton Antitrust Act included price discrimination, contractual clauses which prevent purchasers from going to competing sellers, acquisition of another company's stock for the purpose of reducing competition (later amended by the Celler-Kefauver Act of 1950 to prohibit acquisition of other assets), and INTERLOCKING DIRECTORATES among competitors when the assets of either one exceed $1 million. Tighter control was also established over holding companies, as well as other forms of business which had been established since the Sherman Antitrust Act and therefore required express control.

CLEAN AIR ACT. Legislation which established pollution control programs that focus on improving ground-level air quality near the sources of pollution. Although the act contains provisions for a state to notify the Environmental Protection Agency (EPA) if a neighboring state is "exporting" pollution, the EPA's authority to order remedies is limited. The act also required the EPA to set uniform primary and secondary National Ambient Air Quality Standards (NAAQS) for several pollutants that are considered to endanger public health and welfare. The act also deals with stationary sources, mobile sources, hazardous emissions, and other relevant issues.

CLEAN BILL. A BILL OF EXCHANGE that does not require information other than that on its face and which therefore does not have to be processed with additional documents attached. See DOCUMENT BILL.

CLEAN BILL OF LADING. An ordinary BILL OF LADING which does not have any notes of reservation added such as short count, damaged goods, or other reasons why parties to the shipment might want to point out exceptions to their regular liability. See FOUL BILL OF LADING.

CLEAN FLOAT. The ideal form of FLOATING EXCHANGE RATES, in which monetary authorities of a nation do not intervene in the money market. See also DIRTY FLOAT; INTERNATIONAL EXCHANGE.

CLEARING ACCOUNT. Every MEMBER BANK has an account at its Federal Reserve bank (RESERVE BALANCE). Among other reasons, this account is required so that amounts can be added or subtracted during the CHECK CLEARING process. Therefore, a *clearing account* is not a separate account; rather it is the name one uses for the reserve account when considering its check-clearing function.

CLEARINGHOUSE. Refers to an organization of banks, within a relatively small geographic area, which has the purpose of settling payments for the checks each bank receives during the day. In a typical arrangement, representatives from the banks meet about noon for a preliminary settling, and then again after the close of business for a final settling and the transfer of net amounts due. For a description of other methods, see CHECK CLEARING.
In financial economics, the clearinghouse is an orgainization that coordinates the transfer of securities after they have been sold at a stock exchange.

CLEARING OF CHECKS. See CHECK CLEARING.

CLEARINGS. The settling and payment of the net amounts due from payment instruments, such as checks, that have been received. Also called *bank clearings*.

CLEARING THE MARKET. See SUPPLY AND DEMAND.

CLOSE CORPORATION. A corporation whose stock is held by a small group, usually with an agreement that if a member of the group desires to sell any part of the ownership, it must first be offered to the other members of the group. Sometimes called a *closed corporation*.

CLOSE-DOWN CASE. A situation examined in MICROECONOMICS in which a producer loses money on every article made and sold. The least amount that can be lost is at zero output, when the only loss is the FIXED COSTS.

CLOSED SHOP. Agreement between an employer and a union that only union members will be hired. The TAFT-HARTLEY ACT prohibits such arrangements, although it has been unable to prevent the practice; hiring halls such as those used by longshoremen constitute *de facto* closed shops.

CLOSED UNION. A labor union that either directly or indirectly makes it difficult or impossible for anyone to join. The objective is usually to keep the supply of labor short, although other reasons such as better control over the members are sometimes applicable.

CLOSE SUBSTITUTE. An item that performs most of the functions that its substitute does. Close substitute is important in the study of economics because it is part of the explanation of markets and prices; if a product has a close substitute, any significant increase in its price will result in a large decrease in the quantity purchased, and the product is said to have an elastic demand.

COAL ACT (U.K.). Legislation of 1938 which provided for the nationalization of royalties to the owners of coal mines. One of the most significant pieces of legislation in shaping the U.K. economy, this act was a step toward the nationalization of the coal industry. See also COAL INDUSTRY NATIONALIZATION ACT.

COAL INDUSTRY NATIONALIZATION ACT (U.K.). Legislation of 1946 that created the *National Coal Board*, which assumed complete management of coal mining operations, capital investment, and employment. As a result, a series of nationalizations by government takeover of the coal industry was begun. Sometimes shortened to *Nationalization Act*.

COBWEB THEORY. If the quantity demanded depends on current prices but the quantity supplied depends on prices from a previous period, any disturbance from equilibrium conditions (see SUPPLY AND DEMAND) will cause ever-increasing excursions from equilibrium, as shown in the accompanying diagram. With a product that is in production throughout the year but which goes on the market only during a short season every year, such oscillations could occur. Assume the market is at equilibrium and then, for some reason, a larger supply (quantity *Q*1) is produced. According to the indicated DEMAND SCHEDULE, buyers will take that quantity off the market only when the price drops to *P*1. In producing for the next season, suppliers base their plans on the latest price; therefore, according to the SUPPLY SCHEDULE, they will provide only quantity *Q*2. However, at that quantity, a shortage will develop, and buyers will bid the price up to *P*2. Since they obtained that price, suppliers will produce quantity *Q*3 the next season, but buyers will take that quantity off the market only when the price drops to *P*3. The process continues with ever-increasing oscillations. This situation is also called *explosive equilibrium*.

Of course, the preceding description is pure theory and assumes that suppliers do not think; in practice, the cobweb effect occurs to a significant degree but not without limit. Suppliers are not ignorant of the reasons for the preceding season's prices and therefore use some judgment in setting production quantities for the following season.

CODETERMINATION. A practice in some countries whereby major actions, policies, etc., are decided through committees, boards, and even popular voting so that workers as well as management have a large voice in decisions.

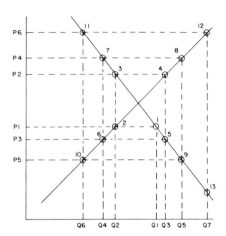

Cobweb theory. When supply decisions are based on prices and quantities of a previous season, the applicable points on a supply-and-demand chart can form a cobweb.

COEFFICIENT OF ACCELERATION. See ACCELERATION PRINCIPLE.

COEFFICIENT OF CROSS-ELASTICITY. The ratio of the percentage change in the *price* of product m to the percentage change in *sales* of product n.

$$E_c = \frac{P_{m2} - P_{m1}}{\frac{1}{2}(P_{m2} + P_{m1})} \bigg/ \frac{Q_{n2} - Q_{n1}}{\frac{1}{2}(Q_{n2} + Q_{n1})}$$

where

E_c = coefficient of cross-elasticity

P_{m1} = original price of product m

P_{m2} = new price of product m

Q_{n1} = quantity of product n when the price of product m is P_{m1}

Q_{n2} = quantity of product n when price of product m is P_{m2}

If products m and n are COMPLEMENTARY GOODS, E_c will be a positive number, and if they are COMPET-ING GOODS, it will be a negative number.

COEFFICIENT OF ELASTICITY. See ELASTICITY.

COEFFICIENT OF VARIATION. A measure of how VOLATILE an economic time series is. It is calculated by expressing the standard deviation as a percentage of the mean.

COIN. Metallic MONEY. Coins are now issued in small denominations only, but when money first became a medium of exchange (see BARTER), all denominations were issued in the form of coins.

COINAGE. The act of forming bullion into coins. See also BRASSAGE.

COINCIDENCE OF WANTS. The situation in which each of two trading partners desires exactly what the other has. See BARTER.

COINCIDENT INDICATOR. A statistic which has no value for predicting purposes because it changes at the same time as the economy in general. For example, many types of sales will peak out and bottom out simultaneously with overall economic conditions. See also LAGGING INDICATOR; LEADING INDICATOR.

COL CLAUSE. Cost-of-living clause, included in many labor contracts. See ESCALATOR CLAUSE.

COLLATERAL. Property or other item of value which a borrower pledges, giving the lender the right to sell it in the event of default.

COLLECTIBLE GOODS. Antiques, works of art, postage stamps, precious metals, precious stones, and other items that have value simply because they are collected. Collectibles usually have no utility value, but they generally hold their value when the value of money declines; in a period of inflation, many people turn to collectibles as a better store of value than money. See SPECULATIVE EXCESSES.

COLLECTION ITEMS. Instruments, accounts, and other items which represent amounts due and are therefore deposited in a bank. However, final crediting of the deposit does not take place until payment is made on the item (until it is collected).

COLLECTIVE BARGAINING. A method or process of determining and maintaining specific conditions of a labor contract—particularly wages, hours, and conditions of work—by direct negotiations between representatives of one or more unions on one hand and an employer or association of employers on the other hand. Although this arrangement meets the definition of monopoly, the courts have ruled that it must be allowed.

COLLECTIVE FARM. In many nations, especially in the Eastern Hemisphere, much of the agricultural sector consists of farms which are owned and operated by a relatively large number of people, sometimes an entire village. Although there are various arrangements for compensation, a common one is to distribute a farm's earnings equally. See also STATE FARM.

COLLECTIVISM. An economic system that is based on central, rather than private, ownership, especially of the major means of production. See also CENTRALLY PLANNED ECONOMY; COMMUNISM.

COLLUSION. Working together of two or more enterprises to defeat the bilateral fairness of competition.

COLOMBO PLAN (U.K.). A plan put forth during a conference in Colombo, Ceylon, in 1950, outlining a multibillion-dollar program for the economic development of Southeast Asia. Since its implementation in 1951, the plan has expanded in size and scope.

COLONIALISM. The premise that a nation can improve its wealth and standard of living by direct ownership and control of another land. Thus, the home country would dictate trade policies and taxes to the colony, would have a captive market at prices demanded or arranged by the seller, and would have a guaranteed source of needed material at prices arranged by the buyer. Modern views do not accept the importance of colonies because of both practical and moral considerations. See also ECONOMIC COLONIALISM.

COMBINATION IN RESTRAINT OF TRADE. An arrangement by two or more economic units (usually sellers) to erect artificial barriers to the free flow of trade and the operation of SUPPLY AND DEMAND. Such arrangements are usually illegal, especially in the U.S. See SHERMAN ANTITRUST ACT.

COMMAND ECONOMY. An economic system in which basic economic decisions, such as what goods and services will be produced, what they will sell for, and who will receive them, are made by central authorities instead of through natural forces such as SUPPLY AND DEMAND. See CENTRALLY PLANNED ECONOMY; CONSUMER SOVEREIGNTY.

COMMEMORATIVE COIN. To commemorate an anniversary or historical event, usually at the local level, special coins are often authorized by acts of Congress, manufactured in limited quantities, and sold at a premium by private organizations sponsoring the issues. About 60 commemorative issues have been authorized, but because they sell at a premium, they are collected and not used in general circulation.

COMMERCIAL BANK. Generally referred to as simply a *bank*. A FINANCIAL INTERMEDIARY whose main characteristic is that it offers checking accounts (demand deposits) and therefore can create MONEY (see MONEY SUPPLY EXPANSION MULTIPLIER). A commercial bank is a *national bank*, if it received its charter from the federal government; if chartered by a state government, it is a *state bank*. National banks are required to join the FEDERAL RESERVE SYSTEM. State banks are allowed to join the FRS if they meet certain requirements.

COMMERCIAL CREDIT COMPANY. An organization that provides liquidity to businesses, either in the form of direct loans or, more often, by purchasing promissory notes and other receivables. Commercial credit companies that concentrate in the latter are also called *factors* or *discount houses* because they purchase the paper at less than face value.

COMMERCIAL LOAN. Originally used for a short-term business loan that was to be liquidated through the sale of the goods for which the loan was made. For example, a toy manufacturer would borrow money to continue operations during the summer and fall and would then repay the loan from the proceeds of toy sales during the holiday season. This type of loan was the principal business of a *commercial bank*. Today, most business loans are referred to as *commercial loans*, and commerical banks have expanded into many areas of banking.

COMMERCIAL LOAN THEORY. A guideline of MONETARY POLICY which holds that limiting credit to short-term commercial paper would automatically result in the appropriate quantity of credit. Although controversial, this theory was followed in varying degrees for several years. When the Banking Act of 1935 authorized FEDERAL RESERVE BANKs to make loans to MEMBER BANKs on any assets the Reserve bank considered satisfactory, the commercial loan theory was finally abandoned as a major guideline.

COMMERCIAL PAPER. Short-term promissory notes used by businesses to obtain money, usually for a specific need. Commercial paper is similar to corporate bonds except that it matures more quickly (usually in six months or less). Commercial paper is often negotiable; buyers can recover their investment earlier than the maturity date by selling the paper to a third party.

COMMERCIAL REVOLUTION. The period from 1500 to the mid-1700s, characterized by the establishment of trade and money systems, the accumulation of wealth, and colonization. Since the Industrial Revolution that followed required large expenditures for CAPITAL GOODS, some historical analysts have said that the accumulation of wealth during the Commercial Revolution made the Industrial Revolution possible.

COMMERCIAL TREATY. An international treaty that concentrates on arrangements for trade, either between the businesses of the nations or between the governments.

COMMERZBANK (Ger.). One of the largest commercial banks in West Germany, with branches throughout the nation.

COMMINGLED INVESTMENT ACCOUNT. A trust arrangement in which a bank, as trustee, pools clients' funds, administers the total fund, and credits each client with a proportionate share. The U.S. Supreme Court ruled in 1971 that commingled investment accounts were directly competitive with mutual funds, and thus banks could no longer offer them.

COMMISSARIAT AU PLAN (Fr.). French government agency responsible for organizing and preparing economic plans. See MONNET PLAN.

COMMISSION. With regard to earnings, a payment for services rendered, in which payment depends directly on the services; for example, when a sales representative is paid a percentage of the sales. Also a committee, especially one formed for a specific purpose such as regulating commodity exchanges.

COMMITTEEMAN. An individual elected by fellow workers in a given shop or plant to deal with grievances and other matters of union business. Called STEWARD in some industries.

COMMODITY AGREEMENT. An agreement among producers, distributors, regulators, and others concerned with a certain commodity. Such agreements are found on an international basis as well

as within a nation. They often include quotas and expansion plans, sometimes covering a relatively long period of time, and differ from COMMERCIAL TREATYs which are mainly concerned with the terms of trade.

COMMODITY EXCHANGE. An organization that coordinates the buying and selling of commodities, generally for future delivery. Some exchanges specialize in one commodity, some in just a few, others trade several items.

COMMODITY EXCHANGE ACT. Legislation that controls financial transactions in commodities such as corn, wheat, and soybeans. Overall responsibility for the act lies with the Commodity Exchange Commission, which in turn created the COMMODITY EXCHANGE AUTHORITY to actually administer the act.

COMMODITY EXCHANGE AUTHORITY (CEA). The organization that has responsibility for administering the COMMODITY EXCHANGE ACT, licensing brokers, and controlling special trades.

COMMODITY EXPORT. See BALANCE OF INTERNATIONAL PAYMENTS.

COMMODITY LOAN. A loan in which the borrower pledges a given amount (or value) of some commodity as collateral. Under the usual commodity loan agreement, the lender has the right, upon default of the borrower, to sell the collateral; any excess from the sale is returned to the borrower, but any deficiency is still due the lender from the borrower.

A variation is found in the *nonrecourse commodity loan* which the U.S. government makes as part of its price support program. Under this arrangement, farmers borrow money, using stored crops, valued at the supported price, as collateral. If the crop's market value is less than the money due the government when the loan is to be repaid, the farmer can turn over the collateral in full and final settlement.

COMMODITY MONEY. A monetary unit that has value aside from its monetary value, such as when beads are used as money or when coins are made of precious metal. One problem with commodity money is that when its value as a commodity exceeds its value as money, it will cease to circulate or function as money. For instance, when the silver in a U.S. dime became worth more than 10 cents, dimes were melted down and the silver was sold. U.S. coinage then shifted to CLAD COINS.

COMMODITY PAPER. Commercial paper representing loans for which a negotiable instrument, such as a warehouse receipt for stored commodities, is the collateral. In case of default, the creditor has the right to take possession of the commodities to sell them for full or part payment of the loan.

COMMODITY STANDARD. A monetary system in which authorities promise to buy or sell, as demanded, a stated commodity at a stated amount per monetary unit. In practice, *commodity standard* usually refers to a commodity other than a precious metal and therefore is of little significance in modern economies.

COMMODITY THEORY OF MONEY. The view that a nation's monetary unit will have an actual value which is a function of the market value of the commodity on which the money is based. For example, when nations were on a gold standard, the true value (purchasing power) of a unit of money was a function of the amount of gold available (supply) and the medical, artistic, scientific, monetary, and other uses for gold (demand).

COMMON CARRIER. A transporter of goods who makes the service available to all. For example, a company that owns a milk tank truck is a common carrier if it offers its services to all who ship milk; it is a contract carrier if, by agreement, it transports milk for just one shipper.

COMMON LAW COPYRIGHT. See COPYRIGHT.

COMMON STOCK. See CAPITAL STOCK.

COMMON TRUST. A fund which is composed of two or more trust funds, usually because the individual funds are too small for efficient buying and selling of securities.

COMMUNISM. In the ultimate form of pure communism (which has never existed, just as pure CAPITALISM has never existed), only the PROLETARIAN CLASS would exist, with each person contributing (labor) to society according to individual ability, and with society providing according to individual need. In this idealistic situation, government withers away because the utopian conditions have eliminated the need for the function it performs.

In a practical sense, communism has come to mean a CENTRALLY PLANNED ECONOMY with government ownership of property, especially the means of production. As with other ideologies, the degree of adherence varies, and each communist nation falls on the continuum from pure capitalism to pure communism.

COMMUNIST LABOR BRIGADE (U.S.S.R.). An award to individuals for their efforts in increasing production, decreasing waste, improving efficiency, etc. Although its objective is to provide nonmaterial incentives, winners are often given wage increases, bonuses, and certificates which can be used as payment in certain facilities such as railroads. A similar award is *Heroes of Socialist Toil*.

COMMUNIST MANIFESTO. Pamphlet written by KARL MARX in 1848, describing abuses by capitalists during the Industrial Revolution and exhorting workers to overthrow capitalism and establish socialism.

COMMUNITY DEVELOPMENT CORPORATION. See HOUSING AND URBAN DEVELOPMENT.

COMMUNITY OF INTEREST. A group of enterprises that have established a pattern of transactions for their mutual benefit, even though they may not even operate in the same industry. For example, the operator of an office building may purchase heating fuel from a company that is a tenant in the building. Nothing illegal is implied in a community of interest, although the economy in general may not benefit, and the parties involved may actually become inefficient because of not considering alternative opportunities.

COMMUNITY PROPERTY. One of several methods by which husband and wife can hold joint title. The details vary from state to state, but generally, all property acquired during the marriage (with certain exceptions) is owned in equal shares by both spouses.

COMPANY STORE. A store provided by an employer especially for the employees' use. A company store is often set up when a company's operations are in a remote location and public shopping facilities are insufficient or completely lacking, or when employees are required or encouraged to purchase items, such as safety shoes, which are not readily available in other stores. Often a company store will extend credit and provide for repayment through payroll deductions. Sometimes, a company store is created because local merchants are treating the employees unfairly. At other times, it has been charged that company stores take advantage of employees because they have a captive market. This situation occurred frequently in the early days of the labor movement, when companies paid in SCRIP which was redeemable only at the company store.

COMPANY TOWN. A residential area in which the employer of all or most of the residents has a heavy financial interest, usually ownership of the homes and the retail establishments. Services such as police protection and sanitation collection are usually provided by the employer. Employees may pay rent to the employer, housing may be provided at no cost as a fringe benefit, or some policy in between may be adopted. Company towns have

usually been created when the company's operations were in a remote area and transportation was inadequate to make use of an existing town.

COMPANY UNION. A labor union which is fostered by an employer. Whether a company union actually represents the workers or whether it merely keeps them from joining an outside union is debatable.

COMPANYWIDE BARGAINING. In labor economics, bargaining on a multiplant basis between an employer operating more than one plant and a union representing workers in all the plants.

COMPARATIVE ADVANTAGE. The situation in which a productive unit, such as a geographical area, a nation, or a group of individuals, is able to produce each of two products at less cost than another productive unit is called *absolute advantage*. However, if the difference in costs is not the same in both productive units, each will have a *comparative advantage* in one of the products. For example, suppose nation A can produce steel at 80 percent of the cost with which nation B can produce steel, and that it can produce wheat at 90 percent of the cost with which nation B can produce wheat. Then, it will pay nation A to concentrate its production on steel and to trade for wheat from nation B (which should concentrate its efforts on producing wheat). Nation A has a comparative cost advantage in steel.

COMPENSATED PRICE CHANGE. See SUBSTITUTION EFFECTS.

COMPENSATING BALANCE. A bank may require that a borrower maintain a certain percentage of the loan amount on deposit (the compensating balance) as a condition for obtaining the loan. Thus, although the person has borrowed one amount and is paying interest on it, he or she actually has the use of only a percentage of that amount, so the *effective* interest rate on the amount really loaned is higher than the apparent rate.

COMPENSATING VARIATION. The amount of money an economic unit would be willing to pay in order to receive a benefit. The amount is usually less than the amount that the same economic unit would require (equivalent variation) before accepting a similar detriment. For example, a group of citizens might be willing to buy out a polluter (they would pay compensating variation), but they would not be willing to accept a polluter for the same amount of money.

COMPENSATION OF EMPLOYEES. In NATIONAL INCOME AND PRODUCT ACCOUNTS, wage and salary disbursements plus salary disbursements plus SUPPLEMENTS TO WAGES AND SALARIES. See also GROSS NATIONAL PRODUCT.

COMPENSATORY DUTY. An import duty established specifically to restore the competitive position of businesses that are put at a disadvantage by a tax which raises their cost.

COMPENSATORY FISCAL POLICY. Planning a government budget so that it will have a countercyclical, full-employment effect, without consideration of whether the result will be deficit, balanced, or surplus. See CONGRESSIONAL BUDGET AND IMPOUNDMENT CONTROL ACT; FISCAL POLICY; FUNCTIONAL FINANCE.

COMPENSATORY PRINCIPLE. The principle that the cost of a government service should be borne by those who are to benefit from the service. See ABILITY-TO-PAY PRINCIPLE; BENEFIT-RECEIVED PRINCIPLE.

COMPETING GOODS. Products which are linked economically so that the increasing sales of one are expected to cause a decrease in sales of the other. For example, if sales of tea increase, many of the new purchasers will be former coffee drinkers; therefore the two items are competing goods. See also COMPLEMENTARY GOODS; SUPPLY AND DEMAND.

There are degrees of competition; for two goods to be fully competing, the total size of the market must remain the same; every customer lost by one must be gained by the other, and every customer gained by one must have previously been a customer of the other.

COMPETITION. Simultaneous attempt by two or more economic units to achieve goals which are to a certain extent mutually exclusive. Thus, if more of a product is available than buyers want at the market price, sellers will compete, and if free-market forces (see MARKETPLACE) are not overridden, the price will drop.

Competition can also apply to buyers, as has been demonstrated whenever there has been less of a product than buyers wanted at the market price. Unless there are controls or other restrictions, buyer competition results in a higher market price.

Pure competition exists when price and quantity are established by just the market forces of SUPPLY AND DEMAND. Three conditions must be present for pure competition:

1. many buyers and many sellers operating independently, where "many" is a number large enough to ensure that no action by any one of them (such as changing the price or stopping production) will change the market. In pure competition, the market determines equilibrium price and quantity, not vice versa.
2. freedom to enter and leave the market. One force that brings price and quantity to their natural equilibrium values is the fact that higher-than-NORMAL PROFIT will attract other suppliers, increase the competition, and lower prices; lower-than-normal profits will induce some suppliers to leave the field, decrease the competition, and raise prices.
3. flow of information. A seller is not competing unless his buyer knows what other sellers are charging.

When the market for a certain product is essentially fixed with regard to most variables, so that a buyer sees only one area of difference among sellers, that difference is used to identify and name the type of competition. See QUALITY COMPETITION for an example.

There are no examples of pure competition, but a major stock exchange comes close. No one of the numerous buyers and sellers could affect the market price by deciding to trade or not to trade (with a few exceptions), and everyone has access to price and quantity information about every sale.

COMPETITIVE FRINGE. When the market for a certain product is dominated by a small number of suppliers (see OLIGOPOLY), the smaller firms that share the minor portion of the remaining market constitute the competitive fringe.

COMPETITIVE WAGE. Workers are sellers, and their labor is the product they have to sell; employers are the buyers, and the usual SUPPLY AND DEMAND situation exists. Competitive wage is the wage an employer must pay in order to attract and hold employees, because there are alternate buyers for their product. Of course, there are unions to change this picture and employers who establish *lock-in packages*, which consist of benefits that increase with seniority and make it costly for employees to change jobs. Both sets of practices change the concept of competitive wage.

COMPLEMENTARY GOODS. Products which are linked economically so that increasing the sales of one is expected to cause increased sales of the other. A common example is cameras and film. For example, if a technological breakthrough allows cameras to be sold at lower prices, more cameras will be sold; it can then be expected that an increase in the sales of film will follow. See also COMPETING GOODS.

There are degrees of complementarity and reversibility; motorcycles and helmets are closely linked, so that a 10 percent increase in motorcycle sales would be coupled with a nearly 10 percent increase in helmet sales. However, although bread and butter are complementary goods, they are not as closely linked. First, an increase in bread sales could be due to an increase in the popularity of bread pudding, and even if the increased sale of bread is due to a demand for sandwiches, many people will use margarine or mayonnaise on them, not butter. See also SUPPLY AND DEMAND.

COMPLETE ELASTICITY. A theoretical market situation in which the demand (or supply) curve is horizontal (parallel to the quantity axis). Actually, complete elasticity has no meaning, but a condition close to it, when the demand (supply) curve is *nearly* horizontal, can be explained: a small change in price will result in an extremely large change in quantity demanded (supplied). Also called *perfect elasticity*. See COMPLETE INELASTICITY.

COMPLETE INELASTICITY. This situation is more likely to be approximated in real life than is complete elasticity. Complete inelasticity (perfect elasticity) is represented by a vertical graph in SUPPLY AND DEMAND, and it means that a certain quantity is demanded (supplied) regardless of the price. A price increase will not cause a drop in sales, and a price decrease will not cause an increase in sales. An example often used in beginning economics texts is insulin. Diabetics stabilize their blood sugar by using a certain amount of insulin; they cannot reduce their purchases, even if the price triples; they are not going to buy more, even if the price is reduced drastically.

COMPOSITE COMMODITY STANDARD. One possible monetary system; the standard to which the monetary unit would be referred is a composite of commodities that would be directly applicable to most residents.

COMPOSITE DEMAND. Total demand; a schedule of total quantity demanded by all sectors, as a function of price. Also called *aggregate demand*.

COMPOSITE SUPPLY. A schedule of total quantity supplied as a function of price. If the ''item'' is picnic needs, it will include everything from picnic baskets supplied by industry to public parks supplied by the government sector. Also called *aggregate supply*.

COMPOSITION OF CREDITORS. An agreement among all the creditors of a certain debtor to accept a selected percentage of the debts as full payment. Usually agreed to when the alternative is likely to result in high costs to the creditors, settlement for an even smaller percentage, or both.

COMPOUND DUTY. An import tariff that is charged according to a formula which is a function of both the value of the item (AD VALOREM DUTY) and some physical characteristic such as weight (SPECIFIC DUTY).

COMPOUND INTEREST. Interest is calculated for a period of time and then added to the principal so that when interest is calculated for the next period, it will include interest earned on previous interest. Usually, a certain number of compounding periods per year, such as four, are specified, and then at the end of each quarter of a year, the interest is calculated and added to the principal. The more frequently interest is compounded, the more the lender actually earns, as shown in the following table for 1 percent:

Compounding period	Equivalent simple interest
Semiannual	1.010025%
Quarterly	1.010038%
Bimonthly	1.010042%
Monthly	1.010046%
Weekly	1.010049%
Daily	1.010050%

The total value after compounding is found from the formula

$$A = P(1 + r)^n$$

where

A = the final amount of compound interest plus the original principal

P = the original principal

r = the interest rate per period; usually the annual interest rate divided by the number of compounding periods in one year

n = the total number of compounding periods

COMPTOIRE NATIONAL D'ESCOMPTE (Fr). One of the largest commercial banks in France, nationalized in 1945.

COMPTROLLER OF THE CURRENCY. An office within the Treasury Department, created by the NATIONAL BANKING ACT in 1864. The comptroller supervises most actions of NATIONAL BANKs (charters new ones, rules on applications for merger and for operating branches, and appoints receivers, etc.). All banks in the District of Columbia are supervised by the comptroller.

COMPULSORY ARBITRATION. A legal requirement that a labor dispute be submitted to an ARBITRATOR whose decision is binding.

COMPULSORY CHECKOFF. In labor economics, an arrangement for paying dues and other assessments to a labor union; with no choice on the employee's part, the employer deducts the amounts from the employee's pay and remits them directly to the union. Also called *automatic checkoff*.

COMPULSORY UNION MEMBERSHIP. See CLOSED SHOP.

CONCENTRATION RATIO. See INDUSTRIAL CONCENTRATION.

CONCILIATION. In labor economics, the attempt of a third party to bring about the settlement of a labor dispute by hearing both parties and then offering (nonbinding) suggestions for a solution.

CONDEMNATION. In a literal sense, an official declaration that premises must not be occupied because they are unsafe. Today, condemnation refers to any removal of private owners when authorities exercise the right of EMINENT DOMAIN.

CONDITIONAL ENDORSEMENT. A special form of RESTRICTIVE ENDORSEMENT in which the transferor, in addition to a signature, adds words to an instrument that make the transfer effective only upon the occurrence of a certain event or the meeting of a certain condition. For example, a transfer may become effective only if a certain financial security is made available on the market. If such a condition is made on the face of the instrument, it is generally not negotiable.

CONDITIONAL SALE. A type of credit transaction in which the buyer takes possession of the property and has certain rights therein but in which full title does not pass until payment is complete. The UNIFORM COMMERCIAL CODE combines many forms of credit sales under the general category *secured transactions*.

CONFEDERATION. A coordinating organization which acts for a group of organizations that have joined it. Refers most often to labor unions, although there are also confederations of employers. In this sense, it has the same meaning as *federation*.

CONFEDERATION GENERALE DE TRAVAIL (CGT; Fr.). The largest organization of labor unions in France. Many unions throughout the nation are affiliated with CGT, which is a member of the Communist World Federation of Trade Unions.

CONFEDERATION OF BRITISH INDUSTRY (CBI; U.K.). An organization of employers in both private and nationalized British industries. In the same way that a labor union represents its members in labor negotiations, CBI represents employers.

CONFEDERATION OF SWEDISH TRADE UNIONS (Swed.). The largest confederation of trade unions in Sweden, it includes unions and union locals which account for nearly all union workers. It concentrates on production and manufacturing workers.

CONFIRMED LETTER OF CREDIT. A document (LETTER OF CREDIT) in which a bank indicates credit approval by stating that, for the named individual, it guarantees acceptance and payment (see ACCEPTANCES) of all drafts. Sometimes a dollar limit is stated in such a letter.

CONGLOMERATE. A business enterprise which operates in several unrelated markets. Prior to the advent of the conglomerate, when one company acquired another it was clearly for the purpose of increased efficiency through the common use of one or more of their functions (such as marketing, distribution, and purchasing); with the conglomerate, the trend switched to the acquisition of companies on no other basis than their present or potential worth or earnings capability.

CONGRESSIONAL BUDGET AND IMPOUNDMENT CONTROL ACT. Signed into law on July 12, 1974, this legislation contains the most radical revisions in congressional budgetary procedures since the *Budget and Accounting Act* of 1921. The new procedures applied during 1976, while the budget for fiscal 1977 was being prepared. The act established a joint *Congressional Committee on the Budget*, composed of a 23-member standing committee from the House of Representatives and a 15-member committee from the Senate. These committees examine, singly and jointly, the budget as a complete document. Under previous procedures, appropriations for expenditures and receipts for revenues were acted upon by entirely separate committees in each house. That procedure frustrated economists because the final budget surplus or deficit was a function of the independent actions of various committees, rather than of deliberate decision as in theoretical MONETARY POLICY.

The budget reform bill also provides for a *Congressional Budget Office* with a director appointed by the Speaker of the House and the president pro tem of the Senate. The staff of the Budget Office will provide information to the Congress pertaining to the budget, appropriations bills, or tax expenditures, as well as receipts, revenue estimates, and changing revenue conditions.

The language of the budget reform bill is quite specific as to the nature and content of each concurrent resolution. It must set forth (1) the appropriate level of total budget outlays and of total new budget authority; (2) an estimate of budget outlays and an appropriate level of new budget authority for each major functional category based upon allocations of the appropriate level of total budget outlays; (3) the amount, if any, of the surplus or deficit in the budget which is appropriate in light of economic conditions and all other relevant factors; (4) the recommended level of federal revenues and the amount, if any, by which the aggregate level of federal revenues should be increased or decreased; (5) the appropriate level of the public debt and the amount, if any, by which the statutory limit on the public debt should be increased or decreased. [Adapted from Federal Reserve Bank of San Francisco, *Business & Financial Letter*, July 26, 1974.]

CONGRESSIONAL BUDGET OFFICE. An organization for providing to the legislative branch information pertaining to the budget, appropriations bills, and tax expenditures, as well as receipts, revenue estimates, and changing revenue conditions. See BUDGET OFFICE; CONGRESSIONAL BUDGET AND IMPOUNDMENT CONTROL ACT.

CONGRESSIONAL COMMITTEE ON THE BUDGET. A committee, composed of a 23-member standing committee from the House of Representatives and a 15-member committee from the Senate, which was created by the CONGRESSIONAL BUDGET AND IMPOUNDMENT CONTROL ACT of 1974 to consider the federal budget as an entity, rather than examining expenditures and appropriations separately, as had been done previously.

CONGRESS OF INDUSTRIAL ORGANIZATIONS (CIO). Prior to 1955, one of two large federations to which much of organized labor belonged. It later merged with the AFL to form the AMERICAN FEDERATION OF LABOR— CONGRESS OF INDUSTRIAL ORGANIZATIONS. Formed in 1936, the CIO was originally called the Committee of Industrial Organizations.

CONSEIL NATIONAL DU PATRONAT FRANÇAIS (Fr.). A French industrial organization whose members are trade associations which, in turn, have companies as members.

CONSENT DECREE. An agreement by the parties to a legal action which in effect settles the dispute out of court. *Consent decree* often refers to an antitrust suit by the U.S. Department of Justice; in a typical decree, the company charged agrees to stop the contested practices.

CONSIGNMENT. In business economics, a shipment of goods by a *consignor* to a *consignee*. In a typical arrangement, the consignee takes possession of the goods for the purpose of reselling them, but does not pay for them until they are sold. Although possession transfers to the consignee, title remains with the consignor.

CONSOL BOND. Short for *consolidation bond*.

CONSOLIDATED STATEMENT OF CONDITION OF ALL FEDERAL RESERVE BANKS. A report released each Thursday afternoon (or on Friday if Thursday is a holiday) by the BOARD OF GOVERNORS (OF THE FEDERAL RESERVE SYSTEM). In the accompanying table, which shows a typical summary of the data from a report, the first

Consolidated Statement of Condition of All Federal Reserve Banks

Item (millions of $)	Eliminations[a]	Wednesday[b] Dec. 17, 1980	Change since 1 week ago (Dec. 10, 1980)	Change since 1 year ago (Dec. 19, 1979)
ASSETS				
1. Gold certificate account		11,161	—	+ 49
2. Special Drawing Rights certificate account		3,368	—	+ 1,568
3. Coin		401	+ 7	− 19
4. Loans		1,616	− 485	+ 55
5. Acceptances (held under repurchase agreements)		327	+ 327	+ 327
6. Federal agency obligations				
bought outright		8,739	—	+ 523
held under repurchase agreements[c]		389	+ 389	+ 389
7. U.S. government securities				
bought outright:				
bills		44,458	+ 4,977	+ 319
certificates—special				
notes		58,718	+ 100	+ 2,224
bonds		16,893	—	+ 2,340
8. total[d]		120,069	+ 5,077	+ 4,883
9. Held under repurchase agreements[c]		2,054	+ 2,054	+ 2,054
10. Total U.S. government securities		122,123	+ 7,131	+ 6,937
11. Total loans and securities		133,194	+ 7,362	+ 8,231
12. Cash items in process of collection	(2,511)	14,122	+ 2,742	− 373
13. Bank premises		458	+ 1	+ 54
14. Other assets[e]		8,151	+ 1,068	+ 3,001
15. *Total Assets*	(2,511)	170,855	+ 11,180	+ 12,511

[a]Made in the consolidating process.
[b]Estimated (Richmond District).
[c]Does not include U.S. government and federal agency securities resold under matched sale-purchase transactions to foreign official and international accounts, of which $0 was outstanding at the end of the latest statement week.
[d]Net of $2,585 million matched sale-purchase transactions outstanding at the end of the latest statement week. Includes $215 million securities loaned—fully secured by U.S. government securities.

(continued)

Consolidated Statement of Condition of All Federal Reserve Banks (*continued*)

Item (millions of $)	Eliminations[a]	Wednesday[b] Dec. 17, 1980	Change since	
			1 week ago (Dec. 10, 1980)	1 year ago (Dec. 19, 1979)
LIABILITIES				
16. Federal Reserve notes		123,333	+ 271	+ 10,969
17. Deposits:				
Depository institutions		31,604	+ 8,307	+ 2,302
18. U.S. Treasury—general account		2,653	+ 1,137	− 408
19. Foreign—official accounts		287	+ 15	+ 13
20. Other		403	− 63	+ 100
21. Total deposits		34,947	+ 9,396	+ 2,007
22. Deferred availability cash items	(2,511)	7,580	+ 1,134	− 225
23. Other liabilities and accrued dividends[f]		2,349	+ 319	− 36
24. *Total Liabilities*	(2,511)	168,209	+ 11,120	+ 12,715
CAPITAL ACCOUNTS				
25. Capital paid in		1,202	+ 3	+ 58
26. Surplus		1,145	—	+ 67
27. Other capital accounts		299	+ 57	− 329

28. MATURITY DISTRIBUTION OF LOANS AND SECURITIES, DECEMBER 17, 1980[g]

	Loans	Acceptances	U.S. government securities		Federal agency obligations	
			Holdings	Weekly changes	Holdings	Weekly changes
Within 15 days	1,573	327	5,011	+ 2,826	389	+ 389
16 to 90 days	43	—	22,888	+ 3,772	595	—
91 days to 1 year	—	—	31,210	+ 533	1,530	—
Over 1 year to 5 years	—	—	34,657	—	4,837	—
Over 5 years to 10 years	—	—	13,355	—	1,092	—
Over 10 years	—	—	15,002	—	658	—
Total	1,616	327	122,123	+ 7,131	9,128	+ 389

[e]Includes assets denominated in foreign currencies, revalued monthly at market exchange rates.

[f]Includes exchange-translation account reflecting the monthly revaluation at market exchange rates of foreign exchange commitments.

[g]Acceptances and securities held under repurchase agreements are classified as maturing within 15 days in accordance with maximum maturity of the agreements.

column of figures gives, to the nearest million dollars, the condition of the 12 FEDERAL RESERVE BANKs at the end of the previous business day (Wednesday). The next column reports the change from the previous Wednesday, and the last column shows the change from the Wednesday 52 weeks earlier.

See other entries in this dictionary for further explanations.

CONSOLIDATION. A joining of two or more corporations, which results in a new organization. See MERGER.

CONSOLIDATION BOND. A BOND sold for the purpose of obtaining funds for retiring two or more other issues in order to make a debt more orderly. Also known as a *consol bond* or a *unifying bond*.

CONSORTIA BANKS. Several European banks which have become allied with U.S. and/or other foreign banks in the establishment of medium-term lending institutions.

CONSPICUOUS CONSUMPTION. Spending, usually for luxury items, in a manner intended to give others the impression of superior spending power or income. There is a countervailing tendency today to take pride in a background of poverty so as to stress economic achievement. Conspicuous consumption can take place on an individual level or on a national level such as when the citizens of one nation attempt to impress the citizens of another nation.

CONSTANT-COST INDUSTRY. An industry whose unit costs for the FACTORS OF PRODUCTION do not have a long-run dependence on the amount of the industry's output. A more likely situation is the DECREASING-COST INDUSTRY, because many items can be produced more efficiently on a larger scale.

CONSTANT COSTS. See FIXED COSTS.

CONSTANT DOLLARS. An economic statistic (or series) which is given in *con-stant dollars* is derived by dividing CURRENT DOLLAR estimates by an appropriate PRICE INDEX. The result shows how many dollars would have been involved if the dollar had a constant purchasing power equal to the purchasing power it had in the base year (which must be given along with the series if complete information is to be conveyed).

CONSTANT RETURNS TO SCALE. No change in MARGINAL COST as production quantity is changed. See also ECONOMIES OF SCALE; CONSTANT-COST INDUSTRY.

CONSULAR INVOICE. In international trade, an invoice which has been cleared through the consulate of the importing nation.

CONSUMER COOPERATIVE. A retail organization that is owned and/or operated by a group of consumers with the objective of saving an intermediary markup in prices. It usually requires a certain amount of volunteer work from its members. Cooperatives have met with varying success; some have accomplished their purpose whereas others have concluded that the markup is amply justified by the services retailers perform.

CONSUMER CREDIT. Debts accumulated by consumers when purchasing goods and services. It may develop from direct borrowing of money or from accepting goods and services with a promise to pay later. Consumer credit is important to economic analysts because it is an indication of consumer optimism as well as ability to make future purchases.

CONSUMER CREDIT PROTECTION ACT. Legislation of 1968 which launched the TRUTH-IN-LENDING Act and led to numerous consumer protection acts such as the Equal Credit Opportunity Act, the FAIR CREDIT REPORTING ACT, the FAIR CREDIT BILLING ACT, and the ELECTRONIC FUNDS TRANSFER ACT.

CONSUMER DETERMINISM. See CONSUMER SOVEREIGNTY.

CONSUMER DURABLES. Consumer goods, such as major appliances, that are expected to have a useful lifetime of several years. Some sources draw the line between durables and nondurables at a specific time period such as 1 year or 3 years; others identify items as durable if they are not for immediate consumption.

CONSUMER ECONOMICS. The entire subfield of economics dealing with the end objective of an economy: that is, consumer goods and services. It is concerned with SUPPLY AND DEMAND, satisfaction, and income levels and distribution, as well as interfaces with other subfields, such as government activities, and labor economics.

CONSUMER EXCESS BURDEN. See EXCESS BURDEN.

CONSUMER FINANCE COMPANY. See FINANCE COMPANY.

CONSUMER GOODS. Items that are used directly by consumers, as opposed to PRODUCER GOODS which are used by industry to produce other goods. Consumer goods are usually separated into DURABLE GOODS and nondurable goods.

CONSUMERISM. Recognition of the fact that the consumer SECTOR comprises many small economic units, all acting independently, and therefore it is at a disadvantage when dealing with the industrial and government sectors. Even though CONSUMER SOVEREIGNTY is a significant force, it has been held that consumers needed additional help in the form of legislation and changed attitudes in business.

A number of steps have been taken voluntarily by business but it is difficult to report them because their voluntary nature means they are not widely coordinated. New policies such as posting unit prices, including complete instructions, holding off the market those items that tend to be harmful to individuals or the environment, liberal refund policies, and rainchecks on advertised sale items are some examples. On the the legislative side there have been federal measures such as the Fair Packaging and Labeling Act, Flammable Fabrics Act, CONSUMER CREDIT PROTECTION ACT, FAIR CREDIT BILLING ACT, ELECTRONIC FUNDS TRANSFER ACT, Equal Credit Opportunity Act, and FAIR CREDIT REPORTING ACT. There has also been relevent legislation by states.

CONSUMER PRICE INDEX (CPI). One of the most frequently used and probably the least understood statistical series in economics. The present CPI for Urban Wage Earners and Clerical Workers, formerly called the "Cost of Living Index," was initiated during World War I for use in wage negotiations. Since then the CPI has undergone major revisions, in 1940, 1953, and 1964, and several partial revisions.

Despite the many changes and improvements in statistical procedures, the CPI continues to be what it has always been—a statistical measure of changes in prices of goods and services bought by urban wage earners and clerical workers, including families and single persons. The CPI measures only changes in prices, it tells nothing about changes in the kinds and amounts of goods and services bought, or the total amount spent for living, or the differences in living costs in different places. Other indicators are required to measure these facts.

Description. The CPI is based on prices of 398 items which were selected to represent the movement of prices of all goods and services purchased. The CPI "market basket" is divided into five major categories: food (105 items), housing (81 items), apparel and upkeep (77 items), transportation (34 items), and health and recreation (101 items). Each item is weighted to reflect its relative importance in the CPI budget. The weights differ among cities, reflecting buying habits, and are revised periodically to account for changes which occur over time.

The CPI covers prices of everything people buy for living: food; clothing; automobiles; homes; house furnishings; household supplies; fuel; drugs; recreational goods; fees to doctors, dentists, lawyers, beauty shops; rent; repair costs; transportation fares; public utility rates; etc. It deals with prices charged to consumers, including sales and excise taxes. Also included are real estate taxes on homes, but not income or personal property taxes.

The complex job of measuring changes in consumer prices is performed by the U.S. Department of Labor's Bureau of Labor Statistics. The national CPI is computed monthly from data gathered in 56 urban areas across the U.S. Food pricing is done monthly in all areas, but a complete monthly survey is conducted in only the five largest standard metropolitan statistical areas (SMSAs), including Chicago, Detroit, Los Angeles, New York, and Philadelphia. The remaining areas are surveyed four times a year, in such a way that an equal number of areas are included each month.

An increase in the CPI means a general increase in prices and a decrease in the value of the dollar. Therefore, the purchasing power of the dollar is the reciprocal of the CPI.

Uses and limitations. The CPI is used extensively in labor-management contracts to adjust wages. Automatic adjustments based on changes in the CPI are incorporated in many wage contracts as well as in some business contracts, such as long-term leases. In addition, the CPI is used as a measure of the purchasing power of the dollar for such diverse purposes as adjusting royalties, pensions, welfare payments, and occasionally, alimony payments. It is also used widely as a reflection of inflationary trends in the economy.

The CPI is designed to reflect the price movements of a fixed quantity and quality of goods and services relating to a well-defined group of consumers. Therefore it does not truly measure overall changes in living standards or cost of living because both are responsive to many factors. Living costs may vary with changes in family size, age, income, tastes, and place of residence and for other reasons not directly related to price fluctuation.

Individual area indexes do not show whether living costs are higher in one area than another; they just show how much the costs have changed in each area since a stated base year. The CPI is also subject to sampling errors, which cause it to deviate somewhat from the results which would be obtained if actual records of all retail purchases could be used to compile it.

[Adapted from Security Pacific National Bank, *Monthly Summary of Business Conditions in Southern California* (April 1971).]

CONSUMERS' CAPITAL. CONSUMER DURABLES. See PRODUCERS' CAPITAL.

CONSUMER SECTOR. See BUSINESS SECTOR.

CONSUMER SOVEREIGNTY. The concept that in a MARKET ECONOMY it is the consumer SECTOR that actually determines what items will be produced, how they will be distributed, what will be paid, and other questions. The essence of any free-will business transaction is that both parties benefit: the buyer will not make the purchase unless the product promises more UTILITY UNITS, or satisfaction, than the money he surrenders; the seller will receive more benefit from the exchanged money than from the product. Therefore, consumers spend their money in a way that will bring them the greatest satisfaction, and producers who are guided by this principle will have neither shortages nor unsold surplus.

CONSUMERS' SURPLUS. The result of subtracting the amount consumers actually pay for an item from the maximum they are willing to pay for it. When this surplus exists, consumers will continue buying the item, while DIMINISHING MARGINAL UTILITY results in less satisfaction obtained from each purchase; eventually, the marginal utility obtained from the item will be the same as that of all other items, and consumer surplus will disappear. See also ALFRED MARSHALL.

CONSUMPTION. The using up of goods and services by consumers. Although, in a general sense, a factory may "consume" raw materials, economists consider those materials to become part of the factory's output; therefore, only a consumer can consume. It is in this economic sense that GROSS NATIONAL PRODUCT is composed of *consumption* expenditures plus INVESTMENT expenditures plus government purchases of goods and services plus NET EXPORTS.

CONSUMPTION FUNCTION. The level of consumption expressed as a function of DISPOSABLE PERSONAL INCOME, or DISPOSABLE INCOME (DI). OTHER THINGS BEING EQUAL is assumed here, so it is important *not* to interpret this function as a means of predicting how consumption will change as DI changes over the years. Instead, the consumption function is a series of "if" points, showing, at a given time and under given conditions, what consumption would be if DI were each of the values considered. In the end, only one of the points will apply for the given time and conditions.

At each income, the difference between DI and consumption is *saving*. When the consumption function extends down to very low values of DI (even to zero), it will be found that consumption exceeds income (even at zero income, it is necessary to have some consumption), and therefore there will be a negative saving, or DISSAVING.

CONSUMPTION TAX. A tax that is assessed in proportion to the amount a taxpayer spends. Economists sometimes disagree on whether certain levies are actually consumption taxes; a sales tax, even if charged separately, is not necessarily a consumption tax, as the seller may reduce

the price of the product in order to compete with another product. Since it is intended that consumers pay consumption taxes, a *direct consumption tax* is one paid directly to the government by filing a tax return, and an *indirect consumption tax* is one paid to the merchant for transmittal to the government.

CONTINENTAL BILL. A BILL OF EXCHANGE that is payable in Europe. See also DOMESTIC BILL; FOREIGN BILL.

CONTINGENCY DUTY. An import duty established specifically to restore the competitive position of businesses that are put at a disadvantage by a tax which raises their costs. More often called a *countervailing duty*.

CONTINGENT ASSET. In financial economics, an asset whose value (if any) is unknown at the present time because it depends on a future event or situation.

CONTINGENT LIABILITY. In financial economics, a liability which is currently recognized, although the actual amount is unknown because it depends on a future event or situation.

CONTINGENT LIABILITY ON ACCEPTANCES PURCHASED FOR FOREIGN CORRESPONDENTS. With regard to the CONSOLIDATED STATEMENT OF CONDITION OF ALL FEDERAL RESERVE BANKS, this item includes the total liability of FEDERAL RESERVE BANKs for ACCEPTANCES purchased for the accounts of foreign central banks. This potential liability arises from the Reserve banks' guarantee that such acceptances will be paid at maturity.

In 1917 the Federal Reserve agreed to purchase U.S. acceptances for the account of the Bank of England and have the Bank of England buy British acceptances for the System's account. Guaranteeing acceptances purchased for foreign CENTRAL BANKs was a standard feature of agreements between the Bank of England and its foreign correspondents. The Federal Reserve adopted the same policy.

One reason for adopting the policy was that the System could not evaluate foreign acceptances and considered it important to obtain a guarantee from the central bank of any nation whose acceptances were being purchased for the Federal Reserve. Another was that the System could not expect such a guarantee if it were not prepared to reciprocate.

Until 1921 the Federal Reserve did not charge central banks for its guarantee (which in effect was an insurance service). Maintaining a demand deposit with the Federal Reserve was considered sufficient compensation. This policy was changed when the Netherlands Bank contended that maintaining a demand deposit was an arbitrary form of payment. Since then a commission has been charged for the guarantee. From 1921 to 1926 the charge was 0.25 percent on the face amount of the acceptance; since 1926 it has been 0.125 percent.

While the Federal Reserve no longer has foreign central banks buy acceptances for the its account, it does feel a "moral" obligation when it purchases acceptances for another central bank and has never altered its guarantee policy.

The Federal Reserve has had to make only one payment under the guarantee. During the U.S. banking crisis in 1933, the System assumed the liability for $634,000 of unpaid acceptances from foreign accounts. These acceptances were all collected in full in 1933 and 1934. The Federal Reserve's loss consisted of $136.50 in uncollected protest fees and $6.00 in interest.

Although this item appears below "capital accounts" on the consolidated statement, it is really a memorandum item not included when balancing "total assets" with "total liabilities and capital accounts."
[Adapted from Federal Reserve Bank of New York, *Glossary: Weekly Federal Reserve Statements.*]

CONTINUED BOND. A bond which will continue earning interest beyond the maturity date if not brought to the issuer for redemption. The rate of interest is either the same as before maturity or according to a prior arrangement.

CONTINUOUS MARKET. A situation in which transactions in a good or service take place almost constantly, with the result that prices fluctuate in response to the forces of SUPPLY AND DEMAND. Most stocks traded at the major exchanges provide a good example of a continuous market.

CONTINUOUS VARIABLE. In analytic economics, a variable which can be changed in any amount, no matter how small, as opposed to a DISCRETE VARIABLE, which can be changed by designated steps only. Also called *infinitely variable*.

CONTRACT CARRIER. A transporter of goods who, by agreement, carries goods for just one shipper. See COMMON CARRIER.

CONTRACT CLAUSE. That part of Article 1, Section 10, of the U.S. Constitution that prohibits states from passing laws which impair the obligation of contracts.

CONTRACTIONARY. Tending to slow down economic activity or to reduce the total output of goods and services. Usually used to describe a policy, such as when it is said that raising taxes is a contractionary FISCAL POLICY. See also EXPANSIONARY.

CONTRACTION OF MONEY SUPPLY. See MONEY SUPPLY EXPANSION MULTIPLIER.

CONTRACT LINE. In a graph showing the allocation of two types of goods between two consumers, the *contract line* is a locus of points which offer no improvement in the lot of one consumer without worsening the lot of the other. Also known as PARETO OPTIMUM.

CONTRACT RENT. Actual amount of payment for the use of land (in the sense of an ECONOMIC RESOURCE). *Con-*

tract rent is sometimes used to avoid confusion with ECONOMIC RENT.

CONTRIBUTORY. Description of pension plans and other funds to which contributions are made by both employee and employer. When the entire cost of a plan is paid by the employer, it is noncontributory.

CONTRIBUTORY NEGLIGENCE. In legal economics, a factor in determining the liability for personal injury, especially with respect to on-the-job injuries. For example, if a high-voltage wire is exposed and employees are warned to stay away from it, the doctrine of contributory negligence would say that any employee who is injured is guilty of such negligence and therefore not all liability falls on the employer. This doctrine is similar to the doctrine of last clear chance, which holds that, although the employer was wrong in allowing the dangerous condition to exist, the injured employee could have avoided the accident by being careful. These doctrines have been superseded in the U.S. by WORKMEN'S COMPENSATION LAWS, which make an employer liable for injuries to employees, with very few exceptions.

CONTROL GROUP. As with any scientific experiment, experiments in economics (such as determining the effects of various welfare plans) have value only when one group, the control group, is exposed to standard conditions and then evaluated in the same way as the group(s) exposed to the experimental methods. Such research is more difficult in economics, and other social sciences, because it is impossible to maintain all variables constant except the one being tested; nevertheless, the experimenter should make every attempt to have all of the factors in the control group as nearly as possible the same as those in the other group(s).

CONTROLLED ECONOMY. An economy in which a significant amount of end results is due to the deliberate decision of government bodies rather than to consumer choice plus forces of SUPPLY AND DEMAND. All economies are controlled to some extent; a CENTRALLY PLANNED ECONOMY is more controlled than a capitalist economy (see CAPITALISM). Also called a *directed economy*.

CONTROLLED MONEY SUPPLY. A nation's MONEY SUPPLY that is determined by deliberate human decision rather than by a natural measure, such as the amount of gold or other precious metal which is available. Most modern economies use a controlled money supply because it is a tool of MONETARY POLICY and because there is a need for short-term adjustments to satisfy transaction demands. Also called a *managed money supply*. See also MONEY SUPPLY EXPANSION MULTIPLIER.

CONTROLLED MONOPOLY. See MONOPOLY.

CONTROLLING COMPANY. A company that owns a significant percentage of the CAPITAL STOCK of another corporation and therefore has the votes to exert management control over it. See also HOLDING COMPANY.

CONVENIENCE DEMAND. See LIQUIDITY PREFERENCE.

CONVENTIONAL WISDOM. An expression seen frequently in economics writings, referring to familiar and acceptable ideas, many of which are questionable over a period of time. The expression was popularized in *The Affluent Society* (1958) by John Kenneth Galbraith (3rd ed., New York: New American Library, 1978). Conventional wisdom is similar to "they say" statements, for which no one seems to know who "they" are.

CONVERSION PRICE. The price at which the option on a CONVERTIBLE BOND or a CONVERTIBLE STOCK can be exercised.

CONVERTIBLE BOND. A BOND whose owners have the privilege of converting it into a stated number of shares of stock or into some other security. Because the owners have a choice of actions, they have a better probability of improving their profit, and therefore the rate of interest on such bonds is usually lower than for identical bonds without the conversion privilege.

CONVERTIBLE CURRENCY. Currency that can be exchanged freely, sometimes into gold, sometimes into other currencies. In times of international monetary crises, nations will suspend convertibility; that is, they will not exchange their currency, and holders of that currency are encouraged to spend it in the nation which issued it.

CONVERTIBLE STOCK. CAPITAL STOCK for which the rights of ownership include an option to exchange it for a stated amount of another security. For example, an issue of *preferred stock* may include an agreement that any time between 5 and 10 years after issue an owner can elect to exchange any number of shares of preferred stock for the same number of shares of *common stock*.

COOLING-OFF PERIOD. The time which must elapse before a strike or lockout may begin. See TAFT-HARTLEY ACT.

COOPERATIVE ASSOCIATION. An organization formed voluntarily by individuals or other organizations for the purpose of advancing certain economic goals of the members.

COOPERATIVE BANK. An organization that performs many banking functions but is operated in a manner similar to a CONSUMER COOPERATIVE.

COPE. See CURRENCY MANUFACTURE.

COPYRIGHT. The right granted to the creator of an artistic work to prevent others from copying or making unfair use of the work. In the U.S., a *common law copyright* exists the moment such a work is created, and remains in effect until the work is published or exhibited. Upon publication, a *statutory copyright* can be ob-

tained to provide protection for 28 years, renewable for another 47 years.

CORE INFLATION RATE. The long-run inflationary trend of a nation.

CORNER ON THE MARKET. Ownership of such a significant percentage of a particular security or commodity that prices can be influenced.

CORN LAWS. Any legislation which regulates price quantity, or other factors pertaining to corn. Usually refers to English laws between 1436 and 1846 which attempted to keep the domestic producers wealthy by reducing or eliminating imports. During those years the corn laws were subject to many amendments and for a while the protection was extended to wheat and other grains. These controversial laws were used repeatedly in political maneuvering.

CORPORATE BOND. An instrument of indebtedness issued by a corporation, as opposed to a public bond which is sold by some level of government. For more details, see BOND.

CORPORATE INCOME TAX. A tax on the earnings of corporations. Corporate income tax is imposed in the U.S. by the federal government and by most of the states. This tax, which yields about 15 percent of the federal government's revenue, is controversial. It is a clear form of double taxation: the corporation pays the tax on its earnings, and then stockholders pay PERSONAL INCOME TAX on the DIVIDENDS that are distributed. The incidence of this tax is also debated (see INDIRECT TAX); it is frequently said that corporations raise their prices by an amount at least equal to their tax liability, and therefore consumers actually pay the corporate income tax.

CORPORATION. See FORMS OF BUSINESS ORGANIZATION.

CORRELATION COEFFICIENT. An index number which indicates the degree of correlation between sets of data or between a function and a set of data. See

MATHEMATICAL REGRESSION in the appendix.

CORRESPONDENT BANK. A bank that performs certain banking functions for another bank; these functions can be as simple as holding deposits or as complex as collecting checks and handling international transactions. Some small banks depend greatly on correspondent banks; most banks use correspondents to some extent. See also INTERBANK FLOAT.

COSIGNER. A person, other than the main borrower, who agrees in writing to accept secondary liability for the repayment of a loan.

COST. In economics, *cost* has little meaning by itself because there are many types of costs. See AVERAGE FIXED COSTS; AVERAGE TOTAL COST; AVERAGE VARIABLE COSTS; FIXED COSTS; MARGINAL COST; TOTAL COSTS; TOTAL FIXED COSTS; TOTAL VARIABLE COSTS; VARIABLE COSTS.

COST ACCOUNTING. A branch of accounting that specializes in identifying FIXED COSTS and VARIABLE COSTS associated with the production of goods and services.

COST EFFECTIVENESS. A type of subjective analysis that can be conducted even when it is not possible to put a dollar sign on the benefits—by ranking the relative economic efficiency of alternatives. By using this method, originally developed for military programs, the costs of different ways to accomplish an objective can be estimated, and least-cost solutions can be identified. This approach is particularly useful in dealing with programs to reduce personal hazards. Instead of being concerned with such a difficult conceptual question as the economic value of human life, it identifies regulatory approaches that would maximize the number of lives saved for a given amount of resources.

COST FUNCTION. A graph or schedule of costs as a function of the level of production. A complete cost function considers totals (TOTAL COSTS, TOTAL FIXED COSTS, and TOTAL VARIABLE COSTS) as well as averages (AVERAGE FIXED COSTS, AVERAGE TOTAL COSTS, and AVERAGE VARIABLE COSTS).

COST-OF-LIVING ADJUSTMENT (COLA). See ESCALATOR CLAUSE.

COST OF LIVING INDEX. See CONSUMER PRICE INDEX.

COST-OF-SERVICE PRINCIPLE. In the economics of PUBLIC FINANCE, the concept that the cost of a service provided by a government should be borne by those who receive the benefit of the service. This principle is most applicable to items such as highways (to the extent that they are financed by the tax on gasoline, which is purchased by those who use the highways), does not apply to welfare payments, and is partially applicable to services such as national parks (which charge an admission fee that covers only part of the cost of maintaining the park). Similar to *benefit-received principle*.

COST-PLUS PRICING. A contractual arrangement used when it is impossible to make a reasonable prediction of what performance of a certain contract will cost. For example, most technology development contracts involve certain components that have never been made before (otherwise, the item would not have to be developed); thus, if a fixed price had to be quoted, the seller would make it high enough to cover all contingencies. In cost-plus pricing, the buyer agrees to pay whatever costs are *plus* a fee, which is the seller's profit. There are various ways of figuring the fee:

Percentage fee. Few contracts are written to give a fee which is a fixed percentage of total costs, because the seller would then be motivated to make the costs as high as possible.

Fixed fee. Many contracts are written on a cost-plus-fixed-fee (CPFF) basis. Suppose the seller estimates costs to be

$100,000, and a $10,000 fee is agreed upon; if costs are kept to the estimated amount, the $10,000 fee represents a 10 percent profit, but if costs go to $200,000, the fee (still $10,000) represents a profit of only 5 percent.

Incentive fee. Several versions of cost-plus-incentive-fee (CPIF) are being tried because it is believed that the declining percentage profit of CPFF is not a sufficient incentive to minimize costs. The incentive fee is usually arrived at by a formula which considers such objectives as costs, schedule, and quality.

COST-PULL DEFLATION. A deflationary spiral that begins with a decrease in costs, followed by a decrease in prices which leads to a decrease in NATIONAL INCOME and a lowering of the "buy" pressures.

COST-PUSH INFLATION. An inflationary spiral in which departure from stability originates with an increase in the cost of one or more of the FACTORS OF PRODUCTION, which is followed by the costs being passed on to consumers. See also DEMAND-PULL INFLATION. Unless there is a specific reason, such as wartime shortages, there is considerable disagreement during most inflationary periods regarding how it started. Also known as *sellers' inflation*.

COTTAGE INDUSTRY. Nonspecialized manufacture, which was almost the only method of production prior to the Industrial Revolution. Its characteristics are that most labor is individual or in a family group, most production is done at the worker's home, and there is little specialization. Also called *domestic production, home industry*, or *household industry*.

COUNCIL FOR ECONOMIC ASSIST-ANCE. A 1949 organization of communist nations, intended to coordinate the exchanging of goods, services, and knowledge. It was considered the counterpart of the EUROPEAN RECOVERY PROGRAM sponsored by the U.S.

COUNCIL OF ECONOMIC ADVISORS (CEA). The CEA serves the president of the U.S. in a strictly advisory capacity. It consists of three members, one of whom is designated as chairman. It is expected that the president will select individuals whose philosophy is consistent with that of the administration. On the other hand, the Joint Economic Committee is composed of elected members of Congress.

COUNCIL OF MINISTERS (U.S.S.R.). A high-level council which has policy responsibility in the field of economic development, maintaining such development within the legal framework established by the Supreme Soviet.

COUNTERCYCLICAL. Tending to return the economy to stability, as opposed to PROCYCLICAL, or tending to push the economy further from stability in whatever direction it starts to go. Countercyclical forces are both natural and artificial; an example of the latter is a PROGRESSIVE TAX (usually an income tax) which dampens runaway expansions by taking larger and larger *percentages* from the public, thereby reducing its ability to spend.

COUNTERFEIT MONEY. Paper or metal which is made to resemble CURRENCY but is not authorized by government or monetary officials.

COUNTERPRODUCTIVE. Tending to result in less output for the same (or more) inputs. For example, a wage increase is ordinarily considered *productive* because it provides an incentive for workers to work harder. However, there is evidence that when people reach a certain level of affluence they would rather have more free time than more money, and therefore a wage increase can be *counterproductive* to the extent that it results in workers taking more time off from their jobs.

COUNTERVAILING DUTY. An import duty established specifically to restore the competitive position of businesses that are put at a disadvantage by a tax which raises their costs.

COUNTRY BANK. See DESIGNATION OF BANKS.

COUPON BOND. A BOND having a block of coupons attached so that the owner can remove a coupon each time an interest payment is due and present it to a bank or other collection agent to obtain payment. The issuer does not have to keep track of who owns its coupon bonds (as it does with REGISTERED BONDs), because it is up to the owner to seek payment by presenting the coupons.

COVER. As used in financial economics, the final settlement of a transaction. See SHORT SALE.

COVERED DOLLARS. Throughout most of the late 1960s, and particularly before the economic policy measures taken by the Nixon administration in August 1971, swap drawings of foreign currencies by the FEDERAL RESERVE SYSTEM enabled it to give a temporary exchange-value guaranty to foreign CENTRAL BANKs accumulating dollars, and thereby to delay or avoid additional foreign requests for gold sales by the U.S. Treasury. In such cases, the Federal Reserve used the foreign currency immediately to buy the additional dollars accumulated by the foreign central bank. Thus, the foreign central bank's additional holdings of "uncovered" dollars were replaced by dollar assets that were "covered" or protected against exchange risk.

COVERED INTEREST ARBITRAGE. See INTERNATIONAL INTEREST ARBITRAGE.

CRAFT UNION. A labor union whose membership is restricted to those who possess a particular skill used in a certain job. Few unions today are true craft unions. In trying to expand their membership they have sometimes gone far afield; as a result, a union of truck drivers might now include office workers. Also known as a *trade union.* See INDUSTRIAL UNION.

CRASH. Usually, the STOCK MARKET CRASH which began in October 1929.

CRAWLING PEG. See SLIDING PEG.

CREATION OF MONEY. See MONEY SUPPLY EXPANSION MULTIPLIER.

CREATIVE DESTRUCTION. Phenomenon in which the rapid expansion of an economy automatically brings into play forces that terminate the expansion and lead to a following period of contraction. This contribution to explaining ECONOMIC FLUCTUATIONS was made by Joseph Alois Schumpeter.

CREDIT. The situation that arises when a debt is created, regardless of whether money is borrowed directly or whether goods and services are bought under a promise to pay later. In double-entry bookkeeping, credit refers to entries on the right-hand side of a T ACCOUNT.

CREDIT AGRICOLE (Fr.). A French organization that obtains funds from depositors, bonds, and the government and supplies money for credit organizations that make agricultural loans within their local jurisdiction.

CREDIT BILL. A BILL OF EXCHANGE which has been previously cleared by establishing the credit standing of the buyer.

CREDIT CARD. A card, usually wallet-sized, indicating that the person named on it is entitled to make purchases on credit. Some cards are metal or heavy plastic, and a few have a magnetic strip on which information is recorded. When a credit card is used, there is sometimes a provision for it to be inserted into a machine which reads the information; at other times sales clerks merely copy information from the card to a credit memorandum. Some credit cards are issued by a company, for use only in buying from that company; others are issued by a central credit organization, such as a group of banks, for use with participating sellers. See also TRAVEL AND ENTERTAINMENT CARD.

CREDIT CONTROL. The part of MONETARY POLICY that deals directly with the amount of credit outstanding or available. To the extent that the availability of credit influences prices and other factors of economic activity, it is felt that credit control is an important tool in the control of an economy.

CREDIT CONTROL ACT. Legislation of 1969 which includes as one of its main features, "Whenever the President determines that such action is necessary or appropriate for the purpose of preventing or controlling inflation generated by the extension of credit in an excessive volume, the President may authorize the Board [BOARD OF GOVERNORS OF THE FEDERAL RESERVE SYSTEM] to regulate and control any and all extensions of credit."

CREDIT CRUNCH. A situation in which potential borrowers DEMAND more MONEY than is available at existing interest rates. When interest rates (the price of money) do not perform the rationing function, a true shortage exists. Also called *money crunch*.

CREDIT FONCIER (Fr.). A French organization that obtains funds from deposits, bonds, and the government, and makes medium-term loans for housing, taking first mortgages as security. Its ownership and control are similar to that of the U.S. FEDERAL RESERVE SYSTEM (i.e., it is privately owned but controlled by directors appointed by the government); its function is similar to that of U.S. SAVINGS AND LOAN ASSOCIATIONs.

CREDIT LYONNAIS (Fr.). One of the largest commercial banks in France, nationalized in 1945.

CREDIT MOBILIER. An organization formed in the U.S. prior to the Civil War which had as its goal the dominance of the credit business. After the war it was weakened by scandal and eventually disappeared from the scene.

CREDIT MONEY. Generally, money that is not fully backed by a precious metal. Most of the world's currencies today are credit money. Also called *fiduciary money*.

CREDIT MULTIPLIER. The relationship between a given reserve base (see BANK RESERVES) and the credit superstructure (see MONEY SUPPLY EXPANSION MULTIPLIER).

CREDIT NATIONAL (Fr.). A French organization that obtains funds from the government and makes loans to private industry in order to stimulate, control, and direct capital investment.

CREDITOR. The party to whom a debt is owed. In the case of a loan, the lender is the creditor.

CREDITOR NATION. In international settlements (see BALANCE OF INTERNATIONAL PAYMENTS), a nation that exports more than it imports. It therefore has a net amount owed to it (either to its government or to its businesses).

CREDIT POLICY. See BANKING POLICY.

CREDIT RATING. The result of an investigation and analysis of a potential borrower, indicating the likelihood that a debt will be paid. A lender often checks a credit rating before loaning money, and a seller often checks a credit rating before selling goods on credit.

CREDIT THEORY. One reason often proposed to explain why the economies of nations and of the world in general do not run on a smooth trend line. According to this theory, debtors go into debt further than some natural desirable point, thus bringing consumption to an unusually high level. As the inertia of that trend relaxes, debtors, in the aggregate, reduce the amount of outstanding debt, resulting in a slowdown of economic activity. See ECONOMIC FLUCTUATIONS.

CREDIT UNION. A depository-type FINANCIAL INTERMEDIARY, which provides many banking services for an identifiable group of individuals. Credit unions have traditionally been available to employees of a certain employer, members of a certain labor union, or participants in a nonprofit function. However, recently the definition of "identifiable group" has been expanded so that membership may be available, say, to all residents of certain cities, or all persons of a certain religion. In 1934 Congress passed the Federal Credit Union Act, providing for federal charters to credit unions that applied and were qualified. Credit unions, SAVINGS AND LOAN ASSOCIATIONs, and MUTUAL SAVINGS BANKs are known collectively as *thrift institutions*.

CREEPING INFLATION. A theoretical concept of a stable economy in which prices of products and resources increase at a fairly steady rate of 2 to 3 percent a year. Those who hold that creeping inflation is a desirable goal claim that it encourages investment and consumer spending because loans are repaid with inflated money, thus helping debtors at the expense of creditors. However, especially with a constant inflation, creditors adjust for their loss of purchasing power by charging higher rates of interest. Therefore, although debtors pay back inflated dollars, they pay back more of them and are not helped by inflation. A bigger objection to creeping inflation is that all prices do not rise evenly. Thus, groups are always trying to catch up, and so they apply pressure for ever-growing price increases; creeping inflation is not a stable situation and eventually turns into *galloping inflation*.

CROP INSURANCE. Indemnification against the loss of an agricultural crop through natural hazards. The U.S. government has arranged for such protection through the Federal Crop Insurance Corporation.

CROSS-ELASTICITY. See COEFFICIENT OF CROSS-ELASTICITY.

CROSS OF GOLD SPEECH. A famous speech delivered by Williams Jennings Bryan in 1896, during debates over a gold standard, silver standard, bimetalic standard, and other forms of money system. Bryan won the attention of the silver forces with a speech that ended, "You shall not press down upon the brow of labor this crown of thorns; you shall not crucify mankind upon a cross of gold."

CROSS-PICKETING. The result of a JURISDICTIONAL DISPUTE in labor economics—picketing by two or more labor unions in an effort to obtain recognition as the representative of the workers in question.

CROSS-RATES. Paired exchange rates among three or more bases. See TRIANGULAR ARBITRAGE for an example.

CROSS-SUBSTITUTION EFFECT. See SUBSTITUTION EFFECTS.

CROWDING-OUT EFFECT. A MONETARIST view which holds that FISCAL POLICY loses some of its effect because, even though government expenditures may stimulate an economy, such expenditures must be financed and, at least in the long run, that financing reduces the ability of the private SECTOR to spend.

CRUDE OIL WINDFALL PROFIT TAX OF 1980. See WINDFALL PROFITS.

CULLOM ACT. See ACT TO REGULATE COMMERCE.

CUM RIGHTS. In financial economics, a CAPITAL STOCK often gives its owner certain purchase rights—usually the right to buy a given amount of the same or another security at a stipulated price. When the stock is sold prior to a specified cutoff date, the rights go with it to the new owner, and it is said to be sold *cum rights*; after that, it is sold *ex rights*.

CUMULATIVE DIVIDEND. The dividend on cumulative preferred stock; it must be paid before dividends can be paid to common stockholders. See CAPITAL STOCK.

CUMULATIVE PREFERRED. See CAPITAL STOCK.

CUMULATIVE VOTING. A type of voting for members of a corporation's board of directors that gives each stockholder a number of votes equal to the number of shares he or she owns times the number of director positions to be filled.

CURB EXCHANGE. When the AMER-ICAN STOCK EXCHANGE was first organized, it did not occupy a building—transactions were conducted in the street. Hence, it was originally called the Curb Exchange.

CURB STOCK. An expression sometimes used to refer to issues that are traded at the AMERICAN STOCK EXCHANGE.

CURRENCY. To an economist, *currency* means paper money and coins, but popular usage of the word makes it synomous with paper money.

CURRENCY BILL. Legislation of February 15, 1900, which set the U.S. on the GOLD STANDARD, established the value of a dollar at 25.8 grains of gold, declared it the duty of the secretary of the treasury to maintain all forms of money at parity with gold and one another, and provided that all government paper money would be redeemable in gold. Also known as the *Gold Standard Act*.

CURRENCY CONTROLS. Rules which make government authorities responsible for the exchange of currencies with other nations. All buying and selling of foreign money is through a designated government agency, and usually the rates are set to favor products the government feels are desirable and industries which it believes should have some protection. When currency controls are used, the currency is *inconvertible*.

CURRENCY MANUFACTURE. Paper currency, the principal product of the U.S. Bureau of Engraving and Printing, is printed by the line-engraved process on high-speed, sheet-fed, rotary presses. The most modern presses use two and four plates of 32 notes (or subjects) each and are capable of printing 9,000 sheets per hour. Each sheet is forced, under extremely heavy pressure, into the fine engraved lines of a plate to pick up the ink. The backs of the notes are printed with green ink on one day, and the faces are printed with black ink the following day.

The use of a special formula, fast-drying, nonoffset ink has eliminated the time-consuming task of tissuing or interleaving between sheets. The inks and distinctive paper used are produced under specifications designed to deter counterfeiting. After the printing operation, each stack of 32-subject sheets is cut into 16-subject size and examined for defects in preparation for numbering and processing on currency overprinting and processing equipment (COPE).

The final printing operation for paper currency consists of overprinting the Treasury Seal, serial numbers, and the appropriate Federal Reserve district seal and number. This operation is accomplished on COPE, which overprints the 16-subject sheets, gathers them into units of 100 sheets, and conveys them to cutting knives. The sheets are cut into two-subject units and then into individual notes. Units of 100 notes each are banded and packaged into "bricks" containing 40 units. Each brick contains 4,000 notes and weighs approximately 8.5 pounds.

CURRENCY OVERPRINTING AND PROCESSING EQUIPMENT (COPE). See CURRENCY MANUFACTURE.

CURRENT ACCOUNT. In accounting for the BALANCE OF INTERNATIONAL PAYMENTS, the United States keeps a *current account* which shows the value of all the goods and services imported or exported as well as the payment and receipt of dividends and interest.

CURRENT ASSET. In accounting, an item of value which will be converted to cash within a short time, usually defined as one year. For example, short term credit which has been extended is a current asset. When an installment loan is granted, that portion which is to be repaid within the year is transferred, each year, to a current asset account.

CURRENT DOLLARS. An economic statistic or series is said to be given in *current dollars* if the amounts given are in the dollars of the year indicated, without correction for changes in the purchasing power of money. For example, when GROSS NATIONAL PRODUCT is given in current dollars (as it usually is), it shows the actual amount of goods and services produced in the indicated year; if identical goods and services were produced in two different years and prices were 10 percent higher in one of the years, GNP in current dollars would be 10 percent higher in that year. See also CONSTANT DOLLARS.

CURRENT LIABILITY. A debt that is to be repaid within a short period, usually within a year.

CURRENT POPULATION SURVEY (CPS). A sampling survey conducted by the Bureau of the Census every month during the calendar week which contains the 19th of the month. This household survey, a principal source of information from which the CIVILIAN LABOR FORCE and the UNEMPLOYMENT RATE are calculated, uses a sample of 50,000 households chosen in 449 sample areas, for a sampling rate of about 1 in 1,300. For purposes of the CPS, the U.S. is divided into 1,913 primary sampling units (PSU), each generally containing an entire county or a number of adjoining counties. A little over half of all STANDARD METROPOLITAN STATISTICAL AREAs are included in the PSUs. The PSUs are then grouped into 357 strata, each containing a group of PSUs with populations relatively similar in terms of race, age, sex, education, occupation, and other characteristics. The actual geographical area surveyed is the Census Enumeration District (ED), which averages somewhat less than 300 households. The EDs within a chosen PSU are sampled in such a manner that the probability of any ED being chosen is equal to its share of the total population in the last census.

The CPS relates to individuals. Another important source of data concerning employment, hours, and earnings (related to jobs) is the ESTABLISHMENT SURVEY.

[Adapted from Herbert Runyon, ''Counting the Jobless,'' *Federal Reserve Bank of San Francisco Monthly Review* (September 1972).]

CURRENT RATIO. A ratio test conducted to determine the financial soundness of an enterprise. This ratio is defined as CURRENT ASSETs divided by CURRENT LIABILITIES, so that the ratio will be largest for those organizations with small current liabilities. Analysts have established desirable values for this ratio, as a function of the industry, size of organization, and other factors.

CURRENT TAX PAYMENT ACT. Legislation of 1943 which defined income tax liability to the federal government as arising immediately upon the earning of income, rather than once a year when tax returns are filed. Under this system, employers remit to the federal government from each employee's earnings an amount which is likely to meet the tax liability of that employee. It resulted in what is commonly called *withholding*.

CURRENT YIELD. The amount earned on an investment, based on the market value of, or the amount paid for, the investment, rather than on maturity or face value. For example, if a $1,000 BOND (maturity value) pays 10 percent interest it will pay $100 every year; if an investor buys the bond for $900, the $100 he receives will represent 11.1 percent, which is the current yield.

CUSTODIAN. One who has custody of an item, as when a bank is given possession of securities and is responsible for protecting them and collecting amounts due on them.

CUSTOMS DUTY. Taxes on either imports or exports, although in practice most often on imports. See also TARIFF.

CUSTOMS BROKER. A person whose business is helping importers pass their goods through customs.

CUSTOMS UNION. An arrangement among nations by which they remove trade restrictions on each other and adopt a common policy toward all other nations. Also called FREE TRADE AREA.

CUTTHROAT COMPETITION. An economically unhealthy form of competition in which fairness is disregarded, usually for the purpose of driving competitors out of the market. Because the fight is generally among industrial giants, the public too often condones it, looking only at the reduction in prices it pays for goods and services. Actually, the benefits are transitory—after competition is eliminated and a monopoly remains, prices will increase rapidly.

CYCLICAL FLUCTUATIONS. That component of ECONOMIC FLUCTUATIONS which repeats at fairly regular intervals. It is generally felt that fluctuations are due to the algebraic sum of cyclical fluctuations, random fluctuations, and a SECULAR TREND.

CYCLICALLY BALANCED BUDGET. After it was recognized that the ANNUALLY BALANCED BUDGET tends to reinforce a departure from stability, attempts were made to balance surpluses and deficits over a complete cycle of the economy instead of every year. This cyclically balanced budget turned out to be impractical for several reasons including the following:

1. The beginning and ending of a cycle can be identified long afterwards, but there is little agreement at the time as to where the economy is in the cycle.
2. Excursions above and below the trend line during a cycle are seldom equal.
3. Realities of the political world rule out all but an occasional surplus budget unless absolutely mandated.

CYCLICALLY EXCESS CAPACITY. A condition of EXCESS CAPACITY in an industry which is strongly affected by BUSINESS CYCLES, such as durable goods.

CYCLICALLY PERVERSE. Tending to amplify ECONOMIC FLUCTUATIONS by turning economic slowdowns deeper toward recessions and economic expansions into runaway booms. Also called *procyclical*. See also COUNTERCYCLICAL.

CYCLICALLY SENSITIVE. Tending to vary more widely than the economy in general. GROSS NATIONAL PRODUCT (GNP) is usually the measure of general economic conditions, so an industry that regularly grows faster than GNP during an economic expansion and declines faster than GNP during a contraction is cyclically sensitive.

D

DAS KAPITAL. See KAPITAL, DAS.

DAWES PLAN. Reparations payments by Germany after World War I caused gold to cycle through Germany and the recipient nations in such a way as to make termination of the famous inflations of the 1920s impossible. The plan, named for General Charles Dawes of the reparations committee, called for reorganization of the obligation and was a major factor in restoring stability to the German economy.

DAYS OF GRACE. Some savings accounts pay interest from a stated date even if the money is not deposited until some days later. The usual arrangement is to pay interest from the first of the month on all money deposited any day from the first to the tenth of the month—the days of grace. Some accounts require that the money be left in a stated length of time, usually a quarter, in order to earn days-of-grace interest. See INTEREST DATES for other methods of figuring interest.

DEADHEAD. A train, locomotive, truck, or other vehicle which is moved empty. For example, tank cars which take petroleum from oil fields are not equipped to carry any goods back to the field; therefore, they deadhead back. As a result, such products must, on the average, pay transportation rates that will cover the carrier's costs of a round trip.

DEAD RENT. Rent based on the value of the mineral or other natural products removed from the rented property, plus a fixed amount.

DEAD TIME. In managerial economics, time during which an expense continues even though there is no benefit or output obtained from the item. Applies to machines that are not producing due to breakdown or other reasons, as well as to labor that is idled while its pay continues.

DEADWEIGHT LOSS. See EXCESS BURDEN.

DEAR MONEY. Describes a period when money has relatively high purchasing power or when the cost of money (interest rates) is high. It is the opposite of *cheap money*.

DEBASEMENT. An official reduction in the specified amount of precious metal, usually gold or silver, in a nation's coins. See also OVERVALUED CURRENCY.

DEBENTURE. A debt instrument which is secured by the credit standing of the issuer, rather than by specific property. Also called a *debenture bond*.

DEBENTURE STOCK. *Preferred stock* (see CAPITAL STOCK).

DEBIT. In double-entry bookkeeping, a debit is an entry on the left side of a T ACCOUNT, as opposed to a *credit*, which is on the right side.

DEBIT CARD. A card that customers use to make purchases through a POINT OF SALE terminal. The machine-readable card allows the electronic transferal of money from the customer's checking or savings account to the merchant's account.

DEBT. An obligation that a *debtor* owes to a *creditor*. In economics, debts are usually amounts of money, but they can also involve a payment in the form of goods or services. A debt to be paid in money may arise from direct borrowing of money, from acceptance of goods or services with the understanding that payment will be made later, or from a later agreement, such as a court judgment.

DEBT CEILING. A legal limit on the size to which the federal debt may accumulate. In actual practice, the ceiling serves only to bring about frequent reviews of government spending, because whenever the debt approaches the ceiling (sometimes more than once a year), Congress votes to raise it.

DEBT, EXTERNAL. See EXTERNAL DEBT.

DEBT, INTERNAL. See INTERNAL DEBT.

DEBT MANAGEMENT. In industry as well as government, a debt is not just a passive bookkeeping entry, but a situation which must be actively administered. Large debts consist of several instruments. Sometimes, each instrument is issued in several series, and each can have different maturity dates. All parts of the debt must be watched constantly for refunding possibilities at the best terms possible.

DEBT MONETIZATION. An increase in the ratio of the CURRENCY in circulation to the amount of government securities outstanding, such as when an official change in RESERVE REQUIREMENTS results in an increase of currency in circulation.

DEBTOR. The party who owes a debt. In the case of a loan, the borrower is the debtor.

DEBTOR NATION. A nation that imports more than it exports, resulting in a net ouflow of its money. See also BALANCE OF INTERNATIONAL PAYMENTS.

DEBT SERVICE. In reference to PUBLIC DEBT, usually the payment of currently due amounts of interest and principal.

DECENTRALIZATION. In managerial economics, the establishment of autonomous units or divisions. For example, when it is said that "debt acquisition is decentralized among the subsidiaries," it is meant that each subsidiary can create debt in its own name and pursue a policy which is optimum for itself, rather than follow a policy dictated by headquarters for all subsidiaries.

DECERTIFICATION. Removal of recognition by authorities of a collective bargaining organization as officially representing a certain group of workers. Depending on the state or jurisdiction, there is a procedure to be followed by workers who feel that they no longer benefit from being organized or that they no longer want that particular union to represent them.

DECLINING MARGINAL EFFICIENCY OF CAPITAL. A theory holding that, after an optimum level of use is reached, each successive increment of added CAPITAL GOODS yields a smaller return on investment. Also called *falling rate of profit* theory.

DECREASING. Numerous expressions in economics can be treated in a special or restricted sense by beginning them with the word *decreasing*. For explanations of such expressions, look under the main part of the expression; for example, *decreasing marginal utility* is explained under MARGINAL UTILITY.

DECREASING COST INDUSTRY. An industry in which, for each producer, unit costs decline as the level of output increases. This condition suggests instability because the first producer to become of such a size that it has a competitive advantage will be able to expand still further, and in the theoretical limit would become a MONOPOLY.

DECREASING RETURNS. Given some mixture of FACTORS OF PRODUCTION in which one of the factors is in less than optimum quantity, adding a certain percentage of that factor will increase output by more than that percentage until the optimum is reached. After that point, called the *point of decreasing (or diminishing) returns*, adding more of that factor will result in smaller percentage increases in output. This is a very important concept, so an example will be given.

Consider a factory with a large amount of machinery and natural resources but no workers. Adding one unit of labor will increase output from zero to a significant amount, and adding a second worker (increasing labor by 100 percent) will probably increase output by more than 100 percent. As more labor is added, employees work in teams, and efficiency continues to increase up to a certain point. Let us assume that when the 101st worker is added (an increase of 1 percent), output increases by over 1 percent, but when the 102nd worker is added (an increase of 0.99 percent), output increases by less than 0.99 percent. It is then said that this factory is in the area of decreasing returns. If carried to ridiculous extremes, we could find a negative change in output resulting from increasing one of the factors.

DEDICATE. To transfer ownership from private to public, as when a developer builds homes, streets, etc. in an area and then *dedicates* the streets. The developer gives up all ownership claims as well as responsibility for maintenance.

DEDUCTION. An amount by which a taxpayer may reduce taxable income. The amount of tax actually saved is equal to the percentage the taxpayer pays times the amount of the deduction. See also TAX CREDIT.

DEFALCATION. Misuse of money or property with which one has been entrusted, especially if the misuse is intended to personally benefit the trustee. Also called *embezzlement*.

DEFENSE STAMPS. To help finance World War II and to reduce inflationary pressures during and after the war by taking excess spending power from the public, the U.S. government strongly urged citizens to buy government bonds. The smallest bond had a maturity value of $25 and sold for $18.75, a significant amount of money in the early 1940s. However, defense stamps sold for as little as 10 cents. When a person accumulated $18.75 worth of stamps, he or she could exchange them for a bond.

DEFERRED ANNUITY. An ANNUITY for which payments to the annuitant do not begin before a specified date.

DEFERRED AVAILABILITY. Bookkeeping entry of an item which is to be paid out shortly. See FLOAT for an example.

DEFERRED AVAILABILITY CASH ITEMS. With regard to the CONSOLIDATED STATEMENT OF CONDITION OF ALL FEDERAL RESERVE BANKS, this item includes checks and other cash items that, although received by the FEDERAL RESERVE BANKS, are not due to be credited for another day or two to the accounts of the depositing banks. The Reserve banks defer credit according to a schedule that allows time for out-of-town checks to be mailed or carried to the banks on which they are drawn. After a maximum of two business days, the member bank's reserve account is credited whether or not the item is collected from the bank on which it is drawn. [Adapted from Federal Reserve Bank of New York, *Glossary: Weekly Federal Reserve Statements.*]

DEFERRED BOND. BOND on which the payment of interest does not begin until some time in the future, as provided in the indenture.

DEFERRED COST. A cost which will be borne at a later time. Deferred cost is often used in connection with a government project—for example, when the cost of a war is to be paid by future generations. Many times the *cost* is nonmonetary, such as deterioration of the environment.

DEFERRED DEMAND. DEMAND, in the economic sense, which would have existed earlier except for some condition that was present, such as a major shortage.

DEFERRED INCOME. In accounting, payment which has been received prior to the performance that will earn the payment; for example, a magazine publisher usually receives payment for subscriptions and then earns it over a period of time by sending out magazines at regular intervals.

DEFICIT. In a government budget, expenditures in excess of income over a period of time, usually a year. Officials have a choice of creating money or borrowing it to make the expenditures. Because a budget deficit raises total spending above the level where it would be with a balanced budget, it is generally EXPANSIONARY and inflationary. See also ANNUALLY BALANCED BUDGET; BALANCED BUDGET; SURPLUS.

DEFICIT FINANCING. The obtaining of funds for expenditures by creating a debt. Often used in referring to government expenditures.

DEFINITIVE. In financial economics, refers to a formal certificate issued as evidence of ownership of a security, usually to emphasize that it replaces an interim certificate issued earlier or because a basic change in finances made the second certificate desirable.

DEFLATION. A general decline in prices in both the PRODUCT MARKET and the RESOURCE MARKET. Deflation is often associated with a contraction of the economy, although there have been periods of stability accompanied by falling prices. There are redistributive effects which are the opposite of those due to

INFLATION, but if either inflation or deflation persisted for a long period of time, anticipatory actions would become automatic and the actual effects would be illusory. See also CREEPING INFLATION.

DEFLATIONARY GAP. A condition of insufficient aggregate spending (total spending by consumers, industry, and government) for goods and services relative to the spending that would be consistent with a full-employment stable economy. The gap is actually the *amount* of change in spending which would lead to stability, and therefore the MULTIPLIER effect must be considered.

DEFLATOR. A factor by which a figure in CURRENT DOLLARS is related to the same figure in CONSTANT DOLLARS (of a stated period). Probably the best known deflator is the *implicit price deflator*; it is obtained by taking each component of GROSS NATIONAL PRODUCT (GNP), in as fine detail as possible, and deflating it from current data. Once deflated, the components are again aggregated to obtain GNP in constant dollars; then the aggregate GNP deflator is found by dividing constant-dollar GNP (of an identified base year) into GNP in current dollars. See also PRICE INDEX.

DEGRESSIVE TAX. A tax system whose *rate* increases as the tax base increases (therefore it is a PROGRESSIVE TAX), although each increase in the rate is smaller than the previous increase. For example, an income tax would be degressive if the rate charged on incomes of $5,000 to $5,999 were 5 percent higher than that charged on $4,000 to $4,999 while that charged on $6,000 to $6,999 is 4 percent higher than that charged on $5,000 to $5,999. See also PROPORTIONAL TAX; REGRESSIVE TAX.

DEL CREDERE AGENT. A person who sells goods or services for another while guaranteeing to the latter that the buyer will make payment. This arrangement is seen most often in international transactions.

DELANEY CLAUSES. Anticancer clauses of the 1958 food additives amendment to the Federal Food, Drug, and Cosmetics Act. They prohibit the use as a food additive of any chemical in any amount if it has been found, by appropriate tests, to induce cancer in people or laboratory animals.

DELINQUENCY CHARGE. A payment that is added to the basic charge because a debt was not paid when due. A delinquency charge is frequently made by governments when taxes are paid late.

DELINQUENT-LOAN RATIO. The dollar amount of mortgage loans and contracts delinquent 60 days or more as a percentage of the total mortgages and contracts held at the end of each month by the lender.

DEMAND. In economics, *demand*, used as a verb, means ready, willing, and able to buy. As a noun, *demand* refers to the quantity of goods and services which buyers are ready, willing, and able to take, such as when it is said that the demand for ice cream cones is 6 million a day. Demand can also refer to a DEMAND SCHEDULE. See also SUPPLY AND DEMAND.

DEMAND BILL. A BILL OF EXCHANGE which is due immediately upon presentation, rather than at a specified date in the future, as with a TIME BILL.

DEMAND DEPOSIT. MONEY which is credited to a checking account. There are two basic types of demand deposit: (1) a *primary deposit*, which results from money that a depositor takes into a bank or other financial institution that offers checking accounts, and (2) a *derivative deposit*, which results from a bank's creating it in exchange for a nonmoney asset (e.g., when the bank loans money in exchange for a promissory note).

Since a primary deposit in effect changes one form of money into an equal amount of another form, it has no effect on the

nation's MONEY SUPPLY. However, a derivative deposit *creates* money and therefore increases the money supply. See also MONEY SUPPLY EXPANSION MULTIPLIER; TIME DEPOSIT.

DEMAND FOR MONEY. See LIQUIDITY PREFERENCE.

DEMAND LOAN. A loan that is in principle for one day but is often extended on a day-to-day basis at the same interest rate. In effect it then becomes a short-term loan for which repayment can be demanded on 24 hours' notice. Also known as a *call loan*.

DEMAND MANAGEMENT. Influence over the wants of buyers, usually consumers. Advertising is one form of demand management, and government exhortation, such as an effort to have citizens conserve energy, is another. Putting certain goods in consumers' hands so that they will buy more of a COMPLEMENTARY GOOD (e.g., giving away flashlights to stimulate the sale of batteries) is another example of demand management.

DEMAND-PULL INFLATION. An inflation in which the departure from stability originates on the demand side, with buyers wanting to buy increasing amounts of the nation's output at every level of prices. Unless the economy is operating considerably below capacity, stepping up production to meet the additional demand will entail higher unit costs, and an inflationary spiral will be under way. See also COST-PULL DEFLATION; COST-PUSH INFLATION. Also known as *buyers' inflation*.

Since the use of these expressions is tantamount to assigning blame for an inflation, the same inflationary period is often described by one analyst as *demand-pull* and by another as *cost-push*.

DEMAND SCHEDULE. A description, in tabular or graphical form, of the relationship between the price of an item and the quantity that would be demanded at that price. A demand schedule describes an inverse function; changes in price and changes in quantity demanded move in opposite directions. A demand schedule should be interpreted under the OTHER THINGS BEING EQUAL assumption; at a specified time and under specified conditions, price and quantity demanded will be as indicated. It should *not* be inferred that if prices rise at some time in the future, the indicated quantity will be demanded. See SUPPLY AND DEMAND.

DEMAND SHIFT. See SUPPLY AND DEMAND.

DEMAND THEORIES. Theories developed to explain why a DEMAND SCHEDULE has the shape it has. In general, the theories are based on the fact that buyers make rational decisions in their own self-interest, to maximize their satisfaction, and that each buyer has limited funds available.

DEMOCRACY, INDUSTRIAL. See INDUSTRIAL DEMOCRACY.

DEMOCRATIC SOCIALISM. An economic system which is closer to socialism with regard to ownership of the means of production (i.e., it includes some private and some state ownership) and closer to democracy with regard to politics and individual choice. Also called *liberal socialism*.

DEMOGRAPHIC FACTORS. Characteristics of a population, such as age, work experience, and marital status.

DEMONETIZE. To remove something from within the definition of MONEY; for example, to take certain types of currency out of circulation or to remove a precious metal as the backing of a monetary system.

DEMONSTRATION EFFECT. The desire of an individual (or group) to have a benefit which others are seen enjoying.

DEMURRAGE. Carriers usually include in their rates an amount that covers the cost of having their trucks, boxcars, or other pieces of equipment out of service for a reasonable length of time while being unloaded at the destination. If the equipment is detained beyond that stipulated length of time, a charge called *demurrage* is made.

DENOMINATIONS. Units of MONEY outstanding in a nation. The accompanying table lists portraits and back designs on the paper currency now being produced at the Bureau of Engraving and Printing.

Denom-ination	Portrait	Back
$　1	Washington	Obverse and reverse of the Great Seal of the U.S.
$　2	Jefferson	Signing of the Declaration of Independence
$　5	Lincoln	Lincoln Memorial
$　10	Hamilton	U.S. Treasury Building
$　20	Jackson	White House
$　50	Grant	U.S. Capitol building
$100	Franklin	Independence Hall

Federal Reserve notes are the only class of currency printed today. Printing of Federal Reserve bank notes, gold certificates, and, most recently, silver certificates has been discontinued. However, some notes from each of these classes are still in circulation. The largest denomination ever printed was the $100,000 gold certificate of 1934, which featured a portrait of President Wilson. Designed for official transactions only, it did not circulate outside Federal Reserve banks. In addition to the denominations now in use, higher denomination notes were issued prior to 1969: a $500 note with a portrait of McKinley, a $1,000 note with Cleveland, a $5,000 note with Madison, and a $10,000 note with Chase (secretary of the treasury during the Civil War). All of these notes have ornate back designs featuring the denomination. The $2 Federal Reserve note, issued on April 13, 1976, is the latest permanent addition to the denominations of U.S. currency. In 1969, it was decided that no currency notes larger than $100 would be printed. All larger denominations are retired when returned from circulation.

DE NOVO. New, as in a *de novo bank.*

DENVER INCOME MAINTENANCE EXPERIMENT (DIME). A sociological experiment which was conducted in conjunction with the Seattle Income Maintenance Experiment. Together they studied approximately 4800 families with below-median incomes. One of the main purposes of the experiment was to compare several forms of the NEGATIVE INCOME TAX proposals with the existing Aid to Families with Dependent Children program. A description and results of the experiments can be found in "Welfare and Youth Unemployment: Evidence from a Controlled Experiment" in the winter 1980 issue of *Economic Review* by the Federal Reserve Bank of San Francisco.

DEPLETION ALLOWANCE. An estimate of the reduction in the value of exhaustible natural resources such as minerals and timber as they are extracted. A tax allowance of varying size, depending on the particular resource, is extended to owners of the resources. Unlike DEPRECIATION CHARGES, the depletion allowance is not used in NATIONAL INCOME AND PRODUCT ACCOUNTS and is not included in CAPITAL CONSUMPTION ALLOWANCES.

DEPOSIT. (1) In commerce, an amount of money paid to a seller to take an article off the market until final arrangements are made for the sale. The agreement should specify whether the deposit is refundable if the sale is not completed, as well as whether the deposit is to be applied to the purchase price. (2) In banking, an amount of money delivered to a depository-type FINANCIAL INTERMEDIARY to be credited to a savings, checking, certificate, or other account.

DEPOSIT AND SAVINGS BANKS (Mex.). See MEXICAN BANKING SYSTEM.

DEPOSIT CEILING RATES OF INTEREST. Maximum interest rates that can be paid on savings and time deposits at federally insured commercial banks, mutual savings banks, savings and loan associations, and credit unions. Ceilings are established by the Federal Reserve Board, the Federal Deposit Insurance Corporation, the Federal Home Loan Bank Board, and the National Credit Union Administration. Present legislation (see DEPOSITORY INSTITUTIONS DEREGULATION AND MONETARY CONTROL ACT) calls for deposit interest-rate ceilings to be phased out by 1986 under direction of the Depository Institutions Deregulation Committee (DIDC).

DEPOSIT CREATION. See MONEY SUPPLY EXPANSION MULTIPLIER.

DEPOSIT CURRENCY. That portion of the nation's MONEY SUPPLY which represents money loaned to customers by crediting their checking accounts (see DEMAND DEPOSIT) with the amount of the loan.

DEPOSIT INSURANCE. Insurance which protects depositors of banks and other institutions against loss due to the failure of the deposit institution. See FEDERAL DEPOSIT INSURANCE CORPORATION; FEDERAL SAVINGS AND LOAN INSURANCE CORPORATION.

DEPOSIT MONEY. Demand deposits in commercial banks other than deposits of the U.S. government and the commercial banks themselves. The FEDERAL RESERVE SYSTEM uses the expression *deposit money* in its reports because these demand deposits are included in the calculation of the nation's MONEY SUPPLY.

DEPOSIT MULTIPLIER. See MONEY SUPPLY EXPANSION MULTIPLIER.

DEPOSITORY. A bank, vault, or other entity which is made responsible for the safekeeping of money or other valuables.

DEPOSITORY FINANCIAL INTER-MEDIARY. A FINANCIAL INTER-MEDIARY which obtains some or all of its capital funds by accepting deposits, which then become liability items in its accounts. A COMMERCIAL BANK is an example of a depository financial intermediary.

DEPOSITORY INSTITUTIONS DE-REGULATION AND MONETARY CONTROL ACT. One of a series of deregulation actions to remove excess government control from the economy, this legislation of 1980 provided for raising interest rate ceilings on time and savings deposits over a period of six years and then abolishing the ceilings completely. It also permitted depository institutions to offer NEGOTIABLE ORDER OF WITHDRAWAL (NOW) accounts, and certain state usury ceilings were preempted. In addition, uniform reserve requirements on transactions liabilities at all depository institutions are being phased in, and the FEDERAL RESERVE SYSTEM has begun charging banks for certain services previously provided without charge.

DEPOSIT RUNOFF. Withdrawals from savings, time, and demand accounts—at a rate not fast enough to be called a panic, but fast enough to be of concern to banks and other depositories.

DEPOSITS: FOREIGN. With regard to the CONSOLIDATED STATEMENT OF CONDITION OF ALL FEDERAL RESERVE BANKS, accounts including DEMAND DEPOSITs of foreign governments, CENTRAL BANKs, and the BANK FOR INTERNATIONAL SETTLEMENTS. While transactions for these accounts are handled by the Federal Reserve Bank of New York, the deposit liabilities are allocated among all Reserve banks, and corresponding adjustments are made in their respective gold certificate accounts. [Adapted from Federal Reserve Bank of New York, *Glossary: Weekly Federal Reserve Statements.*]

DEPOSITS: OTHER. With regard to the CONSOLIDATED STATEMENT OF CONDITION OF ALL FEDERAL RESERVE BANKS, demand balances maintained by nonmember commercial banks for check-clearing purposes; demand balances of international organizations such as the International Monetary Fund (IMF), United Nations, and International Bank for Reconstruction and Development (World Bank); the special checking account of the Exchange Stabilization Fund; the special gold account of the secretary of the treasury; demand balances of EDGE ACT (international banking and financial) corporations held as reserves; and demand balances of certain U.S. government agencies. [Adapted from Federal Reserve Bank of New York, *Glossary: Weekly Federal Reserve Statements.*]

DEPOSITS: U.S. TREASURER—GENERAL ACCOUNT. With regard to the CONSOLIDATED STATEMENT OF CONDITION OF ALL FEDERAL RESERVE BANKS, demand balances in the general checking account of the Treasury with Federal Reserve banks and branches. Virtually all of the U.S. government's disbursements are made from these accounts.

The Treasury maintains the bulk of its operating cash balance in "tax and loan" accounts at more than 12,800 commercial banks. Most tax receipts and funds from the sale of new Treasury obligations are deposited by the Treasury in these accounts to minimize the impact of Treasury borrowing and tax collections on bank reserves. As funds are needed for disbursements, the Treasury issues "calls" to commercial banks, through district Reserve banks, directing them to transfer funds to the Treasury's account at the Reserve banks.
[Adapted from Federal Reserve Bank of New York, *Glossary: Weekly Federal Reserve Statements.*]

DEPRECIATION CHARGE. A realistic way of looking at a long-life piece of equipment purchased by a business is to recognize that a part of it is "consumed" every accounting period during its lifetime. Therefore, a depreciation charge is the transfer to an expense account of a portion of the cost of capital equipment. The charge may or may not be close to the actual reduction in value of the equipment as it ages or is used. For the manner in which depreciation enters NATIONAL INCOME AND PRODUCT ACCOUNTS, see CAPITAL CONSUMPTION ALLOWANCES.

DEPRECIATION OF CURRENCY. The loss of the PURCHASING POWER of a nation's money. The currency is said to be depreciated whether a given amount buys less domestic product or less of imported products. See also OVERVALUED CURRENCY; UNDERVALUED CURRENCY.

DEPRESSION. A major slowdown in an economy. (A minor slowdown is a *recession*.) The word is often used to refer to the GREAT DEPRESSION of the 1930s, although there have been 11 identified depressions in the U.S. since 1790.

DERIVATIVE. In mathematics (calculus), used in the analysis of a graph. If a curve is thought of as an extremely large number of tiny straight line segments, the derivative at any point on the graph is the slope of the segment at that point. Because slope is defined as change in y divided by change in x, mathematically inclined economists often refer to a MARGINAL rate as the derivative of the function.

DERIVATIVE DEPOSIT. See DEMAND DEPOSIT.

DERIVED DEMAND. A DEMAND for a product that exists only because of a demand for another product. For example, the demand for workers with a special trade exists only as long as there is a demand for the product they make.

DESCRIPTIVE ECONOMICS. Branch of economics which examines developed situations with the objective of explaining them, usually without relating them to basic causes or eventual results.

DESCRIPTIVE LABELING. In consumer economics, product identification by a manufacturer or intermediary, without the use of industrywide or government standards. It is contrasted with *grade labeling*, which is based on accepted or mandated standards.

DESIGNATION OF BANKS. Until 1962, MEMBER BANKS were designated, for purposes of reserve requirements (see BANK RESERVES), as (1) *central city banks* (larger New York and Chicago banks), (2) *Reserve city banks* (most banks located in 46 centers designated by the BOARD OF GOVERNORS [OF THE FEDERAL RESERVE SYSTEM] as reserve cities), and (3) *country banks* (all other banks). On July 28, 1962, the New York and Chicago banks were changed to Reserve city banks, leaving only two levels.

Since November 9, 1972, a new criterion has been used to designate Reserve cities, and requirements for reserves against net demand deposits of member banks were restructured to provide that each member bank will maintain reserves related to the size of its net demand deposits: a bank having net demand deposits of more than $400 million is considered to have the character of business of a Reserve city bank, and the presence of the head office of such a bank constitutes designation of that place as a Reserve city. Cities in which there are Federal Reserve banks or branches are also Reserve cities. Any banks with net demand deposits of $400 million or less are considered to have the character of business of banks outside of Reserve cities and are permitted to maintain reserves at ratios set for banks not in Reserve cities.

DESTRUCTIVE COMPETITION. Competition that, contrary to the traditional view, does not improve the position of consumers. For example, in their concentration on beating out the competition, sellers might decrease their service or the quality of their product, or in some other way lower the standards that had been established.

DEUTSCHE ANGESTELLTEN GE-WERKSCHAFT (DAG; Ger.). A large labor union in West Germany which represents mostly industrial white-collar workers.

DEUTSCHE BANK (Ger.). One of the largest commercial banks in West Germany, with branches throughout the nation.

DEUTSCHE BUNDESBANK (Ger.). The CENTRAL BANK of West Germany, created in 1957 as a publicly owned organization. It is responsible for West German MONETARY POLICY, much as the FEDERAL RESERVE SYSTEM is in the U.S.

DEUTSCHE GEWERKSCHAFTS-BUND (DGB; Ger.). The confederation of labor unions which accounts for nearly all unionized workers in West Germany.

DEUTSCHER BEAMTENBUND (DB; Ger.). A large labor union in West Germany which represents civil servants.

DEUTSCHER LANDER (Ger.). Name of CENTRAL BANK in Germany during reorganization from the close of World War II until the DEUTSCHE BUNDES-BANK was created in 1957. See REICHSBANK.

DEVALUATION. See OVERVALUED CURRENCY.

DEVELOPMENT AREA (U.K.). An area which, because of unemployment, loss of a main industry, or other undesirable condition, is subject to special consideration for government assistance in developing industrial employment.

DEVISE. Property, other than real property, that is given through a will.

DIAGONAL EXPANSION. Enlargement of a business' base by adding manufacturing capability for products which are different from those previously manufactured but which have a significant common element, such as those made from the same raw material. See also CONGLOMERATE; HORIZONTAL COMBINATION; VERTICAL COMBINATION.

DICTATORSHIP OF THE PROLE-TARIAT. In communist theory, a transitional stage from capitalism to communism. In this stage, the state, in the interest of the PROLETARIAN CLASS, works toward eliminating the capitalist class. When its task is completed and it is no longer needed, government will wither away.

DIFFERENTIAL DUTY. A duty whose amount is based, not on the product being imported, but on the place of shipment. Also called *discriminating duty* or *preferential duty*.

DIFFERENTIATED PRODUCTS. Products which, to the public, appear not to be identical. The differences may be real, or they may be in the mind, usually created by advertising. See PRODUCT DIFFERENTIATION.

DIFFUSION INDEX. A statistical measure of the overall behavior of a group of ECONOMIC TIME SERIES, indicating the percentage of the group that is expanding. If one-half of the series in the group are rising over a given time span, the diffusion index is 50. As an analytic measure, the diffusion index is helpful in indicating the spread of economic movements from one industry to another and from one economic process to another. Cyclical changes in a diffusion index tend to lead those of the corresponding aggregate (see LEADING INDICATOR).

DIFFUSION THEORY OF TAXATION. In social economics and public finance, the view that in the long run all taxes except personal taxes cause adjustments to prices charged in the MARKET-PLACE. Therefore, all functions of government are financed by consumers, regardless of who actually writes the check that pays a tax liability. See INDIRECT TAX; NEUTRAL TAX.

DIGITAL COMPUTER. An electronic computer which operates in discrete values of variables, as compared to an AN-

ALOG COMPUTER, which uses continuous values. Modern technology has provided digital computers with billions of bits of memory, capable of operations in billionths of a second. The resultant flexibility has increased the use of digital computers to the point that today most people think of a computer as a digital computer.

DIMINISHING. Numerous expressions in economics can be treated in a special or restricted sense by starting them with *diminishing*. Some are defined in the next few entries; for others, look under the main part of the expression (to understand *diminishing marginal product*, begin by looking up MARGINAL PRODUCT). *Diminishing* adds the concept of reducing the dependent variable's value as the independent variable increases. For example, *diminishing unit price* means that unit price declines as quantity increases.

DIMINISHING MARGINAL UTILITY. Credited to ALFRED MARSHALL, the principle which holds that as an individual earns more and more income or wealth, each added dollar brings less satisfaction (see UTILITY UNITS) than the previous dollar. One of the claims for high PROGRESSIVE TAX rates is that the loss to the high-tax payer is small but the gain in happiness to the small-tax payer is large.

DIMINISHING PRODUCTIVITY. The situation in which, to a given amount of labor and capital, each addition of land (see ECONOMIC RESOURCES) results in a smaller increase in output (sometimes an actual decrease in output) than the preceding addition of land.

DIMINISHING RETURNS. See DECREASING RETURNS.

DIMINISHING UTILITY. The situation in which successive acquisitions (of a good, service, wealth, etc.) yield less satisfaction (see UTILITY UNITS) than the previous acquisition of the same item. For example, a couple buys an electric drill for their home workshop and they

are excited about all the things it can do. If they buy a second drill, they might be mildly happy, planning to keep one at each end of the workshop for convenience; however, a third drill would bring less than mild happiness, and a fourth might even bring unhappiness in the form of concern over where to keep them all. Sometimes called *law of diminishing utility*.

DINGLEY ACT. Legislation in effect from 1897 to 1909 which reduced international trade by increasing PROTECTIONISM.

DIRECT CONTROL. Degrees of control by authorities fill the continuum from absolutely direct (such as quotas or prohibitions) to several stages of indirect (such as taxing a specific item so that it will cost consumers more, they will buy less, the industry will decline, and a COMPETING GOOD's sales will increase). The dividing line that separates direct control from indirect is difficult to define, but a control is more likely to be considered direct if it is near that end of the continuum.

DIRECT COSTS (DC). Costs which depend directly, but not necessarily linearly, on the quantity of a product being produced, as opposed to FIXED COSTS, such as real estate taxes which are constant regardless of the level of production (within limits). Also called *variable costs*. See COST for a listing of the various types of costs.

DIRECTED ECONOMY. An economy in which a significant number of end results are due to the deliberate decision of government bodies rather than to consumer choice or to the forces of SUPPLY AND DEMAND. All economies are directed to some extent, but a CENTRALLY PLANNED ECONOMY is usually at the other end of the continuum from a capitalist economy (see CAPITALISM). Also called *controlled economy*.

DIRECT FINANCING. Obtaining funds directly from investors, without involving an UNDERWRITER or intermediary. Small corporations sometimes use direct financing when there is a small number of investors and they are known by management; larger corporations have been known to advertise directly to the investing public.

DIRECTION. An action by MONETARY AUTHORITIES which has greater economic impact on selected industries or sectors than on others. Also called *selective control.*

DIRECTLY RELATED. Two variables are directly related if an increase in one is consistent with an increase in the other, such as in a supply schedule (see SUPPLY AND DEMAND). See also INVERSELY RELATED.

DIRECTOR. In management economics, a member of the BOARD OF DIRECTORS.

DIRECT PRODUCTION. The production of final products without the intermediate step of making capital equipment (which would have eventually made production of final products more efficient). For example if a company is to start making flags, direct production would mean supplying employees with the materials and having them make flags; INDIRECT PRODUCTION would mean a delay in the beginning, while employees first made or obtained flag-making machines.

DIRECT STRIKE. In labor economics, a large scale refusal to work by employees whose complaint is directly against their employer. See also CROSS-PICKETING; JURISDICTIONAL DISPUTE.

DIRECT TAX. See INDIRECT TAX.

DIRTY FLOAT. Situation in which a nation purports to be letting its monetary unit float (seek its own value in international markets while MONETARY AUTHORITIES take no action to control its value) but in which authorities are actually intervening in the market. An objection to FLOATING EXCHANGE RATES is that they become dirty floats

in practice. See also CLEAN FLOAT; INTERNATIONAL EXCHANGE.

DISABILITY COMPENSATION. Provisions for paying some or all of the wages a disabled individual would receive if able to work. Applies to non-work-related disabilities.

DISAGGREGATE. Divide a statistic into its component parts.

DISCLOSURE STATEMENT. The statement that must be given by the lender to the debtor, as required by the TRUTH-IN-LENDING Act. Included must be the total finance charge, the effective annual rate of interest, and several other facts.

DISCONTINUITY. A result which, due to the fairly rapid introduction of a new or changed factor, is clearly not a projection of the previous trend. For example, there is a discontinuity in PERSONAL INCOME on the day an increase in TRANSFER PAYMENTS becomes effective.

DISCOUNT. (1) In consumer economics, a reduction in price from the regular or list price. (2) When a payment is made for goods or services, a reduction in price for special treatment such as early payment or cash payment. (3) When a security is sold at a price lower than its face value, it is said to be sold at a *discount* (e.g., when a $1,000 bond sells for $900. (4) When a lender withholds interest, actually turning over only the net amount, the loan is said to be a *discounted loan.* See also DISCOUNT RATE.

DISCOUNT HOUSE. A COMMERCIAL CREDIT COMPANY that concentrates on providing liquidity to businesses by purchasing promissory notes and other receivables. It pays less than face value because of the time value of money and because some of the paper might be uncollectible.

DISCOUNTING EFFECT. Usually applied to the price of securities, but also applied to other prices, the result of the way in which an event can influence a price and the way in which buyers anticipate an event. For example, if there are rumors that a certain company has increased its profits, the probability that its stock will, in fact, be worth more induces some investors to buy the stock, and the increased DEMAND results in a higher price. If the price of the stock does not jump when increased profits are officially announced, it is said that the price was already where the new profit position would place it because investors had "discounted the news."

DISCOUNT MARKET. Not a physical location, but rather all transactions which involve the trading of COMMERCIAL PAPER and other instruments of finance and funding.

DISCOUNT RATE. The cost of member-bank borrowing is set by each FEDERAL RESERVE BANK's discount rate, that is, the rate of interest established by its board of directors, subject to review by the BOARD OF GOVERNORS (OF THE FEDERAL RESERVE SYSTEM). As envisioned in the original Federal Reserve Act, each Reserve bank would set a discount rate in accord with its regional banking and credit conditions. In the early years of the System, it was assumed that in its review process the Board would look particularly to regional banking conditions, but over the years the progressive integration of regional credit markets into a fluid national market gradually produced a national perspective for discount rate determination. Establishment by Congress of national economic goals in the EMPLOYMENT ACT OF 1946 further enhanced the role of national considerations in proposals for changes in reserve Bank rates and in the Board's determinations with respect to proposed changes.

Because the discount rate establishes the cost to members of reserves borrowed from Reserve banks, it plays a significant role in the decisions that a bank makes about whether to borrow at the DISCOUNT WINDOW. Although bankers may be reluctant to borrow from the Federal Reserve and may do so only to cover

temporary adjustment needs, a low discount rate in relation to other rates on money-market claims makes it more likely that a bank will seek funds at the discount window instead of using alternative sources.

To help control the volume and profitability of borrowings at the discount window, the Federal Reserve adjusts the discount rate from time to time to relate it more closely to other money-market rates. On occasion, however, changes in the discount rate may be used to signal the Federal Reserve's concern over unfolding economic developments and a possible intent to alter current and future policy accordingly. Reactions of the financial community to such signals—*announcement effects*—may exert a significant impact on securities markets because market participants will tend to adjust their investment strategies in anticipation of coordinated System actions via other policy instruments. Changes in the discount rate, therefore, must be interpreted in terms of how they complement, or are likely to be complemented by, other policy actions.

DISCOUNT STORE. In retail economics, a store that charges consumers less than the LIST PRICE, generally providing less service. A discount store may serve just the retail trade, or it may be combined with a wholesale operation.

DISCOUNT WINDOW. A figurative reference to loans made by a FEDERAL RESERVE BANK to a commercial bank, at a rate of interest called the DISCOUNT RATE. Technically, a MEMBER BANK has two ways of borrowing funds from its Reserve Bank: by discount or by advance. Although the two methods are quite different, it has become customary to refer to both as *discounting*.

A discount, in a technical sense, entails the sale of "eligible paper" to the Reserve bank; all such paper carries the member bank's endorsement. An advance is a loan evidenced by a promissory note of the borrowing bank and secured by adequate collateral. At one time, discounts were a much more important means of access to

Federal Reserve credit, but today virtually all funds flow through the discount window by means of advances.

DISCRETE VARIABLE. In analytic economics, a variable that can take on certain values only and cannot take values in between. For example, if one of the variables in an equation is *year*, that variable can assume only integer values (e.g., 1983, 1984), as opposed to a continuous variable which could have values of 1,983.001, 1,983.00001, etc.

DISCRETIONARY FISCAL POLICY. Policy regarding that part of government taxing and spending which can be controlled by authorities. Nondiscretionary items, such as interest on the national debt, are committed and therefore beyond the control of authorities.

DISCRETIONARY TRUST. A TRUST arrangement in which the trustee has discretionary powers regarding portfolio changes; transactions can be undertaken without the specific approval of the trustor. General approval is usually obtained annually. Also called a *managing agent* trust. See also ADVISORY AGENT.

DISCRIMINATING DUTY. A duty whose amount is based, not on the product being imported, but on the place of shipment. Also called *differential duty*, or *preferred duty*.

DISCRIMINATORY TAX. A tax whose burden falls more on one industry or group than on others, as when an INVENTORY TAX costs manufacturing and retailing industries more than it does service industries. See also NEUTRAL TAX.

DISECONOMIES OF SCALE. The increase in unit cost as one producer makes larger quantities of a product. Such increases are due to the manufacturer's operating beyond its optimum point, into the region where MARGINAL COST increases with each additional unit produced. See also ECONOMIES OF SCALE.

DISEQUILIBRIUM. A transitory situation in which forces are created by a change; the forces are not in balance, so change continues until a stable point is reached where the forces are in balance. For example, if sellers try to put a quantity of their product on the market, at a certain price, in excess of the quantity consumers want at that price, SUPPLY AND DEMAND analysis shows that a surplus results; then sellers will reduce price and quantity until equilibrium is reached.

DISGUISED UNEMPLOYMENT. Potential workers who are not employed but do not qualify as part of the CIVILIAN LABOR FORCE and therefore are not counted officially as unemployed. For example, a self-employed person in a seasonal industry is not counted as part of the labor force during the off-season if he or she is not looking for work.

DISHOARDING. Returning an item to either the REAL FLOW or the MONEY FLOW so that it can be circulated, consumed, or otherwise used in its intended function. When an item (e.g., money, coins, food, any product) is merely held or stored, it is said to be hoarded. Hoarding of a manufactured item increases its DEMAND without increasing its consumption; dishoarding causes an increase in consumption without increasing the demand for its manufacture. Statistically, the effect is similar to a reduction in inventories by business.

DISINFLATION. Opposite of INFLATION. Whereas depression and recession involve a slowing down of the economy and may even occur along with inflation, disinflation identifies a general lowering of prices (an increase in the purchasing power of the nation's monetary unit).

DISINTERMEDIATION. Aggregate transfer of funds from financial institutions, usually into money-market instruments. For example, legal limits on interest rates paid by banks (see DEPOSITORY INSTITUTIONS DEREGULATION AND MONETARY CONTROL ACT) have at times made it more attractive for the public to shift its savings out of banks and into other EARNING ASSETS.

DISINVESTMENT. Situation in which CAPITAL CONSUMPTION ALLOW-ANCES exceed GROSS INVESTMENT, or capital goods are being consumed (used up or worn out) faster than they are being replaced. Under these conditions, net investment is a negative number. Also called *negative investment*.

DISMAL SCIENCE. A term used by Thomas Carlyle to describe the field of economics.

DISMISSAL PAY. An amount of money paid to employees when circumstances other than their own conduct or quality of work require that they be laid off. Many labor contracts and employers' policies dictate the amount of such pay according to a formula, usually based on duration of employment; some employers have a blanket policy, such as two weeks pay for every terminated employee. Also called *termination pay*, or *severance pay*.

DISORDERLY MARKET. A condition of erratic fluctuations in international exchange rates.

DISPERSION OF UNEMPLOYMENT. Differences in unemployment rates among the identifiable groups which are component parts of the work force (see CIVILIAN LABOR FORCE).

DISPOSABLE PERSONAL INCOME. Income remaining to persons out of PERSONAL INCOME, after payment of PERSONAL TAXES. It is recognized that many obligations remain to be paid out of disposable personal income, and therefore it is not meant to indicate the amount of discretionary income available to persons. Also called *disposable income (DI)*. See GROSS NATIONAL PRODUCT.

DISSAVING. Reduction of savings; negative saving. In the U.S. in 1932 DISPOSABLE PERSONAL INCOME was $48.7 billion and PERSONAL OUT-LAYS were $49.3 billion, leaving PERSONAL SAVING of $ − 0.6 billion.

DISTORTION. Reallocation of FACTORS OF PRODUCTION, methods of production, mixture of outputs, or other measures in such a way that society as a whole receives less UTILITY from the economy. For example, if the price of natural gas is fixed at a level which causes return on investment to be less than it would be for alternative uses, too little natural gas will be produced in relation to demand.

DISTRIBUTION. In statistical economics, either the absolute or the relative number of a certain event or occurrence. For example, a *functional distribution* of wage earners gives the numbers who earn their livings from farming, dividends, wages, and royalties. The numbers of individuals who earn from $10,001 to $11,000, from $11,001 to $12,000 etc. are a *personal distribution. In marketing economics, distribution* refers to the DISTRIBUTION CHAIN. See also FREQUENCY DISTRIBUTION; FUNCTIONAL DISTRIBUTION OF INCOME.

DISTRIBUTION CHAIN. The path by which goods move from manufacturer to ultimate user. For example, a consumer good may be distributed by passing from manufacturer to distributor to wholesaler to jobber to retailer to consumer.

DISTRICT BANK. Each of the 12 FEDERAL RESERVE BANKs, so called because each serves as headquarters for one of the 12 Federal Reserve districts. See the table under FEDERAL RESERVE CITY.

DISUTILITY. Whereas UTILITY is a qualitative measure of the degree to which a good or service satisfies human wants, disutility is a measure of the degree to which a good or service causes unhappiness or dissatisfaction. For example, an artist provides utility because people derive more satisfaction from a finished painting than from the materials (canvas, tubes of paint, etc.) that it started from;

a criminal provides disutility because people are made unhappy by the function he performs, and the total economy would have a higher value without him.

DIVERSIFICATION. Extension of a firm's product line into several fields or industries. Firms diversify for several reasons. (1) The demand for their other products is such that further expansion in that direction will yield little or no profit; (2) their other product(s) are nearing the end of their technological life-cycle(s); (3) their other product(s) are seasonal, and a product with the opposite seasonal characteristics is needed to smooth out employment and revenues, etc. A CONGLOMERATE is a firm with an extremely large diversification into unrelated products.

DIVIDENDS. In NATIONAL INCOME AND PRODUCT ACCOUNTS, cash payments made by corporations organized for profit to stockholders who are U.S. citizens. Capital gains distributions by mutual funds and dividends in the form of additional shares of stock are not included. See CAPITAL STOCK; GROSS NATIONAL PRODUCT.

DIVISION OF LABOR. In labor economics, the separation of an overall task into separate tasks so that each individual involved performs only a part of the overall task. Usually involves SPECIALIZATION.

DOCTRINE THEORY. One of the MONOCAUSAL THEORIES used to explain economic history, a theory which holds that all major changes in history resulted from the introduction of new doctrines, such as religions, political systems, and economic systems.

DOCUMENT BILL. A BILL OF EXCHANGE that is handled together with a group of other documents. The other papers generally carry backup information or explanations which apply to the processing of the bill.

DOLE. Providing money or goods without receiving anything in exchange.

DOLLAR BLOC. A group of nations whose currencies are pegged to the U.S. dollar and whose international tradings are interrelated.

DOLLAR DEFICIT. In international economics, situation in which the net result of American purchases of imports, sales of exports, and government transactions is that more dollars are flowing out than in. Also called *dollar gap*. See BALANCE OF INTERNATIONAL PAYMENTS; MERCHANDISE ACCOUNT.

DOLLAR EXCHANGE. International transactions in which the U.S. dollar is cited as the base of payment; even if payment is made in another currency, it is equated to the exchange rate of the dollar at the time.

DOLLAR-EXCHANGE BILL. An acceptance used to finance goods stored in or shipped between points in the U.S. and to finance the extension of dollar-exchange credits in foreign countries. This type of financing is especially attractive to foreign banks located in countries whose exports to the U.S. are highly seasonal. Through the dollar-exchange acceptances, foreign banks obtain dollars to be used in financing their customers' imports during periods when export earnings are low and dollars are in short supply; when exports expand, the acceptances are paid off. Dollar-exchange bills and bills to finance goods stored or shipped in the U.S. constitute a small fraction of total acceptances outstanding.

DOLLAR GAP. DOLLAR DEFICIT.

DOLLAR GLUT. A large amount of U.S. dollars circulating in other parts of the world, because of a continuing deficit in the BALANCE OF INTERNATIONAL PAYMENTS. The dollar is then an OVERVALUED CURRENCY.

DOLLAR SHORTAGE. An impediment to world trade caused by an insufficient amount of U.S. dollars circulating in the rest of the world. This situation can arise when the U.S. exports considerably more than it imports, although such periods are infrequent.

DOLLAR VOTES. In a MARKET ECONOMY, basic questions such as what items should be produced are answered by simply recognizing that sellers will provide the items which they can most easily sell to buyers. Therefore, it is said that every time consumers buy an item, they are casting a dollar vote for what they want the market to provide.

DOMEI (Jap.). The Japanese Confederation of Labor. As the second largest confederation of labor unions in Japan, it organizes mostly public employees.

DOMESTIC BILL. A BILL OF EXCHANGE in which the drawer and drawee are in the same state (U.S.) or in the same nation. See also CONTINENTAL BILL; FOREIGN BILL.

DOMESTIC PRODUCTION. In a broad sense, items produced within a nation as opposed to an international industry. In a narrower sense, the nonspecialized manufacture which was almost the only method of production during the *cottage industry* (or *household industry*) period prior to the Industrial Revolution.

DONATED STOCK. Shares of stock owned by the issuing corporation because the previous owners gave them to the corporation. Such a donation is usually made for the purpose of strengthening the financial position of the corporation.

DOUBLE COUNTING. A statistical error in which an item is counted within its primary grouping, and then counted again as part of a larger or smaller group to which it also belongs.

DOUBLE EAGLE. A U.S. $20 gold coin. See EAGLE for related denominations.

DOUBLE-ENTRY BOOKKEEPING. A method of maintaining accounting records in which every transaction results in an increase in one account and a decrease in another—a debit entry and a credit entry. At all times, the total of debits must equal the total of credits, and the fun-

damental accounting equation—Assets = Liabilities + Ownership—must always balance.

DOUBLE INDEXING. Ordinary INDEXING ties some item, such as a cost, to a specific part of the economy, such as the CONSUMER PRICE INDEX; double indexing overcompensates for changes in a specific part of the economy. The following example is from the ECONOMIC REPORT OF THE PRESIDENT, 1982:

In 1972 the Congress sought to index [social security] benefits to inflation, in part to discourage discretionary increases that had been raising benefits faster than inflation. However, the Congress effectively ''double-indexed'' them through a technical flaw in the indexing procedure. As a result, nominal social security benefits continued to rise faster than consumer prices.

DOUBLE STANDARD. In monetary economics, the dual use of two commodities as a standard for a money system, for example, when gold and silver, in a stated ratio, are jointly used as the standard. (When two metals are used, the expression BIMETAL STANDARD applies.)

DOUBLE TAXATION. Taxation of the same base twice. An example often cited is corporate dividends; a corporation is taxed on its profits, yet if it distributes part of those profits as dividends to its stockholders, those individuals must pay personal income tax on the dividends.

DOWNTIME. The time during which no output appears from a production unit (e.g., an entire factory, an assembly line). Downtime can occur at regular or irregular times and can be deliberate (as for maintenance) or unexpected (as when electric power fails).

DOWNWARD SLOPING. Describes a graph in which a change in one variable is consistent with a change in the opposite direction in the other variable. For example, a normal DEMAND SCHEDULE plots as a downward sloping graph because an *increase* in price will result in a *decrease* in the quantity demanded. It is also said that the variables are inversely related.

DOW THEORY. In investment economics, a method of predicting price changes of securities, based on several fundamental guidelines; for example, securities in a general rising trend have short-term peaks and valleys, and each succeeding peak and valley should be higher than the preceding peak and valley.

DRAFT. A financial instrument in which a *drawer* orders a *drawee* to pay a sum of money to a *payee*. This method of paying is generally used in international commerce. Also known as a *bill of exchange* or *acceptance*.

DRAW. A regular salary paid to workers whose total pay is determined by commission. A draw is usually based on the average or expected amount of commissions the worker will earn. Periods when commissions are less than the draw (overdraft) are expected to be offset by periods when commissions exceed the draw. Most employers arrange for the draw to be recalculated periodically as the worker's commissions change. Formerly called a *drawing account*.

DRAWBACK. An amount of money which is collected as a customs duty on imported goods and then refunded when the goods are reshipped as exports.

DRAWEE. The bank or other financial institution which has the account on which a check is written.

DRAWER. The party that has the account against which a check is written.

DRAWING ACCOUNT. See DRAW.

DRAYAGE. A payment made for the transportation of goods.

DRESDNER BANK (Ger.). One of the largest commercial banks in West Germany, with branches throughout the nation.

DRUMMER. Until the early part of the 20th century, used to identify a seller of goods, especially one who traveled constantly to find customers.

DUAL BANKING SYSTEM. A banking system such as that in the U.S., whereby banks may be chartered and regulated by either state or federal agencies.

DUALISTIC SOCIETY. A society which consists mostly of two distinct groups— a wealthy elite and a very poor mass— with a negligible middle class.

DUMMY INCORPORATOR. State laws specify the minimum number of individuals who may act for a new corporation in obtaining the articles of incorporation; a person who is officially one of the incorporators but who actually just lends his or her name to the papers, planning to resign and leave the corporation to the intended owners, is sometimes called a dummy *incorporator*.

DUMPING. Providing the market with a large amount of an item at an unjustifiably low price. Dumping is used most often in international economics when, for various economic or political reasons, a nation floods the markets of the world (or a specific nation) with dumped goods.

DUOPOLY. Situation in which only two sellers are competing. See also COMPETITION; MONOPOLY; OLIGOPOLY.

DUOSONY. Situation in which only two buyers are in competition. See also MONOPSONY.

DURABLE GOODS. Goods which are not intended for consumption immediately or at one time. The time limit which separates durable from nondurable goods is defined in many different ways, and NATIONAL INCOME AND PRODUCT

ACCOUNTS defines durable goods as those with a normal life expectancy of three years or more.

DUTCH AUCTION.   Auction in which the seller starts at a high price and offers successively lower prices until one of the buyers accepts. Some people believe that the seller obtains a higher price with a Dutch auction because each buyer is eager to obtain the article before the other buyers do.

DUTY.   Generally, an import tax (customs duty). Also an export tax or a CONSUMPTION TAX.

E

EAGLE. A United States $10 gold coin, first minted in the late 1700s. Related coins were the double eagle ($20), half eagle ($5), and quarter eagle ($2.50).

EARMARKED GOLD. Gold which, although held by the CENTRAL BANK of one nation, is actually owned by another central bank. The gold may eventually be shipped to its owners or, because of international transactions, may become the property of the nation where it is held.

EARNED INCOME. Income which is received in exchange for goods and services provided. For a further explanation, see UNEARNED INCOME.

EARNED SURPLUS. That portion of an organization's profits which are not paid to owners as dividends but which are held by the organization for growth or other uses. Modern usage generally replaces this expression with *retained earnings*.

EARNING ASSETS. In money and banking, assets (such as bonds and other debt instruments) which, in themselves, earn money. In contrast, assets such as cash earn no money, and assets such as capital equipment may result in earnings but do not in themselves earn money.

EARNINGS OF FACTORS OF PRODUCTION. See FACTOR EARNINGS.

EASEMENT. Applied to real property, a right owned by one person while another person has possessory or ownership rights to the same property. For example, although an individual owns a house and yard, a utility company may have an easement which allows its employees access to the grounds for power line maintenance.

EASY MONEY. Opposite of *tight money*. When MONETARY POLICY is expansionary, and monetary authorities take steps to increase the rate of growth of the MONEY SUPPLY, they are said to be following an easy money policy.

ECCLESIASTICAL CORPORATION. An organization associated directly or indirectly with a church or religious group and that operates under a charter as a nonprofit corporation. A nonreligious incorporated enterprise is a *lay corporation*.

ECONOMETRIC MODEL. See MODEL.

ECONOMETRICS. The branch of economics which specializes in the use of sophisticated mathematical, statistical, and other analytic methods to make quantitative economic analyses. Econometricians work with *economic models*, which are sets of related equations used to depict the essential quantitative relationships that determine the behavior of output, income, employment, prices, and other variables. Such models are used for forecasting, for estimating the impact of alternative assumptions or government policies, and for testing various propositions about the way the economy works. See also MODEL.

ECONOMICAL. Generally, low in price; a wise purchase. *Economical* has little to do with the study of economics, but is often confused with it. See also HOME ECONOMICS.

ECONOMICALLY INDEPENDENT. Not dependent on others for any required ECONOMIC RESOURCES. A nation, or even an area of a nation, can be economically independent, although world economies today are so complex that few if any areas are fully independent. Sometimes, an area is economically independent with regard to a certain item or group of items. Even nations which could have a certain degree of economic independence usually find it to their advantage to specialize in an area in which they are most efficient, and to trade with other nations for other products. See COMPARATIVE ADVANTAGE.

ECONOMIC AND SOCIAL DEVELOPMENT PLAN (Jap.). A detailed economic plan for the years 1964 to 1968, designed to ensure to Japan smooth economic growth while controlling the inflation that resulted during the NATIONAL INCOME DOUBLING PLAN. The success of this plan was one of the reasons Japan received international recognition for its industrial growth.

ECONOMIC COLONIALISM. Unofficial domination of the economy of one nation by another, such as when one nation builds a large manufacturing facility in another and, because it is the largest employer in the area, has almost unilateral control over wages and other employment conditions. Sometimes, the foreign-owned industry is so influential in the colonized nation that even politics and overall economic policy are largely determined by the dominating nation.

ECONOMIC COUNCIL (Jap.). The committee responsible for the develop-

ment of Japan's economic plans for achieving growth, stability, balance, and other objectives. Appointments, from both the public and private sectors, are made by the prime minister.

ECONOMIC DEPENDENCY RATIO. Ratio of the portion of the population that does not work to the portion that does, often expressed as a percentage. The economic dependency ratio has always been over 100 percent because the numerator of the fraction (which includes those both too old and too young to work, as well as homemakers and others not employed) is larger than the denominator.

ECONOMIC DETERMINISM. The theory that economic forces determine the course of history.

ECONOMIC DEVELOPMENT. Some writers use *economic development* interchangeably with economic growth. Others [e.g., J. D. Gould, *Economic Growth in History* (London: 1972), Methuen & Co., Ltd.] use *growth* in connection with sustained increase in real per capita incomes, and *development* in connection with sustained structural change of an economy.

ECONOMIC EFFICIENCY. There are two aspects of economic efficiency: (1) the selection of the proper products to manufacture so there will be no waste, and (2) the arrangement of the FACTOR MIX which results in the lowest cost for a given level of production. In practice, economists recognize that efficiency must be tempered with other goals, some of which may be even more desirable, such as maintaining aggregate spending capability.

ECONOMIC FLUCTUATIONS. Variations above and below the trend line of an economy. These variations have long been referred to as *business cycles*, but because they are not limited to the business sector of an economy and because *cycle* suggests a regularity which most investigators cannot find, many writers today use the expression *economic fluc-*

tuations. Many theories are given to explain these fluctuations. Wars, of course, have a major influence on an economy, as do natural disasters such as storms and droughts. More subtle forces include changes of governments, the irregularity of major innovations, the phasing-out of products, and population growth. One theory has indirectly related economic fluctuations to sunspots because of their effect on weather. Another explanation is the time lags between, for instance, an increase in the demand for a product and the industry's buildup of capital equipment to meet the demand. See also ACCELERATION PRINCIPLE.

The accompanying chart, reprinted with permission of AmeriTrust, Cleveland, Ohio, shows the path of the U.S. economy, along with some significant events. The solid line represents commodity prices.

ECONOMIC GOOD. Something which has value because its acquisition requires a sacrifice (a decision among alternatives). Therefore, all goods and services are considered economic goods; anything which is freely available (such as seawater to an islander) is a *free good*, not an economic good. Of course, certain items may be free goods in some situations and economic goods in others. For example, a zoo, located even a short distance from the ocean, must pay the cost of pumping seawater to its seal tanks; therefore seawater is an economic good to the zoo.

ECONOMIC GROWTH. See ECONOMIC DEVELOPMENT.

ECONOMIC HARMONIES. As described by Adam Smith, the natural forces that rule an economy when people are free of government interference. When each person acts in a logical manner with regard to his or her interests, fundamental questions such as what shall be produced, and in what quantities, are answered by the INVISIBLE HAND.

ECONOMIC IMPERIALISM. Expansion of influence or direct control over other nations for the purpose of controlling economic factors such as raw materials.

ECONOMIC INDICATORS. A monthly publication of the Council of Economic Advisors, prepared for the Joint Economic Committee of Congress. *Economic Indicators* is available to the public on an individual or subscription basis. The document comprises about 37 pages of tables and charts on various aspects of the economy.

ECONOMIC LIBERALISM. An expression used to identify the CLASSICAL SCHOOL of economic thought. The expression is appropriate because, relative to doctrines of the past, classicalists were liberals seeking a change.

ECONOMIC MAN. A hypothetical person whose economic decisions are perfectly logical and objective. Economists of the CLASSICAL SCHOOL examined the economic man vicariously to formulate theories.

ECONOMIC MOBILIZATION. The organization of the ECONOMIC RESOURCES of a nation in order to accomplish a major goal, as when a war requires a concentration on the production of essential goods and services. Economic mobilization usually involves an expansion of the labor force, a considerable amount of overtime work, and the use of CAPITAL GOODS to their fullest.

ECONOMIC MODEL. A representation of an economy, or some part of it, usually for the purpose of determining the effect of a proposed change. See MODEL. Most models in economics are mathematical models.

ECONOMIC MOMENTUM. See J CURVE.

ECONOMIC PLANNING. Predicting and taking action to influence economic events. All economies practice economic planning and budgeting to a degree, but when all or most of the fundamental economic questions are answered by direction from planning authorities rather than

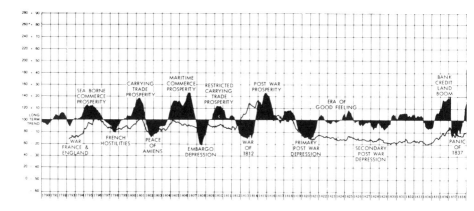

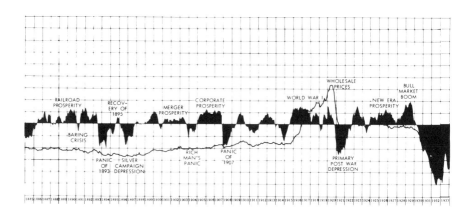

Economic fluctuations. American business activity from 1790 to 1981.

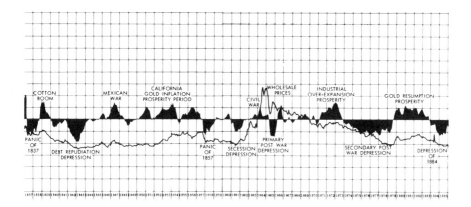

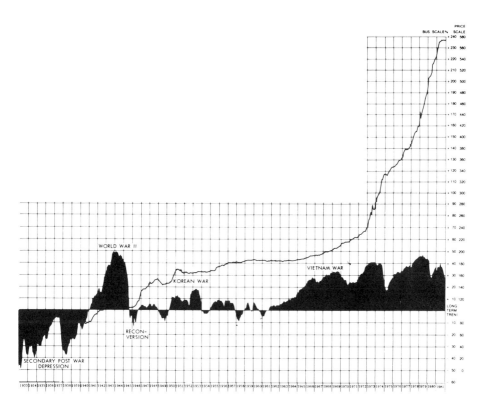

by consumer choice, the economy is a CENTRALLY PLANNED ECONOMY.

ECONOMIC PROFIT. Profit in excess of NORMAL PROFIT. Under conditions of *pure* COMPETITION, economic profit can be earned during a transitory period only; if such profit is being earned, other suppliers will enter the market, and prices will then fall until only normal profit is being earned by the suppliers.

The word profits must be looked at carefully when examining the writings of economists and of noneconomists. In economics, normal profits are considered a cost of doing business, whereas accountants and the general public view all profits as revenues minus costs (and those costs do not include normal profits). Also called *pure profit*.

ECONOMIC RECOVERY TAX ACT. Legislation of 1981 which makes significant changes in the U.S. tax structure for the purpose of putting the economy on a sounder path with higher potential. The act provides for INDEXING of the income tax structure beginning in 1985 in order to reduce the effects of BRACKET CREEP. In addition, the act allows every worker to contribute up to $2,000 to a tax-sheltered INDIVIDUAL RETIREMENT ACCOUNT (IRA).

The act includes several provisions favorable to business. The accelerated cost recovery system (ACRS), for example, allows faster depreciation of capital equipment. New leasing rules provide the same investment incentives to businesses with temporarily low taxable income as they do to other businesses. In addition, the investment tax credit is increased for certain types of equipment, and small businesses are allowed to classify as an expense up to $5,000 of new investment in 1982 and 1983.

ECONOMIC RENT. Sometimes called *economic surplus*. A payment received by an owner of a FACTOR OF PRODUCTION in addition to the payment that owner would require to provide the factor for that use. Such a payment can arise from the fact that the quantities provided according to a SUPPLY SCHEDULE are not MARGINAL, but total, quantities as shown by the following example. See also SUPPLY AND DEMAND.

As shown in the accompanying table, a change in price from $5 to $10 induces suppliers to produce an additional 10,000 units. If they first produced 50,000 units, sold them for $5 each, and then produced 10,000 more and sold them for $10 each, they would receive a total of $5(50,000) + $10(10,000), or $350,000. However, the market seldom operates that way, and it is more realistic to consider that suppliers receive $10 each for all 60,000 units, for total receipts of $600,000. Suppliers receive an economic rent of $5 for each of the first 50,000 units

This concept, originally developed to apply to land, is now applied to all factors of production. *Economic rent* is usually used in connection with continuing payments for use, such as with land, and the *economic surplus* means the same but is applied to a one-time payment as in this example.

If tennis rackets sold for	Suppliers would provide
$ 5	50,000
10	60,000
15	70,000
20	80,000
25	90,000

ECONOMIC REPORT OF THE PRESIDENT. An annual publication of the U.S. Government Printing Office, giving the president's summary of the preceding year plus objectives and current and planned measures. The report includes the president's own message followed by the annual report of the Council of Economic Advisors, which provides a full analysis of specific problems. The last 100 or so pages are tables of statistics on the GROSS NATIONAL PRODUCT, population, income, prices, finance, and related subjects. The report, which was mandated by the EMPLOYMENT ACT of 1946, is published every February.

ECONOMIC RESOURCES. The basic inputs or component parts of an economy. They have long been recognized as land, labor, and capital; modern writers usually include entrepreneurial ability as a fourth economic resource.

Land includes everything provided by nature such as the land itself, air, sea, water power, and wind power. *Labor* includes all effort provided by humans, such as manual laborers, craftsmen, managers, professionals. *Capital* includes everything manufactured for the purpose of helping humans in their productive efforts, such as machines, buildings, and roads. Also called *capital goods*.

Entrepreneurial ability includes everything that helps put life into a grouping of other economic resources, such as management, innovation, risk-taking, and applications analysis. Although this resource is not as visible as the others, it is essential because combinations of land, labor, and capital are not in themselves productive, and, other things being equal, an economy with a larger amount of entrepreneurial ability has more productive potential. Some writers refer to this resource as *management*, but others say it is much more than this word implies.

Labor and entrepreneurial ability are often referred to as the human resources whereas land and capital are called non-human resources. The entire field of economics is based on the fact that resources are limited (some writers say *scarce*) and therefore a price must be paid to obtain them.

ECONOMIC ROYALIST. A wealthy person, especially one born to a wealthy family.

ECONOMICS. In most definitions, the examination of the allocation of limited resources for the satisfaction of the UNLIMITED WANTS of humans. Economics draws on all other fields: elements of psychology, sociology, physics, mathe-

matics, politics, and others are essential to economic studies. A small number believe that economics should be limited to whatever concerns money; however, many other economists feel that everything— individual happiness, wars, morals, etc.— should be considered when examining the allocation of limited resources; others prefer a middle ground in determining what the field should embrace.

ECONOMIC SANCTIONS. Measures, such as boycotts and embargoes, which are aimed at changing the policies of a nation or other economic unit through pressures on its economy.

ECONOMIC STABILIZATION ACT. Legislation of 1970 which gives the president standby powers to declare a wage-and-price freeze if necessary to combat spiraling inflation.

ECONOMIC STRIKE. In labor economics, a strike which results from a dispute in which the issue is other than an unfair labor practice.

ECONOMIC SURPLUS. See ECONOMIC RENT.

ECONOMIC TIME SERIES. A set of quantitative data collected over regular time intervals (such as weekly, monthly, quarterly, or annually) which measures an aspect of economic activity. The series may measure a broad aggregate such as GROSS NATIONAL PRODUCT, or a narrow segment such as the sales of tractors or the price of copper.

ECONOMIC UNIT. A source of single action, for purposes of economic analysis. The composition of an economic unit has no universal definition; it depends on the use it serves and the type of analysis. For example, in an investigation spending, a household, a small firm, or a division of a large firm would be considered an economic unit; in a determination of reaction to fiscal policy measures, it is more likely that individuals would be the economic units.

ECONOMIC WARFARE. Nonviolent activities aimed at making one nation's economy dominant over that of another nation. The weapons of such a war include ECONOMIC SANCTIONS, DUMPING, and TARIFFs.

ECONOMIES OF SCALE. The reduction in unit cost as a producer makes larger quantities of a product. Such reductions result from a decreasing MARGINAL COST due to increasing specialization, the use of capital equipment, the benefits of quantity purchasing, and other economies. Also called *economies of mass production*. See also CONSTANT RETURNS TO SCALE; DISECONOMIES OF SCALE.

ECONOMY OF PLENTY. The conditions for economic analysis when productive capability is sufficient to satisfy the basic wants of a nation; the main problem is to maintain DEMAND so that an economic slowdown does not follow. A BUYERS' MARKET can result when there is a surplus of goods and services being produced.

ECONOMY OF SCARCITY. The conditions for economic analysis when the basic DEMANDs of a nation are larger than its productive capability. Shortages develop, and a SELLERS' MARKET results.

EDGE ACT. Named for Walter Edge (governor of New Jersey from 1917 to 1919, U.S. senator from 1919 to 1929), this 1919 amendment to the Federal Reserve Act empowers the BOARD OF GOVERNORS (OF THE FEDERAL RESERVE SYSTEM) to charter corporations for the purpose of engaging in foreign banking business. Edge Act corporations are granted certain powers subject to the rules and regulations described in regulation K, first issued by the Board in 1920. The regulation specifies that the deposits of such corporations are subject to Reserve requirements and their required reserves must be held in cash or in demand balances at Federal Reserve banks. [Adapted from Federal Reserve bank of New York, *Glossary: Weekly Federal Reserve Statements.*]

EDGE BANK. A COMMERCIAL BANK that engages in international banking under a federal charter.

EDGE CORPORATION. A corporation formed by a U.S. bank for the purpose of engaging in foreign banking and financing. The BOARD OF GOVERNORS (OF THE FEDERAL RESERVE SYSTEM) acts upon applications by member banks to establish Edge Act corporations. It also examines such corporations and their subsidiaries.

EFFECTIVE ANNUAL RATE. The annual rate of interest which when used in the simple-interest-rate formula equals the amount of interest payable in other calculation methods. The concept of the effective annual rate came about with the TRUTH-IN-LENDING act, which resulted from the variety of methods used to calculate interest on debt, making it difficult for debtors to make comparisons among lenders. Also known as *annual percentage rate (APR)*.

EFFECTIVE COMPETITION. In certain industries it is not feasible to have competing suppliers (see NATURAL MONOPOLY), so the government grants regulated monopoly status. The supplier is then regulated so that the consumer obtains the benefits of competition, and the result is *effective competition*.

EFFECTIVE DEMAND. The desire or the ability to obtain goods offered on the market has no economic significance; analysts ask how many are *ready, willing, and able* to take action in the MARKETPLACE. Several writers use the phrase *effective demand* to emphasize that all of this is implied when *demand* is mentioned.

EFFECTIVE RATE OF INTEREST. The rate of interest paid on a security, based on the actual purchase price rather than on the face or maturity value. Thus, if an investor paid $600 for a bond which pays $60 interest every year, he or she would receive an effective rate of 10 percent. This rate compares to the *nominal rate*, which is based on the face value; if the bond has a face value of $1,000, this $60 interest represents a nominal rate of 6 percent.

EFFICIENT. Describes an an economy in which it is impossible to make anyone better off without making someone else worse off. That is, there is no possible rearrangement of ECONOMIC RE-SOURCES which would improve anyone's position without simultaneously harming someone else.

ELASTICITY. A measure of the degree to which a change in quantity (demanded or supplied) is dependent on a change in price.

Elasticity of demand is the ratio of a change in the quantity demanded to the associated change in price. In the accompanying figure (its basis is explained under SUPPLY AND DEMAND), demand curve D1 has low elasticity (is highly *inelastic*), meaning that it takes a large change in price to have any significant effect on the quantity demanded. Necessities typically have inelastic demand schedules; competition, not buyer resistance keeps prices from being higher. Curve D3 shows a highly elastic demand schedule; a small change in price has a large effect on the quantity demanded, as would be expected of luxuries and items with close substitutes.

Elasticity of supply. Curve S1 is highly inelastic, and S3 is highly elastic. Under assumptions of COMPETITION, when firms are free to enter and leave the market, elasticity of supply is most meaningful in the short run. For example, the rapid rise of meat prices in the early 1970s has been attributed to an increased demand. Due to the nature of the product, however, it was not possible to increase the size of beef herds quickly; so even though the increased demand brought forth higher prices, the quantity supplied could increase very little in the short run.

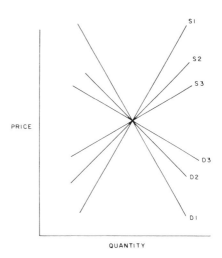

Elasticity. Highly elastic means a small change in price has a large effect on quantity.

The ratios of percentage change in quantity to associated percentage change in price are also called *coefficients of elasticity* (of demand and supply).

ELASTIC MONEY SUPPLY. In a money system, a MONEY SUPPLY whose size can be expanded or contracted by MONETARY AUTHORITIES. In contrast, in a system backed by gold, the only way to expand the money supply is to obtain more gold. See TOOLS OF MONETARY POLICY.

ELECTRONIC DATA PROCESSING (EDP). Working of accounts and other data by means of computers and other automatic machines. In addition to numerical calculations, EDP can include operations such as sorting (alphabetically, numerically, or in some planned combination), merging, selecting, collating, and formatting.

ELECTRONIC FUNDS TRANSFER (EFT). The transfer of ownership of money through electronic signals, without physical movement of cash or checks. Some reasons for the development of EFT are convenience, speed, and cost (it costs the banking system from 30 to 50 cents to clear a check).

Automated teller machine (ATM). An ATM is a 24-hour banking terminal that allows consumers to make deposits, pay bills, transfer funds, and perform other banking operations at their convenience. They use a plastic debit card, along with a code called a *personal identification number* (PIN).

Point-of-sale (POS) *terminal.* In some parts of the U.S., electronic terminals located in shopping areas allow the transfer of funds from a customer's account to a merchant's. To pay for a purchase, the consumer inserts an EFT card into the terminal and punches in the amount; the transfer is made electronically.

ELECTRONIC FUNDS TRANSFER ACT. A considerable amount of insecurity accompanied the growth of ELECTRONIC FUNDS TRANSFER (EFT), thus leading to this legislation. It gives consumers the right to get a written receipt when using an AUTOMATIC TELLER MACHINE and to have electronic transfers shown on a periodic statement. When automatic payments have been made, the party receiving payment is named on the statement, and any fees are shown, along with the opening and closing balances. The act also specifies consumers' rights with regard to errors, information, and the loss or theft of the EFT card.

ELECTRONIC MONEY. Money which exists only as a recording in a computer; transfers of ownership and transfers from one account to another are accomplished by electronic means. In the ultimate arrangement, in the opinion of many planners, there will be no physical movement of money or checks—also called the *cashless/checkless society*. It is generally recognized that something short of that ideal is the practical limit, sometimes called the *less-cash/less-check society*.

ELEEMOSYNARY CORPORATION. A nonprofit corporation which is chartered for charitable purposes.

ELIGIBLE LIABILITIES (U.K.). The base for reserve ratio requirements. Eligible liabilities consist basically of sterling deposits of two years or less from outside the banking sector, plus foreign currency deposits that have been switched into sterling. See also RESERVE ASSETS.

ELIGIBLE PAPER. Assets which FEDERAL RESERVE BANKs will accept as collateral for loans made to commercial banks. The types of instruments that are included as eligible paper have varied over the years; the Federal Reserve Act of 1913 was very restrictive, stating that it "shall not include notes, drafts, or bills covering merely investments issued or drawn for the purpose of carrying or trading in stocks, bonds, or other investment securities, except bonds and notes of the Government of the United States." See COMMERCIAL LOAN THEORY.

ELIGIBLE RESERVES. The DEPOSITORY INSTITUTIONS DEREGULATION AND MONETARY CONTROL ACT specifies that reserve requirements can be met with funds deposited directly at the Federal Reserve, funds held at the Federal Reserve that are passed through a correspondent, and VAULT CASH. A depository institution that is a member of the Federal Reserve System must hold its required reserves directly with the Federal Reserve. A nonmember institution may deposit its required reserve balance directly with the Federal Reserve or pass its required reserve balance through a correspondent. Such a correspondent may be a Federal Home Loan Bank, the National Credit Union Administration Central Liquidity Facility, a depository institution that holds a reserve balance with the Federal Reserve, or certain depository institutions that are not required to hold a reserve balance if authorized by the BOARD OF GOVERNORS (OF THE FEDERAL RESERVE SYSTEM).

EMBARGO. An official government stand of not trading with another nation, sometimes as a war measure, an ECONOMIC WARFARE measure, or an economic measure to force certain concessions. Embargo also means the preventing of a certain nation's ships from entering a port.

EMBEZZLEMENT. The unauthorized appropriation or conversion of property by one to whom it has been entrusted.

EMBOURGEOISEMENT. The process of adopting, by blue collar workers, the living standards previously available only to the more affluent of the white collar workers.

EMERGENCY BANKING RELIEF ACT. Passed as one of the NEW DEAL measures on March 9, 1933, this legislation officially reopened the nation's banks (see BANK HOLIDAY), made credit more available, placed an EMBARGO on exporting gold, called in all domestically held gold and gold certificates, and took steps to strengthen banks that were insolvent or on the verge of insolvency.

EMERGENCY BOARD. In labor economics, a board appointed by the president, under the authority of the Railway Labor Act, when interstate commerce is threatened by a labor dispute. This procedure now applies to airlines as well as railroads.

EMERGENCY COMPENSATION AND SPECIAL ASSISTANCE EXTENSION ACT. Legislation of 1975 that terminated the Federal Supplemental Benefits (FSB) program as of March 31, 1977; extended other programs; and rearranged the federal responsibilities of unemployment benefit programs. A good description of the act is included in *Unemployment Insurance: Programs, Procedures, and Problems*, by the Federal Reserve Bank of Kansas City (1977).

EMERGENCY CREDIT. Money made available by FEDERAL RESERVE BANKs to individual banks or groups of banks facing financial stringency due to adverse local, regional, or national financial developments. In such operations, the Federal Reserve serves its traditional role as the ultimate provider of liquidity—the "lender of last resort."

EMERGENCY DISPUTE. In labor economics, a dispute which is likely to endanger the health and safety of the public if it leads to a work stoppage. Under provisions of the TAFT-HARTLEY ACT, the president can obtain an injunction to postpone a work stoppage while a board of inquiry investigates.

EMERGING NATION. A nation whose economy is developing toward the living standards of the more advanced nations. *Emerging nation* sometimes implies a change from colonial status to advancing independence.

EMINENT DOMAIN. The power of a government (and certain private units such as utilities) to take ownership of private property without the owner's consent. Such action is justified when it is deemed that society, overall, will realize a net benefit (see SPILLOVER)—for example, when land is taken to build a highway. Statutes require that the owner be compensated in a fair manner.

EMOLUMENT. Compensation for labor or services performed, including money, benefits, privileges, and perquisites. When an emolument is money, it is simply called *salary* or *wages*.

EMPIRE PREFERENCE SYSTEM (U.K.). The policy of Great Britain which gives favorable treatment to certain goods in order to encourage trade among members of the British Empire.

EMPIRICAL EVIDENCE. Evidence based on observation of a result, rather than on a source. The danger of drawing conclusions based on empirical evidence is acute in economics because each result is due to many influences (see OTHER THINGS BEING EQUAL). For example, suppose welfare roles are expanded, and the next year the crime rate falls. Before using this empirical evidence as the basis for saying that liberalizing welfare reduces crime, a careful analyst would check into other possible causes (such as increased police patrols).

EMPLOYED. The Bureau of Labor Statistics defines a person as *employed* if that person worked at least 1 hour during the week as a paid employee or in his or her own profession, business, or firm; worked at least 15 hours as an unpaid worker in a family enterprise; or had a job or business but was not at work because of illness, bad weather, vacation, labor dispute, or personal reasons. For collecting and interpreting statistics, it is important to have a definition of who is considered employed.

EMPLOYEE BENEFIT TRUST. A trust arrangemment, usually arising from pension and profit-sharing plans, but also including trusts set up under stock bonus plans, as well as under plans for stimulating employee savings and aiding disabled workers. Such trusts may be administered by business enterprises, labor and religious organizations, educational and charitable institutions, and state and local governments.

EMPLOYEE RELATIONS. A department in an organization, generally responsible for the same functions as INDUSTRIAL RELATIONS.

EMPLOYEE REPRESENTATION SYSTEM. A GRIEVANCE COMMITTEE or other group that examines and discusses issues. Employees, by a ballot, usually elect one or more of their group to represent them on the committee.

EMPLOYERS' ASSOCIATION. A voluntary nonprofit organization of business competitors established to promote the common interest.

EMPLOYMENT ACT OF 1946. During the GREAT DEPRESSION the policy of LAISSEZ-FAIRE was increasingly questioned as more and more people wanted the government to "do something." However, the federal government's responsibility to take a hand in general economic matters was not clearly identified.

Then World War II interrupted the controversy. Soon after the war, the employment act was passed, making it clear that it was the government's responsibility to use FISCAL POLICY and MONETARY POLICY as necessary to keep the economy growing and employment at the highest level consistent with stable growth. The act also created the COUNCIL OF ECONOMIC ADVISORS and required annual reporting via the ECONOMIC REPORT OF THE PRESIDENT.

EMPLOYMENT MULTIPLIER. Ratio of change in total employment which results from the addition of one job in a selected industry. For example, if a manufacturing industry multiplier is 1.5 in a certain city, then for every two persons added to manufacturing employment, total employment in that city will increase by three. Information on employment multipliers will help a government decide where its efforts are likely to be most effective. See also INPUT-OUTPUT TABLE.

EMPORIUM. A store, usually one specializing in high-quality goods of a particular specialty.

ENCLAVE ECONOMY. The economy of a nation which is dominated by, and dependent on, the economy of a nation that surrounds it.

ENCLOSURE MOVEMENT. That period in each nation's history when the erection of fences caused a change in agricultural methods and in economic activities such as transportation. A common sequence was unoccupied, open land; scattered occupation; and denser occupation that led to property boundary identification. Overall economic functions changed gradually with this sequence, but the next step, erection of fences, caused rapid, and sometimes violent, changes.

END MONEY. In certain industries, contingency funds that are held aside in order to allow the completion of a project if costs exceed estimates.

END OF MONTH (EOM). In a sales contract for continuing sales, a stipulation that the seller will continue to ship goods as ordered throughout the month; then, at the end of the month, the seller will bill the buyer for all goods shipped.

ENDOGENOUS. Coming from or controlled from within. When predicting sales, an organization has control over such items as selling price and advertising expenditures, which are endogenous variables, but not over competitor prices and weather, which are exogenous variables.

ENDOGENOUS THEORY OF BUSINESS CYCLES. Theory which holds that the *major* causes of ECONOMIC FLUCTUATIONS in a nation are found within that nation, and that only minor causes originate in other parts of the world. Also called the *internal theory of business cycles*. Some of the internal causes are information lags, overinvestment, and PROCYCLICAL industries. See also EXOGENOUS THEORY OF BUSINESS CYCLES.

ENDORSEMENT. Writing one's name on a negotiable instrument (such as a check or bond) to signify transfer of title to another. In many legal areas (such as the UNIFORM COMMERCIAL CODE), it is spelled *indorsement*. See also ALLONGE; BLANK ENDORSEMENT; CONDITIONAL ENDORSEMENT; QUALIFIED ENDORSEMENT; RESTRICTIVE ENDORSEMENT; SPECIAL ENDORSEMENT.

ENDOWMENT. An amount of money or other wealth which provides the basic financing for a nonprofit organization. For example, many universities have an endowment which, when added to tuitions, gifts, and other sources of income, allows them to operate. It is generally desirable to draw on the earnings that result from investment of the endowment and to leave the principal untouched, or to enlarge the principal by additions from its earnings.

ENDOWMENT OF HUMAN CAPITAL. The present value of the after-tax income that a household would earn if it was interested solely in maximizing its labor earnings.

END PRODUCT. Some economics writers use *end product* in strict reference to a consumer product. Others interpret it to mean the final form of output from any producer; thus the end product of one manufacturer might be the raw material of the next manufacturer.

ENGELS, FRIEDRICH. Associate of KARL MARX, Engels carried on socialist activities after Marx died; in fact, the second and third volumes of their famous work, DAS KAPITAL, were put in final form by Engels prior to publication. Born of wealthy parents in Germany, he later moved to England to manage a factory owned by his family.

ENGEL'S LAWS. In 1857 Ernst Engel, director of the Bureau of Statistics in Prussia, published a paper which showed that, OTHER THINGS BEING EQUAL, family income and percentage of income spent on food are inversely related. Later, that conclusion was called the first of Engel's laws. The others are: (2) the percentage of income spent on clothing does not change; (3) the percentage spent on housing and housing operations does not change; (4) the percentage spent on items such as leisure, education, and personal care increases as income increases.

ENTREPRENEURIAL ABILITY. See ECONOMIC RESOURCES.

E PLURIBUS UNUM (Lat.). "Out of many, one." Official motto of the U.S., this phrase is used in the Great Seal of the U.S., on coins, and other official items. The phrase contains 13 letters and therefore is symbolic of the original 13 states.

EQUAL EMPLOYMENT OPPORTUNITY COMMISSION. Organization responsible for policing public and private employers to prevent discrimination based on color, race, religion, sex, or national origin. It was created by the Civil Rights Act of 1964.

EQUALIZATION OF ASSESSMENTS. A program conducted over an entire taxing jurisdiction for the purpose of adjusting inequitable rates and methods of collecting property taxes. Inequities usually occur as a result of unplanned growth or a rearrangement of jurisdictional boundaries.

EQUALIZING DIFFERENCES. Differences in pay received by workers because of the different attractiveness of jobs. For example, a teacher may accept a job in a private school at less money than public schools pay because less time is spent on discipline and more on teaching, which gives the teacher a more satisfied feeling about work. Or, to look from the other side, a teacher who spends the day maintaining discipline derives little satisfaction from the job and therefore will keep it only if the pay is high.

EQUALIZING WAGE DIFFERENTIALS. Official differences in wages paid to workers as compensation for some special condition of their assignments, such as danger, undesirable hours, or undesirable conditions. In contrast, EQUALIZING DIFFERENCES refers to *de facto* differences; for example, a teacher is not told that "this part of your salary is for putting up with an unruly class." See also PREMIUM PAY.

EQUAL PAY ACT. Legislation of 1964 requiring that equal pay be given for equal work, regardless of whether a male or female is performing the work.

EQUATION OF EXCHANGE. Expresses the relationship among MONEY SUPPLY, prices, VELOCITY of money, and quantity of GOODS AND SERVICES in the market. The equation has the form

$$MV = PQ$$
$$= \text{the sum over } i \text{ of } p_i q_i$$

where

M = money supply
V = velocity of money
P = general price level
Q = total quantity of goods and services
p_i = price of product i
q_i = quantity of product i

While most economists agree that this equation or one similar to it correctly describes parts of the economy, they disagree widely on the interpretation of the terms. A MONETARIST generally feels that velocity is constant. If both velocity and quantity are considered constant (as in the quantity theory of money), the result is

$$P = (V/Q)M$$
$$= kM$$

where k is a constant. The conclusion of this theory is that prices are exactly proportional to the money supply. Modern theories take into account other factors such as population, and various definitions of MONEY.

EQUILIBRIUM. A stable economic condition with no forces to prevent its continuation. Equilibrium is not the same as a static condition; the growth of an economic series is in equilibrium if it is changing according to its long-run pattern *and can continue to do so*, whereas *static* implies no change at all. For an example of equilibrium, see SUPPLY AND DEMAND.

EQUILIBRIUM PRICE. In SUPPLY AND DEMAND analysis, the price at which the supply schedule crosses the demand schedule. Also called *market price* because it is the price for CLEARING THE MARKET; there will be neither a shortage nor a surplus.

EQUIPMENT TRUST BOND. A BOND for which security in the form of various properties is held by the trustee.

EQUITABLE DISTRIBUTION OF INCOME. The proportions of an income measure (such as NATIONAL INCOME) which go to different groups or individuals constitute the distribution of income. The question of when that distribution is equitable is probably answered in as many ways as there are individuals—some say that equal distribution is equitable; others say that those who contribute the most should receive the most; etc.

EQUITY. The standard meaning of *equity*—fairness—is carried into economics, especially the social aspects of economics. See EQUITABLE DISTRIBUTION OF INCOME.

In another sense, economics uses a definition borrowed from the field of finance: claims to ownership. For example, the assets of a corporation are subject to many claims: creditors for accounts payable, employees for accrued wages, lenders such as bondholders, stockholders for those assets not subject to the claims of outsiders. Stockholders are the owners of the corporation, and their claims are known as *equity* claims.

EQUITY TRADING. See TRADING ON THE EQUITY.

ERRORS AND OMISSIONS. See BALANCE OF INTERNATIONAL PAYMENTS.

ESCALATOR CLAUSE. A provision in a labor contract that requires periodic adjustments of wages so as to maintain constant purchasing power per hour of work. These adjustments are independent of other wage changes, such as scheduled changes during the life of the contract. Most escalator clauses use a formula which is based on the CONSUMER PRICE INDEX. Also called *cost-of-living adjustment (COLA)*.

ESCAPE CLAUSE. Prior to the effective date of mandatory provision (such as employees having to remain members of a labor union), contracts sometimes include an escape clause, which allows the affected individuals a specified length of time to remove themselves from the obligation.

ESCROW. Temporary placing of money or other property with a third party. A real estate transaction frequently involves escrow until it is completed.

ESSAY ON THE PRINCIPLE OF POPULATION, AN. Often referred to as *Investigation into the Poverty of Nations*, a book published by THOMAS MALTHUS in 1798 and kept in print through seven editions until 1826. One of Malthus's main conclusions was that the world's population growth would eventually become an economic problem, which would lead to a time of bare subsistence for the human race. His reasons included the famous observation that population grows geometrically $(2, 4, 8, 16, \ldots)$ while food production grows arithmetically $(2, 4, 6, 8, \ldots)$.

ESTABLISHMENT SURVEY. A survey, conducted in conjunction with the CURRENT POPULATION SURVEY. The latter is taken directly from workers; the *establishment survey* is taken from employer payroll records and thus is frequently referred to as *payroll data*. Establishments are classified as to size and industry. Large establishments, which in most industries are those with 250 or more employees, are automatically included in the sample. When an industry is characterized by large establishments, the sampling of smaller facilities is less frequent than it is for industries (such as retail trade or services) with many small establishments. Altogether, more than 157,000 establishments are included in the nationwide sample.

Both full-time and part-time employees, and both permanent and temporary employees, are counted if they receive any pay during the reference period. Workers on paid sick leave or on paid holiday or vacation are also counted. Persons on the payroll of more than one establishment (about 5 percent of all workers) are included in the tally of each. Proprietors, self-employed persons, unpaid family workers, and domestic household workers are excluded. [Adapted from ''Counting the Jobless,'' by Herbert Runyon, in the *Federal Reserve Bank of San*

Francisco Monthly Review (September 1972).]

ESTATE TAX. A tax on the estate of a deceased person. It is similar to a property tax in that it is levied on the donor rather than on the recipient. As a result, the total estate determines the tax bracket. Because the estate tax is figured as a PROGRES-SIVE TAX, it is in a higher tax bracket than each portion would be if it were first divided among heirs. In the U.S. the federal government and some of the states levy an estate tax. See also GIFT TAX; INHERITANCE TAX.

EURODOLLAR CERTIFICATE OF DEPOSIT (Euro CD). A dollar-denominated instrument evidencing a time deposit with a bank at an agreed upon rate of interest for a specific period of time. Unlike a domestic CD, however, a Euro CD is issued abroad, either by the foreign branch of a U.S. bank or by a foreign bank. The market for Euro CDs is centered in London and is therefore frequently called the *London dollar CD market*.

EURODOLLARS. Deposits denominated in U.S. dollars at banks and other financial institutions outside the U.S. Although the name *eurodollars* is derived from the large amounts of such deposits held at banks in Western Europe, similar deposits in other parts of the world are also called eurodollars.

EUROPEAN MONETARY AGREE-MENT (EMA). A successor to the EU-ROPEAN PAYMENTS UNION, the EMA came into being in 1958. Its purposes included financing international debts, preventing large imbalances in international payments, and providing for the convertibility of major currencies. One of the operating tools of the EMA was the newly created European Monetary Fund, which served as the financing agency.

EUROPEAN MONETARY FUND (EMF). The financial agency created to make possible the workings of the EUROPEAN MONETARY AGREE-MENT.

EUROPEAN PAYMENTS UNION (EPU). An outgrowth of the EURO-PEAN RECOVERY PROGRAM (created by most of the same nations). During its lifetime, from 1950 through 1958, the EPU worked to expand trade among all nations rather than to acomplish a limited number of reciprocal arrangements. It was followed by the EUROPEAN MONE-TARY AGREEMENT.

EUROPEAN RECOVERY PROGRAM (ERP). A program that helped restore the economies of Europe after the devastation of World War II. The required legislation went through Congress as the Foreign Assistance Act of 1948. The U.S. made about $12 billion in grants and loans before the ERP ended and the Mutual Security Program was implemented. Also known as the *Marshall Plan*, after Secretary of State George C. Marshall, who received the 1953 Nobel Peace Prize for his role in developing the program.

EVEN-KEEL OBJECTIVE. A policy of the FEDERAL RESERVE SYSTEM which calls for avoiding overt actions that might undermine a Treasury financing. In OPEN MARKET OPERATIONS, actions which the market might interpret as reflecting a change in MONETARY POL-ICY are avoided. For the same reasons, the DISCOUNT RATE and RESERVE REQUIREMENTS are kept unchanged during a major Treasury financing. Even keel is not maintained on all Treasury financings; it has been limited principally to the large quarterly refundings and to a few other offerings involving longer-dated coupon issues.

EVOLUTIONARY SOCIALISM. Socialism which replaces capitalism gradually, over a period of years, as opposed to the violent overthrow urged in the writings of Karl Marx.

EXCESS BURDEN. The BURDEN that results when ECONOMIC RESOURCES are diverted from the private sector to the government sector, causing a less efficient economy (efficiency being defined as closeness to PARETO OPTIMUM). Loss of efficiency may appear as a less efficient mixture of FACTORS OF PRODUC-TION (factor excess burden), a less efficient organization of production (production excess burden), or a less-than-optimum consumer demand (consumer excess burden). Also called *deadweight loss*.

EXCESS CAPACITY. In the BUSINESS SECTOR, the ability (through the accumulation of plant and equipment) to produce more than is demanded. Only modern equipment is counted; equipment which is idle because it is obsolete or inefficient does not contribute statistically toward excess capacity. (Thus, in an emergency the business sector could produce over 100 percent of capacity.) When referring to an industry, such as the durable goods industry, that is strongly affected by ECONOMIC FLUCTUA-TIONS, the expression *cyclically excess capacity* is often used. Also called *redundant capacity*.

EXCESS DEMAND. The shortage that results when a product is selling at less than its equilibrium (see SUPPLY AND DEMAND), and buyers want a larger quantity than suppliers are willing to provide. Ordinarily, the price will rise, and equilibrium will be attained. However, sometimes the price can't rise, usually because of a government-imposed price ceiling, and then some form of RA-TIONING is instituted, often accompanied by a BLACK MARKET.

EXCESSIVE CONDEMNATION. The power of EMINENT DOMAIN when it seems to have been exercised beyond the point at which society as a whole receives maximum benefit.

EXCESS PROFITS. Quantitatively, an amount (or rate) above which a SURTAX is levied. In a more qualitative sense, *excess profits* is used by economists to describe ECONOMIC PROFIT.

EXCESS RESERVES. See BANK RE-SERVES.

EXCESS SUPPLY. Surplus that occurs when a product is priced at more than its equilibrium price (see SUPPLY AND DEMAND), and buyers do not want as much of the product as suppliers are providing. Ordinarily, the suppliers will lower their prices, more buyers will be interested, and equilibrium will eventually be reached.

EXCHANGE ARBITRAGE. See AR-BITRAGE.

EXCHANGE CONTROL. Official limitations on the buying and selling of currencies of foreign nations. The U.S. has used many degrees of control, including an outright prohibition against dealing in foreign exchange except through the government.

EXCHANGE, EQUATION OF. An equation that expresses the relationship among MONEY SUPPLY, VELOCITY, prices, and quantities. See EQUATION OF EXCHANGE.

EXCHANGE OPPORTUNITIES LINE. A MODEL (also called the *production possibilities exchange*) which is extremely simplified but nevertheless useful for analyzing certain economic behavior. It assumes that an economic unit (individual, firm, nation, etc.) can produce just two different items and that all its productive facilities are being used to capacity. If all facilities are used to make product A, U_a quantity of that product will be produced; if all facilities are used to make product B, U_b will be the quantity. If the market for these two items is *perfect*, the two points can be joined by a straight line and the economic unit can make an exchange any place along the line; for example, it can choose to make $U_a/2$ units of product A and $U_b/2$ units of product B. However, markets are actually *imperfect*, and thus the exchange opportunities line will bend as shown by the dotted line in the accompanying figure. The line curves because some of the facilities are

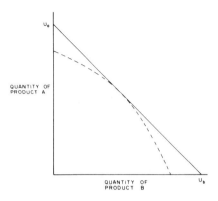

Exchange opportunities line. Simplified model of the possible mixes for an economy that produces just two products.

more efficient at producing product A and others are more efficient at producing product B. Therefore the closer we approach to making just one product, the more we pull in facilities that are inefficient in the production of that item.

When a fixed amount of money can be used to buy a mix of two products, a similar diagram can be drawn but the expression *budget line* is used.

EXCHANGE RATES. Rates at which the monetary unit of each nation exchanges with the unit of other nations. See INTERNATIONAL EXCHANGE.

EXCHANGE STABILIZATION FUND. See SPECIAL DRAWING RIGHTS CERTIFICATE ACCOUNT.

EXCHANGE VALUE GUARANTY. See SWAP NETWORK.

EXCISE TAX. A tax on the sale or manufacture of a specified product, usually with the expectation that it will cause an increase in price and therefore be passed on to the ultimate buyer (see INDIRECT TAX). An excise tax is often also a SUMPTUARY TAX, intended to decrease consumption of the product.

EXCLUSION PRINCIPLE.   Principle stating that the benefits of consumption of certain goods accrue only to those who

partake of them directly; this principle helps separate PRIVATE GOODS from SOCIAL GOODS. For example, the exclusion principle applies to chewing gum because only the person who consumes it derives any benefit. It does not apply to police protection because everyone, not only those who have been rescued from a criminal, benefits from living in a safer environment.

EXCLUSIVE UNIONISM. The practice of creating a shortage in the supply of a specific type of labor in order to put upward pressure on wages. One of the methods used is to restrict union membership to those with certain skills (see CRAFT UNION). Other effective methods include long apprenticeship periods, high initiation fees, and other practices that effectively restrict membership to a relatively small number.

EX DIVIDEND. In financial economics, the sale of a corporate stock with the understanding that the previous owner will receive the dividend that was recently declared.

EXECUTIVE TRADE AGREEMENTS. Pacts that allow the executive branch of the government to reduce import tariffs up to a stipulated maximum if international trading partners reciprocate. Also called *reciprocal trade agreements*.

EXECUTOR. A person authorized by the will of the deceased to oversee the execution of its terms. If no one is named, a court can appoint an *administrator*. The general term for either executor or administrator is *personal representative*.

EXEMPTION. An item which reduces taxable income. The actual saving in taxes is a fraction of the exemption, as explained under TAX CREDIT.

EXIMBANK. EXPORT IMPORT BANK.

EXOGENOUS. Coming, or controlled, from the outside. In management science, *exogenous* describes variables which, even if predictable, are not under the control of an organization. When predicting sales, the organization has control over such items as selling price and advertising expenditures, which are endogenous variables, but not over competitor prices and weather, which are exogenous variables. The division between exogenous and endogenous is not always clear. Some analysts might consider consumer demand exogenous and others might consider it endogenous, depending on how directly influenced by advertising each analyst considers consumer demand to be.

EXOGENOUS THEORY OF BUSINESS CYCLES. Theory which holds that the *major* causes of ECONOMIC FLUCTUATIONS within a nation are found in the economies of other nations. Some of these external causes are prices of imports, control of international exchange rates, and military activities. See also ENDOGENOUS THEORY OF BUSINESS CYCLES. Also called the *external theory of business cycles.*

EXPANDED INTERNATIONAL MONETARY FUND (XIMF). See BANCOR.

EXPANSIONARY. Tending to speed up the economy; tending to increase employment and the output of goods and services. Usually describes a policy, such as when it is said that lowering taxes is an *expansionary* FISCAL POLICY. See also CONTRACTIONARY.

EXPANSION OF MONEY SUPPLY. See MONEY SUPPLY EXPANSION MULTIPLIER.

EXPECTED COST. As in elementary statistics, a quantity equal to the sum of the probability of each outcome times the cost associated with it. For example, if the probability of an item's costing $75.90 is 0.88 and the probability of its costing $73.29 is 0.12, then the expected cost is 75.90(0.88) + 73.29(0.12), or $75.59. It is important that all outcomes be included so that the probabilities add up to 1 (it is assumed that the two prices used here are the only prices the item could have).

EXPEDITER. A person who checks on the flow of material needed. An expediter will concentrate on items that may arrive late or whose lateness would most disrupt the overall process.

EXPENDABLE. Describes an item which is totally consumed during its ordinary use, as opposed to an item, such as capital equipment, which is considered permanent.

EXPENDITURES. When used in connection with a government budget, money actually spent. In contrast, APPROPRIATIONS are amounts authorized for spending.

EXPENDITURES MULTIPLIER. The ratio of the change in the equilibrium point of a graph of total spending vs. total income of the economy to the change in spending of one sector. Change in total spending = Multiplier × Change in spending in selected sector. For example, if the multiplier has a value of 2, and businesses increase their expenditures for capital equipment by $10 billion, total spending in the economy will be at equilibrium at a point $20 billion higher than before the capital spending increase.

In its simplest form, the multiplier is given a value of 1/MPS (see MARGINAL PROPENSITY TO SAVE). However, the practical multiplier always has a lower value than this because of LEAKAGES such as imports and the distributional nature of expenditures, as well as second order effects such as a change in interest rates caused by the expenditures.

EXPERIENCE RATING. A rating that makes an employer pay unemployment insurance taxes in accordance with its layoff history. Records are kept, and employers whose exemployees collect the most unemployment benefits are charged the highest rates.

EXPLICIT COST. An actual payment to a FACTOR OF PRODUCTION, as opposed to an IMPLICIT COST, which is the use of a factor without a corresponding charge being recorded.

EXPLICIT DEBT. A debt that is a legal obligation, such as principal and interest on the NATIONAL DEBT. In contrast, *implicit debt*, such as social security payments, is not a legal obligation.

EXPLOSIVE EQUILIBRIUM. See COBWEB THEORY.

EXPORT. To send out to another economic unit, usually because of a sale of goods. Generally applied to international trade, but *export* is also used for a geographic area within one nation.

EXPORT BOUNTY. Money paid by government to exporters of a product as a means of encouraging the particular industry to compete in world markets.

EXPORT-IMPORT BANK. Originally established in 1934 to finance U.S. exporters in order to increase domestic employment during the Great Depression. The bank now makes loans to trading partners outside the U.S., especially less developed nations. Also known as *Eximbank*.

EXPORT LICENSE. A license that exporters must obtain before shipping goods. It is usually required when a government wants to control the amount of a particular item which is exported, or the amount of trade which is transacted with a particular nation.

EXPORT POINT. See GOLD POINTS.

EXPROPRIATE. To take over, by a government. Expropriation, which applies to property of all kinds owned by citizens of other nations, does not imply mutual agreement. The history of expropriations shows payments to previous owners ranging all the way from zero to the fair value of the property.

EX RIGHTS. In financial economics, when a COMMON STOCK is sold without the transfer of certain purchase rights. See CUM RIGHTS.

EXTENDED BOND. A BOND issued with a specified maturity date, but the bondholders have agreed to postpone the maturity.

EXTENDED FAMILY. A situation, found especially in less developed areas, in which several generations of a family, as well as distant relatives, are supported by one or more family members who have fairly regular employment.

EXTERNAL DEBT. A debt in which the debtor and creditor are essentially separate economic units, so that creation or termination of the debt will change the aggregate wealth in both economic units. For example, corporate debt is external because, even though some part of it may be held by individuals who are also stockholders (owners), repayment would change the aggregate wealth of the corporation and the creditors. On the other hand, the federal government debt is internal because most of it is held by U.S. citizens and repayment would not change the nation's aggregate wealth.

EXTERNALITY. External benefit or external cost. See SPILLOVER.

EXTERNAL THEORY OF BUSINESS CYCLES. See EXOGENOUS THEORY OF BUSINESS CYCLES.

EXTRACTIVE INDUSTRY. An industry that removes natural resources from the earth, such as the mining industry.

EXTRAPOLATE. In mathematics, to assume data points in addition to those points that are known, such as in extending a graph to project future results. Many errors in predictions are due to extrapolations into a region where conditions change, and therefore it may not be valid to extend such a graph. See also INTERPOLATE.

F

FACT-FINDING. An agreement between parties to a dispute (usually a labor-management dispute) that they will use the services of a third party to ascertain the facts and make an objective recommendation. The results of fact-finding are not binding on either party. See also ARBITRATION; COMPULSORY ARBITRATION; MEDIATION.

FACTOR. In commercial economics, (1) a person who receives goods for resale but who does not take title to them and does not pay for them until they are resold. (2) A person who buys ACCOUNTS RECEIVABLE from businesses that prefer immediate cash and then has the responsibilities (and risks) involved in collecting the accounts. See also FACTORS OF PRODUCTION.

FACTOR COST. That part of the cost of an item which can be traced directly to a cost which is paid to a FACTOR OF PRODUCTION. Many other costs, such as excise taxes, also increase the cost of the product but are not considered factor costs.

FACTOR DEMAND. Demand for a FACTOR OF PRODUCTION. Because factors of production exist not for themselves, but for the ultimate products they manufacture, factor demand is a DERIVED DEMAND. Also called *derived demand*.

FACTOR EARNINGS. Payments made to the owners of FACTORS OF PRODUCTION for their use. There are four categories of factor earnings:

1. LAND. Earnings are *rent*, including all payments made for the use of earth, air, water, and everything provided by nature.
2. LABOR. Earnings are *wages*, including hourly pay, salaries, commissions, bonuses, and all other pay in return for a service or work provided.
3. CAPITAL. Earnings are *interest* (return on investment).
4. ENTREPRENEURIAL ABILITY. Earnings are *profits*.

Some writers believe that a fifth category—MANAGEMENT—exists, in which the factor earnings are *wages*.

FACTOR EXCESS BURDEN. See EXCESS BURDEN.

FACTOR MARKET. Not a physical marketplace, but simply the transactions in which FACTORS OF PRODUCTION are bought and sold (with the factors being in the supply side of SUPPLY AND DEMAND). Also called *resource market*. See CIRCULAR FLOW OF MONEY.

FACTOR MIX. The relative amounts of land, labor, capital, and entrepreneurial ability used for a given level of production. See also ECONOMIC RE-SOURCES.

FACTOR MOBILITY. The ease with which FACTORS OF PRODUCTION are physically moved from one location to another. Since there are alternative ways that each factor can be used, as well as alternative mixes of factors to produce a given result, the FACTOR MARKET is characterized by competition of both buyers and sellers. However, anything short of complete factor mobility represents an imperfection in the competitiveness of the factor market.

FACTORS OF PRODUCTION. The same as ECONOMIC RESOURCES (land, labor, capital, and entrepreneurial ability), *factors of production* is the proper expression to use when emphasizing that the resources are viewed as inputs to an economy's production process.

FACTOR SUPPLY. A SCHEDULE of the amount of a given FACTOR OF PRODUCTION which will be offered under certain conditions. For example, a schedule may give the amounts of labor which will be offered, under stated conditions, at a series of wage rates. Then, if one of the conditions is changed—say, income taxes are raised—the schedule is no longer valid.

FACTORY ECONOMY. An economy in which a large percentage of all production is performed by individuals using relatively large amounts of CAPITAL GOODS and whose work has some degree of specialization. *Factory economies* describes the economies in developed nations. For a contrast, see COTTAGE INDUSTRY.

FAILURES, BUSINESS. See INDEX OF NET BUSINESS FORMATION.

FAIR CREDIT BILLING ACT. Legislation that specifies the rights of the consumer in dealings with creditors. It set up procedures for promptly correcting billing mistakes, for allowing the consumer to refuse credit card payments on defective goods, and for promptly rec-

ognizing payments to a consumer credit account.

FAIR CREDIT REPORTING ACT. Legislation giving an individual the right to examine information in his or her own credit file. The act includes procedures for having errors corrected and for handling disagreements regarding the facts in a file.

FAIR DEAL. Name used by the Truman administration to describe the social programs presented to Congress after the election of 1948.

FAIR DEBT COLLECTION PRACTICES ACT. Legislation of March 20, 1978, designed to correct abusive practices by certain debt collectors. The act applies to any debt incurred for personal, family, or household purposes but does not apply to banks, other lenders, or businesses which collect their own accounts, using their own names. It sets down rules for locating and contacting a debtor, and it prohibits harassing, threatening, or abusive conduct in connection with collection of a debt. An informative pamphlet is available from the department of consumer affairs of the Federal Reserve Bank of Philadelphia.

FAIR EMPLOYMENT PRACTICES. Various codes, laws, acts, etc. which have been enacted by different levels of government for the purpose of eliminating hiring and other employment practices that are determined by factors other than ability or value on the job.

FAIR EMPLOYMENT PRACTICES COMMISSION. There are agencies with this or a similar name at each level of government. They enforce laws which prohibit discrimination in hiring, promoting, paying, job assignments, etc. for reasons other than ability. See also EQUAL EMPLOYMENT OPPORTUNITY COMMISSION.

FAIR LABOR STANDARDS ACT. Legislation of 1938 which established the standard workweek at 40 hours; required that at least 50 percent additional be paid for all work in excess of 40 hours (with exceptions, such as salaried workers); set 16 years as the minimum age for regular employment (with exceptions); and established a minimum rate that must be paid to all employees. At first, the law covered only nonagricultural workers employed directly in interstate commerce, but over the years the courts have interpreted more and more work as being a part of interstate commerce. The dollar amount of the minimum wage clause is frequently amended upward by Congress. See MINIMUM WAGE for arguments for and against this feature, which has remained the most controversial part of the act. Also known as the *Wage and Hour Law*.

FAIR RETURN. An economic concept that is especially applicable in a MIXED ECONOMY, one in which (1) some production facilities are privately owned and operated competitively, (2) some are privately owned but under direct government control (see MONOPOLY), (3) some are government owned, and (4) there are various other arrangements. Consider, for example, the first two arrangements; it is not necessarily true that those who invest in an electric power company are entitled to the same rate of return on their money as those who invest in a company that sets its own prices—risk, ease of selling the ownership shares, prospects for the future, and many other factors must also be taken into account. When all factors are considered, fair return is the rate of return that will attract the necessary amount of capital funds.

FAIR TRADE LAWS. Legislation in various states which allows suppliers to require retailers to maintain minimum prices on certain products. This practice is also called *resale price maintenance*, or *vertical price fixing*. When such practices were first tested in the courts (Beech-nut Packing Company, 1922), they were held to be in violation of the SHERMAN ANTITRUST ACT. Then some states passed legislation which validated resale price maintenance, and in 1936 the Supreme

Court ruled (in Dearborn Distributing Company v. Seagram Distilleries), that manufacturers have the right to protect an image they wish to project, thereby upholding some state "fair-trade" laws. In 1937 Congress passed the Miller-Tydings Act, which resolved the question of restraint of trade by specifically exempting resale price maintenance from the Sherman Antitrust Act and by providing that such laws be enforceable on a state-by-state basis when not inconsistent with state law. The Supreme Court ruled in 1951 (in Schwegmann Brothers v. Calvert Distillers Corp.) that only those retailers who signed a fair-trade agreement with the supplier were bound. However, in 1952, Congress passed the McGuire Act (also called the *McGuire-Keogh Act*), which compelled all retailers in a state to observe the minimum price if any one retailer signed the agreement. Recently, the entire fair-trade movement has fallen into disfavor with sellers as well as consumers, and little is heard of it.

FALLACY OF COMPOSITION. A wrong conclusion reached by taking a known fact about individuals and projecting it to apply to the entire population. For example, giving an individual more money makes that individual better off, but giving more money to everyone will not make anyone better off (except, possibly, the money printer).

FALLING RATE OF PROFIT THEORY. Theory which holds that, after an optimum level of use is reached, each successive increment of added CAPITAL GOODS yields a smaller return on investment. Also called the *declining marginal efficiency of capital theory*.

FAMILY ALLOWANCES. Several nations have a plan by which households receive payments from the government, based on the size of the family. Sometimes, as in the U.K., allowances are financed out of the general fund; in France, the *allocations familiales* are financed through a tax on employers, and the payments are tax-free.

FAMILY ECONOMY. An economy which is influenced significantly by traditions regarding family life, especially as it applies to the production of goods and services. See also COTTAGE INDUSTRY; FACTORY ECONOMY.

FAMILY QUOTIENT SYSTEM (Fr.). An arrangement in personal income tax laws which allows a taxpayer to figure income as if the total amount were earned in equal shares by all members of the family. In a PROGRESSIVE TAX structure, a person with a large family thus receives the benefit of using a lower rate.

FANNIE MAE. Popular name for FEDERAL NATIONAL MORTGAGE ASSOCIATION.

FARM BLOC. Cooperative influence among those concerned with legislation regarding agriculture. *Farm bloc* is often used to describe government representatives (e.g., in Congress) who act in unison on legislation that affects agriculture.

FARM CREDIT ADMINISTRATION (FCA). An agency of the federal government that provides loans to farmers, both directly and through private banks and other lenders.

FARMERS HOME ADMINISTRATION. A government bureau which, along with the Rural Electrification Administration, is responsible for originating the bulk of off-budget direct loans to farmers.

FARM MORTGAGE FORECLOSURE ACT. One of the NEW DEAL measures passed during the GREAT DEPRESSION, this 1934 legislation provided for loans to enable farmers to regain the farms which they had lost through foreclosure due to their inability to make mortgage payments.

FARM PROGRAM. Generally, legislation that affects farm income, land use, crop plantings, livestock decisions, and other parts of agriculture. Over the years,

such programs have taken the form of government purchases of farm commodities which did not sell on the open market at or above a predetermined price; government payments to farmers; and absolute limits on the acreage planted to certain crops.

FARM RELIEF AND INFLATION ACT. Legislation passed with the objective of inflating prices by restricting agricultural production. Farmers were paid for taking land out of production in order to create shortages. Also known as the First AGRICULTURAL ADJUSTMENT ACT (FIRST AAA), it was part of the NEW DEAL program during the GREAT DEPRESSION.

FASB-8. The controversial Statement No. 8 of the Financial Accounting Standards Board, designed to standardize procedures for reporting the foreign-currency positions of U.S. multinational corporations. Prior to FASB-8, accounting practices of such companies varied considerably, particularly regarding translation rates (current versus historical) for inventory and long-term debt. More important, most companies employed ''reserve accounts'' to absorb the impact of variations in the dollar value of balance-sheet items due to exchange-rate fluctuations, thereby preventing such changes from appearing on quarterly income statements. The dollar value of these changes, plus or minus, could be accumulated over time and reported out on the income statement when the impact was as small as possible, thereby minimizing the impact of exchange-rate changes on reported net earnings. Because many multinational corporations became accustomed to using reserve accounts in this fashion to stabilize reported earnings, the storm of protest which greeted FASB-8 is not surprising.

FASCISM. An economic and political system in which a strong central government administers the means of production, most of which are privately owned.

FAVORABLE BALANCE OF PAYMENTS. The BALANCE OF INTER-

NATIONAL PAYMENTS is said to be favorable for a nation when the net flow of money from bilateral and unilateral international transactions is into the nation.

FEASIBLE SET. In economic analysis, a set that includes all combinations of goods and services whose total cost is equal to or less than consumer disposable income. Spending of less than that amount represents saving; spending of more represents DISSAVING.

FEATHERBEDDING. Creating a position in the labor force and employing workers in that position, even though nothing is produced by that position. The expression became well known when railroads were switching from steam engines to diesel; the unions insisted that firemen be retained, and the railroads insisted that, since firemen no longer had to shovel coal, keeping them on would be pure featherbedding and would increase transportation costs.

FED. In financial circles and the press, the FEDERAL RESERVE SYSTEM.

FEDERAL ADVISORY COUNCIL. A group of 12 citizens, each elected by the board of directors of a FEDERAL RESERVE BANK, usually from among bankers of the district. Meets at least four times a year to confer with the BOARD OF GOVERNORS (OF THE FEDERAL RESERVE SYSTEM) on business conditions and to make recommendations regarding matters of concern to the FEDERAL RESERVE SYSTEM.

FEDERAL AGENCY OBLIGATIONS. With regard to the CONSOLIDATED STATEMENT OF CONDITION OF ALL FEDERAL RESERVE BANKS, *federal agency obligations* belong to two categories:

Bought outright. Federal agencies established by law, primarily to implement the U.S. government's farm and home lending programs, and issue obligations to finance the activities of those programs. Most agency securities are not guaranteed

by the U.S. government; rather, they are obligations of the agency alone. However, these agencies have the authority to borrow directly from the U.S. Treasury in the event of a cash shortage.

In 1977 the FEDERAL OPEN MARKET COMMITTEE restricted System Open Market Account purchases of federal agency securities to agencies that aren't eligible to borrow from the Federal Financing Bank, which began operations in 1974.

Securities eligible for System purchase are issues of agencies such as Federal Home Loan Banks, Federal National Mortgage Association, Federal Land Banks, Federal Intermediate Credit Banks, and the Banks for Cooperatives. Securities of the Federal Financing Bank itself are also eligible for purchase.

Held under repurchase agreements. Federal agency obligations bought under repurchase agreements with dealers in U.S. government securities. These agreements are used to provide a temporary and self-reversing injection of reserves into the banking system.

FEDERAL CREDIT UNION ACT. See CREDIT UNION.

FEDERAL CROP INSURANCE CORPORATION (FCIC). An organization that provides indemnification against loss of an agricultural crop through natural hazards.

FEDERAL DEPOSIT INSURANCE CORPORATION (FDIC). A government-owned organization which insures the accounts of depositors in participating banks. Because of the nation's FRACTIONAL RESERVE BANKING SYSTEM, a large increase in the number of people wanting to withdraw their funds would force banks to liquidate some of their less-liquid assets at a discount; if the process continued, it would become a run on the bank, and the bank would be forced to sell less and less liquid assets at more and more of a loss from face value. The failure of many banks in the early 1930s could be traced to a similar sequence: each depositor knew that, once a run started, the last depositors to try withdrawing would find the bank had no way to pay them.

With the creation of the FDIC, a run on a participating bank no longer makes sense; depositors know that, if a run on a bank (or any other event) caused the bank to fail, they still receive the full amount of their deposits from the FDIC. See also BANK HOLIDAY.

FEDERAL FUNDS. Short-term loans of immediately available funds, such as funds that can be transferred or withdrawn during one business day. They include deposits at FEDERAL RESERVE BANKS and collected liabilities of commercial banks and other depository institutions. *Federal funds* is occasionally used in a broader sense by members of the financial community to refer to all funds which are immediately available and not subject to reserve requirements, such as in a RE-PURCHASE AGREEMENT.

FEDERAL GOVERNMENT PURCHASES OF GOODS AND SERVICES. In NATIONAL INCOME AND PRODUCT ACCOUNTS, both defense and nondefense expenditures. National defense purchases include Department of Defense military functions, military assistance to other nations, development and control of atomic energy, and stockpiling of strategic materials. Nondefense purchases include the purchase of agricultural commodities under price support programs, and investment of GOVERNMENT ENTERPRISEs.

FEDERAL HOME LOAN BANK ACT. Congressional legislation of 1932 which enabled the creation of savings institutions that would channel funds into building loans. Building and Loan Associations (later called SAVINGS AND LOAN ASSOCIATIONS) and other thrift institutions developed as a result of this act.

FEDERAL HOME LOAN BANK BOARD (FHLBB). An administrative organization created for the purpose of supervising SAVINGS AND LOAN AS-SOCIATIONS and other thrift institutions which are controlled by the FEDERAL HOME LOAN BANK ACT. The FHLBB performs some of the functions for these thrift institutions that the BOARD OF GOVERNORS (OF THE FEDERAL RESERVE SYSTEM) performs for COMMERCIAL BANKs. The board's top officials are government appointed

FEDERAL HOME LOAN BANK SYSTEM. Banking system composed of 12 regional Federal Home Loan banks and a supervisory body, the FEDERAL HOME LOAN BANK BOARD, which is an independent agency of the executive branch of the U.S. government. The FHLBs make loans, called *advances*, to member institutions. The demand for these advances is especially large during periods of DIS-INTERMEDIATION, which occur when open-market interest rates are high relative to the interest rate ceilings placed by regulation on time and savings deposits (see DEPOSITORY INSTITUTIONS DEREGULATION AND MONETARY CONTROL ACT). Consequently, the amount of funds raised by the FHLBs in the money and capital markets rises sharply in periods of high interest rates. Advances are also made to meet seasonal mortgage demand, as well as to expand overall mortgage lending consistent with the FHLBs' goal of fostering homeownership. Most FHLBs make advances with maturities of up to five years, and some offer maturities of up to ten years.

FEDERAL INSTITUTE FOR PRICES (Yugo.). The Yugoslavian government agency which is responsible for the administration of price control. Not all items are controlled, and the trend has been to reduce the list of items that are controlled.

FEDERAL INTERMEDIATE CREDIT BANKS. Twelve banks created by the Agricultural Credit Act of 1923 for the purpose of making short-term agricultural loans. Funds are obtained by selling debt instruments to the public.

FEDERALLY SUBSIDIZED HIGH-WAYS. Ever since World War II acts of Congress have provided federal money for highway construction to state governments that spend a stipulated amount of their own money. The objective of federal subsidization is to encourage states to build highways, especially interstate connections, so that the nation might have a complete network of roads. In 1956, a long-range plan for the construction of nearly 50,000 miles of *interstate highways* was instituted, with the federal government agreeing to pay 90 percent of the costs.

FEDERAL MEDIATION AND CONCILIATION SERVICE (FMCS). Created by the TAFT-HARTLEY ACT, the FMCS provides professional mediators when requested by parties to a labor dispute that has or might have a large effect on the overall economy.

FEDERAL NATIONAL MORTGAGE ASSOCIATION (FNMA). Popularly known as *Fannie Mae*, FNMA is the largest federally sponsored agency. Since its inception in 1938 under the name National Mortgage Association of Washington, FNMA has undergone several reorganizations to reach its present status as a private corporation. The federal government maintains limited control over the agency through the Department of Housing and Urban Development.

Under its current charter, the function of FNMA is "to provide supplemental assistance to the secondary market for home mortgages by providing a degree of liquidity to mortgage investments thereby improving the distribution of investment capital for home mortgage financing." To accomplish this function, FNMA has been authorized to purchase and sell FHA, VA, and other conventional loans from banks, savings and loan associations, mortgage bankers, and other organizations that meet its requirements. In general, FNMA increases its purchases of mortgages when the supply of funds to the mortgage market from other sources is declining. As a result, FNMA's demand

for funds in the financial markets typically rises sharply in periods of high interest rates and DISINTERMEDIATION at the thrift institutions.

FEDERAL OPEN MARKET COMMITTEE (FOMC). THE FEDERAL RESERVE SYSTEM's most important policymaking body, composed of the seven members of the BOARD OF GOVERNORS (OF THE FEDERAL RESERVE SYSTEM) plus the president of the Federal Reserve Bank of New York and presidents of four other Federal Reserve banks. Its main responsibility is to establish continuing policy regarding open market operations—that is, the extent to which the System buys and sells government and other securities. It also oversees the System's operations in foreign exchange markets.

The manager of the System open market account is referred to as the *account manager*, and the *trading desk* of the Federal Reserve Bank of New York is called the *desk*. Government securities bought outright are prorated among the 12 Reserve banks according to a formula based upon the reserve ratios of the banks (see BANK RESERVES). Similarly, the foreign department of the Federal Reserve Bank of New York acts as the FOMC's agent in foreign exchange transactions. Foreign currencies purchased in these operations are also prorated among the 12 district banks.

FEDERAL RESERVE ACT. Legislation which, in 1913, created the FEDERAL RESERVE SYSTEM as the nation's CENTRAL BANK. One reason for the passage of this act was recurring money panics, especially the severe one of 1907.

FEDERAL RESERVE BANK. Also called a Reserve bank, a corporation chartered by Congress to operate in the public interest. There are 12 regional Reserve banks (with a total of 24 branches), one for each of the 12 Federal Reserve districts (see FEDERAL RESERVE CITY). Thus, the FEDERAL RESERVE SYSTEM is considerably more decentralized than

CENTRAL BANKs of other nations. The corporate structure of Reserve banks resembles that of commercial banks. All issue stock, have boards of directors elect their officers, have similar official titles and departments, and obtain earnings largely from interest on loans and investments.

There are three main differences, however, stemming from Reserve banks' responsibilities to the public. First, although the capital stock of each Reserve bank is owned by the MEMBER BANKS in the district, such ownership does not bring the full privileges and powers ordinarily connected with stockholders. Second, although they do earn large profits, Reserve banks are not profit motivated. Expenses and member-bank dividends absorb some earnings, but most earnings are turned over to the U.S. Treasury as "interest" on Federal Reserve notes. In 1970, dividends totaled $41 million, and payments to the Treasury ran almost $3.5 billion. Third, if the Reserve banks should ever be liquidated, the federal government would receive any assets remaining after the stock was paid off at par.

Each Reserve Bank has nine directors: three class A directors who represent member banks, three class B directors who are engaged in pursuits other than banking and are elected by the member banks in the district, and three class C directors. The BOARD OF GOVERNORS (OF THE FEDERAL RESERVE SYSTEM) appoints the latter, and it designates one as chairman and another as deputy chairman. No class B or C director may be an officer, director, or employee of a bank, and class C directors must not be stockholders of a bank. Each *branch* of a Reserve bank has its own board of directors of five or seven members. A majority (three or four, as the case may be) is appointed by the head-office directors, and the others are appointed by the Board of Governors.

In addition to their regular duties in overseeing the operations of their Reserve banks, the boards of directors have certain duties in the field of MONETARY POLICY. First, they establish, subject to the approval of the Board, the DISCOUNT RATE each Reserve Bank charges on short-term loans to member banks. Second, they elect five of the presidents of the banks to serve as members of the FEDERAL OPEN MARKET COMMITTEE. Third, they provide the Reserve bank presidents and the Board with an invaluable source of grass-roots information on business conditions.

Reserve banks hold the bulk of cash reserves of member banks, provide checking accounts to the Treasury, issue paper currency (FEDERAL RESERVE NOTES), collect checks (see CHECK CLEARING), supervise member banks, handle issuance and redemption of government securities, and act in other ways as fiscal agent for the federal government.

[Much of this description was taken from *The Federal Reserve at Work*, published by the Federal Reserve Bank of Richmond. That publication includes a description of the Federal Reserve System, economic history including FISCAL POLICY and monetary policy, and a section on the pros and cons of monetary policy.]

FEDERAL RESERVE CITY. A city in which a FEDERAL RESERVE BANK is located. The following table lists the 12 Federal Reserve cities.

District	City
1	Boston, MA
2	New York, NY
3	Philadelphia, PA
4	Cleveland, OH
5	Richmond, VA
6	Atlanta, GA
7	Chicago, IL
8	St. Louis, MO
9	Minneapolis, MN
10	Kansas City, MO
11	Dallas, TX
12	San Francisco, CA

FEDERAL RESERVE COMMUNICATIONS SYSTEM (FRCS). An electronic means of transferring funds among

FEDERAL RESERVE BANKS and their branches. The banks are equipped with data communications terminals which can be connected through a central switching station. When immediate payment is desired, MEMBER BANKs can transfer funds through the FRCS. Nonmember banks, firms, and individuals can make use of this service through member banks. These wire transfers of funds are especially attractive for large transactions. Also called *Fedwire*.

FEDERAL RESERVE FLOAT. When a MEMBER BANK sends checks for collection to the FEDERAL RESERVE BANK in its district, the latter credits the depositing bank's reserve account within a maximum of two business days, even though it may take three or more days to collect checks from the banks on which they are drawn. As a result, the Reserve banks customarily show on their books more dollars due from member banks on which checks have been drawn than dollars due to member banks which have deposited checks for collection. On a typical day, due from items in the process of collection might total $12 billion, while due to might total $8.5 billion. The difference of $3.5 billion is called the *Federal Reserve float*, or sometimes just *the float*. See also CHECK CLEARING; INTERBANK FLOAT. [Adapted from Paul Meek, *Open Market Operations* (New York: Federal Reserve Bank of New York), page 8.]

FEDERAL RESERVE NOTES. Except for some notes of the $100 denomination (see UNITED STATES NOTES), all U.S. paper currency issued today is in the form of Federal Reserve notes. They are issued in denominations of $1, $2, $5, $10, $20, $50, and $100. At one time, Federal Reserve notes were also available in $500, $1000, $5000, and $10,000 denominations, but, because of insufficient demand, they were discontinued by the BOARD OF GOVERNORS (OF THE FEDERAL RESERVE SYSTEM) on December 27, 1945. The FEDERAL RE-

SERVE BANKs continued to issue remaining supplies of these large-denomination notes until July 14, 1969, when their issuance was finally terminated. In addition, $100,000 gold certificates of 1934 were once printed, for official transactions only, and none were ever circulated outside Federal Reserve banks. Federal Reserve notes make up over 99 percent of the dollar amount of paper currency in general circulation in the U.S. today.

With regard to the CONSOLIDATED STATEMENT OF CONDITION OF ALL FEDERAL RESERVE BANKS, this item means the total amount of all such notes in circulation, including those held in COMMERCIAL BANK vaults and those held by the U.S. Treasury in "cash depots" maintained in Washington, Puerto Rico, Hawaii, and certain U.S. possessions for the distribution of currency to the public. This item excludes notes held in the vaults of Reserve banks and branches and canceled notes forwarded to the Treasury for destruction. (In the Consolidated Statement, the notes of one Reserve bank held by another Reserve bank are eliminated. The amount appears in parentheses to the left of the weekly figures.)
[Adapted from *Glossary: Weekly Federal Reserve Statements*, by the Federal Reserve Bank of New York.]

FEDERAL RESERVE SYSTEM. The United States' CENTRAL BANK. Often referred to as *The Fed*. Like other central banks throughout the world, its chief responsibility is to regulate the flow of money and credit in order to promote economic stability and growth. It also performs many service functions for commercial banks, the Treasury, and the public. Its objective is to provide MONETARY POLICY favorable to the realization of four objectives: (1) a high level of employment, (2) stability in overall price levels, (3) economic growth, and (4) a sound BALANCE OF INTERNATIONAL PAYMENTS.

As economic conditions shift, the System at times must shift the emphasis it

places on each of the objectives, but all are continually considered. The four goals are closely interdependent. Without high employment, an economy can neither remain prosperous nor can it grow. With persistent inflation, business and government practices become wasteful, speculation replaces productive activity, excesses leading to economic collapse may develop, and balance-of-payments problems are apt to arise. Chronic deficits in the balance of payments can so tie the hands of fiscal and monetary authorities that they cannot pursue as actively as would be desirable policies designed to stimulate employment or facilitate economic progress. Achievement of high employment, a stable price level, and a sound balance of payments, however, promotes the kind of savings incentives and enterprise needed in a growing economy. Hence, System policies contributing to these three objectives also produce a monetary environment conducive to long-term growth.

The Federal Reserve System has several important functions, which are explained in separate entries such as MEMBER BANK; FEDERAL RESERVE BANK; BOARD OF GOVERNORS (OF THE FEDERAL RESERVE SYSTEM); FEDERAL OPEN MARKET COMMITTEE; FEDERAL ADVISORY COUNCIL.

Two good sources for details of the System, economic history, policy action descriptions, and similar information are *The Federal Reserve at Work* by the Federal Reserve Bank of Richmond, and *The Federal Reserve System Purposes and Functions* by the Board of Governors.

FEDERAL SAVINGS AND LOAN ASSOCIATION. A SAVINGS AND LOAN ASSOCIATION which has a federal, rather than a state, charter. Such associations are required to join the FEDERAL HOME LOAN BANK SYSTEM; others may join if they qualify.

FEDERAL SAVINGS AND LOAN INSURANCE CORPORATION (FSLIC). The organization which insures deposits

at SAVINGS AND LOAN ASSOCIATIONs, in much the same way as the FEDERAL DEPOSIT INSURANCE CORPORATION insures deposits at COMMERCIAL BANKs.

FEDERAL TRADE COMMISSION (FTC). The organization of the federal government which is responsible for enforcing laws that relate to maintaining COMPETITION in business practices, advertising, and related issues.

FEDERAL UNEMPLOYMENT TAX ACT (FUTA). Legislation which established a federal-state unemployment insurance system. Originally a provision of the Social Security Act, FUTA was later incorporated as part of the Internal Revenue Code. Under the law, each state was free to join the system and to adopt coverage and benefit provisions as it saw fit. To "encourage" the states to join, the law provided that certain categories of employers with eight or more workers must pay a federal tax equal to 3 percent of their payroll. This tax was due the federal government whether or not a state had an unemployment insurance law; however, employers covered by both the federal law and a state law meeting certain federal requirements could deduct 90 percent of the 3 percent payroll tax (2.7 percent of payroll) by paying it to the state for use in the payment of unemployment claims. The remaining 10 percent (0.3 percent of payroll) went to the federal government to pay the administrative costs of the program.

At their option, states could offer broader or narrower coverage than that specified by the federal law. But since narrower state coverage penalized uncovered employers (who were still liable for the federal tax) without benefiting the state, there was little incentive to adopt this option. Thus, the choice available to the states was whether to join an unemployment system which they had to pay for anyway. As a result, by 1938 every state and the District of Columbia had joined the system; Puerto Rico joined in 1960.

FEDERATION. A coordinating body which acts for a group of organizations that have joined it. *Federation* refers most often to labor unions, although there are also federations of employers. In this sense, the word has the same meaning as confederation.

FEDERATION OF ECONOMIC OR-GANIZATIONS (Keidenran) (Jap.). The largest of several business organizations to which Japanese companies and other associations belong. Its main purposes include the correlation of business activities and the influence of economic policies.

FEDERATION OF INDEPENDENT UNIONS (Churitsu Roren) (Jap.). A confederation of Japanese labor unions. It is about one-fourth the size of the largest confederation.

FEDWIRE. The Federal Reserve Communications System. An electronic communications network connecting the Federal Reserve offices, the Board of Governors, depository institutions, the Treasury, and other government agencies. Fedwire is used for transferring reserve-account balances of depository institutions and government securities, as well as for transmitting Federal Reserve administrative, supervisory, and monetary policy information.

The computerized central relay point for messages transmitted between Federal Reserve districts on the Fedwire is located in Culpeper, Virginia. There, messages moving billions of dollars of funds and securities daily are processed in electronically coded form. They originate from depository institutions, are sent to Reserve banks, and then are transmitted to Culpeper, where they are switched to other Reserve banks and, in turn, to other depository institutions.

FIAT MONEY. Ordinarily, when monetary authorities issue money, there is asset backing either in the form of precious metal or promises to pay or exchange. However, there have been examples of *printing press money* or *fiat money* which

is printed without any backing at all. During the Civil War, the greenbacks were fiat money.

FIDELITY BOND. An indemnity contract in which the insurer promises to pay as agreed if a person in a position of trust causes a loss by violating that trust. Many employers of individuals who handle money, securities, or other valuables require a fidelity bond on all those employees.

FIDUCIARY. Refers to an arrangement involving financial trust. A party—individual, group, company, etc.—upon whom another party is dependent is the fiduciary. Many laws are written to describe the high degree of probity and subjugation of self-interest required of a fiduciary.

FIDUCIARY MONEY. Generally, money that is not fully backed by a precious metal but is controlled by MONETARY AUTHORITIES. All money in circulation in the U.S. is fiduciary money. Also called *credit money*.

FIDUCIARY MONEY SYSTEM. A money system in which the monetary unit itself, rather than gold or some other precious metal, is the reference for the system.

FINAL ESTIMATE. See ADVANCE, PRELIMINARY, AND FINAL ESTIMATE.

FINAL OUTPUT. Goods and services which reach the terminal point in their distribution, regardless of which SECTOR that terminal point is in. For example, a piece of machinery purchased as capital equipment by the business sector is part of the final output; however, raw material which that machine will process for resale is not included in final output until it is processed and reaches its ultimate user, who may be a consumer or a member of the government or business sector.

FINAL SALES. The portion of current GROSS NATIONAL PRODUCT sold to ultimate users. Included are consumption expenditures of the private and government SECTORs, plus FIXED INVESTMENT and NET EXPORTS. Not included is CHANGE IN BUSINESS INVENTORIES, since inventories are not yet in the hands of ultimate users. Final sales are derived by subtracting the change in business inventories from the GNP in current dollars.

FINANCE CHARGE. The total dollar amount a consumer pays to use credit. It includes interest costs, and sometimes other costs such as service charges, credit-related insurance premiums, appraisal fees, and other charges that would not be made in a cash transaction. See also TRUTH-IN-LENDING ACT.

FINANCE COMPANY. A FINANCIAL INTERMEDIARY which specializes in small loans to individuals. Its risk, and therefore the rates it charges, are usually higher than those of other lenders, such as banks. Since its capital is obtained by issuing stock and by selling COMMERCIAL PAPER, a finance company is a *nondepository* financial intermediary. It is also known as a *personal finance company* or a *consumer finance company*.

A *sales finance company* loans money specifically for the purpose of buying goods. It usually works with retailers, sometimes buying promissory notes from them after they have actually extended a loan to the consumer. Sometimes a sales finance company makes loans directly to consumers. See also DISCOUNT HOUSE.

FINANCE, FUNCTIONAL. See FUNCTIONAL FINANCE.

FINANCIAL INSTITUTION. In general, a FINANCIAL INTERMEDIARY.

FINANCIAL INTERMEDIARY. A business organization which buys claims against others (i.e., makes loans, provides LIQUIDITY), using funds obtained by selling claims against itself. There are two general types: (1) *depository* financial intermediaries, which consist of the

"banking industry" and include banks, savings and loan associations, credit unions, and similar institutions that obtain most of the money they loan by accepting deposits, and (2) *nondepository* intermediaries, which include life insurance companies, mutual funds, private pension funds, and others.

SAVINGS AND LOAN ASSOCIATIONS, MUTUAL SAVINGS BANKS, and CREDIT UNIONS are known collectively as *thrift institutions*.

FINANCIAL INVESTMENT. Investment in its everyday meaning—the buying of goods or securities with plans to sell them later at a higher price, or to receive earnings from them (as opposed to the economists' definition of investment—the purchase of CAPITAL GOODS).

FINANCIAL LOAN AND INVESTMENT PROGRAM (Jap.). In Japan, the source of funds for public corporations, as well as for certain housing, transportation, and industry development programs.

FINANCIERAS (Mex.). See MEXICAN BANKING SYSTEM.

FINE. (1) A punitive nontax payment to a government. DISPOSABLE PERSONAL INCOME is calculated by subtracting personal tax payments, as well as nontax payments such as fines and penalties from PERSONAL INCOME. (2) With respect to precious metals, a measure of the purity.

FINE TUNING. The use of MONETARY POLICY and FISCAL POLICY to attempt to smooth out small irregularities in an economy. Some individuals believe that fine tuning is desirable; others contend that only the major fluctuations are a problem and that time delays in the results of fine tuning actions can, in fact, cause small fluctuations to become major disruptions.

FIRST AGRICULTURAL ADJUSTMENT ACT (First AAA). See FARM RELIEF AND INFLATION ACT.

FIRST BANK OF THE UNITED STATES. The first attempt of the young nation to have a CENTRAL BANK. It was given a 20-year charter in 1791, and during its lifetime there were many political and economic arguments over exactly what its functions and authorities were. When its charter was allowed to expire without renewal in 1811, the nation returned to uncoordinated state banking until the Second Bank of the United States was chartered in 1816. That charter also expired after 20 years, and finally, in 1913, the FEDERAL RESERVE SYSTEM was created as the nation's central bank. Sometimes the first two central bank attempts are referred to as the *First National* and *Second National* banks.

FIRST DOLLAR COVERAGE. A reimbursement, such as certain types of insurance, that does not impose a deductible; the first dollar spent or lost will be repaid.

FIRST FRENCH PLAN. See MONNET PLAN.

FIRST IN, FIRST OUT (FIFO). In accounting economics, the bookkeeping system which records the cost of items brought out of inventory in the chronological order in which they entered inventory. Suppose 10 gross of bolts costing $0.12 each are placed in inventory and then another 5 gross costing $0.14 each are added. If 8 gross are used, all 8 would all be costed at $0.12 each under FIFO. This is the "pipeline" system, with items put in at one end and taken out in the same order at the other end.

The choice of whether to use FIFO or *last in, first out* (LIFO) becomes important when prices are changing, such as during an inflation; it involves the question of whether prices should reflect how much was paid for an item or how much it will cost to replace it.

FIRST NATIONAL BANK. A COMMERCIAL BANK which obtains its charter from the federal government is required to use the word *National* in its name; as a result, a large number of banks across

the nation use the name *First National Bank of. . .*, adding the name of the city or area where they operate. *First National Bank* is also used to refer to the FIRST BANK OF THE UNITED STATES.

FIRST ORDER EFFECTS. See INTERDEPENDENCE.

FIRST SHIFT. The work schedule that begins in the morning and ends in the afternoon. Also called the *day shift*. The *swing* (second) shift is the one that follows, ending about midnight, and the *graveyard* (third) shift spans daybreak.

FIRST WORLD. The most developed, industrialized nations.

FISCAL AUTHORITIES. Individuals in the federal government who are responsible for determining the level of taxation, the forms of taxation, the level of government spending, the forms it will take, and the methods of financing any resultant deficit. These actions together are FISCAL POLICY.

FISCALIST. An economist who believes that employment, prices, and other measures of the economy are controlled mainly through FISCAL POLICY. See also MONETARIST.

FISCAL MONOPOLY. A monopoly owned and operated by some level of government for the purpose of obtaining revenue for the government.

FISCAL MULTIPLIER. A multiplier derived through economic analysis under the assumption that MONETARY AUTHORITIES take perfect accommodating action and therefore interest rates remain constant.

FISCAL POLICY. Control of the economy through revenues and expenditures of the GOVERNMENT SECTOR. An excess of revenues over expenditures (a budget surplus) is the general rule when the economy is above its POTENTIAL GNP and inflation is the major problem; this is a *contractionary policy*. An excess of expenditures over revenues (a budget deficit) is the general rule when the economy is below its potential GNP and the need is for economic growth; this is an *expansionary* policy. A person who favors fiscal policy to cure economic problems is a FISCALIST. See also MONETARY POLICY.

FISCAL RESTRAINT. A tendency toward a less expansionary FISCAL POLICY, especially with regard to a reduction in government spending.

FISCAL STIMULUS. A government's providing for additional spending power in the economy by reducing taxes, increasing its spending, or both. This action is part of expansionary FISCAL POLICY.

FISCAL YEAR (FY). A period of time, usually one year but sometimes varying as much as a couple of weeks, which an economic unit designates as its accounting year. For example, a business might select its fiscal year as November 1 to October 31; a school system might choose September 1 to August 31. The selection is usually made for convenience or economy; thus a retailer might end its accounting year at the time inventory is always at its lowest point.

FISHER'S INDEX. A response to the biases in the LASPEYRES and Paasche indexes. This index is found by taking the geometric average (the square root of the product) of the other two; it will always yield a value closer to the lesser of the other two. Also called *ideal index*.

FIT CURRENCY. The condition of currency in circulation is described as *fit*, *unfit*, or *new*. *Fit* currency does not show enough wear to require withdrawal from circulation; *unfit* currency is sufficiently worn to require withdrawal and replacement. New currency is issued by the Treasury (see UNITED STATES NOTES) or by the FEDERAL RESERVE SYSTEM (see FEDERAL RESERVE NOTES) and then goes into circulation.

FIVE-ANTI CAMPAIGN (CHINA). In 1951 and 1952, during the early days of communist rule in China, one step toward the nationalism of industry was the Five-

Anti Campaign, which denounced tax cheating, other fraud against the government, bribery of all kinds, theft (especially of government property), and disclosure of official economic data. Punishment, generally a monetary fine or a CAPITAL LEVY, transferred a considerable amount of private assets to the government. See also THREE-ANTI CAMPAIGN.

FIVE-YEAR PLAN (U.S.S.R.). Communist leadership in the Soviet Union has relied heavily on intermediate-range plans, starting with its first five-year plan of 1928 to 1932. These plans, worked out in great detail, specify the INPUTs to be allocated and the goals which they will strive for. Sometimes goals have not been met; sometimes they have been far exceeded.

FIXED ASSET. An ASSET that is permanent or will be used continually for several years.

FIXED COSTS (FC). Costs which are independent of the quantity of a product being produced. In applied economics, a fixed cost is considered to be independent of quantity up to a certain quantity; then that cost becomes fixed at a new level for another range of output quantities. For example, the cost of heating a factory does not increase as factory output increases; however, when output reaches a certain level a larger factory will be required, and then heating cost will remain fixed at a higher level until that factory is no longer sufficient.

Since fixed costs are independent of quantity, a large output will allow each unit to bear a smaller share of fixed cost allocation (see AVERAGE FIXED COSTS).

One definition of LONG RUN is the length of time it takes for all costs to become VARIABLE COSTS; there are no fixed costs in the long run. See COST for a listing of the various types of costs. Also called *constant costs*.

FIXED COSTS PER UNIT. *Average fixed costs;* the sum of all FIXED COSTS divided by the quantity of goods produced. Since fixed costs are a constant, the larger the quantity produced, the smaller the allocation to each unit will be.

FIXED INVESTMENT. A purchase of durable equipment, construction, or both by business and nonprofit organizations. Fixed investment expenditures are reflected in GROSS NATIONAL PRODUCT in two ways: (1) capital investment increases GNP by the value of the asset in the period in which the investment is made, and (2) the effect of the previous year's investment appears in the products produced with the help of that investment in CAPITAL GOODS. These products are of all types: consumer goods, additional capital goods, exports, and government purchases.

FIXED RATES. In INTERNATIONAL EXCHANGE, the rates that result when nations fix the price at which their money converts into a standard such as gold; the rates at which their monies convert to each other is then automatically established. See also FLOATING EXCHANGE RATES.

FLAT. In financial economics, describes the sale of a bond without an adjustment of the price for interest which has accrued and will be paid to the buyer.

FLEXIBLE RATES. In INTERNATIONAL EXCHANGE, rates that result when MONETARY AUTHORITIES set upper and lower limits to exchange rates and act to control the rates only when they threaten to move outside the limits. The limits are usually changed only when there are large inequities in the rates; alternatively, they can be changed in small, frequent increments by means of a SLIDING PEG. See also SNAKE IN THE TUNNEL.

FLIGHT FROM. The expression ''flight from [a certain nation's monetary unit]'' means that speculators are selling their holdings of that money. For example, in 1973 there was a flight from U.S. dollars; that is, speculators preferred to hold marks, yens, or some other unit. The desire to

hold fewer dollars in effect increases the supply of dollars in the market, and as with any transaction, when supply increases, equilibrium price declines (see SUPPLY AND DEMAND). In such a case, if monetary authorities want to maintain a constant exchange ratio, they must enter the market to buy up the excess that is offered in order to keep the law of supply and demand from operating to lower the exchange rate of the monetary unit.

FLOAT. See CHECK CLEARING; FEDERAL RESERVE FLOAT; INTERBANK FLOAT.

FLOATING DEBT. Nominally short-term debt which is extended in practice when the issuing corporation or government sells new short-term debt in order to obtain funds to retire previous short-term debt as each issue becomes due.

FLOATING EXCHANGE RATES. Exchange rates that occur when a nation's monetary authorities do not act to affect the rate at which its monetary unit is traded in the money markets. According to the BRETTON WOODS agreement, each nation is committed to take action as necessary to keep the market rate of its monetary unit (relative to the U.S. dollar) within plus or minus 1 percent of an established parity rate. The range was modified in 1971 to 2.25 percent. See also CLEAN FLOAT; DIRTY FLOAT.

FLOOR PRICE. Usually established by the government, the smallest price that a seller is allowed to charge. A true floor price is usually established by government, and a true floor price means that sellers can charge more, but not less. If the floor price is less than the equilibrium price (see SUPPLY AND DEMAND), it is ineffective because the market will stabilize at the equilibrium price; if the floor price is above equilibrium, a surplus will develop.

FLOOR TRADER. In an organized stock exchange, a member who works on the trading floor, conducting transactions at the posts.

FLOWCHART. A pictorial or verbal diagram showing normal and alternative flows of events. In computer programming, a flowchart can be used to show how a program will progress through its steps and checks; in management economics, a flowchart can show the operation of a business system, such as the route taken by a purchase requisition from original writer through approvals.

FLOWS. See MONEY FLOW; REAL FLOW.

FOOD, IMPUTED VALUE OF. See IMPUTATION.

FORCED SAVING. An involuntary foregoing of present consumption; the intention is that the resultant saving will be redistributed for consumption later. Government retirement plans (such as social security) are a form of forced saving, as are private retirement plans in which participation is not voluntary.

FORCES, MARKET. See MARKET FORCES.

FORECLOSURE. In a secured transaction of the mortgage type, the action of the mortgagee to regain possession and title upon default of the mortgagor.

FOREIGN ASSISTANCE ACT OF 1948. See EUROPEAN RECOVERY PROGRAM.

FOREIGN BANK (Vneshtorgbank) (U.S.S.R.). In the Soviet Union, the financial enterprise which specializes in international accounts and in financing enterprises that deal with international trade.

FOREIGN BILL. A BILL OF EXCHANGE in which the drawer and drawee are in different states (if within the U.S.) or in different nations. See also CONTINENTAL BILL; DOMESTIC BILL.

FOREIGN DESK. At the Federal Reserve Bank of New York open market purchases and sales of government securities are made at "the desk"; transactions in the foreign exchange market are made at "the foreign desk."

FOREIGN DOLLAR BALANCES. See BALANCE OF INTERNATIONAL PAYMENTS.

FOREIGN EXCHANGE. International BILL OF EXCHANGE used for a settlement between a buyer (importer) in one nation and a seller (exporter) in another.

FOREIGN EXCHANGE BANK (Jugoslovenska Banka Za Spoljnu Trogovina) (Yugo.). One of the specialized banks within the commercial banking system of Yugoslavia. Its function is to assist domestic and foreign traders with financing transactions which involve an exchange of currency. This assistance usually takes the form of exchange credit.

FOREIGN EXCHANGE DESK. The foreign exchange trading desk at the Federal Reserve Bank of New York. It undertakes operations in the exchange markets for the account of the FEDERAL OPEN MARKET COMMITTEE (as agent for the U.S. Treasury) and as agent for foreign CENTRAL BANKs.

FOREIGN EXCHANGE MARKET. An organized market in which the monies of various countries are exchanged. Rates of exchange are the prices of currencies quoted in terms of other currencies. As with other organized markets, transactions are either *spot* (for prompt settlement) or *future* (contracted for settlement at a stated future date). The financial instruments exchanged are all current: money in the form of notes and coin, bank deposits denominated in different currencies, or NEAR MONEY in such forms as bank drafts and bills of exchange.

FOREIGN INVESTMENT. The provision of CAPITAL FUNDS by the government or citizens of one nation, for use in another nation. Such funds flow out of the nation providing them and are therefore a negative item in the INTERNATIONAL BALANCE OF PAYMENTS. However, because they also include a claim (either debt or ownership), it is expected that when the production they finance becomes effective, funds will flow in the other direction.

FOREIGN TRADE ZONE. An area, sometimes found in large ports, where provision is made for reshipping imported goods without taking them through customs. Also called a *free port*.

FORMATION, BUSINESS. See INDEX OF NET BUSINESS FORMATION.

FORMS OF BUSINESS ORGANIZATION. The three main forms of organization are sole proprietorship, partnership, and corporation. The following descriptions are general because details vary from one nation to another and even from one state to another.

Sole proprietorship. This is the simplest form because one person owns the business and it is not necessary to first obtain approval of any government agency. Of course, certain types of businesses are required to obtain a license or other type of permit, but basically a sole proprietorship is started by the owner's simply opening for business. About 80 percent of all businesses in the U.S. are sole proprietorships; mostly small businesses, they account for only about 14 percent of all sales. One significant disadvantage is that the firm's assets are limited by the personal wealth of the owner.

Partnership. About 8 percent of all businesses in the U.S. are partnerships, firms owned by more than one person. They account for about 5 percent of all sales. However, the firm's size remains limited because all general partners are liable for all the debts of the partnership, and therefore it is difficult to attract money from a large number of people. In the U.S., partnerships are governed by the Uniform Partnership Act (UPA). A special kind of partnership, the *limited partnership*, allows limited partners to invest money without being liable for the partnership's debts, but it also requires that one or more general partner(s) be fully liable. The rules for this arrangement are in the Uniform Limited Partnership Act (ULPA).

Corporation. Although less than 13 percent of the business firms in the U.S. are corporations, they are mostly "big business"—over 80 percent of all sales are through corporations. In a corporation, ownership shares are sold to persons whose direct voice in the management of the firm is limited, usually to voting for members of the board of directors and to approve or disapprove certain major issues. There is no provision for stockholders (owners) to participate in day-to-day management. More important, they are not liable for debts of the corporation; they are protected by the concept of limited liability. As a result, large numbers of people are willing to buy shares of ownership (CAPITAL STOCK), and organizations can grow to the optimum size for ECONOMIES OF SCALE.

FORM UTILITY. The level of satisfaction which a given tangible object or good can yield in various forms. See UTILITY UNITS. For example, one ton of seawater has a certain value, but when available as separate quantities of iodine, gold, other minerals, distilled water, and other items, that ton will yield more utility.

FORTY-FIVE DEGREE LINE. In general, a line which bisects the axes of a graph and passes through the origin; $x = y$ at every point on the line. Economists often use the expression *45-degree line* in connection with a graph of spending versus income. In that application, the 45-degree line is the locus of all points where spending equals income (i.e., where there is no aggregate saving or dissaving). These points are significant because when total spending equals total income the economy is neither inflationary nor recessionary. However, not every point along the 45-degree line is desirable; other factors such as the level of employment must be considered.

FORWARD CONTRACT. See SWAP NETWORK.

FORWARD EXCHANGE CONTRACT.
An agreement to deliver (or to accept delivery of) an amount of a foreign currency at a specified date in the future. In a variation, the *option contract*, customers are given the option of delivering the foreign exchange to their bank (or receiving delivery) at any time within a specified period—typically a ten-day period at the beginning, middle, or end of a month. See also SPOT EXCHANGE CONTRACT.

FORWARDING AGENT. One who deals with both the shipper and the carrier, receiving shipments directly from shippers and taking responsibility for placing them properly with carriers. The forwarding agent usually receives relatively small shipments and combines them for more efficient handling and lower rates. See CARLOAD.

FORWARD RATE. With regard to three-month Treasury bills, the interest rate two quarters ahead that would be required to equalize expected returns on six- and nine-month bills over a nine-month holding period.

FOUL BILL OF LADING. A shipping document (see BILL OF LADING) on which one of the parties to the shipment notes some irregularity, such as short count, damaged goods, or other reason for an exception to its usual liability.

FRACTIONAL CURRENCY. Units of currency less than the basic denomination of a nation's money system. In the U.S. the dollar is the basic unit, and therefore fractional currency consists of pennies, nickels, dimes, quarters, and half-dollars.

FRACTIONAL RESERVE BANKING SYSTEM. System of commercial banking in the U.S. and most other nations, in which banks are allowed to reduce the reserves they keep for immediate use to a fraction of their total deposit liabilities. See BANK RESERVES.

FRANCHISE. Usually found in retail trade, an arrangement whereby one party (a *franchisee*) pays another party (a *fran-*

chisor) for the right to operate a business under the latter's name. Many franchisors supply franchisees with equipment, facilities, training, and other assistance, and they provide at least part of the operating inventory. Another advantage to the franchisee is that he or she does not have to work for a long period to become known in the trade, because the franchisor is already well known and is often a national advertiser. Advantages to the franchisor include expansion with a minimum of working capital.

In another type of franchise, a level of government grants a party (such as a local bus line) the right to operate a business, usually as a monopoly.

FRANCHISE TAX. A recurring charge paid by a franchisee to the government body that issued it a franchise to operate.

FRANK. To mark mail for sending, rather than affix a stamp. Many public officials and government bureaus have the privilege of franking their mail.

FRAZIER-LEMKE BANKRUPTCY BILL. One of the NEW DEAL measures passed during the GREAT DEPRESSION, this legislation gave farmers the right to repurchase, over a period of six years at 1 percent interest, farms they had lost through bankruptcy. It was declared unconstitutional; Congress then passed it again with minor modifications.

FREE BANKING ACT. Legislation passed in New York in 1838, enabling banks to be chartered without a special act of the legislature provided they met certain requirements, including the deposit of specified types of securities with the state comptroller, who could sell them to redeem notes in case the bank failed. The act permitted free entry into banking, but regulations were imposed to make note issues safe.

FREE COINAGE. A condition in which a government agrees to mint coins in whatever quantity will consume the precious metal (such as gold) that is offered to it at a specified price. *Free* is used here in the sense of *unlimited*, rather than indicating that no charge is made to cover the cost of minting. See also GRATUITOUS COINAGE; BRASSAGE.

FREE ENTERPRISE. A business which is privately owned and in which decisions are the result of market forces (see MARKETPLACE) rather than government control. In practice, no firm has the theoretical ultimate in freedom, and therefore *free enterprise* actually describes a privately owned firm which operates according to SUPPLY AND DEMAND, with a minimum of government influence. *Free enterprise system, capitalism, market economy*, and many other expressions refer to noncommunist economies which are guided by CONSUMER SOVEREIGNTY.

FREE ENTRY. The fact that firms may enter or leave a given market. They will enter if profits are above normal (see ECONOMIC PROFIT), thereby tending to reduce profits in the industry to normal; they will leave the industry if profits are below normal, thereby providing the long-term tendency for profits of those firms remaining to become normal. Freedom to enter and leave a market is one of the basic principles of COMPETITION, and economists believe that one of the main purposes of government is to see that that freedom is not taken away by firms that want to maintain a MONOPOLY or OLIGOPOLY position for themselves.

FREE FUNDS. In Eastern European economies, liquid assets which are not allocated for a specific purpose—similar to the Western expression *excess liquidity*. [Adapted from George Garvey, *Money, Banking, and Credit in Eastern Europe* (New York: Federal Reserve Bank of New York, 1966), p. 18.]

FREE GOOD. An item which has value and is available at no cost (whoever uses it does not have to decide what other expenditure to forego). With the growth in world population, free goods have practically disappeared; one cause of environmental pollution is disregarding the

social cost of certain items (see SPILLOVER) and treating them as free goods.

FREE LIST. A list of items which are not subject to customs duties.

FREE MARKET. Transactions conducted under conditions of a MARKET ECONOMY.

FREE PORT. Area sometimes found in large ports where provision is made for reshipping imported goods without taking them through customs. Also called a *foreign-trade zone*.

FREE RESERVES. See BORROWED RESERVES.

FREE TRADE. Freedom from government regulations in conducting trade, especially international trade. Because it is difficult or impossible to find a total absence of government control today, *free trade* describes those areas or transactions which are *relatively free* of control and regulations.

FREE TRADE AREA. An arrangement in which participating nations remove trade restrictions on each other while maintaining their original tariff policies toward all other nations. Also called *customs union*.

FREE TRADER. A person who feels that trade (usually international trade) should be determined by the forces of SUPPLY AND DEMAND and COMPARATIVE ADVANTAGE rather than be restricted by tariffs, quotas, and other artificial barriers. See also PROTECTIONISM.

FREIGHT FORWARDER. A person whose business is collecting relatively small shipments from others and combining them into larger shipments in order to obtain a more efficient price from the carrier. See CARLOAD.

FREQUENCY DISTRIBUTION. A display of events (or results) and the number of times each occurs. For example, a bar chart showing income ranges along one axis and the number of workers in each of the ranges along the other axis is a frequency distribution.

FRICTIONAL UNEMPLOYMENT. Unemployment that is of a short-term nature because the individuals involved are between jobs, have jobs they will return to in the near future, or are looking for their first jobs. Also called *natural unemployment* because it is the rate of *full employment* in a healthy economy. See also STRUCTURAL UNEMPLOYMENT.

FRINGE BENEFITS. Benefits other than wages received by employees including low-cost group insurance, vacation pay, subsidized company cafeterias, and many other "fringes." Of the total cost of labor, fringes are accounting for an increasing percentage. One reason for the popularity of fringe benefits is that workers do not pay income tax on them; if wages were increased enough to allow workers to buy the benefits, the workers would be taxed on the higher wages.

FROZEN. A holding of value which is difficult to convert into cash. A frozen asset is said to be *illiquid* (see LIQUID ASSET).

FUEL, IMPUTED VALUE OF. See IMPUTATION.

FULL COST PRICING. The practice of setting a selling price by first determining a desired mark-up and then adding that value to the actual total costs of the item. Also called *cost-plus pricing* or *markup pricing*.

FULL EMPLOYMENT. The maximum practical utilization of ECONOMIC RESOURCES consistent with a stable economy, rather than absolute 100 percent usage. Regarding nonhuman resources, the most efficient units will be used first, and there will always be some that could be used but at a decrease in efficiency. Regarding human resources, it is recognized that at any time there are individuals counted in the CIVILIAN LABOR FORCE who, for various voluntary and involuntary reasons (e.g., seasonal work, population shifts, production changes), are not employed. Even during

World War II, when there was demand for more of all resources, the lowest annual unemployment rate reached was 1.2 percent (670,000 unemployed in 1944). Therefore, full employment, as applied to the EMPLOYMENT ACT OF 1946, was considered to exist when only 4 percent of the labor force is unemployed. That figure has never had universal acceptance, however, and 5 percent has had more acceptance recently. See also POTENTIAL GNP.

For an analysis of the 4 percent view, see Robert A. McMillan, in *Economic Review, Federal Reserve Bank of Cleveland* (March-April 1973). McMillan examines the origin of the 4 percent target and the positions of those who believe it should be changed; he then considers the implications of some alternative definitions of full employment.

FULL EMPLOYMENT AND BALANCED GROWTH ACT. Legislation of 1978 that details procedures for working toward the goals of full employment and balanced economic growth. One section of the act establishes more specific targets for money growth. Also known as the *Humphrey-Hawkins Act*.

FULL EMPLOYMENT DEFICIT (SURPLUS). See HIGH EMPLOYMENT DEFICIT (SURPLUS).

FULL EMPLOYMENT EQUILIBRIUM. An economic situation in which total demand is equal to total supply (i.e., is neither inflationary nor recessionary) at the same time that FULL EMPLOYMENT exists. One of the main reasons for MIXED CAPITALISM, rather than *pure* CAPITALISM, is that although the natural forces of the latter may bring about stability, that stability may not coincide with acceptable levels of unemployment. However, planned economic policies can find other points of stability (see FORTY-FIVE DEGREE LINE) with lower levels of unemployment.

FULL EMPLOYMENT GNP. Total output of goods and services (GROSS NATIONAL PRODUCT) which would result if an economy were at its defined level of FULL EMPLOYMENT.

FULL EMPLOYMENT UNEMPLOYMENT RATE (FEUR). The rate of unemployment that could exist if an economy were operating at the POTENTIAL GNP rate.

FULL FAITH AND CREDIT BOND. A BOND issued by some level of government, and backed by the full taxing authority of that government. Interest payments and repayment of principal are taken from general funds. Also called *general obligation* bond. See also REVENUE BOND.

FULL STOCK. CAPITAL STOCK which has a PAR VALUE of $100. See also HALF STOCK.

FULLY INVESTED. The condition of a bank or the banking system when *actual reserves* are just sufficient to satisfy *required reserves*; there are no *excess reserves* and therefore loans are difficult to obtain. Also called *loaned up*. See BANK RESERVES.

FUNCTIONAL DISTRIBUTION OF INCOME. Disaggregation of income data into type of income, or methods of earning. NATIONAL INCOME is composed of compensation of employees, proprietors' income, net interest, rental income of persons, and corporate profits. See also PERSONAL DISTRIBUTION OF INCOME.

FUNCTIONAL FINANCE. Planning of a government budget so that it will have a COUNTERCYCLICAL, full employment effect, without consideration of whether the result will be deficit, balanced, or surplus. This policy is generally considered the opposite of an ANNUALLY BALANCED BUDGET, whereby government revenues and expenditures are equalized over a fiscal year, regardless of the macroeconomic effect. See FISCAL POLICY.

FUNCTIONS OF MONEY. The barter system suffers from three main weaknesses; since a money system is designed specifically to overcome them, they are called the *functions of money*. These functions—*standard of value*, *standard of deferred payments*, and *medium of exchange*—are explained under BARTER.

FUNDAMENTAL ACCOUNTING EQUATION. Modern accounting recognizes three general categories of accounts in the following relationship:

Assets = Liabilities + Ownership

Assets represents the total value of everything an organization has. On the right-hand side of the equation, all assets are subject to the claims of either outsiders (liabilities) or those who own the enterprise (ownership).

FUNDAMENTALIST. In financial economics, a follower of the securities markets whose decisions are based mostly on the strength, earning power, and similar characteristics of the issuing company. This position is opposed to that of a *chartist*, who holds that the price of a security is mostly a function of past and present movements of prices, volume of trade, and other statistics.

FUND, IMPREST. See IMPREST FUND.

FUNNY MONEY. Informally, COUNTERFEIT MONEY.

G

GALLOPING INFLATION. Inflation that is proceeding at an undesirably high rate. See also CREEPING INFLATION; HYPERINFLATION.

GANTT CHART. In managerial economics, a scheduling chart that shows each of the tasks to be performed and the period of time during which each will take place. Analysts can then determine which tasks are critical to the overall schedule, and management can identify checkpoints at which to measure actual progress relative to predicted results.

GAP, GROSS NATIONAL PRODUCT. See POTENTIAL GNP.

GENERAL AGREEMENT ON TARIFFS AND TRADE (GATT). An agreement signed at the Geneva Trade Conference in 1947, which was attended by representatives of 23 nations, including all important industrial nations outside the communist bloc. One outcome of the conference was the *most favored nation* principle, which provides that all parties to GATT must be given any tariff reduction (i.e., tariff concession) which is given to any other member. In 1962 the U.S. passed the *Trade Expansion Act*, giving President Kennedy discretionary authority to reduce any tariff by as much as 50 percent; that act was the basis for the Kennedy round (one of several rounds in a continuing series of international negotiations which began in 1947).

GENERAL CONTROL. An action by government or monetary authorities which exerts control of the economy nonselectively through all sectors and components. Addition of a NEUTRAL TAX can be a general control associated with FISCAL POLICY.

GENERAL COUNCIL OF TRADE UNIONS OF JAPAN (SOHYO). The largest and most aggressive confederation of labor unions in Japan, SOHYO is committed to socialist doctrines and the promotion of class struggle.

GENERAL OBLIGATION BOND. A BOND issued by some level of government, and backed by the full taxing authority of that government. Interest payments and repayment of principal are taken from general funds. See also REVENUE BOND.

GENERAL PARTNER. In a partnership (see FORMS OF BUSINESS ORGANIZATION), a partner who has unlimited liability for debts of the firm. *General partner* is used mostly in connection with a *limited partnership*, in which there are also *limited partners* who have limited liability.

GENERAL THEORY OF EMPLOYMENT, INTEREST, AND MONEY. Book by JOHN MAYNARD KEYNES, published in 1936 during the GREAT DEPRESSION. It revolutionized economic thinking by calling for a concentration on aggregate spending and for government to increase or decrease its spending as necessary to maintain total spending at the desired level. Usually shortened to *General Theory*. See FISCAL POLICY; EXPENDITURE MULTIPLIER.

GENEVA TRADE CONFERENCE. A meeting in Geneva, Switzerland, in 1947, attended by representatives of 23 nations, including all important industrial nations outside the communist bloc. The GENERAL AGREEMENT ON TARIFFS AND TRADE (GATT) was signed at that conference.

GEOGRAPHIC MONOPOLY. A selling area in which a seller has no COMPETITION, although there may be sellers of the same product in other areas.

GEOMETRIC MEAN. The nth root of the product of n terms. See FISHER'S INDEX for an example. See also AVERAGE.

GEOMETRIC PROGRESSION. A series of numbers each of which was obtained by multiplying the preceding number by a constant. See MALTHUS, THOMAS, for an example in economics. See also ARITHMETIC PROGRESSION.

GERMAN CONFEDERATION OF EMPLOYERS ASSOCIATION (Ger.). Organization of employers in West Germany, formed to handle labor negotiations with unions.

GI BILL OF RIGHTS. See SERVICEMEN'S READJUSTMENT ACT.

GIFFEN GOOD. See INCOME EFFECT.

GIFT TAX. A tax levied on the *giver* of a gift which exceeds a specified amount. If it were not for gift taxes, individuals could avoid ESTATE and INHERITANCE TAXes by simply giving their property to their heirs prior to death.

GILT-EDGE SECURITY. A BOND or other security which involves negligible risk for its owner.

GINNY MAE. A popular name, especially among investors, for GOVERNMENT NATIONAL MORTGAGE ASSOCIATION.

GIRO SYSTEM. A checking account method, used in several European countries, in which the DRAWER prepares a check in the traditional way but then, instead of sending it to the PAYEE, sends it to the DRAWEE. The drawee might be a commercial bank or, as in some countries, the post office system. Upon receipt of the order to pay, the drawee transmits the *information* to its branch nearest to the payee; then the branch notifies the payee that the amount has been credited to its account. In some giro systems the payment order, or a copy of it, is actually sent to the office at which the payee finally receives payment; in others, only the information is transmitted, usually by wire.

GIROZENTRALEN (Ger.). West German organizations of the GIRO SYSTEM. They act in many ways as bankers' banks.

GLASS-STEAGALL ACT. One of the NEW DEAL measures with long-lasting effect, this legislation of June 16, 1933, which required that commercial banking operations be separate from investment banking, restricted the use of bank credit for speculative purposes, limited MEMBER BANKs' dealings in foreign securities, and increased the authority of the FEDERAL RESERVE SYSTEM. The GLASS-STEAGALL ACT also created the FEDERAL DEPOSIT INSURANCE CORPORATION. On the liberal side, it clearly stated that NATIONAL BANKs could establish branches in states which allowed the practice.

GNP GAP. See POTENTIAL GNP.

GNP IMPLICIT PRICE DEFLATOR (GNPIPD). The overall correction factor for price changes, as opposed to the CON-

SUMER PRICE INDEX, the farm price index, and several other measures that show price changes in selected parts of the economy. GROSS NATIONAL PRODUCT in CURRENT DOLLARS divided by GNPIPD is equal to the GNP in constant dollars of the year on which the deflator is based. Also known as GNP price deflator, and GNP deflator. See also DEFLATOR.

GOING VALUE. Current market price; amount for which similar items are selling.

GOLD ACCOUNT. In accounting for BALANCE OF INTERNATIONAL PAYMENTS, the U.S. keeps this account, in which is recorded all official purchases or sales of gold. The import and export of gold for commercial accounts are entered in the CURRENT ACCOUNT.

GOLD ARBITRAGE. The simultaneous buying and selling of gold in two different markets when the price of gold is different in each. See ARBITRAGE.

GOLD BULLION. An ingot or bar (rather than coins or other monetary units) of gold in a very pure form.

GOLD BULLION STANDARD. A money system which is backed by gold in that its currency can be exchanged upon demand for gold bullion.

GOLD CERTIFICATE. A form of paper currency, formerly in circulation in the U.S., bearing a notation of redeemability in gold. Today gold certificates are used only between the U.S. Treasury and the FEDERAL RESERVE SYSTEM; the most recent method of gold transfer is simply through bookkeeping entries, which are also referred to as *gold certificates*. See also FEDERAL RESERVE NOTES; SILVER CERTIFICATE.

GOLD CERTIFICATE ACCOUNT. An account in the CONSOLIDATED STATEMENT OF CONDITION OF ALL FEDERAL RESERVE BANKS, it includes two items:

Gold certificate credits in the INTERDISTRICT SETTLEMENT FUND. The Federal Reserve banks maintain a gold-certificate fund in Washington—the Interdistrict Settlement Fund—which is used to settle daily amounts due one another. Each Reserve bank keeps as credits in the Interdistrict Settlement Fund a substantial part of the gold certificates it holds. The books of the fund are maintained by the BOARD OF GOVERNORS (OF THE FEDERAL RESERVE SYSTEM) but the U.S. Treasurer is custodian of the fund. The fund settles amounts due by increasing or decreasing the gold-certificate balances held by each Reserve bank, thus redistributing but not changing the total credits held by all 12 Reserve banks.

Gold certificates held by the Federal Reserve banks. When the Treasury purchases gold and needs to replenish its dollar balances, it *monetizes* the gold—it issues gold-certificates credits to the Federal Reserve banks, and an equal amount in dollars is credited to its account at the Reserve banks. If the Treasury wishes to sell gold that has already been monetized, it must free the gold by redeeming gold certificates issued to the Reserve banks. When redeeming gold certificates, the Treasury "returns" an equal amount of dollars to (reduces its balances at) the Reserve banks for gold certificates received.

Some credits are pledged with *Federal Reserve agents*, the Board of Governors' representatives at each Reserve bank. [The Federal Reserve Act (Section 4) specifies that the Board of Governors must designate one of the three Class C directors of each Federal Reserve bank (one of the directors appointed by the Board) as chairman of the Board and Federal Reserve agent. The agent is responsible for the custody of the bank's unissued Federal Reserve notes. To obtain notes from the agent, the bank must pledge collateral at least equal to the amount of notes it wishes to issue.] These credits are collateral against Federal Reserve notes issued. Statutory minimum gold-reserve requirements against Federal Reserve deposit liabilities and notes were abolished on March 3, 1965, and March 19, 1968, respectively. However, each Reserve bank must maintain collateral equal to the amount of its Federal Reserve notes outstanding. This collateral may be gold certificates or SPECIAL DRAWING RIGHTS certificates, U.S. government securities, or collateral received in making loans. [Adapted from *Glossary: Weekly Federal Reserve Statements*, by the Federal Reserve Bank of New York.]

GOLD CLAUSE. A clause in a contract providing for payment in gold or in money equated to gold.

GOLDEN AGE OF AGRICULTURE. In the U.S., the years from 1910 until 1914, when World War I began in Europe. It is generally agreed that during those years western population shifts, farm technology, overall demand, and several other factors all worked in the direction of improving per capita REAL INCOME on farms.

GOLDEN HANDCUFFS. Benefits provided by employers that make it costly for employees to change jobs, thereby removing the competitive advantage individuals would otherwise have in selling their labor. See LOCK-IN BENEFITS.

GOLD EXCHANGE STANDARD. The standard of the U.S. international monetary system prior to August 1971. Under the gold-exchange standard, the U.S. freely bought gold from and sold gold to monetary authorities of other nations at $35 an ounce, according to its basic commitment under rules of the INTERNATIONAL MONETARY FUND (IMF). At the same time, all other nations met their IMF obligations by an exchange of dollars and sometimes other currencies.

GOLD POINTS. The upper (export point) and lower (import point) boundaries to which the currency of nation A can fluctuate inside nation B, if both currencies are tied to gold. If nation A's monetary unit (let's call it *boikles*) trades in nation

B for $2.00, there must be twice as much gold in a boikle as there is in a dollar. Now assume that the total cost of shipping a boikle's worth of gold including packing, insurance, transportation, and OPPORTUNITY COST, is $0.03. The export point is then $2.03, the import point is $1.97, and the exchange rate of a boikle will not fluctuate outside these boundaries.

GOLD POOL. A group of eight major nations that agreed to stabilize the price of gold at $35 an ounce by buying or selling any amounts that were demanded or offered. In March 1968 the gold pool was terminated because the nonmonetary users of gold (i.e., private users and speculators) had been buying so much that supplying the market was endangering the gold reserves of the participating nations. At that time international agreement called for monetary authorities and CENTRAL BANKs to continue to buy and sell gold at $35 an ounce but not to the private market. Therefore the private market could be supplied only by nonmonetary sources and, in effect, became a separate market. This became known as the *two-tier gold system*.

GOLD REPEAL JOINT RESOLUTION. NEW DEAL legislation which made a sweeping cancellation of GOLD CLAUSEs in existing contracts, both public and private, and stated that payment in LEGAL TENDER must be accepted.

GOLD RESERVE ACT. Legislation of 1934 that terminated the use of gold coins and withdrew the offer to exchange currency for gold. The act drastically changed the U.S. monetary system.

GOLD SETTLEMENT FUND. A fund maintained by the FEDERAL RESERVE SYSTEM to facilitate CHECK CLEARING. The fund was established through an assessment on all 12 FEDERAL RESERVE BANKs. By paying in with gold certificates, the banks created the fund with MONEY that already existed rather than by creating new money.

GOLD STANDARD. There are three parts to a gold standard:

1. A nation defines its monetary unit as being equal to a given amount of gold.
2. The monetary authorities of that nation buy all the gold that is offered and sell all the gold that is demanded, at the defined rate. Therefore, the worldwide value cannot change.
3. Anyone can exchange money for gold and can sell gold to the financial authorities of any nation.

No nation has been on a true gold standard since the mid-1930s, but some nations still attempt to define their monetary unit in terms of gold. Other precious metals, especially silver, have been used at times as the standard for a nation's money.

GOLD STANDARD ACT. Legislation of February 15, 1900, which set the U.S. on the GOLD STANDARD; established the value of the dollar at 25.8 grains of gold; declared it the duty of the secretary of the treasury to maintain all forms of money at parity with gold and with one another; and provided that all government paper money would be redeemable in gold. Also known as the *Currency Bill.*

GOOD, GIFFEN. See INCOME EFFECT.

GOOD MONEY. Money in a period of relatively low prices. See also CHEAP MONEY; GRESHAM'S LAW.

GOODS AND SERVICES. Everything produced by an economy is either a good or a service. The two categories together account for *all* the output of a nation. Goods and services are often categorized as *consumer* or *industrial* and as *final* or *intermediate* (see FINAL OUTPUT). Goods, the tangible products, can be further divided into *durables* and *nondurables* (see DURABLE GOODS). Services are intangible commodities such as medical care, haircuts, personal transportation, and the use of housing.

GOSBANK (U.S.S.R.). The state bank of the Soviet Union. More than a CENTRAL BANK, it performs all functions of a banking system (including BANK OF ISSUE, MONETARY POLICY, commercial banking, and other functions as applicable to the Soviet economy). A bank of this type is referred to as a *monobank.*

GOSPLAN (U.S.S.R.). Soviet agency which coordinates economic planning, especially the series of five-year plans, and provides economic information to the COUNCIL OF MINISTERS. There is a central Gosplan as well as Gosplans at intermediate and local levels, all coordinated toward the goal of balanced growth.

GOTEBORGS BANK (Swed.). One of the largest commercial banks in Sweden. It is privately owned.

GOVERNMENT. Usually, economists use *government* to mean all levels of government collectively. In the U.S. the three levels are federal, state, and local. Local refers to all governments below state level, such as county, city, and township. This usage developed because all levels together constitute the public SECTOR and therefore have many characteristics in common. However, it is recognized that government actions must be disaggregated for many analyses because their objectives are not identical. For example, only the federal government is specifically given responsibility for FISCAL POLICY.

GOVERNMENT BILL OF LADING. A shipping document (see BILL OF LADING) used when the government is the shipper; usually the government is also the consignee.

GOVERNMENT CONSUMPTION. Official reports distinguish between government expenditures for consumption and for investment. Consumption expenditures include items for promoting education, training, research and development, etc. and activities that contribute to economic growth. Government investment expenditures are for capital goods, which are not for immediate consumption, and mainly comprise purchases of military hardware and structures.

GOVERNMENT ENTERPRISE. A government activity that is financed primarily by the sale of a good or service rather than through taxes. A state-operated liquor store is a government enterprise.

GOVERNMENT MONOPOLY. A government owned enterprise which, by dictate or circumstance, has no COMPETITION.

GOVERNMENT NATIONAL MORTGAGE ASSOCIATION (GNMA). An organization that sells its securities to investors as a means of obtaining funds for guaranteeing mortgages. Its objectives include stimulating the homebuilding industry by channeling funds within the investment community. The organization is sometimes known, especially among investors, as *Ginny Mae*.

GOVERNMENT PURCHASES OF GOODS AND SERVICES. In NATIONAL INCOME AND PRODUCT ACCOUNTS, the net expenditures for goods and services by the three levels of government—federal, state, and local—and the gross investment of GOVERNMENT ENTERPRISEs. Among the items included are compensation of government employees; construction of highways, bridges, and schools; and net purchases of equipment and supplies from business and abroad. Excluded are purchases for the acquisition of land, government interest, subsidies, and transactions in financial claims.

GOVERNMENT SECTOR. See BUSINESS SECTOR.

GOVERNMENT SECURITIES CLEARING ARRANGEMENT. An arrangement which records gross and net changes in the holdings of U.S. Treasury securities by the FEDERAL RESERVE SYSTEM and by dealers. The arrangement achieved a considerable reduction in the physical movement of such securities, thus expediting open market operations (see

FEDERAL OPEN MARKET COMMITTEE).

GOVERNMENT SPENDING MULTIPLIER. See MULTIPLIER.

GRACE DAYS. See DAYS OF GRACE.

GRADE LABELING. In consumer economics, product identification by a manufacturer or intermediary, using accepted standards or standards mandated by industry associations or government bodies. *Descriptive labeling*, in contrast, is not based on widely used standards.

GRADUALISM. Situation in which MONETARY POLICY, FISCAL POLICY, or both are planned so as to return the economy slowly to the desired long-term trend line. There are two general advantages to gradualism: (1) it reduces the possibility of overshooting the desired point, and (2) it reduces the monetary and nonmonetary costs of returning the economy to the target point. Among the disadvantages of gradualism are that (1) as slow changes are made, the public adapts to them, partially canceling their intended effects, and (2) it increases the costs of remaining off target.

GRADUATE. Status of a LESS DEVELOPED COUNTRY which has progressed from financial dependence on larger, developed countries to unsubsidized participation in international capital markets.

GRANDFATHERED ACTIVITIES. In general, a practice that is allowed to continue for those who were engaged in it prior to the passage of a law that forbids it. In the FEDERAL RESERVE SYSTEM, grandfathered activities are bank activities which are normally not permissible for bank holding companies and foreign banks in the U.S., but which were acquired or engaged in before a particular date. Such activities may be continued under the grandfather clauses of the BANK HOLDING COMPANY ACT and the International Banking Act.

GRANT-IN-AID. Money paid by one level of GOVERNMENT to a lower level of government. It is usually determined as a percentage of the cost of an identified public project. For example, the federal government may want a certain highway constructed, but it has no authority to order a state to construct it; hence the federal government often encourages the state to proceed with construction by offering to pay 90 percent of the cost.

GRATUITOUS COINAGE. Conversion by financial authorities of precious metals (such as gold or silver) into coins without charging for the service, as when $1,000 in gold is made into coins and the owner receives the full $1,000 in coins. See also FREE COINAGE.

GRATUITY. A payment made as an expression of gratitude, rather than as a required or agreed-upon price.

GRAVEYARD SHIFT. The work shift that begins about midnight. Also called the *third shift.* See also FIRST SHIFT; SWING SHIFT.

GRAY MARKET. During a period of shortages and scarcities, describes transactions in which individuals profit from the situation through actions that, while legal, are definitely not for the good of the entire economy. See also BLACK MARKET.

GREAT DEPRESSION. One of the deepest and longest in history, this depression was worldwide; exact dates cannot be defined because it began and ended, and was felt with varying levels of severity, at different times in each nation. In the U.S. it lasted from 1930 until 1940, when the demands of World War II strained the productive capacity of the nation. Some analysts identify several depressions within that period that collectively constitute the Great Depression. One of its long-lasting outcomes was the NEW DEAL program, which led to a steadily increasing role of government in the economy.

GREAT LEAP FORWARD (China). After experimenting with the First Five-Year Plan, in 1958 the communist leaders of China instituted a program aimed at improving the utilization of human resources instead of producing a more CAPITAL INTENSIVE economy. For more details on this many-sided program, see Schnitzer and Nordyke, *Comparative Economic Systems* (Cincinnati, Ohio: Southwestern Publishing Co., Inc).

GREENBACK. A less formal word for FIAT MONEY. Specifically, paper money printed with no asset backing during the U.S. Civil War is referred to as greenbacks.

GRESHAM'S LAW. Named for Sir Thomas Gresham, sixteenth century financier, although it is generally recognized that others applied the principle before him. This law states that bad money drives good money out of circulation. In other words, if two issues of the same denomination are given different backings, the one with the larger backing value will be held by the public in hopes of appreciation or it will be used in foreign transactions. In either case, only the money of lesser backing value will remain in circulation within the nation.

GRIEVANCE. In labor economics, a claim by an employee that management has committed either a direct violation of the labor agreement or an unfair practice which, even if not expressly identified in the contract, is considered to be within the intent of the contract. Most labor contracts include a *grievance procedure* which details the methods for resolving grievances, including ARBITRATION, boards, and committees.

GRIEVANCE COMMITTEE. A group appointed, usually jointly by labor and management, for the purpose of reviewing GRIEVANCEs and ruling on them.

GROSS. The full amount, without adjustment for offsetting quantities or amounts. A sales representative's *gross income* might be $25,000; however, if, in order to receive that income, he or she had to pay out $4,000 for travel, samples, and similar expenses, a better measure of income is the NET of $21,000.

GROSS AUTO PRODUCT. Sum of the value of autos produced within a nation, plus the net value added by the distribution of new, used, and imported autos.

GROSS INCOME. The full amount of income received. See TAXABLE INCOME.

GROSS INVESTMENT. Short for GROSS PRIVATE DOMESTIC INVESTMENT, the absolute value of expenditures on new capital equipment, not adjusted for CAPITAL CONSUMPTION ALLOWANCES.

GROSS NATIONAL PRODUCT (GNP). The market value, as determined from NATIONAL INCOME AND PRODUCT ACCOUNTS, of all goods and services produced in a year. If GNP is given for a period of time other than one year, it is usually given on an ANNUAL RATE basis. GNP is a *gross* measure because no deduction is made to reflect the wearing out of machinery and other CAPITAL used in production. A measure that may be more meaningful in certain applications is Net National Product (NNP), which is defined as GNP minus allowances for the consumption of capital during the period.

Unless otherwise specified, the GNP is given in CURRENT DOLLARS; for any year indicated, the total of goods and services is given in dollars of that year, with no correction for a change in the purchasing power of the dollar. Thus, if the nation had identical output for two years, but prices were 10 percent higher in one of those years, GNP would be 10 percent higher that year. If a correction is made, the resultant measure is usually called GNP in CONSTANT DOLLARS; it is meaningful only when a base year is included.

The accompanying figure shows the component parts of GNP, most of which are further explained in separate entries.

GROSS PRIVATE DOMESTIC INVESTMENT (I_g). Often shortened to *gross investment*. In NATIONAL INCOME AND PRODUCT ACCOUNTS,

the sum of FIXED INVESTMENT and CHANGE IN BUSINESS INVENTORIES. Since I_g is a *gross* measure, it is not adjusted for investment goods that are used up while producing goods and services (CAPITAL CONSUMPTION ALLOWANCES); the adjusted term is *net private domestic investment* (I_n).

GROSS PROFIT. Often, the same as MARKUP—that is, the difference between selling price and basic cost, without accounting for other costs of doing business.

GROUND RENT. Payment made to the owner for the use of a piece of land. (Note that the word RENT in economics has a meaning quite different from its everyday usage.)

GROUP BANKING. The actual control of a group of ostensibly independent banks by an organization which may or may not be another bank. Also called *chain banking*. See also BANK HOLDING COMPANY.

GROUP PROFIT MAXIMIZATION. See JOINT PROFIT MAXIMIZATION.

GROWTH. See ECONOMIC DEVELOPMENT.

GROWTH RECESSION. A period of time during which real economic growth is larger than zero but less than normal.

GUARANTEED ANNUAL WAGE (GAW). In labor economics, an agreement by an employer to pay employees who are on the payroll a minimum agreed-upon wage over a period of a year. One purpose is to remove the incentive for employers to have large variations in the number of employees, especially when seasonal layoffs are involved.

GUARANTEED BOND. A BOND which is issued by one corporation although payment of principal and/or interest is guaranteed by another corporation. Also known as an *assumed bond* or an *endorsed bond*.

GUARANTEED STOCK. CAPITAL STOCK which is issued by one corpo-

Gross National Product

	Consumer expenditures (*C*)
plus	Gross private domestic investment (I_g) = Net investment (I_n) + Depreciation
plus	Government purchases of goods and services (*G*) = Total expenditures − Transfers, interest, and subsidies
plus	Net exports (X_n) = Gross exports (X_g) − Imports
EQUALS	Gross National Product (GNP) (on expenditure basis)
minus	Capital consumption allowances = Depreciation
EQUALS	Net National Product (NNP)
minus	Indirect business tax (sales, customs, excises, etc.) and nontax liability
minus	Current government enterprise surplus
minus	Business transfer payments
minus	Statistical discrepancy
plus	Subsidies
EQUALS	National Income

$$NI = \text{Compensation of employees}^a + \text{Proprietors' income} + \text{Net interest} + \text{Rental income of persons} + \text{Corporate profits}$$

Proprietors' income = Farm^b income + Business and professional income

Corporate profits = Profits before taxes + Inventory valuation adjustments

minus	Wages payable
minus	Corporate profits
minus	Social insurance contributions
plus	Dividends
plus	Interest paid by consumers and net paid by government
plus	Business transfer payments and government transfer payments to persons
EQUALS	Personal Income (PI) = Wage and salary disbursements^c + Other labor^{c,d} + Proprietors' income + Personal interest income + Rental income of persons + Transfer payments − Personal contributions for social insurance + Dividends
minus	Personal tax and nontax^e payments
EQUALS	Disposable Personal Income
minus	Personal outlays = personal consumption expenditures + Interest paid by consumers + Transfer payments to foreigners
EQUALS	Personal saving

---

^{a}Includes employer contributions for social insurance.
^{b}Excludes farm profits of corporations engaged in farming.
^{c}Excludes employer contributions for social insurance and the excess of wage accruals over wage disbursements.
^{d}Consists of employer contributions to private pension, health, and welfare funds; compensation for injuries; directors' fees; military reserve pay; and a few other minor items.
^{e}Fines, penalties, etc.

ration but which includes a guarantee by another corporation that dividends will be paid.

GUARANTOR. A person who makes himself or herself liable in the event another person defaults on a debt.

GUIDELINES. Voluntary restraints encouraged by the government as a means of solving a specific economic problem while avoiding direct government intervention. One example is *wage guidelines* provided by some U.S. administrations; wage increases within those guidelines should be noninflationary because they would match productivity increases. The use of voluntary guidelines is controversial, and many economists have offered statistics to show that they fail completely. See also MORAL SUASION.

H

HALF EAGLE. A $5 U.S. gold coin. See EAGLE for related denominations.

HALF STOCK. An expression sometimes used for CAPITAL STOCK which has a PAR VALUE of $50. See also FULL STOCK.

HALLMARK. A mark of quality. This word has its origins in the official mark stamped into gold and silver items, in Goldsmiths' *Hall*, in England, to identify the fineness of the metal.

HANDICRAFT ECONOMY. An economy in which a majority of production units are individuals, usually working right on their own property. About the same as *cottage industry*. See also FACTORY ECONOMY.

HANDS-OFF ECONOMICS. See LAISSEZ-FAIRE.

HARD-CORE UNEMPLOYED. The individuals who have the most difficulty finding steady employment, even when the UNEMPLOYMENT RATE is low. The causes of hard-core unemployment include lack of physical ability, job skills, communication skills, and social adjustment.

HARD MONEY. Generally, coins that contain precious metal; sometimes money of an economy that is stable and therefore retains its purchasing power. See also SOFT MONEY.

HARD SELL. A selling technique in which the salesperson is relentless, disregards the buyer's actual needs and financial position, and takes advantage of the buyer's weaknesses. Often the methods used are of questionable legality. In the opposite tactic, *soft sell*, the intended buyer is given the price and other facts, but is left to make up his or her mind without further influence. Hard sell is significant in the study of economics because it brings about a certain amount of DEMAND that is not coupled with actual needs or desires.

HARGREAVES' JENNY. A spinning machine invented by James Hargreaves in the 1760s that made it possible to spin as many as 80 threads at the same time. The spinning jenny is of interest to economists because (1) it helped to bring about the Industrial Revolution through the increased productivity of textiles, and (2) it led to one of the earliest demonstrations of workers destroying machinery because they were afraid its greater productivity would reduce employment. See AUTOMATION.

HARMONIES. The various forces in an economy that are held to complement each other. CLASSICAL SCHOOL writers believed that each person, acting in his or her own self-interest, would produce the net effect of an economy that efficiently manufactures the goods and services which are most desired, at prices which are fair to all; modern economic thinking recognizes harmonies to a much smaller degree, if at all.

HAWLEY-SMOOT TARIFF. In the early days of the GREAT DEPRESSION, as unemployment began to rise, the first wave of sentiment was for reducing imports, which were supposedly taking away from domestic employment. Despite the fallacy of this reasoning, as pointed out by many economists, the Hawley-Smoot Tariff was passed in 1930, creating record high tariff rates. Of course, other nations retaliated, and the amount of international trade was pinched down (adding unemployment in the shipping industry to the original problem). The first step toward expanding world trade was the RECIPROCAL TRADE AGREEMENT ACT of 1934.

HEAD TAX. A tax levied in a fixed amount on every person (or sometimes on every male), with certain exceptions such as indigent persons. Collection of a head tax is sometimes facilitated by combining it with a common function such as voting. Also called a *capitation tax* or a *poll tax*.

HEALTH MAINTENANCE ORGANIZATION (HMO). An insurer that provides complete medical coverage for a flat premium. It is intended that HMOs should have built-in incentives to encourage the public to use medical facilities efficiently while enjoying better health. As stated in the 1982 *Economic Report of the President*, "The incentives for efficient use of health resources rest with the HMOs, not with the patients, and health maintenance organizations appear to have succeeded in reducing hospitalization use among their members."

HEROES OF SOCIALIST TOIL (U.S.S.R.). Award given to Soviet citizens for their efforts in increasing production, decreasing waste, improving efficiency, etc. Although the award ostensibly provides nonmaterial incentives, winners are often given wage increases, bonuses, and certificates which can be used as payment in certain facilities

such as railroads. A similar award is *Communist labor brigade*.

HIDDEN INFLATION. If in two different years a family (or a nation) purchases identical goods and services, inflation for them can be measured by simply noting the difference in prices paid. However, when prices increase, many consumers lower their standard of living by purchasing goods of lower quality. For example, a family may buy a deluxe washing machine during a period of stable prices; yet if the appliance needs replacement during or after an inflationary period, the family may buy an economy model. To the extent that this practice is followed, *hidden inflation* adds to the inflation cost shown by price indexes

HIDDEN TAX. A tax that is not charged as a separate amount to the ultimate consumer. All taxes paid by industrial organizations that cause the price of their products to increase are hidden taxes. See also INDIRECT TAX.

HIGGLING. All negotiating in the MARKETPLACE; although *higgling* usually refers to bargaining by individuals when price is the only question. The buyer wants to obtain a product at as low a price as possible and the seller wants to receive as high a price as possible.

HIGH EMPLOYMENT DEFICIT (SURPLUS). An estimate of the DEFICIT (or SURPLUS) that would result from a fixed government budget structure if the economy were to operate at a low level of unemployment. This result has also been called *full employment surplus*, but because of a lack of agreement regarding the definition of FULL EMPLOYMENT, *high employment* is used more often.

HIGHEST QUARTERLY WAGE (HQW). A typical method of determining unemployment payments bases them on the quarter (13 weeks) during the previous year in which the individual had the highest earnings.

HIGH GRADE BOND. See BOND RATINGS.

HIGH-POWERED MONEY. CURRENCY on hand at banks (VAULT CASH), plus money that banks have in their accounts at Federal Reserve banks (RESERVE BALANCEs). Even though these items are not counted as part of the nation's MONEY SUPPLY, they are called *high powered* because they constitute the legal reserves which in turn determine how much can be created in DEMAND DEPOSITs. Moreover, they are the major component of our money supply. See MONEY SUPPLY EXPANSION MULTIPLIER.

HIGH-PRESSURE SELLING. A selling technique in which the salesperson is relentless and takes advantage of the buyers' weaknesses. High-pressure selling influences an economy because it brings about a certain amount of DEMAND for the nation's output which does not reflect actual needs or desires. Also called *hard sell*.

HISTOGRAM. A bar graph drawn with no space between the bars.

HISTORIC COST. Usually applicable in a regulated industry (see MONOPOLY) where selling price and other terms are dictated by government, with the desire to allow a fair return on investment. The regulating body determines the value of the present investment by starting with the accumulated amounts actually paid (i.e., the historic cost) and adjusting for CAPITAL CONSUMPTION ALLOWANCES and other additions and subtractions. Also called *original cost*.

HOARDING. Removing an item (money, coins, food, or any product) from the REAL FLOW or the MONEY FLOW so that it is merely held or stored. Hoarding of a manufactured item causes an increase in DEMAND for the item without increasing its consumption; DISHOARDING causes an increase in the consumption of an item without increasing the demand for its manufacture.

HOLDING COMPANY. A business enterprise which uses its CAPITAL FUNDS to purchase ownership shares of other companies, usually for the purpose of exerting management control over those companies. In contrast, an INVESTMENT COMPANY purchases ownership shares for the purpose of realizing dividends or appreciation. See also BANK HOLDING COMPANY.

HOME ECONOMICS. The field that includes information for shoppers, kitchen management, making and buying clothes and other fabric items, personal finances, and related topics. Many high schools and colleges offer home economics courses, although not usually within the economics department.

HOME INDUSTRY. The nonspecialized manufacture which was almost the only method of production prior to the Industrial Revolution. In home industries, most of the labor used comes from individuals or families; most of the production is done at the workers' homes, and there is very little specialization. Also called *cottage industry* or *domestic production*.

HOMEWORK. That part of regular industrial work which is performed by individuals in their homes; for example, a company might provide beads that are packaged by individuals in the home, or a person might be paid (but not hired) to type in the home. *Homework* does not usually refer to the work of self-employed individuals who regularly work at home, such as writers.

HORIZONTAL COMBINATION. A joining of firms which are on the same level of the distribution chain. Because competition generally applies to firms which serve the same customer, such mergers are most likely to be questioned or challenged under antitrust laws (see CLAYTON ANTITRUST ACT; SHERMAN ANTITRUST ACT).

HORIZONTAL LABOR UNION. A labor union which is restricted in membership to those who possess a particular skill used in a certain job. Few unions today are true horizontal unions; they usually try to expand their membership and sometimes go far afield in doing so, such as when a union of truck drivers includes office workers. Also called a *craft union*, or *trade union*.

HORIZONTAL PRICE-FIXING. Agreement among firms on the same level of the distribution chain (e.g., retailers), to avoid competition by charging the same prices. Such agreements are unlawful, although *vertical price fixing* (also known as FAIR TRADE LAWS), in which the selling price is controlled through more than one level of distribution, such as manufacturer and retailer, is generally allowed.

HOT CARGO. In labor economics, a shipment of goods which for some reason is felt to hurt the cause of organized labor. The reason may be connected with the manufacture or the distribution of the goods.

HOUSEHOLD. Can be as small as a single person or as large as an entire family; the significance is that it operates as a single economic unit. Although the amount of goods and services consumed by a household varies somewhat with the size of the household, it does not vary as much as it would if the individuals were separate households; a household of five people might have more refrigerators than a household of one person, but it usually would not have as many refrigerators as five households of one person each.

HOUSEHOLD FORMATION. Net increase in the number of HOUSEHOLDs. Economists are interested in this figure, as well as the manner in which households are formed—whether owing to increase in population, tendency for young adults to live away from family, etc.

HOUSEHOLD INDUSTRY. The nonspecialized manufacture which was almost the only method of production in pre-Industrial Revolution days. Also called *cottage industry* and *domestic production*.

HOUSEHOLD SURVEY. A survey in which the interviewer asks questions relating to the economics of the home, as opposed to a payroll survey that is concerned with employment data. For further information, see "Counting the Jobless" [*Monthly Review of the Federal Reserve Bank of San Francisco* (September 1972)].

HOUSING AND URBAN DEVELOPMENT (HUD). An act passed in 1970 because of congressional concern over problems of the "patterns of urban development" and the impact of the rising population on the economic and environmental balance. The legislation envisioned new communities as one device for achieving a more balanced growth, which would in turn "preserve and enhance both the natural and urban environment." To implement the act, a new Community Development Corporation was created within the Department of Housing and Urban Development (the initials HUD usually refer to this department) to determine eligibility standards for new-town proposals and to serve as a vehicle for extending various forms of assistance.

HOUSING STARTS. The number of new housing units in residential buildings on which construction has started. A *construction start* is defined as the beginning of the excavation for footings or the foundation. A *new housing unit* is a single room or a group of rooms intended for occupancy as separate living quarters by a family unit. All housing units in an apartment building are individually counted as started when excavation for the building is begun. *New housing units* exclude dormitories, mobile homes, hotels, motels, and housing units in primarily non-residential buildings.

HOUSING UNIT. A housing unit consists of a single room or a group of rooms occupied as separate living quarters. It must have at least one of the following: (1) direct access from the outside or through a common hall; or (2) a kitchen, or cooking equipment for the exclusive use of the occupant(s).

HR-10. See KEOGH PLAN.

HUMAN CAPITAL. Spending for education, health, and other services that increases the usefulness of labor (i.e., the ECONOMIC RESOURCE called *labor*). There is disagreement over whether a greater increase in GOODS AND SERVICES is achieved through investment in human capital or in the economic resource *capital*.

HUMAN OBSOLESCENCE. As technology becomes obsolete, so do the workers whose specialty is that technology. Machines are replaced when they are obsolete; the best way for humans to avoid the same treatment is through education.

HUMAN RESOURCES. *Labor* and *entrepreneurial ability* (see ECONOMIC RESOURCES).

HUMPHREY-HAWKINS ACT. See FULL EMPLOYMENT AND BALANCED GROWTH ACT.

HUNT COMMISSION. See PRESIDENT'S COMMISSION ON FINAN-CIAL STRUCTURE AND REGULATION.

HYPERINFLATION. An extremely high rate of inflation. Hyperinflation destroys an economy because money ceases to perform its traditional functions (i.e., standard of value, store of value, and reliable medium of exchange); larger and larger amounts of the nation's capability are shifted from productive efforts toward speculation. See also RUNAWAY INFLATION.

HYPOTHECATION. In the securities business, the turning over of possession, but not title, of securities as a means of providing security for a debt.

HYPOTHESIS. In ECONOMETRICS, a relationship which is assumed for the purpose of statistical evaluation. For example, an analyst may say that a certain tax on corporations is really paid by consumers through higher prices (see INDIRECT TAX); the analyst then uses statistical means to prove (or maybe disprove) this hypothesis by finding the degree of correlation between the tax and consumer prices.

I

IDLE MONEY. Bank deposits that are available as backing for creating additional money, but which are not so used. Technically, idle money is not a part of the nation's MONEY SUPPLY. See BANK RESERVES; MONEY SUPPLY EXPANSION MULTIPLIER.

IMPACT TEST. During the wage-price freeze of the Nixon administration, price-increase applications were rejected if their threatened impact on an associated index (e.g., CONSUMER PRICE INDEX, Farm Price Index) was more than 0.1 percent. Immediately after its inception, the impact test was applied in the shoe industry; it was ruled that shoemakers could pass increased leather costs on to consumers on a dollar-for-dollar basis.

IMPAIRMENT OF CAPITAL. In financial economics, a reduction in the value of a corporation below the legal value which must be maintained.

IMPERFECT COMPETITION. A market situation which is ruled by forces other than those of SUPPLY AND DEMAND; neither *pure.* COMPETITION nor MONOPOLY. See MONOPOLISTIC COMPETITION; MONOPSONY; OLIGOPOLY; OLIGOPSONY.

IMPERFECTIONS IN JOB MARKETS. See NORMAL UNEMPLOYMENT.

IMPLICIT COST. Economists recognize that FACTORS OF PRODUCTION have many possible uses and that therefore their use in a certain productive effort, even if their owner has provided them at no recorded charge, should be counted as a cost. This is the implicit cost (also called *imputed cost*), as opposed to an *explicit cost*—any payment to an external owner. For example, the owner of a business often works in the business but does not charge it for that labor. See also OPPORTUNITY COST.

IMPLICIT DEBT. Usually spoken of in regard to government debt, implicit debt, such as social security benefits, is a promise to pay but not a legal commitment. On the other hand, *explicit debt*, such as interest and principal on a government bond, is a legal commitment. [Adapted from *1982 Economic Report of the President*, p. 105.]

IMPLICIT PRICE DEFLATOR. See DEFLATOR.

IMPORT. Purchase of goods and services which originate in another nation, including expenditures made by U.S. tourists while in other countries. Although the following is obvious, it must be stated because of its significance: The total amount of imports worldwide equals the total amount of exports. Because exports and imports are direct opposites, imports are often called *negative* exports. See BALANCE OF INTERNATIONAL PAYMENTS.

IMPORT LICENSE. When the government controls the amount and kinds of products that can be imported, individuals engaged in importing must obtain an import license, giving them authorization for the transaction.

IMPORT POINT. See GOLD POINTS.

IMPORT QUOTA. A form of government control which establishes a limit to the amount of items that can be imported. The quota may be specified in money value of the imported item or in physical amount; it may apply to all imports of a certain item, or it may apply only to imports from a specific nation.

IMPOST. A tax on an imported item.

IMPOUNDMENT CONTROL ACT. See CONGRESSIONAL BUDGET AND IMPOUNDMENT CONTROL ACT.

IMPREST FUND. In accounting economics, an account or fund that is provided for making cash purchases. As those responsible for its use make purchases, management replenishes the fund. It is used for those transactions that are urgently needed or that are too small to stand the expense and delay of processing through regular channels. Sometimes called a *petty cash fund*.

IMPROVEMENT FACTOR. In labor economics, a contract provision by which the employer periodically raises wages during the life of a contract, based on the assumption that machines and methods are going to improve and therefore lower costs will provide a source of additional payments to workers.

IMPUTATION. An estimate which makes possible the inclusion in NATIONAL INCOME AND PRODUCT ACCOUNTS of certain types of income and product flows that do not take measurable monetary form. The general procedure for counting these nonmonetary flows is to value them as if they were paid for.

The four major imputations made in National Income and Product Accounts are for wages and salaries paid in kind

(e.g., food, clothing, lodging); the rental value of owner-occupied houses; food and fuel produced and consumed on farms; and interest payments by FINANCIAL INTERMEDIARIES which do not otherwise explicitly enter the accounts (as with a DEMAND DEPOSIT for which no interest is paid). The National Income Division assigns, as additional interest income to persons, an amount equal to the value of the services rendered.

IMPUTED COST. See IMPLICIT COST.

IMPUTED RENT. The amount of RENT which an owner-occupant would pay for the use of the property if it were owned by someone else.

INACTIVE STOCK. An issue of CAPITAL STOCK which is not bought and sold in large quantity and which may not be traded at all for several days. In contrast to an active stock, for which the price is easily established by the last trade, the "price" of an inactive stock is more subjective.

INCENTIVE PAY. Payments to the human FACTORS OF PRODUCTION, based on production rather than on a fixed rate per time unit worked. Commission payments, a common method of compensating sales persons, are a typical form of incentive pay. In factories where individual output is easily measured and quality is controlled, PIECEWORK is often used. Where group effort, rather than individual output, is measurable, bonus plans using various formulas are common. Incentive pay is sometimes based on quality rather than quantity, such as when a person's pay depends on the absence of rejections by assembly-line inspectors.

INCENTIVE TAX. A tax that is planned to affect the economic actions of the taxpayers; for example, the levying of an excess profits tax on businesses with the objective of encouraging them to lower prices. The recent trend has been *incentive deductions*, such as fast write-offs in order to encourage businesses to buy capital equipment. See ECONOMIC RECOVERY TAX ACT of 1981; NEUTRAL TAX.

INCIDENCE OF TAXATION. See INDIRECT TAX.

INCOME. See MONEY INCOME; PSYCHIC INCOME.

INCOME BOND. Most bonds carry a promise, or even a secured backing, that interest will be paid throughout the bond's life; the indenture for an income bond, however, provides that interest payments will be omitted if the current earnings of the issuer do not supply the necessary funds.

INCOME EFFECT. Change in quantity demanded as a function of income. A commodity is said to be a *superior good* (sometimes called a *normal good*) if increased income results in increased demand; it is an *inferior good* (or a *Giffen good*) if increased income results in decreased demand. Applied to income taxation, the income effect is positive when, as a result of the addition of, or the increase in, a tax, workers work more to restore the spending power they lost to taxation; the effect is negative if workers realize how little they benefit from extra work and therefore they exert less effort. See also SUBSTITUTION EFFECTS

INCOME ELASTICITY OF DEMAND. The change in demand (see SUPPLY AND DEMAND) which results from a change in income, divided by that change in income. This coefficient is not a constant but varies as a function of previous level of income as well as position on the demand curve.

INCOME MAINTENANCE. In welfare economics, the policy of reducing the multiplying effect of an increase in unemployment. That is, when one person loses his or her job, that person loses spending power in the marketplace; the resultant decrease in suppliers' sales causes them to lay off other workers, who will then lose spending power, etc. Income maintenance includes programs such as unemployment compensation, which keeps the temporarily unemployed in the marketplace and thus may prevent a cumulative slowing down of the economy.

INCOME REDISTRIBUTION. Change in the aggregate amount of income which is enjoyed by each of several identified blocks of individuals. One typical measure of income redistribution considers all wage earners arranged in order of income and then looks at the earnings of each 20 percent. If everyone had the same income, each 20 percent of the workers would earn 20 percent of the aggregate income; however, the top 20 percent receives more than 20 percent of the total income. The trend for a number of years shows a steady diminishing of this difference, especially if after-tax income is examined. Income redistribution is usually thought to be the result of tax policies, such as PROGRESSIVE TAXes, but there are other causes, such as inflation (which often causes redistribution in the direction of greater differences among the 20-percent blocks).

INCOMES INFLATION. After one group achieves an increase in income and prices have increased as a result, others see a decline in the purchasing power of their incomes, so they will demand wage increases, which raise prices and cause others to lose purchasing power, etc.

INCOMES POLICY. Direct government action for economic control, such as controls on wages and limitations on corporate profits. An incomes policy is usually favored when it is believed that the less direct methods of FISCAL POLICY and MONETARY POLICY would cause unintended hardships while accomplishing their goals.

INCOME STATEMENT. In accounting economics, a balance sheet showing a company's income and expenditures for a given period.

INCOME TAX. A tax whose amount is a function—usually a graduated function (see PROGRESSIVE TAX)—of the taxpayer's income. Income taxes are levied against individuals and corporations by governments at all levels. In 1982, 48 percent of the U.S. federal government's budget receipts were obtained through individual income tax, and 7 percent through corporate income tax.

INCONVERTIBLE CURRENCY. Money of a nation which is not freely exchangeable into a standard, such as gold, or into money of other nations. See also CONVERTIBLE CURRENCY; CURRENCY CONTROLS.

INCREASE IN DEMAND (SUPPLY). See SUPPLY AND DEMAND.

INCREASE IN QUANTITY DEMANDED (SUPPLIED). See SUPPLY AND DEMAND.

INCREASE, WAGE. See ACROSS-THE-BOARD INCREASE; MERIT INCREASE.

INCREASING-COST INDUSTRY. An industry which cannot step up its rate of production without paying more per unit of output for the FACTORS OF PRODUCTION it uses. As a result, selling prices will be raised if there is an increase in demand. Such a situation might occur if the industry is working at capacity; increasing its output would require considerable expense. Most industries are in a *decreasing cost* situation.

INCREASING RETURNS. A situation in which adding to the quantity of FACTORS OF PRODUCTION that are being used results in more than a proportionate increase in output. For instance, there are increasing returns if enlarging the work force of a company by 10 percent results in an increase of 12 percent in total output.

INCREMENTAL CAPITAL-OUTPUT RATIO. See CAPITAL-OUTPUT RATIO.

INCREMENTAL COSTS. Costs incurred by the manufacture of a given unit but that were not incurred by manufacture of the preceding unit. The incremental cost of producing the nth unit is equal to total costs after n units minus total costs after $n - 1$ units. See MARGINAL COST; VARIABLE COSTS.

INDEMNIFY. To guarantee against financial loss in the event of a physical loss; for example, when an insurance policy promises to pay a stated amount of money if a certain shipment is destroyed.

INDENTURE. In financial economics, the agreement drawn up by an organization that is selling an issue of BONDs to the public. The indenture gives information regarding the price of the bonds, interest rates and payments, uses of the funds so obtained, collateral, provisions for repayment, etc.

INDENTURED SERVANT. A person who receives a benefit with the understanding that he or she will work for the giver of the benefit until the obligation is paid. Many of the early settlers in America became the indentured servants of those who paid their transportation from Europe.

INDEPENDENT. In statistics, describes two or more items that have no influence on each other. For example, the amount of snow falling in Alaska and the amount of cotton harvested in Alabama are independent, but the size of the government deficit and the rate of inflation are not. A large part of mathematical economics (ECONOMETRICS) concerns itself with proving dependence or independence.

INDEPENDENT UNION. A labor union which is not affiliated with a central organization. In the U.S., unions not affiliated with the AFL-CIO are considered independent.

INDEXING. Arranging an economy for frequent adjustments in an effort to reduce the inequities that result from persistent inflation. Nations which use indexing provide for legally enforced adjustments to assets, incomes, contracts, and other items or transactions which are affected by inflation. Beginning in 1985, U.S. income tax tables are indexed to prevent BRACKET CREEP, the situation in which an inflationary increase in national income automatically means that the government takes a larger percentage of that income.

INDEX OF NET BUSINESS FORMA-TION. A measure of the net number of new businesses formed each month, compiled from data on new business incorporations and the number of business failures. The statistics include new businesses which are incorporated, existing businesses which have changed from noncorporate to corporate form, existing corporations which have been given certificates of authority to operate in another state, and transfers of existing corporations to new states. Also included are cases in which the promotion of a projected corporation was not completed and the charter, although issued, was never exercised.

Data on the number of business failures, which are compiled monthly, include businesses that (1) ceased operations following assignment or bankruptcy; (2) ceased with loss to creditors, after such actions as execution, foreclosure, or attachment; (3) voluntarily withdrew, leaving unpaid obligations; (4) were involved in court actions such as receivership, reorganization, or arrangement; and (5) voluntarily compromised with creditors out of court.

INDICATOR. A statistic which can be used, usually with others, to reach a conclusion regarding the economy. A LEADING INDICATOR (the most useful for making predictions) is one whose changes are usually followed by certain changes in the overall economy, a COINCIDENT INDICATOR changes at the same time as the overall economy, and a LAGGING INDICATOR is useless for prediction because it changes after the economy in general has changed.

INDIFFERENCE CURVE. A graph which shows combinations of quantities of two different products or services such that the consumer of those products or services is equally happy (receives equal UTILITY) at any point on the curve. The

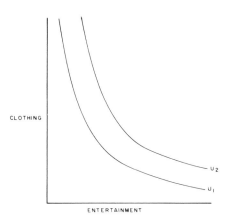

CLOTHING

ENTERTAINMENT

Indifference curve. U2 represents a higher level of satisfaction than U1.

accompanying figure shows that if an individual has a large quantity of bread and very little wine, he or she is willing to exchange a large quantity of bread to obtain only a slight increase in wine. However, if the individual has moderate quantities of both types of goods, he or she would give up the same quantity of bread only if a larger quantity of wine could be obtained in return. Indifference curves always have this general shape, and they are made with the basic assumption of OTHER THINGS BEING EQUAL. If other factors should change, such as the individual's income or general attitude, then the entire indifference curve moves (e.g., from U1 to U2). Also called *isoutility curve*.

INDIFFERENCE MAP. A presentation of several INDIFFERENCE CURVEs on the same graph, with each curve showing the locus of constant utility when a given set of conditions is held constant and one variable, such as income, is changed. The curve which comes the closest to the origin represents the least utility; each curve beyond that represents a higher level of utility. Only ordinal, not cardinal, numbers can be attached to the curves because we cannot say *how much* more utility difference there is from one curve to another and the amount of space between adjacent curves should not be relied on as significant.

INDIGENT. Financially poor, usually in need of assistance.

INDIRECT BUSINESS TAX AND NON-TAX LIABILITY. In NATIONAL INCOME AND PRODUCT ACCOUNTS, INDIRECT TAX liabilities paid by business, which specifically excludes employer contributions for social insurance and corporate income taxes, but includes nontax items such as fines, copyright and processing fees, royalty payments, and penalties. Sales, excise, and real property taxes paid by businesses are the principal types of indirect taxes.

INDIRECT CONTROL. MONETARY POLICY, FISCAL POLICY, debt management, and other controls of an impersonal nature, which are directed at controlling the economy through control of motivations, incentives, and logical actions of economic units. Indirect controls work through, rather than cancel, the basic market mechanisms of SUPPLY AND DEMAND. *Direct controls* include price ceilings, wage freezes, rationing, allocations, and other measures which work directly, rather than through incentives. In general, *indirect controls* are aimed at correcting problems, and direct controls are limited to eliminating symptoms.

INDIRECT COST. An expense that must be incurred but which cannot be associated directly with the production of a specific product. For example, if an employer subsidizes a cafeteria for employees, the cost would be indirect.

INDIRECT DEMAND. See FACTOR DEMAND.

INDIRECT PRODUCTION. The manufacturing of CAPITAL equipment which will then make final products or other capital equipment. Although it involves a large extra step, indirect production is more efficient than direct production in the long run because the former benefits from the higher productivity of capital equipment. An example from elementary economics looks at Robinson Crusoe when he first arrives at the island. Suppose he wants to capture rabbits for food. The direct method is to run after them and catch them, a way by which he may or may not keep from starving. The indirect way is to first make traps. The final output of his initial productive efforts will be zero rabbits, but when he puts his traps (capital equipment) to work, they will produce more rabbits in the long run than he will need. Also called *roundabout production*.

INDIRECT TAX. A tax whose burden is borne by an economic unit other than the one which makes payment of the tax, in contrast to a direct tax whose burden is not passed on. For example, if a business must pay a certain tax and raises the price of its product to cover the tax, that tax is indirect, and its *incidence* is on the customer (unless that customer is not the ultimate consumer and is also able to pass the tax on).

Categorizing taxes as direct and indirect is controversial because it is difficult to know exactly what the long-run terms of trade would have been without the tax. Perhaps, in the preceding example, the business actually sells less because of the higher price after it includes the tax; in such a case, the tax is then costing the business, as well as its customers, because its total profits are down. It is generally considered that sales taxes, excise taxes, and real property taxes paid by businesses are indirect and that personal income taxes are direct. However, it is sometimes claimed that employees have demanded and received higher wages than they would have if there were lower (or no) personal income taxes, and those higher wages may be passed along in the form of higher prices.

An indirect tax is *shifted forward* when prices are raised so that customers pay the tax; it is *shifted backward* when the taxpayer is able to reduce the amount paid to the FACTORS OF PRODUCTION so that the incidence really falls on them.

INDIVIDUALIST SCHOOL. The CLASSICAL SCHOOL of economic thought. *Individualist* was applied because classicalists opted for removal of government intervention in the form of trade restrictions such as the CORN LAWS.

INDIVIDUAL PROPRIETORSHIP. The simplest form of business enterprise, in which there is just one owner and for which, except for certain licenses and other special requirements, no permission from a government agency is required. See FORMS OF BUSINESS ORGANIZATION. Also called *sole proprietorship*, or *proprietorship*.

INDIVIDUAL RETIREMENT ACCOUNT (IRA). A 1974 change in the U.S. tax laws, which allows individuals not covered by group retirement plans (such as many employers and unions have) to deposit up to 15 percent of their income a year (up to a stipulated maximum— then $1,500) into a special fund. IRAs provide two tax advantages to contributors. First, contributions are deductible from current taxable income; second, earnings on IRAs accumulate tax-free as long as the funds are not withdrawn from the account.

In 1981, significant tax legislation extended the opportunity to use IRAs to all workers. Under the new law, each worker may contribute up to $2,000 to these accounts regardless of whether he or she is already covered under an employer-sponsored pension plan. One-earner couples can contribute up to $2,250.

INDORSED BOND. A BOND which is issued by one corporation, while the payment of principal, or interest, or both is guaranteed by another corporation. Also known as an *assumed bond* or a *guaranteed bond*.

INDORSEMENT. A spelling common in many legal areas (such as the UNIFORM COMMERCIAL CODE) of ENDORSEMENT (the popular spelling).

INDUCED DEMAND. DEMAND for goods and services that arises because increased spending (usually spending for CAPITAL GOODS) in one sector of the economy has resulted in more money in the hands of consumers, through increased employment and payments to other FACTORS OF PRODUCTION. See *spending multiplier* under MULTIPLIER.

INDUCED INVESTMENT. CAPITAL ACCUMULATION in response to an increased demand for output, as opposed to capital spending to replace worn-out or obsolete capital equipment. See ACCELERATION PRINCIPLE.

INDUCTIVE REASONING. In economics, as in other fields, arriving at a HYPOTHESIS through the examination of observations from the past, followed by a critical check of the hypothesis.

INDUSTRIAL BANK. A depository-type FINANCIAL INTERMEDIARY that functions in much the same way as a COMMERCIAL BANK except that its loans are smaller, are made to individuals, and are usually repaid in installments.

INDUSTRIAL BOND. An instrument of indebtedness issued by a corporation. In contrast, a *public bond* is an instrument of indebtedness issued by some level of government. Also called a *corporate bond*.

INDUSTRIAL CONCENTRATION. The degree to which large producers dominate an industry. There are several definitions of *concentration ratio*; one frequently used is the percentage of total output (of the industry) which is provided by the four largest producers in the industry. An industry is said to be highly concentrated if this ratio is 50 percent or higher; concentration is low when the ratio is less than 20 percent. See also MARKET CONCENTRATION; OLIGOPOLY.

INDUSTRIAL DEMOCRACY. A situation in which workers have a voice in the affairs of the corporation, especially affairs that directly affect working conditions. Issues are sometimes put directly to the workers for a vote; at other times, the employer holds meetings with a council composed of representatives elected from the ranks of workers. See also CO-DETERMINATION.

INDUSTRIAL INSURANCE. Life insurance bought by individuals, usually for $500 or less. Whereas most life insurance has the purpose of providing an income for surviving dependents, the purpose of industrial insurance is to pay for funeral expenses.

INDUSTRIAL RELATIONS. Generally, those functions that affect employer-employee relations, employee morale, work incentives, etc. The industrial relations department of a large company administers and coordinates group insurance, vacation scheduling, safety equipment, the company store, and many other related functions.

INDUSTRIAL REVOLUTION. The time during which the developed nations changed their manufacturing methods from individual production by hand to factory production which emphasized specialization and the use of machinery (capital equipment). It is generally considered to have spanned the late 1700s through the early 1800s.

INDUSTRIAL SECTOR. That portion of the economy which consists of privately owned enterprises. Also known as the BUSINESS SECTOR.

INDUSTRIAL UNION. A labor union which represents workers in an entire industry, regardless of their skills. In contrast, a CRAFT UNION covers workers of a certain skill, regardless of the industry in which they work.

INDUSTRIE KREDITBANK (Ger.). Financial organization owned and operated by the West German government for the purpose of making INVESTMENT money available to industry.

INDUSTRY. Privately owned, profit-seeking manufacturing establishments. The word is also used to identify a segment of the business world, such as the textile industry or publishing industry.

INDUSTRY ASSOCIATION. An organization whose members are companies in the same INDUSTRY. There are tens of thousands of such associations in the U.S., representing all industries and branches within industries. They have many purposes, including setting standards, cooperative advertising, and the interchange of information (technical, methods, marketing, etc.). Some industry associations comprise companies only, whereas others provide for individual memberships. Also called *trade association* or *trade organization*.

INDUSTRY SUPPLY SCHEDULE. A schedule of the aggregate amount of a product which an entire industry will supply at various prices. See SUPPLY AND DEMAND. Also called *market supply schedule*.

INDUSTRYWIDE BARGAINING. In labor economics, the practice of a union negotiating simultaneously with all employers in an industry. The union may obtain faster, higher settlements because (1) the entire supply of that industry's goods or services is withheld from the public (if a strike is involved), thereby creating public pressure to reach a settlement, and (2) each employer knows that its competitive position will not be affected by the size of the settlement. On the other hand, employers often prefer industrywide bargaining because, if there is a strike, no supplier will lose customers to its competitors. See also KEY CONTRACT.

INELASTIC DEMAND. See ELASTICITY.

INELASTIC SUPPLY. A SUPPLY SCHEDULE which shows that sellers do not provide a much larger (or smaller) quantity when the price increases (or decreases). For example, when world-wide demand for meat increased in 1972 and 1973, the additional demand caused an increase in prices; with other products, suppliers would have increased their production and prices would have stabilized. But the size of herds cannot be increased quickly (meat supply is inelastic in the short run), and therefore the shortage caused rapid increases in the price of meat but had little effect on the quantity available in the market.

INFANT INDUSTRY ARGUMENT. Despite *absolute advantage*, COMPARATIVE ADVANTAGE, and other analyses which show that international specialization and trade will lead to increased total consumption, several arguments support the use of protective tariffs and other barriers to international trade. In the infant industry argument, it is said that the nation now making a certain product is making it efficiently only because that nation has an established manufacturing capability; if another nation could get started, it could make the product competitively. Therefore, some protection (such as import duties or quotas) should be provided so that this infant industry can become established; then, presumably, the new industry will willingly support removal of the protection.

INFERIOR GOOD. See INCOME EFFECT.

INFINITE ELASTICITY. A theoretical market situation in which the supply (or demand) curve is drawn parallel to the quantity axis (see SUPPLY AND DEMAND); price is not a function of quantity. Also called *perfect elasticity*. The concept is easier to understand for a situation *approaching* perfect elasticity—for example, a DEMAND SCHEDULE whose graph has a slight upper-left-to-lower-right slope. The interpretation is that a small change in price results in a very large change in the quantity demanded.

INFINITELY VARIABLE. See CONTINUOUS VARIABLE.

INFLATION. There are many definitions of inflation, usually worded for completeness and technical accuracy. For most practical applications it is sufficient to consider that inflation is a decrease in the PURCHASING POWER of a nation's

monetary unit, in both the PRODUCT MARKET and the RESOURCE MARKET. Prices go up, and "the dollar buys less."

INFLATIONARY GAP. A condition of excess aggregate spending (for consumer, investment, and government goods and services) relative to the spending that would be consistent with a full-employment stable economy. The gap is actually the *amount* of change in spending which would lead to stability, and therefore the MULTIPLIER effect must be considered. See also POTENTIAL GNP.

INFLATIONARY SPIRAL. When workers demand and receive more pay (or other benefits that increase costs for their employers), their employers must raise the price of their product; then other workers see their wages buying less, so they demand wage increases, which cause the price of other products to increase; then other workers see...; etc. The inflationary spiral demonstrates the interdependence of cause and effect in regard to inflation.

INFLEXIBILITY. See PRICE RIGIDITY.

INFORMATIONALLY EFFICIENT. Describes one of the advantages of a MARKET ECONOMY. In this economy, manufacturers determine the quantity to produce by directly observing what consumers decide to buy. By contrast, in a CENTRALLY PLANNED ECONOMY, the government tells manufacturers what quantity to produce.

INFRASTRUCTURE. The enabling sector of an economy. It includes utilities, communication networks, transportation systems, and other organizations that make it possible for manufacturers of final goods and services to operate. Some parts of the infrastructure (such as roads) are operated by government; others can be either public or private. When examining the problems of the LESS DEVELOPED COUNTRY, one finds that one big impediment to growth is the lack of an infrastructure. Sometimes called *social overhead capital*.

INHERITANCE TAX. A tax levied against a person who receives money or property from a deceased person. In contrast, an ESTATE TAX is levied against the overall estate prior to distribution to inheritors.

INJUNCTION. A court order prohibiting a party from doing or continuing to do a specified act. In economics, *injunction* usually applies to labor—for example, the president may obtain an injunction to prevent a strike which would tend to endanger national health and safety (see TAFT-HARTLEY ACT).

INNOVATION. A significant step forward in technology, management, thinking, etc.; something more than a mere extension or improvement of present methods. One of the functions of *entrepreneurial ability* (see ECONOMIC RESOURCES) is innovation. In economic history, some innovations are significant enough to be considered as the cause of ECONOMIC FLUCTUATIONS, especially if two or more major innovations are bunched in time. The growth of a LESS DEVELOPED COUNTRY can sometimes be traced to innovation.

INPUT. Everything that goes into the production of goods and services; the total amounts of FACTORS OF PRODUCTION which are used in the productive efforts of an economy. The goods and services that result are referred to as *output*.

INPUT-OUTPUT TABLE. A matrix which shows the way in which industries or SECTORs interact. It generally shows, for each industry, the amount of that industry's output that goes to each other industry as input (as raw materials or as semifinished products), as well as the amount that goes to the final markets of the economy. The table may also indicate each industry's consumption of the products of other industries, as well as its contribution to the production process, in the form of value added.

Input-output tables are prepared by the U.S. Office of Business Economics for the nation as a whole and by other levels of government for their own regions. The tables permit the tracing of the industrial repercussions, direct and indirect, of changes in consumer demand and investment-goods demand, of imports and exports, and of government purchases. Some input-output tables include an EMPLOYMENT MULTIPLIER for each industry so that officials can determine where government assistance would be most effective for employment growth.

INQUIRY INTO THE NATURE AND CAUSES OF THE WEALTH OF NATIONS, AN. A book by ADAM SMITH published in 1776 in England. It describes the CLASSICAL SCHOOL of economic thinking, showing that the path to economic growth lies, not in amassing a hoard of gold, but in improved productivity, achieved through LAISSEZ-FAIRE and letting natural forces such as SUPPLY AND DEMAND control economic activity. Smith used the expression *invisible hand* in showing that goods and services desired by consumers would be made available in the market, in proper quantities, without the need for any central command or coordination. Often referred to as *The Wealth of Nations*.

INSOLVENCY. Inability to pay debts as they become due. *Insolvency* is often confused with BANKRUPTCY, which is a formal declaration by a court. Insolvency may be a temporary condition that is cured by a resumption of revenues, or it may be a step toward bankruptcy.

INSTALLMENT CREDIT CONTROLS. Regulations by the FEDERAL RESERVE SYSTEM, designed to prevent excessive use of credit. Installment credit controls can specify allowable down payments and other terms. See SELECTIVE CONTROLS.

INSTALLMENT LOAN. A loan which is repaid over a period of time (sometimes years). In contrast, a *single-payment* loan requires the borrower to repay the entire loan at one time. An installment loan always provides for the borrower to make payments of both interest and principal during the life of the loan, and there may or may not be a balloon payment (see PICKUP PAYMENT) at the end; single-payment loans sometimes provide for interest payments during the life of the loan, but sometimes all principal and accumulated interest are paid together.

INSTRUMENT. (1) Financial document such as a BOND or a check; (2) tool—for example, control of DISCOUNT RATE is a *tool* of MONETARY POLICY.

INSURANCE. Payment to avoid financial loss as a result of a physical loss. Life insurance pays an amount to survivors of a deceased person; health insurance pays medical expenses when health is lost; property insurance pays the insured when property is destroyed, stolen, or otherwise decreased in value. The idea behind property and health insurance is to exchange the possibility (and uncertainty) of a large loss for a known amount (the premium).

INSURANCE, INDUSTRIAL. See INDUSTRIAL INSURANCE.

INTAGLIO ENGRAVED PROCESS. The process used to print U.S. paper currency, stamps, and other official documents at the Bureau of Engraving and Printing in Washington, D.C. A characteristic of this process is the detail that can be printed from engraved plates.

INTANGIBLE PERSONAL PROPERTY. Personal property which cannot be seen or held, such as a copyright. Personal property is that which is not land or attached to land—i.e., real property.

INTENDED INVESTMENT. Purchases of CAPITAL GOODS by the business SECTOR. Also called *planned investment*. In contrast, unintended or unplanned investment is defined as an increase in inventories due to lower than expected sales (see CHANGE IN BUSINESS INVENTORIES).

INTERBANK FLOAT. Regarding CORRESPONDENT BANKs, the difference between collected balances and those in the process of collection. See also *float* under CHECK CLEARING.

INTERCHANGEABLE PARTS. Although now accepted as a standard manufacturing technique, it was unheard of prior to the INDUSTRIAL REVOLUTION. When a craftsman made an entire chair by himself, he could make each leg to fit, but when chairs are made in a factory where one person makes all the legs and another assembles them to the seat, it is necessary that all legs be identical (interchangeable). The concept, often credited to Eli Whitney (inventor of the cotton gin), had a significant effect on economic history.

INTERDEPENDENCE. An economy is such a complex phenomenon that even the most elaborate MODEL, run on a large computer, can only claim to be a rough approximation of it. Almost every action or event will cause some other event, and often a chain of events. One of the most elementary interdependences is between income taxes and personal incomes. If an income tax is reduced, people will have money to spend on consumer products; then manufacturers of consumer products will have to hire more workers who will become taxpayers, and eventually the reduction in taxes may result in larger revenues flowing to the government. Obviously, there is an optimum point (for maximizing revenues to the government), because continuing this process to zero taxes will not produce maximum revenue. A rigorous analysis would have to take into account other economic conditions at the time of the tax change, as well as whether government spending changes, and many other variables. The immediate effects are called *first-order effects*, their influence is called a *second-order effect*, and so on. Sometimes interdependence refers to OLIGOPOLISTIC INTERDEPENDENCE. See also INPUT-OUTPUT TABLE.

INTERDISTRICT SETTLEMENT FUND. Transactions among the 12 district banks of the FEDERAL RESERVE

SYSTEM are handled through this fund, which is maintained in Washington, D.C.

INTEREST. The cost of borrowed money. Banks pay interest to depositors because the former have in effect borrowed money from depositors. Investigators and students often question the reasoning behind interest (is it compensation for not spending, payment for risk, etc.?); several theories and explanations have resulted. See also ABSTINENCE THEORY OF INTEREST; COMPOUND INTEREST; LIQUIDITY PREMIUM.

INTEREST BOND. When an organization with fairly fixed debt does not have the necessary liquidity to make certain interest payments when due, it sometimes sells additional debt (BONDs) and uses the proceeds to make interest payments on the first debt. Of course, investors will buy the interest bonds only if they feel that the illiquid situation is temporary and that there will be funds when their own bonds are due to receive interest and to mature.

INTEREST CEILINGS. The BOARD OF GOVERNORS (OF THE FEDERAL RESERVE SYSTEM) regulation Q, has established ceilings on the rate of interest MEMBER BANKs may pay to depositors of time and savings accounts. The rates have been set in consultation with the FEDERAL DEPOSIT INSURANCE CORPORATION, which sets ceilings on rates paid by nonmember insured banks, and with the FEDERAL HOME LOAN BANK BOARD, which sets ceilings on dividend rates payable by its members and by other insured SAVINGS AND LOAN ASSOCIATIONs.

The DEPOSITORY INSTITUTIONS DEREGULATION AND MONETARY CONTROL ACT arranged for the gradual removal of interest ceilings, culminating in complete removal by 1986.

INTEREST DATES. Banks and other institutions that have savings accounts use various methods for figuring the amount of interest earned by depositors. The fairest is *day of deposit to day of withdrawal*

(DD-DW), which simply means that interest is earned by all money all the time it is in the account. At the other extreme, a *low balance* account earns interest on only the lowest amount shown in the account during a period, usually a quarter. With the latter arrangement, new deposits earn no interest until the following period. A *days-of-grace* account earns interest from a stated date, even if the money is deposited some days later. The typical days-of-grace account pays interest from the first of the month for money deposited from the first to the tenth of the month. Some agreements require that the money be left in the account a full quarter in order to earn days-of-grace interest.

INTEREST EQUALIZATION TAX. A tax on foreign investments, for the purpose of curtailing the outflow of private funds. This tax was not levied until 1964, but it was made retroactive to July 1963, the date it was proposed. This tax was part of the CAPITAL CONTROLS PROGRAM, which was terminated in 1974. See also VOLUNTARY FOREIGN CREDIT RESTRAINT.

INTEREST, IMPUTED. See IMPUTATION.

INTEREST RATE. The amount of INTEREST on a debt, expressed as a percentage of the debt, rather than as an amount of money. See COMPOUND INTEREST; TRUTH-IN-LENDING ACT.

INTEREST SENSITIVE. Quality of an industry that declines significantly when interest rates rise. Homebuilding and automobile industries are interest sensitive; they both sell expensive items to the public, and the buyers usually have to borrow money to make such purchases.

INTERLOCKING DIRECTORATES. Corporate boards of directors which have one or more members in common. Although this arrangement is not itself illegal, the CLAYTON ANTITRUST ACT prohibits it when the companies are competitors and each company has assets of over $1 million.

INTERMEDIATE GOODS. An expression sometimes used for CAPITAL GOODS in order to emphasize that the end objective of all economics is to provide goods and services to consumers. The purpose of manufacturing a capital good such as an industrial stamping machine is to manufacture consumer goods more efficiently. The machine has a finite lifetime, and therefore it might be considered that some part of each intermediate good becomes a part of the final product it manufactures. See also CAPITAL CONSUMPTION ALLOWANCES; FINAL OUTPUT.

INTERMEDIATION. Use of a ''middleman'' (the intermediary) in debt. Instead of a debtor borrowing money directly from individual consumers who have saved some money, the debtor borrows from a bank, and the bank borrows from individuals by holding their savings accounts. Banks, savings and loan associations, and similar organizations are called *financial intermediaries*.

INTERNAL COST. A cost which is recognized and borne by the producer, as opposed to an external cost (see SPILLOVER), which is borne by someone other than the producer and therefore does not add to the price of the product. Environmental pollution is an example of an external cost.

INTERNAL DEBT. Debt in which the debtor and creditor are essentially the same economic unit so that creation or termination of the debt would not change the aggregate wealth of either unit. For example, corporate debt is an *external debt* because its repayment changes the wealth of the corporation and of the creditors; federal government debt is *internal debt* because (to the extent that government bonds are held within the U.S.) repaying it would not change the amount of money within the U.S.

INTERNAL REVENUE SERVICE (IRS). The branch of the U.S. Treasury Department that is responsible for administering federal tax laws and collecting taxes. The IRS is a regulatory agency, with powers to write laws, interpret them, and administer them—in many ways, it acts as all three branches of the federal government (executive, legislative, and judicial). A few cases are taken into Federal courts, but most are settled within the IRS system.

INTERNAL THEORY OF BUSINESS CYCLES. See ENDOGENOUS THEORY OF BUSINESS CYCLES.

INTERNATIONAL BALANCE OF PAYMENTS. See BALANCE OF INTERNATIONAL PAYMENTS.

INTERNATIONAL BANK FOR RECONSTRUCTION AND DEVELOPMENT (IBRD). Usually called the *World Bank*, an organization created at the BRETTON WOODS conference. It was capitalized at $10 billion for the purpose of lending funds for the reconstruction of economies ravaged by World War II, and for economic development. Although it was expected that the World Bank's function would be to guarantee loans by private investors, the uncertainties of the postwar period made lenders hesitant, and the World Bank functioned more as a direct lender than it had been expected to.

Having accomplished its original purposes—reconstruction—the World Bank has, since 1956, concentrated on economic development. With the creation that year of the International Finance Corporation—mandated to promote private-sector enterprise in developing countries—and with the establishment in 1960 of the International Development Association (IDA) to lend on highly concessional terms to the poorest countries, the World Bank group was formed.

In July 1982, the World Bank changed its policy of lending at fixed interest rates; it now adjusts rates on outstanding loans every six months. At the same time, it changed policy regarding the funds it borrows; money, which had never been borrowed for less than 12 months, can now be borrowed in the short-term market.

INTERNATIONAL ECONOMICS. Economics which recognizes the interrelationships among the economies of various nations, rather than treating any one nation as a closed economy. It includes such topics as absolute advantage, COMPARATIVE ADVANTAGE, FOREIGN EXCHANGE, importing, exporting, and other topics.

INTERNATIONAL EXCHANGE. The area of economics that deals with exchange rates—that is, the rates at which the monetary unit of one nation trades with the monetary units of other nations. Rates have been established by several means:

1. *Fixed rate.* When nations fix the price at which their money converts into a standard such as gold, the rates at which their monies convert into each other are automatically established.
2. *Flexible rate.* Exchange rates with upper and lower limits set by MONETARY AUTHORITIES who take no action while the rate fluctuates within those limits. Both fixed and flexible rates are generally kept unchanged unless large inequities develop, but sometimes a SLIDING PEG provides small, frequent changes.
3. *Floating rate.* There are two kinds of floating rate. If monetary authorities take no action, but simply let the forces of the open market determine exchange rates, the condition is a *clean float.* However, monetary authorities do intervene to some extent, which results in a *dirty float.*

See also OVERVALUED CURRENCY; UNDERVALUED CURRENCY.

INTERNATIONAL FINANCE CORPORATION. Originally created to facilitate operation of the INTERNATIONAL BANK FOR RECONSTRUCTION AND DEVELOPMENT, the International Finance Corporation has become the funnel through which the money flows to assist LESS DEVELOPED COUNTRIES.

INTERNATIONAL INTEREST ARBITRAGE. Simultaneous buying and selling of similar financial instruments in two countries, for the purpose of benefiting from differences in interest rates. When the exchange risk in such a transaction is eliminated with a FORWARD EXCHANGE CONTRACT, the operation is called *covered interest arbitrage.* See ARBITRAGE.

INTERNATIONAL MONETARY FUND (IMF). Created at the BRETTON WOODS Conference, the IMF's purpose is to stabilize currencies in order to maintain an orderly market in world trade. Competitive depreciations of currencies following World War I had been given part of the blame for the worldwide GREAT DEPRESSION.

Subscriptions to the IMF were paid with a combination of gold and each member's currency. The fund operates by buying and selling currencies of various nations, providing statistical information on international trade, establishing policy on exchange rates and the movement of gold, and other activities.

Currently, the IMF provides a framework in which governments can consult and cooperate in determining the structure and functioning of the international monetary system. In particular, the IMF extends technical assistance and temporary balance-of-payments financing to members, often conditional on their implementing economic policy measures to correct the factors underlying their balance-of-payments problems. In addition, the IMF monitors the exchange-rate arrangements and policies of member governments. Finally, it reviews the adequacy of international liquidity and supplements reserves, when necessary, through the allocation of SPECIAL DRAWING RIGHTS.

INTERPOLATE. To assume additional data points between existing points. For example, suppose a company knew how much of a product was sold when it spent $100,000, $120,000, $135,000, and $160,000 on advertising. It could plot those points on a graph and see from the graph (or *interpolate*) the amount it could expect to sell if it spent $150,000 on advertising. See also EXTRAPOLATE, and Mathematical Regression in the Appendix.

INTERSTATE COMMERCE. Trade in the PRIVATE SECTOR which involves parties in more than one state. Interstate commerce is significant because there are many areas in which the federal government has no jurisdiction unless this type of trade is involved.

INTERSTATE COMMERCE ACT. See ACT TO REGULATE COMMERCE.

INTERSTATE HIGHWAY SYSTEM. A long-range program initiated in 1956 to coordinate the construction of about 50,000 miles of highways across the U.S. See FEDERALLY SUBSIDIZED HIGHWAYS.

INTERVENTION. (1) Actions by monetary authorities which affect international exchange rates and prevent them from floating freely. See DIRTY FLOAT. (2) Any government action which causes a deviation from pure MARKETPLACE forces.

INTRASTATE COMMERCE. Trade within the PRIVATE SECTOR involving parties within a single state.

INTRINSIC VALUE. The value an item would have in the absence of emotional and social considerations. It is sometimes difficult for economists to explain why, although salt is essential to life, we can purchase all the salt we need for less than it costs to buy a necktie, which has little intrinsic value.

INVENTORY. Assets used in pursuit of an enterprise's business. Items in an inventory vary from raw material received and waiting to be used, to finished products waiting for shipment.

INVENTORY CONTROL. Management of inventory so as to maximize long-term profits through minimizing costs. If too little is carried in inventory, shortages will result, causing expenses of idle time, lost sales, and others; if too much is carried, spoilage, loss of cash flow, and other expenses will result. Therefore, inventory control establishes policies regarding the average level to maintain, when to order, what quantity to order, etc.

INVENTORY PROFITS. When goods are moved from an inventory account to a product account, such as WORK IN PROCESS, the eventual cost of the product depends on whether FIRST IN, FIRST OUT or LAST IN, FIRST OUT is the accounting rule used. During a period of inflation, it is possible for items to increase in value while in inventory; total cost will depend on whether the items from inventory are entered at purchase price or current value (replacement price).

INVENTORY RECESSION. A slowdown in economic activity, led by the manufacturing sector because output has outpaced consumption and inventories throughout the nation are large. Until inventories are taken down to normal, orders to manufacturers will be smaller than usual.

INVENTORY TAX. A tax, assessed by some states, whose base is the value of inventory held by a business on the day of record. One of its main drawbacks is that it causes a distortion of optimum inventory policy.

INVENTORY VALUATION ADJUSTMENT. An adjustment applied to profits before taxes in order to exclude the gains or losses due to differences between the replacement cost of goods taken out of inventory and their recorded acquisition cost. Such an adjustment is necessary because many business firms do not keep their books in terms of current market prices, but rather at original cost or some other basis. In addition, the adjustment is required to prevent overstatement or understatement of earned profits in periods of changing prices. Generally, it carries a negative sign during periods when prices are rising, and a positive sign when prices are falling. See GROSS NATIONAL PRODUCT.

INVERSELY RELATED. Two variables are inversely related if an increase in one is consistent with a decrease in the other, as with a demand schedule. See SUPPLY AND DEMAND. See also DIRECTLY RELATED.

INVESTIGATION INTO THE POVERTY OF NATIONS. See ESSAY ON THE PRINCIPLE OF POPULATION, AN.

INVESTMENT. Spending by industry for CAPITAL GOODS. In studying economics, it is important to separate this definition from the commonly accepted one, that of putting funds into a form that is intended to increase in value. To an economist, putting money in a savings account is not investment. See GROSS PRIVATE DOMESTIC INVESTMENT.

INVESTMENT ADVISER. A person who helps people make decisions regarding the use of their savings. Although investment advisers are generally thought of in connection with SECURITIES, they also provide advice on other investments, such as real estate and insurance, and on taxes.

INVESTMENT BANK (Jugoslavenska Investiciona) (Yugo). One of the specialized banks within the commercial banking system of Yugoslavia. It provides funds to industry for purposes of capital investment.

INVESTMENT BANK (U.S.S.R.). The *Stroibank*, which obtains funds mostly from government grants and provides financing for a wide range of activities including industrial enterprises, schools, hospitals, and housing.

INVESTMENT BANKING. That part of the financial community that trades in SECURITIES. In contrast, *deposit bank-*

ing involves the functions ordinarily considered part of banking.

INVESTMENT BANK OF SWEDEN (Sveriges Investeringsbank) (Swed.). A Swedish financial institution which obtains funds by selling bonds to the NATIONAL PENSION FUND and uses the money to finance long-term industrial investment.

INVESTMENT BANKS (Mex.). See MEXICAN BANKING SYSTEM.

INVESTMENT BILL. A BILL OF EXCHANGE which is negotiated to a new holder prior to the payment-due date. The new holder pays less than the face amount (i.e., buys it at a discount), intending to profit by collecting the face amount on the due date.

INVESTMENT COMPANY. A business enterprise that uses its CAPITAL FUNDS to purchase securities (stocks, bonds, commercial paper, etc.) for the purpose of realizing dividends and appreciation. Some investment companies specialize in certain industries or even certain types of securities within an industry, while others are more diversified. The objective of investment companies is to pool the investments of many individuals for efficient trading administered by professionals. Also known as a *mutual company*.

INVESTMENT, FOREIGN. See FOREIGN INVESTMENT.

INVESTMENT FUNCTION. See INVESTMENT SCHEDULE.

INVESTMENT MULTIPLIER. See MULTIPLIER.

INVESTMENT, PLANNED. See PLANNED INVESTMENT.

INVESTMENT PORTFOLIO. An inventory of the securities owned by an investor.

INVESTMENT RESERVE (Swed.). Swedish businesses are provided with tax incentives for (1) adding funds to the investment reserve during economic expansion and (2) drawing from the investment reserve for capital investment when the economy needs a stimulus. Called an *economic expansion tank*, it is analogous to a hydraulic expansion tank, which smooths pressure in the main flow by compressing air during pressure increases and releasing compression during pressure decreases.

INVESTMENT SCHEDULE. A schedule showing the relationship between PLANNED INVESTMENT and GROSS NATIONAL PRODUCT or another measure of total spending or total income. Because investment planning is a long-term process, the amount spent on CAPITAL GOODS (i.e., invested) in any given year is fairly independent of income that year, and a first-order analysis would use a fixed investment schedule. Also called *investment function*.

INVESTMENT TAX CREDIT. An income tax provision which allows corporations to take a TAX CREDIT equal to a percentage of expenditures for CAPITAL GOODS during the tax period. See also ACCELERATED COST RECOVERY SYSTEM.

INVISIBLE GOODS AND SERVICES. In international economics (see BALANCE OF INTERNATIONAL PAYMENTS), items which cannot be held or seen, such as services bought by tourists in other countries, interest due to foreigners, and insurance charges.

INVISIBLE HAND DOCTRINE. A term used by ADAM SMITH in INQUIRY INTO THE NATURE AND CAUSES OF THE WEALTH OF NATIONS, AN (1776). It is the doctrine that the fundamental questions of economics are answered without deliberate decision, as if, today, an invisible hand told manufacturers how many batteries to manufacture for transistor radios so that there will be neither a SURPLUS nor a SHORTAGE.

INVISIBLE ITEMS OF TRADE. Costs that are necessary for the efficient operation of international trade but which do not arise directly from the transaction.

Included can be items such as insurance on shipments, and money spent by tourists abroad. See also BALANCE OF INTERNATIONAL PAYMENTS.

INVOICE. Notice that payment resulting from a transaction is due. An invoice usually includes details of the transaction, as well as payment terms and instructions for payment. Also called a *bill*.

INVOLUNTARY   BANKRUPTCY. BANKRUPTCY that results from proceedings initiated by creditors.

IRON AND STEEL ACT (U.K.). During the postwar socialization controversies, there were two significant acts by this name. The 1949 act nationalized most of the British steel industry, and, after a change of government, the 1953 act restored private ownership but retained a high degree of government supervision by creating the *Iron and Steel Board*.

IRON LAW OF WAGES. One of the population problems predicted by DAVID RICARDO, who argued that the REAL INCOME of workers cannot be improved, for any apparent rise in income will result in larger family size and faster population growth. As population grows, there will therefore be increased demand for food and other necessities, causing their prices to increase and canceling the benefits of the wage increase. The wage stalemate was also predicted to arise from the fact that large numbers of potential workers made it possible for factory owners to keep wages at subsistence levels.

IRREDEEMABLE CURRENCY. Money of a nation that is not freely exchangeable into a standard, such as gold, or into money of other nations. Also called *inconvertible currency*. See also CONVERTIBLE CURRENCY; CURRENCY CONTROLS.

IRREVOCABLE LETTER OF CREDIT. A document (LETTER OF CREDIT) in which a bank indicates credit approval by stating that, for the named individual, it will accept drafts through a given date (see ACCEPTANCES).

ISO-. A prefix meaning constant. It appears in economics in words such as isocost, isoprofit, isoutility, and ISOQUANT.

ISOPRODUCT CURVE. See ISOQUANT.

ISOQUANT. A graph drawn with one FACTOR OF PRODUCTION on one axis and another factor on the other; the curve shows the various combinations of the two factors which can produce a given OUTPUT. Therefore, an isoquant is a *constant quantity graph* (sometimes called an isoproduct curve). When such a graph is not a straight line, it indicates that the two factors are not perfectly substitutable throughout the range considered; in fact, an isoquant will always be convex toward the origin because, as the factor mix becomes more and more intensive with fac-tor A, it will take increasingly larger amounts of that factor to replace a given amount of factor B.

ISOUTILITY CURVE. See INDIFFERENCE CURVE.

ISSUE. All of a certain security that is covered by the same agreement. Thus, all the preferred stock (see CAPITAL STOCK) paying $1 dividend by a certain company is one issue; stock paying a different amount is part of another issue.

ISSUED STOCK. The amount of CAPITAL STOCK of a corporation that people are holding. Issued stock does not include the shares of its own stock that a corporation is holding. It can be obtained through purchase, bonus, stock dividend, or other means. See also AUTHORIZED STOCK.

J

JACQUARD'S LOOM. An invention of Joseph Marie Jacquard, first exhibited in 1801, that greatly increased productivity in textiles by enabling one worker to produce the output which previously required several workers. Its economic significance is twofold: (1) it was a factor in bringing about the Industrial Revolution; (2) its introduction elicited protests, and workers often fear for their jobs when new machinery appears, although the weavers' opposition in this instance did not extend to the violence and destruction touched off by the introduction of HARGREAVES' JENNY.

JAPAN DEVELOPMENT BANK (Jap.). An organization created after World War II to assist with funding reconstruction, especially with directing funding in the areas deemed essential for economic growth. Since this bank is owned by the Japanese government, it is an important element in the coordination of various phases of economic policy.

JAPANESE CONFEDERATION OF LABOR (Domei) (Jap.). The second largest confederation of labor unions in Japan, organizing mostly public employees.

JAPANESE FEDERATION OF EMPLOYERS ASSOCIATIONS (Nikkeiren) (Jap.). One of the largest of several organizations in Japan to which companies and other associations belong. Some of their main activities include correlating business activities and influencing economic policies.

JAPAN EXPORT-IMPORT BANK (Jap.). A source of funds for capital investment in Japanese export industries. The loans it makes available are attractive because the interest rates are lower than market rates (the difference is provided by the government). Another function is to accept monies of other nations and in other ways to assist in attracting foreign capital to Japan.

JARVIS-GANN AMENDMENT. See PROPOSITION 13.

JAWBONING. See MORAL SUASION.

J CURVE. An economic function which initially decreases by a relatively small amount and then, as other forces become effective, increases well beyond its original value. For example, when a nation devalues its monetary unit to improve its balance of trade, the immediate decrease in the prices of that nation's products often causes the balance of trade to worsen; then, when the lower prices cause the volume of trade to expand, the balance of trade improves rapidly. For a good example, see Federal Reserve Bank of San Francisco, *Business & Financial Letter*, September 28, 1973.

JOBBER. A middleman who buys goods in large lots, taking title to them for resale in smaller lots further down the distribution chain. Jobbers who supply retailers often go directly to the retailer's place of business, place the goods on shelves, and arrange displays.

JOB CORPS. One of the U.S. programs of the 1960s designed to fight poverty by helping the disadvantaged to upgrade themselves, rather than receive a continuing handout, this program established centers where young people received free training and were paid living expenses during their training.

JOINT BOARD. In labor economics, a group whose representatives are from more than one union. The board thus represents all or a large percentage of affected employees during negotiations. Also called *joint council*.

JOINT ECONOMIC COMMITTEE (JEC). A committee of the U.S. Congress established by the EMPLOYMENT ACT OF 1946 for the purpose of advising the president on economic matters. It occasionally conducts surveys and other studies as it prepares to make recommendations.

JOINT PROFIT MAXIMIZATION. Deliberate action by suppliers to set output and prices at a point which will maximize aggregate profit for the group, just as if it were one supplier. Such action defeats the natural forces of the MARKET ECONOMY, but is claimed to occur to a certain extent under conditions of OLIGOPOLY. Sometimes called *group profit maximization*.

JOINT RETURN. An income tax return on which two people combine their incomes and expenses, filing as one taxpayer. Most married couples file a joint return, the objective of which is to minimize the effects of PROGRESSIVE TAX rates.

JOURNEYMAN. In labor economics, an individual who is fully qualified in his or her trade, usually by virtue of having completed an apprenticeship. When applicable, union contracts establish a journeyman rate, which is the rate for that trade in that area.

JUGOSLOVENSKA INVESTICIONA (Investment Bank) (Yugo). A specialized bank within the commercial banking system of Yugoslavia, it provides funds to industry for purposes of capital investment.

JUGOSLOVENSKA POLJOPRIVEREDNA BANKS (Agricultural Bank) (Yugo.). A specialized bank within the commercial banking system of Yugoslavia that provides funds for the financing of agricultural capital expenditures. It also makes a small number of short-term crop loans.

JURISDICTION. In labor economics, the extent of a union's authority over certain workers or certain actions to be performed.

JURISDICTIONAL DISPUTE. Conflict between two or more labor unions over which will represent a certain group of employees in collective bargaining, or over which union's members will be entitled to do a particular type of work. Picketing that results from this type of labor dispute is called *cross-picketing*.

K

KAPITAL, DAS. Famous presentation of the theories of KARL MARX. Volume 1 was published in 1867, and Volumes 2 and 3, with final editing by Friedrich Engels, were published after Marx's death. The book promotes the LABOR THEORY OF VALUE, which holds that the value of a good is the value of the labor that is put into it. Therefore, the profit obtained by capitalists was said to be exploitation of wage earners, and Marx predicted a revolt of the working classes and an end of the capitalist system. Marx called the difference between the amount paid to labor for an item and the amount received by capitalists *surplus value*.

KEIDENRAN (Jap.). Federation of Economic Organizations, the largest of several business organizations in Japan to which companies and other associations belong. Some of their main activities include correlating business activities and influencing economic policies.

KENNEDY ROUND. See GENERAL AGREEMENT ON TARIFFS AND TRADE.

KEOGH PLAN. A U.S. tax law provision which allows self-employed individuals to put up to a given percentage of annual income (not to exceed a stated amount) into an investment program; income tax on contributions as well as earnings of the program is paid only when that money is drawn out, usually after retirement.

Because of PROGRESSIVE TAX rates, there should be a saving in taxes, since total income is usually lower during retirement, and the taxpayer should thus be in a lower bracket.

KEY CONTRACT. A contract obtained when labor unions direct their action at a single employer instead of engaging in INDUSTRYWIDE BARGAINING. The advantage of this approach to the union is that it can select the employer least able to withstand a strike and thus in the poorest bargaining position. The key contract then becomes the model or goal in negotiations with other employers.

KEY INDUSTRY. An industry that, either because of its size or the essential nature of the goods and services it provides, has a significant influence on the overall economy.

KEYNES CLEARING ARRANGEMENT. A proposal presented at the BRETTON WOODS conference which would have established a world CENTRAL BANK. See BANCOR.

KEYNES, JOHN MAYNARD. English economist (1883-1946) who revolutionized economic thinking with his *new economics*, or *Keynesian economics*. The best known of his writings, *The General Theory of Employment, Interest, and Money* (usually referred to as *General Theory*), was published in 1936 during the GREAT

DEPRESSION, which was felt world-wide. He shifted the concentration of economic policy-making from individual income and expenditures to aggregate concerns (now called MACROECO-NOMICS). Increasing government expenditures was suggested for deflationary periods and reducing government expenditures for inflationary periods, as a means of adjusting total spending (which he felt was the chief cause of depressions). These suggestions are recognized today as FISCAL POLICY or FUNCTIONAL FINANCE.

KICKBACK. In labor economics, a secret agreement by which a worker returns part of his wages to a person, usually a minor union leader, who controls the hiring of workers.

KIND. Goods and services rather than money. When someone is *paid in kind*, that person receives goods and services as pay, often the product in which the employer deals.

KINGSLEY-WOOD BUDGET (U.K.). One of the first government budgets to be planned largely as a tool of FISCAL POLICY, in keeping with the then (1941) new Keynesian economics.

KREDITANSTALT FÜR WIEDER-AUFBAU (Reconstruction Finance Corporation) (Ger.). Financial organization owned and operated by the West German government for the purpose of making investment money available to industry.

KUZNETS CYCLES. Many investigators have produced analyses which purport to demonstrate that there is some predictability to business cycles. One of the most widely acknowledged is Simon Kuznets, who wrote that junctures of major endogenous and exogenous events make the cycles repeat about every two decades. Because most economists see no regularity in business statistics and because the entire economy, rather than just the business sector, is affected, the term ECONOMIC FLUCTUATIONS is often used instead of *business cycles*.

L

LABELING. See DESCRIPTIVE LABELING; GRADE LABELING.

LABOR. See ECONOMIC RESOURCES.

LABOR COURT. In labor economics, a permanent U.S. governmental agency established to deal with industrial disputes.

LABOR FORCE PARTICIPATION RATE (LFPR). Percentage of civilian noninstitutional population 16 years and over that is either working or looking for work (see CIVILIAN LABOR FORCE). In the U.S. this rate was 63.9% in 1982; for males in 1981 it was 77%, and for females it grew from 43.3% in 1970 to 52.1% in 1981.

Another definition is the civilian labor force divided by the civilian noninstitutional population of working age.

LABOR GRADE. Each of the steps defined when an employer establishes a series of positions based on level of skill and other criteria, coordinated with a series of wage rates.

LABOR INTENSIVE. If a relatively large percentage of costs is labor, as in the service industry, the industry is *labor intensive*. Other industries or products might be described as CAPITAL INTENSIVE or LAND INTENSIVE.

LABOR-MANAGEMENT RELATIONS ACT OF 1947. See TAFT-HARTLEY ACT.

LABOR-MANAGEMENT REPORTING AND DISCLOSURE ACT. See LANDRUM-GRIFFIN ACT.

LABOR MARKET. The economic transactions involving the hiring of people on the one side and the selling of one's labor on the other side. *Labor market* does not refer to a physical *marketplace*.

LABOR MOVEMENT. The evolution of labor-management relations, from individual bargaining through guilds to today's strong unions.

LABOR RELATIONS. Generally, the same as INDUSTRIAL RELATIONS, although *labor relations* often implies the resolution of grievances.

LABOR RELATIONS BOARD. One of the many groups of authorities in the U.S., at various levels of government from federal to local, that have responsibilities such as writing labor legislation, interpreting labor legislation, providing for settlement of disputes, and related matters.

LABOR SAVING. Describes technology and management that result in lowering the ratio of labor costs to total costs. See also CAPITAL SAVING.

LABOR SUPPLY CURVE. A graph of the number of individuals who are available for work as a function of the wage rate. An aggregate measure, it refers to the total CIVILIAN LABOR FORCE and to some representative or average wage. Like so many functions in economics, *labor supply curve* is a theoretical function, because it can be obtained by indirect means only. It is difficult to cancel out the millions of other effects and determine how that supply of labor was affected by the wages (see OTHER THINGS BEING EQUAL). However, it is generally felt that the two variables are directly related—an increase in wages brings forth an increase in the supply of labor. This is a general conclusion; there are examples to show that once individuals reach their goals, an increase in their rate of pay will encourage them to offer fewer hours to the labor market.

LABOR THEORY OF VALUE. Theory which holds that the value of a good is the labor that goes into it. Karl Marx used this theory in KAPITAL, DAS, to conclude that profit received by owners of businesses represents exploitation of workers.

LABOR TURNOVER. The percentage of an employer's workers who are replaced because of voluntary or involuntary leaving, usually figured on an annual basis.

LAG. A time delay between two economic occurrences which are related. One theory of ECONOMIC FLUCTUATIONS is that lags are a major contributing factor, as might be shown by the following sequence:

1. Retailers experience unusually high demand for a certain item.
2. They place orders for extra quantities from the factory.
3. There are lags all along the distribution channels between retailers and factories, plus the time required to manufacture the items (and, perhaps, for the factories to place orders for their raw material).
4. By the time the factory gears up for larger production and the items reach the retailers, conditions change and the retailers are left with a surplus inventory (and the factory is left with surplus capacity).

LAGGED RESERVE ACCOUNTING (LRA). The method currently used in figuring outstanding bank liabilities for the purpose of determining reserve requirements (see BANK RESERVES). Under this rule the requirements in any given week are based on outstanding liabilities two weeks previously. In the article "Short-Run Monetary Control Under Alternative Reserve Accounting Rules," *Economic Review Supplement* [Federal Reserve Bank of San Francisco (Summer 1980)], a thorough comparison is made of the results of this method, contemporaneous reserve accounting (using liabilities of the current week), marginal reserve accounting (using LRA rules plus 100 percent of the change in deposits over the preceding two week period), and reserve lag accounting (identical to contemporaneous reserve accounting, except that the reserves which can be used to meet requirements are those held in the preceding week).

LAGGING INDICATOR. A statistic which does not change until after the economy in general has changed. For example, the value of construction completed is a lagging indicator because the main effect on the economy occurred when plans were announced and contracts let and during the peak of construction activity. See also COINCIDENT INDICATOR; LEADING INDICATOR.

LAISSEZ-FAIRE. Economic policy which calls for government to let the economy run itself. It is an extreme form of MARKET ECONOMY, said to be self-regulating through the forces of SUPPLY AND DEMAND. Actually there has never been a real laissez-faire economy; see MIXED CAPITALISM.

LAND. See ECONOMIC RESOURCES.

LANDESZENTRALBANKEN (Ger.). Central banks of states. See REICHSBANK.

LAND GRANT. Land which is given by the government to private ownership, usually for a specific objective, such as settling an unpopulated area or establishing a nonprofit or charitable enterprise.

LAND GRANT COLLEGE ACT. Legislation of 1862 providing for the establishment of colleges in areas of the U.S. where population was growing. Also called the *Morrill Act*.

LAND INTENSIVE. Indicates that a relatively large percentage of the costs of an item are land costs; farming in a LESS DEVELOPED COUNTRY is land intensive. Other industries or products might be described as LABOR INTENSIVE or CAPITAL INTENSIVE.

LAND REFORM. Programs of reassignment of land for agricultural use, usually from large holdings of wealthy individuals to small holdings by a large number of individuals.

LANDRUM-GRIFFIN ACT. 1959 legislation aimed at preventing some of the corruption within unions disclosed during U.S. Congressional hearings and at providing protection for the individual union member from his or her own union. Provisions include the prohibition of convicted felons and certain others from holding union offices and the requirement of secret ballots in voting by rank and file. Also known as the *Labor-Management Reporting and Disclosure Act*.

LASPEYRES INDEX. Index used by the U.S. CONSUMER PRICE INDEX. The cost of a given MARKET BASKET in a past period is the denominator of this ratio, and the cost of the *same* market basket in a later period is the numerator. In contrast, the *Paasche index* uses the later period as the base and still puts it in the numerator. The numerator is then the cost of a given market basket determined in the later period, and the denominator is the cost of *that* market basket in the earlier period. Since the difference between the two indexes is the period in which the

market basket is determined, the results can vary as a result of shifts in consumer spending patterns. A good analysis is made in "Indexes, Inflation and Public Policy" [Federal Reserve Bank of San Francisco, *Economic Review* (Spring 1981)].

LAST CLEAR CHANCE. In legal economics, a doctrine holding that the person creating a dangerous condition is less liable if the injured person could have avoided being injured. See CONTRIBUTORY NEGLIGENCE.

LAST IN, FIRST OUT (LIFO). In accounting economics, the bookkeeping system which records the cost of items brought out of inventory in reverse chronological order from that in which they entered inventory. It is analogous to putting plates on a stack and, when one is needed, taking it from the top of the stack. If 1,000 gallons of cleaning compound costing $0.50 per gallon are put into inventory, then another 1,000 gallons costing $0.60 per gallon are added to inventory, and then 500 gallons are used, the cost entered under LIFO would be $0.60 per gallon. See also FIRST IN, FIRST OUT.

LATENT DEMAND. A need that is not now being satisfied but is expected to be satisfied when some condition is met in the future. For example, during a major war there is spending power and desire but a lack of goods to purchase; during a recession there may be goods and desire but a lack of spending power. Sometimes a technological advance can change latent demand into actual demand. Also called *potential demand*.

LAWFUL MONEY. Generally, the same as LEGAL TENDER.

LAW, GRESHAM'S. See GRESHAM'S LAW.

LAW OF DEMAND. See SUBSTITUTION EFFECTS.

LAW OF DIMINISHING RETURNS. Principle that, as more and more cost is expended on a given objective, the benefits per unit of cost decrease. For example, one person working a farm of a given size might be inefficient, and adding one more person would double the labor cost but more than double the output. If adding still another person (adding another 50 percent to the labor cost) resulted in increasing output by less than 50 percent, then the law of diminishing returns would have set in.

LAW OF DIMINISHING UTILITY. Phrase denoting that a consumer obtains a considerable amount of satisfaction (see UTILITY) from the first of an item acquired, but that after a certain number have been acquired, the object's value to the consumer declines. For example, a professor might be willing to pay quite a bit for a new attache case; he might even pay a certain (smaller) amount for a second or even a third case because he knows he might forget where he left one of them. Beyond a certain quantity he would buy another only if the price were very low, and eventually he would have so many that he would not buy another at any price. A large enough quantity could even bring the professor negative utility if he had to find a place to keep them. Of course, we are examining a simplified situation of a consumer and are not considering that the attache cases can be resold. Also called *law of satiation*.

LAW OF LARGE NUMBERS. In statistics or ECONOMETRICS, law holding that if an action is repeated a large number of times, the percentage occurrence of each possible result will tend toward the statistical probability of each of those results. For example, if a magazine advertisement produces one sale for every seven persons who read it, any single running of the advertisement may produce a wide range of results, but as the ad is used a larger and larger number of times the aggregate results will show less and less variation above and below the long-run tendency of one sale per seven readers.

LAW OF SATIATION. See LAW OF DIMINISHING UTILITY.

LAW OF SUPPLY. The fact that producers will be willing to divert more of their productive efforts to a given product when its market price is high than when it is low, OTHER THINGS BEING EQUAL. Therefore, there is a direct relationship between price and quantity supplied. See SUPPLY SCHEDULE.

LAW OF VARIABLE PROPORTIONS. Principle that the relationship between INPUT and OUTPUT is not linear. As relative amounts of input (see FACTORS OF PRODUCTION) are changed, the output will change, but as the total amount of input is changed, output will not necessarily change in the same proportion. See LAW OF DIMINISHING RETURNS; ECONOMIES OF SCALE.

LAW OF WAGES. See IRON LAW OF WAGES.

LAY CORPORATION. Any incorporated enterprise except a religious one; the opposite of an *ecclesiastical corporation*, which is owned and operated by a church.

LEADER THEORY. One of the MONOCAUSAL THEORIES used to explain economic history. According to it, the world proceeds with very little change until a strong leader or thinker influences the course of history.

LEADING INDICATOR. A statistic valued for predicting purposes because its movement is generally followed by a certain movement of the economy in general. Building permits obtained is often used as a leading indicator. Economists sometimes refer to a *short list*, which is a composite of 12 leading indicators that have correlated particularly well with economic changes that have followed. Average weekly work hours, unemployment claims, and corporate profits are included in the short list. See also COINCIDENT INDICATOR; LAGGING INDICATOR.

LEAKAGES. Practical side effects which cause actual workings of the economy to differ from predictions that are based on elementary idealized models or formulas. For example, an elementary model would show the MONEY SUPPLY increasing by the reciprocal of the reserve ratio (see BANK RESERVES; MONEY SUPPLY EXPANSION MULTIPLIER), but in practice the money supply would expand by less than that amount because of several leakages (slippages), such as borrowers who take their loans in CURRENCY (cash drain) and banks which do not respond immediately to changes in the reserve ratio.

LEANING AGAINST THE WIND. A figurative identification of economic countercyclical policies, especially applied to MONETARY POLICY. Countercyclical methods imply EXPANSIONARY moves when the economy is moving toward a below-trendline phase of the cycle (see ECONOMIC FLUCTUATONS) and CONTRACTIONARY moves when an unstable rate of growth threatens. The objective of leaning against the wind is to maintain a steady, healthy rate of economic growth.

LEASE. A contract which gives one person possession of another's property for a specified length of time. If the agreement is terminable at will, it is usually called a *rental agreement*.

LEAST SQUARES. A method of comparing a graph or function to a set of data. The distance of each data point from the curve (distance in one orthogonal component, usually *y*) is measured, squared, and added to the sum of squared distances from all other data points. The curve which has the least sum of squared errors is the best fit by this definition. See Mathematical Regression in the appendix.

LEGAL PERSON. A person in the eyes of the law; one who can act for himself and in his own name. Thus, all natural individuals are legal persons, and for most actions corporations are legal persons.

LEGAL RATE OF INTEREST. A rate of interest not in excess of the maximum

allowed by law for the type of debt in question. See also USURY.

LEGAL TENDER. In the U.S., paper MONEY and coins; that is, when a debtor offers paper money and coins in settlement of a money debt, he fulfills his obligation. It is generally necessary that a nation give legal tender status to some form of money, because one main requirement of a money system is that it be accepted by parties to a transaction.

LEGAL TENDER NOTES. See UNITED STATES NOTES.

LENDER OF LAST RESORT. The FEDERAL RESERVE SYSTEM, which, by extending credit to depository institutions or other entities in a national or regional emergency, can avert a severe adverse impact on the economy.

LESS-CASH/LESS-CHECK SOCIETY. The practical limit of what was once thought would be an ultimate payments system, the CASHLESS/CHECKLESS SOCIETY.

LESS DEVELOPED COUNTRY (LDC). A country other than the leading industrialized ones. There is no universally accepted measure for identifying LDCs; many writers say a nation is less developed if a large percentage of its work force is engaged in agriculture, a large percentage of its industry is LABOR INTENSIVE, and/or much of its trade is by barter. Other criteria include level of education, per capita use of utilities, per capita income, and bathtubs per capita.

Many expressions have been used to label LDCs. For example, *underdeveloped country* (UDC) was used for a while but is generally not favored now because it implies a judgment as to how developed a nation *should* be, whereas LDC merely says that the country in question is not as developed as the most industrialized ones and does not rule out the conclusion that the latter are overdeveloped.

For a complete discussion of the subject, see W.W. Rostow, *The Stages of*

Economic Growth (New York: Cambridge University Press.)

LESS THAN CARLOAD (LCL). A shipment of goods that is placed in a railroad car along with other shipments, as opposed to a *carload* (CL) shipment, which occupies an entire car. The significance to the shipper is that a CL shipment is handled at a lower price because the car can be sealed so as to require no internal handling until it reaches its destination. See FREIGHT FORWARDER.

Economists are interested in the percentage of total shipping that goes by LCL as an indication of the types of goods and services being produced and of the size of sales being made.

LESS THAN TRUCKLOAD (LTL). A shipment of goods that is carried in a truck along with other shipments. See further discussion under LESS THAN CARLOAD.

LET IT WORK ITSELF. See LAISSEZ-FAIRE.

LETTER OF CREDIT (LOC). A document in which a bank indicates credit approval by stating that, for the named individual, it will accept drafts (see ACCEPTANCES). Such letters usually include stipulations that give them descriptive names such as CONFIRMED LETTER OF CREDIT; IRREVOCABLE LETTER OF CREDIT; REVOCABLE LETTER OF CREDIT; REVOLVING LETTER OF CREDIT; STRAIGHT LETTER OF CREDIT; UNCONFIRMED LETTER OF CREDIT.

LEVEL OF RESOURCE UTILIZATION. The percentage of ECONOMIC RESOURCES which are being used. Of most concern is the level of *human resources* utilization, because unemployment hurts individuals as well as the entire economy. See also MANUFACTURING CAPACITY.

LIABILITIES. That portion of an organization's total assets which is claimed by or will be due to outsiders, such as debts and DEFERRED INCOME. See

FUNDAMENTAL ACCOUNTING EQUATION.

LIABILITY COMPOSITION. In the banking industry, usually the ratio of time and savings deposits to total deposits. Economic analysts, with *liability composition* and other statistics, can forecast items such as the MONEY SUPPLY. See also MONEY SUPPLY EXPANSION MULTIPLIER.

LIABILITY MANAGEMENT. Arranging to obtain the best long-run terms from debts.

LIBERAL SCHOOL. An expression used to identify the CLASSICAL SCHOOL of economic thought, whose adherents held beliefs that, relative to doctrines of the time, were liberal. These economists sought changes in the system.

LIBERAL SOCIALISM. An economic system which inclines more toward socialism with regard to ownership of the means of production (some private and some state ownership), and toward democracy with regard to politics and individual choice. Also called *democratic socialism.*

LIBERTÉ CONTROLÉE (Fr.). Under general price controls in France, describes those industries which are required to obtain approval from authorities for any established prices they change, or for prices they set on new items.

LIBERTÉ SURVEILLÉE (Fr.). Under general price controls in France, describes those industries in which the government sets prices directly.

LIBERTÉ TOTALE (Fr.). Under general price controls in France, describes those industries which are entirely or mostly free of control.

LIBERTY BOND. Bonds sold by the U.S. government during the first World War.

LICENSE. Evidence of approval of a certain activity by authorities. A government generally requires a license for one or a combination of the following reasons:

1. to raise revenue for government
2. to maintain quality—an examination or inspection is required to obtain and to renew the license
3. to make it easier to have the operation discontinued—the government agency has only to withdraw the license or refuse to renew it.

Private parties also issue licenses. For example, the owner of a copyright or invention may give others the right to produce the protected product.

LIEN. A claim against property preventing the owner from having free and clear title until a debt is settled.

LIFE ANNUITY. An ANNUITY in which payments continue throughout the life of the annuitant.

LIMITED LIABILITY. The corporate form of enterprise (see FORMS OF BUSINESS ORGANIZATION) offers *limited liability* because the corporation is a legal entity, separate from its owners (the stockholders). Therefore large amounts of money can be accumulated to run a corporation, because people who are not in a position to control the actions of the corporation can buy a part of the ownership (shares of stock) without fear of being held responsible for debts and other liabilities of the corporation.

LIMITED PARTNER. A partner (see FORMS OF BUSINESS ORGANIZATION) who, by agreement, is not liable for the debts of the firm beyond the amount he has personally invested in it. In the U.S. the Uniform Limited Partnership Act states that a limited partnership cannot be formed without at least one general partner who will have unlimited liability.

LIMITED RESOURCES. One of the basics of economics is that ECONOMIC RESOURCES are not freely available in unlimited quantities. Although some economists use the word *scarce*, many prefer to say that resources are *limited*, because they may be around us in large quantities but, relative to the world's population and our desired level of con-

sumption, they are limited in quantity. That choices must therefore be made among alternatives is a description of the field of economics.

LINEAR. In reference to a graph, all spacings having equal value. For example, if the distance from 100 to 110 on the scale is the same as the distance from 200 to 210, the scale is linear. One of the most common *nonlinear* scales is the logarithmic scale, in which the distance from 10 to 100 is the same as the distance from 100 to 1000.

LINEARLY RELATED. Describes two functions whose graph is a straight line. That is, changing one function by a factor of x results in changing the other function by the same factor (e.g., doubling one results in doubling the other).

LINE OF REGRESSION. See Mathematical Regression in the appendix.

LINKAGE. Tie-in, or connection, between two or more variables. For example, an analysis of the effect that interest rates have on the rate of saving would be a study of the linkages between interest rates and saving.

LIQUID ASSET. There are degrees of LIQUIDITY; a completely liquid asset is MONEY, because it exists as wealth in a form for immediate spending. A highly, although not completely, liquid asset is an item which can be converted to money quickly and with little or no loss of value, such as a government security. See also QUICK ASSET.

LIQUIDATE. To convert assets or items of value to LIQUID ASSETS. In the business world, *liquidate* often means to terminate a business enterprise and sell the assets. Liquidation may be planned, or it may be the result of a BANKRUPTCY.

LIQUIDITY. Ease with which an asset can be spent or exchanged for another asset; the most liquid asset is cash. NEAR MONEY has recognized value and can easily be exchanged for money. There is a continuum of degrees of liquidity, from completely liquid to "tied-up" (having no liquidity at all).

LIQUIDITY BASIS. See BALANCE OF INTERNATIONAL PAYMENTS.

LIQUIDITY PREFERENCE. The aggregate desire of economic units to hold their assets in the form of MONEY (currency in circulation plus demand deposits) rather than in other forms which usually earn interest. Four reasons are identified for this preference:

1. *Transactions demand.* There may be a need to have money available for known expenses, recognizing that income is not received at exactly the time each expense must be paid.
2. *Precautionary demand.* Liquidity may be maintained for unknown expenses (or opportunities).
3. *Speculative demand.* During times of falling prices, money increases in purchasing power but other assets are worth less as time goes on. When prices are rising, this demand has a negative value and influences people to hold less money for other purposes. (It is also true that interest rates are usually higher during a period of rising prices.)
4. *Convenience demand.* A certain amount of liquidity is kept simply because the alternatives do not earn enough to make it worth the effort of converting money to other forms (see LIQUDITY TRAP).

LIQUIDITY PREMIUM. The part of total interest on a long-term debt instrument which investors demand as compensation for their holding assets with little LIQUIDITY. See ABSTINENCE THEORY OF INTEREST. This premium is not an identifiable separate payment, but rather a component that an analyst might show during a determination of why certain values of interest rates were found.

LIQUIDITY RATIO. The ratio of the quantity of cash and certain liquid assets to total (or sometimes selected) bank li-

abilities. In several European nations, authorities set requirements on the liquidity ratio as a tool of MONETARY POLICY—sometimes in place of, and sometimes in addition to, setting reserve requirements (see BANK RESERVES).

LIQUIDITY TRAP. In a graph of stable points relating interest rates to total income (LIQUIDITY PREFERENCE equals MONEY SUPPLY), the lower limit reached at which fairly large increments in money have very little effect on interest rates. The accompanying figure shows this effect where the graph becomes nearly horizontal.

LISTED SECURITY. A security traded at one of the organized exchanges, such as the NEW YORK STOCK EXCHANGE or the AMERICAN STOCK EXCHANGE.

LISTED STOCK. An issue of CAPITAL STOCK which is on the list of securities traded at one of the major STOCK MARKETs, as opposed to an *over-the-counter* stock, whose sales are coordinated by a network of brokers without using a stock market.

LIST PRICE. The price charged to buyers who do not qualify for a lower price through discounts, memberships, or other provisions; in retail trade, usually the price

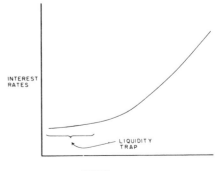

Liquidity trap. An economy is in the liquidity trap when a decrease in interest rates does very little to stimulate the economy.

suggested by the manufacturer, and generally the highest price charged (although a few retailers may charge more than list) at a full-service store. Often the same goods can be purchased by any customer at a *discount store* for a lower price.

LIVESTOCK BILL OF LADING. A BILL OF LADING that is prepared especially to document the shipment of livestock.

LIVING STANDARD. The amount of goods and services consumed. Thus, a family that goes to restaurants more often than another, other things being equal, has a higher standard of living. It is difficult to compare standards of living because, of course, all other things are not equal. For example, one family owns a boat and another family goes to Europe for vacations; perhaps both families spend the same amount of money on recreation. Their living standards cannot be compared. Also called *standard of living*.

LOANABLE FUNDS. Amounts available for loans; some of the amounts exist as MONEY, and others will be counted as money only after they are loaned. The former come from savers who make their savings available for others to borrow; the latter amounts are loaned by banks (see MONEY SUPPLY EXPANSION MULTIPLIER).

LOAN ASSETS. Bank assets which consist of money loaned to borrowers.

LOANED UP. The condition of a bank or the banking system when *actual reserves* are just sufficient to satisfy *required reserves* (see BANK RESERVES). Also called *fully invested*.

LOAN, INSTALLMENT. See INSTALLMENT LOAN.

LOANS. In the CONSOLIDATED STATEMENT OF CONDITION OF ALL FEDERAL RESERVE BANKS, credit granted by the FEDERAL RESERVE BANK—as authorized and limited by the Federal Reserve Act and regulated by the Board of Governors' regulation A—almost exclusively to MEMBER BANKS, at the borrower's initiative.

Loans in this very special sense are discounts or advances. *Discounts* are made when a member bank presents customers' short-term commercial, industrial, agricultural, or other business papers for rediscounting. *Advances* are loans made on the borrowing bank's own promissory note secured by government obligations, paper eligible for discounting, or other satisfactory collateral. A maturity distribution of loans outstanding on the statement date appears directly below the Consolidated Statement. Virtually all loans appear in the first maturity category "within 15 days." A more refined distribution would show the bulk of borrowings maturing in one or two days, reflecting the borrowing pattern of the large city banks which account for most of the dollar volume. As a separate group, the borrowing of smaller banks clusters at seven or eight days.

The following types of loans may be made by Federal Reserve banks to member banks: (1) advances secured by the bank's promissory note, maximum maturity 15 days; (2) discounts of eligible paper, maximum maturity 90 days; (3) advances secured by eligible paper or by U.S. government securities or any other obligations eligible for Federal Reserve bank purchase, maximum maturity 90 days; (4) discounts of certain bankers' acceptances, maximum maturity 6 months; (5) discounts of agricultural paper, maximum maturity 9 months; (6) advances secured to the satisfaction of the Federal Reserve bank, maximum maturity 4 months. The interest rate charged on such loans cannot be less than one-half percentage point higher than the prevailing discount rate.

The following types of loans may be made by Federal Reserve banks to other banks: (1) advances to foreign governments, CENTRAL BANKs, or monetary authorities, secured by gold, with no maximum maturity specified in the Federal Reserve Act; (2) advances to individuals, partnerships, or corporations secured by U.S. government or agency obligations, maximum maturity 90 days [the interest rate charged on such loans is fixed by each Reserve Bank, subject to review and determination by the BOARD OF GOVERNORS (OF THE FEDERAL RESERVE SYSTEM)]; (3) in unusual and exigent circumstances, discounts to individuals, partnerships, or corporations of paper that would be eligible for discounting if presented by member banks, with no maximum maturity.

Banks usually borrow on their own promissory notes secured by U.S. government securities. Under continuing lending agreements instituted by the Reserve banks in February 1971, member banks need not physically present a promissory note. Borrowers may request an advance by telephone or wire. Many member banks keep government securities at their Reserve bank or branch, thus making sure collateral is always immediately available. Reserve banks may grant an advance even without physical possession of the collateral if distance or poor transportation facilities would make actual delivery difficult. In these cases, member banks may pledge as collateral securities held in a safekeeping account at another member bank.

The interest rate the Reserve banks charge on loans is called the DISCOUNT RATE and is payable when the loan is repaid. The discount rate is always expressed in annual terms, but interest charges are computed on the number of days funds are actually borrowed. Thus, charges on a 24-hour loan would amount to 1/365 of the discount rate.
[Adapted from Federal Reserve Bank of New York, *Glossary: Weekly Federal Reserve Statements.*]

LOAN SHARK. A person who loans money at illegally high rates of interest (see USURY), often enforcing collections by violence or threats of violence.

LOCAL MAXIMUM. A point in a mathematical function such that changing the operating conditions a small amount in either direction causes a decrease in the dependent variable. A large change in operating point *may* lead to another local

maximum, which may or may not be a higher one.

For example, suppose factory size, market size, and other variables dictate that production of 1,000,000 units per month results in a unit profit of $100. If that level of production is a local maximum, then producing a few units more or a few units less than 1,000,000 will result in a unit profit of less than $100. However, if a gross change is made, say to 3,000,000 units per month, another local maximum might be found, and possibly the unit profit at that point will be $105.

LOCAL MINIMUM. A point in a mathematical function such that changing the operating conditions a small amount in either direction causes an increase in the dependent variable. A large change in operating point *may* lead to another local minimum, which may or may not be a lower one.

For example, suppose factory size, machinery in place, and other variables dictate that total unit costs of producing 1,000,000 units per month are $100. If that level of production is a local minimum, then producing a few units more or a few units less will result in unit costs larger than $100. However, if a gross change is made, say to a production level of 3,000,000 per month, we might find another local in which could be less than $100 per unit.

LOCKBOX TECHNIQUE. A method to reduce the paperwork (and resultant costs) involved in widespread business activities. A company establishes post office boxes (lockboxes) at major mail distribution centers, and customers are instructed to mail payments to a specified post office address. The company opens an account with a bank in each of the cities in which it has a lockbox, and the bank takes care of emptying the lockbox and crediting the company's account.

LOCK-IN BENEFITS. Benefits provided by employers, usually not including ordinary wages, which accumulate with seniority. Such arrangements are made ostensibly to reward loyal service, but the effect is actually to make it more costly for an individual to change jobs; the employer is then under less immediate pressure to keep wages and other conditions up to competitive levels.

Managements prefer lock-in benefits because, although the various benefits have a cost involved, the overall labor bill is lowered as a result of the reduction in ability of the employees to sell their labor competitively. Labor unions also like to see employees locked in because their decreased individual bargaining position makes them even more dependent on collective bargaining for increased benefits. Often referred to as *golden handcuffs.*

LOCKOUT. In labor economics, management's equivalent of a strike; a work stoppage initiated by employers. If the union tactic is to strike one part of an industry, obtain a high wage settlement because the struck company is afraid of losing customers, and then use that settlement for negotiating with the rest of the industry (see KEY CONTRACT), the entire industry may choose to call a lockout. This method is very seldom used.

LOCUS. A path made up of all the points that meet a certain criterion—therefore, in economics, a graph.

LOGARITHMIC SCALE. In a graph, one or both scales may be logarithmic, instead of LINEAR, in order to give a more meaningful representation of the data. When both scales of a graph are logarithmic, it is called a *log-log graph.* See RATIO SCALE.

LONDON CLEARING HOUSE (U.K.). An organization which handles drafts, exchanges checks, and assists with other banking functions. The large commercial banks are members of the clearing house.

LONDON DOLLAR CD MARKET. The market, centered in London, for Eurodollar CDs. Like a domestic U.S. certificate of deposit (CD), a Eurodollar CD is a dollar denominated instrument ev-

idencing a time deposit placed with a bank at an agreed-upon rate of interest for a specific period of time. Unlike a domestic CD, however, a Eurodollar CD is issued abroad, either by the foreign branch of a U.S. bank or by a foreign bank. The market for Eurodollar CDs is centered in London and is therefore frequently called the London dollar CD market.

LONG RUN. Not an absolute length of time, but an amount of time sufficient for a change in output capacity. A firm, therefore, sees the long run as the time necessary for changing the amount of any selected FACTOR OF PRODUCTION (building additional plant capacity usually takes the longest time); an industry sees it as the time necessary for firms to enter or leave the industry. All costs are VARIABLE COSTS in the long run. See also SHORT RUN.

LOOPHOLE. A provision of tax laws allowing selective reduction of income tax. It is a legal DEDUCTION or TAX CREDIT, with no official distinction from any other deduction or tax credit, except that the fewer individuals who are eligible for a certain credit or deduction, the more likely it is to be referred to as a loophole. It is said that the reductions a person claims are justified, but those that others take are loopholes.

LORENZ CURVE. A continuous curve of percentage of all income as a function of percentage of earners, demonstrating graphically that everyone does not receive the same income. If every 5 percent increment of earners received the same income, the graph would be a straight line from the origin; however, in any real economy the Lorenz curve will bow toward the lower right because the highest earners have more income than the lowest earners.

LOSS LEADER. In retail trade, an item sold at a loss in order to attract a large number of customers to the store; the retailer accepts the loss and feels that sales of more profitable items will increase as a result of the mere presence of customers.

LOSS MINIMIZATION. A factor in profit maximization. *Loss minimization* emphasizes that a firm seeking to maximize its profits must think in the algebraic sense; when loss is inevitable, the smallest negative profit (loss) is a form of profit maximization.

LOW BALANCE. Refers to savings accounts in which interest is figured on the lowest amount in the account during a period, usually a quarter. See INTEREST DATES for other methods of figuring interest on savings accounts.

LOW GRADE BOND. See BOND RATINGS.

LUDDITES. A group of English textile workers who, between 1811 and 1816, stormed factories and destroyed machinery which they felt was a threat to their jobs. The name probably derives from Ned Lud, a feebleminded man responsible for smashing two textile frames around 1780.

LUXURY TAX. A tax on luxury items, imposed on the theory that people of low incomes do not buy luxuries and that therefore the government obtains money only from the wealthy. In practice, there is considerable disagreement over the definition of luxury and many feel that poor and middle-income families are paying most of the luxury taxes.

M

M1, M2, M3. See MONEY.

McFADDEN-PEPPER ACT. This 1927 U.S. legislation, and amendments, permits NATIONAL BANKs to establish branches if state law permits STATE BANKs to establish branches, subject to the same restrictions on location as those imposed by state law on state banks.

McGUIRE-KEOGH ACT. Congressional action in 1952 which compelled all retailers in a state to observe a fixed minimum selling price if any one retailer signed an agreement with the manufacturer. See FAIR TRADE LAWS.

MACROECONOMICS. Study of an entire closed economic system. Although no nation is a completely closed system, study of a nation's economy is generally considered to be macroeconomics. Also known as *aggregative* economics. See also MICROECONOMICS.

MAGNETIC INK CHARACTER RECOGNITION (MICR). Information written in magnetic ink on checks and other documents to speed up processing. Electronic equipment sorts and tabulates at speeds in excess of 15 items per minute.

MAINTENANCE OF MEMBERSHIP. A form of union security used in contract formation; the employee is not required to join a union but agrees to remain a member of the union for the duration of the contract if he is already a union member or does join the union during the life of the contract.

MAKE-WORK. The policy of creating jobs solely to place individuals on a payroll when there is no actual need for that work to be performed. FEATHERBEDDING is one example; another is avoidance of PIGGYBACK transportation and insistence that a truck's contents be unloaded, loaded into a railroad car, unloaded at their intermediate destination, and reloaded into another truck for transportation to their final destination. If the entire truck trailer can be carried on a railroad car, with the goods protected from breakage and pilferage, requiring all the extra handling keeps productivity down and contributes to inflation.

MALTHUS, THOMAS. An English ordained minister and economist (1766-1834) and author of *An Essay on the Principle of Population.* The book was first published in 1798, and the seventh edition was published in 1826. One of its best known parts has become known as the Malthusian theory of population. This theory states that population will grow geometrically (2, 4, 8, 16,. . .), but food supply will increase arithmetically (2, 4, 6, 8,. . .); therefore the human race will eventually settle out at subsistence levels. The theory states that increases in real wages are followed by a general increase in family size, returning wage earners to their previous low standard of living. Another of his books, *Principles of Political Economy*, never reached the same level of popularity. See IRON LAW OF WAGES.

MANAGED MONEY SUPPLY. Occurs when the size of a nation's MONEY SUPPLY is a function of deliberate human decision rather than of some natural measure, such as the amount of gold or other precious metal which is available. Most modern economies use a managed money supply because it is a tool of MONETARY POLICY and because there is need for short-term adjustments to satisfy transaction demands. Also called *controlled money supply*. See also MONEY SUPPLY EXPANSION MULTIPLIER.

MANAGEMENT SCIENCE. Application of analytic methods to management functions. The purpose is to make management decisions more objective and less subject to hunch and emotion. For many reasons the mathematics involved becomes very cumbersome, so the development of computers has increased the interest in management science.

MANAGER OF THE SYSTEM OPEN MARKET ACCOUNT. A senior officer of the Federal Reserve Bank of New York, appointed annually by the FEDERAL OPEN MARKET COMMITTEE to conduct *open market operations*. The manager is concurrently the senior vice president in charge of the securities and acceptance departments.

MANAGING AGENT. A TRUST arrangement in which the trustee has full discretionary powers regarding portfolio changes; transactions can be undertaken without prior approval. Approval is usually obtained on an annual basis. See also ADVISORY AGENT.

MANCHESTER SCHOOL. School of economic thought which coincided roughly with the latter part of the CLASSICAL SCHOOL (early to mid-1800s). Adherents of the Manchester school concentrated on those doctrines of the classical

school which differed from the MERCANTILIST school and therefore worked actively for repeal of trade restrictions such as CORN LAWS.

MANIFEST. A list of all items being transported by a carrier, usually a ship.

MANOR. Important in the study of economic history as the center of all economic activity in medieval Europe. Each manor was largely economically self-sufficient; when cities took their place as economic centers, they were more dependent on trade with other cities. Today, a nation is recognized as an economic unit, and it coordinates or affects many economic activities, even though not directly involved in them.

MANPOWER CONTROL. Government control of the quantity, quality, and location of various portions of the CIVILIAN LABOR FORCE.

MANPOWER DEVELOPMENT AND TRAINING ACT (MDTA). A U.S. program begun in 1962 to train (or retrain) the unemployed. One objective was to break the chain which kept the HARDCORE UNEMPLOYED from realizing opportunities. The program has trained millions, some through formal training programs and some with ON THE JOB TRAINING.

MANUFACTURERS' NEW ORDERS. The dollar volume of net new orders received by all manufacturers. These orders are further classified as durable and nondurable goods and by industry.

MANUFACTURERS' SALES AND INVENTORY EXPECTATIONS. The subject of a quarterly survey of manufacturing firms conducted by the U.S. Office of Business Economics. This survey collects data on sales and inventory expectations for the next two quarters. It also collects data on actual sales for, and inventories held at the end of, the most recent quarter.

Manufacturers' sales (or shipments) include receipts, billings, or the value of the products shipped, less discounts, returns, and allowances. Shipments for export as well as those for domestic use are included. *Manufacturers' inventories* refer to book values of stocks and include materials and supplies, goods in process, and finished goods. In general, inventories are reported as valued by manufacturers.

MANUFACTURERS' UNFILLED ORDERS. A measure of the dollar value of all orders that have been received by all manufacturers but have not yet passed through the manufacturers' sales accounts at the end of each month. Unfilled orders at the end of the reporting period are therefore equal to unfilled orders at the beginning of the period, plus net new orders received during the period, minus net sales. The data are classified by durability and by industry, although DURABLE GOODS account for approximately 95 percent of the total.

MANUFACTURING CAPACITY. The output a plant is capable of producing when its FACTORS OF PRODUCTION are fully utilized. Generally, the figure is given as a percentage of maximum capacity, or *utilization rate.* From 1960 through 1981 the figure has varied from a low of 72.9 percent in 1975 to a high of 91.1 percent in 1966. This statistic is of interest to economists because it helps them find correlations, trends, and other information for building models.

MARGINAL. Relating to *changes* in value, rather than *absolute* value. For an example, see MARGINAL COST. Actually, *marginal* refers to *small* changes— one unit if discrete items are being analyzed, an infinitesimal change if the function is continuous.

The everyday interpretation of the word, something that is insecure or subject to failure, is seldom used in economics.

MARGINAL ANALYSIS. Economic analysis which concentrates on *changes* in economic variables. For example, instead of examining what percentage of NATIONAL INCOME is saved, marginal analysis would examine what per-

centage of an incremental change in national income would be saved. See also MARSHALL, ALFRED.

MARGINAL BORROWER. One who feels that the next incremental increase in the interest rate (the price of borrowed money) will raise the price beyond the point at which he or she would consider borrowing.

MARGINAL BUYER. A person who will voluntarily buy an item at its current price but will no longer be willing to buy if the price is raised. In SUPPLY-AND-DEMAND analysis there are marginal buyers at every price, and the more inelastic (see ELASTICITY) the demand schedule, the more buyers will drop out as the price is raised.

MARGINAL COST (MC). The additional cost incurred by producing one more unit of a product. FIXED COSTS are not included, so, for example, the marginal cost of the 1,001st unit consists of only the material, direct labor, etc. that would not be required for the 1,000th unit. Building rent, interest on bonds, and other costs that "would have to be paid anyway" are not part of marginal cost. See COST for a listing of the various types of costs.

MARGINAL COST PRICING. A policy, used to minimize selling price or to lower costs to keep a business operating during a period of poor sales, by which the firm charges, for each unit sold, only the addition to TOTAL COSTS which results from manufacturing that unit— usually just material and direct labor. For example, if a firm that has developed a new airplane on a government contract owns the design rights, it might sell a commercial version for only the manufacturing cost, because development costs are already paid. In another situation, a firm might be temporarily unable to sell its products for a profit but wants to keep its workers ready for the expected upturn. Its FIXED COSTS such as building maintenance and rent have to be paid whether the the employees are laid off or not, so if it manufactures and sells a product for just marginal cost, its loss during that period will be no higher than if it lays off the work force and manufactures nothing.

MARGINAL EFFICIENCY OF CAPITAL (MEC). The change in earnings which will result from a change in expenditure on capital equipment. Also called *marginal efficiency of investment.*

MARGINAL LAND. Agricultural land whose yield is such that its use is profitable now but would not be if agricultural commodity prices were lower. As world population increases, marginal land is constantly being brought under cultivation, providing one of the major causes for inflation.

MARGINAL MANUFACTURER. A manufacturer who finds it profitable to produce a given item at current prices, but who, if costs increase or selling price decreases, will find it more profitable to make other use of available funds.

MARGINAL PHYSICAL PRODUCT (MPP). The same as MARGINAL PRODUCT.

MARGINAL PRODUCT (MP). The increase in output which results from using one additional unit of a FACTOR OF PRODUCTION while holding the other factors constant. The usual pattern is that when small amounts of a certain factor are used (see FACTOR MIX), adding another unit of that factor will bring about a large increase in output (increasing marginal product); but as more of that factor is added, the rate of increase in its product will decline and a point will be reached where marginal product begins to fall (diminishing marginal product). Also called *marginal physical product.* See also LAW OF DIMINISHING RETURNS.

Sometimes marginal product is identified for each of the factors of production; there is a *marginal productivity of land*, *marginal productivity of labor*, etc., but each figure is valid only in the specified circumstances.

MARGINAL PROPENSITY TO CONSUME (MPC). The probability that a group will consume, rather than save, the next dollar of income. The word *next* is significant; the MPC does not represent an average value over all income, but just the next (marginal) dollar. Therefore, the value of MPC is a function of the portion of the income curve being considered.

Since consuming and saving are the only two possibilities, the sum of MPC and MARGINAL PROPENSITY TO SAVE (MPS) must always equal 1.

MARGINAL PROPENSITY TO SAVE (MPS). The probability that a group will save, rather than consume, the next dollar of income. See MARGINAL PROPENSITY TO CONSUME.

MARGINAL RATE OF SUBSTITUTION (MRS). The rate, at any point on an INDIFFERENCE CURVE, at which the individual concerned is willing to trade one product for the other.

MARGINAL RATE OF TECHNICAL SUBSTITUTION (MRTS). The number of units of one FACTOR OF PRODUCTION that must be employed to replace one unit of another factor, in order to maintain a constant output. Thus suppose x bushels of a certain crop are produced with four men, using 1 ton of fertilizer on a given number of acres; if the amount of fertilizer is reduced by 500 pounds and it is found that five men are then required in order to maintain output at x bushels, the MRTS of labor for this reduction of capital is one man per 500 pounds.

MARGINAL RATE OF TRANSFORMATION (MRT). In an EXCHANGE OPPORTUNITIES LINE, the rate at which one FACTOR OF PRODUCTION can be substituted for the other while maintaining constant output.

MARGINAL RESERVE ACCOUNTING (MRA). A method of figuring outstanding bank liabilities for the purpose of determining reserve requirements (see BANK RESERVES). See LAGGED RE-

SERVE ACCOUNTING for other methods and a reference.

MARGINAL REVENUE (MR). The addition to total revenue which will result from selling one more unit.

MARGINAL REVENUE PRODUCT (MRP). The additional revenue which results from adding one unit of one FACTOR OF PRODUCTION while holding the other factors constant. MRP equals the product of MARGINAL PRODUCT times MARGINAL REVENUE.

MARGINAL SELLER. A person who is willing to sell at the current price but not at a lower price. In SUPPLY-AND-DEMAND analysis, marginal sellers are those who, at any given price, will not be in the market at the next lower price.

MARGINAL TAX RATE. The tax rate applied to a certain level of income but not to lower incomes. For example, if rate r is levied on incomes up to $20,000 and rate s (a higher rate) on incomes over $20,000, a person whose taxable income is $20,500 will pay r percent of $20,000 plus s percent of $500. Marginal tax tables ensure that a person's takehome pay (after taxes) is not reduced when that person receives an increase in before-tax income.

MARGINAL UTILITY. The degree of satisfaction or benefits which a buyer obtains from each dollar spent. Presumably the first dollar will be spent on a life-giving necessity such as food, and therefore that expenditure yields a large marginal utility (see UTILITY UNITS). After that want is satisfied, the buyer spends the next dollar on what he has the next strongest desire for. The theory of *decreasing marginal utility* holds that each dollar buys less utility than the previous dollar; this theory provides part of the justification for PROGRESSIVE TAXation. See also BALANCING MARGINS.

MARGINAL UTILITY SCHOOL. A branch of economic thinking in which analyses are based on MARGINAL UTILITY. The significance of this school is that it answers many questions which once puzzled economists, such as why gold, which is not important to the instinct of self-preservation, brings prices so much higher than corn. Also called the *Austrian school*, after the nation where it was made popular, it explains that price is a function of need, scarcity, and the satisfaction the item brings to individual purchasers.

MARGIN REQUIREMENTS. The minimum percentage of purchase price that a buyer in the stock market must provide in cash; the rest of the purchase price can be borrowed if the purchaser and lender agree. This requirement is set by the BOARD OF GOVERNORS (OF THE FEDERAL RESERVE SYSTEM) and is a form of SELECTIVE CONTROL of the economy; increased margin requirements reduce speculative stock market trading and therefore are CONTRACTIONARY.

MARGIN TRADING. In the securities market, buying of a security by paying cash for only part of the purchase and borrowing the rest from the seller or broker. See TOOLS OF MONETARY POLICY.

MARKET. Sometimes refers to buying and selling of securities. See also MARKETPLACE; MONEY MARKET; PRODUCT MARKET; RESOURCE MARKET.

MARKETABLE SECURITIES. SECURITIES which have no contractual prohibition against change of ownership and therefore can be bought and sold at a price agreed upon between buyer and seller.

MARKET BASKET. See CONSUMER PRICE INDEX.

MARKET, BLACK. See BLACK MARKET.

MARKET CLEARING. See SUPPLY AND DEMAND.

MARKET CONCENTRATION. The degree to which large sellers dominate a market. A particular product might not have significant competition (that is, it might have a high degree of market concentration) in one geographical area, but might have active competition (low concentration) in other areas. See also INDUSTRIAL CONCENTRATION.

MARKET ECONOMY. An economy in which basic economic decisions, such as what should be produced, in what quantities, and at what prices, are made automatically and freely in the MARKETPLACE rather than by deliberate government direction. CAPITALISM implies a market economy plus private ownership.

MARKET, FACTOR. See FACTOR MARKET.

MARKET FAILURE. Situations in which the natural forces of a market economy produce results that are not best for consumers or the economy in general. For example, a considerable amount of our pollution and deterioration of the environment can be traced to the pressures of competition, and free public education would not appear through forces of SUPPLY AND DEMAND. Market failure is the justification for MIXED CAPITALISM—a mixture of free enterprise and government controls.

MARKET FORCES. See MARKETPLACE.

MARKET, GRAY. See GRAY MARKET.

MARKET MECHANISMS. See MARKETPLACE.

MARKET MODEL. A description of the functioning of the market in which certain products are traded. One of the market models is PURE COMPETITION, meaning large numbers of sellers and buyers acting independently. Other models are OLIGOPOLY, OLIGOPSONY, MONOPOLY, MONOPOLISTIC COMPETITION, and MONOPSONY.

MARKETPLACE. In economics, the occurrence of transactions, rather than a physical location. Thus, all transactions

(sales of goods and services, store sales, catalog sales, sales in the customer's home, etc.) are said to occur in the marketplace.

The *marketplace* leads to expressions such as *market forces*, or *market mechanisms*, which refer to all the determinants, except direct government action, which help to answer the basic economic questions, such as what quantity should be provided and what should the price be. Because these market forces are free and not centrally planned, CAPITALISM is often called a *market economy*.

MARKET PRICE. Same as MARKET VALUE.

MARKET, RESOURCE. See FACTOR MARKET.

MARKET SHARE. The percentage of total sales of a product which one seller has. For example, if the total market for a product is 1,000,000 and one manufacturer sells 50,000, his share of the market is 5 percent. Market share is important because it is possible for a manufacturer to increase sales every year and still be a shrinking firm if the total market is increasing faster than his sales (his share is declining). Also called *share of the market*.

MARKET SHARING. Agreement among sellers who would otherwise be competitors for each to sell exclusively in a certain part of the market. The division may be by geography, price, product, time, or other criteria which reduce competition. Such agreements are generally illegal.

MARKET SUPPLY SCHEDULE. A schedule of the aggregate amount of a product which an entire industry will supply at various prices. See SUPPLY AND DEMAND. Also called *industry supply schedule*.

MARKET VALUE. The price that can be obtained by selling an item. With some items, such as NONDURABLE consumer goods, market value is generally set by the seller and changes infrequently; other items may be negotiated, and market value is known only after a transaction has taken place. See also BOOK VALUE.

MARKUP. The difference between what a merchant pays for an item and what he receives when selling it. Markup is often confused with profit, which is the amount remaining out of markup after expenses, such as wages, rent, advertising, and interest on debt, are subtracted. Sometimes called *gross profit*

MARKUP INFLATION. A period of rising prices triggered by some firms' increasing their MARKUP rates. It is difficult if not impossible to pinpoint a start to and cause for inflation, but labels such as this one, COST-PUSH, and DEMAND-PULL are helpful for purposes of analysis and corrective action.

MARKUP PRICING. A policy by which a fixed increase (usually a fixed percentage) is added to the purchase price of an item in order to determine the selling price. This policy often sets a target price, which is then adjusted according to competition.

MARSHALL, ALFRED. A professor of economics at Cambridge University whose background in mathematics led to advances in analytic methods of economic analysis. Marshall's writings, such as *Principles of Economics* (1890), were instrumental in the formation of the NEOCLASSICAL SCHOOL of economic thought. During his lifetime (1842-1924), he also developed the concepts of CONSUMERS' SURPLUS, DIMINISHING MARGINAL UTILITY, and MARGINAL ANALYSIS.

MARSHALL PLAN. See EUROPEAN RECOVERY PROGRAM.

MARX, KARL. Best known for socialist theories and for the pamphlet *The Communist Manifesto* (1848) and the book DAS KAPITAL (1867). The latter was written in collaboration with Friedrich Engels; Marx (1818-1883) died after Volume 1 was released and Engels did the final editing and oversaw the release of Volumes 2 and 3. These writings held

that capitalists were reaping the benefit of workers' labor and they predicted and encouraged uprisings and the violent overthrow of capitalism. Marx's writings were based on the small time period he observed—the period of the Industrial Revolution, when social and economic systems were in transient conditions, seeking stability.

MASS MARKETING. Advertising, packaging, pricing, and other promotional activities designed to appeal to large numbers of consumers. It is expected that large numbers of sales will result with little or no additional help from sales personnel, as when a certain brand of toothpaste is mass marketed and then consumers select that item from retailers' shelves.

MASS PICKETING. Appearance of large numbers of strikers (who may or may not be employees of the employer being picketed), usually in excess of the number legally allowed.

MASS PRODUCTION. Production of a large quantity of an identical item. There are two points of significance to this expression: (1) production methods can be studied and standardized, with heavy use of manual and automatic machinery (see AUTOMATION; CAPITAL INTENSIVE; ECONOMIES OF SCALE); (2) MASS MARKETING techniques must be used to create or continue final demand for a large quantity of these identical products.

MATCHED SALE-PURCHASE TRANSACTION. As part of their open market operations (see FEDERAL OPEN MARKET COMMITTEE—FOMC), the Federal Reserve may sell TREASURY BILLs for cash and simultaneously purchase the same issue of bills for delivery a day or more later. By this technique they can absorb reserves temporarily and in very large volume without affecting NONBORROWED RESERVES for more than a few days. These transactions, plus REPURCHASE AGREEMENTs, enable the FOMC to affect reserves with much less impact on interest rates of securities than if the same amount of reserves was absorbed or supplied by outright sales or purchases.

MATHEMATICAL ECONOMICS. When a significant amount of advanced mathematics and statistics are used in economic studies, the field is called *econometrics.* See also MANAGEMENT SCIENCE and the appendix.

MATURE ECONOMY. In the study of economic development, an economy is generally considered *mature* when its productive capability can provide sufficient necessities and further growth will be concentrated in services and an improved standard of living.

MATURITY. Completion of the period for which a debt was created. For example, when a bond is to mature in ten years, the creditor can at that time return his bond to the debtor for return of the face value.

MATURITY VALUE. The value which a BOND will return to its owner when the bond is bought back by its issuer at the end of the stated length of time. During the time it is outstanding, the bond's market value might vary considerably if interest rates vary (see EFFECTIVE RATE OF INTEREST), but the market value will approach maturity value as the maturity date approaches.

MAXIMIZING BEHAVIOR. Each ECONOMIC UNIT acting in a rational and logical manner. If an item is available at two different prices, and such behavior is assumed, it is expected that, other things being equal, a buyer will buy the lower-priced one. See also SELF-INTEREST.

MAXIMUM INTEREST RATES. See INTEREST CEILINGS.

MEAN. See AVERAGE.

MEASURED INCOME. See PERMANENT INCOME.

MEASURE OF ECONOMIC WELFARE (MEW). A problem with GROSS NATIONAL PRODUCT (GNP) is that it is often misinterpreted as a measure of economic well-being or as an amount that is added to the nation's total value or net worth. Actually, it includes no corrections for losses; if a building is put up, destroyed, and replaced in one year, GNP will record the value of two buildings. Even NET NATIONAL PRODUCT (NNP) subtracts only capital goods which are used up. One of many suggestions is the MEW, to be used in conjunction with GNP. It would modify GNP primarily in three ways: (1) by subtracting estimates of certain costs such as pollution from the NATIONAL INCOME total; (2) by excluding some services, such as police services, since it is possible that the size of police budgets is a function of the level of crime, and actually represents a loss of well-being; (3) by adding to GNP some activities, such as household activities (housework, home repairs, etc.) and leisure, which reflect standard of living. [Adapted from "National Income Accounting and Economic Welfare: The Concepts of GNP and MEW," *Federal Reserve Bank of St. Louis Review* (April 1974), p. 18.]

MEASURE OF VALUE. One of the basic functions of MONEY. Also known as *standard of value.* See BARTER.

MECHANISMS OF THE MARKETPLACE. See MARKETPLACE.

MECHANIZATION AND MODERNIZATION. An agreement in October 1960 between the Pacific Maritime Association (an employer organization) and the International Longshoremen's and Warehousemen's Union. By the mechanization portion of this agreement, new machines and techniques of cargo handling were allowed; *modernization* here means relaxing of some restrictive work rules and practices. Employers agreed to pay $5 million a year for 5½ years into a fund to provide retirement pay and a wage guarantee.

MEDIAN. See AVERAGE.

MEDIATION. A form of settling labor disputes in which an outside agency or person acts as a go-between for the two parties attempting to reach a settlement. When both labor and management are convinced that the mediator is a disinterested party, it is likely they will accept his recommendations.

MEDIUM OF EXCHANGE. One of the basic functions served by MONEY. See BARTER.

MEMBER BANK. Nearly half the commercial banks in the United States are members of the FEDERAL RESERVE SYSTEM, and these banks account for about 79 percent of all bank deposits. National banks, which are chartered by the Comptroller of the Currency (an official of the Department of the Treasury) are required by law to be members of the System. Banks chartered by any of the states may elect to become members if they meet the requirements laid down by the BOARD OF GOVERNORS.

MENSHEVIK (U.S.S.R.). Revolutionaries who wanted to achieve Marxist goals by first replacing the Russian government with another by the BOURGEOISIE, expecting the latter to be replaced in a revolution of the PROLETARIAN CLASS. Bolsheviks, on the other hand, were in favor of moving directly to a DICTATORSHIP OF THE PROLETARIAT.

MERCANTILE AGENCY. A business organization whose "product" is information relating to the financial position of other businesses, usually for the purpose of evaluating credit worthiness.

MERCANTILIST. An economist who puts great emphasis on increasing a nation's holdings of precious metals such as gold and silver. This view was popular in the general period of the early 1700s to 1800. Policies were favored for each nation which tended to bring gold into *that* nation, and one of the main functions of government was considered to be legislating duties

and other actions which would promote this flow.

MERCHANDISE ACCOUNT. In international economics, the trade that takes place between nations. It usually appears as *balance of payments on merchandise account*, which is another expression for *balance of trade*. See BALANCE OF INTERNATIONAL PAYMENTS for more details.

MERCHANDISE TRADE BALANCE. The difference between the value of domestically produced goods exported to other countries and foreign-produced goods imported. The trade balance is generally regarded as favorable when exports exceed imports—a trade surplus.

MERGER. A combining of business enterprises in which all but one cease to exist as business entities. For example, if companies A, B, and C join together and will be known as company B, they have joined by merger.

A *horizontal merger* occurs when the combining members were performing the same function in the same product lines; a *vertical merger* occurs when the combining members were at different levels in the manufacture and distribution of a product; and a CONGLOMERATE merger occurs when the combining members were in unrelated fields.

MERIT INCREASE. A raise in pay granted to an individual, based on a review of his or her performance and the needs for the skills that person possesses, as compared to an ACROSS-THE-BOARD INCREASE, which is not based on individual merit.

METHODS OF FIGURING INTEREST. See INTEREST DATES.

MEXICAN BANKING SYSTEM. The CENTRAL BANK (Banco de Mexico) has been the focal point of the Mexican monetary system. On the one hand, it performs the traditional duties of a central bank, such as issuing currency, supervising the banking system, and advising the government on monetary and credit policy. In addition, it has assumed the nontraditional function of redirecting the flow of credit to specific sectors. Some activities, such as agriculture, have received this preferential treatment because their role in fulfilling the government's goal of development is generally regarded as essential.

The most important reallocation of credit, however, is a result of the central bank's position in financing government deficits. Through the mechanism of legal reserve requirements, the central bank allocates government domestic debt in the banking system. Funds placed on deposit at the central bank for reserve requirement purposes are used to purchase high-yield government bonds. The central bank extends the procedure to the reserves of investment banks as well as to commercial banks. As a result, funds available to the government through reserve requirements represent about 25 to 30 percent of total liabilities of the system. (Nonbanking institutions are another source of funds for financing government debt. Insurance companies and trust fund organizations, for example, are required by law to hold a certain portion of their financial assets in some form of public debt instruments.)

As is probably evident, the allocation and availability of credit are the primary concerns of the central bank. Unlike monetary policy in the United States, the cost of credit is not given a great deal of attention in Mexico. As a result, the level of interest rates in Mexico is not a very reliable indicator of central bank activity.

The National Credit Institutions are those financial intermediaries either partly or wholly owned by the government. Although considerably less important than they were 20 years ago, these institutions still play a fundamental role in the economy. They were originally established to give special priority in the allocation of domestic and foreign credit. Their funds have been directed mainly to agriculture, to infant industries, and for the promotion of Mexican exports.

These institutions compete with private commercial and investment banks for the savings of the public. In addition they are allowed to issue debt to the foreign public, for which there is government assurance of payment. The funds received are allocated at lower interest rates and longer maturities than those prevailing in the market, which is generally reflected in a lower profitability for these banks. Losses incurred by these institutions are covered in the government's budget.

Private financial intermediaries, which account for about 70 percent of total banking liabilities, are divided into the following functional categories: (1) deposit and savings banks; (2) investment banks; (3) mortgage loan banks; (4) capitalization banks; and (5) trustee institutions. All these institutions operate under the jurisdiction of the Ministry of Finance through the National Banking Commission. The Banco de Mexico is, however, the primary bank regulator.

1. Deposit and savings banks constitute the framework of the private banking system in Mexico. Their functions are similar to those of a commercial bank in the United States. Reflecting the demand for the relatively simple instruments which these institutions supplied, the deposit and savings banks experienced substantial growth between 1940 and 1955. Today the banking structure has changed and these banks have lost importance in relative terms. However, they still hold a high volume of savings in absolute terms.

2. During the early 1970s the investment banks, or *financieras*, attained a spectacular growth. Originally the financieras issued long-term paper, but the strong preference of the public for LIQUID ASSETs resulted in the issuance of sight-payable bonds carrying an 8.5 percent interest rate. As public confidence grew, it was possible to issue paper with longer maturities and high yields, such as *certificados financieros*. These instruments matured in 10 years, and their acceptance rose rapidly through 1960 to 1969. Instability of the international monetary markets after 1969 created a greater domestic demand for highly liquid paper with high yields. This development pushed

the financieras back on the money market, instead of the capital market for which they were originally intended.

3. The mortgage banks are similar in function to U.S. SAVINGS AND LOAN ASSOCIATIONs. The main instruments employed by these banks are bonds and *cedulas* hipotecarias. The latter are a form of mortgage secured not only by real estate, but also by the guarantee of issuing mortgage banks. These instruments offer a combination of high liquidity and moderate yield.

4. The capitalization banks, originally developed to act as savings banks, have been unable to compete effectively for funds. As a result, they have not grown in either number or total assets.

5. The Mexican banking system is supplemented by a number of financial institutions, such as insurance companies and social security trust funds, that either issue financial claims or facilitate the flow of financial resources between the various sectors of the economy. [Adapted from "Present Structure of the Mexican Banking System," *Federal Reserve Bank of St. Louis Review* (June 1973), p. 21.]

MEXICAN CENTRAL BANK. See BANCO DE MEXICO.

MEXICAN MIRACLE. Sustained economic growth in Mexico from the early 1960s through the early 1970s. During that time growth was exceeded only by Japan, and the rate of inflation was a constant low value.

MICROECONOMICS. Study of some portion of an economy, such as individuals, a company, an industry, or a SECTOR. See also MACROECONOMICS.

MILL, JOHN STUART. English economist and philosopher (1806-1873) who described himself as loyally in the CLASSICAL SCHOOL, saying that his writings were reworkings of those of earlier economists. However, it can be seen that he contributed some original ideas which redirected economic thought more than he realized. He showed that many kinds of work other than manufacturing and agriculture could be productive. He agreed with predictions of problems due to overpopulation (see MALTHUS, THOMAS), but he felt that they were avoidable. Some of his ideas were expanded upon by KARL MARX.

During his one term as a member of Parliament, Mill worked for the enfranchisement of women. His best-known contribution to economics is the book *Principles of Political Economy*, published in 1848, in which he claimed that there should be less dependence on natural forces and more reliance on deliberate actions by government. He felt that technology and planning could defeat the IRON LAW OF WAGES.

He also wrote *On Liberty*, stressing individual rights and the need to protect them from loss to the majority. An earlier book, *System of Logic*, published in 1843, demonstrated his versatility—by 3 years of age he was studying Greek and Latin and by 10 he had mastered algebra and geometry.

MILLER-TYDINGS ACT. See FAIR TRADE LAWS.

MINIMIZATION OF LOSS. An expression which recognizes that a firm seeking to maximize its profits must do so in the algebraic sense; the smallest negative profit (loss) is a form of profit maximization when loss is inevitable.

MINIMUM WAGE. A legally defined minimum which must be paid to all employees, regardless of management's analysis of their contribution. The objective is to raise the standard of living of those with fewer skills. This legislation is controversial because it is claimed that: (1) it adds to the unemployment problem of the less skilled because employers feel that although such workers may not be worth the minimum wage, they would be hired at a lower wage ("Would you rather be unemployed at $4 an hour or employed at $3.75 an hour?"); (2) it is inflationary because it raises costs, and so, although people with limited skills earn more money, they are no better off because prices are forced up. See also FAIR LABOR STANDARDS ACT.

MINOR COIN. A coin not made of the precious metal that standardizes the monetary system.

MINT. As a verb, to make metal into coins; as a noun, the place where coins are minted. In the U.S. the Bureau of the Mint is responsible for operating mints and for related functions. See also BUREAU OF ENGRAVING AND PRINTING.

MINTAGE. The amount charged by authorities for minting coins. It differs from *brassage* in that the latter is the actual cost, which may or may not be the amount charged.

MINT PRICE. The set amount, in terms of a nation's money, for which its monetary authorities buy precious metal (usually gold or silver).

MINT RATIO. The ratio at which a nation whose monetary system is on a BIMETAL STANDARD evaluates the two metals.

MIXED CAPITALISM. An economic system between pure CAPITALISM and pure COMMUNISM, but closer to capitalism, in which some personal property and some means of production are privately owned and some are owned by government. *Mixed capitalism* also implies that government exerts some influence over economic decisions in the consumer and industrial sectors; it also manipulates distribution of income and other measures of wealth. All capitalist nations today have some degree of mixed capitalism.

MIXED ECONOMY. An economy characterized by elements of various economic systems.

MIX, FACTOR. See FACTOR MIX.

MOBILITY, FACTOR. The ease with which FACTORS OF PRODUCTION are physically moved from one location to another. Since there are alternative ways that each factor can be used, as well as

alternative mixes of factors to produce a given result *factor substitution*, the FACTOR MARKET is characterized by competition of both buyers and sellers. However, anything short of complete factor mobility represents an imperfection in the competitiveness of the factor market.

MODE. See AVERAGE.

MODEL. A representation of some part of the real world which is being studied, usually for the purpose of determining the effect of certain changes that are being considered. In economics a model is almost always understood to be a mathematical model; some are as simple as an elementary equation, and others can comprise dozens of equations with nonlinear and interdependent terms. The more complex models have become practical only since the development of computers.

An economist develops a model by using a combination of logic, historical data, and sophisticated statistical techniques. Then, when the model has been tested and is in operation, it might be used by changing one of the variables (e.g., rate of change of MONEY SUPPLY) and observing the model's predictions of other variables (such as unemployment). See also ECONOMETRICS.

MONETARIST. An economist who holds the view that changes in the growth rate of money have important effects on spending, prices, production, and employment. According to this view the trend in the growth of money over extended periods (say, 4 years or longer) has a dominant effect on the trend of prices. Marked changes in the growth rate of money around this trend lasting about three quarters or more have effects on production and employment; but once a trend in the growth of money is reflected in prices, the production and employment effects vanish.

However, this monetary approach does not neglect the role of federal budget developments. Changes in government spending, in particular, have transitory effects on total spending in the economy for several quarters. These effects tend to be positive initially, and then are reversed as a CROWDING-OUT EFFECT of the financing of government expenditures results in reduction in private outlays. In addition, government taxing and spending actions can alter the allocation of income, affect long-term economic growth rates, and influence monetary growth rates.

In simpler terms, a monetarist believes that the most effective way to control a nation's economy is through MONETARY POLICY; employment, inflation, growth, and other characteristics are highly influenced by changes in the money supply. See also FISCALIST; SCHOOLS OF ECONOMIC THOUGHT.

[Adapted from "1973—A Year of Inflation" by Norman N. Bowsher, *Federal Reserve Bank of St. Louis Review* (December 1973).]

MONETARY AUTHORITIES. Individuals responsible for formulating and implementing MONETARY POLICY; in the U.S., principally the BOARD OF GOVERNORS (OF THE FEDERAL RESERVE SYSTEM) and the U.S. Treasury.

MONETARY BASE. Net monetary liabilities of the U.S. Treasury and FEDERAL RESERVE SYSTEM held by COMMERCIAL BANKs and the nonbank public. These monetary liabilities are MEMBER BANK reserves and currency in the hands of the public.

MONETARY POLICY. Exerting influence over the economy through control of money and interest rates. In the U.S. the FEDERAL RESERVE SYSTEM has basic responsibility for monetary policy, using three general tools:

1. *Open market operations.* Transactions of the FEDERAL OPEN MARKET COMMITTEE (FOMC) consist largely of buying and selling government securities from and to COMMERCIAL BANKs. Because transactions between commercial banks and Federal Reserve banks

are through reserve accounts (see BANK RESERVES), buying securities from commercial banks has expansionary tendencies (see MONEY).

2. *Reserve ratio.* See BANK RESERVES.

3. DISCOUNT RATE.

See also FISCALIST; MONETARIST; TOOLS OF MONETARY POLICY.

MONETARY RESTRAINT. Holding down the rate of growth of the MONEY SUPPLY or, in general, using contractionary MONETARY POLICY.

MONETARY TARGET. The variable which is actually measured and watched by MONETARY AUTHORITIES to determine the effectiveness of actions taken as part of MONETARY POLICY. The objective of monetary policy actions is smooth economic growth and a high level of employment, but these results are subject to delays and to many other influences. Therefore, when a policy action is taken (see TOOLS OF MONETARY POLICY), authorities select monetary targets, such as BANK RESERVES, MONEY SUPPLY, interest rates, and other measurable items, to determine whether they should continue, increase, or reverse their actions.

MONETARY UNITS. The accompanying table gives the names of some major currency units. Although some exchange rates change rapidly, some are given here (equivalent number of U.S. cents) for reference. These are the December 1979 figures from the *Federal Reserve Bulletin* (January 1980, p. A68).

Nation	Currency	Value (U.S. cents)
Australia	dollar	110.30
Austria	shilling	8.0039
Belgium	franc	3.5423
Canada	dollar	85.471
Denmark	krone	18.618
Finland	markka	26.830

Nation	Currency	Value (U.S. cents)
France	franc	26.614
Germany	deutsche mark	57.671
India	rupee	12.350
Ireland	pound	212.76
Italy	lira	.12329
Japan	yen	.41613
Maylasia	ringgit	45.931
Mexico	peso	4.3768
Netherlands	guilder	52.092
New Zealand	dollar	98.100
Norway	krone	20.092
Portugal	escudo	2.0036
South Africa	rand	120.79
Spain	peseta	1.5039
Sri Lanka	rupee	6.4300
Sweden	krona	23.935
Switzerland	franc	62.542
United Kingdom	pound	220.07

MONETIZE. To bring into the money system: When some item, say clam shells, is made the base of a monetary system, it is said that clam shells are monetized.

MONETIZED GOLD. The total value of gold certificates issued by the U.S. Treasury to the FEDERAL RESERVE BANKs.

MONEY. Economists have several definitions of what constitutes a nation's money supply. The suitability of each definition depends on the purpose of evaluating the money supply, such as evaluation of business potential, interest rates, stability of credit extensions, and many others. The following definitions were used prior to January 1982.

M1A included checking accounts and currency and coin in circulation (outside the U.S. Treasury, the Federal Reserve banks, and commercial bank vaults).

M1B included M1A plus negotiable order of withdrawal (NOW) and automatic transfer service (ATS) accounts at commercial banks and thrift institutions, credit union share draft accounts, and demand deposits at mutual savings banks.

M2 included all of M1B plus savings and small-denomination time deposits at

all depository institutions, certain overnight repurchase agreements and Eurodollar deposits, and money-market mutual fund shares.

M3 included all of M2 plus large time deposits and term repurchase agreements.

L included all of M3 plus other liquid assets.

In January 1982 the Federal Open Market Committee changed to a single M1 figure with the same coverage previously defined for M1B. M1 is often referred to as the *narrowly defined money supply*.

The United Kingdom uses similar definitions:

M1. Currency in circulation plus sterling demand deposit liabilities to the U.K. private sector. It does not include transit items or deposit liabilities to nonresidents.

M2. M1 plus time deposits at the clearing banks, certain other domestic deposit banks, and the discount houses. It does not include time deposits at the accepting houses, British overseas banks, and foreign banks.

M3. M1 plus time deposit liabilities to the U.K. private sector in both sterling and foreign currencies plus deposits of the U.K. public sector. It does not include deposit liabilities to nonresidents.

In "Britain's New Monetary Control System" by Dorothy B. Christelow [*Monthly Review of the Federal Reserve Bank of New York* (January 1974, p. 15)], the following explanation is given:

M2 has been rendered obsolete by institutional changes associated with monetary reforms. . . . Prior to 1971, time deposits at clearing banks, certain other domestic deposit banks, and discount houses were of very short maturity, generally seven day's notice, whereas time deposits at accepting houses, British overseas banks, and foreign banks were for longer maturities. Beginning in 1971, the clearing and other deposit banks offered deposit facilities similar to those offered by other banks, destroying the validity of the distinction between M2 and M3.

There are two types of demand deposits: (1) *primary deposits*, which result from a depositor's taking money into a bank and depositing it in his account, and (2) *derivative deposits*, which result from the bank's making loans by crediting borrowers' accounts with the amount loaned (bank-created money). A bank can loan in this manner an amount equal to its excess reserves (see BANK RESERVES); then, when checks written against the derivative deposit are cleared, the bank will neither have excess reserves nor be deficient in reserves. If checks so written become primary deposits for other banks, those banks will be able to make additional loans and the entire money supply can be expanded by a multiplier whose value is the reciprocal of the required reserve ratio (see MONEY SUPPLY EXPANSION MULTIPLIER). In actual practice the multiplier has a value less than that because of LEAKAGEs, such as borrowers' taking cash instead of demand deposits.

MONEY BALANCE. See REAL MONEY BALANCE.

MONEY COST. The burden of some action or policy, measured in monetary units, as opposed to costs which are not easily measured in money, such as health, leisure, convenience, and others.

MONEY CREATION. See MONEY SUPPLY EXPANSION MULTIPLIER.

MONEY CRUNCH. A situaton in which potential borrowers DEMAND more MONEY than is available at existing interest rates. When interest rates (the price of money) do not perform the rationing function that price usually performs, a true SHORTAGE exists. Also called *credit crunch*.

MONEY FLOW. Tracing of payments for transactions as goods and services move through one or more sectors of an economy. See CIRCULAR FLOW OF MONEY; REAL FLOW.

MONEY, FUNCTIONS. See FUNCTIONS OF MONEY.

MONEY ILLUSION. Perception of a relation between dollars of income and well-being, without regard to other costs or to changes in the value of dollars.

MONEY INCOME. The amount of income a person actually receives, measured in current dollars. This quantity, like most statistics in economics, is generally used for making comparisons with money income at other times or other places; there are several ways that such a comparison can be misleading. First, dollars change in value, so any comparison involving different times requires a correction (see CONSTANT DOLLARS). The comparison must also take into account the changes in the environment during those years, but after making corrections for the differences in dollar purchasing power in two different times, how does the analyst correct for differences in population density, quality of air and rivers, medical care, security, etc.?

When making comparisons involving different nations, the usual method is to determine how much one of the incomes would convert to in the other nation's money (see INTERNATIONAL EXCHANGE). But again, stopping the analysis at that point disregards the questions raised in the preceding paragraph. The entire way of life in the two nations can be so different that money incomes, even if adjusted for international exchange rates, would give little or no indication of comparative well-being.

Another item to consider is *psychic income*, which is the amount of money a person imputes to nonmonetary factors, such as enjoyable work and security. By this measure it is recognized that nonidentical wages between employers are not necessarily inequitable, because employees, consciously or subconsciously, attach monetary equivalents to nonmonetary benefits that are not identical between employers. If the cost to the employer of providing the nonmonetary benefit is less than the psychic income as perceived by the employee, the employer's total labor cost will decrease. For example, when office buildings do not have windows and the additional wages required to obtain an equivalent level of work force are higher than the saving due to the windowless building, the total cost of labor is higher than if the psychic income (attractive work area) had been provided.

MONEY MARKET. Not a physical marketplace, but the entire part of the business SECTOR which deals with credit and LIQUIDITY. The securities traded fall into two general categories: *Negotiable instruments* are short-term credit instruments such as U.S. Treasury bills, commercial paper, bankers' acceptances, negotiable certificates of deposit (CDs), loans to security dealers, repurchase agreements, and federal funds. *Nonnegotiable instruments* are short-term loans to government securities dealers, loans of reserves among depository institutions, and Federal Reserve discount window loans to depository institutions.

MONEY MARKET CERTIFICATE. A CERTIFICATE OF DEPOSIT (CD) in a minimum denomination of $10,000 with a maturity of six months. The interest rate on money-market certificates is related to the yield on six-month Treasury bills, in accordance with regulations issued by the U.S. Depository Institutions Deregulation Committee.

MONEY MULTIPLIER. Ratio of the MONEY SUPPLY to the MONETARY BASE.

MONEYNESS. Closeness to being MONEY; ease with which an asset can be spent or exchanged for another item; LIQUIDITY.

MONEY STOCK. Same as MONEY SUPPLY.

MONEY SUPPLY. The amount of money a nation has, according to a certain definition of what money is. When a number is given in newspapers without further qualification, it is probably M1 (see MONEY for different measures). The accompanying table shows, for selected dates, the sizes of United States' SEA-

SONALLY ADJUSTED money supply as given by the 1982 *Economic Report of the President.*

	M1	M2	M3
1975	291.8	1024.4	1373.5
1976	311.1	1169.4	1302.3
1977	336.4	1296.4	1462.5
1978	364.2	1404.2	1625.9
1979	390.5	1525.2	1775.6
1980	415.6	1669.4	1965.1
1981	441.9	1841.2	2187.2

MONEY SUPPLY EXPANSION MULTIPLIER. One tool of MONETARY POLICY is discretionary control over the reserve ratio (see BANK RESERVES) by the FEDERAL RESERVE SYSTEM. Also called *deposit multiplier*. This ratio specifies the minimum percentage of amounts which a bank has in demand deposits that it must keep in reserves. Basically, a bank can create money by loaning out any amount it has in excess of this minimum (excess reserves); if the borrower deposits his loan in another bank, that second bank will then have additional reserves and can loan out some percentage of what was deposited; that borrower can deposit his loan in a third bank, and the process can be repeated as shown in the accompanying table, which is based on a hypothetical reserve ratio of 0.2 (20 percent).

The table shows that if one bank acquires excess reserves of $100,000, the entire banking system will be able to create another $400,000 and the total amount which can be loaned out will be $500,000. The *money supply expansion multiplier* in this example is 5; it can be demonstrated mathematically that the multiplier is equal to the reciprocal of the reserve ratio.

This calculation gives a theoretical maximum value for the multiplier; in practice the value is reduced by such LEAKAGES as borrowers' taking their loans in cash (cash drain) and banks' not loaning out the full amount they are allowed to.

A similar multiplying effect works (in reverse) during contraction of the money

Money Supply Expansion Multiplier

Cycle	Bank . . .	has excess reserves of . . .	and loans the entire amount to a borrower who deposits it in bank . . .	which must increase its reserves by 20% of the new deposit, or . . .	and 80% of the borrowed amount becomes excess reserves which can be loaned out to start a new cycle:
1	A	$100,000	B	$20,000	$ 80,000
2	B	80,000	C	16,000	64,000
3	C	64,000	D	12,800	51,200
4	D	51,200	E	10,240	40,960
5	E	40,960	F	8,192	32,768
6	F	32,768	G	6,654	26,214
7	G	26,214	H	5,242	20,972
8	H	20,972	I	4,195	16,777
9	I	16,777	J	3,355	13,422
10	J	13,422	K	2,685	10,737
11	K	10,737	L	2,147	8,590
12	L	8,590	M	1,718	6,872
13	M	6,872	N	1,374	5,498
14	N	5,498	O	1,100	4,398
15	O	4,398	P	880	3,518
16	P	3,518	Q	703	2,815
17	Q	2,815	R	563	2,252
18	R	2,252	S	451	1,801
19	S	1,801	T	360	1,441
20	T	1,441	U	288	1,153
21	U	1,153	V	231	922
22	V	922	W	184	738
Sum of other cycles		3,690			2,952
		$500,000			$400,000

supply, when MONETARY AUTHORITIES follow a restrictive policy.

MONEY WAGES. See MONEY ILLUSION; MONEY INCOME; REAL INCOME.

MONNET PLAN (Fr.). The first in a series of four- and five-year plans to develop the French economy systematically after World War II. The first plan, which covered the years 1947 to 1953, was designed to expand development of six basic industries; later plans applied to the econ-

omy in general, showing increasing concern about inflation, and to social issues. Also called the *First French Plan.*

MONOBANK. Usually applied to the Soviet Union's state bank (GOSBANK), this term refers to a bank which functions as a CENTRAL BANK and performs functions of a commercial banking system and other banking activities.

MONOCAUSAL THEORIES. Some investigators claim to have found a single type of occurrence that explains the overall course of economic history. For example, there is the *leader theory*, which holds that the world proceeds with very little change until a strong leader or thinker influences the course of history. Other monocausal theories are the *doctrine theory* (all major changes in history resulted from the introduction of new doctrines, such as religions, political systems, and economic systems), *political theory* (changes in governments explain major turns in history), and *war theory* (major directions in history occur only in connection with wars).

MONOCULTURE. A nation in which the citizens are of the same general background and have similar demands and interests. Economic development is generally difficult under such conditions because a cross-fertilization of ideas is lacking, and innovation is unlikely. In addition, a nation that depends on exports or a single product is vulnerable to embargoes, quotas, and other trade barriers if its product has competition from other exporters.

MONOMETALISM. Use of one precious metal (usually gold) as a standard for a nation's monetary system. See also BIMETAL STANDARD.

MONOPOLISTIC COMPETITION. A significant but not major departure from *pure* COMPETITION, where the latter is characterized by many independent buyers, many independent sellers, and free flow of market information. The last characteristic is usually missing or reduced in monopolistic competition, as when firms practice PRODUCT DIFFERENTIATION.

MONOPOLY. A MARKET MODEL in which there is just one seller of a product. Although a capitalist economy is based on the belief that COMPETITION will bring about the goods and services that are most desired, at the fairest price, it is recognized that competition can sometimes cause waste and inefficiency (MARKET FAILURE). For example, if a city were to be served by a large number of electric power companies, the extra cost of multiple distribution systems so that each consumer could have a choice of suppliers would more than offset any possible price reductions due to competition; there would also be a loss of ECONOMIES OF SCALE. The solution, under MIXED CAPITALISM, has been to have the government authorize companies to operate *controlled monopolies*; each such company is the only supplier in an identified market, but those suppliers are not free to set their own prices or the quality of their product. Usually a government agency is given responsibility for establishing prices, ruling on price change requests, ensuring a defined standard of service, and other controls. A business in this position is also called a *regulated monopoly*. See also GEOGRAPHIC MONOPOLY; SHERMAN ANTITRUST ACT.

MONOPSONY. A market condition in which there is just one buyer (as compared to monopoly, where there is just one seller). Monopsony, like competition, never occurs in a pure form but can be approximated—for example, when a large manufacturer buys all the output from certain mines (this is a geographical monopsony, because if the mine looked far enough, it could find other customers). Another example would be that of a large firm hiring all of the engineers (or all of any specialty) in an area (it is the only buyer of that product). Also called a *buyer's monopoly*. See also COMPETITION; OLIGOPOLY.

MONTHS FOR CYCLICAL DOMINANCE (MCD). An estimate of the time span required to identify significant cyclical movements in a monthly ECONOMIC TIME SERIES. Some time series, even seasonally adjusted ones, are quite erratic and therefore single month-to-month changes can be misleading when seeking information on cycles. MCD indicates the point at which fluctuations in the SEASONALLY ADJUSTED series are dominated by cyclical rather than irregular or erratic movements.

For quarterly series, a similar measure—quarters for cyclical dominance (QCD)—is used.

MOODY'S RATINGS. See BOND RATINGS.

MOONLIGHTING. Working at a full- or part-time job by a person who has another regular job. This item is important in economic analysis, mostly for the confusion it causes. For example, the UNEMPLOYMENT RATE depends on a careful definition of the amount of work that qualifies an individual as EMPLOYED, and a person holding two jobs is not counted as two employed persons. For some investigations it would be important to know how many of the employed have more than one full-time job.

MORAL SUASION. A form of economic control in which authorities explain a problem to the public and point out that actions of the public are contributing to the problem. The objective is to achieve voluntary cooperation, although moral suasion sometimes includes threats of direct government action if public cooperation does not result. One example is the use of GUIDELINES for reducing the inflationary impact of rapidly increasing labor costs. Also called *jawboning*.

MORATORIUM. A specified time during which a creditor cannot exercise his rights if a debtor is in default, or a specified time during which payments are not due. When payments are resumed, the amount due usually includes interest for the moratorium period. During economic disruptions, governments often declare moratoriums on certain debts in order to avoid having major effects of the disruption fall on a small number of individuals.

MORRILL ACT. Legislation of 1862 providing for establishment of colleges in areas of the U.S. where population was growing. Also called the *Land-Grant College Act*.

MORRILL TARIFF. Introduced by Senator Justin Smith Morrill in 1861, this legislation provided much of the revenue for financing the U.S. Civil War.

MORRIS PLAN BANK. A FINANCIAL INTERMEDIARY that specializes in personal loans but, unlike a FINANCE COMPANY, obtains funds by accepting deposits in the same way as a commercial bank.

MORTGAGE. A secured transaction in which title transfers to a buyer but the property is used as collateral for the loan with which the property was purchased.

MORTGAGE BANKS (Mex.). See MEXICAN BANKING SYSTEM.

MORTGAGE BOND. A BOND secured by tangible property, often real property. This instrument is contrasted to a DEBENTURE, which is backed by the general credit worthiness of the issuer rather than by specific property.

MORTGAGEE. The person to whom money is owed in a mortgage arrangement; the creditor.

MORTGAGE POINTS. Extra charge that mortgage lenders sometimes require the borrower to pay in addition to the interest. This extra charge is calculated as a certain percentage of the mortgage amount. For example, if two points are charged on a $50,000 mortgage, then 2 percent of $50,000, or $1,000, must be paid in addition to the stated interest. The borrower is therefore paying a higher price than if points were not charged! The effective rate of interest is higher than stated. In order to determine the true effective rate of interest when points are charged, it is necessary to deduct the dollar amount resulting from the point calculation from the mortgage amount and add it to the interest amount to be paid. The borrower is viewed as having the mortgage amount less the point charge amount, rather than the entire mortgage amount.

MORTGAGOR. The person who borrows money to purchase property, and pledges the property as security; the debtor in a mortgage transaction.

MOST FAVORED NATION (MFN) PRINCIPLE. See GENERAL AGREEMENT ON TARIFFS AND TRADE.

MOTOR CARRIER ACT OF 1980. Part of the deregulation policy of the federal government, this act changed the regulatory framework for the motor carrier industry. A large number of applications for authority to provide service were granted, the geographical and commodity authority in new certificates was broadened, and price reductions occurred in both the TRUCKLOAD and LESS THAN TRUCKLOAD sectors. The 1982 *Economic Report of the President* says, "The industry, although not fully deregulated, appears to be much more competitive than in the past."

MULTIBANK HOLDING COMPANY. A HOLDING COMPANY which uses its CAPITAL FUNDS to purchase capital stock of several banks for the purpose of exerting management control.

MULTIEMPLOYER BARGAINING. Labor negotiations involving a union and one or more employers.

MULTINATIONAL COMPANY. A firm with headquarters in one nation and significant operations in one or more other nations.

MULTIPLE CONTRACTION (EXPANSION) OF THE MONEY SUPPLY. An expression often used to emphasize that commercial banks create money, and therefore actions which create reserves can result in a multiplied effect. See MONEY SUPPLY EXPANSION MULTIPLIER.

MULTIPLE EXPANSION OF CREDIT. Creation of MONEY through the flow of newly created loans into deposits in banks. See MONEY SUPPLY EXPANSION MULTIPLIER.

MULTIPLIER. Any functioning of the economy such that magnified results are obtained from an original action. Some frequently used multipliers are the following.

Employment multiplier. The factor by which total employment will increase when one person is hired in a given industry or area. For example, in a certain city, statistics may show that when one person is hired in construction the increased spending by that person and his employer will result in another 0.3 new jobs in the city; the employment multiplier would be 1.3. The multipliers usually have values between 1.05 and 1.5, although numbers outside this range do occur.

Multiplier for money supply expansion. See MONEY SUPPLY EXPANSION MULTIPLIER.

Spending multiplier. When there is an increase in aggregate spending, the economic units who receive that money can respend it, and the spending power continues to flow in a circular path. However, each unit probably saves a percentage of what it receives [see MARGINAL PROPENSITY TO SAVE (MPS)] and therefore an amount originally spent would not continue indefinitely through the loop. If each unit saves an amount equal to the amount it receives times its MPS, the total contributed by the original spending of D dollars will be D times the reciprocal of MPS. This reciprocal is the spending multiplier. Also called *expenditure multiplier.*

Although there are several more multipliers, when the word is used without a qualifier, it usually refers to the spending multiplier, which is often broken into its component parts; an *investment multiplier* and a *government spending multiplier.* See also MONEY MULTIPLIER.

MUNICIPAL BOND. A BOND issued by a level of government lower than the federal, it can be a GENERAL OBLIGATION BOND or a REVENUE BOND. The significant feature is that interest earned is not taxable by the U.S. government.

MUNICIPAL ENTERPRISE. Essentially a business organization, but one that is owned by a city government and usually earns a profit or is self-supporting. Utilities, bus lines, and some recreation facilities are examples.

MUTUAL COMPANY. See INVESTMENT COMPANY.

MUTUAL INTERDEPENDENCE. Two or more economic units (usually nations), each of which provides something essential to the other(s). By working together, each economic unit benefits.

MUTUAL SAVINGS BANK. A nonprofit depository type of FINANCIAL INTERMEDIARY which obtains all its funds from deposits (issues no capital stock), and invests mostly in real estate. Earned surplus is distributed among depositors, and in years when there are losses they are shared by depositors through deductions from their accounts. Deposit insurance is available from the FEDERAL DEPOSIT INSURANCE CORPORATION and other organizations. The expression *savings bank* usually refers to a mutual savings bank.

N

NARODNA BANKA JUGOSLAVIJE (Yugo.). The CENTRAL BANK of Yugoslavia. See NATIONAL BANK OF YUGOSLAVIA.

NARROWLY DEFINED MONEY SUPPLY. See MONEY.

NATION. Since early in the 20th century communication technology has enabled an entire nation to function and be coordinated as an economic unit. See MANOR.

NATIONAL AMBIENT AIR QUALITY STANDARDS (NAAQS). Primary and secondary standards established by the U.S. Environmental Protection Agency, as required by the CLEAN AIR ACT. Primary NAAQS are set at levels judged to be adequate to protect the public health, with a margin of safety. Secondary standards are set at levels that protect the public welfare, and cover such things as property damage.

NATIONAL ASSOCIATION OF SECURITIES DEALERS (NASD). An organization whose members are individuals and companies that provide dealer and broker services in OVER-THE-COUNTER STOCKs. One of the functions of the organization is to license individuals to work in the industry, after they pass a competency test.

NATIONAL BANK. A COMMERCIAL BANK which has a federal charter; it is required that the word *national* be used in the bank's name. National banks, like STATE BANKs, are prohibited from operating in more than one state, although they may have branches in other countries. See also McFADDEN-PEPPER ACT.

NATIONAL BANKING ACT. This legislation of 1863 was an early step toward establishing a stable and uniform currency. This act required that all national banks meet uniform regulations, back their note issues by government bonds, limit the total amount issued to their paid-in capital, and maintain a fund of lawful money in the U.S. Treasury for their redemption.

In 1864 another National Banking Act was passed as a reform measure to replace the inadequate bill of 1863; it provided for a system of NATIONAL BANKs to supplement STATE BANKs, which had previously composed the entire banking system. The office COMPTROLLER OF THE CURRENCY was created by this act. Also called the *National Currency Act.*

NATIONAL BANK OF YUGOSLAVIA (Narodna Banka Jugoslavije). The CENTRAL BANK of Yugoslavia, completely government owned and operated. It is not as much a part of the total banking system as is the central bank of other communist nations, but unlike the situation in western nations, its responsibility goes far beyond administration of MONETARY POLICY.

NATIONAL BOARD FOR PRICES AND INCOMES (U.K.). An organization created by the NATIONAL PLAN to administer anti-inflation measures.

NATIONAL COAL BOARD (U.K.). The organization created by the Coal Industry NATIONALIZATION ACT of 1946 to manage coal mining.

NATIONAL COMMISSION ON SOCIAL SECURITY REFORM. A commission appointed to examine problems of the social security system and propose solutions to both the short-run and the long-run problems by January 1983. As expected, the result was a combination of an increase in retirement age, a decrease in benefits relative to prior earnings, and an increase in contribution rates.

NATIONAL CREDIT COUNCIL (Fr.). An organization created after nationalization of the CENTRAL BANK (Bank of France) in 1946 to work for regulation of commercial banks and for MONETARY POLICY. Members of the Council are drawn from private as well as public sources.

NATIONAL CREDIT UNION ADMINISTRATION (NCUA). The U.S. government agency that supervises, charters, and insures federal credit unions. NCUA also insures state-chartered credit unions that apply and qualify for insurance, and operates a credit facility for member credit unions.

NATIONAL CURRENCY. An early form of paper currency in the U.S., no longer issued.

NATIONAL CURRENCY ACT. Original name for the NATIONAL BANKING ACT.

NATIONAL DEBT. The algebraic sum of DEFICIT (+) and SURPLUS (−) spending by the federal government, assuming that surpluses are used to retire some debt and that deficits are financed by borrow-

ing. There is considerable disagreement about the benefits and dangers of a national debt. Some argue that, since most of the debt is owed to citizens of the U.S., it is an internal debt and therefore not the same as a business or personal debt. Proponents also argue that the debt gives a means of providing social goods, provides the means for most of MONETARY POLICY (see FEDERAL OPEN MARKET COMMITTEE), and makes FISCAL POLICY possible. Opponents of permanent debt argue that deficit spending makes excessive government spending too convenient, that debt and interest payments cause an undesirable redistribution of income and remove flexibility from fiscal policy, and that coercive methods are used to sell debt instruments to employees of the government and its contractors.

NATIONAL EMERGENCY DISPUTE. Labor-management negotiations which, if deadlocked, could result in a strike endangering national safety, health, or welfare. See TAFT-HARTLEY ACT.

NATIONAL FEDERATION OF INDUSTRIAL ORGANIZATIONS (Jap.) (Shinsanbetsu). A confederation of labor unions, about one-sixtieth the size of the largest confederation.

NATIONAL HEALTH SERVICE (NHS) (U.K.). The social agency that provides government-paid medical care for U.K. citizens. It is financed through general funds as well as payroll taxes levied on employers and employees.

NATIONAL INCOME (NI). In U.S. NATIONAL INCOME AND PRODUCT ACCOUNTS this item represents aggregate earnings which arise from current production of goods and services, inclusive of taxes on those earnings. NI consists of compensation of employees, profits of incorporated and unincorporated enterprises, net interest, and rental income of persons. Profits of government enterprises are not included; they are treated as charges against the value of output not attributable to any particular FACTOR

OF PRODUCTION. However, wages earned by government employees are included in NI.

NATIONAL INCOME AND PRODUCT ACCOUNTS (NIA). A detailed description of the overall U.S. economy. These accounts depict in dollar terms the volume, composition, and use of the nation's output of goods and services. There are two principal points of view: (1) the value of all goods and sevices produced (product side of the account); (2) the costs incurred and payments received in producing all goods and services (income side of the account).

Because the National Income and Product Accounts offer a total picture, these accounts are basic tools used in analyzing past and current performance of the economy and also in forecasting future economic developments. Furthermore, this quantitative framework makes these accounts of great importance in the formulation of national economic policies.

All entries except WAGE AND SALARY DISBURSEMENTS are on an accrual basis. See also GROSS NATIONAL PRODUCT. The accompanying table gives a summary of the accounts; most terms in the table are explained in entries throughout this dictionary.

National Income and Product Accounts

Charges against Gross National Product	Gross National Product
Compensation of employees Wages and salaries: Disbursements Wage accruals less disbursements Supplements to wages and salaries: Employer contributions for social insurance Other labor income	*Personal consumption expenditures* Durable goods Nondurable goods Services
Proprietors' income	*Gross private domestic investment* Fixed investment: Nonresidential structures Producers' durable equipment
Rental income of persons	Residential structures
Corporate profits and inventory valuation adjustment Profits before tax: Profits tax liability Profits after tax dividends undistributed profits Inventory valuation adjustment	Change in business inventories Net exports of goods and services: Exports Imports
Net interest	*Government purchases of goods and services* Federal: National defense Other
National income	State and local
Business transfer payments *Indirect business tax and nontax liability* less: *Subsidies less current surplus of government enterprises* *Capital consumption allowances* *Statistical discrepancy*	

NATIONAL INCOME DOUBLING PLAN (Jap.). A detailed economic plan for the years 1961-1970, which began with increased investment incentives intended to bring about an overall growth of the Japanese economy and eventually a doubling of national income. The results were mixed, exceeding the goal rate of growth in some areas but falling short in others, exceeding money income growth in some areas but falling short in others, and creating an undesirable degree of inflation. In 1967 a five-year plan, the ECONOMIC AND SOCIAL DEVELOPMENT PLAN, became the official plan.

NATIONAL INDUSTRIAL RECOVERY ACT (NIRA). One of the NEW DEAL measures, this legislation created the NATIONAL RECOVERY ADMINISTRATION.

NATIONAL INSURANCE (U.K.). A compulsory program for every citizen of working age, financed by payroll taxes on employers and employees as well as by the general fund. Payments are made for sickness, maternity, retirement, death, and other losses.

NATIONALIZATION. Transfer from private to public ownership, sometimes with consent of the private owners, but more often without consent; sometimes with fair compensation to former owners, sometimes with no payment. Nationalization has been applied to bits of property and to entire industries. One frequent occasion for nationalization is when a new government assumes control of a nation and seeks to increase public feeling by nationalizing industries owned by foreigners.

NATIONALIZATION ACT (U.K.). Short name for COAL INDUSTRY NATIONALIZATION ACT of 1946 by which the coal mining industry was nationalized.

NATIONAL LABOR RELATIONS ACT. The main piece of U.S. labor legislation from July 5, 1935, until it was included in the TAFT-HARTLEY ACT on June 23, 1947. One of the continuing acomplishments was creation of the National Labor Relations Board (NLRB), which has authority for writing and interpreting labor legislation, CERTIFICATION, and more. Officially known as the *Wagner Act*, this legislation specifically gave labor the right to organize and required that management recognize collective bargaining units.

NATIONAL MONETARY COMMISSION. After ten years in which there was only one relatively minor panic, the U.S. was disrupted by the panic of 1907, and so the Aldrich-Vreeland Act enabled the appointment of this commission in 1908. Its purpose was to make a thorough study of the monetary and banking system and to make recommendations for remedying the defects discovered. The report, called the *Aldrich Plan* and published in 1911, included several features that became part of the FEDERAL RESERVE SYSTEM, which was created in 1913.

NATIONAL PENSION FUND (Swed.). A financial organization that obtains funds from taxes which are assessed specifically for pensions; it uses the money mostly to purchase government bonds. The fund is operated by a board with membership from industry, unions, and government.

NATIONAL PLAN (U.K.). A wide-based design, sent to Parliament in 1965, aimed at alleviating some chronic economic problems. Some of the domestic goals were redeployment of industry for a more satisfactory overall national development, achievement of greater efficiency in labor through manpower mobility, geographically and between skills; increased efficiency through more use of capital equipment; and control over inflation. The major international concern was unfavorable balance of trade. As part of the anti-inflation measures a *prices and incomes policy* and a *National Board for Prices and Incomes* were created, with only advisory powers at first and punitive powers later.

NATIONAL PRODUCT. See GROSS NATIONAL PRODUCT.

NATIONAL RECOVERY ADMINIS-TRATION (NRA). An agency created by the National Industrial Recovery Act of June 1933 as one of the NEW DEAL measures. The objective was to start business on its return to economic growth by using measures such as industrywide codes of fair competition (over 500 were approved by the NRA in one year) and minimum standards regarding working hours, conditions, and wages. In effect, many antitrust requirements were temporarily overlooked. The act was declared unconstitutional in 1935.

NATIONAL SECURITY EXCHANGE. An exchange where SECURITIES of many companies are traded, regardless of the location of the company, as opposed to a regional security exchange, where only companies in that geographical area are listed.

NATIONAL TAX ADMINISTRATION (Fr.). The central tax authority which arranges and approves nearly all taxes, including those that will provide revenue to local governments. The administration collects national taxes and most of the local ones, then turns over those that are marked for local use.

NATURAL CAPITAL. ECONOMIC RESOURCES are generally identified as land, labor, capital, and entrepreneurial ability, where the two nonhuman resources, land and capital, are, respectively, the resources provided by nature and the items made by man to help in his productive efforts. Another view is that both of these nonhuman resources are capital; land is *natural capital*; tools, machines, and other items made by humans are *artificial capital*.

NATURAL GAS POLICY ACT (NGPA). Natural gas regulation was changed substantially with passage of this 1978 act. A small amount of (high cost) new gas was deregulated under NGPA almost immediately, and the price of between 40 and 60 percent of all gas was scheduled for deregulation on January 1, 1985. The price of a smaller volume of gas was scheduled for deregulation on July 1, 1987. Under NGPA, price controls were extended to gas sold in intrastate markets. About 20 categories of gas were created, each with its own ceiling price and inflation adjustment or other escalation factor.

NATURAL MONOPOLY. A MONOPOLY that is created because it is impractical to have COMPETITION, as when the position of consumers would not be improved by having 30 water companies offering their services to every household in a certain city. The extra cost of installing 30 sets of pipes would more than offset any possible price reduction brought about by competition. In the U.S., most natural monopolies are *regulated* monopolies, including privately owned utility companies.

NATURAL RATE OF UNEMPLOY-MENT. See NORMAL UNEMPLOYMENT.

NEAR MONEY. A measure of wealth one step away from being used directly in a transaction. The most generally accepted definition of MONEY includes only DEMAND DEPOSITs plus paper currency and coin in circulation; those are the items that a person can take into a store and use to make a purchase. Many financial assets (dollars) are also held in the form of savings accounts, government bonds, and similar forms; dollars in those forms are called *near money* because, for most transactions, it is first necessary to convert them to money.

NEGATIVE. In economics, many actions are understood to be effective in either direction, and it is common practice to consider one direction as positive and the other as negative. For example, deposits in a savings account are considered positive savings, but withdrawals are considered negative savings. The reason for this system is that algebraic addition of the positive and negative numbers will show the amount that is in the savings account. Several other examples are shown in the next few entries. See also NET.

NEGATIVE CORRELATION. Statistical connection between two variables such that an increase in the size, value, etc. of one is consistent with a decrease in the other. For example, quantity demanded and income level are negatively correlated for an inferior good (see INCOME EFFECT).

NEGATIVE EXPORTS. Imports. The negative expression is used because a sale of goods or services to another nation (an actual export) is a credit item in the balance of trade, and a purchase from another nation has a negative effect on balance of trade. *Net exports* is equal to actual exports minus imports (the algebraic sum of positive exports and negative imports).

NEGATIVE INCOME TAX. A general name for plans which are in effect in some nations and have been proposed in numerous forms in the United States. All such plans have one thing in common: Those who earn above a certain level *pay* income tax, and those below a certain level *receive* payments according to some formula. These receipts are the negative income tax.

NEGATIVE INVESTMENT. When CAPITAL CONSUMPTION ALLOWANCES exceed GROSS INVESTMENT, or when capital goods are wearing out faster than they are being replaced, investment will be a negative number. Also called *disinvestment*.

NEGATIVE SAVING. Reduction of savings. In the U.S. in 1932, DISPOSABLE PERSONAL INCOME was $48.7 billion and PERSONAL OUTLAYS were $49.3 billion, leaving PERSONAL SAVINGs of *negative* $0.6 billion. The conclusion is that during the GREAT DEPRESSION people spent some of the money they had saved during prosperous times. Also called *dissaving*.

NEGOTIABLE ORDER OF WITHDRAWAL (NOW). Originally an ar-

rangement for MUTUAL SAVINGS BANKs in Massachusetts and New Hampshire permitting depositors to earn interest on their accounts and still make withdrawals by a form of check. Since 1982, all accounts which pay interest on checking accounts, in banks as well as thrift institutions, are called NOW accounts.

NEGOTIABLE CERTIFICATE OF DEPOSIT (Negotiable CD). A time deposit liability issued by a U.S. bank in large denominations (greater than $100,000), and evidenced by a written instrument or certificate. The certificate specifies the amount of the deposit, the maturity date, the rate of interest, and the terms under which interest is calculated.

NEGOTIABLE SECURITY. A security, such as a BOND, which will be redeemed to any holder in due course; therefore a negotiable security can be sold before maturity.

NEIGHBORHOOD EFFECT. See SPILLOVER.

NEIGHBORHOOD YOUTH CORPS. One of the U.S. programs of the 1960s designed to fight poverty by helping the disadvantaged to upgrade themselves rather than by providing a continuing handout. This program provided subsidies to employers who hired unskilled youth from low-income families and trained them on the job.

NEOCLASSICAL SCHOOL. A school of economic thought that began in the mid- to late 1800s and is characterized by a reevaluation of the ideas of the CLASSICAL SCHOOL and an updating of technical methods of analysis. One of the main deviations from the classical school is a decreasing dependence on LAISSEZ-FAIRE, or leaving an economy entirely to natural forces. ALFRED MARSHALL (1842-1924) and his book *Principles of Economics* (1890) are associated with this area of economic thought. Among the changes it espoused was development of MARGINAL ANALYSIS, shifting the concentration from overall effects to individuals and segments. Also called *Cambridge School.*

NEOCOLONIALISM. The situation of politically independent nations' having their economies dominated by financial interests of other nations. Sometimes it is claimed that aid, both public and private, actually tends to exploit the workers and the natural resources of third world nations.

NET. Adjusted, usually by subtracting certain amounts from gross. Thus, net weight is the weight of the contents of a container, obtained by subtracting the weight of the container from the gross weight of the container with contents; net income is gross income minus certain expenses involved in obtaining that income; net national product measures what was put into the economy after subtracting from GROSS NATIONAL PRODUCT (GNP) the amount that was used in making that GNP.

NET BORROWED RESERVES. See BORROWED RESERVES.

NET BUSINESS FORMATION. See INDEX OF NET BUSINESS FORMATION.

NET CAPITAL FORMATION. Algebraic sum of expenditures on new CAPITAL GOODS (positive) and capital goods worn out and otherwise replaced in the manufacturing process (negative). The same as NET INVESTMENT.

NET EXPORTS (X_n)**.** The algebraic sum of exports (positive) and imports (negative) of all goods and services. It includes merchandise trade as well as *invisible* items, such as shipping charges, income on investments, rents, royalties, payments on insurance, donations, and travel costs.

Exports of goods, often referred to as *merchandise exports*, are valued to include all costs incurred up to the point of loading the goods on a vessel at a domestic port. Exports of services include items such as ocean and air fares paid to U.S. carriers, insurance, profits earned by U.S. business firms operating abroad, and earnings received from other U.S.-owned public and private assets located abroad.

Imports of goods are valued to exclude U.S. import duties, ocean freight, and marine insurance. Imported services include such items as military expenditures by U.S. service personnel abroad, travel expenses, ocean freight and marine insurance paid to foreign carriers and firms, and earnings of foreigners on their investments in the U.S.

NET FOREIGN INVESTMENT. See BALANCE OF INTERNATIONAL PAYMENTS.

NET INTEREST. In NATIONAL INCOME AND PRODUCT ACCOUNTS, the excess of interest payments made by the domestic business sector over its interest receipts from other sectors, plus net interest received from abroad. Interest paid by one business firm to another is not included because there is no net effect in the business sector. The same is true of interest payments within other sectors, as from one individual to another or one government agency to another.

NET INVESTMENT. Short for NET PRIVATE DOMESTIC INVESTMENT, result of subtracting CAPITAL CONSUMPTION ALLOWANCES from total expenditures on capital equipment (GROSS INVESTMENT). If capital equipment is being used faster than it is being replaced, net investment will be a negative number, called *disinvestment.*

NET NATIONAL DEBT. Adjusted value of NATIONAL DEBT after subtracting certain amounts, such as that part which is held by other government levels and agencies.

NET NATIONAL PRODUCT (NNP). See GROSS NATIONAL PRODUCT.

NET PRICE. The resultant price after LIST PRICE has been adjusted by discounts, allowances, and other credits.

NET PRIVATE DOMESTIC INVESTMENT (I_n). The adjusted figure obtained by subtracting CAPITAL CONSUMPTION ALLOWANCES from GROSS PRIVATE DOMESTIC INVESTMENT. Usually shortened to *net investment*.

NET REPRODUCTION RATE (NRR). The number of childbearers in one generation divided by the number in the preceding generation. When this ratio is 1.0 the population is steady (zero population growth), and when it is larger than 1.0 the population is increasing.

NET YIELD TO MATURITY. The total return on a bond from the time it is bought to the time it matures and is redeemed by its issuer. This yield will take into account the EFFECTIVE RATE OF INTEREST as well as any difference between the price paid and the amount returned by the issuer at maturity. Sometimes called simply *yield to maturity*.

NEUTRALITY OF MONEY. A proposition which holds that, although a change in the quantity of money may cause relative shifts in the types of goods and services purchased, the long run would find all prices changed in the same proportion and relative quantities returned to where they were before the change in quantity of money.

NEUTRAL MONEY. (1) Money supply whose size and availability is arranged so as to *allow* a planned result to take place, as contrasted to money which is used as a POLICY INSTRUMENT.

(2) Unit of money whose material content has the same value as the monetary unit it represents. For example, if $1 worth of gold is stamped into a $1 coin, the result is neutral money, also called a *full-bodied coin*. See also COMMODITY MONEY.

NEUTRAL TAX. A tax which affects every part of the economy to the same extent. It therefore does not cause a shift in spending, utilization, mix, or any other variable—just an overall reduction in the amount of money in the private sector.

For example a neutral tax that removes 10 percent of the nation's spending power will cause spending on milk, guns, automobiles, medical care, yachts, and every other product to be reduced by 10 percent. No tax is completely neutral; in fact, very few taxes are even intended to be neutral. A SUMPTUARY TAX is meant to be nonneutral, but a REVENUE TAX might be intended as neutral.

NEW DEAL. Name used by President Roosevelt to identify the series of programs and measures instituted during his administration in an attempt to end the GREAT DEPRESSION and its effects. Measures such as the FARM RELIEF AND INFLATION ACT and the EMERGENCY BANKING RELIEF ACT were just two of hundreds of steps taken in the early 1930s. The social security system was created during that time, along with significant labor legislation. In general, it is considered that the New Deal was the beginning of large increases in the size of government and the national debt.

NEW ECONOMIC POLICY (NEP). (1) In August 1971 President Nixon announced a New Economic Policy for the purpose of combating unemployment, inflation, and a balance of trade which had just turned negative. This policy had elements in three areas: As a FISCAL POLICY measure, Congress was asked to reduce government spending by nearly $5 billion and to reduce taxes by $7 billion to $8 billion.

In international trade, existing authority was exercised to put a SURTAX on imports, and buying and selling of gold in settlement of international accounts was ended.

Wages and prices were frozen at existing levels for a period of 90 days in hopes of breaking the momentum of inflation.

These actions were the beginning of a series of phases (I through IV) designed to improve the economy; the phases officially ended April 30, 1974, when the standby power expired.

(2) In a completely different sense, New Economic Policy identifies a program of economic reorganization in the U.S.S.R. from 1921 to 1928. NEP is generally thought of as a retreat from the ideology of COMMUNISM and terrorist revolutionary practices. It had become recognized that it was going to take many years longer than had been hoped for the ultimate form of communism to come about.

NEW YORK STOCK EXCHANGE (NYSE). Located in New York City, the nation's largest organization that provides a marketplace for buying and selling stocks, bonds, and other securities. See also AMERICAN STOCK EXCHANGE.

NIKKEIREN (Jap.). Japanese Federation of Employers Associations, one of the largest of several organizations to which companies and other associations belong. Some of their purposes include correlation of business activities and influence of economic policies.

NISHO (Jap.). Chamber of Commerce and Industry, one of the largest of several Japanese business organizations to which companies and other associations belong. Some of their main activities include correlating business activity and influencing economic policy.

NO LOCKOUT CLAUSE. Provision in a labor contract whereby the employer pledges not to shut his plant in order to force workers to agree to his conditions or to give up their demands.

NOMINAL PRICE. An amount which is associated with a product, although discounts, extra charges, and others may make the actual selling price higher or lower than the nominal price.

NOMINAL RATE. The rate of interest paid on a security, based on the face value of the security. Thus, if a bond with $1,000 maturity value pays $60 interest annually, the nominal rate is 6 percent. This rate compares to the *effective rate*, which is based on the amount actually paid; if an investor paid only $600 for the bond, the

$60 he receives would represent an effective rate of 10 percent.

NONASSESSABLE STOCK. CAPITAL STOCK whose owners are not liable for any amounts to the issuing corporation or its creditors.

NONBORROWED RESERVES. Reserves (see BANK RESERVES) which are owned outright by banks or are supplied by the FEDERAL RESERVE SYSTEM through open market operations. The opposite is *borrowed reserves*, which are supplied through temporary loans from the DISCOUNT WINDOW of the Federal Reserve.

NONCASH CIRCUIT. Flow of money in the form of book entries. The term has most significance in Eastern European economies where intermingling of monies in the noncash circuit and the cash circuit is less likely. For additional information see *Money, Banking, and Credit in Eastern Europe* by George Garvy (Federal Reserve Bank of New York, 1966).

NONCASH ITEM. In banking, instruments of value that will be converted to cash, such as drafts, notes, bonds, warrants, and coupons.

NONCONTRIBUTORY. Describes pension plans, insurance plans, and other employee benefits the entire cost of which is borne by the employer; *contributory* plans involve some payment by employees.

NONDEPOSITORY FINANCIAL INTERMEDIARY. A FINANCIAL INTERMEDIARY which does not obtain any of its capital funds by accepting deposits, as a bank does. One example is a personal FINANCE COMPANY.

NONDISCRETIONARY TRUST. Type of TRUST such that the trustee has little if any latitude in handling the funds, especially with regard to specific securities that the fund may purchase.

NONDURABLES. See DURABLE GOODS.

NONEQUALIZING WAGE DIFFER-ENTIALS. Wage differentials due to artificial forces, such as union power, rather than to natural forces, such as the SUPPLY AND DEMAND of labor, economic value of a worker, or skill required. A worker in a strong union may earn more than another worker of identical skills and who may be making the same contribution to the nation's productive effort. When skills are not identical, the analysis is more difficult, but in many situations it is obvious that the relative amounts earned by individuals of two skill levels are the reverse of what they would be in the absence of monopoly forces.

NONINSTITUTIONAL POPULA-TION. Total population minus those individuals who are in institutions, such as prisons or homes for the aged.

NONMEMBER DEPOSITORY INSTI-TUTION. A depository institution (commercial bank, mutual savings bank, savings and loan association, credit union, or U.S. agency or branch of a foreign bank) that is not a member of the FEDERAL RESERVE SYSTEM. Nonmember depository institutions that offer transactions accounts or nonpersonal time deposits are subject to reserve requirements set by the Federal Reserve, and they have access to the DISCOUNT WINDOW and Federal Reserve services on the same terms as member banks.

NONMONETIZED GOLD. That portion of total gold stock against which no gold certificates have been issued by the U.S. Treasury. From 1956 to 1972 the monetary (or Treasury) gold stock included gold sold to the U.S. by the INTERNATIONAL MONETARY FUND (IMF) with the right of repurchase. During this period, the IMF occasionally sold gold to the U.S. for dollars that were then used to purchase income-earning U.S. Treasury securities. Under the terms of these sales, the same quantity of gold could be repurchased by the IMF upon termination of the investment. In February 1972 both parties agreed to end this arrangement,

and the U.S. sold back to the IMF the $400 million in gold (at $35 an ounce) acquired under these transactions.

From 1965 to 1972 the monetary or Treasury gold stock included the $144 million gold deposit with the IMF at the Federal Reserve Bank of New York. In February 1972, that gold deposit was also turned back to the IMF.

NONPARTICIPATING PREFERRED STOCK. Preferred stock (see CAPITAL STOCK) whose ownership rights include a promise of a stated amount of annual dividend. If earnings are especially good, the corporation may distribute large amounts to holders of common stock, but holders of nonparticipating preferred stock will receive just their promised dividend. On the other hand, holders of *participating* preferred stock share, along with holders of common stock, dividends from unusually profitable years.

NONPRICE COMPETITION. When similar goods and services of several firms sell at or near the same price and SHAREs OF THE MARKET are not fixed, sellers compete by providing real or illusory differences among the products of each firm. Real differences can take the form of services, for example, an airline may have more frequent flights. Illusory differences (see PRODUCT DIFFERENTIATION) can be seen when one competitor advertises that you will be better off buying from him because he is large, while another advertises that you will be better off buying from him because he is small.

NONPRODUCTIVE INVESTMENT. Investment in CAPITAL GOODS that do not increase the firm's output, such as pollution control devices.

NONRECOURSE COMMODITY LOAN. A variety of the COMMODITY LOAN which the U.S. government makes as part of its price support programs. Under this arrangement, farmers borrow money, using stored crops valued at the supported price as collateral. If the crop's market value when the loan is to be repaid is less than the money due the government, the farmer can turn over the collateral in full and final settlement.

NONRECURRING EXPENSE. An expense that is expected to occur only one time, such as the initiation fee of a professional society. The repair or replacement of items that usually do not require it, such as a burned-out transformer, are sometimes considered nonrecurring expenses. This category can include predictable and nonpredictable expenses as well as accidental and deliberate expenses.

NONRESIDENTIAL FIXED INVESTMENT. In NATIONAL INCOME AND PRODUCT ACCOUNTS an item that includes capital expenditures by the business SECTOR for (1) new and replacement construction and (2) producers' durable equipment (such as machinery, office equipment, and motor vehicles).

NONRESIDENTIAL STRUCTURES. In NATIONAL INCOME AND PRODUCT ACCOUNTS, all new and replacement business expenditures on buildings such as factories, warehouses, and retail stores; expenditures on farm structures, schools, and hospitals; and all public utility expenditures on items such as railroad tracks and stations, and telephone, electric, and gas distribution systems. It also includes petroleum and gas well-drilling and exploration expenditures.

NONSIGNERS' CLAUSE. See FAIR TRADE LAWS.

NO PAR. Describes CAPITAL STOCK to which no stated value has been assigned. See PAR VALUE.

NO RAIDING AGREEMENT. In labor economics, an agreement among unions not to try to obtain members from each other.

NO STRIKE CLAUSE. An agreement in a labor contract that the union will not authorize a strike during the term of a contract.

NORMAL COSTS. The payments which, in a competitive economy, must be made to the FACTORS OF PRODUCTION in order to buy their inputs. Each factor receives its own type of payment (see FACTOR EARNINGS), and each can be further identified by adding the word *normal*; there are normal wages, normal rents, normal interest, and normal profits. Economists consider each of these a cost because without them there would be no output.

NORMAL DISTRIBUTION. The statistical distribution that results when the final outcome is due to random selection of a large number of variables. For example, the intelligence of an individual is the result of heredity, diet, environment, health, and literally millions of experiences; if a large number of individuals is checked, the distribution of their intelligences will follow a normal distribution. Because the graph of this distribution looks like the silhouette of a bell, it is often called a *bell-shaped curve*.

NORMAL GOOD. See INCOME EFFECT.

NORMAL PRICE. The price at which an item will trade if no unusual influences affect the price. See EQUILIBRIUM PRICE; SUPPLY AND DEMAND.

NORMAL PROFIT. The return that is required in order to keep a firm producing in a competitive economy (actually paid to the FACTOR OF PRODUCTION called *entrepreneurial ability*). Such profit is the theoretical amount which is achieved under conditions of pure competition over a long period of time. Any earnings less than normal profit encourage firms to leave the industry, creating forces that return profits to normal. If the industry's profits are higher than normal, the additional profit is called *economic profit*, or *pure profit*, and will encourage other firms to enter the industry, creating forces that will bring profits back down to normal.

Note the difference between economists' and accountants' definitions of profit. The former consider that normal profit is a cost of doing business, but accountants think of both normal profit and pure profit as profit.

NORMAL UNEMPLOYMENT. The UNEMPLOYMENT RATE which exists because of imperfections in job markets. Imperfections are such factors as absence of costless job information, lack of perfect mobility, membership limitation by unions, and licensing for purposes of restricting quantities of workers. Also called *natural rate of unemployment*.

NORRIS-LA GUARDIA ACT. This U.S. legislation of 1932 significantly strengthened the position of labor unions. Two of the best-known provisions (1) greatly restricted the conditions under which an employer can obtain an injunction ordering striking workers back to their jobs and (2) outlawed employment contracts in which workers are not hired unless they agree in writing not to take part in union activities (yellow dog contracts). Also known as the *Anti-injunction Act*.

NOTES PAYABLE. In accounting, liabilities which consist of PROMISSORY NOTEs that are due for payment during the accounting period.

NOTES RECEIVABLE. In accounting, assets which consist of PROMISSORY NOTEs whose payment is expected during the accounting period.

Nth CURRENCY PROBLEM. In international exchange it is a mathematical fact that if there are N countries with N currencies, there can be no more than $N-1$ independently determined exchange rates. One of the countries must be passive in its exchange rate to all the others. In addition, once $N-1$ countries fix their exchange rates with the Nth (or passive) currency, then their own exchange rates with each other—if they are to be consistent—are fully determined. See TRIANGLE ARBITRAGE.

NUISANCE TAX. A tax whose revenue just about equals the costs of administering the tax and therefore provides for little or nothing in the way of the SOCIAL GOODS that are expected of government.

O

OBSOLESCENT. Becoming out of date; as opposed to *obsolete*, which means currently out of date and clearly inefficient or even useless. Obsolescence is thus a transitional state. Its economic significance is that a part of our national worth (especially in capital goods) is obsolescent. In a period of optimism much of it would be replaced; at other times it would be continued in service. Therefore, a large amount of obsolescent equipment would be CYCLICALLY PERVERSE, tending to cause a reduction in AGGREGATE spending when the economy is slowing down and vice versa. In addition, productivity during an economic slowdown would decrease; it would increase after an economic expansion was well established.

OCCUPATIONAL SAFETY AND HEALTH ADMINISTRATION (OSHA). A U.S. regulatory agency that establishes standards for work environments. Many changes in safety rules and equipment have been implemented since this agency was created.

OCEAN BILL OF LADING. A shipping document (see BILL OF LADING) used for shipping goods between nations by water routes.

ODD LOT. In financial economics, CAPITAL STOCK is usually traded in *round lots,* which are almost always defined as 100 shares; any trade of less than a round lot is an odd lot. Most stock exchanges operate in round lots only, and therefore an individual who wants to buy or sell an odd lot must use the services of an *odd lot broker,* who trades from odd lots in his own PORTFOLIO.

OFFICE OF ECONOMIC OPPORTUNITY (OEO). Part of the U.S. *War on Poverty* announced by the federal government in 1964. This office coordinated economic programs aimed at improving the condition of the poor through improved health and education.

OFFICE OF MANAGEMENT AND BUDGET (OMB). Formerly the U.S. *Bureau of the Budget,* the OMB is operated within the executive branch to administer the federal budget and coordinate appropriations. See CONGRESSIONAL BUDGET AND IMPOUNDMENT CONTROL ACT.

OFFICIAL RESERVE TRANSACTIONS BASIS. See BALANCE OF INTERNATIONAL PAYMENTS.

OFFICIAL TRANSACTIONS (U.K.). One of the measures of economic activity, especially in the banking sector, official transactions consists of transactions on the London Stock Exchange by the BANK OF ENGLAND, the National Debt Commissioners, and various government departments.

OIL SHOCK. For decades business and consumer spending patterns reflected relatively stable prices of petroleum products, and so when the prices of those products took large jumps in 1973-1974 and again in 1979-1981, many short- and long-run adjustments, ranging from not using the extra gasoline required to stop for a hitch-hiker to creating whole new industries related to saving energy, were made.

OKUN'S LAW. Named for Arthur Okun, the economist who evaluated the relationship in 1962, an empirical rule which holds that, at unemployment levels higher than FULL EMPLOYMENT, each *change* of 1 percent in the unemployment rate will cause a *change* of 3 percent in the nation's total output.

OLD LADY OF THREADNEEDLE STREET (U.K.). Term used in the press and elsewhere to refer to the BANK OF ENGLAND.

OLIGOPOLISTIC INTERDEPENDENCE. Because OLIGOPOLY is defined as the departure from *pure* COMPETITION which results when there are so few suppliers that the actions of each will have some effect on the market, it follows that there is a significant amount of interdependence among oligopolistic firms. For example, the number of automobiles which firm A will manufacture in a certain year will be affected by the number manufactured by firm B, the price charged by firm B, the amount of advertising by firm B, and many other factors.

OLIGOPOLY. A market situation in which there are few large suppliers, in contrast to pure COMPETITION, in which there are a large number of small suppliers. On the continuum that runs from pure competition to MONOPOLY, oligopoly is near the latter.

OLIGOPSONY. A market situation in which there are only a small number of buyers, each relatively large, in the market. Quite often a firm which has an OLI-GOPOLY position with regard to its customers will be in an oligopsony position with regard to its suppliers.

OMNIBUS BUDGET RECONCILIATION ACT. U.S. legislation of 1981, planned by the administration to work together with the ECONOMIC RECOVERY TAX ACT, intended to restrain the growth of many open-ended entitlement programs. Another part of this act contributed to the deregulation of broadcasting; it extended the length of television licenses from three to five years and radio licenses from three to seven years, while establishing a lottery to determine who will get new licenses.

ONE-FIRM INDUSTRY. A MONOPOLY.

ONE PERCENT RULE. Guideline to an adequate level of aid for LESS DEVELOPED COUNTRIES, established in 1968 by the United Nations Conference on Trade and Development. It recommended that advanced nations should provide aid equal to 1 percent of their GROSS NATIONAL PRODUCTs. This aid was requested from both public and private sources.

ON LIBERTY. See MILL, JOHN STUART.

ON THE JOB TRAINING (OJT). A plan in which a person is hired and placed on the payroll with the understanding that he will learn the work he is to do by actually doing it. The usual method has been to begin with close supervision and gradually to lessen the supervision to levels normally found on the job. Sometimes these plans include a period of straight instruction, but generally the instruction consists of directions given at the work station.

OPEN ACCOUNT. With regard to a credit transaction, it is said that the account is open until final payment is made; the account is then closed. Sometimes the term *open account* is used to refer to a revolving charge account, where new charges and payments are continually being made.

OPEN-END CONTRACT. A contract providing an unspecified amount of goods or services over a period of time, which may or may not be specified. For example, a factory may sign a contract to purchase all its heating oil from supplier ABC, but at the time the parties sign the contract they do not know how severe the winter will be, so no quantity is specified.

OPEN-END CREDIT. A line of credit that may be used repeatedly up to a stated limit. It includes credit cards, charge plates, and check-overdraft accounts that allow for writing checks for more than one has in the checking account. TRUTH IN LENDING requires that creditors disclose the method of calculating finance charges and when finance charges will begin. Also called *revolving credit* or a *charge account.*

OPEN-END LEASE. A lease that may invlove a *balloon payment*—a payment based on the value of the property when it is returned at the end of the lease.

OPEN MARKET. Generally, a lack of restrictions as to which buyers and sellers can participate, what products are traded, what price may be used, what policies apply on credit, etc. However, *open market* has various meanings, depending on context.

OPEN MARKET COMMITTEE. See FEDERAL OPEN MARKET COMMITTEE.

OPEN MARKET OPERATIONS. See FEDERAL OPEN MARKET COMMITTEE.

OPEN MARKET PAPER. Negotiable financial instruments that are bought and sold by investors, providing financing (usually short term) for business and government organizations.

OPEN SHOP. An employment situation in which union membership is not a condition for employment.

OPERATING PROFIT. Profit of a business organization that results from operations which are the main purpose of that

particular business's existence. For example, if a textile mill sold its plant for more than it cost, the difference would be included in their profit but would not be operating profit; if a company whose purpose was real estate investment sold that plant at a profit, it would be operating profit.

OPERATIONS RESEARCH (OR). Use of analytical methods to develop empirical and theoretical relationships among variables in business and government. Mathematics, statistics, graphs, computers, and many other tools are used in OR. See also MANAGEMENT SCIENCE.

OPERATION TWIST. An informal identification of open market operations (see FEDERAL OPEN MARKET COMMITTEE, FOMC) of the early 1960s. Prior to that time, open market purchases had been limited, except in unusual circumstances, to short-term bills; in 1960 purchases were made of securities with maturities up to 15 months, and over the next several years the FOMC extended its practice of buying securities with longer maturities, some running beyond five years. It was hoped that this practice would help to hold up short rates (thus reducing the outflow of liquid funds) and to restrain the rise in long rates (thereby contributing to domestic economic recovery).

OPPORTUNITY COST. The amount a FACTOR OF PRODUCTION could have earned in some alternative use. One example often brought out in elementary economics texts is the total cost of a person's attending college full time: In addition to such expenses as tuition and books, there is the opportunity cost of the money the student could have earned if employed.

Businesses must recognize this as a real cost when making decisions regarding uses of funds. One weakness in the U.S. economy before the GREAT DEPRESSION was that high interest rates in the money market induced many large corporations to loan out their working capital rather than use it for expansion—the opportunity cost of using the money for expansion was too great to be disregarded. Also called *alternative cost*.

OPTIMUM POPULATION. If the world's population were extremely small, even though advanced technological techniques might be known, it would not be economically feasible to have such goods and services as large jet airliners, networks of highways, and inexpensive frozen dinners. Such items depend on mass production and large-scale usage. On the other hand, with a population as large as today's, attempts to derive pleasure and satisfaction cause displeasure to others, pollution, decreases in health, and many other negative effects. Optimum population is that number of individuals who can derive the greatest amount of per capita pleasure and satisfaction from life. Of course, there will be little agreement among economists as to a quantitative definition of optimum population.

OPTION. See STOCK OPTION.

OPTION CONTRACT. (1) Generally, a legal arrangement by which a prospective buyer pays consideration to the offeror and in exchange receives a binding promise to keep the offer open for a stated length of time. (2) In international exchange, an arrangement in which the customer is given the option of delivering the foreign exchange to (or receiving delivery at) his bank at any time within a specified period, typically a ten-day period at the beginning, middle, or end of a month. See also FORWARD EXCHANGE CONTRACT; SPOT EXCHANGE CONTRACT.

ORDER BILL OF LADING (OBL). A BILL OF LADING that is negotiable because each holder can assign his rights to another holder (*order* that his rights be transferred).

ORDINARY ASSET. A property of value which is expected to last for a relatively long time and is an item in which the

individual regularly deals. See also CAPITAL ASSETS.

ORDINARY RENT. Payment made to the owner for the use of a piece of land with CAPITAL GOODS or improvements attached. See RENT.

ORGANIC. Describes an approach to government in which it is assumed that the leaders have the desire and the ability to determine what is best for society as a whole.

ORGANIZATION FOR ECONOMIC COOPERATION AND DEVELOPMENT (OECD). Under the name of Organization for European Economic Cooperation this organization was created by Western nations in 1948 for the purpose of rebuilding the economies of Europe after World War II. The name was changed in 1960.

ORGANIZATION FOR EUROPEAN ECONOMIC COOPERATION (OEEC). See ORGANIZATION FOR ECONOMIC COOPERATION AND DEVELOPMENT.

ORGANIZED LABOR. That portion of the work force which belongs to unions.

ORIGINAL COST. Term usually applicable in a regulated industry (see MONOPOLY) where selling price and other terms are dictated by government in order to allow a fair return on investment. The regulating body determines the value of present investment by starting with the accumulated amounts actually paid (*original cost*) and adjusting for CAPITAL CONSUMPTION ALLOWANCES and other additions and subtractions. Also called *historical cost*.

ORIGINAL ISSUE STOCK. CAPITAL STOCK purchased directly from the issuing corporation rather than from a previous owner.

ORTHODOX SCHOOL. An expression sometimes used to identify the CLASSICAL SCHOOL of economic thought.

OTHER ASSETS. With regard to the CONSOLIDATED STATEMENT OF CONDITION OF ALL FEDERAL RESERVE BANKS, miscellaneous assets including accumulated interest and other accounts receivable, premiums paid on securities bought, and assets denominated in foreign currencies such as those acquired through the SWAP NETWORK. [From Federal Reserve Bank of New York, *Glossary: Weekly Federal Reserve Statements.*]

Accumulated interest represents the daily accumulation of accrued interest earned on government securities owned, government securities held under REPURCHASE AGREEMENTs, loans made to member banks, loans made to CENTRAL BANKs, and foreign currency investments.

Premiums represent the amount paid by the Federal Reserve above the face value of the securities it has purchased. Each day part of this amount is amortized into earnings. (This item is decreased and the OTHER CAPITAL ACCOUNTS decreased by an equal amount.) This amortization is at a uniform rate calculated to exhaust the premium on the maturity date of each security. A security purchased at a premium is treated on the books in this way because at maturity the Federal Reserve collects only the face amount of the security (i.e., over the life of the security its value gradually declines). The premium paid on securities bought under repurchase agreements is not amortized; it is paid back to the Federal Reserve when the securities are purchased by the dealer.

A *swap drawing* is a reciprocal credit exchange between the Federal Reserve and a foreign central bank where the latter exchanges on request its own currency for dollars up to a maximum amount over a limited period of time, such as three or six months. In a swap drawing, the *other assets* item is increased and the DEPOSITS: FOREIGN liability item increased by an equal amount.

OTHER CAPITAL ACCOUNTS. With regard to the CONSOLIDATED STATE-

MENT OF CONDITION OF ALL FEDERAL RESERVE BANKS, unallocated net earnings since the last payment of dividends to stockholders (dividends are paid in semiannual installments, on the last business days in June and in December) and payment of interest to the Treasury on Federal Reserve notes outstanding.

Each Reserve bank pays part of its accumulated net earnings to the Treasury as "interest on Federal Reserve notes outstanding" on the sixth business day of each month except January, when payments are made on the first business day. The payments reduce this account and increase the U.S. Treasurer's general account at the Reserve banks. Section 16 of the Federal Reserve Act grants the Board of Governors authority to levy an interest charge on outstanding Federal Reserve notes not fully covered by gold certificate reserves. This authority has been used since 1947. The purpose of the interest charge is to transfer to the Treasury any excess earnings of the Reserve banks after expenses, dividends, and adjustments that are necessary to make surplus equal to paid-in capital. Prior to 1933, each Reserve bank was required to pay a franchise tax to the government, which accomplished the same end. From 1933 to 1946 the Reserve banks did not transfer excess earnings but used them to restore their surplus accounts, which had been depleted by mandatory purchases of the capital stock of the FEDERAL DEPOSIT INSURANCE CORPORATION in 1933. [Adapted from Federal Reserve Bank of New York, *Glossary: Weekly Federal Reserve Statements.*]

OTHER DEMAND DEPOSITS. Demand deposits which the U.S. government maintains in commercial banks, and demand deposits which commercial banks maintain with each other. This expression is used in reports of the FEDERAL RESERVE SYSTEM because these deposits are not included in the MONEY SUPPLY.

OTHER LIABILITIES AND ACCRUED DIVIDENDS. With regard to the CON-

SOLIDATED STATEMENT OF CONDITION OF ALL FEDERAL RESERVE BANKs, this item includes liabilities for statutory dividends on paid-in FEDERAL RESERVE BANK capital stock (all owned by member banks) accrued between semiannual payment dates (the last business day of June and December), unearned discount on securities bought outright [as explained below], sundry items payable, and accrued expenses. [From Federal Reserve Bank of New York, *Glossary: Weekly Federal Reserve Statements.*]

The *unearned discount* is the amount paid by the Federal Reserve below the maturity value of the securities and bankers' acceptances it has purchased. Each day part of this amount is transferred to the earnings account to eliminate the discount on the maturity date. This item is decreased, and the *other capital accounts* increased by an equal amount.

A security or acceptance purchased at a discount is treated on the books this way because at maturity the Federal Reserve collects more than it paid for the instrument. Thus, the difference between what it paid and what it will receive at maturity represents a discount not yet earned.

The discount on securities bought under REPURCHASE AGREEMENTs is not accumulated into earnings. It is paid back to the dealer when he repurchases the securities from the Federal Reserve.

The discount on acceptances bought under repurchase agreements is treated differently. It is accumulated daily into earnings—the other capital accounts item—to eliminate the discount on the termination date of the repurchase agreement. If the dealer repurchases the acceptance before termination, he receives a rebate of the remaining discount from the Federal Reserve.

OTHER THINGS BEING EQUAL. An important simplification by which the relationship between two variables is examined while it is assumed that nothing else of economic significance in the universe is changing. For example, in a DE-

MAND SCHEDULE we look at a series of points which show the relationship between price and quantity demanded, but that relationship is valid only if incomes, fashions, taxes, inflationary expectations, related products, and innumerable other variables do not change. This concept, often called *ceteris paribus*, is necessary because of the large number of direct and indirect influences which affect every event, the interactions among them, and the fact that the economic universe is never static.

OUT-OF-POCKET COSTS. Costs that are paid as they occur, or soon afterward—as opposed to costs that accumulate or do not relate directly to the action being taken, such as wear and tear or insurance premiums.

OUTPUT. Goods and services produced in an economy. Everything that results from productive efforts is referred to as output, and all the FACTORS OF PRODUCTION used are the input.

OUTSIDE BROKER. A stock broker, or brokerage firm, that does not have a SEAT on the exchange with which it is dealing; such a broker must employ the services of another broker.

OVERALL BALANCE ON LIQUIDITY BASIS. See BALANCE OF INTERNATIONAL PAYMENTS.

OVERDRAFT. A written order (check) for a bank to pay a stated sum which is in excess of the funds available in the writer's account. Ordinarily the bank will mark the check "insufficient funds" and return it unpaid, but many banks now provide *overdraft protection* by agreeing to pay the check, in effect making a loan to the writer of the check. One objection to this protection is that such an easy way to obtain a loan may encourage excessive debt.

OVERHEAD COST. An actual cost of doing business, that cannot be associated directly with the production of a certain product. For example, in a mercantile establishment the salary of the company's attorney would be an overhead cost. Often called simply *overhead*.

OVERHEATED ECONOMY. Economic expansion at a rate which cannot be sustained. Such economic growth is usually accompanied by inflation and other conditions that lead to instability.

OVERINVESTMENT. In either macro- or microeconomics, the purchase of CAPITAL GOODS in excess of the amount required for the actual OUTPUT at the desired level of MANUFACTURING CAPACITY. It can result from each manufacturer's overestimating either the total market or his SHARE OF THE MARKET. Some theorists hold that recurrent overinvestment, leading to excess capacity, is the dominant reason for ECONOMIC FLUCTUATIONS.

OVERLYING BOND. A BOND such that the claims of its owners are subordinated to the claims of owners of other bond issues of the same company. It is the opposite of an *underlying bond*, whose owners have a superior claim to pledged property.

OVERNIGHT MONEY. FEDERAL FUNDS which are lent out on one day and repaid the following morning.

OVERPRODUCTION. Manufacture of more than is demanded at the intended price. The usual result of overproduction is a reduction in price to bring about an increase in quantity demanded (see SUPPLY AND DEMAND).

OVERSAVING. Saving in excess of investment demands, resulting in an economic slowdown because money is being removed from the CIRCULAR FLOW OF MONEY.

OVERSAVING THEORY. An attempt to explain ECONOMIC FLUCTUATIONS: Some economists claim that during prosperity there is a considerable amount of CAPITAL ACCUMULATION, followed by a period of large incomes which allow large values of MARGINAL PRO-

PENSITY TO SAVE, causing less need for the capital equipment, and leading to an economic slowdown.

OVERSTATE. To cause statistics, reports, or other presentations to be misleading by using methods which give results larger than if more realistic methods had been used. For example, in a period of inflation, corporate profits often reach record highs, but to the extent that INVENTORY PROFITS contribute to these records, it is often said that profits are overstated.

Another example is found in the 1982 *Economic Report of the President:*

> In recent years, at least, the method of computing the CPI (Consumer Price Index) has caused it to overstate increases in the cost of living. In October 1981 the Bureau of Labor Statistics announced its intention to correct these technical deficiencies. The correction will first affect Federal outlays in fiscal 1985. The cumulative effect of mismeasurement may have increased the real level of benefits paid by as much as $10 billion in 1981 alone.

OVER-THE-COUNTER (OTC). Describes stock whose sales are coordinated by a network of brokers without using a STOCK MARKET, as opposed to a *listed stock*, which is on the list of securities traded at one of the major stock markets.

OVERTIME WAGES. The U.S. Fair Labor Standards Act of 1938 established the 40-hour week as the standard in interstate commerce and required that a premium rate (time and a half is typical, although double time and other arrangements are used) be paid for work in excess of that standard. Exceptions include professional people, who are usually paid a fixed salary rather than an hourly rate.

OVERVALUED CURRENCY. When the monetary unit of nation B exchanges with other nations' monetary units at a rate such that imports to nation B sell to the citizens at an unusually low price, the currency of nation B is said to be overvalued. Nation B then has an unfavorable balance of trade (see MERCHANDISE ACCOUNT) because imports exceed exports. This imbalance can be corrected by *devaluation* of the currency of nation B, meaning that B will exchange more of its money for a given quantity of other money. See also BALANCE OF INTERNATIONAL PAYMENTS; UNDERVALUED CURRENCY; ARBITRAGE.

OWN-PRICE SUBSTITUTION EFFECT. See SUBSTITUTION EFFECTS.

P

PAASCHE INDEX. See LASPEYRES INDEX.

PACESETTER. (1) A company that is emulated by others within the industry with regard to efficiency, earnings, sales, introduction of new products, or other measures. (2) In labor relations, an individual worker whose rate of output is used as the standard when establishing quotas, bonuses, piecework rates, etc. In this application, the expression is often used in a derogative sense, by unions which claim that the fastest worker is used as the pacesetter.

PAPER CURRENCY SIZE. Until July 1929, U.S. currency was 7.42 by 3.13 inches, now described as the "old, large-size," or *blanket*, bills. Currency printed since 1929 is 6.14 by 2.61 inches.

PAPER PROFIT AND LOSS. Change in the value of an asset, such as a security, while it belongs to one owner. Such profit or loss becomes actual profit or loss only when the asset is sold. The significance of a paper profit or loss is that it can never be counted as firm because the value of the asset could always reverse so that a profit could become a loss. Sometimes a person has such a large block of a security with a paper profit that it is impossible for him to realize an actual profit; if he started to sell, his very act of selling would cause the market price to drop and his paper profit would vanish.

One of the reasons for PROPOSITION 13 (in California) was that paper profit on real estate, although bringing no benefit to the homeowner, was the basis for collecting property taxes.

PARADOX OF THRIFT. If one person saves a large part of his income, he will have more money to spend and enjoy in later years, but if everyone wants to save a large part of his income, the resultant decrease in spending will reduce economic activity, causing a depression, and no one will be able to save. See CIRCULAR FLOW OF MONEY; OVERSAVING.

PARETO OPTIMUM. A condition such that the well-being of one individual (group, class, etc.) cannot be improved without decreasing the well-being of another. For a development of Pareto optimum, see Chapter 2 of *Government Finance Economics of the Public Sector*, 5th ed. (Homewood, Ill.: Richard D. Irwin, 1973).

PARIS CLUB. An informal arrangement whereby representatives of the major Western creditor countries meet with a debtor country, at the latter's initiative, to consider postponement of servicing obligations on certain portions of the debt owed to those governments. [From Security Pacific National Bank, *Economic Report* (Winter 1981-1982).]

PARITY PRICE. A price which is sought or maintained. For an agricultural product, quantity of the goods and services which could have been purchased with the proceeds of a given amount of the product in a reference period is determined; parity exists today if the proceeds from the same amount of that product can purchase the same goods and services

PARTIAL ANALYSIS. An analysis of less than an entire economy. Beginning economics courses always use partial analyses to show the workings of various parts of the economy before it is possible to tie it all together in an overall analysis. But partial analyses are not limited to beginning courses; advanced studies also use them because even a small part of an economy is so complex that the entire economy cannot be considered in every study.

PARTIAL MONOPOLY. A market situation which approaches a monopoly in that there are very few sellers, each with a significant influence over the market. Also called *oligopoly*.

PARTICIPATING BOND. Ordinarily a bondholder is promised that he will receive regular interest payments, but on the other hand, he also knows that he will not receive any additional amount, even in years when the issuer makes extraordinary profits. A participating bond, also known as a *profit-sharing bond*, has a special provision that allows such additional payments.

PARTICIPATING PREFERRED STOCK. Ordinarily, preferred stock (see CAPITAL STOCK) is sold with the promise that a certain dividend will be paid periodically, while common stock carries no promise. However, if a corporation is particularly profitable, dividends on preferred stock may remain at the promised amount while dividends on common stock are increased to reflect the company's improved financial position. To make ownership of preferred stock more attractive, an arrangement is sometimes made whereby, after holders of common stock

are paid a stated amount, any additional distribution of dividends will include holders of *participating preferred stock*.

PARTICIPATION. Advancing of funds by a bank to its correspondent bank so that the latter may complete a large loan which it is currently unable to handle.

PARTICIPATION RATE. The percentage of eligible persons who take advantage of a given opportunity. For example, the *labor force participation rate* is the percentage of the total eligible population who work, are looking for work, or are otherwise counted in the CIVILIAN LABOR FORCE.

PARTI COMMUNISTE FRANÇAIS (Fr.). The communist party in France. Holding about 20 percent of the popular vote, it is a significant political force.

PARTNER. See GENERAL PARTNER; LIMITED PARTNER.

PARTNERSHIP. See FORMS OF BUSINESS ORGANIZATION.

PAR VALUE. When applied to CAPITAL STOCK, a stated amount of money by which the stock is known for accounting and tax purposes. The market value of the stock (price at which it trades in the open market) seldom bears any relationship to its par value. Stock which does not have a stated value is called *no-par stock*. When applied to BONDs, par value is sometimes used interchangeably with maturity value.

PASSBOOK. The record given to the depositor in a depository type of FINANCIAL INTERMEDIARY such as a COMMERCIAL BANK or a SAVINGS AND LOAN ASSOCIATION. The depositor presents the passbook when making deposits and withdrawals, which are recorded, along with interest credited, to show how much is in the account.

PATERNALISM. The policy of a government that assumes responsibility for providing a large number of SOCIAL GOODS and services. Since such goods and services must be paid for through taxes, the government is, in effect, deciding for its citizens how their incomes will be spent.

PATTERN BARGAINING. In labor economics, collective bargaining in which the union tries to apply the same terms to a number of employers in the same industry although the employers bargain individually and not through an association. The result is a *pattern settlement*, sometimes a KEY CONTRACT.

PAYABLE TO BEARER. A phrase used on negotiable instruments when it is intended that anyone in possession can convert them to cash. Instruments of this type are only slightly safer than cash. See BEARER.

PAYEE. The party who is receiving money when a check is written.

PAYMENT BILL. A BILL OF EXCHANGE is referred to as a *payment bill* when it is due and brought in for payment, to distinguish it from a *new bill* which is brought in for acceptance signature.

PAYMENTS MECHANISM. System designed for the movement of funds, payments, and money between financial institutions throughout the nation. The FEDERAL RESERVE SYSTEM plays a major role in the nation's payments mechanism through its distribution of currency and coin, check processing, wire transfers, AUTOMATED CLEARING-HOUSEs, and securities transfer. Federal Reserve payments mechanism services are made available to both member banks and nonmember depository institutions on the basis of uniform pricing schedules. Various private associations also perform many payments mechanism operations.

PAYMENTS TO FACTORS OF PRODUCTION. See FACTOR EARNINGS.

PAY, RETROACTIVE. See RETROACTIVE PAY.

PAYROLL STATISTICS. Data taken from payroll records of establishments. An establishment is defined as ''an economic unit which produces goods or services, such as a factory, mine, or store.'' These data provide the principal source of state and metropolitan-area labor statistics. Further details can be found in ''Counting the Jobless,'' *Monthly Review of the Federal Reserve Bank of San Francisco* (September 1972). Also called *establishment statistics*.

PAYROLL TAX. A tax which is a direct function of the size of an employer's payroll.

PECUNIARY. Refers to money or interests in money.

PEG. A reference to which some price is correlated. Thus the currency of some nation may be ''pegged to'' the U.S. dollar or salaries in a certain company ''pegged to the CONSUMER PRICE INDEX.'' See also SLIDING PEG.

PENSION FUND. A holding of money, usually in the form of a TRUST, which is established for the purpose of providing payments to individuals after they retire. These funds are FINANCIAL INTERMEDIARIES because they buy debt in the MONEY MARKET, thereby providing LIQUIDITY for others. Governments as well as private organizations may establish pension funds for employees. Pension funds have considerable, and growing, influence in the economy because they work with the accumulated funds of many individuals and their transactions are usually large. Formerly, investors used to watch certain wealthy individuals to see what action they were taking in the stock market; now it is more common to watch what the funds are doing.

PEOPLE'S BANK OF CHINA. The CENTRAL BANK of China, owned and operated by the government. In addition to the MONETARY POLICY responsibilities which other central banks have, this bank coordinates expenditures of enterprises with economic plans.

PER CAPITA. Per person. Many statistics are meaningless on an aggregate basis, especially if the population is changing, so they are expressed in per capita form.

For example, the change in total wages earned in California from 1982 to 1983 does not say a thing about whether workers' pay is increasing—but if both numbers are divided by the population of California in those years, to obtain average per capita wages, the statistic begins to have meaning.

PER DIEM. For each day. For example, an employer may pay a given amount per diem to employees traveling on company business. In general, there are two methods: per diem and expense account—with the former, a reasonable amount is paid and it is up to the employee to spend it carefully so as not to have the business travel cost him from his own money— with an expense account the employee is reimbursed for actual amounts spent. Some employers prefer per diem because it is simple (no receipts are required) and because they feel that employees might live lavishly while traveling if all expenses were to be reimbursed. Others feel that per diem may not be fair to either party because it is an average; thus sometimes the employer pays more than necessary whereas at other times it costs the employee money to travel.

PERFECT COMPETITION. The idealistic form of COMPETITION, in which there are a large number of sellers acting independently, a large number of buyers acting independently, freedom for sellers and buyers to leave the market, and a complete flow of information. Also called *pure competition*.

PERFECT ELASTICITY. A theoretical market situation in which the supply (or demand) curve is drawn parallel to the quantity axis (see SUPPLY AND DEMAND)—price is then not a function of quantity. Also called *infinite elasticity*. See ELASTICITY.

PERFECT INELASTICITY. A theoretical market situation in which the supply (or demand) curve is drawn parallel to the price axis (see SUPPLY AND DEMAND)—quantity is then not a function

of price. Also called *complete inelasticity*. See ELASTICITY.

PERFECTLY SUBSTITUTABLE. If an EXCHANGE OPPORTUNITIES LINE is straight (if the ratio of one INPUT to the other remained constant throughout the range of exchange possibilities), the two inputs are said to be *perfectly substitutable*.

PERFECT MARKET. See EXCHANGE OPPORTUNITIES LINE.

PERIL POINT. The point at which, in the view of protectionists (see PROTECTIONISM), any further reduction in protective tariff will be harmful to domestic industry.

PERMANENT INCOME. Most simply, expected average lifetime income. It is a good measure of economic well-being because it is presented without the temporary ups and downs. A laborer who is working his way through medical school has a higher permanent income than do co-workers whose present, or *measured*, income is the same as his is today.

PERMISSIBLE NONBANK ACTIVITIES. Financial activities closely related to banking that may be engaged in by a BANK HOLDING COMPANY, either directly or through nonbank subsidiaries. Examples are owning finance companies and engaging in mortgage banking. The BOARD OF GOVERNORS (OF THE FEDERAL RESERVE SYSTEM) determines which activities are closely related to banking. Before making such activities permissible, the Board must also determine that the performance of the activities by bank holding companies is in the public interest.

PERPETUAL BOND. A BOND which pays agreed-upon interest indefinitely; it has no maturity date.

PERQUISITE. A work benefit other than wages; it also provides incentive to workers. Perquisites can range from use of a company automobile to having a secretary, working in an attractive atmosphere, or having an "executive size" waste-basket. Also referred to as a *perk*.

PERSONAL AGENCY ACCOUNT. A trust arrangement in which title to the assets is not vested in the trustee; the agency terminates automatically upon the death of the client.

PERSONAL CONSUMPTION EXPENDITURES (PC). In general, outlays by consumers other than for interest payments or for transfer payments to foreigners. In NATIONAL INCOME AND PRODUCT ACCOUNTS this item is defined as the market value of goods and services purchased by individuals and nonprofit institutions or acquired by them as income in KIND. The rental value of owner-occupied dwellings is included, but not the purchase price of dwellings. Purchases are recorded at cost to consumers, including excise and sales taxes, and in full at the time of purchase, whether made with cash or on credit. See also the chart with GROSS NATIONAL PRODUCT.

The accompanying table has been prepared as an aid in studying shifts of U.S. consumption patterns. Numbers in the second column are in billions of dollars, and all columns that follow are in percentage of the second column. Columns 3, 4, and 5 are the three categories that form PC, so those three columns add to 100 percent (except for rounding in some rows). The last three columns are selected categories, just for the purpose of noting trends. One measure of economic growth is a decreasing requirement for expenditures on necessities such as food, leaving an increasing portion of our income for spending on luxuries; the table shows a steady trend in that direction.

PERSONAL DISTRIBUTION OF INCOME. A statistical description of how much (or what percentage) of the nation's income is received by people earning in each of several income brackets. For example, the distribution may show how much was received by those earning $5,000 to $10,000, how much by those earning

$10,000 to $15,000, etc. This distribution compares to a *functional distribution* of income, which shows how much was received through wages, how much through receipts of rents, how much through receipts of interest, etc.

PERSONAL FINANCE COMPANY. See FINANCE COMPANY.

PERSONAL INCOME. Total income received by individuals from all sources—wage and salary disbursements, other labor income, proprietors' income, rental income, dividends, personal interest income, and transfer payments—minus personal contributions for social insurance. See GROSS NATIONAL PRODUCT.

PERSONAL INCOME TAX. A tax on incomes of individuals, imposed by most nations—in the U.S. by the federal government, most states, and some cities. One of the main arguments in favor of this method of obtaining government revenues is that it is generally a PROGRESSIVE TAX and therefore takes relatively more from those with larger incomes (see ABILITY-TO-PAY PRINCIPLE). By taking relatively more from high incomes and returning benefits equally (or in even larger proportion to the poor), this tax works toward redistribution of income. Also, because of their progressivity, income taxes are one form of BUILT-IN STABILIZER.

PERSONAL OUTLAYS. The sum of personal consumption expenditures, interest paid by consumers, and personal transfer payments to foreigners. When personal outlays are subtracted from DISPOSABLE PERSONAL INCOME the remainder is *personal saving*. See also GROSS NATIONAL PRODUCT.

PERSONAL PROPERTY. Property other than REAL PROPERTY which is subject to ownership rights. It can be tangible, such as clothing and tools, or intangible, such as patents and copyrights.

PERSONAL REPRESENTATIVE. One who oversees the execution of the terms

Personal Consumption Expenditures

Year	Personal consumption expenditures (billions of U.S. $)	Durable goods (%)	Nondurable goods (%)	Services (%)	Motor vehicles and parts (%)	Food (%)	Housing (%)
1940	71.0	11.0	52.1	36.9	3.9	28.5	13.7
1941	80.8	12.0	53.1	34.9	4.3	29.0	12.9
1942	88.6	7.8	57.3	35.0	0.8	32.1	12.6
1943	99.4	6.5	59.0	34.5	0.8	33.4	11.9
1944	108.2	6.2	59.4	34.3	0.7	33.9	11.4
1945	119.5	6.7	60.2	33.1	0.8	34.0	10.7
1946	143.8	11.0	57.5	31.5	2.9	33.0	9.9
1947	161.7	12.6	56.2	31.2	4.1	32.3	9.9
1948	174.7	13.1	55.3	31.7	4.6	31.0	10.2
1949	178.1	14.0	53.3	32.7	6.0	29.5	11.0
1950	192.0	16.0	51.1	32.8	7.1	28.1	11.3
1951	207.1	14.4	52.5	33.1	5.9	29.2	11.7
1952	217.1	13.4	52.5	34.1	5.2	29.2	12.4
1953	229.7	14.1	50.7	35.1	6.1	28.0	13.0
1954	235.8	13.5	50.0	36.5	5.5	27.7	13.7
1955	253.7	15.2	48.4	36.3	7.0	26.5	13.5
1956	266.0	14.2	48.5	37.3	5.9	26.3	13.8
1957	280.4	14.0	48.2	37.8	6.1	26.2	14.0
1958	289.5	12.7	48.3	39.0	5.1	26.4	14.5
1959	310.8	13.6	47.1	39.2	6.1	25.5	14.5
1960	324.9	13.3	46.5	40.2	6.1	25.0	14.8
1961	335.0	12.4	46.4	41.2	5.3	24.8	15.3
1962	355.2	13.1	45.5	41.4	6.1	24.1	15.4
1963	374.6	13.7	44.6	41.7	6.5	23.4	15.5
1964	400.5	14.1	44.2	41.7	6.5	23.1	15.3
1965	430.4	14.6	43.8	41.5	7.0	23.0	15.2
1966	465.1	14.6	44.0	41.4	6.5	22.9	14.9
1967	490.3	14.3	43.4	42.3	6.1	22.4	15.1
1968	536.9	15.0	43.0	42.1	6.8	22.1	14.9
1969	581.8	14.7	42.6	42.7	6.7	21.9	15.0
1970	621.7	13.7	42.7	43.6	5.8	22.3	15.1
1971	672.2	14.5	41.5	44.1	6.8	21.5	15.3
1972	737.1	15.1	40.8	44.1	7.1	21.0	15.3
1973	812.0	15.2	41.1	43.7	7.0	21.2	15.2
1974	888.1	13.7	42.0	44.3	5.7	21.8	15.5
1975	976.4	13.5	41.7	44.8	5.7	21.9	15.3
1976	1,084.3	14.5	40.7	44.8	6.7	21.3	15.4
1977	1,205.5	14.8	39.7	45.4	7.1	20.8	15.5
1978	1,348.7	14.8	39.3	45.9	7.0	20.5	15.8
1979	1,510.9	14.1	39.9	46.1	6.3	20.7	16.0
1980	1,672.8	12.7	40.4	46.9	5.4	20.7	16.3
1981	1,858.1	12.5	40.0	47.5	5.3	20.6	16.5

of a will. He can be either an executor (named in the will) or an administrator (named by a court when none is named in a will).

PERSONAL SAVING. The residual obtained by subtracting PERSONAL OUTLAYS from DISPOSABLE PERSONAL INCOME. See the chart with GROSS NATIONAL PRODUCT.

PERSONAL SAVING RATE. The ratio of PERSONAL SAVING to DISPOSABLE PERSONAL INCOME. Sometimes expressed as a percentage.

PERSONAL TAXES. Taxes levied directly on individuals, such as state and federal income taxes, as well as property and school taxes.

PERVERSE INCENTIVES. Conflicts in a person's decision-making processs when there are strong points to be made for each possible choice. For example, suppose a government official must decide whether or not to approve a new drug. If it is approved too quickly, it may turn out to have side effects that hurt some people; if approval is delayed, some people who might have been helped could suffer or die. See also CYCLICALLY PERVERSE.

PETTY CASH. Liquid funds which an organization keeps for immediate use to purchase items that cannot be handled efficiently through regular purchasing channels, such as meals for guests or one pencil of a special color. Depending on the organization's policy, receipts may or may not be required in order for an employee to be reimbursed from petty cash for expenditures.

PHILLIPS CURVE. The relationship between price changes and unemployment, published with empirical evidence by Alban William Housego Phillips in 1958. The curve shows an inverse relationship; *low* rates of unemployment go with *high* rates of price change (inflation). Much has been written describing further analyses; the following, adapted from the March 8, 1974, *Business & Financial Letter* of

the Federal Reserve Bank of San Francisco, is typical:

One cure which has been used for unemployment is the adoption of fiscal and monetary policies which are generally inflationary. However, in considering the Phillips curve as a policy guide most economists believe that the trade-off between unemployment and inflation is a short-run phenomenon—one which arises due to unforeseen inflation or other sources of misinformation and vanishes as soon as expectations adapt to inflationary experience. They suggest, for example, that labor unions in the long-run are not subject to MONEY ILLUSION in their wage negotiations; that workers actively seek to protect the purchasing power of their wages from erosion by inflation.

PHYSICAL CAPITAL. The ECONOMIC RESOURCE called *capital*—sometimes *physical* is included to emphasize that the writer or speaker is not referring to HUMAN CAPITAL.

PHYSIOCRACY. A school of economic thought in the 1700s which held that agriculture is the sole contributor to real growth and productivity: Manufacturing is simply a rearrangement of existing goods, but a farmer takes seeds and, through his efforts, brings forth a large crop plus more seeds. This view should be contrasted with today's recognition of FORM UTILITY, PLACE UTILITY, TIME UTILITY, and other methods of increasing the real value of goods. Economists associated with the Physiocratic school include François Quesnay and Anne Robert Jacques Turgot.

PICKUP PAYMENT. In a consumer credit contract, a final payment which is larger than the regular payments. Some consumers have found the arrangement satisfactory because it reduces the size of each regular payment; others complain that they are unable to make the large final payment and are therefore forced to default or refinance. Also called a *balloon payment.*

TRUTH IN LENDING does not prohibit pickup payments, but it requires that if such payment "is more than twice the amount of an otherwise regularly scheduled payment, the creditor shall state the conditions, if any, under which such 'pickup' may be refinanced if not paid when due."

PICTOGRAPH. A form of graphical display in which quantities are represented by whole and fractional pictures, usually silhouettes.

PIECE WORK. Work for which the pay is entirely or partially dependent on the amount of work produced. Such arrangements work best in factories where large amounts of a standard product are produced and where the quality is easily measured and controlled.

PIGGYBACK. Carrying an entire truck trailer or semitrailer on a railroad car. Some of the advantages are a reduction of unnecessary labor costs for multiple loading and unloading (see MAKE-WORK), of losses to dishonesty, of accidental breakage, and of documentation work.

PIGOU EFFECT. See WEALTH EFFECT.

PIT. In securities exchanges, especially where commodities are traded, an area where traders meet to conduct their trades in a particular commodity.

PLACE UTILITY. The value added to an item by moving it. For example, a head of lettuce is worth more money in a store than on the farm.

PLANCHET. A round blank that is punched from a strip of metal as the first step in making a coin.

PLANNED ECONOMY. See CENTRALLY PLANNED ECONOMY.

PLANNED INVESTMENT. Purchases of CAPITAL GOODS by the business SECTOR, as opposed to unplanned (or unintended) investment, which is increases in inventories due to lower-than-expected sales (see CHANGE IN BUSINESS INVENTORIES). Also called *intended investment.*

PLANNING COMMISSARIAT. See COMMISSARIAT AU PLAN.

POINT. (1) In financial economics, stock prices as well as the indexes are often quoted in points, where a point is exactly the same as a dollar. Thus, an index that "rose 12 points" went up 12 dollars. In bond prices, one point is 10 dollars, so a bond selling for $950 would be quoted at 95 points.

(2) In mortgages and some other loans, an extra amount of the loan fee that is sometimes charged. Points represent finance charges which are paid in addition to the monthly interest charge. Each point equals 1 percent of the amount financed, so one point on a $50,000 mortgage would be an additional charge of $500.

POINT ELASTICITY. ELASTICITY is a measure of the degree to which a change in quantity (demanded or supplied) is dependent on a change in price. As the "change-in" amount becomes smaller, in the limit approaching zero, the resultant elasticity is called *point elasticity.* This concept is the same as the derivative in calculus.

POINT FOUR PROGRAM. See ACT FOR INTERNATIONAL DEVELOPMENT OF 1950.

POINT, IMPORT. See GOLD POINTS.

POINT OF INDIFFERENCE. The point between DECREASING RETURNS and INCREASING RETURNS, where increased spending on inputs (FACTORS OF PRODUCTION) is just offset by an increase in net income, causing neither an increase nor a decrease in profit.

POINT OF SALE (POS). A system that allows for the transfer of funds between accounts, authorization of credit, verification of checks, and provision of related services at the time of purchase. POS terminals are located in some shopping areas and allow customers of participating financial institutions to effect transactions through the use of machine-readable debit cards.

POLICY INSTRUMENT. Any action which is available to an economic policymaker. Those responsible for MONETARY POLICY use such policy instruments as control of the RESERVE RATIO, DISCOUNT RATE, and MARGIN REQUIREMENTS, as well as other techniques. Also called *tools of monetary* (or *fiscal*) *policy*.

POLITICAL BUSINESS CYCLE. An example would be government spending projects or programs which are initiated just before an election although the resultant higher taxes or inflation do not occur until after the election.

POLITICAL THEORY. A MONOCAUSAL THEORY of economic history.

POLL TAX. A tax levied in fixed amount on every person (sometimes on every male), with certain specified exceptions, such as indigent persons. Collections have sometimes been facilitated by combining them with a common function such as voting. Also called a *capitation tax* or a *head tax*.

POLYMETALISM. An extension of the BIMETAL STANDARD to include three or more precious metals as the backing for a nation's money.

PORTAL-TO-PORTAL PAY. In labor economics, an agreement by the employer to allow workers time at the start or end of the shift for tasks such as changing clothes, washing up, and other preparatory or closing-out tasks.

PORTFOLIO. In economics, the securities an individual or an organization owns. Thus if an individual owns 100 shares of ABC Corporation, 500 shares of XYZ Corporation, and $10,000 in government bonds, that inventory of holdings is his portfolio.

PORT OF ENTRY (POE). The place where imported goods enter the nation. Many prices are quoted POE, meaning that the person who buys from the importer must pay all costs (transportation, insurance, etc.) from that point.

PORTRAITS. The following table shows the portraits and the scenes which are on paper currency now being produced and issued by the U.S.

Denomination	Portrait	Back
$1	Washington	Obverse and Reverse of Great Seal of U.S.
$2	Jefferson	Signing of the Declaration of Independence
$5	Lincoln	Lincoln Memorial
$10	Hamilton	U.S. Treasury Building
$20	Jackson	White House
$50	Grant	U.S. Capitol Building
$100	Franklin	Independence Hall

POSITIVE CORRELATION. Statistical connection between two variables such that an increase in the size, value, etc. of one is consistent with an increase in the other. For example, quantity demanded and income level of buyer are positively correlated for a normal good (see INCOME EFFECT). See also NEGATIVE CORRELATION.

POSSESSION UTILITY. The increase in ability of a good or service to satisfy human wants when it is made available for distribution. For example, boxed cereals kept in the manufacturer's warehouse have no utility value (cannot be used to satisfy human wants), but when they become available, their utility value increases.

POST OFFICE SAVINGS BANK (Swed.) (Postsparbanken). An arrangement for accepting savings of individuals and making the funds available for real estate loans.

POTENTIAL DEMAND. A need that is not now being satisfied but is expected to be satisfied when some condition is met in the future. For example, during a major war there is spending power and desire but a lack of goods to purchase; during a recession there may be goods and desire but a lack of spending power. Sometimes a technological advance can change potential demand into actual demand. Also called *latent demand*.

POTENTIAL GNP. A calculated value of GROSS NATIONAL PRODUCT (GNP) assuming "full" utilization of the nation's productive resources and existing technology. This figure allows for some margin of unused resources due to population shifts, transition between jobs, and incomplete utilization of less efficient productive facilities. (See ECONOMIC RESOURCES.) Regarding human resources, 4 percent unemployment has long been the official level of "full" employment, but today economists are increasingly recognizing 5 percent as more reasonable. See FULL EMPLOYMENT.

When actual GNP is less than potential GNP, the difference, called *GNP gap*, represents incomplete or inefficient use of resources. GNP above the potential level is not desirable either, because a level that high is not sustainable and will lead to inflation, probably followed by a recession or depression.

POTENTIAL STOCK. That portion of AUTHORIZED STOCK which has not yet been sold or otherwise issued by the corporation.

PREAUTHORIZED TRANSFER. A method of automatically withdrawing or depositing funds to or from an individual account under authority given to the bank or to a third party (such as an employer) by the account holder. For example, consumers can authorize direct electronic deposit of wages, social security checks, or dividend payments to their accounts; or they can authorize financial institutions to pay recurring bills such as insurance, mortgage, utility, and others.

PRECAUTIONARY DEMAND. See LIQUIDITY PREFERENCE.

PRECLUSIVE BUYING. Buying of goods whose supply is limited, not for one's direct use, but to prevent another from obtaining them. Sometimes called *cornering the market*, it is one form of hoarding.

PREDATORY COMPETITION. An economically unhealthy form of competition in which fairness is disregarded, usually for the purpose of driving competitors out of the market. Because the fight is generally among industrial giants, the public too often condones it, or encourages it, looking only at the immediate reduction in the prices of goods and services. Actually, the benefits are transitory; after competition is eliminated and a monopoly remains, prices will increase rapidly.

PREFABRICATE. To manufacture part of an assembly so that final assembly consists of attaching the prefabricated items. In economics, these subassemblies have various names, such as *unfinished goods inventory* and *work in process*. When a subassembly is finished in one year but not included in the complete assembly that year, it is counted in figuring GROSS NATIONAL PRODUCT; the following year the finished assembly is counted, but the subassembly is subtracted so that it is not counted twice. Also called *preassemble*. See DOUBLE COUNTING.

PREFERENCE STOCK. Preferred stock. See CAPITAL STOCK.

PREFERENTIAL ARRANGEMENT. A labor contract which, while it does not require that all employees be union members, specifies that certain benefits, such as overtime at PREMIUM PAY, be offered to union members first.

PREFERENTIAL DUTY. A duty whose amount is based, not on the product being imported, but on the place of shipment. Also called *differential duty* or *discriminating duty*.

PREFERRED INCOME. Income for which no income tax is paid, such as the interest on MUNICIPAL BONDs.

PREFERRED STOCK. CAPITAL STOCK which carries a promise to pay a stated amount of dividend.

PRELIMINARY ESTIMATE. See ADVANCE, PRELIMINARY, AND FINAL ESTIMATE.

PREMIUM. Usually an extra amount paid, for example, a $1,000 BOND may be bought for a figure such as $1,005, or a worker may be paid 1.5 times the regular rate. Also means the payments to an insurer. In retailing, *premium* is sometimes used to identify high-quality goods.

PREMIUM, LIQUIDITY. See LIQUIDITY PREMIUM.

PREMIUM PAY. Wages higher than the regular rate, as compensation for special work, such as overtime, holiday, hazardous, and others. The time which earns the higher rate is called *premium time*.

PREPAID EXPENSE. In accounting, an asset account in which is recorded an amount paid for a good or service that is yet to be received, such as payment made for a fire insurance policy. Payment is made immediately, and the asset the company has in place of the cash is financial protection, which will be used up day by day while the policy is in force.

PRESENT VALUE. The amount of money today which will become a given amount at a stated time in the future. For example, at 10 percent interest $100 will grow to $110 in one year; therefore the present value of $110 one year from now at 10 percent is $100. If the end product is a series of payments, the present value is the amount that will result in the sum of that series.

PRESIDENT'S COMMISSION ON FINANCIAL STRUCTURE AND REGULATION. Commonly known as the *Hunt Commission*, this group issued a report and recommendations toward the end of 1971. The report influenced several pieces of legislation over the years. One of the major proposals was to offer bank-type powers to THRIFT INSTITUTIONs

if they also assume approximately the same regulatory and tax burdens as COMMERCIAL BANKs. See NEGOTIABLE ORDER OF WITHDRAWAL.

PREVIOUS BALANCE METHOD. A method for figuring the base on which interest will be charged in consumer credit. By this method the base is the balance at the end of the previous billing period, so payments that might have been made during the present billing period do not reduce the balance on which interest is charged.

PRICE. Economists consider the price paid in a transaction to be more than just the money that changes hands—that is, more than just the *price* that is entered in the accounts. It is often more meaningful to think of the BARTER system with regard to price, because our funds are limited, and when we spend for a certain item, we have less left for other items. For example, if an automobile and a swimming pool each cost $10,000, and a family with just one $10,000 to spend buys an automobile, it might be considered that the price of the automobile was one swimming pool. See OPPORTUNITY COST.

The examination of price can be carried further: Suppose a young woman has $10,000 after high school and buys a car with it instead of going to college. The price of that car could be a college education, which could then be converted to the money she could have earned as a doctor or the President.

PRICE COMPETITION. In its pure form, a practice that exists when sellers have *identical* products (the product itself, service, reputation of seller, and every tangible and intangible is identical); a lower price is then the only benefit any of the sellers can offer as a reason buyers should prefer one seller over the others. In practice, PRODUCT DIFFERENTIATION reduces the effects of price competition, and it is often difficult for consumers to determine the best buy.

PRICE CONTROL. Establishment of prices by authorities rather than by competitive forces or by SUPPLY AND DE-

MAND. Such control could set the exact price to be charged, but usually (in a MARKET ECONOMY) price controls are used only to control inflation and therefore sellers are free to sell for less than the stated price. For an example of the use of price control to set minimum selling prices, see PRICE FIXING.

PRICE DEFLATOR. See DEFLATOR.

PRICE DISCRIMINATION. The practice of a seller's charging different prices to different buyers when the cost of selling is identical; quantity discounts to businesses while consumers pay list price are *not* instances of discrimination because many additional costs are involved in selling small amounts to consumers. However, practices such as youth fares on airlines, or a discount to the first 100 customers *are* price discrimination. It should not be inferred that this practice is always illegal or covert, or that there is no economic justification for it. The test of legality usually asks whether the practice violates the rules of fair competition.

PRICED OUT OF THE MARKET. A DEMAND SCHEDULE shows, at every price, how many sales there will be of the item in question, and it is reasonable that a larger quantity will be demanded when the price is low than when it is high. Therefore, when the price is raised from any point to a higher point, a certain number of MARGINAL BUYERs no longer want to buy the item—they are *priced out of the market*.

Sometimes the expression is used from the seller's point of view: If a seller raises prices and loses customers, it is said that he priced himself out of the market.

PRICE EFFECTS. See SUBSTITUTION EFFECTS.

PRICE ELASTICITY. The change in quantity (demanded or supplied) which results from a given change in price. The schedule is highly elastic if a small change in price causes a large change in quantity;

it is inelastic if price has little influence on quantity. See ELASTICITY.

PRICE FIXING. An arrangement which results in all sellers' charging the same prices (elimination of PRICE COMPETITION). This practice can range from the strictly illegal method of collusion among direct competitors (horizontal price fixing), to regulated monopolies (see MONOPOLY), government-mandated prices (e.g., a state says that milk shall be sold at a stated price), or manufacturer-administered arrangements (vertical price fixing; see FAIR TRADE LAWS).

PRICE INDEX. A factor which relates purchasing power of money in two identified periods of time. The U.S. government compiles many indexes, such as the *farm price index* and the *implicit price deflator* (see DEFLATOR). See CONSUMER PRICE INDEX for an example of one of the best-known price indexes.

PRICE LEADER. A seller who dominates to the extent that when it changes prices, its competitors make similar changes. Such a practice could not occur under *pure* COMPETITION; it depends on the price leader's knowing that if he raises prices, buyers will not switch to his competitors. Competitors also know this, so they see no advantage in keeping their prices unchanged.

PRICE, MARKET. See MARKET PRICE.

PRICE RIGIDITY. In an economy ruled by the forces of SUPPLY AND DEMAND, a decrease in the quantity demanded will result in a lower price, and equilibrium will be reestablished at a quantity which is lower than at the original price—although not as low as if the original price had not changed in response to the decrease in quantity demanded. In the latter situation, the price is said to be *rigid*. For many years the trend has been away from free market forces toward control of prices and quantities. One result has been price rigidity, causing equilibrium quantities to vary considerably.

For example, suppose there were an increase in unemployment. With pure market forces, people would be willing to work for slightly less, and at that lower wage (the wage is the *price* of labor) the employer would be willing to keep a larger work force. Unemployment would change little or not at all, and recessionary pressures would be lessened. However, when the wage rate is rigid, a drop in employment results in a complete loss of some jobs and complete loss of spending power for those individuals, causing wider swings in the economy.

PRICES AND INCOMES POLICY (U.K.). An anti-inflation portion of the NATIONAL PLAN, sent to Parliament in 1965.

PRICE SETTER. See PRICE LEADER.

PRICE SUPPORT. Government action for the purpose of keeping prices of certain items at or above a certain level. The action may consist of governments' buying large quantities to create a shortage, buying a surplus if the supported price was above equilibrium (and therefore more was put on the market than buyers wanted; see SUPPLY AND DEMAND), direct subsidies, or any of a number of other actions.

PRICE SYSTEM. Essentially, the free economy system. There are two elements to a price system: (1) producers' questions as to what and how much to produce, what prices to charge, etc. are answered by determining what the buyers will want; (2) buyers' decisions as to how to spend their limited funds are answered by consciously or subconsciously seeking the largest amount of pleasure (see UTILITY UNITS). See also MARKET ECONOMY.

PRICE TAKER. A party to a transaction in which the price was determined by natural forces of competition. The seller wanted a higher price, while the buyer wanted a lower price; neither could influence the price because it was determined by the market. One example is the

stock market. If a person has some shares of XYZ Corporation and wants to sell them when the market price is $52, he cannot set the price at, say, $56 and make a sale.

PRICING POLICY. The method by which a seller establishes his selling price. The policy may be a fixed MARKUP, a percentage markup, a copy of the PRICE LEADER's price, or any number of other methods or a combination of them. See FULL-COST PRICING.

PRIMARY BOYCOTT. A BOYCOTT in which the party refusing to transact business is doing so in order to obtain some action or change from the other party, as opposed to a *secondary boycott*, in which the objective is to have the second party exert some influence over a third party.

PRIMARY DEPOSIT. See DEMAND DEPOSIT.

PRIMARY MARKET. Selling of securities by the issuer. The buyer may be an investor intending to keep the securities, or he may be buying them for the purpose of selling to other investors in the *secondary market*.

PRIMARY RESERVES. Funds which a bank keeps for immediate use, as opposed to *secondary reserves*, which are not for immediate use but can be quickly converted to MONEY. See BANK RESERVES.

PRIMARY WORKERS. That portion of the CIVILIAN LABOR FORCE which has skills, professions, or other factors that make them most in demand. Unemployment rates for primary workers are generally lower than for the economy as a whole; it is not uncommon to find shortages of certain skills during a recession. See also SECONDARY WORKERS; DISPERSION OF UNEMPLOYMENT; HARD-CORE UNEMPLOYED.

PRIME BILL. A BILL OF EXCHANGE in which the parties have high credit ratings. The bill therefore involves little risk and is easily negotiable at low discount.

PRIME COSTS. VARIABLE COSTS— those costs which depend on the level of production.

PRIME RATE. The rate of interest banks charge on the lowest-risk loans they make. Usually after one of the large New York banks makes a change in its prime rate, the others follow (see PRICE LEADER); sometimes others do not follow, since the banking industry is competitive and each bank will act in the way which is best for itself.

PRIMING. See PUMP PRIMING.

PRIMOGENITURE. Literally, the passing of family wealth, position, etc. exclusively to the oldest child, although the oldest male child is usually meant.

PRINCIPAL. (1) The basic amount of a loan, the amount of a loan which is used for figuring interest, or the amount in a savings account. (2) In legal terms, a party who employs an AGENT to stand in his place and transact business in his behalf.

PRINCIPLE OF . . . . Many laws, rules, and hypotheses in economics are identified with the word *principle*. Several are found in this dictionary under the main part of the expression; *principle of marginal utility* is found under MARGINAL UTILITY.

PRINCIPLES OF ECONOMICS. A book presenting the NEOCLASSICAL SCHOOL of economic thought. It was written by ALFRED MARSHALL and published in 1890

PRINCIPLES OF POLITICAL ECONOMY. A book by JOHN STUART MILL, published in 1848, in which he claimed that there should be less dependence on natural forces and more control by government.

PRINCIPLES OF POLITICAL ECONOMY. See MALTHUS, THOMAS.

PRINCIPLES OF POLITICAL ECONOMY AND TAXATION. A book written by DAVID RICARDO, published in 1817.

PRINTING PRESS MONEY. Paper money which is issued without relation to assets held by the issuing authority and without a promise to redeem. Technically known as FIAT MONEY.

PRIOR STOCK. Preferred stock. See CAPITAL STOCK

PRIVATE DEBT. Debt owed by the PRIVATE SECTOR—individuals and business—that is, not including debts of any level of government.

PRIVATE ENTERPRISE. The aggregate of business organizations owned by individuals rather than by some level of government. The degree of control exercised by government over such businesses depends on the industry. Sometimes *private enterprise* refers to the entire economic system known as CAPITALISM, the market economy, and other descriptive names.

PRIVATE GOODS. Goods owned by individuals or by businesses—that is, goods not owned by government.

PRIVATE OWNERSHIP. Ownership by individuals or by organizations which are owned by individuals, as opposed to *public ownership*, in which some level of government is the owner.

PRIVATE SECTOR. That portion of the total economy which does not directly involve any level of government, as opposed to the *public sector*, which includes all operations of all levels of government. See SECTOR; BUSINESS SECTOR.

PROCYCLICAL. An economic force which tends to amplify ECONOMIC FLUCTUATIONS—tends to turn economic slowdowns into deep recessions and economic expansions into runaway booms. Also known as *cyclically perverse*. See also COUNTERCYCLICAL.

PRODUCER GOODS. Goods manufactured for use in making other goods but which do not themselves continue through the manufacturing stream and are not used directly by consumers. See CONSUMER GOODS.

PRODUCER PRICE INDEX (PPI). The oldest continually published index of prices, calculated on a 1967 base and currently covering about 2,800 commodities. Its purpose is to measure both price levels and changes in prices of items at the stage of their most important commercial transaction. Goods sold at retail by producers or producer-owned establishments, and interestablishment transfers of goods within firms are also excluded from the index. Formerly called *wholesale price index (WPI)*.

The Producer Price Index uses base value weights that have been updated since the original base period. The weights used are expenditures for items measured by net value of shipments of producers in particular industries and sectors. Currently, weights are based on the net selling value of commodities in 1972 as reported in *Census of Manufacturers* and *Census of Mineral Industries*, as well as on certain other data provided by the U.S. Department of Agriculture, Bureau of Fisheries, and Bureau of Mines, the Edison Electric Institute, and the U.S. Department of Commerce.

One of the main significances of the Producer Price Index is that movements in this index often portend changes in prices of consumer goods, although the indexes differ considerably in design and coverage.

A good source of more detail is the book *Measuring Price Changes*, by the Federal Reserve Bank of Richmond.

PRODUCERS' CAPITAL. A term sometimes used to emphasize that the goods under discussion are used in industry and not by consumers. Actually, the precise meaning of *capital* is goods used to assist people in their productive efforts, and therefore the word *producers'* is a tautology. However, some writers say that everything of value is capital, and therefore they use qualifiers on the word, such as *consumers' capital* (roughly the same as what is generally called CONSUMER DURABLES) and producers' capital.

PRODUCERS' DURABLE EQUIPMENT. In NATIONAL INCOME AND PRODUCT ACCOUNTS, fixed-investment expenditures on producers' durable equipment, including purchases of new and replacement automobiles, trucks, machinery, and other equipment used by the PRIVATE SECTOR. The three largest components of this category are electrical machinery; trucks, buses, and truck trailers; and office, computing, and accounting machinery.

PRODUCT DIFFERENTIATION. In MICROECONOMICS, actions taken by suppliers to produce a difference in the consumer's mind between products that are exactly or essentially the same. The purpose is to obtain a higher price than could be obtained if it were understood that the products were substitutes for each other. For example, suppose company ABC is selling a product X, which is identical to product x being sold by many other companies; if ABC advertises, ". . . in the distinctive blue box, made by ABC Company, a name you can trust," it is creating product differentiation. When the practice is successful it raises the price by reducing competition; to the extent that the public feels the product is different from the others, there is no other supplier of the differentiated product. Although the other products are SUBSTITUTE GOODS, they are not completely substitutable in the public's mind.

PRODUCTION EXCESS BURDEN. See EXCESS BURDEN.

PRODUCTION FUNCTION. A schedule, graph, or other representation of OUTPUT as a function of some INPUT or of a combination of inputs. For example, a production function may show a pair of curves on a graph to demonstrate total output as a function of FACTORS OF PRODUCTION used for a CAPITAL INTENSIVE arrangement and for a LABOR INTENSIVE arrangement.

PRODUCTION POSSIBILITIES LINE.
See EXCHANGE OPPORTUNITIES
LINE.

PRODUCTIVITY. The ratio of real GNP
to total hours worked in the nation, where
real GNP is GROSS NATIONAL PROD-
UCT expressed in constant dollars (adjusted for inflation). Productivity is loosely
defined as the output of an average worker
over a period of one year. As automated
equipment allows workers to produce more,
productivity increases; as work rules become more restrictive, a counterforce tends
to reduce productivity. See also FEATH-
ERBEDDING; MAKE-WORK.
    Productivity is watched by economists
as one key to fighting inflation; increases
in productivity reduce costs, and the only
way to improve the income of *everyone*
(not just those who receive wage increases) is through increases in productivity. The long run average increase in
productivity in the United States is 3 percent, but it has averaged only 0.7 percent
from 1973 through 1981.

PRODUCT MARKET. Transactions in
which the nation's output of goods and
services are sold (are on the supply side
of SUPPLY AND DEMAND). See CIR-
CULAR FLOW OF MONEY.

PRODUCT SUPPLY SCHEDULE. A
schedule of the aggregate amount of a
product which an entire industry will supply at various prices. Also called *industrial supply schedule*. See SUPPLY AND
DEMAND.

PROFESSIONAL ASSOCIATION. A
nonprofit organization whose membership is limited to, or especially solicited
from, individuals or businesses operating
in the same profession. Such organizations have meetings, symposia, professional journals, and other means of com-
municating for mutual improvement of
their professional abilities.

PROFIT. In general, receipts from sales,
minus costs. This definition shows that
when cost exceeds receipts the resultant

loss is mathematically a *negative profit*.
Actually, this definition is too broad to
be of much use to economists; more descriptive expressions such as NORMAL
PROFIT, pure profit, and monopolistic
profit, are used.
    One important point is that *profit* and
markup are not synonymous; the latter is
simply the amount a seller adds to the
price he paid for an item; many costs,
such as store rent, employee salaries, telephone expenses, and advertising must be
subtracted from markup to arrive at profit.

**PROFIT AND LOSS STATEMENT
(P&L).** A formal presentation by the
company's accountant showing gross income, expenses, profit (or loss), and various other items plus footnotes. Most
companies issue a complete P&L once a
year and a shorter (sometimes unaudited)
statement at the end of each quarter.

PROFIT MAXIMIZATION. It is sim-
plistic to say that a business's goal is to
reduce costs to a minimum and raise prices
to a maximum so as to earn maximum
profit. There are fewer objections to the
statement if it is understood to refer to
the very long run, although even then it
must be recognized that there are motivations other than profit which influence
business decisions. The list could include
growth, stability, prestige, security, safety,
convenience, and many other goals.

PROFIT SHARING. Plans whereby part
of an employee's compensation is a function of the financial success of the employer. These plans can be true profit
sharing—in which a percentage of profits
is distributed to employees—or they can
be some form of quasi profit sharing. In
the latter cases, the employer includes as
a cost a certain amount for profit sharing;
this amount is distributed regardless of
how much or how little profit the company
makes that year.

PROFIT SHARING BOND. Ordinarily a
bondholder is promised regular interest
payments, regardless of how much or how
little profit the company makes. The in-

denture for a profit sharing bond instead provides that additional payments can be made to holders of these bonds if company profits are large. Also known as a *participating bond*.

PROFIT SYSTEM. An economic system in which the promise of profit is the incentive that influences economic decisions. Usually a profit system implies private ownership. Therefore, the only difference from a PRICE SYSTEM is a desire, on the part of the person using the word, to emphasize the role of profits.

PROFIT TAKING. In the economics of investments, the selling of a security which now has a market value larger than when it was bought. Sometimes a leveling off or a decline in the stock market after several days of increases is explained as profit taking, meaning that many investors have paper profits (see PAPER PROFIT AND LOSS) and want to realize an actual profit by selling their securities; SUPPLY-AND-DEMAND analysis shows that market price will decline any time there is an increase in the quantity that is offered for sale.

PROGRAM. A sequence of commands given to a computer, programmable calculator, or similar device.

PROGRAM EVALUATION AND REVIEW TECHNIQUE (PERT). A tool of managerial economics used both in planning a project and in monitoring it. A PERT chart shows each task to be performed, the time each will require (sometimes three time estimates are given—worst case, most likely, and most optimistic), the tasks that are prerequisites for each task, and various other information. Some PERT charts are programmed into a computer for monitoring. Sometimes called *program evaluation research task*.

PROGRESSION. See ARITHMETIC PROGRESSION; GEOMETRIC PROGRESSION.

PROGRESSIVE TAX. A tax levied at *rates* that increase as the base increases.

Income taxes are usually progressive; those with higher incomes pay larger *percentages* of their income as taxes than those with smaller incomes. See also DEGRESSIVE TAX; PROPORTIONAL TAX; REGRESSIVE TAX.

PROLETARIAN CLASS (PROLETARIST). This class comprises the working class (dependent on the sale of its labor) and the propertyless. It constitutes the majority of the population. According to Marxist doctrine, this class will eventually overcome the dominance of the BOURGEOISIE and COMMUNISM will ultimately prevail.

PROMISSORY NOTE. An instrument which states that the debtor owes a certain amount and gives the terms of repayment. Such notes are usually negotiable, meaning that the holder can transfer his right to receive payment to another.

PROMOTER. One who is active in obtaining financing and a charter for a new corporation.

PROPENSITY. Tendency or inclination. Several propensities are used in economics, including MARGINAL PROPENSITY TO CONSUME and MARGINAL PROPENSITY TO SAVE.

PROPENSITY TO CONSUME. See AVERAGE PROPENSITY TO CONSUME; MARGINAL PROPENSITY TO CONSUME.

PROPENSITY TO SAVE. AVERAGE PROPENSITY TO SAVE. See AVERAGE PROPENSITY TO CONSUME; MARGINAL PROPENSITY TO SAVE.

PROPERTY TAX. A tax based on the amount of property a taxpayer owns. In the U.S. this source of revenue is left to state and local governments, and the methods of taxation differ considerably around the nation. Some governments tax only real property, and some tax all possessions. One of the many criticisms of this form of taxation is that the incentives it provides are counter to most economic goals—a tax based on the value of real property discourages the owner from maintaining and improving it (see PROPOSITION 13); a tax on durable goods encourages spending of a type that does not build a base of goods with significant value.

PROPORTIONAL. In constant ratio, or multiplied by the same number. Thus, if some percentage change in one variable (say, a 10 percent change in price) produces the same percentage change in a related variable (say, a 10 percent change in SUPPLY), it is said that the changes are proportional.

PROPORTIONAL TAX. A tax whose rate is a fixed percentage of the tax base, regardless of the size of the base. See also DEGRESSIVE TAX; PROGRESSIVE TAX; REGRESSIVE TAX.

PROPOSITION 13. A ballot issue approved by California voters in 1978. As a major battle in the taxpayer revolt, it was joined in the same year by tax- or spending-limitation measures overwhelmingly approved by voters in five Western states. Also known as the *Jarvis-Gann Amendment*, or *Jarvis-Gann Initiative*.

One factor that led to Proposition 13 was the rapid rise in real estate prices in Southern California. Although a home, when sold, brought a large price, the homeowner who did not want to sell did not benefit. Although the value of the home had gone up, it was only a paper profit for the homeowner. However, property taxes were based on neighborhood selling prices, so the family that wanted to remain in its home found its property taxes increasing at a rapid rate. Proposition 13 puts a limit on the amount by which an assessment can increase until the property is sold, at which time it is assessed at the selling price.

The legislation (1) restricts the property tax rate to no more than 1 percent of assessed value; (2) sets the assessed value of a property that has not been transferred since 1975-1976 equal to its 1975-1976

fair market value plus 2 percent per year (compounded)—or, in case of subsequent transfer, sets assessed value equal to market value at time of sale plus the 2 percent growth factor; (3) requires that new taxes or increases in existing taxes (except property taxes) receive the approval of two-thirds of the legislature in the case of state taxes, of the electorate in the case of local taxes. The last item was included because an additional goal was to reduce the rate of government growth; the provision was adopted to prevent state officials from simply increasing other taxes in order to continue the rapid rate of government growth.

PROPRIETORSHIP. The simplest form of business enterprise. There is just one owner and, except for certain special requirements, such as health licenses, no permission is necessary for opening the business. See FORMS OF BUSINESS ORGANIZATION. Also called *sole proprietorship*.

PROPRIETORS' INCOME. In NATIONAL INCOME AND PRODUCT ACCOUNTS, all earnings of unincorporated businesses (proprietorships, partnerships, and producers' cooperatives) from current business operations. It does not include supplementary income of individuals derived from renting property. Capital gains and losses are also excluded, and no deduction is made for depletion. See also RENTAL INCOME OF PERSONS; GROSS NATIONAL PRODUCT.

PROSPECTUS. In financial economics, a document describing a securities issue to provide those interested with information on which to base their decision whether to invest.

PROTECTIONISM. The feeling that government should protect domestic sellers from competition with imported goods and services by the use of taxes, quotas, import prohibitions, and other means. Protectionists offer several arguments to justify their position:

1. *Maintaining the standard of living.* If wages are low in another country, allowing their imports to compete with domestic production would lower the standard of living at home and provide less incentive for the other nation to raise its standard.
2. *Infant industry argument.* The rules of pure COMPETITION can be extended to an international basis only if there is complete freedom to enter and leave all markets, but the existence of low-priced imports makes it practically impossible for a domestic producer to enter the market. Import restrictions are demanded, at least until the domestic industry is mature enough to compete.
3. *National defense.* A nation can become so dependent on foreign sources that in time of war or other emergency it would be impossible to begin domestic production.

PROTESTANT ETHIC. The philosophy that hard work is good; self-indulgence is bad; success is to be admired. These views have their roots in Calvinist doctrines.

PRUDENT MAN RULE. In a TRUST arrangement, one of the frequent limitations on the trustee's action; it states that the trustee may make investments "only in such securities as would be acquired by prudent men of discretion and intelligence in such matters who are seeking a reasonable income and the preservation of their capital." [This wording of the rule, used in the statutes of a number of states, was copied from the *Monthly Review of the Federal Reserve Bank of New York* (October 1972, p. 259).]

PSYCHIC INCOME. See MONEY INCOME.

PSYCHOLOGICAL CAUSES. Some economists trace the causes of ECONOMIC FLUCTUATIONS to aggregate feelings; it is argued that, collectively, popular feelings cycle through optimism, unbounded optimism, restraint, and all stages between.

PUBLIC CORPORATION. An enterprise organized as a corporation (see FORMS OF BUSINESS ORGANIZATION) with a GOVERNMENT at some level being the only stockholder (owner).

PUBLIC DEBT. Debt which is owed by all levels of GOVERNMENT combined. Sometimes only the national debt (debt of the federal government) is meant.

PUBLIC DOMAIN. Belonging not to any one individual but to everyone collectively—for example, when a copyright on a book expires and no one has any further right to stop others from publishing it.

PUBLIC FINANCE. That branch of economics which deals with financing the PUBLIC SECTOR—all levels of government. This area includes studies of budgets, DEBT MANAGEMENT, taxes, welfare economics, SPILLOVERs, and many other topics.

PUBLIC GOOD. Usually, items provided by government for consumption by the public in general. A public good has two distinctive characteristics: (1) Consumption of the good by one party does not reduce consumption of the good by others. (2) There is no effective way to restrict the benefits of such goods to those who directly pay for them. The standard example of a public good is national defense. See also SOCIAL GOODS.

PUBLIC INTEREST. The aggregate benefits and costs to all. It is often said that a certain practice is prohibited because it is not in the public interest, meaning that the aggregate cost of that practice (see UTILITY UNITS) to all concerned has been weighed and found to be negative, or more negative than some alternative practice. It is related to an expression formerly in use, "the greatest good for the greatest number."

PUBLIC LANDS. Land owned by the government (but not necesarily open to the public).

PUBLICLY CONTROLLED INDUSTRY. See PUBLIC REGULATION.

PUBLIC OWNERSHIP. Ownership by some level of government, as opposed to *private ownership*, in which an individual or an organization owned by individuals is the owner. See also PUBLIC CORPORATION.

PUBLIC REGULATION. Some enterprises are privately owned, profit seeking, and competitive, and have other characteristics of capitalism but have less than the normal amount of freedom in conducting their business. The reason may be that they have been given a MONOPOLY position (as in the case of utilities) and therefore have not been allowed to charge monopoly prices; that public safety is so involved that the government does not wish to let competitive pressures affect certain decisions (as with airlines and maintenance schedules); or that the industry is so vital to the economy that regulation is deemed advisable (as with banking). There can be any number of other reasons. The present trend is to examine the reasons for government regulation and to deregulate when it is found that doing so is in the PUBLIC INTEREST.

PUBLIC RELATIONS (PR). Efforts by an organization or individual to present a favorable image to the public. Sometimes the purpose is to sell more of a product, sometimes to gain public sympathy in a legal battle, sometimes to acquire long-term good will.

PUBLIC SECTOR. That portion of the total economy which involves any level of GOVERNMENT, whether in strictly governmental functions such as police protection, or in business functions such as operating retail outlets. Other sectors are the consumer sector and the business sector, often combined and called the *private sector*.

PUBLIC SERVICE COMMISSION. Every state as well as the federal government has a board that is responsible for overseeing business enterprises that are vital to the public interest, such as public utilities. The names of the boards vary, as do their responsibilities. See PUBLIC REGULATION.

PUBLIC UTILITY. An enterprise which provides a good or service that the community is dependent on. Today a public utility is almost always a provider of gas, electricity, or water. All are either government owned or (if they are privately owned) controlled monopolies (see MONOPOLY).

PUBLIC WORKS. Projects undertaken by the PUBLIC SECTOR with the expectation of producing long-lasting SOCIAL GOODS such as roads, and bridges.

PUBLIC WORKS ADMINISTRATION (PWA). Created along with the NATIONAL RECOVERY ADMINISTRATION, a program that handled many construction projects for the purpose of putting people to work during the GREAT DEPRESSION. Although over $4 billion was spent, the program had little effect on unemployment and the economic situation and was replaced in 1935 with the WORKS PROJECTS ADMINISTRATION.

PUMP PRIMING. An analogy to a water pump, which does not raise water until it is first primed by the introduction into its valves and piping of some water. Government spending during a recession is sometimes called *pump priming* to indicate that the spending is for the purpose of putting money into the economic stream so that spending power will continue and economic expansion will follow.

PURCHASE TAX (U.K.). A tax on consumer goods, levied at the wholesale level. It is both a SUMPTUARY TAX and a REVENUE TAX—the former because different rates are used, depending on the degree of luxury represented by the item, and the latter because about 7 percent of total taxes are obtained from this source.

PURCHASING POWER. A ratio of the amount of goods and services which a given amount of money will currently buy to the amount it would have bought in a specified base year. When consumer items are being considered, purchasing power is the reciprocal of the CONSUMER PRICE INDEX. Sometimes *purchasing power* is used simply as a qualitative reference to the amount of goods and services a certain amount of money will buy.

PURCHASING POWER PARITY. An exchange rate adjustment that changes a currency's foreign purchasing power after there has been a change in that currency's domestic purchasing power.

PURE COMPETITION. The idealistic form of COMPETITION, in which there are a large number of sellers acting independently, a large number of buyers acting independently, freedom to enter and leave the market, and complete flow of information. Also called *perfect competition.*

PURE INTEREST. That portion of total interest which the lender would demand in the absence of other factors, such as inflation. Also called *true interest.*

PURE PROFIT. See NORMAL PROFIT.

PUT. In the field of SECURITIES, an option to sell a given amount of an identified security within a stated time period. The investor purchases this option, and if the price of the security goes down, he exercises his option to sell at the higher price; if the price goes up, he allows his option to expire unused, losing only the amount he paid for the option. See also CALL.

PYRAMIDING. When a consumption tax is charged at more than one level between manufacturer and consumer, and each seller sets his price by a percentage markup, the resultant *pyramiding* causes the cumulative markup paid by the consumer to be higher than the cumulative tax paid along the line.

Q

QUALIFIED ENDORSEMENT. On a negotiable instrument, the signature of the transferor along with words which limit or remove the liability of the endorser as regards payment on the instrument. A qualified endorsement would include the words *without recourse* and the signature. It is usually used when someone who is clearly involved in the transaction as a mere handler of the funds, such as an agent, is named on the instrument and therefore must endorse it. See also BLANK ENDORSEMENT; CONDITIONAL ENDORSEMENT; RESTRICTIVE ENDORSEMENT; SPECIAL ENDORSEMENT.

QUALITATIVE CONTROLS. Tools of MONETARY POLICY which seek to correct the path of the economy through control of a specific part of the economy. See SELECTIVE CONTROLS.

QUALITY COMPETITION. Market situation in which all other variables on which a buyer bases a purchase decision are fixed, and therefore the choice goes to the seller who offers the highest quality. For example, if two airlines had parallel flights at the same price, and all other factors were identical, it is likely that their advertising would stress safety, on-time operations, and other factors relating to the quality of their service.

QUALITY OF CREDIT. Credit is considered high quality when it functions to increase the smooth, unobstructed movement of goods from producer through the channels of distribution to the ultimate users—as opposed to *speculative credit*, which is not productively used. The latter type of credit usually increases during an inflationary period and is one of the factors making it difficult to return to a stable economy.

QUANTITATIVE CONTROLS. Tools of MONETARY POLICY which are aimed at control of the economy in general (as opposed to SELECTIVE CONTROLS) through affecting reserves of the commercial banking system and the MONEY SUPPLY. Quantitative controls consist of the reserve ratio and discount rate. See FEDERAL OPEN MARKET COMMITTEE.

QUANTITY THEORY OF MONEY. Theory holding that the overall level of prices is proportional to the size of the MONEY SUPPLY. This theory, which stems from the EQUATION OF EXCHANGE, is one of the bases of a group of economists called monetarists. Many monetarists moderate their stand by saying that money supply is the most important factor in determining prices but that prices will not change in direct proportion.

QUARTER. One-fourth of a year; three months; 13 weeks. Economic and business statistics, especially those which are aggregates of many series (such as GROSS NATIONAL PRODUCT), are usually compiled and released quarterly. Even when statistics for many years past are presented, they are often given by quarters to show more detail than would be shown if the entire year were averaged.

There are several ways to indicate the applicable quarter on a graph or schedule. Some ways to indicate the period April through June of 1984 are 1984(2), 1984(II), 1984-2Q, and 1984-Q2.

QUARTER EAGLE. A $2.50 U.S. gold coin. See EAGLE for related denominations.

QUARTERS FOR CYCLICAL DOMINANCE (QCD). See MONTHS FOR CYCLICAL DOMINANCE.

QUARTER STOCK. An expression sometimes used for CAPITAL STOCK which has a PAR VALUE of $25.

QUASI RENT. Generally, a rent is a continuing series of payments for a certain use; quasi rent, in contrast, can also be a single payment, as for a purchase. What distinguishes this type of payment is that a change (possibly through negotiation or changed market conditions) caused an amount that was previously an ECONOMIC PROFIT to be identified as *quasi rent*. For example, suppose a retailer has a contract to buy product A from its manufacturer for $10, knowing that it can retail the item for an amount sufficient to earn NORMAL PROFIT. If consumers are so anxious to buy the item that they pay a higher retail price than expected, the retailer makes an economic profit because he continues to buy at the original low price. However, when the contract expires, the manufacturer will maximize his profit by raising the price to the retailer; then the amount that was formerly economic profit to the retailer becomes quasi rent (a cost), and his profits return to normal.

QUESNAY, FRANCOIS. French economist (1694-1774) and founder of the school of economic thought known as PHYSIOCRACY. Among his contributions were a theory on distribution of income and the tableau économique—a mathematical representation of France's economy generally recognized as the world's first macroeconomic MODEL.

QUICK ASSET. An asset which can be converted to cash rather easily and with little or no sacrifice in value. This expression is sometimes preferred to *liquid asset* because of its more precise meaning; the latter includes both cash and quick assets.

QUOTA. One of the most direct controls. A quota sets the maximum, minimum, or both for participation by an ECONOMIC UNIT. Within an economy a quota can be used to answer one of the basic questions, Who will receive the output of a certain product? Ordinarily in a MARKET ECONOMY price does the rationing, but if a price control has been established below the equilibrium price (see SUPPLY AND DEMAND), one way to resolve the resultant shortage is to set a quota on the amount each economic unit can buy.

In international economics, a quota can establish the maximum amount of a product which a nation allows to enter its borders (see PROTECTIONISM; IMPORT QUOTA).

R

RACK RENT. If each payment to the owner for the use of property is a very large percentage of the total value of the property, the payment is called *rack rent*.

RANDOM NUMBER. In many applications of mathematics to economics (see ECONOMETRICS) it is necessary to select a random number, meaning that every number has an equal probability of being selected and that every selection must be independent of all previous selections. Most computers have the ability to generate sequences of random or quasi-random numbers, and many books include a random number table.

RATE. Many figures in economics are *rates*, meaning that they are in terms of a certain quantity *per* some base (often time). Thus, if one company increased its employment by 100 workers and another by 150 workers, we know almost nothing about their relative growths until we can convert those numbers into at least two rates: First we would want to know how many employees each company had originally (the rate we would then calculate with this base is the *percentage* increase). Next, we would want to know the periods of time over which those increases took place (then we would work up a figure such as employment increase *per month*, or some other unit of time). See also ANNUAL RATE.

RATE OF RETURN. Earnings of an enterprise as a percentage of, usually, money put into the firm. This figure is of special interest to authorities responsible for regulated monopolies (see MONOPOLY): Without the benefit of the natural forces of the MARKETPLACE, these authorities must establish charges, services, and other items at levels such that management will have incentives to be efficient, profits will be reasonable but not excessive, and new capital will be attracted.

RATE OF SUBSTITUTION. See MARGINAL RATE OF SUBSTITUTION.

RATE OF TIME PREFERENCE. The interest rate at which consumers are willing to forgo present consumption in order to save, presumably for future consumption. This rate implies riskless saving, and therefore actual market rates will be higher. See PURE INTEREST.

RATIO. Simply a fraction; "the ratio of A to B" means a fraction with A as the numerator and B as the denominator.

RATIO CHART. See RATIO SCALE.

RATIONAL WAGE DIFFERENTIALS. The extra amount paid to workers as compensation for some special disadvantage in connection with their assignment, such as danger, undesirable hours, or undesirable location. Also called *equalizing* *wage differentials.* See also PREMIUM PAY.

RATIONED CREDIT. When demand for borrowed funds exceeds supply, but interest rates (for various legal, business, or other reasons) do not rise enough to bring about equilibrium, a shortage of funds (see CREDIT CRUNCH) occurs and lenders must ration funds according to some plan. Some common plans are raising lenders' standards of credit worthiness, requiring larger down payments, and requiring larger COMPENSATING BALANCEs. Marginal borrowers who consequently cannot obtain credit even though they are willing to pay existing rates are referred to as the *unsatisfied fringe of borrowers.*

RATIONING. A determination of who is to receive the output of certain goods and services, especially when quantity demanded exceeds quantity supplied.

Rationing by plan. When there is a shortage—that is, the product is selling at less than its equilibrium price (see SUPPLY AND DEMAND)—buyers want to take more off the market than suppliers are willing to provide, so someone other than the buyers often decides who will be permitted to buy. Often a government makes the decision, rationing according to a plan, such as limiting every person to a fixed amount (during World War II nearly all consumer items were rationed this way) or limiting the availability to only certain groups (during an epidemic, medicines are sometimes given only to the very old, the very young, or pregnant women). Sometimes the suppliers do the rationing according to a plan such as first come first served, a limited amount per customer, only regular customers served, or random number selection. One of the problems with rationing is the tendency for a BLACK MARKET to develop.

Price rationing. One of the basics of economics is that wants are unlimited while the goods and services available for satisfying wants are limited. If the price is at or above equilibrium, everyone who wants to buy at the price can find a

seller, and it is said that the price does the rationing. Such a price can be established by market forces (see MARKETPLACE) or by plan of a government or suppliers. Shortages are ended in this way: When a shortage develops, sellers increase their price and then some buyers are no longer interested; there is no longer a shortage when the price finds a level such that the quantity of buyers still in the market equals the quantity of the good available.

Unplanned rationing. Distribution of some products can be thought of as rationed by such unplanned methods as chance, physical power, proximity, association, and many other methods.

RATIO SCALE. Graphs one or both scales of which have logarithmic spacing rather than even (linear) spacing; they are called *ratio scales* because changes of equal ratio will have the same slope and are therefore easier to compare. For example, the distance from 1 to 2 and from 100 to 200 will be the same on a ratio scale, since both represent a doubling. The typical logarithmic scale is marked in decades, with each decade receiving the same length along the scale: If 1 inch represents 10 to 100, then 100 to 1,000, as well as 100,000 to 1,000,000 and all other changes resulting from multiplying the lower number by 10 (decades), are also marked 1 inch apart. Another reason for the popularity of ratio scales is that a constant-percentage change is graphed as a straight line, whereas the same constant percentage change approaches a vertical line at high numbers on a linear scale.

REAGANOMICS. In the press, the economic policies of President Reagan. In general these policies were planned to produce a stronger economy in a few years, even if an economic slowdown has to occur first. Another characteristic of Reaganomics is a decrease in the government sector and a corresponding increase in the private sector.

REAL. Usually, adjusted for changes in the purchasing power of the dollar. For example, real wages are actual current wages which have been adjusted so as to be expressed in CONSTANT DOLLARS. Sometimes *real* refers to non-money items, as in REAL INCOME.

REAL DISPOSABLE PER CAPITA INCOME. A U.S. Commerce Department series, based on total PERSONAL INCOME less income taxes (federal and state), social security, and other social insurance contributions. The series is adjusted by the price DEFLATOR for personal consumption expenditures, and the result is divided by the total population.

REAL EFFECTIVE EXCHANGE RATE. Nominal effective foreign exchange value of the dollar (a trade-weighted exchange rate) multiplied by the RATIO of the U.S. CONSUMER PRICE INDEX to the foreign consumer price index. PURCHASING POWER PARITY holds when the real effective exchange rate is 100. Below 100 the dollar depreciates in real terms; above 100 the dollar appreciates in real terms.

REAL FLOW. The movement of goods and services through one or more sectors of an economy. Each time there is a transfer or transaction, payment takes place and therefore money flows in the direction opposite to that of goods and services. Because the eventual purpose of an economy is to provide goods and services for consumption, they constitute the real flow, and the rest of the transaction, which is actually only the "lubricant" of the transaction, is the *money flow*.

REAL GROSS NATIONAL PRODUCT. GROSS NATIONAL PRODUCT measured in CONSTANT DOLLARS; adjusted for inflation since a specified base year.

REAL INCOME. The amount of goods and services a person can buy with his MONEY INCOME. Real incomes are difficult to compare because individuals prefer to buy different mixes of products with their incomes, but the general rule is that a person's real income declines if

his money income remains constant and prices of goods and services increase. See SUBSTITUTION EFFECTS.

REAL INVESTMENT. The buying of CAPITAL GOODS, in contrast to the everyday use of *investment*—the buying of securities and other property which are expected to increase in value to the investor. The word *real* is added to remove any doubt as to which investment is being considered.

REALIZED INVESTMENT. The sum of FIXED INVESTMENT and CHANGE IN BUSINESS INVENTORIES. Also called *actual investment*. The word *realized* is used to emphasize that both PLANNED INVESTMENT and UNPLANNED INVESTMENT are taken into account. See also GROSS PRIVATE DOMESTIC INVESTMENT.

REAL MONEY BALANCE. MONEY SUPPLY in CONSTANT DOLLARS divided by a price index. For example, the U.S. money supply was $291.8 billion in 1975 and $415.6 billion in 1980; the IMPLICIT PRICE DEFLATORs for those years were 125.56 and 177.36, respectively. Dividing the money supply of each year by its deflator, we find that real money balances changed from $232.40 in 1975 to $234.33, for a change of 0.83 percent; the change in current dollars (without adjusting by deflators) was 42.43 percent. (The implicit price deflator is given on the basis of 1972 equals 100, and therefore, to be mathematically rigorous, the deflators for both years should be divided by 100 to become 1.2556 and 1.7736. However, the 100s would cancel in the fraction, and even if that step is omitted, the percentages will calculate to the values given.)

It can be seen that the absolute size of a real money balance has meaning only when the base year of the associated index is given, but changes in real money balance are meaningful even if the base year is not given—although it is always necessary to use the same base year for all calculations in the comparison.

REAL PRODUCT. Another expression for GROSS NATIONAL PRODUCT in CONSTANT DOLLARS of a specified year.

REAL PROPERTY. Land, buildings, and certain items attached to land.

REAL SPENDABLE WEEKLY EARNINGS. A U.S. Labor Department series, derived from the average hourly earnings of all private nonfarm production (and nonsupervisory) workers listed on payrolls, multiplied by the average weekly hours of those workers. The weekly tax liability (payroll and federal income tax, computed on the assumption that these earnings are realized throughout the year and that the worker is married, has three dependents, and has no other income) is subtracted from weekly earnings to obtain net weekly earnings, which are then deflated by the CONSUMER PRICE INDEX to obtain the final figure.

REAL WAGES. The amount of goods and services a person can buy with his MONEY INCOME; same as REAL INCOME.

REASONING, INDUCTIVE. See INDUCTIVE REASONING.

REBATE. A refund due because of a business arrangement such as a discount or overpayment. There are several reasons why manufactures' rebates have become so popular in recent years: (1) They have been accepted, and the public likes them. (2) The procedure leaves retailers more freedom to offer discounts and other arrangements of their own. (3) A few consumers lose their sales receipt or for other reasons never apply for the rebate. (4) The manufacturer receives an interest-free loan: If the net selling price (after rebate) is established and then a $5 rebate is added on, every $5 paid by consumers provides an interest-free loan until the manufacturer mails the rebate.

RECALL. In labor economics, a list of former employees who have been laid off but who will be notified when the employer is hiring again. Some recall arrangements automatically offer a job to the former employee; others simply notify him that he will be considered along with other applicants. A former employee on recall may be completely separated from the employer, or everything—such as group insurance, seniority accumulation, and retirement plan—except pay may be allowed to continue. If the employee is notified that jobs are now available, and he chooses not to return, then a complete separation is effected, except for vested rights such as any retirement plan. Recall periods are always of a definite, stated duration, usually 1 or 2 years, although they are sometimes extended at the end of that time.

RECESSION. A slowdown in economic activity, less severe than a depression. When unemployment increases in a recession, basic SUPPLY AND DEMAND analysis indicates that product prices will decline, mitigating the effects of the recession. However, most economies today are characterized by PRICE RIGIDITY in products as well as labor, and the natural forces that tend to bring the economy out of the recession have been weakened.

Many economists say that a recession occurs when for two consecutive QUARTERs there is a decline in REAL GROSS NATIONAL PRODUCT.

RECESSION, INVENTORY. See INVENTORY RECESSION.

RECIPROCAL BUYING. Transactions in which two parties to another transaction reverse their roles as buyer and seller. For example, a printing company uses a certain trucking company for all its shipments, and then when the trucking company needs printed forms it buys them from that printer. The reason for reciprocal buying may be that each offers the best buy to the other, convenience, or simply an agreement that each will buy from the other. If the last reason applies, managerial economics usually warns that reciprocal buying may be convenient but is probably not the most efficient alternative because no element of competition is involved.

RECIPROCAL TRADE AGREEMENTS. Agreements that allow the executive branch of government to reduce import tariffs up to a stipulated maximum if international trading partners reciprocate. Also called *executive trade agreements*.

RECIPROCAL TRADE AGREEMENTS ACT. U.S. legislation of 1934 that followed the record high tariff rates of the HAWLEY-SMOOT TARIFF. The president was given authority to negotiate bilateral tariff reductions of up to 50 percent. See also GENERAL AGREEMENT ON TARIFFS AND TRADE.

RECIPROCITY. Reduction in import tariffs in one nation because of the good will generated by similar reductions in another nation.

RECOGNITION. In labor economics, an official agreement between an employer and a union recognizing the latter as the bargaining unit for a certain group of employees. See CERTIFICATION.

RECONSTRUCTION FINANCE CORPORATION. (1) (Ger.) (Kreditanstalt Fuer Wiederaufbau) Financial organization owned and operated by the West German government for the purpose of making investment money available to industry. (2) (RFC) A NEW DEAL program enacted during the GREAT DEPRESSION for the purpose of getting credit money flowing in order to stimulate industry and agriculture. It made loans directly and took assignments of loans that FINANCIAL INTERMEDIARIES and others had made.

RECOVERY. The state of an economy while it is moving from a recessionary period toward fuller utilization of its resources.

RED DOG. Name used for state bank notes about the time of the U.S. Civil War, indicating the lack of faith citizens had in that form of money.

REDISCOUNT RATE. It was once general policy that commercial banks borrowed from Federal Reserve banks by turning over promissory notes and other commercial paper which they had already discounted. The Federal Reserve bank would deduct interest charges and loan the balance, so it was said that the paper was *rediscounted*. Under current practice, several kinds of loans are made to commercial banks; although *discount* no longer correctly describes the loan procedures, it is still used. See DISCOUNT RATE for additional description of this tool of MONETARY POLICY.

REDISTRIBUTION OF INCOME. Change in the aggregate amount of income which is received by each of several identified blocks of income recipients. See INCOME REDISTRIBUTION.

REDUNDANT CAPACITY. The ability among producers (accumulation of plant and equipment) to produce more than is demanded. See EXCESS CAPACITY.

REEDING. Ridges on the rim of a finished coin.

RE-EXPORT. To ship out of the nation certain goods that were recently imported. The phrase usually implies that the goods are reshipped without being changed and without payment of customs duty.

REFLECTIONS ON THE FORMATION AND DISTRIBUTION OF RICHES. Book of the economic school of PHYSIOCRACY, written by ANNE ROBERT JACQUES TURGOT and published in 1766.

REFUND. (1) The paying of a debt with funds obtained by selling new debt. In this sense the U.S. national debt is constantly "refunded" through selling of new government bonds in order to obtain the funds with which to pay bonds that are constantly maturing. (2) In the everyday sense, the return of the purchase price when a buyer returns merchandise and cancels the sale.

REFUNDING BOND. A BOND sold for the purpose of obtaining funds to retire old debt. Many organizations, private as well as government, have what is considered to be a permanent debt. As each unit of debt matures these organizations repay it as promised, but they sell new debt to obtain the funds. Bonds which are sold for the purpose of obtaining funds to retire old debt are called refunding bonds.

REFUSAL TO NEGOTIATE. In labor economics, a breakdown of negotiations because one party to a labor dispute has simply made an offer and does not consider any counteroffers. By federal law both parties must negotiate in good faith; refusal is a violation and is grounds for legal remedies.

REGIONAL CHECK PROCESSING CENTER (RCPC). A facility in a "community whose trade, business and financial activities are substantially related" ["RCPCs—Transitional Step," *Federal Reserve Bank of San Francisco Business Review* (July/August 1973)], established to reduce the handling, transportation, and time required for CLEARING OF CHECKS. It is considered that RCPCs are a transitional step toward ELECTRONIC MONEY.

REGIONALISM. Removal of trade barriers among economic units of a certain region. *Regionalism* usually refers to the agreement by a group of nations to allow free trade among themselves, usually while maintaining restrictions against all other nations.

REGIONAL SECURITY EXCHANGE. An exchange where SECURITIES of companies within the geographical area are traded, as opposed to a national securities exchange, which lists securities regardless of the location of the company.

REGISTERED BOND. A BOND whose ownership is recorded by the issuer; interest payments are sent automatically. Selling of a registered bond must involve the issuer because the latter is required to have the name and address of the new owner. See also COUPON BOND.

REGRATE. Purchasing items for the specific purpose of reselling them in a short time in another market.

REGRESSION, MATHEMATICAL. Synthesizing a mathematical expression whose locus is a best fit for a series of available data points, where *best fit* can be defined in various ways but is usually defined by the LEAST SQUARES criterion. See the appendix.

REGRESSIVE TAX. A tax levied at *rates that decrease* as the the tax base *increases*. Many sales tax arrangements provide for not taxing food in order to avoid being regressive; because high-income families spend a small percentage of their incomes on food, while low-income families spend a large percentage of their incomes on food. Such a sales tax is a PROGRESSIVE TAX because those with low incomes pay a smaller percentage of their incomes to the tax than do those with larger incomes. See also DEGRESSIVE TAX; PROPORTIONAL TAX.

REGULAR DELIVERY. In the buying and selling of government securities as part of *open market operations* (see FEDERAL OPEN MARKET COMMITTEE), transactions which call for payment and delivery on the following business day; transactions for payment and delivery the same day are called *cash* delivery.

REGULATED INDUSTRY. An industry which is subject to a considerable amount of direct control by government authorities and is influenced very little by the natural forces of SUPPLY AND DEMAND. See MONOPOLY; PUBLIC REGULATION.

REGULATION Q. Most of the FEDERAL RESERVE SYSTEM regulations are directed at the banking industry and therefore never come to the public's attention. However, regulation Q is often referred to in newspapers; it is the regulation which puts the ceilings on interest rates that commercial banks may pay to depositors. See TOOLS OF MONETARY POLICY.

REGULATION Z. Official designation of the legislation popularly known as TRUTH IN LENDING.

REGULATORY AGENCIES (REGU-LATORY COMMISSIONS). Every state and the federal government has a board which is responsible for overseeing business enterprises that are vital to the public interest, such as public utilities. The names of the boards vary from jurisdiction to jurisdiction, as do the scopes of their responsibilities. See PUBLIC REGULATION.

REGULATORY IMPACT ANALYSIS (RIA). Since February 1981, U.S. regulatory agencies have been directed, to the extent permitted by law, to use BENEFIT-COST ANALYSIS when promulgating new regulations, reviewing existing regulations, or developing legislative proposals concerning regulation. In the case of *major rules*, the agencies must publish preliminary and final RIAs which set forth the benefit-cost balance and feasible alternatives. (Major rules consist of those that will have any of the following three effects: an annual effect of $100 million or more, a major increase in costs or prices, or a significant adverse effect on a specific industry or on the economy in general.)

An RIA includes (1) a description of the potential costs and benefits of the proposed rule; (2) a determination of its potential net benefits; and (3) a description of feasible cheaper alternatives with an explanation of the legal reasons why such alternatives, if proposed, could not be adopted.

REICHSBANK (Ger.). First CENTRAL BANK of Germany, created in 1876. It lost its power and true function during the Nazi years and was replaced by the DEUTSCHE BUNDESBANK in 1957. In the years between World War II and 1957 the bank was reorganized and renamed the Deutscher Lander; at the same time, state central banks (*Landeszentralbanken*) were given control over issue of bank notes.

REINSURANCE. The practice by which one insurer accepts a policy and then sells all or part of it to another insurer. For example, one insurer might sell insurance to several shippers who are all using the same ship; sinking of that ship could be a single disaster which would cause considerable loss to the insurer, so he might sell some of the policies to other insurers for cash, or they might trade policies.

RELATIVE FACTOR PRICES. The ratio of the price of one economic factor (FACTOR OF PRODUCTION) to another, usually with regard to a specific product or job, but may also be a reference to index prices of the factors.

RELATIVE MONEY BALANCE. The amount of MONEY demanded by the public relative to the level of national income. Equilibrium is constantly being adjusted by devices such as interest rates which rise (fall) when relative money balance is high (low). Stability of this balance is the basis of the MONETARIST position.

RENT. (1) Earnings which accrue to the owners of land and capital (see ECONOMIC RESOURCES; FACTOR EARNINGS). (2) In popular usage gross payments by the users of any item owned by another; *ordinary rent* is all inclusive, *ground rent* refers to payments made for the use of land only, and *capital rent* is payment for the use of a CAPITAL GOOD.

RENTAL AGREEMENT. See LEASE.

RENTAL, IMPUTED VALUE OF. See IMPUTATION.

RENTAL INCOME OF PERSONS. In NATIONAL INCOME AND PRODUCT ACCOUNTS, the money earned by persons from the use of their real property, such as a house, store, or farm. It also includes the imputed net rent of owner-occupants of nonfarm dwellings, as well as royalties received by persons from patents, copyrights, and rights to natural resources. The income received by persons primarily engaged in the real estate business is excluded but is included in PRO-

PRIETORS' INCOME. Also excluded are rent and royalties received by corporations and governments. See GROSS NATIONAL PRODUCT.

REORGANIZATION BOND. An industrial BOND sold with the specific intention of using the proceeds to reorganize the debt and financial structure of a firm. Also called *adjustment bond.*

REPARATIONS. Payments by an aggressor nation for damage caused.

REPLACEMENT DEMAND. DEMAND which results not from expansion of the economy, but from a need to replace durable items so as to keep the economy at a constant level. (In an economic analysis, the cause of a certain statistic is often more important than the size of the statistic.)

REPO. Expression sometimes used for REPURCHASE AGREEMENT.

REPORTING PAY. The minimum which an employer promises to pay an employee who is asked to report to work. For example, if, because of a special meeting, a guard is asked to come from home to unlock a gate, it would not be fair to pay the guard for just the 30 seconds it takes to unlock the gate, so a minimum reporting pay is established, typically two hours. Also called *call-in pay.*

REPRESENTATION ELECTION. In labor economics, voting by employees to determine if a sufficient percentage desire to be represented by a certain union. See CERTIFICATION. Such elections are usually supervised by a LABOR RELATIONS BOARD.

REPRESENTATIVE. See PERSONAL REPRESENTATIVE.

REPRESENTATIVE MONEY. Paper money and coins each unit of which represents a given amount of precious metal (usually gold or silver) held by authorities. The theory is that, instead of the inconvenience and loss (see ABRASION) involved in circulating the metal itself, the

same function can be achieved by storing the metal and circulating the receipts.

REPRESSIVE TAX. A tax which effectively provides negative incentive for production and therefore reduces total output and has a contractionary effect on the economy. It is difficult to determine precisely the effect of a tax, and many feel that a large number of U.S. taxes are repressive.

REPURCHASE AGREEMENT (RP). In the financial markets, an acquisition of funds through the sale of securities with a simultaneous agreement by the seller to repurchase them at a later date. Basically they are a secured means of borrowing and lending short-term funds. RPs are most frequently made for one business day (overnight RP). Other RPs are arranged for 30 days or other periods mutually agreed upon. A special type of RP is the *continuing contract*, which consists of a series of overnight loans that are automatically renewed each day until terminated by either party to the transaction. The greatest share of all RP transactions consists of repurchase agreements involving U.S. government or federal agency securities.

For example, suppose the treasurer of a large corporation calculates the firm's cash position for the day and determines that the firm has funds that are not required immediately but will probably be needed in a day or two. The treasurer, wishing to earn interest on these excess funds for a day, arranges to purchase a government security from a commercial bank with an accompanying agreement that the bank will repurchase the security on the following day. Other RPs are arranged for 30 days or other periods mutually agreed upon.

REQUIRED DEPOSIT BALANCE. A certain percentage of a loan that a bank sometimes requires a borrower to leave on deposit with the bank. The borrower then does not have the use of the entire loan amount, but only the loan amount minus the required balance. One result is that the effective rate of interest is greater than it would be if no deposit balance were required. Also called a *compensating balance*.

For example, suppose $1,000 is borrowed at 15 percent from a bank, to be paid back at the end of 1 year. Suppose further that the bank requires that 10 percent of the loan amount be kept on deposit. The borrower therefore has the use of only $900 ($1,000 less 10 percent), on which interest of $150 is charged (15 percent of $1,000 for 1 year). Interest of $150 on $900 is actually an effective rate of 16.67 percent. If the $100 is placed in an account that earns, say, 5 percent, the net interest paid by the borrower is $145 and the overall effective rate is 16.11 percent.

REQUIRED RESERVES. See BANK RESERVES.

RESALE PRICE MAINTENANCE. See FAIR TRADE LAWS.

RESERVATION PRICE. The highest price which a seller will *not* accept; that seller *will* accept if the offered price is raised incrementally. See MARGINAL SELLER.

RESERVE ASSETS (U.K.). Those funds which constitute reserves in the U.K. (see BANK RESERVES); they are defined to include non-interest-bearing deposits at the BANK OF ENGLAND, government securities within a year of maturity, local authority bills eligible for rediscount at the Bank of England, commercial bills (limited to 2 percent of ELIGIBLE LIABILITIES), tax reserve certificates (only through 1974), and money at call with the discount houses.

RESERVE BALANCE. The amount of money a MEMBER BANK has in its account at its Federal Reserve bank. See BANK RESERVES.

RESERVE BANK. See FEDERAL RESERVE BANK.

RESERVE BANK CREDIT. The amount of credit extended by FEDERAL RE-

SERVE BANKs, consisting of holdings of U.S. government securities (either bought outright or under REPURCHASE AGREEMENT), loans (mostly to COMMERCIAL BANKs), FEDERAL RESERVE FLOAT, and miscellaneous assets.

RESERVE CITY BANK. See DESIGNATION OF BANKS.

RESERVE DEFICIENCY. The amount by which a bank's reserve account is below its required level. See BANK RESERVES; RESERVE RATIO.

RESERVE, INVESTMENT. See INVESTMENT RESERVE.

RESERVE LAG ACCOUNTING. A method of figuring outstanding bank liabilities for the purpose of determining reserve requirements (see BANK RESERVES). See LAGGED RESERVE ACCOUNTING for other methods and a reference.

RESERVE POSITION. See BALANCE OF INTERNATIONAL PAYMENTS.

RESERVE RATIO. The fraction of demand deposit money which a COMMERCIAL BANK must keep in its reserve account. This ratio determines the maximum amount a bank may loan out, and therefore it indirectly affects the size of the nation's MONEY SUPPLY. See BANK RESERVES; MONETARY POLICY.

RESERVE REQUIREMENTS. Reserves that must be held against customer deposits of banks and other depository institutions. The reserve requirement ratio affects the expansion of deposits that can be supported by each additional dollar of reserves. The BOARD OF GOVERNORS (OF THE FEDERAL RESERVE SYSTEM) sets reserve requirements, within limits specified by law, for all depository institutions (including commercial banks, savings and loan associations, credit unions, and U.S. agencies and branches of foreign banks) that have transaction accounts of nonpersonal time

deposits. A lower reserve requirement allows more deposit and loan expansion and a higher reserve ratio permits less expansion. See MONETARY POLICY.

RESERVES AVAILABLE FOR PRIVATE NONBANK DEPOSITS (RPD or RPDs). Total MEMBER BANK reserves (see BANK RESERVES) less reserves required against U.S. government demand deposits and net interbank deposits. It has been held that RPDs give more meaningful information for guiding MONETARY POLICY, than total reserves, because short-run fluctuations in government and interbank deposits are sometimes large and difficult to predict and usually are not of major significance for policy. This definition and a very good explanation of the meaning of reserves is in "RPDs and Other Reserve Operating Targets" by Charlotte E. Ruebling [*Federal Reserve Bank of St. Louis Review* (August 1972)].

RESERVE TRANSACTIONS. See BALANCE OF INTERNATIONAL PAYMENTS.

RESIDENTIAL STRUCTURES. In NATIONAL INCOME AND PRODUCT ACCOUNTS, private investment expenditures on residential structures reflecting completed construction of new single-family houses, apartments, or other space in which people can maintain separate households. In addition to housing units, residential structures include non-housekeeping quarters such as hotels, and dormitories and farm as well as urban dwelling units. Also included are expenditures for additions and alterations made to these structures.

Mobile homes are not in this category; they are included in PERSONAL CONSUMPTION EXPENDITURES as durable goods if occupied by the owner, in PRODUCERS' DURABLE EQUIPMENT if rented.

These estimates differ from the residential construction figures published by the U.S. Census Bureau in that they include brokers' commissions on the sale of structures, net purchases of used structures from government, and farm residences.

RESOURCE MARKET. Transactions in which ECONOMIC RESOURCES are sold (are on the supply side of SUPPLY AND DEMAND). Also called *factor market*. See CIRCULAR FLOW OF MONEY.

RESOURCES. See ECONOMIC RESOURCES.

RESTRAINT. See FISCAL RESTRAINT.

RESTRAINT OF TRADE. Actions which tend to reduce the quantity of trade below that which would be conducted through natural forces of SUPPLY AND DEMAND. See CLAYTON ANTITRUST ACT; COMPETITION; SHERMAN ANTITRUST ACT.

RESTRICTION OF NUMBERS. In labor economics, the practice of many unions whereby membership is controlled to maintain a shortage of labor in that trade.

RESTRICTIVE ENDORSEMENT. On a negotiable instrument, the signature of the transferor along with words that limit the purpose for which the instrument may be applied. A typical restrictive endorsement is "for deposit only," meaning that no one in possession of the check can obtain cash for it. See also BLANK ENDORSEMENT; CONDITIONAL ENDORSEMENT; QUALIFIED ENDORSEMENT; SPECIAL ENDORSEMENT.

RESTRICTIVE POLICY. Actions taken by authorities which tend to cause a decrease in the rate of growth of spending and prices, either in the overall economy or in some segment of it, usually as an anti-inflation measure. Such actions are taken by the authorities responsible for FISCAL POLICY or for MONETARY POLICY. See also EXPANSIONARY.

RETAILER. The last seller in the distribution chain from manufacturer to consumer. Each handler in this chain adds a markup to cover costs (economists define the cost of doing business as including normal profit), so the *retail price* is the highest price in the chain.

RETAIL PRICE MAINTENANCE. An agreement, involving more than one level of the distribution chain (usually a manufacturer and his retailers), not to sell for less than a certain price. Also called *vertical price fixing*. See FAIR TRADE LAWS.

RETAINED EARNINGS. The amount of profits a business enterprise keeps—hence the remainder of profits after payment of taxes and dividends. Retained earnings is the amount by which a business is growing and is the source of funds for expanding without borrowing or selling additional ownership shares. Also called *undistributed profits*.

RETALIATORY TARIFF. When one nation increases tariffs on goods imported from another nation, the objective is usually to increase domestic economic activity and employment by discouraging imports. However, the nation whose exports are now going to decline will want to restore its position, so it might increase tariffs to discourage the imports it was buying from the first nation. The latter increase is a retaliatory tariff, and its inevitability is one of the arguments against PROTECTIONISM and high tariffs. See also HAWLEY-SMOOT TARIFF; RECIPROCAL TRADE AGREEMENTS ACT.

RETROACTIVE PAY. If a labor contract expires and workers agree to continue working during negotiations, there is usually a tentative agreement that any settlement will be made effective as of the date the previous contract expired. Where there is no such tentative agreement, it is usually made one of the negotiation issues. The resultant money, which will be paid later, is retroactive pay.

RETURN, RATE OF. See RATE OF RETURN.

REVALUATION. See UNDERVALUED CURRENCY.

REVENUE. Income other than personal income. In the BUSINESS SECTOR, revenue comes from sales, as well as from such other sources as capital gains and investments; in the PUBLIC SECTOR, revenues are obtained by taxes, fines, license fees, user charges, and other means.

REVENUE BOND. A BOND issued by some level of government or by an agency of the government to finance a specific project which will yield revenues, such as a bridge on which tolls will be collected. Interest and repayment of principal are dependent on revenues from the project. See also GENERAL OBLIGATION BOND.

REVENUE SHARING. Voluntary distribution of income from a powerful collector to others with recognized needs but less ability to collect. The expression usually refers to the federal government's sending to state and local governments a percentage of the federal tax collected. The reasoning is that state and local governments compete for businesses, residents, and other revenue sources, and are not free to act in the overall best interest. In contrast, those who can flee from federal taxation are insignificant and therefore taxes can be assigned at the federal level in the over all best interest. Thus the federal government can collect taxes and give to state and local governments the amounts which are optimum for their responsibilities. Any controversy centers on these questions:

1. Should the central government distribute funds with no restrictions on their uses?
2. What are the respective responsibilities of local and central governments?
3. Should government at any level be free of the competitive pressures which affect industry?
4. If people in one area expect less from their government and want to be taxed less, is it right that a na-

tional standard should be set for them?

REVENUE STAMP. A stamp affixed to certain products to show that the required revenue has been paid.

REVENUE TARIFF. A tariff whose main purpose is raising REVENUE for the operation of a government, as opposed to a tariff whose main purpose is control or regulation (see INFANT INDUSTRY ARGUMENT). When the U.S. first became a nation, tariffs provided almost all income for the government, but one of the main problems with depending on such a source of money was that in time of war, when expenditures were highest, international trade decreased or stopped.

REVENUE TAX. A tax whose main purpose is raising REVENUE for operation of a government, as opposed to a SUMPTUARY TAX, which is mainly for control. The dividing line between these two types of taxes is not sharp, since most, if not all, taxes provide some control and some revenue; only a tax which is strictly a NEUTRAL TAX could be considered a pure revenue tax.

REVERSE REPOS. See TOTAL U.S. GOVERNMENT SECURITIES.

REVERSE SPLIT. See SPLIT-UP.

REVISIONIST. A person who believes that socialism is the eventual desired goal of mankind; unlike a Marxist, however, a revisionist wants to see an evolutionary approach rather than a revolutionary defeat of capitalism. Revisionism starts with Marxist doctrines and revises them according to faults which have already been demonstrated, other weaknesses, and more philosophical considerations. See SCHOOLS OF ECONOMIC THOUGHT.

REVOCABLE LETTER OF CREDIT. A document (LETTER OF CREDIT) in which a bank indicates credit approval by stating that it will accept drafts (see ACCEPTANCES), for the named individual, but further states that the promise can be revoked at any time, without prior notice.

REVOLVING CHARGE ACCOUNT. A credit arrangement in which the debtor is allowed to make purchases on credit at any time, adding the new amount to the balance owed. Each time the balance is increased, the repayment schedule changes.

REVOLVING LETTER OF CREDIT. A document (LETTER OF CREDIT) in which a bank indicates credit approval by stating that it will accept drafts (see ACCEPTANCES) for the named individual up to a stated limit, and that as the individual makes payments the limit will automatically be reestablished.

RICARDO, DAVID. Originally a businessman and broker on the London stock exchange, Ricardo (1772-1823) retired wealthy from business in 1815 and spent his time studying, mostly economics. Most of his thinking was related to agriculture, especially corn. He even spoke of wages and profits in units of corn. He is identified with the later period of the CLASSICAL SCHOOL—favoring free trade and LAISSEZ-FAIRE. But one division in the classicists involved those who claimed complete harmony among the classes and those who did not; Ricardo was among the latter. He developed the IRON LAW OF WAGES, arguing that workers will never be better off because wage increases tend to encourage larger families.

Ricardo's main literary contribution was *Principles of Political Economy and Taxation*, first published in 1817. As a FREE TRADER, he opposed the CORN LAWS. To demonstrate the economic advantages of international trade, he developed COMPARATIVE ADVANTAGE, an analysis that is still used today.

RIGGING THE MARKET. Actions, usually by sellers, to raise prices in the MARKETPLACE higher than they would be if controlled by the natural forces of SUPPLY AND DEMAND.

RIGHT-TO-WORK LAW. Legislation in some states which holds that no one should be required to join (or not join) a union as a condition of employment.

RIGIDITY. See PRICE RIGIDITY.

RISING EXPECTATIONS. The desire of an individual or of a group to have some benefit which others are observed enjoying. One of the difficulties holding back economic growth (see LESS DEVELOPED COUNTRY) is that a growing nation must direct a relatively large part of its productive efforts toward the production of capital (see ECONOMIC RESOURCES) and less toward the production of goods for present consumption. If the desire for a higher standard of living is strong, the people want it *now*, not a generation from now, and therefore the rate of economic growth will be quite limited. More often referred to as the *demonstration effect*.

RISK. When a debt security such as a BOND is purchased as an earning asset, there are three types of risk:

1. *Default risk*. There are two ways in which the debtor can default: failure to make interest payments when due, and failure to repay the principal upon maturity of the debt.
2. *Trading risk*. If interest rates on similar securities rise before the bond matures, anyone who buys the bond in the market will demand a discount so that the interest payments he receives will yield a return on his investment equal to what he can receive on similar securities.
3. *Purchasing power risk*. The face amount of the bond, when returned at maturity, may not buy the same amount of goods and services that were forgone to buy the bond.

RISK PREMIUM. The part of an interest charge which is due to uncertainty about future inflation. For example, if a lender, having considered all factors related to a loan and the borrower, would, in a time of stable prices charge 12 percent interest, but charges 15 percent because he does not know what the money will be worth

when it is repaid, the risk premium is 3 percent.

ROLLBACK. A return of prices to a previous level after thay have been raised by one or more sellers. This action sometimes follows pressure from consumer groups, or it can follow pressure, direct or indirect, from government.

ROLLING STOCK. In the railroad industry, those assets that operate along the rails—railroad cars, service equipment, locomotives, etc.

ROUNDABOUT PRODUCTION. See INDIRECT PRODUCTION.

ROUND LOT. The quantity in which CAPITAL STOCK is normally traded, almost always 100 shares. Any quantity less than a round lot is an *odd lot*.

ROYALTY. Payment for the use of a property covered by a copyright, patent, or similar claim.

RULE OF 78s. See SUM OF DIGITS.

RUN. An accelerating clamor to exercise an economic privilege before it is withdrawn either by choice or by economic necessity. A *run on a bank* occurs when depositors feel that because other depositors are withdrawing their funds the bank might become unable to continue honoring requests for withdrawal; the fear becomes self-fulfilling as large numbers of depositors attempt to obtain their funds before other depositors make the bank insolvent. See FEDERAL DEPOSIT INSURANCE CORPORATION.

A *run on a currency* can have two meanings. It can mean that holders of large amounts of a nation's money are demanding that authorities exchange it as promised for the precious metal that backs the money. (Prior to 1971 the U.S. balanced international accounts by exchanging gold. A *run on the dollar* then meant that foreigners were choosing to exchange dollars for gold rather than hold onto the dollars.) The second meaning is simply that holders of a nation's money want to exchange it for money of almost any other nation.

RUNAWAY INFLATION. INFLATION which is difficult to control because it has reached the point where the fact of inflation causes further inflation. For one example, consumers know that during an inflation their money decreases in value but many products increase in value; if an inflation has continued for a period of time, consumers will accelerate their purchasing plans in order to beat price rises, but this action causes an *increase in demand* (see SUPPLY AND DEMAND), which is one of the causes of an inflation. The next step after runaway inflation is HYPERINFLATION, and economic collapse can be expected to follow.

One of the main arguments against CREEPING INFLATION is that it is not a stable condition; it is easy for it to drift into runaway inflation.

RUNAWAY RATE. PIECEWORK is intended to provide an incentive because normal pay is given for normal amounts of production, while those who are unusually productive receive higher pay. Setting of the piece rates is difficult, and sometimes *runaway rates* become established such that workers in one area of the shop can earn much more with the same amount of effort than workers in another area.

RUNAWAY SHOP. In labor economics, an expression used by unions to describe a business which moves despite union objections that the new location gives management a better bargaining position.

RURAL ELECTRIFICATION ADMINISTRATION (REA). A U.S. government bureau which administers the extension of electricity to rural areas where it is generally not commercially feasible, usually by supplying low-interest loans. It was most active in the 1930s and 1940s, but even today this bureau and the Farmers Home Administration originate the bulk of federal government off-budget direct loans.

S

SADDLE POINT. In a graph in two dimensions, a LOCAL MINIMUM—a point from which the curve rises in both directions. On a three-dimensional graph, a saddle point is a local minimum in one plane and a LOCAL MAXIMUM in a plane perpendicular to it.

SAFETY FUND ACT. Legislation passed in New York in 1829 requiring each bank to contribute a certain amount to a guarantee fund to be used in meeting the liabilities of banks that failed. The fund continued in existence for many years, and can be thought of as the forerunner of the FEDERAL DEPOSIT INSURANCE CORPORATION.

SALARY. Compensation for labor or services performed, usually for executives and professionals who receive a monthly or yearly salary, as opposed to hourly earnings, which are governed by the FAIR LABOR STANDARDS ACT and must change to a premium rate after 40 hours per week. In economics, the word *wages* is understood to mean all compensation for labor or services performed, and there is no distinction between salary and wages.

SALES FINANCE COMPANY. See FINANCE COMPANY.

SALES TAX. Usually, a tax assessed on retail sales by adding a stated percentage to the purchase price at the time of sale. The seller therefore collects the tax and at certain times (often quarterly) remits the collections to the government assessing the tax. One objection to a sales tax is that, since a low-income family spends 100 percent of its income, the sales tax it pays represents a higher percentage of its total income than the sales tax paid by a wealthy family. For this reason, sales tax is sometimes called a REGRESSIVE TAX. A popular technique for removing that objection is to exempt food from the sales tax; then, since the low income family spends a large percentage of its income on food, it pays relatively little tax.

The federal government has left this form of taxation for use by state and local governments, and it has become a significant source of revenue in most states. There are many variations, in the percentage, items excluded, methods of collecting, and other factors. In some areas the sales tax is charged by several levels of government so that a certain part goes to the state, a certain part to the county, and a certain part to the city. Some arrangements allow the retailer to deduct a small part before remitting to the government, as compensation for the extra labor and bookkeeping costs involved in collecting and remitting the money.

SALLIE MAE. See STUDENT LOAN MARKETING ASSOCIATION.

SAMPLE. In statistical economics, a series of data inputs smaller in quantity than the entire group of actual inputs. For example, if it is desired to determine what percentage of a tax increase is being paid for out of savings accounts across the nation, an analyst might check in detail the financial arrangements of a few hundred taxpayers; he would then draw conclusions regarding the entire population of the nation. A sample is usually selected very carefully to include various categories in the same proportions as they appear in the total population; if 5 percent of the nation's taxpayers are agricultural workers, an ideal sample would contain 5 percent agricultural workers, etc.

Almost all statistics in economics are obtained through samples, because obtaining data from the entire population would be unreasonably expensive. The technique is to take a census every ten years, using the entire population, and then use that information to select representative samples for other statistics. If the sample is not a faithful miniature of the population, but the differences are known, weightings and other statistical techniques can be used to correct the results.

SANCTIONS. Measures taken with the intention of coercing others to implement changes. The measures can range all the way from physical blockades to subtle steps that are hardly noticed, but in economics the measures are usually import quotas, taxes, and other means of controlling international trade. Sometimes sanctions are in retaliation for other sanctions, and there can be an escalation of sanctions, which is often referred to as *economic warfare*.

SANDWICH COIN. A coin made from sheets of different kinds of metal bonded together. See CLAD COINS.

SATIATION, LAW OF. See LAW OF DIMINISHING UTILITY.

SATISFACTION. In economics, that which a party to a transaction expects to receive. There are degrees of satisfaction, and one of the basics of economics is the quest to maximize the satisfaction of unlimited wants with limited resources. See UTILITY UNITS.

SAVING. In general, income minus expenditures. By this definition, all income is either spent or saved; these are the only two categories, and therefore saving plus expenditures must equal income. See PERSONAL SAVING.

SAVING, FORCED. See FORCED SAVING.

SAVINGS. Wealth that is accumulated through SAVING. Correct interpretation of certain economic writings depends on the distinction between the singular and plural forms of this word.

SAVINGS AND LOAN ASSOCIATION (S&L). A depository type of FINANCIAL INTERMEDIARY that accepts savings and time deposits and makes loans primarily for real estate and construction. They were formerly known as building and loan associations. Although technically not banks, they are generally considered part of the banking industry, and many people refer to them as banks. As the accompanying table shows, there are many similarities.

Until 1982 one of the main distinctions was that banks offered checking accounts but S&Ls did not. In 1980, banks were allowed to pay interest on some checking accounts, and then in 1982 S&Ls were allowed to offer similar accounts. To be precise, "checking with interest" accounts are NEGOTIABLE ORDER OF WITHDRAWAL (NOW) accounts. Commercial customers must still use traditional checking accounts that do not pay interest.

Bank	Savings and Loan
Can be chartered by state or federal government; if the latter, must use the word *National* in firm name.	Can be chartered by state or federal government; if the latter, must use the word *Federal* in firm name.
Administered by FEDERAL RESERVE SYSTEM	Administered by FEDERAL HOME LOAN BANK BOARD
Deposits insured by FEDERAL DEPOSIT INSURANCE CORPORATION	Deposits insured by FEDERAL SAVINGS AND LOAN INSURANCE CORPORATION
Many types of personal and commercial loans	Loans mostly for real estate

SAVINGS BANK. See MUTUAL SAVINGS BANK.

SAVINGS BOND. A debt instrument of the federal government planned for convenient sale to individuals and the general public. They are usually of small maturity value, starting as low as $25; purchase through payroll deduction plans is strongly encouraged and is sometimes made all but mandatory.

SAVINGS FUNCTION. The relationship between income and the amount of income which is saved (not spent). The figures are sometimes presented in a table, referred to as a *savings schedule*.

SAVINGS SCHEDULE. See SAVINGS FUNCTION.

SAY'S LAW. Named after French economist J. B. Say, a rule generally stated as "supply creates its own demand." In other words, the fact that goods and services were produced means that FACTORS OF PRODUCTION received payments (which to the producer were costs), and those who received the payments will be able to buy the goods and services which were produced. An increase in production automatically puts more purchasing power in buyers' hands, and therefore the CIRCULAR FLOW OF MONEY is self-adjusting.

The more modern view is closer to "demand creates its own supply." Welfare and various other programs in many countries provide purchasing power to consumers; that power results in demand for goods and services. Industry will see that those items are produced and in so doing will continue the cycle by putting more spending power in the hands of the public. See CIRCULAR FLOW OF MONEY.

SCAB. A name of derision applied by union members to those who do not agree with the majority, especially to those who wish to work when others wish to strike.

SCARCE RESOURCES. One of the basic tenets of economics is that ECONOMIC RESOURCES are not freely available in unlimited quantities. Although some economists use the word *scarce*, many prefer to say that resources are *limited*, because even when they are around us in abundance, that they are not free means that we must choose among alternatives. That, very briefly, is the problem that economics seeks to solve.

SCARCITY VALUE. That part of the price of an item that is attributable, not to the cost of producing it, but to the fact that buyers are bidding up the price because there is a shortage of the item.

SCATTER CHART. A graph on which data are plotted. The expression is used because actual values of one variable as a function of another seldom fall on a smooth curve, especially in economics, where each data point is the result of large numbers of influences. One step which frequently follows the plotting of a scatter chart is to use mathematical regression (see the appendix) to develop an equation for the line which best fits the data points.

SCHEDULE. A presentation of the relationship between two variables. See DEMAND SCHEDULE.

SCHOOLS OF ECONOMIC THOUGHT. The various philosophies or theories as to how to solve the basic questions of economics. Some actually bear school (university) names because a professor at that university originated the thoughts; others are named for individuals or have descriptive names. A few are described in this dictionary; see CLASSICAL SCHOOL; JOHN MAYNARD KEYNES; LIBERAL SCHOOL; MERCANTILIST; MONETARIST; PHYSIOCRACY; REVISIONIST; SOCIALISM; CAPITALISM; COMMUNISM.

SCRIP. A medium of exchange other than LEGAL TENDER and therefore redeemable at very few locations. During the period of labor abuses in the 1800s, employers sometimes paid wages in scrip, redeemable only at the COMPANY STORE; employees complained that the captive market thus created enabled the employer to overcharge and therefore employees did not receive fair compensation for their labor.

SCRIP DIVIDEND. A certificate stating that at some time in the future the issuing corporation will exchange it for a cash dividend. This form of dividend was common during the GREAT DEPRESSION because cash became more valuable the longer it was held.

SEASONAL BORROWING PRIVILEGE. A 1973 change in the conditions under which banks are allowed to borrow from the FEDERAL RESERVE SYSTEM. The change recognizes that seasonal peak demands vary among banks: The peak business activity for a rural bank may be at a different time from that at which business peaks for an urban bank. It was noted in the report of a special committee that without an assured source of seasonal credit, smaller banks typically accumulated short-term securities as a pool of liquidity on which they could draw to meet peak seasonal needs for funds. To the extent that bank resources were tied up in this way during the off-peak season, there was a danger that some local credit

needs for desirable projects would not be adequately accommodated. As a result of the 1973 changes in the regulation, which permit the Reserve banks to supply credit to smaller banks to tide them over periods of peak seasonal need, banks are now able to use resources that they had previously placed in liquid assets to meet local needs.

To be eligible for the seasonal borrowing privilege, a member bank must (1) lack reasonably reliable access to national money markets, (2) have a seasonal need that arises from a recurring pattern of movement in deposits and loans that persists for at least eight weeks, (3) meet from its own resources that part of the seasonal need equal to at least 5 percent of its average deposits over the preceding calendar year, and (4) arrange with its Reserve bank for seasonal credit in advance of the actual need for funds.

Small banks that do a substantial volume of loan business in farm or resort areas are examples of institutions that may need to use the seasonal borrowing privilege, but they by no means exhaust the possibilities. For some banks, seasonal credits may remain outstanding for a number of months.

SEASONAL FLUCTUATIONS. Variations in economic statistics which are regular and due to the time of year. For example, the UNEMPLOYMENT RATE increases in early summer because many students and recent graduates seek employment. See ECONOMIC FLUCTUATIONS; SEASONALLY ADJUSTED.

SEASONALLY ADJUSTED (SA). Adjusted for comparison with previous identical periods in a cycle so that long-term trends can be identified. For example, comparison of unadjusted retail spending data for November and December of one year would yield little useful information: The fact that sales increased in December does not mean that the economy is expanding; it means that Christmas is coming. Seasonal adjustment takes out the change *normally* expected between November and December, and so it can be determined whether or not there is a changing trend. Adjustments can also be made for exogenous variables such as weather, so that resultant data are a better indication of long-term trends.

SEASONAL UNEMPLOYMENT. Variations in the employment statistics which are due to natural effects of the time of year. For example, the UNEMPLOYMENT RATE can be expected to be higher in January than in December because many people were hired temporarily for the holiday rush. See SEASONALLY ADJUSTED.

SEASONED SECURITY. In the economics of investment, a security which has been favored by investors for a relatively long period of time.

SEAT. In the economics of investment, the right to trade directly on the floor of a major securities exchange. The number of seats is fixed (and fairly small), so when a person wants to buy a seat he must buy it (sometimes for hundreds of thousands of dollars) from someone who presently owns one. Traders who do not own a seat deal through someone who does.

SEATTLE INCOME MAINTENANCE EXPERIMENT (SIME). A sociological experiment which was conducted along with the DENVER INCOME MAINTENANCE EXPERIMENT. Some description and a reference is included with that entry.

SECONDARY BOYCOTT. A BOYCOTT in which group A refuses to conduct business with group B, not because the former has any complaint directly against the latter, but because group B is in a position to exert pressure on group C to take some action or make some changes which group A wants. For example, nation A might refuse to buy goods from nation B unless the latter uses its influence to stop nation C from supplying arms to a certain part of the world. When results are sought directly from the second party, the boycott is a *primary boycott*.

SECONDARY MARKET. Selling of securities by one investor to another investor, rather than by the original issuer as in the *primary market*.

SECONDARY RESERVES. Funds which a bank keeps in a fairly liquid form (see LIQUIDITY) for easy, but not immediate, conversion to MONEY. In some instances banks are allowed to count all or part of their secondary reserves toward meeting RESERVE REQUIREMENTS, but MEMBER BANKs in the U.S. are limited essentially to vault cash plus the amount in their reserve accounts, known as their *primary reserves*. See also BANK RESERVES.

SECONDARY STRIKE. An ordinary labor walkout except that the participants act not to obtain benefits for themselves at the time, but to demonstrate support for others who are having a labor dispute. Also called *sympathy strike*.

SECONDARY WORKERS. That portion of the work force which, because of lack of appropriate skills, is in less demand while PRIMARY WORKERS are available. See also DISPERSION OF UNEMPLOYMENT, WORK FORCE.

SECOND BANK OF THE UNITED STATES. Unlike many older nations, which had a more coordinated banking system as well as a CENTRAL BANK, the U.S. had an unreliable arrangement of state banks after the FIRST BANK OF THE UNITED STATES ceased to exist in 1811. To meet the needs of centralization, control, and regulation, this second bank was chartered in 1816, but like the First Bank, its charter was allowed to expire 20 years later and the U.S. was again without a central bank until the FEDERAL RESERVE SYSTEM was created in 1913. Sometimes the expression *Second National Bank* is used when referring to this bank of 1816.

SECOND NATIONAL BANK. A COMMERCIAL BANK which obtained its charter from the U.S. government is required to use the word *national* in its name;

as a result, several banks around the country have taken the words "Second National Bank" of and added the name of the city or area where they operate, especially if there is already a "First National Bank of . . ." in the area.

Second National Bank is also sometimes used as a reference to the SECOND BANK OF THE UNITED STATES.

SECOND-ORDER EFFECTS. Changes in the economy due, not directly to an action that was taken, but to the effect that an action had on another part of the economy. See INTERDEPENDENCE.

SECOND SHIFT. The work shift that ends about midnight. See also GRAVEYARD SHIFT. Also called *swing shift.*

SECTOR. Economists divide the economy into three main sectors—consumer, business (also called the *industrial sector*), and government (also called the *public sector*). While it is recognized that economic units in all three sectors have much in common (all buy and sell; have inputs, outputs, and budgets; and consume goods and services), grouping according to goals and motivations is highly significant because of its effect on economic decisions. Sometimes a subgroup is referred to as a sector—we might read about "the transportation sector of our economy" in a newspaper.

Consumer sector. This sector comprises individuals and households, and supplying it is the overall purpose of the economy. Characteristics of this sector are that it sells FACTORS OF PRODUCTION, it buys goods and services, and it is motivated by the desire to increase UTILITY UNITS. The consumer sector is not noted for efficiency or objectivity in decisions.

Business sector. This sector includes nonprofit organizations as well as regular firms. It buys factors of production and uses them to produce goods and services, which it sells to all three sectors. Motivations are complex and include long-run growth, survival, and filling a need in society, as well as profits. Although there

are exceptions, the business sector is characterized by efficiency and objectivity in its decisions.

Government sector. This sector includes all levels of government—federal, state, city, etc. Although some of its income comes from sales of goods and services, most of it is from direct and indirect taxes. In the field of economics, government is needed to establish and enforce the rules of competition and to ensure that parties adhere to the rules of fairness.

SECTORAL INFLATION. An inflation which has resulted from a shortage in a particular SECTOR of the economy. If the output of that sector cannot be bypassed, the shortage will cause price increases, which are then passed on to buyers and which cause other shortages until a general inflation results. Also called *bottleneck inflation.*

SECULAR. In economics, refers to long periods of time. On page 66 of the 1982 *Economic Report of the President* we read that "procyclical growth in money was accompanied by a secular growth," where the latter growth is the fairly steady growth line about which there are short-term variations.

SECULAR STAGNATION. Lack of growth, or even decline in an economy, that has persisted for a period of time long enough to indicate that the problem is not going to cure itself.

SECULAR TREND. Long-term average of a statistical series, usually understood to cover at least three or four generations. There will be short-term variations above and below this trend.

SECURED TRANSACTION. In the Uniform Commercial Code (UCC) a credit transaction in which the seller retains a security interest in the property even though the buyer may take possession and/or title.

SECURITIES. Stocks, bonds, and other instruments of ownership or debt used to finance large operations in the business and the government sectors. Also property which is used to ensure payment in a secured transaction.

SECURITIES ACT. U.S. legislation of 1933 requiring businesses to register and provide information on securities offered for sale to the public. Enforcement of this act is one of the responsibilities of the SECURITIES AND EXCHANGE COMMISSION.

SECURITIES AND EXCHANGE COMMISSION (SEC). An agency of the U.S. government, created by the SECURITIES EXCHANGE ACT for the purpose of enforcing that and several related acts.

SECURITIES EXCHANGE ACT. A compromise between the minimum control preceding the STOCK MARKET CRASH and the Sale of Securities Act, with its heavy liabilities of underwriters. This U.S. legislation of June 1934 required the registration, along with detailed financial information, of securities to be sold to the public, banned many of the practices which affected securities prices, established various standards, and created the Securities and Exchange Commission (SEC).

SECURITIES, MARKETABLE. See MARKETABLE SECURITIES.

SECURITY. Usually refers to property that is pledged in a credit transaction. See SECURITIES.

SECURITY, GILT-EDGED. A BOND or other security which involves negligible risk for its owner.

SECURITY INTEREST. As used in the UNIFORM COMMERCIAL CODE (UCC), refers to property rights retained by a creditor to minimize his risk in case the debtor defaults. For example, if the seller in a credit sale retains the right to repossess the merchandise if the buyer defaults on his debt, it is said that the seller retains a security interest. Such a transaction is referred to as a *secured transaction*.

SEIZURE. Government takeover of management and control of a private enterprise. In the U.S. this action occurs sometimes during a labor dispute to avoid prolonged interruption of an essential industry.

SELECTIVE CONTROLS. Tools of MONETARY POLICY which aim at control of specific industries or sectors of the economy. The selective control used most often is authority of the BOARD OF GOVERNORS (OF THE FEDERAL RESERVE SYSTEM) to change MARGIN REQUIREMENTS in the stock market, that is, to establish the amount that must be paid with a purchase in the stock market, allowing the rest to be borrowed. In the 1950s selective controls also included restrictions on consumer credit for purchasing durable goods and real estate. See also QUANTITATIVE CONTROLS.

SELECTIVE CREDIT CONTROLS. A subgroup of SELECTIVE CONTROLS, designed specifically for controlling consumer installment credit. During and after World War II and in the Korean War period the Federal Reserve was given the additional responsibility for selective regulation of consumer installment credit, and in the Korean War this responsibility was extended to real estate credit as well. The objective of both types was to encourage postponement of spending on durable goods as a means of releasing scarce national resources for war production and of minimizing inflationary pressures on prices and wages. The controls established for consumer credit set minimum down payments and maximum maturities on installment purchases of consumer durable goods; those on real estate credit set maximum maturities and maximum loan-to-value ratios on mortgage-financed purchases of housing. As of mid-1974 no such controls were authorized, but the Credit Control Act of 1969 does provide that "whenever the President determines that such action is necessary or appropriate for the purpose of preventing or controlling inflation generated by the extension of credit in an excessive volume, the President may authorize the Board [of Governors of the Federal Reserve System] to regulate and control any and all extensions of credit.''

In some other countries the CENTRAL BANK's authority extends to programs that grant favorable credit terms to certain classes of borrowers, such as exporters, farmers, and small businesses, because these borrowers are at a disadvantage in competing for credit funds with large businesses through usual market channels and because the well-being of such borrowers in the economy is considered to warrant a special financing subsidy.

SELECTIVE EMPLOYMENT TAX (U.K.). A payroll tax which uses several rates, one of the variables being the industry; by granting a rebate to manufacturing industries, authorities are trying to increase the ratio of manufacturing expenditures to service industry expenditures. The reason is that the latter are LABOR INTENSIVE and therefore not conducive to improvements in productivity through technological advances. Since economic growth occurs through productivity improvements, an economy with a large amount of manufacturing is more likely to grow. About 11 percent of all taxes are obtained from this source.

SELF-INTEREST. It is often said that one of the basics of a MARKET ECONOMY is that each ECONOMIC UNIT acts in its own self-interest. What is meant here is not a rapacious following of self-interest, but merely adherence to rational and logical thinking; an individual faced with several buyers of some item he is selling will sell to the highest offer, other things being equal.

SELF-LIQUIDATING DEBT. A debt that is expected to be paid off through action of the function for which the debt was created. For example, if a farmer borrows money to pay people to harvest his crop, harvesting and selling of the crop will enable him to pay off the loan. See also COMMERCIAL LOAN.

SELF-SUFFICIENT. Not dependent on others for required ECONOMIC RE-SOURCES. A nation, or even an area of a nation, can be spoken of as self-sufficient, although world economies today are so complex that very few if any areas are fully self-sufficient. Sometimes an area is self-sufficient with regard to a certain item (the area can survive without importing any food), although complete functioning of its economy might require imports of other items. Also called *economically independent*.

SELLERS' INFLATION. See COST-PUSH INFLATION.

SELLERS' MARKET. A market or a period of time in which shortages exist. Because of the shortages buyers are more anxious to buy and competition among buyers will be intense; prices will be bid up and/or sellers will discontinue certain services. See SUPPLY AND DEMAND for an explanation of the sequence that raises prices when a shortage occurs.

SELLER'S SURPLUS. The amount received by a seller above the amount which would have just convinced him to make the sale. In everyday transactions this situation is seen: A person wants to sell his car for $1,000, he asks $1,200 for it; someone offers $1,100. If the sale is concluded there, the seller's surplus is $100. See also BUYER'S SURPLUS.

SELLING SHORT. See SHORT SALE.

SEMIDEVELOPED. Describes a nation whose economy is further advanced than that of a LESS DEVELOPED COUNTRY but not as advanced as that of the industrial nations. Such a country may remain semideveloped, or it may pass through that stage on its way to further development.

SEMILOG. The full word is *semilogarithmic*, and it describes a graph which has one scale in logarithmic units and the other in linear units. One purpose of such a graph is, since logarithms have a compressing effect, to portray data which cover a large range: If a statistic (such as GROSS NATIONAL PRODUCT) changed by a factor of, say, 100 over many years, a linear scale that showed the present (large) value would not be able to show details at the small end. With a logarithmic scale, the same percentage of detail can be shown throughout the range. See RATIO SCALE.

SENIORITY. Rights which are built up for no other reason than that the person continues to be employed by the same employer. For example, many labor union contracts apply the *seniority rule* to layoffs, meaning that, if layoffs become necessary, the individual who has been with the employer for the shortest period of time will be the first to be discharged, regardless of his worth to the employer. Other rights, such as amount of paid vacation, choice of work location, and promotion, can also be functions of seniority.

SENSITIVE MARKET. In investments, the prevailing condition on days when prices of securities fluctuate by considerable amounts in response to encouraging and discouraging news.

SERIAL BOND. A BOND issued with the intention that it will be redeemed according to a schedule based on its serial number. The indenture provides that a certain range of serial numbers will be redeemed in a specified year, another range the next year, etc.

SERRANO V. PRIEST. A very significant case decided by the California Supreme Court in 1971. It led to a number of other court decisions with the general theme that the traditional system of financing public school districts by local property taxes was unconstitutional.

SERVANT, INDENTURED. See INDENTURED SERVANT.

SERVICE CHARGE. A component of some finance charges, such as the fee for triggering an overdraft checking account into use.

SERVICE INDUSTRY. Any of the industries whose OUTPUT is an intangible service rather than a tangible good. Services can include gardening, medical care, and any other output which adds value but does not produce a product. One reason service industries are of interest to economists is that they are LABOR INTENSIVE and therefore not subject to productivity increases that come about through improved CAPITAL GOODS and automation. Another point is that employment in service industries provides one measure of economic growth, since the percentage of the total economy in service industries is small in LESS DEVELOPED COUNTRIES and is larger in developed, industrial nations. See also GOODS AND SERVICES.

SERVICEMEN'S READJUSTMENT ACT. Popularly known as the GI Bill (or GI Bill of Rights), this U.S. legislation of 1944 eased the problem of servicemen returning to civilian life after World War II. The bill provided benefits for education, unemployment payments, assistance toward home ownership and improvement, business loans, and other items. Other international hostilities led to similar legislation for those involved, and the GI Bill has gone through many changes in times of peace as well as war.

SERVICE UTILITY. When a person receives *service utility*, a need or a want is satisfied through someone's performing a service for him. Because that service was performed, he has gained some satisfaction or utility (see UTILITY UNITS).

SETTLEMENT FUND. See INTERDISTRICT SETTLEMENT FUND.

SEVERANCE PAY. Money paid to employees who are terminated through no fault of their own—for example, because an employer loses a contract or, for some reason, work slows below normal. Many labor agreements call for severance pay based on a formula which includes length of time on the job; some employers give every discharged worker two weeks' pay. Workers who are hired with the understanding that the job is temporary are seldom given severance pay. Also called *dismissal pay* or *termination pay*.

SEVERANCE TAX. A tax whose base is the amount of a natural resource removed from the land (where *land* is used here as an ECONOMIC RESOURCE).

SHADOW PRICE. Each price developed in the intermediate steps when an economic model is being iterated, or worked through successive improvements toward optimum. See Linear Programming in the appendix.

SHARE. In financial economics, usually one unit of ownership of a corporation (one share of stock). Many large corporations have issued millions of shares of stock, each share representing a proportional part of ownership.

In a more general sense, any pooling of ownership results in ownership of shares; when individuals pool their money to invest in the stock market, each owns a certain number of shares of the value of their cooperative.

SHARE OF THE MARKET. A very important concept in evaluating the growth (or lack of growth) of an organization: The *percentage* of total sales of a product which one seller or manufacturer has. For example, if the total industry sales of a certain product are 1,000,000 and one manufacturer sells 50,000, its share of the market is 5 percent. It is possible for an organization to increase sales every year and still be a shrinking firm; if the total market is increasing faster than that firm's sales, its share of the market is declining.

SHARING, REVENUE. See REVENUE SHARING.

SHERMAN ANTITRUST ACT. A very effective piece of U.S. legislation passed July 2, 1880, to curb the concentrations of economic power that had been growing with industrialization of the nation. Its two general prohibitions (restraint of trade and monopolizing) are found in Section 1, "Every contract, combination in the form of a trust or otherwise, or conspiracy, in restraint of trade or commerce among the several states, or with foreign nations,

is declared to be illegal," and Section 2, "Every person who shall monopolize, or attempt to monopolize or combine or conspire with any other person or persons to monopolize any part of the trade or commerce among the several states, or with foreign nations, shall be deemed guilty of a misdemeanor." See also CLAYTON ANTITRUST ACT.

SHIFT. When an enterprise is in operation each day for longer than about eight hours, employees are usually assigned to work separate *shifts*. The *first shift*, or *day shift*, the one most people work, usually starts within about an hour of 8 a.m. The *second shift*, or *swing shift*, starts about the time the day shift ends, and often ends soon after the new day "swings in." The *third shift*, or *graveyard shift*, starts about midnight and continues until the day shift returns.

SHIFT IN DEMAND (SUPPLY). Refers to a relocation of the demand (or supply) schedule, rather than to a movement along an existing schedule. For example, if a televised Ping Pong match makes the game more popular, Ping Pong paddles are going to be in more demand, and at every price, people will buy more than they previously did. On the other hand, a *change in quantity demanded* (or supplied) means that other things remained the same (popularity of the item did not change) and the reason for increased sales is simply that the seller lowered the price. See SUPPLY AND DEMAND.

SHIFTING OF TAX. A tax is fully *shifted forward* if it is paid by a seller who then raises his prices by the amount of the tax; it is fully *shifted backward* if it is paid by a buyer who is able to reduce, by the full amount of the tax, the price he pays to one or more FACTORS OF PRODUCTION. For example, if the government taxes the manufacturer of a certain product, and if the manufacturer merely raises the selling price of the product by the amount of the tax, then it is really the buyer who is paying the tax, and it has been shifted forward. Actually, the higher price will probably cause some reduction in sales, and therefore both parties pay—the seller through reduced profits and the buyer through a higher price. Continuation of the analysis shows that there is another party who bears a cost due to the tax—previous buyers who are now priced out of the market (see MARGINAL BUYER). Their "cost" is not being able to buy the product, or having to substitute a less desirable product. See INDIRECT TAX.

SHINPLASTER. During the U.S. Civil War, widespread hoarding of coin led to the issuance of paper money in 3-cent, 5-cent, 10-cent, 25-cent, and 50-cent denominations to substitute for metallic coins. These fractional currency notes became known as *shinplasters*.

SHIN-SANBETSU (Jap.). National Federation of Industrial Organizations, a confederation of Japanese labor unions about one-sixtieth the size of the largest.

SHIP MORTGAGE BANK (Swed.). A financial institution that obtains funds by selling medium- and long-term bonds to the public and makes the money available for long-term loans to finance shipbuilding, taking mortgages on the ships as security.

SHOE LEATHER COSTS. One of the hidden and subtle costs of inflation. In periods of stable prices, consumers and businesses follow established shopping patterns because they have determined where they can buy various items at prices they have accepted. However, during inflation, individual prices are unpredictable, and part of the cost to consumers and businesses is the time spent checking prices, waiting in lines—in general, making investigations they do not have to make when prices are stable.

SHOPPING CENTER. A location where several stores provide customers with a large variety of goods and services within a short distance, usually with one parking of the car. A shopping center commonly includes a SUPERMARKET (usually the main tenant of the center), a drugstore, a hardware store, a restaurant, and other shops. These complexes reflect changing conditions of the economy in that they began to proliferate as (among other things) ownership of autos became common, credit became available to the masses, and consumers became more affluent.

SHOP STEWARD. In labor economics, the worker who is the first link in the communications chain between workers, their union, and their management. One function of th˄ shop steward is to receive GRIEVANCEs from other workers and pass them on through the system that has been established. The shop steward is often responsible for originating reports on violations of labor contracts.

SHORTAGE. Less product available than buyers are demanding at the market price. Generally a shortage cannot occur in a product whose price is not controlled by government (except temporary shortages due to miscalculation, storm, etc.), because price will rise (causing a decrease in quantity demanded, and probably an increase in quantity supplied) until demand equals supply. See SUPPLY AND DEMAND. When a shortage develops in a free market, it is because sellers, for a variety of reasons, have *chosen* not to raise prices even though buyers would pay the higher price.

SHORT-DATED BILL. See TAX ANTICIPATION BILLS.

SHORT LIST. A composite of 12 economic series which have correlated well with changes in the general economy that follow a relatively short time later. See LEADING INDICATOR.

SHORT RUN. Not an absolute length of time; rather, an amount of time sufficient for a firm to alter the utilization rate of its existing plant (as by hiring more labor), but not long enough for it to change its plant capacity (as by building or by putting more capital equipment in place). See also LONG RUN.

SHORT SALE. In the economics of financial investing, a sale in which a person sells a security before owning it—in effect, borrowing it for the sale. At some time in the future the seller will have to *cover* by purchasing the security to replace the one borrowed. A person who sells short hopes that the price will decline so that he can cover at a price lower than that at which he sold.

SHRINKAGE. Technically, decline in weight and volume due to aging of an item. Shrinkage is also used for any decline in weight, volume, or quantity that occurs for any reason (such as through pilfering) except intended use.

SICKOUT. The concept of sick pay was established in response to the problem of workers reporting to work when they are sick because they do not want to lose pay. Some groups of workers have abused this benefit by arranging for all employees (or a large number of them) to call in sick as a form of strike.

SIGHT BILL. A BILL OF EXCHANGE which is due immediately upon demand to the holder, rather than at a specified time in the future, as with a TIME BILL.

SIGHT DRAFT. A DRAFT whose payment is due upon presentation to the drawee.

SILENT PARTNER. A person who is known to the public as a partner (see FORMS OF BUSINESS ORGANIZATION) but actually takes no part in managing the business.

SILVER BULLION. An ingot or bar (rather than coins or other monetary units) of silver in a very pure form.

SILVER CERTIFICATE. The form of U.S. paper currency issued prior to the present FEDERAL RESERVE NOTES. They were issued in $1, $5, and $10 denominations, and accounted for virtually all of the $1 notes in circulation until November 26, 1963, when the $1 Federal Reserve notes were issued. See also GOLD CERTIFICATE; UNITED STATES NOTES.

SILVER PURCHASE ACT. A NEW DEAL measure to induce price inflation, this 1934 legislation had the objective of increasing the monetization of silver toward a goal of one-fourth of the value of the nation's money stock. Although a considerable amount of silver was purchased, the program never approached its goal.

SILVER STANDARD. A monetary standard. A pure silver standard comprises three elements: (1) The nation defines its monetary unit as being equal to a given amount of silver. (2) The monetary authorities of that nation buy all the silver that is offered, and sell all that is demanded, at the defined rate, so the worldwide value cannot change. (3) Anyone can exchange money for silver and can sell silver to the authorities or to other nations. No nation is completely on a silver standard today. Other precious metals, especially gold, have been used at times as the standard for a nation's money.

SIMPLE INTEREST. Interest which is not added to the principal as it is earned; therefore interest in the following period will be figured on the original principal, rather than on original principal plus interest previously earned, as it would be with COMPOUND INTEREST.

SIMULATION. Running a situation or event on its mathematical MODEL, usually to test a proposed change. A simulation typically uses random numbers over a selected interval, with their distribution shaped the same as the conditions they represent. For example, if it is known that 17 percent of the customers in the store being simulated use credit cards, then the random numbers which represent customers entering the store will be arranged so that 17 percent of them initiate the sequence of events associated with a credit purchase.

SINGLE-PAYMENT LOAN. A loan in which the borrower keeps the entire amount, repaying principal and interest at one time. See INSTALLMENT LOAN.

SINGLE STANDARD. A monetary system that is based on one commodity, such as a precious metal (usually gold). Also called *monometalism*.

SINGLE TAX. A system of obtaining revenue for government by levies on just one source, such as a single product. Such systems have not been found to be very successful, and they are particularly distasteful to economists because of the high distortion they introduce into the allocation of FACTORS OF PRODUCTION. See also NEUTRAL TAX.

SINKING FUND. An account which is established to accumulate funds to be used for retiring a debt, such as a bond issue, when due.

SIT-DOWN STRIKE. A labor tactic in which the workers remain inside the plant but refuse to work. Such strikes were common during the 1930s, when workers in effect took over and prevented employers from operating the plant with supervisory personnel or newly-hired workers. A considerable amount of press coverage was obtained when families brought food and passed it through plant windows. Sit-down strikes are now illegal in the U.S.

SKANDINAVISKA BANKEN (Swed.). One of the largest commercial banks in Sweden. It is privately owned.

SKEW. A deviation from symmetry; for example, a certain DISTRIBUTION is centered about some value, but at equal distances from the center we do not find equal amplitudes to the distribution curve.

SLACK LABOR MARKET. A period of relatively high unemployment, when it is difficult to find jobs. Opposite is *tight labor market*, when it is difficult for employers to fill positions.

SLIDING PEG. A form of INTERNATIONAL EXCHANGE in which MONETARY AUTHORITIES make frequent small changes in the rate at which the nation's monetary unit officially trades with others. Some nations which have used the sliding peg (also called *crawling peg*) established a formula that triggered a change when certain conditions were reached; other nations took steps to ensure that the changes would be made at random intervals to discourage speculation.

SLIPPAGES. LEAKAGES which prevent MONETARY POLICY from achieving its theoretical maximum effectiveness. For example, when the reserve ratio (see BANK RESERVES) is changed, banks may not immediately expand or contract earning assets accordingly (see MONEY SUPPLY EXPANSION MULTIPLIER). In addition, even if banks responded promptly, shifts in monetary velocity might partly offset changes in the MONEY SUPPLY.

SLOPE. The angle at which a graph rises (positive slope) or falls (negative slope). Quantitatively, slope between two points on a graph is defined as change in ordinate (*y* or vertical axis coordinate) divided by change in abscissa (*x* or horizontal axis coordinate).

SLOW ASSET. In the economics of business finance, an asset that cannot be easily converted to cash without a significant loss, in contrast to a QUICK ASSET. See also LIQUID ASSET.

SLOWDOWN. A tactic of labor unions to force concessions from an employer by curtailing output without the employees' losing pay, as they would in a regular strike. In a slowdown the employees agree among themselves to use whatever means they can to reduce the work they accomplish without giving the employer cause to discharge them. Sometimes the slowdown consists of applying literally various work rules that under normal conditions are interpreted in a more lenient way.

SMALL BUSINESS ADMINISTRATION (SBA). A U.S. government department created in 1953 to provide assistance to small businesses, usually in the form of management guidance, but also in the form of indirect—and sometimes direct—loans. (In indirect loans, the SBA does not loan the money, but it guarantees repayment, making it easier for a small business to obtain a loan from a commercial lender.)

SMALL BUSINESS FINANCE CORPORATION (Jap.). A government-owned organization which provides funds for expansion of industries and businesses that do not qualify for financing from other lenders.

SMALL SAVER CERTIFICATE. A CERTIFICATE OF DEPOSIT (CD) offered by banks and thrift institutions to individuals with a minimum maturity of 2.5 years. The interest rate on these certificates is related to the average yield on 2.5 year U.S. Treasury securities, in accordance with regulations issued by the Depository Institutions Deregulation Committee. There is no minimum denomination required by federal law on these certificates.

SMITH, ADAM. Scottish economist (1723-1790) responsible for much of the organized economic thinking and analyses we use today. He was a prominent member of the CLASSICAL SCHOOL of economic thought, which was responsible for displacing the MERCANTILIST school, which advocated government action in the form of protectionism in the belief that the nation with the largest gold hoard was the wealthiest. The classicists were in favor of free trade and LAISSEZ-FAIRE in general. In 1759 Adam Smith published *Theory of Moral Sentiments*, but it was his 1776 book, AN INQUIRY INTO THE NATURE AND CAUSES OF THE WEALTH OF NATIONS, that became popular and is still cited frequently.

SMITHSONIAN MEETING. In August 1971 the U.S. announced several changes which were generally considered to end international monetary arrangements as they had been since the BRETTON WOODS agreement. As a result, the Smithsonian meeting, attended by most industrialized nations, was held in December 1971 in Washington, D.C. to discuss new arrangements. One of the out-

comes was a widening of the range through which a nation's currency could drift before MONETARY AUTHORITIES were required to take action (see FLOATING EXCHANGE RATES)—from 1 percent to 2.25 percent. Another outcome was a devaluation of the U.S. dollar, changing the price of gold from $35 an ounce to $38 an ounce. (However, the U.S. continued not to sell gold at the official price, and by that time the market price was so high that no one would offer to sell gold to the U.S. at that price.)

SMUGGLING. Any importing of goods which is in violation of laws. Of most interest to economists is the smuggling which avoids payment of customs duties and which affects legitimate markets in the U.S.

SNAKE IN THE TUNNEL. Situation in which a nation maintains the exchange rates of its currency within a narrower band than required for all currencies according to international agreement: For example, in March 1972 the member nations of the Common Market agreed to keep their currencies from varying relative to one another by more than 1.125 percent up or down, while each of their currencies could vary as much as 2.25 percent up or down against the U.S. dollar. The name developed because, on a graph, the line connecting the outer limits of the wide variation forms the tunnel, and the smaller variations form the snake.

SOCIAL BENEFIT OR COST. See SPILLOVER.

SOCIAL GOODS. Those goods (economists use this expression to include goods and services) which benefit society as a whole rather than just those who participate directly in their use. One of the main examples is an armed service: Every citizen benefits from the fact that such services provide protection and make possible the very existence of the nation. See EXCLUSION PRINCIPLE; PRIVATE GOODS.

SOCIAL INSURANCE. A general expression used to identify government programs which provide protection against financial losses such as that due to unemployment or injury on the job.

SOCIAL LEGISLATION. Government action in the form of laws, codes, acts, etc. that aims to improve the well-being of the residents. Most such legislation is directed toward a specific segment of society, such as the young, the elderly, or the disabled, while other legislation attempts to make overall improvements, such as maintaining the quality of air.

SOCIALISM. A type of economic system one of whose main characteristics is that government owns the major means of production, which are used according to central planning (see CENTRALLY PLANNED ECONOMY). As an entire system of economics, socialism cannot be explained in a few words; a book such as *Comparative Economic Systems* by Martin C. Schnitzer and James Nordyke (Cincinnati, Ohio: South-Western Publishing Company, 1971) gives a good description.

SOCIALIZED MEDICINE. In general, an arrangement whereby medical care for civilians is paid for by the government. No national government is completely out of the medical picture. All pay for at least indigent cases, and many pay all or some of the cost of medical care for the aged. There is a continuum of arrangements, from the minimal coverage to payment of all medical bills for everyone.

In deciding what coverage a nation should provide, one side of the debate holds that no one should have to consider the cost of health; if an individual pays for medical care, then that individual is going to forgo certain treatment because it involves a choice between that treatment and alternative uses of the money. On the other hand, taxpayers ask whether it is the government's responsibility to pay for false teeth, detoxification, reducing salons, body builders, toupees, in-patient care, doctor's office visits, cold remedies, etc.

SOCIAL OVERHEAD. The OPPORTUNITY COST of goods and services which are produced, not specifically for consumption, but rather for widespread benefit. Social overhead is found in the private sector as well as the government sector, and includes items such as transportation and communications.

SOCIAL SECURITY. The basic method in the U.S. of providing a continuing income to families whose earnings are reduced or stopped because of retirement, disability, or death. Nine out of ten workers earn protection under social security. Nearly one out of every seven persons receives monthly social security checks. Nearly all of the nation's 26 million people 65 and over have health insurance under Medicare. Another 2 million disabled people under 65 have been covered by Medicare since July 1, 1973.

Through the years since social security was enacted in 1935, there have been many changes to the protection it gives workers and their families. At first, social secruity covered only the retired workers, but in 1939 the law was changed to pay survivors, as well as certain dependents, upon retirement. Disability insurance was added in 1954 to give workers protection against loss of earnings due to total disability.

Social security originally covered only workers in industry and commerce, but in the 1950s, coverage was extended to include most self-employed persons, most state and local employees, household and farm employees, members of the armed forces, and the clergy. Today, almost all jobs in the U.S. are covered.

The social security program was expanded again in 1965 with the enactment of Medicare, which ensured hospital and medical insurance protection to people 65 and over. Since July 1, 1973, Medicare coverage has been available to people under 65 who have been entitled to disability payments for two years or more and to people with severe kidney disease who need dialysis or kidney transplants. As a result of legislation enacted in 1972, social security benefits will increase automatically in the future as the cost of living goes up.

SOCIAL VALUE. Refers to benefits to society as a whole for a certain expenditure, regardless of how many or how few participate directly in the good or service provided. See SPILLOVER.

SOCIAL WEALTH. An indication of all the things of value possessed by a nation, used to compare the well-being of the people in two different time periods. In any time period the measure will include obvious things of value, such as spending power and material objects; in addition, economists performing a serious analysis will include such items as security of income, general level of health, morals, freedom of choice, absence of war, and numerous other factors which affect well-being. Of increasing importance late in the 20th century is the quality of the environment, over-population, crime, terrorism, and related factors. Without considering *social wealth* it would appear that all people are better off than their ancestors because inventions and innovations are constantly adding to the goods we use; serious investigators, using the concept of social wealth, balance goods such as automobiles against the polluted atmosphere and the deaths they cause.

SOCIÉTÉ GÉNÉRALE (Fr.). One of the largest commercial banks in France, nationalized in 1945.

SOFT MONEY. Generally, money other than coins containing precious metal, as opposed to *hard money*. It can also refer to money of any economy that is not stable and whose value is therefore likely to fluctuate.

SOFT SELL. The selling technique in which the intended buyer is given price and other information and is left to make a decision without further influence. See also HARD SELL.

SOGO SHOSHA (Jap.). Japanese general trading company involved in every stage of economic activity from manufacturing to consumption. It gathers information, raises funds, performs market research, locates materials, coordinates international trading, and performs many other functions.

SOHYO (Jap.). The General Council of Trade Unions of Japan, committed to socialist doctrines and promotion of class struggle. It is the largest confederation of labor unions in Japan.

SOIL CONSERVATION. An expression which identifies any of several programs or plans aimed at maintaining the productivity of soil. Methods include saving the soil itself from losses such as erosion, and saving the chemical and organic content from depletion.

SOIL CONSERVATION AND ALLOTMENT ACT. A NEW DEAL measure of 1936 that appropriated $500 million to preserve soil, improve fertility, work against wasteful soil exploitation, and protect rivers and harbors from soil erosion.

SOLE PROPRIETORSHIP. The simplest form of business enterprise; there is just one owner, and, if certain special requirements (such as a health certificate for handling food) are satisfied, no permission is necessary for opening the business. Also called *proprietorship*. See FORMS OF BUSINESS ORGANIZATION.

SOLVENT. The financial condition of being able to pay bills and other expenses as they become due. See also BANKRUPTCY; INSOLVENCY.

SPAN OF CONTROL. The maximum number of subordinates that a manager can control effectively. One objective of management analysts is to increase the span of control at all levels so that the organizational pyramid can be wider, with fewer levels of management, and less cost will be devoted to management and more to direct productivity.

SPECIAL ASSESSMENT. Usually, a tax that is levied on a certain group in addition to the taxes that are paid by all. For example, in local government finance it is sometimes said that property owners in the vicinity of an improvement such as a park will receive more benefit from the park than other taxpayers within that local government, and therefore they should pay an extra assessment (usually a one-time payment) in addition to the property taxes paid by everyone. It is then said that a *special assessment district* is created.

In the PRIVATE SECTOR, the expression generally refers to a charge which all members of an organization (such as an INDUSTRY ASSOCIATION or a labor union) are to pay for a specified purpose (such as an advertising campaign).

SPECIAL DEPOSITARY. A bank in which the U.S. Treasury deposits the proceeds of sales of federal securities.

SPECIAL DEPOSITS (U.K.). A variable cash ratio consisting solely of deposits of commercial banks with the BANK OF ENGLAND. This ratio was first applied in 1960, with the objective of making calls for *special deposits* whenever it was desired to put pressure on banks' liquid assets; banks were expected to sell liquid assets to obtain deposits demanded by the CENTRAL BANK.

SPECIAL DRAWING RIGHTS (SDRs). A type of international money created by the INTERNATIONAL MONETARY FUND (IMF) and allocated to its member nations. SDRs are an international reserve asset, although they are only accounting entries (not actual coin or paper, and not backed by precious metal). Subject to certain conditions of the IMF, a nation that has a balance of payments deficit can use SDRs to settle debts to another nation or to the IMF.

SPECIAL DRAWING RIGHTS CERTIFICATE ACCOUNT. In the CONSOLIDATED STATEMENT OF CONDITION OF ALL FEDERAL RESERVE BANKS, Special Drawing Rights certificate credits held by the FEDERAL RE-

SERVE BANKs. It is a Federal Reserve asset item closely related to the gold certificate account. These rights may be transferred, somewhat like gold, from one national monetary authority to another.

SDRs received by the U.S. government are first placed in the Exchange Stabilization Fund by the Treasury. From time to time the Treasury may MONETIZE SDRs by issuing SDR certificates to the Reserve banks. When this occurs, the SDR certificates thus acquired by the banks are credited to the SDR certificate account. Since the first SDRs were created in 1970, the Federal Reserve banks' reserve assets have included small amounts of SDR certificate credits.

Transfers of SDRs to and from the monetary authorities of other countries against payment in dollars have up to now been made only in small volume. These transfers have utilized unmonetized SDRs, or have added to the Stabilization Fund's holdings, without effect on the Federal Reserve banks' holdings of SDR certificate claims.

Total Treasury holdings of SDRs by the Treasury's Exchange Stabilization Fund on May 16, 1973, amounted to $1,949 million, of which $400 million was obligated to the SDR certificate account held by the Reserve banks. On that date the total U.S. gold stock was $10,487 million, of which $10,303 million was owed to the gold certificate account; the remainder—unmonetized—was held by the U.S. Treasury ($107 million) and by the Exchange Stabilization Fund ($77 million).

Most of this information is from *The Federal Reserve System Purposes and Functions* by the Board of Governors of the Federal Reserve System (6th ed., 3rd printing, December 1980).

SPECIAL ENDORSEMENT. On a negotiable instrument, the signature of the transferor along with words indicating to whom the instrument is being endorsed. For example, a BLANK ENDORSEMENT of a check would consist of just the name of the holder who is negotiating the check to someone else; a special endorsement could say "Pay to the order of . . ." and include the name of the next holder. See also CONDITIONAL ENDORSEMENT; QUALIFIED ENDORSEMENT; RESTRICTIVE ENDORSEMENT.

SPECIALIST. In the economics of investments, a specialist is an individual responsible for maintaining an orderly market in certain specified securities. He buys and sells for his personal PORTFOLIO as necessary to maintain control of a security.

SPECIALIZATION. Narrowing the capability of a FACTOR OF PRODUCTION so as to make it more efficient in the remaining capabilities. With regard to the human resource, we all specialize to some extent, but when the practice is carried to extremes on assembly lines it is often condemned as "dehumanizing the work," or taking all the interest out of the job.

SPECIAL MANAGER. A senior officer of the Federal Reserve Bank of New York, who serves on the staff of the FEDERAL OPEN MARKET COMMITTEE by reporting on foreign exchange operations and other developments.

SPECIAL STOCK. In financial economics, an issue of CAPITAL STOCK that is sold to obtain money for a specific purpose such as refunding a debt. If the issue is not retired within a few years, it becomes merely outstanding stock (it may retain its identity because of its class— see CLASSIFIED STOCK), and the original purpose for its issue is no longer significant.

SPECIAL UNEMPLOYMENT ASSISTANCE (SUA). Title II, of the U.S. Emergency Jobs Unemployment Assistance Act of 1974 as amended and extended by the Emergency Compensation and Special Unemployment Assistance Act of 1975. It was a temporary, two-year program of federal benefits for workers not

eligible for regular state benefits. The amount of benefit was based on applying the state benefit formula to the individual's employment, disregarding the difference between covered and noncovered work. Maximum duration was 39 weeks. The program ended December 31, 1976, with last benefits payable March 31, 1977.

SPECIE. Coins, although sometimes specifically coins which have a precious metal (such as gold or silver) content equal to each coin's monetary value.

SPECIFIC DUTY. An import tariff that is charged according to a physical characteristic, such as volume, rather than according to value, as would be done with an AD VALOREM DUTY. See also COMPOUND DUTY.

SPECULATION. In its fullest sense, the incurring of an expense with the objective of later receiving a profit on the reverse transaction. Two forms of speculation are (1) the purchase of property (real estate, securities, or any other property) with the intention of reselling it later at a higher price; and (2) investment of a valuable, such as time (as when a person writes a book and hopes to receive satisfactory financial return). In practice, *speculation* is often reserved for those transactions that involve a relatively high degree of risk. See also the next few entries.

SPECULATIVE CREDIT. Credit on which the borrower hopes to make a profit but without the economy's realizing any additional output of goods and services. See QUALITY OF CREDIT.

SPECULATIVE DEMAND. See LIQUIDITY PREFERENCE.

SPECULATIVE EXCESSES. There is no distinct line separating normal speculative activity from speculative excesses, but the latter are generally considered to exist when some condition of the economy results in a shifting of a significant amount of effort from productive uses to nonproductive speculation. For example, during rapid rises in real estate prices a certain amount of money will be diverted from investment in factories and capital equipment to the buying and selling of real estate for profit. In addition to shifting economic resources, this practice can itself contribute to the rise in real estate prices.

SPEEDUP. The charge, often made by labor unions, that an employer has contrived to obtain more work from its employees for the same amount of pay, for example, by increasing the pace of an assembly line.

SPENDABLE EARNINGS. The amount of income a worker has for discretionary spending, after deductions and after fixed payments (such as rent) and required payments (such as utilities). There is no universal agreement on the parts of this definition (as to what a ''fixed payment'' is, etc.), and therefore this expression is of little use in economics. See also TAKEHOME PAY.

SPENDING MULTIPLIER. See MULTIPLIER.

SPENDING UNIT. The buyer of an item. For a stick of chewing gum the spending unit is an individual; for furniture it might be a family; for a metal-forming machine it might be a large corporation. Identification of the spending unit is important in advertising, and cures to specific weaknesses in an economy are sought in government efforts to change the relative position of certain spending units as a group. For example, when low retail sales cause a problem for the economy, government might take measures to put more money in the hands of consumers; when capital spending is too low for future growth, government might make it more attractive for businesses to buy capital equipment.

SPILLOVER. A *spillover benefit* occurs when an economic unit that is not directly involved benefits from a transaction or from consumption of a good or service. For example, a civic-minded group collects money and sends neighborhood youths

to summer camp. The group, the youths, and those who donated are directly involved, but if a reduction in crime should result, there would be spillover benefits to unknown individuals who otherwise would have been victims of crime. Also referred to as a *spill-in* or a *social benefit*.

A *spillover cost* occurs when an economic unit is caused to bear a cost from a transaction or from consumption even though it did not participate directly. For example, homeowners (including those who do not own automobiles) as a group have to paint their houses more often because of the corrosive effects of smog. Therefore the automobile industry is paying less than the total amount that automobiles are costing the economy, and there is a spillover cost. Most degradation of the environment involves spillover costs, which are also called *spill-outs*, or *social costs*.

The cost and benefits referred to include UTILITY UNITS as well as monetary units, and therefore it is usually difficult to assess the overall effect of an economic action. For example, considering just the first-order effects, it may be said that a city is justified when it exercises its right of EMINENT DOMAIN and acquires several private properties to build a public park if the cumulative happiness of those who use the park is larger than the cumulative unhappiness of those who lost their private property plus that of those whose payment of taxes made the park possible. But there are also second- and higher-order costs and benefits: The appearance of the neighborhood may be better or worse with the park, someone may be injured during construction, local businesses may gain or lose customers, and air pollution may increase because of people driving to the park.

Because of spillover effects, the equilibrium quantity and price of a product, as determined by individual analysis, may not be the price and quantity which are optimum for society as a whole. For this reason, questions of government action usually involve spillover analysis. Other expressions used are *neighborhood effects* and *externalities*.

SPIRAL, INFLATIONARY. See IN-FLATIONARY SPIRAL.

SPLIT-DOWN. See SPLIT-UP.

SPLIT-UP. In the economics of investments, an increase in the number of shares into which a corporation's ownership is divided. For example, a corporation might have one million shares of CAPITAL STOCK outstanding. If it divides the same ownership into two million shares, each holder of a share of the ''old'' stock will have two shares of the ''new'' stock, and it is said that the corporation had a *two-for-one split*. Each stockholder still owns the same percentage of the corporation as before, and the total value of each stockholder's holding has the same value as before. Other splits, such as three-for-one and five-for-two, are also made.

Much less common is the *reverse split*, or *split-down*, in which a corporation reduces the number of shares into which its ownership is divided. When the word *split* is used alone, it usually refers to a split-up. The reason for both types of splits is to make the market price of the stock fall into a more desired range. For example, most investors do not want to buy stocks that cost more than about $50, so a company whose stock is selling for $120 might declare a three-for-one split, after which a share will be worth $40. On the surface it makes no difference whether a person owns 10 shares worth $120 each or 30 shares worth $40 each; however, if more people are interested in buying the stock at $40, the split will increase demand, and market equilibrium price will be higher than $40 (see SUPPLY AND DEMAND). In the same way, if a stock is selling for just a few dollars, the company might feel that investors do not associate quality and security with the company. If the stock splits down and the price per share (after the split down) is higher, the new corporate image might induce more investors to want to buy shares of that company, and the increased

demand will push the market price still higher.

SPOT DELIVERY. Delivery at the time the contract is made, rather than at a time in the future.

SPOT EXCHANGE CONTRACT. An agreement providing for prompt delivery of a specified amount of foreign currency at an agreed-upon price. Most spot contracts call for delivery in one or two business days (depending on the currency), although some are for *value today*, meaning same-day delivery. International transactions between banks in the U.S.— whether they are forward transactions or spot transactions with value date today, tomorrow, or in two business days—are usually settled in clearinghouse funds.

SPOT PURCHASE. In international exchange market terminology, a present sale of one currency against another. See SWAP NETWORK.

SPREAD. The difference between a buying and a selling price. For example, the broker handling OVER-THE-COUNTER STOCK quotes a *bid* price (he will buy the indicated security at that price) and an *asked* price (he will sell at that price); their difference is the spread. In financial economics, *spread* refers to the difference between the price an UNDERWRITER pays for a security and the amount he receives when selling it.

SPREADING THE WORK. Reducing the hours worked by each person so that all can have some work, rather than allowing some to have full incomes while others are completely out of work. The practice was one of the factors that kept the GREAT DEPRESSION from being more of a disaster, and it is felt by many economists that today's more rigid employment rules would result in a tremendous gap between the haves and the have-nots if another depression should occur.

STABILITY. See EQUILIBRIUM.

STABLE CURRENCY. The monetary unit of a nation in which there is not an unacceptable level of inflation or deflation.

STABLE EQUILIBRIUM. A true EQUILIBRIUM, or point in the economy where any disturbance will result in natural forces which tend to return the economy to that equilibrium point.

STAGFLATION. A word recently coined to describe the simultaneous occurrence of economic slowdown, with its concomitant increased unemployment (stagnation), and rising prices (inflation). Traditionally, these two conditions are corrections for each other, and therefore should not occur simultaneously. However, many prices in today's economy are *downward inflexible*, and so an economic slowdown is less effective in curtailing price rises than it used to be.

STAGGERS RAIL ACT. One of the deregulation acts which were passed in the late 1970s and early 1980s, this U.S. legislation provided the authority to eliminate significant portions of the economic regulation of railroads. The deregulatory provisions of the Staggers Rail Act of 1980 have helped to increase the efficiency of the railroads and to improve their performance. A new standard of revenue adequacy, based on the current cost of capital, gives greater rate flexibility to railroads with inadequate revenues.

Significant changes in Interstate Commerce Commission (ICC) regulation of the rail industry have been implemented as a result of the Staggers Rail Act. Contracts between railroads and individual shippers are now legal and are virtually free of any ICC regulation. Rates and practices for shipping trailers or containers on flatcars are now exempt from regulation. Rates and practices for shipping fresh fruits and vegetables have been exempted since 1979.

STAKHANOVITE MOVEMENT (U.S.S.R.). A program of work incentives in the Soviet Union involving publicizing the names of workers of exceptional productivity, displaying their pictures, awarding them medals, and providing other nonmaterial incentives. The movement is named after a coal miner who far exceeded his quota and was rewarded with many honors.

STALE CHECK. A check written at least six months ago. The UNIFORM COMMERCIAL CODE gives the bank on which the stale check was written the choice of paying the check or refusing to pay. In addition, the writer of a check has the right to name an earlier date at which the check becomes stale, and checks sometimes include such words as "void after 60 days."

STAMP TAX. A tax which is collected by requiring that commercial establishments in a given level of the manufacturing chain buy stamps and affix them to the product.

STANDARD. In monetary economics, the reference relative to which the monetary unit is valued. For example, when nations were on a gold standard, they agreed to buy or sell gold at the stated number of monetary units per ounce.

STANDARD METROPOLITAN STATISTICAL AREA (SMSA). A county or group of counties which contains (1) at least one city of 50,000 inhabitants or more or (2) "twin cities" with a combined population of 50,000. Continuous counties are included in an SMSA if, according to certain criteria, they are socially and economically integrated with the central city. Most numerical data are collected and published with an SMSA as the basic unit.

STANDARD OF LIVING. The amounts of goods and services consumed. This expression is used qualitatively to express the well-being of economic units, from individuals to entire populations. Also called *living standard*.

STANDARD OF VALUE. One of the basic functions of money. When money functions as a standard of value, it allows comparisons of any items in the world, such as a horse and a typewriter. Instead of comparing the horse and the typewriter directly, we can express both the horse's value and the typewriter's value in dollars, and can then determine how many typewriters are worth one horse.

STANDBY LEGISLATION. Legislation that is passed by Congress with the intention of giving some authority (such as the president) the legal power to take a certain action if it is deemed beneficial to the nation. For example, in 1970 the U.S. Congress passed the Economic Stabilization Act, giving the president the power to freeze wages and prices if inflation or other economic conditions became excessive; in August 1971 the president declared a wage-and-price freeze.

STAR NOTE. A UNITED STATES NOTE or FEDERAL RESERVE NOTE printed to replace a note damaged during printing. Star notes are made up with special runs of serial numbers chosen to match exactly the notes they replace, but a star is substituted for one of the serial letters.

STATE. Generally, a nation, but in the U.S., because of the disagreements as to how tightly the original colonies would be bound in one nation, the 50 political subdivisions into which the nation is divided became known as states.

STATE AND LOCAL GOVERNMENT PURCHASES OF GOODS AND SERVICES. An item in NATIONAL INCOME AND PRODUCT ACCOUNTS. That is, state and local government purchases of goods and services are credited to these levels of government *collectively* in GROSS NATIONAL PRODUCT, regardless of who pays for them. For example, expenditures of federal grant money on schools are counted as purchases of goods and services by state and local governments.

STATE BANK. A COMMERCIAL BANK chartered by the state in which it operates.

STATE FARM. A farm which is owned by the government; people are employed and paid wages to work such farms, rather than being self-employed. See also COLLECTIVE FARM.

STATE OF NORTH DAKOTA DOING BUSINESS AS THE BANK OF NORTH DAKOTA. Official designation of the Bank of North Dakota, the only COMMERCIAL BANK in the U.S. which is owned and operated by a state. It functions exactly like privately owned banks except that it makes very few loans to the private sector; most of its loans are to state agencies.

STATIC. Not changing. The word is frequently used in economics to emphasize that certain analyses, such as SUPPLY AND DEMAND, view the world as if frozen at one point in time. See also OTHER THINGS BEING EQUAL.

STATISTICAL DISCREPANCY. Theoretically, GROSS NATIONAL PRODUCT is determined by adding up all that was paid by receivers of goods and services, so we should obtain the same amount as if we had added up all that was received by the sellers of those same goods and services. In practice, the magnitude of the task plus the statistical and sampling nature of the methods tell us that the two methods cannot be expected to yield identical results; the total of expenditures minus the total of receipts is the *statistical discrepancy*, and although usually in billions of dollars, it is a relatively small percentage of the total.

STATUTORY COPYRIGHT. Formal protection granted to the creator of a work of art after it is published. See COPYRIGHT.

STERLING BLOC. Either those nations whose monetary unit is based on sterling, or those nations that are economically dependent on the British Empire.

STEWARD. In labor economics, the worker who is the first link in the communications chain between workers and management. The steward, who receives GRIEVANCEs from other workers and passes them on to those responsible for action, is often responsible for originating reports on violations of labor contracts. Also called *shop steward*, and some industries use the name *committeeman*.

STIMULATIVE. Tending to speed up the economy; tending to increase employment and the output of goods and services. *Stimulative* is usually used to describe an economic policy; for example, lowering taxes is said to be a stimulative FISCAL POLICY. See also CONTRACTIONARY.

STIMULUS. See FISCAL STIMULUS.

STOCK. In financial economics, ownership of a corporation. See CAPITAL STOCK.

STOCK CERTIFICATE. Documented evidence of ownership of CAPITAL STOCK. Certificates usually are elaborately engraved and provide a space for filling in the number of shares that are transferred at the time the certificate is being prepared.

STOCK DIVIDENDS. See DIVIDENDS.

STOCK EXCHANGE. See STOCK MARKET.

STOCKHOLDER. A person who owns shares of CAPITAL STOCK of a corporation.

STOCKHOLDER OF RECORD. The person who is shown in the records of the issuing company as the owner of CAPITAL STOCK. The expression is usually accompanied by a date (stockholder of record as of . . .), and it is used for determining who is to receive a certain benefit. For example, if some shares of stock are sold at about the time a dividend is declared, any question as to whether the new or the old owner is entitled to the dividend is resolved by declaring the dividend payable to stockholders of record as of a specified date.

STOCKHOLM ENSKILDA BANK (Swed.). One of the largest commercial banks in Sweden. It is privately owned.

STOCK MARKET. A place where stocks, bonds, and other securities are bought and sold. The stock market does not buy or sell the securities; it provides the facilities, establishes the rules, and oversees the trading. See NEW YORK STOCK EXCHANGE; AMERICAN STOCK EXCHANGE.

STOCK MARKET CRASH. The rapid decline of prices of stocks and other securities that ended the speculative growth of the 1920s. Although the securities market faltered several times, it is generally agreed that October 24, 1929, *Black Thursday*, was the beginning of a long decline which saw only a few short-lived rallies. A good description of the period is given in *The Great Crash, Nineteen Twenty-Nine*, by John Kenneth Galbraith (Boston: Houghton Mifflin, 1979). The GREAT DEPRESSION of the 1930s followed, but historians are not in agreement as to cause and effect regarding the two events.

STOCK OPTION. A plan giving employees the right to purchase a stated number of shares of CAPITAL STOCK—almost always stock of the corporation for which they work—at a stated price per share. The purpose of the plan is to provide incentives for efficient work; if the stock's market price rises above the price at which the employees have a right to purchase, they can make an immediate profit by exercising the right. Most stock option plans are offered to executives and higher-level management.

STOCKPILING. Buying relatively large quantities of an item for future, rather than immediate, use. For example, if it is likely that there will be a strike in a certain industry, users of that industry's product often stockpile a quantity that they estimate will serve them until production resumes.

STOCK PURCHASE WARRANT. See WARRANT.

STOCKRIGHT. In the economics of investments, a contractual right to purchase a given quantity of a CAPITAL STOCK at a stipulated price. If the stipulated price is lower than the market price, the stockright has value.

STOCK SPLIT. Dividing all outstanding CAPITAL STOCK into a larger number of shares; in a two-for-one split each stockholder is given two new shares for each old share owned, but of course, each new share represents only half as much claim on ownership of the corporation. Therefore the value of the new holding is, on the surface, identical to the value before the split. However, the purpose of the split is to move the price of the stock into a more popular range. If more people are interested in buying it, the laws of SUPPLY AND DEMAND hold that equilibrium price will increase, and it can be expected that the total stock held by an individual will sell for a slightly higher price after the split. See SPLIT-UP.

STOP-LOSS ORDER. In the economics of investments, an order to a broker to sell certain securities if the market price drops to a stipulated level. The reasoning is that if the stock declines to that level, it is likely to continue declining, and it is better to take the loss and use the remaining money to purchase another security that is more likely to increase in price.

STORE OF VALUE. One of the basic functions served by MONEY. See BARTER.

STRAIGHT BILL OF LADING (SBL). A BILL OF LADING which provides that only the named consignee can receive the goods; the instrument cannot be negotiated to another party.

STRAIGHT LETTER OF CREDIT. A document (LETTER OF CREDIT) in which a bank indicates credit approval by stating that, for the named individual and through a stated date, it guarantees acceptance and payment (see ACCEPTANCES) of all drafts. Sometimes a dollar limit is stated.

STRATIFY. In statistical economics, the practice of identifying a SAMPLE as representative of a certain level of possible selections, rather than representative of the entire population from which it might be chosen. For example, in analyzing spending patterns as a function of income, a researcher might select a group to represent the $10,000 to $20,000 range, another in the $20,000 to $30,000 range, etc.

STREET BROKER. A stock broker who deals in OVER-THE-COUNTER stocks.

STREET NAME. When an investor purchases a security but allows it to be registered in the name of the brokerage firm through which he dealt (relying on bookkeeping records to show that he is actually the owner), the security is said to be in *street name*. The reference is to Wall Street (in New York City), which is the center of financial activity in the United States.

STRIKE. Sustained refusal by workers to perform all or some of those acts for which they were hired. Those on strike believe that, although they are losing money by not working, the employer is losing more because of continuing FIXED COSTS, and therefore the employer is expected to yield to employees' demands.

STRIKEBREAKER. A person whose actions strengthen the position of the employer during a strike.

STRIKE FUND. In labor economics, money amassed by a union throughout the year in order to pay the extra expenses of a strike, especially individual benefits to replace wages for all or some of the strikers. The fund sometimes makes direct payment to strikers, sometimes provides food for them, and in general offsets some of the costs of being on strike.

STROIBANK (U.S.S.R.). The Soviet Investment Bank, which obtains funds mostly from government grants and provides financing for a wide range of activities, including industrial enterprises, schools, hospitals, and housing.

STRUCTURAL TRANSFORMATION. Change in the basic makeup of an economy, such as a shift in the main source of employment from agriculture to manufacturing. Structural transformation is often associated with economic development.

STRUCTURAL UNEMPLOYMENT. Unemployment which can be traced to structural shifts in supply and demand in the labor market, such as defense spending cuts that cause a decrease in employment in the aerospace industry, or a large factory moving to another part of the nation. See also FRICTIONAL UNEMPLOYMENT.

STRUCTURES, RESIDENTIAL. See RESIDENTIAL STRUCTURES.

STUDENT LOAN MARKETING ASSOCIATION. Organization, known in the financial world as *Sallie Mae*, established to provide liquidity to lenders engaged in making student loans under the Federal Guaranteed Student Loan Program. Unlike the other federally sponsored credit agencies, Sallie Mae is authorized to borrow funds from the U.S. Treasury through the Federal Financing Bank. Prior to 1981 Sallie Mae raised all its funds from the Federal Financing Bank, and in 1981 it began to sell short-term discount notes directly to investors.

STUMPTAIL. Name used for state bank notes about the time of the U.S. Civil War, to indicate the lack of faith citizens had in that form of money.

SUBSCRIPTION. An agreement by an investor to purchase a certain amount of CAPITAL STOCK at a stipulated price.

SUBSCRIPTION PRICE. The price at which a new issue of CAPITAL STOCK is made available to investors.

SUBSIDIARY. A company that is owned by another company.

SUBSIDIARY COIN. A coin of value less than the basic monetary unit of the nation, such as the dime, quarter, and other coins which are worth less than the basic unit.

SUBSIDIES LESS CURRENT SURPLUS OF GOVERNMENT ENTERPRISES. An item in NATIONAL INCOME AND PRODUCT ACCOUNTS. *Subsidies* are monetary grants by government to private business, primarily in the form of payments to farmers, airlines, shipping companies, and others. The *current surplus* of GOVERNMENT ENTERPRISEs represents the excess of sales receipts over current operating costs of such enterprises as the Commodity Credit Corporation and the Tennessee Valley Authority. No deduction is made for depreciation, and the interest is not included in either receipts or costs.

SUBSIDY. The provision of federal economic assistance to the private sector producers or consumers of a particular good, service, or FACTOR OF PRODUCTION. The government receives no equivalent compensation in return but stipulates a particular performance by the recipient, thereby altering the price or cost of the particular good or service to the subsidy recipient in a way which encourages or discourages the output, supply, or use of the item and the related economic behavior. Assistance may take the form of (1) explicit cash payments; (2) implicit payments through (a) a reduction of a specific tax liability, (b) loans at interest rates below the government borrowing rate or from loan guarantees, (c) provisions of goods and services at prices or fees below market value, (d) government purchases of goods and services above market prices, and (e) certain government regulatory actions that alter particular market prices. [Adapted from Comptroller General of the United States, "Budgetary and and Fiscal Information Needs of the Congress B-115398" (February 17, 1972)].

SUBSISTENCE THEORY. In wage analyses early in the 1800s, investigators such as Thomas Malthus saw little hope that the human race could rise above subsistence levels because, they argued, any increase in REAL INCOME was followed by an increase in family size, which (1) reduced the wage earner's discretionary income and (2) increased the number of individuals who would be competing for jobs in the next generation. It is now generally felt that the technology explosion has led to significant increases in the level of human living, but the tendency toward large families has counteracted many of the possible benefits in the manner predicted by Malthus. In the 1970s the general awareness of the true cost of babies added impetus to the fight for less population growth, but it will be many years before it is known if the change in the tendency in family size is a permanent one. Early in the 1980s the birthrate in the United States was down, but the worldwide population explosion continued; there is reason for concern about the effects of such a large population. The beginnings of serious problems have been seen: rapid increases in real estate prices (the earth's amount of land is fixed, so an increasing number of people are bidding up the price of homes) and a dwindling supply of such natural resources as petroleum and natural gas.

SUBSTITUTE GOODS. Goods which perform the same function or satisfy the same wants. The significance of this category is that a small change in the price of a good may result in a large change in the quantity demanded if there is a close substitute whose price did not change. See also COMPETING GOODS; COMPLEMENTARY GOODS.

SUBSTITUTION EFFECTS. Several assumptions will be made in order to explain these effects. First, assume that we are examining a consumer whose income is I_A and whose market basket (see CONSUMER PRICE INDEX) consists of two products, product X and product Y. The unit price of Y will be designated P_Y and the unit price of X at this time will be P_{XA}. If the consumer spends all his income on product Y, he can buy I_A/P_Y units; if he spends all his income on product X, he will buy I_A/P_{XA} units; or he can buy any combination, as indicated in the accompanying figure by the straight (called the budget line) joining those points on the axes. Now, assume that U0 and U1 are two of his INDIFFERENCE CURVEs, with U1 representing a higher level of utility (see UTILITY UNITS). This consumer can achieve the greatest amount of satisfaction by adjusting his spending so that he reaches the indifference curve with the highest level of utility; his budget line will just touch, or be tangent to, the curve at that point. The figure shows that U1 is the highest level he can reach; this requires buying quantity Q_{XA} of product X and quantity Q_{YA} of product Y.

Now suppose the unit price of product X is raised to P_{XB}. The consumer can still buy quantity I_A/P_Y of product Y, but if he spends all his income on product X he will buy only quantity I_A/P_{XB}, so his new budget line never reaches a higher utility level than U0; his REAL INCOME has declined.

Substitution effects. Simplified model shows the complexity of interrelationships between just two products.

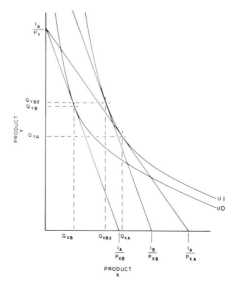

Now assume that his MONEY IN-COME is changed so that his real income becomes as high as it was before the increase in the price of product X. (The price increase is then called a *compensated price change*.) One way to obtain this new income level I_B graphically is to draw a budget line parallel to the latest budget line but passing through the point where the original budget line was tangent to indifference curve U1. Another way is to draw a new budget line parallel to the latest budget line but finding its own point of tangency with U1. We shall use the latter method because the former would produce a line tangent to a still higher indifference curve, representing an overall increase in real income. The figure shows that the consumer can now maximize his satisfaction by buying Q_{XB2} units of product X and Q_{YB2} units of product Y. The changes in the mix of products due to a compensated price change are the *substitution effects*, and there are two of them:

1. *Own price substitution effect:* the change in quantity of product X, from Q_{XA} to Q_{XB}. It is always inversely related to the price change; the price was increased and the quantity decreased. This inverse relationship is the *law of demand*.
2. *Cross-substitution effect:* the change in quantity of product Y due to a compensated change in price of product X. It is always directly related; quantity increases when price increases.

In income taxation, *substitution effect* has a different sense. Here it means that if an individual views taxes as reducing the benefit he obtains from working, he will prefer to spend less time working and more time at leisure. For the opposite result of taxation, see INCOME EFFECT.

SUBSTITUTION, RATE OF. See MARGINAL RATE OF SUBSTITUTION.

SUFFOLK BANK. A bank of significance in U.S. economic history because it agreed to redeem the notes of outlying banks at par if those banks would maintain balances with it for that purpose. Because of that agreement, the notes of New England banks generally circulated at par, or face, value for several years, whereas in other parts of the nation the value of notes was unstable because they were redeemed at a variety of discounts, or not accepted at all.

SUM OF DIGITS. (1) A method of figuring the fraction of total interest which has been paid. It is often used when a consumer wants to pay off a loan early. Because periodic (usually monthly) payments are generally equal, large portions of the first payments are interest, and the last payments are mostly to reduce the debt. Therefore a consumer who wants to pay off a loan after making half the payments will find that more than half the debt is still unpaid.

The first step is to add the number of payments originally planned for the loan. For example, if the loan were to be paid off in 12 installments, we would add

$$1 + 2 + 3 + 4 + 5 + 6 + 7 + 8 + 9 + 10 + 11 + 12 = 78$$

This sum, applicable in the case of a one-year loan, is the reason this method is also called the *rule of 78s*. (Actually, *sum of digits* is misleading, because, for loans with more than nine installments it is actually integers that are being summed, not digits. However, the method is known by this name.)

The borrower pays 12/78 of the total interest the first month, 11/78 the second month, . . . , and 1/78 of the total interest the 12th month. The total amount which would pay off the loan at any time can be determined by looking at the gross amount which would have been paid in 12 regular payments and subtracting the amount of interest that will not have to be paid because the loan will be paid off.

For a large number of payments the formula $S = (n/2)(n + 1)$ is easier to use than actually adding up the numbers of payments. Here S is the sum and n is the number of payments.

SUMPTUARY TAX. A tax whose main purpose is control, as opposed to a tax which is mainly for revenue. The dividing line between a sumptuary tax and a REVENUE TAX is not well defined, since most, if not all, taxes provide some control and some revenue.

SUPERMARKET. A large retail store, generally a large grocery store. One main significance of the supermarket to economists is the way in which its growth has affected retailing; consumers have indicated their preference for lower prices in exchange for less personalized service.

SUPERIOR GOOD. See INCOME EFFECT.

SUPPLEMENTS TO WAGES AND SALARIES. In NATIONAL INCOME AND PRODUCT ACCOUNTS, employer contributions for social insurance, plus such items as employer payments for private pension, health, and welfare funds; compensation for injuries; directors' fees; and pay of the military reserves.

SUPPLY. As a verb, to provide goods and services. As a noun, *supply* refers either to the quantity of goods and services which suppliers are willing to supply or to a SUPPLY SCHEDULE.

SUPPLY AND DEMAND. One of the basic models used in economics. It is built on the logical assumption that buyers want to obtain goods and services at as little cost as is reasonable, and sellers want to obtain as high a price as is reasonable. It is also recognized that buyers want to maximize the MARGINAL UTILITY of their expenditures. The model is most applicable to AGGREGATIVE ECONOMICS (MACROECONOMICS).

Very briefly, a supply-and-demand model is the superposition of a SUPPLY SCHEDULE on a DEMAND SCHEDULE, usually for the purpose of explaining equilibrium price and quantity. Sometimes several schedules are included for the purpose of explaining the effect of nonprice variables. The model may include many other influences, such as quota and ceiling price.

The following example shows a typical application of elementary supply-and-demand analysis. Assume that if tennis rackets were available at prices shown in the following table, consumers would want the indicated quantities.

If tennis rackets sold for	consumers would buy
$ 5	120,000
10	110,000
15	100,000
20	90,000
25	80,000
30	70,000
35	60,000
40	50,000

This table is a *demand schedule*; it does not say that tennis rackets are available at those prices or in those quantities; it simply says that *if* they could be obtained at any of those prices, consumers would be ready, willing, and able to purchase in the quantities shown. Price and quantity supplied are directly related; an increase in one is consistent with an increase in the other.

Next, we have a *supply schedule*, which also does not say what quantities or prices apply; rather it says that *if* any of the prices shown could be obtained (if manufacturers could sell, at the indicated price, all they produced), they would want to provide the quantities shown. Demand and price are inversely related; an increase in one is consistent with a decrease in the other. The supply schedule table for this example is as follows:

If rackets sold for	suppliers would provide
$ 5	50,000
10	60,000
15	70,000
20	80,000
25	90,000
30	100,000
35	110,000
40	120,000

When these two schedules are plotted on the same graph, the point of intersection represents the price and quantity at which the market is in *equilibrium*. It is said that this is a condition for *clearing the market*, because at that price and quantity everyone who wants to buy at that price can obtain the product and everyone who wants to sell at that price can find a buyer. Under the conditions of pure COMPETITION, the market will automatically and naturally settle at the equilibrium point. For example, suppose manufacturers provided 100,000 tennis rackets; as indicated in the schedule, they would want them to sell for $30—but at that price the schedule shows that consumers would buy only 70,000, so there would be a surplus, which would cause the price to drop. Only those manufacturers who were willing to provide tennis rackets at the lower price would remain, so the quantity would also drop and eventually equilibrium would be reached. The same reasoning can be applied to any point on the graph, and it can be seen that natural forces drive the market to equilibrium.

A single supply or demand schedule is based on the assumption of OTHER THINGS BEING EQUAL—*nothing* in the universe which may have an effect on these price-quantity combinations is changing. For an example of what is meant here, assume that supply-and-demand schedules for tennis *balls* are as shown in Figure 1a. Now suppose that manufacturers of tennis rackets develop a new laminating machine which allows them to use a less expensive grade of wood

and still produce tennis rackets which consumers cannot differentiate from the previous ones. If tennis rackets sold for $40 and manufacturers were previously willing to provide 120,000 of them, they would now want to provide more at that price (because they now make more profit)—say 130,000. The same can be said for all of the prices in the original supply schedule.

Figure 1b shows the *new supply schedule* superimposed on the original demand schedule; consumers do not change their views as to how many they buy at each price. However, the equilibrium point changes, and the correct descriptions are as follows:

1. There has been a *change in supply*, or *supply shift* (a new supply schedule has been created because one of the determinants of supply has changed).
2. There has been a *change in quantity demanded* (regarding demand, other

Supply and demand. Figure 1.

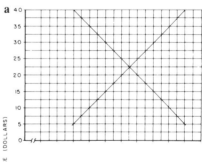

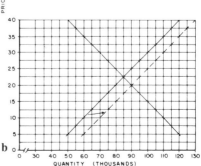

things remain unchanged, so equilibrium is found at a new point on the *same* demand schedule).

Next, assume that supply and demand schedules for tennis balls have been as shown in Figure 2a. Now that consumers have more tennis rackets in their possession it is reasonable to expect that at every price they will buy more tennis balls than they would previously. Therefore a new equilibrium will result, as shown in Figure 2b, and the following can be said:

3. There has been a *change in demand*, or *demand shift* (a new demand schedule has been created because one of the determinants of demand—willingness to buy—has changed).
4. There has been a *change in quantity supplied* (regarding supply, no determinant has changed, so equilibrium is found at a new point on the *same* supply schedule).

Tennis balls and tennis rackets are known as *complementary goods*; a similar analysis (but with different results) could be conducted with *competing goods*, such as zippers and buttons.

SUPPLY, FACTOR. See FACTOR SUPPLY.

SUPPLY SCHEDULE. A description in tabular or graphical form of the relationship between the price of an item and the quantity suppliers will provide. Supply and price are normally directly related; increases in one are consistent with increases in the other. See also BACKWARD BENDING SUPPLY CURVE.

It is important to interpret a supply schedule under the OTHER THINGS BEING EQUAL assumption; at a specified time and under specified conditions the schedule applies. See SUPPLY AND DEMAND.

SUPPLY SHIFT. See SUPPLY AND DEMAND.

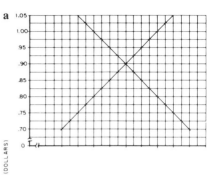
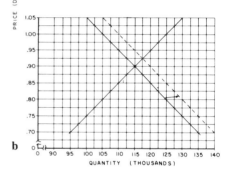

Supply and demand. Figure 2.

SUPPLY-SIDE ECONOMICS. Generally, economic policies and actions that will have long-run benefits even though they may be contractionary in the short run. The expression relates to the CIRCULAR FLOW OF MONEY and the theory that money injected any place in the loop expands the entire economy. *Supply-side economics* generally provides incentives to the business sector so that it will expand and hire increasing numbers of workers; the workers will then be able to buy the output of the business sector, which will continue to expand.

SURETY. A person who makes himself primarily liable for the debt of another.

SURPLUS. In budgeting, an excess of income over outflow. In the context of the federal government budget, a surplus is quite important for the entire economy. Because a surplus budget does not put back into the economy all the money it takes out, it is generally felt to be a CONTRACTIONARY policy, although a budget which is only slightly on the surplus side is often said to be EXPANSIONARY (because it takes in taxes much of the money people would have saved and puts that money into the economy). Actually, the question is much more complex than these few words indicate, partly because a budget that is not running a surplus is likely to run a deficit, and the national debt is an accumulation of deficits. Regardless of any first-order effect a surplus may have on the economy, its use in reducing the national debt can be very important. See also BALANCED BUDGET; BALANCE OF INTERNATIONAL PAYMENTS.

The word *surplus* is also often seen in supply-and-demand analysis, where it refers to the condition of more product available than buyers are demanding at the market price. In a MARKET ECONOMY a surplus is generally transitory because each supplier, in an effort to sell his surplus, will lower his price until the resultant increase in quantity demanded eliminates the surplus. There is a practical limit to price declines: Below that limit suppliers would rather pay inventory costs, salvage the product, rework the product, or in some other way take it off the market.

In accounting, the word is not generally used today because it suggests something extra or left over, but some areas of accounting refer to *earned surplus* (more often called *retained earnings*) and to *paid-in surplus* (often identified with a more descriptive expression such as *capital contribution in excess of par value*).

With regard to the CONSOLIDATED STATEMENT OF CONDITION OF ALL FEDERAL RESERVE BANKs, surplus consists of earnings retained as a reserve against unforeseen losses. Federal Reserve banks are required by law (Federal Reserve Act, Section 7) to maintain such a fund accumulated from their annual earnings after distribution of a cumulative 6 percent dividend on the paid-in capital stock. At the end of 1964 the Board of Governors of the Federal Reserve System concluded that the growth of the capital, accumulated surplus, and net earnings of the Reserve banks warranted halving the surplus of the Reserve banks from the total of subscribed capital (6 percent) to the level of paid-in capital (3 percent). [Adapted from *Glossary: Weekly Federal Reserve Statements*, Federal Reserve Bank of New York.] See CAPITAL PAID IN.

SURPLUS VALUE. As seen by KARL MARX, each worker contributes a certain value to the productive process but employers obtain more than that value when selling the fruits of the worker's labor. *Surplus value* is the difference between what the worker contributes and what he is paid; Marx saw that sum as accruing to capitalists.

SURTAX. A tax which is charged in addition to a tax already on the good or service. Although surtaxes are usually meant to be temporary, they sometimes become a permanent part of the tax structure. A typical surtax might be applied for the purpose of making an adjustment in demand (by reducing consumer purchasing power) or to adjust government revenues. A surtax could be one tool of FISCAL POLICY, used for FINE TUNING of the economy.

SUSPENSE ACCOUNT. An account to which accountants post items temporarily while a decision is being made as to final disposition to a permanent account.

SVENSKAHANDELSBANKEN (Swed.). One of the largest commercial banks in Sweden. It is privately owned.

SVERIGES INVESTERINGSBANK (Swed.). Investment Bank of Sweden, a financial institution which obtains funds by selling bonds to the NATIONAL PENSION FUND and uses the money to finance long-term industrial investment.

SVERIGES KREDITBANK (Swed.). The only commercial bank in Sweden which is owned by the government; the other 15 are privately owned.

SWAP NETWORK. A major feature of the Federal Reserve's foreign exchange operations is the use made of a network of inter-central-bank reciprocal currency arrangements, commonly known as *swap* facilities. In exchange market terminology a *swap* is a pair of transactions between two parties entered into simultaneously: (1) a *spot* purchase or sale of one currency against another, and (2) a *forward* contract to resell or repurchase the currency after a specified period of time at a specified rate. This forward rate may be the same as the rate used in the spot transaction, or it may differ from the spot rate enough to yield the equivalent of interest to one of the parties. In effect, the holder of a currency balance covered by such a forward contract is protected against any risk of a depreciation of the other currency against his own; the holder has what is called an *exchange value guaranty*.

The swap arrangements between foreign central banks and the Federal Reserve have generally provided that if one central bank has initiated a swap transaction with a second central bank, and if that second central bank and its government are about to revalue its currency upward, the swap will be unwound before the revaluation occurs. Under these conditions the debtor central bank (the bank that initiated the swap drawing) will not suffer a loss in obtaining the currency it needs to fulfill the swap contract. Under circumstances in which the dollar floats against other currencies, these provisions may not be applicable. For example, during 1973, when most major currencies were on a floating basis, the Federal Reserve had agreements with certain other central banks specifying that profits and losses from market intervention by the Federal Reserve would be shared equally by the Federal Reserve and the foreign central bank participating in the agreement.

As of mid-1974, the Federal Reserve's swap network included arrangements with 14 foreign central banks and the Bank for International Settlements; together these totaled almost $20 billion. Drawings on a particular swap line may be initiated by either party.

[Adapted from *The Federal Reserve System Purposes and Functions*, by the Board of Governors of the Federal Reserve System.]

SWEATSHOP. A place of employment where the employer exhibits no concern for workers' safety or comfort; the only concern is to obtain as much work as possible from the workers.

SWEDISH EMPLOYERS' CONFEDERATION (Swed.). An organization of employers in private industry, formed mainly to negotiate with confederations of labor unions. There are other employers' confederations, but this one is the largest.

SWING SHIFT. The work shift that ends about midnight. Also called *second shift*. See also FIRST SHIFT; GRAVEYARD SHIFT.

SYMPATHY STRIKE. A labor walkout initiated not to obtain additional benefits at the time but to demonstrate support for others who are striking. Also called *secondary strike*.

SYSTEM CONFERENCE OF LENDING OFFICERS. A committee of Federal Reserve authorities which meets periodically and holds telephone conferences as needed for the purpose of minimizing regional differences of interpretation regarding the regulation of commercial banks.

SYSTEM OF LOGIC. See JOHN STUART MILL.

T

TABLEAU ÉCONOMIQUE (Fr.). A MODEL built on macroeconomic theory in the 1700s. See QUESNAY, FRANÇOIS.

T ACCOUNT. In double-entry bookkeeping, each account has the name of the account on a horizontal line across the top, and then a vertical line separating the debit entries from the credit entries. The lines form a T, giving the name to this type of account.

TAFT-HARTLEY ACT. This U.S. legislation amended the Wagner Act of 1935 because the government protection given to labor by the latter resulted in a significant imbalance of power unfavorable to management, to the detriment of society and the economy in general. Abuses of power by management had been corrected by the Wagner Act, and the Taft-Hartley Act was required to correct the overshoot. One significant feature of the new act was the provision that any strike which was likely to create a national emergency could be postponed for 80 days (called a *cooling off period*) through an injunction by the Attorney General, if requested by the president. When a dispute raises the threat of a national emergency, the president appoints a *Board of Inquiry* to ascertain the facts and make recommendations. Also known as the *Labor-Management Relations Act of 1947.*

TAKEHOME PAY. The amount of money a worker has after his pay is reduced by taxes and other deductions. There is no official definition of exactly what deductions are included (as there is with the clearly defined term DISPOSABLE PERSONAL INCOME) and therefore economic statistics do not include takehome pay. For example, two workers earn the same gross pay. One may have deductions from his pay go directly to his CREDIT UNION to repay an automobile loan; the other worker may be making identical payments on a loan, but if they are not deducted, he will have a larger takehome pay. For these reasons, little information can be inferred about consumer choices, and takehome pay is of little significance in economics. Sometimes called *spendable earnings.*

TANDEM PLAN. A method of allowing flexibility in government action to stabilize the housing market. The plan allows the GOVERNMENT NATIONAL MORTGAGE ASSOCIATION to purchase at or below market interest rates up to a stipulated amount per year in unsubsidized Federal Housing Administration and Veterans Administration mortgages.

TANGIBLE PROPERTY. Material property that can be seen and touched, as opposed to intangible property, such as a patent. The patent certificate can be seen and touched, but the patent itself is merely a right which is granted, so the patent is intangible.

TAPE. Usually, in the economics of investing, TICKER TAPE.

TAP OFFERINGS (U.K.). New issues of treasury bills to which the BANK OF ENGLAND subscribes in full, and that it then resells gradually to the public.

TARGET. See MONETARY TARGET.

TARIFF. A government charge on goods entering the country. In the early days of the U.S., and in some other nations, import tariffs were applied specifically to provide revenue for the government; today most tariffs are mainly for control (to make it more expensive for citizens to buy the goods of other nations), the resultant revenue being incidental. The justification for tariffs is clouded by issues other than economics, such as politics and self-interest.

TARIFF WAR. Economic competition in which the nations involved adjust their tariff laws so as to counteract the effect of each other's tariff laws; the end objective is to obtain a trade advantage over the other nation.

TASK FORCE ON REGULATORY RELIEF. As part of the 1980-1984 administration's economic recovery plan, a series of actions designed to evaluate government regulation of various industries and to deregulate where indicated was included in Executive Order 12291, issued February 17, 1981. To spearhead the administration's regulatory relief efforts, the president created the Task Force on Regulatory Relief, which is chaired by the vice president. The task force reviews proposed regulations, using guidelines established by Executive Order 12291, and assesses existing regulations with an eye toward their revision.

TAX. Payment levied by a government, sometimes in payment for a service provided, but usually the conditions for tax collection do not require that a service first be performed. There are many kinds of taxes, but two main classifications are (1) sumptuary taxes—the main purpose of which is to control consumption; and (2) revenue taxes—the main purpose of which is to raise revenue to finance government operations. The two kinds of taxes blend into each other; most taxes have elements of both revenue and control.

One of the many controversies in the field of taxation has to do with who should pay for government operations: (1) According to the *benefit-received principle*, those who use the service should be the ones who pay for it; for example, highways are built with money collected by taxes on gasoline. (2) The *ability-to-pay principle* states that whoever can afford to pay for a service should be taxed for it, whether or not that taxpayer receives any benefit or uses the service.

Today taxes are generally considered to be a means of controlling the economy as well as to raise money to finance governments—see FISCAL POLICY.

TAXABLE INCOME. The portion of a taxpayer's (corporate or personal) income which forms the base for figuring income tax liability. Gross income is the full amount earned but it does not form the taxable base: (1) Some of that amount can be subtracted as expenses incurred in earning that income, such as the cost of uniforms required on the job, or the cost of advertising. (2) Some of that amount (personal and dependent deductions) is considered by the government to be ordinary expenses of living.

TAX AND LOAN ACCOUNT. An account kept in a commercial bank by the U.S. Treasury. Amounts are transferred from such accounts to Treasury accounts with the FEDERAL RESERVE SYSTEM through treasury CALLS when disbursements are to be made, because Treasury checks are written against Federal Reserve accounts.

TAX ANTICIPATION BILLS (TABs). Bills sold to the U.S. Treasury on an irregular basis prior to the mid-1970s. They were introduced in October 1951 and were designed specifically to help smooth out the Treasury's uneven flow of tax receipts while providing corporations with an investment vehicle for funds accumulated for tax payments. These bills were accepted at par on the tax date in payment for taxes due. They actually matured a week later, usually on the 22nd of the month. Tax anticipation bills did not have to be used for tax payments, and some investors chose to hold them to maturity.

Tax anticipation bills were sold in periods of low Treasury revenues and were scheduled to mature in periods of heavy tax receipts. Since two of the five major tax payment dates fall in the April-June quarter, that quarter generally registers a budget surplus. Because of this pattern, the great majority of the $159.4 billion of tax anticipation bills issued from 1951 through 1974 were sold in the period from July through March and were scheduled to mature in March, April, and June. Of the 83 tax bill auctions carried out through 1974, 19 were scheduled to mature in March, 17 in April, and 36 in June; only 9 were scheduled to mature in September and 2 in December.

No tax anticipation bills have been issued since 1974. In their place the Treasury has raised money on an irregular basis through the sale of *cash management bills*, which are usually "reopenings" or sales of additional amounts of outstanding matured bills. Cash management bills usually have maturities that fall after one of the five major tax dates and, like tax anticipation bills, are designed to help finance the Treasury's requirements until tax payments are received. Thirty-eight issues of cash management bills were sold in the period from 1975 to 1980, with maturities ranging from 2 to 167 days and averaging 51 days. Annual sales of cash management bills varied from $4 billion in 1976 to $45 billion in 1980. Very short-term cash management bills are sometimes referred to as *short-dated bills*.

TAX BASE. The amount that forms the basis for calculating a taxpayer's liability. In the aggregate, the tax base is the sum of such amounts or items. For income taxes the base is the earnings of citizens; for property taxes the base is the value of property.

TAX CREDIT. An amount by which a taxpayer may reduce his tax liability, as opposed to a tax deduction, which provides a reduction in taxable income. If a taxpayer is charged at the rate of 50 percent of his income, a tax credit reduces his tax liability by twice as much as a tax deduction of equal amount.

TAXE SUR LA VALEUR AJOUTÉ (Fr.). See VALUE ADDED TAX.

TAX EXEMPTS. Securities whose earnings are not subject to income tax. U.S. federal income tax is not taken from interest paid on bonds issued by state, county, and local governments.

TAX INCIDENCE. See INDIRECT TAX.

TAX LOOPHOLE. A provision of tax laws allowing the selective reduction of income tax liabilities; a legal DEDUCTION or TAX CREDIT. There is no official distinction between loopholes and any other deduction or tax credit, those provisions that are controversial are most likely to be called loopholes. Those deductions and credits which are criticized most often as loopholes are those which apply or are most significant to the wealthy or to large corporations.

TAX MULTIPLIER. Change in GROSS NATIONAL PRODUCT which results from a change in the amount government takes in taxes. The formula is basically the change in GNP is equal to the negative of change in taxes, times MARGINAL PROPENSITY TO CONSUME, divided by MARGINAL PROPENSITY TO SAVE. It is a negative number because increasing the amount removed from the consumer expenditure stream reduces total output. However, the net effect on GNP depends on government's use of the money received in taxes; see EXPENDITURES MULTIPLIER; BALANCED BUDGET MULTIPLIER.

TAX ON VALUE ADDED. Better known as VALUE ADDED TAX.

TAXPAYER REVOLT. A collective expression for the growing number of legal measures taken by taxpayers to express their feeling that government at all levels is too large a sector of the economy and that more of their income should be left in their hands, to be spent at their discretion. It is generally considered to have begun with PROPOSITION 13 in California in 1978.

TAX SELLING. Planned selling of property (usually securities) so as to reduce the seller's tax liability.

TAX SHELTER. A plan which allows a taxpayer to exempt certain parts of his income from current taxable income. Such arrangements are usually planned to give income after retirement, at which time the individual will pay the income tax. The theory of a tax shelter is that during working years income is relatively high and the taxpayer is in a high tax bracket; after retirement, the taxpayer's total income is smaller and taxes will therefore be less.

TECHNOLOGICAL DETERMINISM. One of the arguments used in the continuing debate over the effects of big business on the economy. On the positive side, technological determinism holds that only large corporations can efficiently use many new innovations—which require either large monetary layouts, a large volume of usage, large numbers of operators, or other factors not likely to be found in a small organization. Those who see technological determinism as a negative item claim that the very presence of such equipment gives large corporations an advantage that makes it increasingly difficult for smaller organizations to compete and

stay in business. This group also holds that technological determinism allows one large corporation to dominate production of an entire product.

TECHNOLOGICAL MONOPOLY. The situation that one manufacturer alone is able to produce and sell a certain item, free of competition. This advantage may be the result of (1) patent, giving the right to prevent others from copying the item or process; (2) company secrets; (3) a technology so complex that, even though there may be no restrictions on competitors, it will take them a significant amount of time to establish production. Technological monopoly is generally of relatively short duration; competitors soon develop variations which circumvent patents, learn trade secrets, or enter the industry if profits are sufficiently high.

TECHNOLOGICAL UNEMPLOYMENT. That portion of total unemployment which is due to changes in technology or in management methods. Economists point out that technological unemployment might explain why a certain individual is out of work, but the overall effect of technology is to shift jobs rather than to create unemployment. For example, no one works as a lamplighter today, but the number of people employed lighting streets electrically far exceeds the number of lamplighting positions which have been eliminated.

TEKHPROMFINPLAN (U.S.S.R.). The operating plan submitted by each Soviet enterprise, showing its technical and economic goals as well as how it will achieve them. Such plans eventually become integrated throughout the nation when a five-year plan is prepared. See also GOSPLAN.

TENANT FARM ACT. Legislation of 1937 designed to spread the ownership of farms in the U.S. to create smaller units. It made long term (40 years) money available for such nonowners as tenant farmers to purchase small farms. Also known as the *Bankhead-Jones Farm Tenant Act.*

TENDER. To offer or make available; one says, for example, that a buyer tenders (offers) payment. See also LEGAL TENDER.

TENNESSEE VALLEY AUTHORITY (TVA). One of the largest projects undertaken by the U.S. government during the 1930s, it had the multiple purposes of providing flood control, supplying electricity, and providing employment. The work was authorized by the Tennessee Valley Authority Act of 1933.

TERM FEDERAL FUNDS. Loans by the Federal Reserve System to commercial banks for a period of more than one day, as opposed to "overnight money," which is loaned just until the next day.

TERMINATION PAY. An amount of money paid to an employee when circumstances other than his own conduct or quality of work require that he be laid off. Many labor contracts and employers' policies dictate the amount of such pay according to a formula, usually based on duration of employment; some employers give every discharged worker a fixed rate, such as two weeks' pay. Also called *dismissal pay* or *severance pay*.

TERMS OF TRADE. In international economics, a barterlike comparison, such as the number of bushels of U.S. wheat that have the same value as a German camera. See also PURCHASING POWER PARITY.

TEST, IMPACT. See IMPACT TEST.

TEXTILE MACHINERY. See HARGREAVES' JENNY; JACQUARD'S LOOM.

THE DESK. The trading desk at the New York Federal Reserve Bank, through which open market purchases and sales of government securities are made. The desk maintains direct telephone communication with major government securities dealers. A "foreign desk" at the New York Federal Reserve Bank conducts transactions in the foreign exchange market. See FEDERAL OPEN MARKET COMMITTEE.

THEORY OF MORAL SENTIMENTS. Early book by ADAM SMITH describing some thoughts on the CLASSICAL SCHOOL of economic thinking. His later book, AN INQUIRY INTO THE NATURE AND CAUSES OF THE WEALTH OF NATIONS, became very popular and is still cited in today's writings.

THIRD COUNTRY BILLS. Bankers' ACCEPTANCES which involve the financing of goods stored in or shipped between foreign countries.

THIRD PARTY INTERVENTION. In labor and other disputes, help from an individual or a group with no direct interest in the final agreement. See also ARBITRATION; MEDIATION.

THIRD SHIFT. The work shift that begins about midnight. Also called *graveyard shift*. See also SWING SHIFT.

THIRD WORLD. All the nations of the world that are classified as LESS DEVELOPED COUNTRIES.

THREE-ANTI CAMPAIGN (China). In the early 1950s, during the transition to communist rule in China, this campaign was instituted to weaken resistance to complete state takeover. It was directed at civil servants serving the middle class, specifically at giantism in government bureaus, corruption, and waste of labor and materials. See also FIVE-ANTI CAMPAIGN.

THRIFT AND LOAN ASSOCIATION (T&L). A depository type financial intermediary that accepts savings deposits and makes loans for mortgage, personal, and small business uses. This form of financial company operates in a minority of states. See also SAVINGS AND LOAN ASSOCIATION.

THRIFT INSTITUTION. A MUTUAL SAVINGS BANK, SAVINGS AND LOAN ASSOCIATION, or CREDIT UNION. See also FINANCIAL INTERMEDIARY.

THROUGH BILL OF LADING. A BILL OF LADING that provides for all handling, from receipt by first carrier to delivery by the last carrier.

TICKER TAPE. In finance and investing, a narrow paper tape that records every transaction at the major stock exchanges. For many years the information was relayed to brokerage houses throughout the nation, where tickers would print additional copies of the tape for viewing by investors either directly or when projected on a screen. The modern method is instead to reconstruct the information at each brokerage house through a matrix of lights.

TIED LOAN. An international loan to a LESS DEVELOPED COUNTRY, in which conditions for use of the money are stipulated. In a typical tied loan the nation receiving the loan might be required to spend the money to buy goods from the nation that makes the loan.

TIE-IN CONTRACT. A contract in which the buyer can purchase certain items in a given ratio only. For example, a soft drink retailer might not be able to purchase a case of flavor X unless he also purchases a case each of flavor Y and flavor Z. Obviously, this scheme can work only if there is large demand for flavor X; the retailer often raises the price of the item with the heavy demand and lowers the other prices so that he can sell the entire mix he is forced to buy. When the seller requires that the buyer carry all of the former's products, the arrangement is called *full line* forcing. Such contracts are generally legal as long as they do not tend to reduce competition.

TIGHT CREDIT. Situation said to exist when interest rates are high—it is then expensive to obtain credit.

TIGHT LABOR MARKET. A period when unemployment is low and it is difficult to find people to fill vacancies. Opposite is *slack labor market*.

TIGHT MONEY. Contractionary MONETARY POLICY. In taking steps to decrease the rate of growth of the MONEY SUPPLY, monetary authorities are said to be following a *tight money*, or restrictive, policy. The opposite of *easy money*.

TILL MONEY. CURRENCY kept on hand in banks for day-to-day needs. Also called *vault cash*. See HIGH-POWERED MONEY.

TIME BILL. A BILL OF EXCHANGE in which payment is not required until a specified date. See also SIGHT BILL.

TIME CERTIFICATE OF DEPOSIT. More commonly known as a CERTIFICATE OF DEPOSIT.

TIME DEPOSIT. The type of account with a DEPOSITORY FINANCIAL INTERMEDIARY in which the latter has the right (sometimes the obligation) to refuse to permit a withdrawal for a stated length of time. Such accounts pay interest, although that fact is not part of the definition of time deposit. See also CERTIFICATE OF DEPOSIT; DEMAND DEPOSIT.

TIME SERIES. Economic data which are taken at various times and are presented as a function of time. For example, a SCHEDULE of NATIONAL INCOME for each of several years is a time series; national income for various nations in a given year is not a time series.

TIME UTILITY. Increase in the value of an item because of its being made available at a more desirable point in time. For example, vegetables which are stored during their regular season will sell in their off-season for a higher price.

TIME VALUE OF MONEY. Because money has earning power, a person who will be paid $100 would rather have the money today than at some time in the future. If money can earn 10 percent per year, then a person who receives $100 today has been given exactly the same spending power as a person who will be given $110 one year later. See also PRESENT VALUE.

TOKEN COIN. A coin whose value as a unit of money is larger than the commodity value of the metal from which it is made. Unless a coin *is* a token coin, it will cease to function as money because people will sell it for its commodity value rather than use it in trade.

TOKYO ROUND. One of a series of international negotiations dealing with tariffs and world trade.

TOOLS OF MONETARY POLICY. The FEDERAL RESERVE SYSTEM has two types of tools with which it can affect the level of domestic economic activity and the basic balance of international payments: quantitative (general credit) and qualitative (selective) controls. *Quantitative controls* influence the MONEY SUPPLY, interest rates, and the overall availability of credit; *qualitative controls* are directed at a particular kind of credit. The principal quantitative tools are changes in the DISCOUNT RATE, changes in reserve requirements (see BANK RESERVES), and open market operations (see FEDERAL OPEN MARKET COMMITTEE). The only qualitative tool which is ordinarily used is changing the MARGIN REQUIREMENTS on securities listed on national exchanges. There are also tools which are partly quantitative and partly qualitative: setting of maximum interest rates payable on time and savings deposits at member banks, and buying and selling of foreign securities in the foreign exchange market. See also MONETARY POLICY.

TOTAL BANK CREDIT. Commercial bank investments and loans adjusted for transactions with affiliates.

TOTAL COSTS (TC). The sum of all FIXED COSTS (costs which are independent of the quantity of a product being made) and all VARIABLE COSTS (costs which depend on the quantity produced). See COST for a listing of various types of costs recognized by economists.

TOTAL FIXED COSTS (TFC). The sum of all FIXED COSTS (costs which do not vary with the number of units being produced).

TOTAL U.S. GOVERNMENT SECURITIES. With regard to the CONSOLIDATED STATEMENT OF CONDITION OF ALL FEDERAL RESERVE BANKS, securities held by the Reserve banks which may be sold to dealers under a matched sale-purchase agreement (so-called reverse repos). The dealers are required to sell the securities back to the Reserve banks on the date specified in the agreement. Typically, these contracts mature in a day or two. Outstanding matched sale-purchase transactions on the date of the statement are indicated in a footnote. If a transaction has not been completed by Wednesday evening, the statistics include the ''sale,'' and the purchase is included the following week. [Adapted from Federal Reserve Bank of New York, *Glossary: Weekly Federal Reserve Statements.*]

TOTAL VARIABLE COSTS (TVC). The sum of all VARIABLE COSTS (those costs which depend on the number of units produced). See COST for a list of various types of costs recognized by economists.

TRADE ACCEPTANCE. A financial instrument in which a *drawer* orders a *drawee* to pay a sum of money to a *payee* and that nonbank entity has accepted. It is similar to *banker's acceptance*, except that the latter instrument is accepted by a bank.

TRADE ADJUSTMENT ASSISTANCE. A federal program which has provided more generous unemployment benefits to workers who have been displaced by foreign competition than to other unemployed workers.

TRADE AGREEMENTS. See RECIPROCAL TRADE AGREEMENTS.

TRADE ASSOCIATION. See INDUSTRY ASSOCIATION.

TRADE BLOC. A group of nations that arrange tariffs, quotas, and other controls for mutual benefit.

TRADE DEFICIT. An excess of imports over exports, resulting in a net outflow of money from a nation.

TRADE DISCOUNT. A single discount or a schedule of discounts used in industrial sales, usually so that effective selling prices can be changed simply by changing a discount instead of changing list prices or printing a new catalog.

TRADE EXPANSION ACT. See GENERAL AGREEMENT ON TARIFFS AND TRADE.

TRADE ORGANIZATION. An organization whose members are companies in the same industry. See INDUSTRY ASSOCIATION.

TRADES UNION CONGRESS (TUC) (U.K.). A federation of British trade unions. About 20 percent of unionized labor belongs to unions which are affiliated with TUC.

TRADE SURPLUS. An excess of exports over imports, resulting in a net inflow of money into the nation.

TRADE UNION. A labor union whose membership is restricted to those who possess a particular skill used in a certain job. Also called a *craft union*. Very few unions today are true craft unions; they usually try to expand their membership and sometimes go far afield to achieve that goal, such as a union of truck drivers that organizes office workers.

TRADE-WEIGHTED EXCHANGE RATE. The nominal effective foreign exchange value of the dollar.

TRADING DESK. See FEDERAL OPEN MARKET COMMITTEE.

TRADING ON THE EQUITY. Borrowing money and using it in a profitable manner so that, even after deducting for interest that must be paid on the borrowed money, there is a net profit.

TRADING RISK. One of the risks to be faced by an investor who purchases a "fixed" investment such as a bond. See EFFECTIVE RATE OF INTEREST; RISK.

TRADING STAMP. A stamp that is purchased by retailers and given to consumers in quantities proportional to the amount spent in the store (usually one stamp for each 10 cents spent). The consumer can then obtain merchandise by trading the stamps back to the company that sold them to the retailer. In the 1960s neighborhood stores gave these stamps as a competitive measure to attract customers, but the procedure became so widespread in the 1970s that it could no longer be viewed as a competitive device, and it is seldom seen in the 1980s.

TRANSACTIONS ACCOUNT. A checking account or similar account from which third-party transfers can be made. Demand deposit accounts, negotiable order of withdrawal (NOW) accounts, automatic transfer service (ATS) accounts, and credit union share draft accounts are examples of transactions accounts at banks and other depository institutions.

TRANSACTIONS DEMAND. See LIQUIDITY PREFERENCE.

TRANSFER AGENT. The person who keeps records of ownership of securities as they are sold among investors.

TRANSFER PAYMENT. An income flow which represents a change in the distribution of national wealth but not compensation for a current contribution to the production process. The primary components of government transfer payments are social security benefits and veterans' pensions. Business transfers include bad debts, charitable contributions, and contest prizes.

TRANSPORTATION INSURANCE. Protection against financial business losses due to damage or destruction of goods while in possession of a carrier.

TRAVEL AND ENTERTAINMENT CARD (T&E). A type of CREDIT CARD, issued by the company which grants the credit, valid in large numbers of establishments that choose to join the system. There is usually an annual charge to the credit card holder, and purchases which are not paid within a billing period are then subject to a FINANCE CHARGE.

TRAVELER'S CHECK. A check that a person obtains by paying the amount of the check to the issuer (sometimes along with a fee for the service). Such checks are more readily negotiable because, since the issuer has already been paid, there are never insufficient funds to clear the check.

The procedure is that the buyer signs his name immediately on the check and then, to negotiate it to another person, signs his name again in front of that person. If the signatures match, the person accepting the traveler's check is guaranteed payment by the issuer. Lost or stolen traveler's checks are replaced by the issuer.

TREASURY BILL. Short-term U.S. Treasury security issued in minimum denominations of $10,000 and usually having original maturities of 3, 6, or 12 months. Investors purchase bills at prices lower than the face value of the bills; the return to the investors is the difference between the price paid for the bills and the amount received when the bills are sold or when they mature. Treasury bills are issued in book-entry form only; that is, the purchaser receives a statement, rather than an engraved certificate. Treasury bills are the type of security used most frequently in open market operations.

TREASURY BOND. Long-term U.S. Treasury security having initial maturity of more than 10 years and issued in denominations of $1,000 or more, depending on the specific issue. Bonds pay interest semiannually, with principal payable at maturity. As is the case with notes, bonds are issued in registered or bearer form.

TREASURY CALL. See TAX AND LOAN ACCOUNT.

TREASURY CURRENCY OUTSTANDING. In official accounts, coins and currency that are obligations of the Treasury Department held by the public, commercial banks, the FEDERAL RESERVE BANKs and the Treasury itself (but excluding gold certificates, series of 1934, which are issued only to Federal Reserve banks and are not in circulation).

The largest part of this item is coin, including a very small amount of standard silver dollars. The only Treasury currency now being issued is United States notes, and they are limited by law to $347 million. Included in Treasury currency outstanding, however, are all outstanding Treasury currencies originally issued by commercial banks but for which the Treasury has legal redemption responsibility. These currencies include Federal Reserve notes issued before July 1, 1929 (large size), Federal Reserve bank notes, national bank notes, gold certificates issued before the 1934 series, silver certificates, and Treasury notes of 1890. [Adapted from Federal Reserve Bank of New York, *Glossary: Federal Reserve Weekly Statements.*]

TREASURY NOTE. Intermediate-term coupon-bearing U.S. Treasury security having initial maturity of 1 to 10 years. It is issued in denominations of $1,000 or more, depending on maturity of the issue. Notes pay interest semiannually, and the principal is payable at maturity. Notes are issued in registered or bearer form.

TREASURY SECURITY. Interest-bearing obligation of the U.S. government issued by the Treasury as a means of borrowing money to meet government expenditures not covered by revenues. Marketable Treasury securities fall into three categories (see TREASURY BILL; TREASURY BOND; TREASURY NOTE). The FEDERAL RESERVE SYSTEM holds more than $100 million of these obligations, acquired through open market operations (see FEDERAL OPEN MARKET COMMITTEE).

TREASURY STOCK. CAPITAL STOCK which was sold by the issuing corporation and then repurchased by the same corporation. Such stock does not carry voting privileges. Corporations sometimes hold treasury stock for use in STOCK OPTION and other plans.

TREND LINE. Long-run average of a fluctuating statistic. There are several ways of locating the trend line. One common way is to locate the line such that the areas under the envelope of actual points are equal above and below the line, another is LEAST SQUARES.

TRIANGULAR ARBITRAGE. If the spot rates among three currencies are disorderly, or inconsistent, ARBITRAGE will occur. For example, consider the following hypothetical set of exchange rates for the French franc (FF), Deutschemark (DM), and U.S. dollar: DM 1 = $0.30; DM 1 = FF 1.5; FF 1 = $0.22. This set of exchange rates is inconsistent because, disregarding transactions costs, one Deutschemark will bring 30 cents if converted directly to dollars but will yield 33 cents if converted first into francs and then into dollars. A foreign exchange trader would simultaneously buy Deutschemarks with dollars, buy francs with Deutschemarks, and buy dollars with francs. Such arbitrage, requiring no capital and carried out on a large scale, would quickly change all three rates so as to make them consistent. In this example, the dollar price of Deutschemarks would rise, the franc price of Deutschemarks would fall, and the dollar price of francs would fall and settle at DM 1 = $0.31; DM 1 = FF 1.476; FF 1 = $0.21. [This example adapted from Federal Reserve Bank of Cleveland, *Economic Review* (April/May 1972), p. 13.]

Triangular arbitrage may also occur in FORWARD EXCHANGE CONTRACTs if there is an inconsistency in the exchange rates of such contracts with identical maturity.

TRIBALISM. A feeling of closeness and loyalty within a local group to the extent that antagonism, discrimination, and even hate are felt toward other tribes or groups. This situation, often found in a LESS DEVELOPED COUNTRY, makes it difficult to achieve the national unity that is necessary for economic growth.

TRIFFIN PLAN. See BANCOR.

TRUCKLOAD. A shipment of goods that occupies an entire truck or trailer. For further explanation see LESS THAN CARLOAD.

TRUST. A fiduciary relationship in which complete or partial control of assets is given to someone (a trustee) other than the owner. Banks often have trust departments that manage investments (such as employee pension funds), administer estates, act as guardian of property of minors, and perform similar functions. See ADVISORY AGENT; MANAGING AGENT.

TRUSTEE. See TRUST.

TRUST FUND BUREAU (Jap.). A depository of funds which will be used for loans, mostly to public enterprises.

TRUST PROPERTY. Items of value that are placed in TRUST.

TRUTH IN LENDING. Officially known as Federal Reserve regulation Z, legislation designed to let borrowers and customers know the cost of credit so they can compare costs of various credit sources and avoid uninformed use of credit. This regulation does not fix maximum, minimum, or any other charges for credit; it merely provides for disclosure and uniform interpretation of pertinent information. It applies to any individual or organization that extends or arranges credit for which a finance charge is or may be payable or which is payable in more than four installments. See also CONSUMERISM.

TURGOT, ANNE ROBERT JACQUES. French economist (1727-1781) of the school of economics known as PHYSIOCRACY, which held that agriculture was the only productive activity. One of his main contributions was the book *Reflections on the Formation and Distribution of Riches*, published in 1766.

TURNOVER. Replacement of a unit or an asset because of the departure or using up of a similar unit or asset. There are various kinds of turnovers in economics. For example, *labor turnover* refers to the percentage of an employer's workers who are replaced because of voluntary or involuntary leaving, usually figured on an annual basis. *Inventory turnover* refers to the replacement of goods that are sold.

TURNOVER TAX. A tax paid by manufacturers each time goods change hands during the manufacturing process. One of the reasons that a VALUE ADDED TAX is more popular than a turnover tax is that the latter allows goods produced by a single vertically integrated manufacturer to be less costly than the same goods produced by a chain of small manufacturers; it is not a NEUTRAL TAX. Also called *cascade tax*.

TWO-TIER GOLD SYSTEM. Prior to March 1968, a GOLD POOL of eight major nations bought and sold gold as required to keep the price at $35 an ounce. When private demands required large-scale selling by the pool, it could be seen that their gold reserves were exhaustible. The gold pool was then replaced with the two-tier system. In gold transactions between monetary authorities and central banks for monetary uses the price would remain at $35 an ounce; the market for private users would be independent, with prices freely determined by ordinary forces of SUPPLY AND DEMAND. In November 1973 the U.S. along with six European nations agreed to abandon the two-tier system.

U

UMPIRE. In labor economics, an individual who is called in as an arbitrator.

UNAUTHORIZED STRIKE. In labor economics, a work stoppage which is not officially called by the union. It may occur because of some event on the job site which the union leaders may not even be aware of, or it may occur because an INJUNCTION has been issued forbidding the strike. There have been examples of an injunction's being followed by a statement by the union "suggesting" a work stoppage but telling the workers not to strike. Unauthorized strikes are also called *wildcat strikes*.

UNCONFIRMED LETTER OF CREDIT. A document (LETTER OF CREDIT) in which a bank indicates credit approval by stating, but not unconditionally guaranteeing (credit could be withdrawn if the person had been arrested) that it will accept drafts (see ACCEPTANCES) for the named individual.

UNCOVERED DOLLARS. Throughout most of the later 1960s, and particularly prior to the economic policy measures taken by the administration in August 1971, swap drawings (see SWAP NETWORK) of foreign currencies by the Federal Reserve enabled the System to give a temporary exchange value guaranty to foreign CENTRAL BANKs accumulating dollars, and thereby to delay or avoid additional foreign requests for gold sales by the U.S. Treasury. In such cases the Federal Reserve used the foreign currency immediately to buy the additional dollars accumulated by the foreign central bank. Thus, the foreign central bank's additional holdings of "uncovered dollars" were replaced by dollar assets that were "covered" or protected against exchange rate risk.

Ordinarily, these covered dollar assets took the form of special nonmarketable U.S. Treasury securities, while the rate protection was afforded by the Federal Reserve's obligation to return a specified amount of national currency to the foreign central bank at the termination of the swap. To fulfill this obligation, the Federal Reserve acquired the foreign currency through subsequent market purchases, or it arranged to buy such currency directly from the foreign central bank. Otherwise, the Federal Reserve had to buy the needed currency from the U.S. Treasury following either a gold sale or an INTERNATIONAL MONETARY FUND drawing through which the Treasury acquired the foreign currency.

Swap drawings of the type just described—to help delay or avoid reductions in U.S. reserve assets—were discontinued after August 15, 1971. As of that date, when the U.S. government suspended convertibility of the dollar into gold or other reserve assets, drawings outstanding amounted to about $3 billion.

UNDERDEVELOPED COUNTRY (UDC). Because this expression seems to imply an arbitrary standard as to just how developed all nations should be, the more acceptable expression today is LESS DEVELOPED COUNTRY.

UNDEREMPLOYMENT. Using FACTORS OF PRODUCTION in an inefficient manner, as when a large computer installation is used to type out reports which a simple printer could do. The really undesirable part of underemployment is that it gives the appearance of working to capacity and hides the potential that exists in the economy. With regard to the human resource, underemployment can take the form of DIRECT PRODUCTION (not taking advantage of machines and technology that could increase productivity) or of FEATHERBEDDING (creating a position and hiring a worker even though nothing is accomplished by that position).

UNDERLYING BOND. Bond giving the claims of its owners priority over the claims of owners of other bond issues. It is the opposite of an *overlying bond*, whose owners have a subordinated claim to pledged property.

UNDERMARGINED. When an investor purchases CAPITAL STOCK by giving the broker a portion of the price and borrowing the rest, the sale is a *margin sale*, and the portion given to the broker is the margin. The FEDERAL RESERVE SYSTEM establishes minimum margin requirements, and when the amount given to the broker no longer meets the margin requirements (regardless of the reason—because the market price of the stock changes, or because the margin requirements were changed), the investor is said to be undermargined.

UNDERSTATE. To cause statistics, reports, or other presentations to be misleading by having numbers smaller than would result from some other method of figuring or by failing to give due consideration to underlying facts whose overall effect would be similar to that of having larger numbers. For example, in a period of falling prices corporate profits may decline, but to the extent that a fall in the

value of inventories on hand is responsible, it is often said that profits are understated.

UNDERUTILIZATION. Less than optimum use of an ECONOMIC RESOURCE. The term is often applied to factories and other means of production if there could be more production without additional investment in the factories. Labor in general is underutilized if more work could be accomplished without increasing the size of the work force, and individuals are underutilized if they are on the payroll but not being used effectively (FEATHERBEDDING).

UNDERVALUED CURRENCY. A monetary unit—say, of nation A—that exchanges with other nation's monetary units at a rate such that exports from nation A sell for an unusually low price in other nations; other nations therefore have an unfavorable balance of trade (see MERCHANDISE ACCOUNT) because of excess of imports over exports. This imbalance can be corrected by *revaluation* of the currency of nation A, meaning that it will exchange less of its money for a given quantity of other money. See also BALANCE OF INTERNATIONAL PAYMENTS; OVERVALUED CURRENCY.

UNDERWRITER. In economics of finance, the middleman for selling and distributing SECURITIES to investors or the public. For many securities issues the underwriter guarantees the entire issue or buys it outright for resale to the public. See also SPREAD.

UNDISTRIBUTED PROFITS. The remainder of corporations' profits after taxes and dividends have been paid.

UNEARNED INCOME. In general economics, inflows, usually money, such as fortuitous gains from an increase in the value of property held. Accountants use *unearned income* to describe payments which have been received prior to the performance that will earn the payments; for example, a publisher receives subscription payments but will be earning them by sending out magazines over a period of time.

UNEMPLOYMENT. See FRICTIONAL UNEMPLOYMENT; HARD-CORE UNEMPLOYMENT; NORMAL UNEMPLOYMENT; STRUCTURAL UNEMPLOYMENT. Information on the collection of unemployment data is found in an excellent article, "Counting the Jobless" [*Monthly Review of the Federal Reserve Bank of San Francisco* (September 1972)].

UNEMPLOYMENT COMPENSATION AMENDMENTS. Amendments to the Unemployment Insurance (UI) system, signed October 21, 1976, by President Ford, making permanent modifications, most of which became effective January 1, 1978. The major area of change is set forth in Title I of the new law, Extension of Coverage. Effective January 1, 1978, coverage of agricultural workers of certain large employers (as determined, in part, by payroll size) is made mandatory under federal law. Coverage is also extended to certain domestic workers and, with some exceptions, to employees of state and local governments and of nonprofit elementary and secondary schools. While some states had already covered agricultural workers, such coverage was not required by federal law. However, because of the limitations imposed on eligibility in the new law, only about 2 percent of farm employers are subject to the FEDERAL UNEMPLOYMENT TAX ACT (FUTA), thereby covering only about 459,000 agricultural workers. Similarly, only domestic workers of employers with a quarterly payroll of at least $1,000 are included, so the new provision extends coverage to about 130,000 workers, or about 11 percent of those in domestic service. Finally, approximately 600,000 jobs in state government and about 7.7 million jobs in local government are thus afforded unemployment compensation protection.

UNEMPLOYMENT INSURANCE BENEFITS (UIB). A plan whereby a person who loses his job receives payments for a certain length of time. The details vary from state to state but it is usually necessary that the job loss not be the fault of the individual and that the person make a continuing effort to find new employment. Most such plans are financed by a payroll tax. Often called *unemployment insurance* (UI).

UNEMPLOYMENT RATE. The number of individuals who are within the CIVILIAN LABOR FORCE but not employed, divided by the total civilian labor force. To determine percentage unemployment, that result would be multiplied by 100.

UNFAIR LIST. In labor economics, a list of firms that some labor group desires to take economic sanctions against, usually by a BOYCOTT of their products.

UNFAVORABLE BALANCE OF TRADE. See BALANCE OF INTERNATIONAL PAYMENTS.

UNFIT CURRENCY. Currency which has been worn sufficiently to justify withdrawing and replacing it. See FIT CURRENCY.

UNIFIED DEFICIT. There are several measures of the federal government's deficit, but the figure generally cited as "the deficit" is the unified deficit. It includes only the deficit arising from on-budget expenditures, even though the federal government borrows to finance off-budget activities as well.

UNIFORM COMMERCIAL CODE (UCC). Legislation which has been adopted, sometimes with variations, by all states except Louisiana. It was prepared by the National Conference of Commissioners on Uniform State Laws in 1952 to standardize the uncoordinated legal environment in which business operated. Its nine main sections are (1) general provisions; (2) sales; (3) commercial paper; (4) bank deposits and collections; (5) letters of credit; (6) bulk transfers; (7) warehouse receipts, bills of lading, and other documents of title; (8) investment securities; (9) secured transactions, sales of accounts, contract rights, and chattel paper.

UNIFORM PRICING CODE (UPC). A system implemented in the U.S. in the early and mid-1970s providing for marking consumer items with bars that can be read by electronic equipment at the cashier's station. When the item is passed over a sensor, price and other information is automatically read and processed. In addition to price, some products are coded to show category, sales tax information, inventory information, and other items.

Advantages include faster and more accurate checkout and reduced inventory and labor costs; also, a detailed cash register receipt can be printed with item descriptions. The main disadvantage is the expense of equipping checkout counters with the electronic devices.

UNIFYING BOND. A BOND sold for the purpose of obtaining funds to retire two or more other issues so as to make the debt more orderly. Also known as a *consol bond* or a *consolidation bond*.

UNILATERAL ACCOUNT. In accounting for BALANCE OF INTERNATIONAL PAYMENTS, the U.S. keeps a *unilateral account* in order to meet the requirements of double-entry bookkeeping with regard to the export of something for which no payment will be received in return. In that account is entered the amount that would have been received if there had been a payment.

UNILATERAL TRANSFERS. See BALANCE OF INTERNATIONAL PAYMENTS.

UNINTENDED INVESTMENT. Increases in inventories due to lower-than-expected sales (see CHANGE IN BUSINESS INVENTORIES), as opposed to planned investment, which is purchases of CAPITAL GOODS by the business SECTOR. Also called *unplanned investment*.

UNION. An organization that represents a group of workers in collective bargaining

with their employer, giving them more power than they would have if negotiating individually with their employer.

UNION LABEL. An identifying mark, sewed into fabric, printed on paper, stamped on hardgoods, etc. for the purpose of showing that the item was produced with unionized labor. Buyers are encouraged by unions to look for the label before purchasing items.

UNION SECURITY CLAUSE. A contract provision fixing the jurisdiction of a union in a plant and its relationship to the workers it represents and their jobs.

UNION SHOP. A place of employment in which every employee must be a member of the recognized union or must join within a stated period of time after being hired.

UNISSUED STOCK. Shares of CAPITAL STOCK which the corporation has received authorization to issue (see AUTHORIZED STOCK) but is holding for possible sale or other issue at a later time. Corporations sometimes hold unissued stock for use in STOCK OPTION and other plans. Also called *potential stock*.

UNIT. In labor economics, the group of workers represented by a single collective bargaining organization. For general application, see ECONOMIC UNIT.

UNIT BANK. A bank which has no branches.

UNIT BANKING LAW. A law in some states which prohibits banks from operating a BRANCH BANK.

UNIT COST. The cost of a single item.

UNITED STATES NOTES. A form of paper money now issued in $100 denomination only. In the modern small size (see PAPER CURRENCY SIZE), they were formerly issued in $1, $2, and $5 denominations. Just a few of the $1 notes were issued, and they disappeared from general circulation many years ago. The $2 denomination was discontinued in 1966 and the $5 in 1968. The $100 note appeared in 1969, although marked Series 1966.

Also called *legal tender notes*, they were issued in the old large size in $1, $2, $5, $10, $50, $1,000, $5,000, and $10,000 denominations. All paper money now issued is FEDERAL RESERVE NOTES.

UNIT ELASTICITY. A schedule in which the coefficient of ELASTICITY is 1; that is, a change of x percent in the price will cause a change of x percent in the quantity demanded or supplied.

UNLIMITED TAX BOND. A BOND issued by some level of government and backed by the full taxing authority of that government, as opposed to a *revenue bond*, in which payment of interest and principal is contingent upon revenue from some operation, such as a toll bridge or a municipal stadium. Interest and principal of an unlimited tax bond are taken from general funds. More often called *general obligation bond*.

UNLIMITED WANTS. One of the basic tenets of economics is that people always want more than is freely available, and therefore economic growth is generally welcomed.

UNLISTED STOCK. CAPITAL STOCK which is not traded at a major STOCK MARKET. Also called *over-the-counter stock*.

UNPLANNED INVESTMENT. Increases in inventories due to lower-than-expected sales (see CHANGE IN BUSINESS INVENTORIES), as opposed to *planned investment*, which is purchases of CAPITAL GOODS by the business SECTOR. Also called *unintended investment*.

UNSATISFIED FRINGE OF BORROWERS. See RATIONED CREDIT.

UNSECURED BOND. A BOND which is secured by the general credit of the borrower rather than by specific property or collateral. Also called a *debenture*.

UNSECURED LOAN. A loan arrangement in which the borrower does not provide any property (collateral) which the creditor may sell if the borrower fails to repay. It can generally be expected that the interest rate on an unsecured loan will be higher than on a secured loan, other things being equal, because there is higher risk for the lender.

UNSTABLE EQUILIBRIUM. Not an EQUILIBRIUM at all, but simply a flat period in economic statistics. When any change occurs, natural forces do not return the economy to this flat point, as they would in a true equilibrium.

UPSET RIM. The raised rim along the periphery of a coin, obtained by putting the PLANCHET through a milling, or upsetting, machine.

USER CHARGE. A payment made by those who use specified goods and services provided by a government, such as admission charges at national parks or charges made for government publications. The user charge may cover the total cost of the item, or part of the cost may be subsidized by the government. See BENEFIT-RECEIVED PRINCIPLE.

USE TAX. A tax which a person must pay before using certain items of his property, such as an automobile, within the jurisdiction of that taxing authority. One of the arguments used by its proponents is that a person may live in another city, and pay taxes in that city, but use the roads and other facilities of the city where he works.

U.S. GOVERNMENT SECURITIES BOUGHT OUTRIGHT. With regard to the CONSOLIDATED STATEMENT OF CONDITION OF ALL FEDERAL RESERVE BANKS, a breakdown of Treasury securities bought by the FEDERAL RESERVE SYSTEM in the open market from primary dealers in government securities, foreign official accounts, and the U.S. Treasury. Except for purchases in exchange for maturing issues, direct purchases from the Treasury are infrequent, for very short periods, and for relatively small amounts.

When the Treasury borrows directly from Federal Reserve banks, it issues *special certificates of indebtedness* to the Reserve banks for the amount of the loan and receives a corresponding increase in its general account. Such borrowing is done infrequently and almost exclusively to cover overdrafts on the Treasury's account with the Federal Reserve banks immediately before quarterly tax payment dates, when the Treasury's balances are low and a large inflow of funds is soon to take place. Such borrowing is recorded on a separate line after the certificate line and would read "certificates—special."

The distinction between bills, certificates, notes, and bonds is based essentially on the maturity of the obligation. *Bills* are the shortest-term Treasury obligation; they are sold at auction on a discount basis, and their maturity may range up to one year. *Certificates*—certificates of indebtedness of the Treasury—also may have maturities that range up to one year but differ from Treasury bills in that they carry an interest coupon. *Notes*, which also carry interest coupons, have maturities of not less than one year nor more than seven years. While bonds can be issued in any maturity time, they are generally issued with maturities in excess of seven years. They are the longest term Treasury obligations. Coupon-bearing issues may be sold at auction or at a set price. A maturity distribution of U.S. government securities held by the System account on the statement date appears directly below the Consolidated Statement.

[Adapted from Federal Reserve Bank of New York, *Glossary: Weekly Federal Reserve Statements.*]

Securities purchased by the Federal Reserve are carried on the books at maturity value. See OTHER ASSETS and its footnotes for the treatment of any premiums paid on securities purchased. See OTHER LIABILITIES AND ACCRUED DIVIDENDS for the treatment of securities purchased at discount.

U.S. GOVERNMENT SECURITIES: HELD UNDER REPURCHASE AGREEMENTS. With regard to the CONSOLIDATED STATEMENT OF CONDITION OF ALL FEDERAL RESERVE BANKS, U.S. government securities purchased from nonbank dealers under an agreement calling for the seller to repurchase them on a specified date (within 15 days) or earlier, at the dealer's or the Federal Reserve's option. [Adapted from Federal Reserve Bank of New York, *Glossary: Weekly Federal Reserve Statements.*]

USURY. Charging a higher rate of interest than the law allows for a certain debt. In the U.S. individual states have usury laws that identify various types of loans and other debts and specify the maximum rate of interest that can be charged for each.

UTILITY. A qualitative measure of the degree to which a good or service satisfies human wants. See FORM UTILITY; PLACE UTILITY; POSSESSION UTILITY; TIME UTILITY.

UTILITY MAXIMIZING RULE. See BALANCING MARGINS.

UTILITY THEORY OF VALUE. The theory which explains why goods or services which are necessary for life are not necessarily more expensive than non-necessities; it holds that whether a product is easily obtainable (like air) is more important in determining the price than whether it is a necessity.

UTILITY UNITS. A hypothetical measure of well-being or satisfaction, especially useful in theoretical analyses such as determining the optimum level of government intervention in an economy. Utility can be given in ordinal numbers only (we can say that, given a choice of higher hourly pay or an extra week's vacation, a certain individual will give first preference to the extra week's vacation and second choice to extra pay), not in cardinal numbers (we cannot say that the individual prefers the extra vacation by an absolute factor, such as 6.83). There is also a difficulty in assigning utility units to different individuals: Individual A may prefer an extra vacation, and individual B extra pay, but we do not know whether the extra vacation provides more utility to A than the extra pay provides to B. One possible analysis would be to add the utility units that the options give the individuals—*if* we could put numbers on utility, it would be easy to decide which benefit to provide. For example, if the extra vacation gave 75 utility units to A and 50 to B, whereas the extra pay gave 40 units of happiness to A and 70 to B, everyone would agree that the extra vacation would provide more total happiness (125 utility units) than the extra pay (110 utility units).

The concept of utility units, even without the use of absolute numbers, is very important in discussions in the field of government finance, taxation, and fiscal policy.

UTILIZATION RATE. See MANU-FACTURING CAPACITY.

V

VALUE ADDED TAX (VAT). A tax which accumulates on goods as they move from raw materials through the production and distribution process. Each processor pays a tax according to the amount by which he has increased the value of items that were raw materials to him. This tax is used in the European Economic Community and has been used and considered in various other nations. Sometimes called *tax on value added* (TVA).

VALUE JUDGMENT. An opinion; a conclusion which is based on an individual's sense of values. Economics is a mixture of facts and value judgments. Thus it is recognized that a government deficit budget increases economic activity while adding inflationary pressures (fact), but a decision as to whether a deficit budget is beneficial depends on the net result of comparing the advantages and disadvantages of each effect (value judgment).

VALUE, LABOR THEORY OF. See LABOR THEORY OF VALUE.

VALUE TODAY. See SPOT EXCHANGE CONTRACT.

VANONI PLAN (It.). A ten-year growth plan (1955-1965) which concentrated on creating employment in the southern part of Italy so as to narrow the gap in per capita income between north and south.

VARIABLE COSTS (VC). Costs which depend directly, but not necessarily linearly, on the quantity of a product being produced, as opposed to FIXED COSTS, such as real estate taxes, which are constant regardless of level of production (within limits). Raw material which goes into a product is a variable cost. See COST for a listing of various types of costs recognized by economists. Also called *direct costs*.

VARIABLE RATE. An arrangement in which a borrower and a lender agree that the rate of interest on the loan will be adjustable periodically according to some formula, which is generally based on the economy or on other interest rates. On the surface, lenders gain through variable rates if interest rates rise during the period of the loan, and borrowers gain if interest rates decline. However, as with all issues in economics, a more thorough examination should be made; one would take into account that if the interest rate is fixed at the time of the loan, the lender is likely to demand a higher rate (for protection) than if the rate were to be adjusted later; therefore, the borrower is likely to gain if interest rates remain constant.

VAULT CASH. U.S. CURRENCY and coin (with the exception of silver and gold coins) owned by a depository institution and that can, at any time, be used to satisfy depositors' claims. It includes (1) U.S. currency and coin in transit to a FED-

ERAL RESERVE BANK or a correspondent depository institution and for which the reporting depository institution has not yet received credit and (2) U.S. currency and coin in transit from a Federal Reserve bank or a correspondent depository institution if the reporting depository institution's account at the Federal Reserve or correspondent bank has been charged for such shipment.

More simply, vault cash refers to coin and paper money kept in a bank (or other depository institution) for daily use. Since 1960, vault cash has been counted as part of BANK RESERVES. See also HIGH-POWERED MONEY.

VELOCITY. The number of times each dollar, on the average, circulates through the economy in a year. A rough evaluation of velocity can be obtained by dividing GROSS NATIONAL PRODUCT by MONEY SUPPLY. However, a more detailed analysis recognizes money in different uses has different velocities—different velocities in the various SECTORs of the economy. In other words, there is a transactions velocity, an income velocity, and others.

VENTURE CAPITAL. Financing which involves a relatively high risk (therefore it might be concluded that the possible returns are high), as opposed to *security capital*, which involves less risk.

VERTICAL COMBINATION. A joining of business enterprises in which the combining members are involved in the same product lines but at different levels of the manufacture and distribution chain. The significance of distinguishing this type of combination is that the enterprises which joined were not direct competitors, although their combining may affect the resultant enterprise's ability to compete with others. See also HORIZONTAL COMBINATION; CLAYTON ANTITRUST ACT; SHERMAN ANTITRUST ACT.

VERTICAL PRICE FIXING. Agreement involving more than one level of the distribution chain (usually a manufacturer and its retailer) not to sell for less than a certain price. See FAIR TRADE LAWS.

VESTING. Making an employee benefit irrevocable on the part of the employer. Vesting is usually used in connection with retirement plans; when an employee is vested in a plan he can draw the expected benefits at retirement age, even if that employment was terminated earlier.

VISIBLE GOODS AND SERVICES. In international economics, those items which can be seen and touched. Those which cannot include insurance charges. See BALANCE OF INTERNATIONAL PAYMENTS; INVISIBLE GOODS AND SERVICES.

VISTA. One of the U.S. programs of the 1960s designed to fight poverty by helping the disadvantaged to upgrade themselves, rather than provide a permanent handout. This program used volunteer, as well as paid, social workers to counsel and otherwise help the poor.

VNESHTORGBANK (U.S.S.R.). The *Foreign Bank*, a financial enterprise which specializes in international accounts and in financing enterprises that deal with international trade.

VOLATILE. Describes an economy, industry, product, etc. which is characterized by changes that are numerically large in relatively short time periods. For example, CONSUMER DURABLES are said to be volatile because a change in the economy of any given percentage usually results in a much larger percentage change in that sector.

VOLUNTARY ARBITRATION. Agreement of the two parties to a labor dispute to accept as binding the decision of a third party over the disputed issues.

VOLUNTARY BANKRUPTCY. BANKRUPTCY that results from proceedings initiated by the bankrupt person.

VOLUNTARY CHECKOFF. In labor economics, an arrangement for paying dues and other assessments to a labor union; the employer deducts the amounts from the pay of each employee who so chooses and remits the amount directly to the union.

VOLUNTARY FOREIGN CREDIT RESTRAINT (VFCR). A program for voluntary restraint of foreign lending, started in 1965 by the FEDERAL RESERVE SYSTEM at the request of the president, with the immediate aim of ameliorating the U.S. balance of payments deficit by holding down the net outflow of bank loans to foreign borrowers and of investments abroad by other financial institutions. Flows to Canada after February 1968, long-term investments in developing countries by nonbank financial institutions, and credits to finance U.S. exports after late 1971 were exempt from coverage. Influenced by this program, by the INTEREST EQUALIZATION TAX, and by high interest rates, the U.S. deficit in BALANCE OF PAYMENTS in 1965 fell to its lowest level since 1957. Along with various other capital control programs administered by the U.S. government, the VFCR program was terminated on January 29, 1974.

W

WAGE ACCRUALS LESS DISBURSE-MENTS. An adjustment item in the NA-TIONAL INCOME AND PRODUCT ACCOUNTS to take into account that wages and salaries are not always received at the same time they are earned. Income is typically recorded in the national accounts in the period it is earned rather than received (accrual basis of accounting), but an exception is made in the wage and salary component of PERSONAL INCOME. It is regularly estimated on a cash receipts basis, following the usual practice of households.

Ordinarily, wage and salary payments disbursed in one quarter but earned in the preceding quarter are approximately offset by those earned in the current quarter but not received until the following quarter, making the adjustment for wage accruals less disbursements small or negligible. See GROSS NATIONAL PRODUCT.

WAGE ADVANCE PLAN. In labor economics, part of an agreement under a GUARANTEED ANNUAL WAGE by which an employer advances wages during a period which is short of regular workdays so that average earnings will be maintained.

WAGE AND HOUR LAW. See FAIR LABOR STANDARDS ACT.

WAGE AND SALARY DISBURSE-MENTS. In NATIONAL INCOME AND PRODUCT ACCOUNTS, all employee earnings, including executive salaries, hourly pay, bonuses, commissions, payments in kind, incentive payments, and tips. This figure is given on a cash receipts basis, following the usual thinking and practice of households. All other entries in the National Income and Product Accounts are made on an accrual basis, in accord with predominant business practice. See WAGE ACCRUALS LESS DISBURSEMENTS for more details regarding this statement. See also GROSS NATIONAL PRODUCT.

WAGE GUIDELINES. See GUIDE-LINES.

WAGE ILLUSION. See MONEY IL-LUSION.

WAGE INCREASE. See ACROSS-THE-BOARD INCREASE; MERIT IN-CREASE.

WAGE-PRICE SPIRAL. Inflation that continues because labor unions obtain increased wages, causing additional costs to producers, who then raise their prices to meet costs, with the result that unions demand further wage increases, etc. Usually each claims that the spiral is due to actions of the other.

WAGE REOPENING. In labor economics, a contract provision which states that the question of wages can be renegotiated prior to expiration of the overall contract;

usually found in contracts of several years' duration.

WAGE RIGIDITY. See PRICE RIGIDITY.

WAGES. The payment to the FACTOR OF PRODUCTION known as labor. In economics *wages* include salaries, hourly pay, commissions, bonuses, and other forms of compensation for the work people performed.

WAGES AND SALARIES, IMPUTED. See IMPUTATION.

WAGNER ACT. Official name for the NATIONAL LABOR RELATIONS ACT, which was the milestone legislation in the U.S. that gave unions an official legal standing. See TAFT-HARTLEY ACT.

WALL STREET. A street in downtown New York City where a very large percentage of the nation's (and therefore the world's) financial activity is centered.

WALSH-HEALEY ACT. This 1935 legislation required that contractors who bid on U.S. government contracts pay their employees according to certain stated minimum standards.

WANTS. The goods and services that people desire. The entire field of economics is based on the thought that resources are limited (see ECONOMIC RESOURCES) and therefore must be allocated among competing uses in response to the unlimited wants of mankind.

WAR ON POVERTY. Name used to identify much of the social legislation of President Lyndon Johnson's administration.

WARRANT. (1) In the economics of investment, a right to purchase a given amount of a security at a given price within a stated time period. If the market price of the security is higher than the price offered by the warrant, the warrant has value to its owner.

(2) In another use of the word, a warrant is a financial instrument which is treated very much the same as a check. The difference is that a check is an order for a bank or other financial institution to pay, whereas a warrant is an order for a non-banking organization, such as a local government or an insurance company, to pay.

WAR THEORY. One of the MONO-CAUSAL THEORIES used by investigators to explain economic history. This theory holds that major wars have been the real determinants of the world's economy; few events of any lasting significance take place at other times.

WASHINGTON AGREEMENT. An economic treaty after World War II between the U.S. and the U.K., canceling billions of dollars of Lend-Lease debt and formalizing a new agreement for a long-term loan.

WASH SALE. A planned sale of a security for the sole purpose of giving the appearance of more activity in the market than there really is, thus causing the price of the security to rise. A wash sale may consist of the owner's selling the security to another person who will shortly sell it back. Most of the investing public sees only that the security is actively traded and its price is increasing.

WASTING ASSET. A natural resource that is removed from nature, reducing the value of the property from which it is removed.

WATERED STOCK. CAPITAL STOCK whose price is higher than the value that a stockholder would receive if the company were liquidated.

WAYBILL. A document which records goods delivered to a carrier for shipment.

WAYS AND MEANS COMMITTEE. A major unit of the U.S. Congress, involved in legislation which affects federal government revenues.

WEALTH EFFECT. A theoretical COUNTERCYCLICAL force which, under an extreme condition, might provide some stimulus to an economy in a depression. This effect works in the following stages: (1) There is an economic slow-

down; (2) underemployment of FAC-
TORS OF PRODUCTION spreads; (3)
prices fall; (4) assets held in the form of
MONEY increase in value (PURCHAS-
ING POWER increases); (5) holders of
money, realizing their relative increase
in wealth, begin spending their money;
(6) this spending provides income for others, who can then spend, and the entire
economy accelerates out of its recession
or depression.

The extreme condition mentioned is
that it would take a very large drop in
prices to bring this effect into play, and
other factors in the economy must be ready
for a recovery.

WEALTH OF NATIONS. Popular name
used for AN INQUIRY INTO THE NA-
TURE AND CAUSES OF THE WEALTH
OF NATIONS. This book by ADAM
SMITH was published in 1776. It describes the CLASSICAL SCHOOL of
economic thinking.

WEEKLY BENEFIT AMOUNT (WBA).
In the field of unemployment compensation, the amount a person receives each
week after it is determined that the person
is eligible for payments. The formula for
calculating WBA is determined by each
state and usually depends on maximum
or average amounts the person earned
while employed.

WEEKLY CONDITION REPORT. A
weekly statement covering most banks in
the U.S. whose total deposits amount to
$100 million or more. It shows the dollar
value of various assets and liabilities at
the close of business on each Wednesday,
and the net change in each type of asset
and liability from the previous Wednesday and from the same week of the previous year. The full title of the report is
*Weekly Condition Report of Large Com-
mercial Banks.*

WEIGHTED AVERAGE. See AVER-
AGE.

WELFARE. Basically, a person's well-
being, as when installation of safety
equipment is said to be for employees'

welfare. Most of the time the word is seen
in introductory economics texts it is used
in this sense.

However, the field of social economics
uses *welfare* in the same sense as in popular usage; maintenance by government
of the real or money income of individuals.

WELFARE ECONOMICS. A specialty
within economics that concentrates on the
effect of different actions on overall and
individual well-being. In its ideal form,
welfare economics maximizes aggregate
UTILITY UNITS available from a given
set of inputs.

WELFARE STATE. A nation in which a
great many goods and services are provided at public expense and little or no
cost is borne directly by the immediate
recipient of the goods and services. As
the incidence of state-supplied goods and
services increases, the number of private
decisions and choices decreases; however, the benefits of a welfare state are
that no one will be denied an essential
service which might be available to someone else.

WELL-BEING. See UTILITY UNITS.

WHIPSAW METHODS. All the efforts
of a labor union applied against one employer, putting him in a poor bargaining
position. After a settlement with large
concessions to the union, the latter can
more effectively use these same tactics
against the next employer.

WHOLESALE PRICE INDEX (WPI).
Former name for PRODUCER PRICE
INDEX.

WHOLESALER. Generally, the party that
supplies RETAILERs, although in many
industries special names are used for each
step along the distribution chain from
manufacturer to consumer.

WILDCAT. Name used for state bank notes
about the time of the Civil War, indicating
the lack of faith citizens had in that form
of money.

WILDCAT BANKING PERIOD. The period which began roughly a few years after expiration of the Second National Bank's charter in 1836 and ended with passage of restrictive legislation in the 1850s. See ANTIBANK MOVEMENT.

WILDCAT STRIKE. In labor economics, a work stoppage not officially called by the union. See UNAUTHORIZED STRIKE.

WINDFALL PROFITS. Profits earned because of some external event rather than by the normal functioning of the business. One recent example is the profits earned by oil companies in the early 1980s as a result of the decontrol of domestic crude oil prices. On June 1, 1979, the U.S. Department of Energy began to implement a program for decontrolling crude oil prices by October 1, 1981; the Reagan administration, in its first major economic policy move, lifted all remaining price controls on domestically produced crude on January 28, 1981. As a result of estimates that producer revenues could be boosted by over $1 trillion during the 1980-1990 period, Congress enacted the Crude Oil Windfall Profit Tax of 1980 to divert to the U.S. Treasury some of the incremental revenues that would otherwise be received by producers through decontrol.

WITHHOLDING. The ongoing subtraction by employers from each employee's earnings of an amount calculated to approximate the employee's accumulating income tax liability to the government. This procedure was established in the U.S. by the CURRENT TAX PAYMENT ACT of 1943.

WITHOUT RECOURSE. Words used with a QUALIFIED ENDORSEMENT.

WORKERS' COUNCIL (Yugo.). In an enterprise, a committee that has direct, and not merely advisory, authority for hiring, firing, establishing wages, and other working conditions, deciding on product, and production methods, and many other functions that are the responsibility of management in other nations. Members of the council are elected by the workers, and care is taken to see that manual, professional, and other categories of workers have proportional representation.

WORK FORCE. See CIVILIAN LABOR FORCE.

WORKING CAPITAL. Properly defined, current assets minus current liabilities. Working capital is also sometimes used to mean CURRENT ASSETs.

WORK IN PROCESS. An asset account or group of accounts which record the accumulation of increases in the value of goods at various stages in the production process.

WORKMEN'S COMPENSATION LAWS. Legislation that provides financial protection for employees injured on the job, superseding doctrines such as CONTRIBUTORY NEGLIGENCE, which required that an injured employee prove that the employer was negligent and that the employee's actions did not contribute to the injury. One objective of making employers liable (with very few exceptions) is to motivate them to provide the safest possible working conditions to ensure that no injury occurs.

WORKS PROJECTS ADMINISTRATION (WPA). A NEW DEAL measure, intended to alleviate the unemployment problem of the GREAT DEPRESSION. Unlike its predecessor, the PUBLIC WORKS ADMINISTRATION, the WPA sponsored many projects other than construction; actors, mathematicians, artists, and others were employed by the WPA. Over $13 billion was spent from 1935 until 1942, when the crash effort to mobilize the U.S. for World War II increased the demand for workers.

WORLD BANK. See INTERNATIONAL BANK FOR RECONSTRUCTION AND DEVELOPMENT.

Y

YELLOW DOG CONTRACT. A contract of employment in which the employee agrees not to take part in union activities; if he does, he is in default on his contract and can be discharged. Such contracts were outlawed by the NORRIS-LA GUARDIA ACT of 1932.

YIELD. In relation to CAPITAL STOCK, the ratio of DIVIDENDS paid by the issuing corporation (per share) to the price paid per share.

YIELD TO MATURITY. Total return on a bond from the time it is bought to the time it matures and is redeemed by its issuer; it takes into account the EFFECTIVE RATE OF INTEREST as well as any difference between the price paid and the amount returned by the issuer at maturity.

YOUTH CORPS. See NEIGHBORHOOD YOUTH CORPS.

Z

ZAIBATSU COMBINE (Jap.). A large complex of Japanese industrial enterprises which is controlled by a small group (usually one or two families) and has considerable influence over the economic situation in which it operates.

ZERO ECONOMIC GROWTH (ZEG). The objective of many people who feel that, because increases in the numbers of goods and services produced usually involve increases in pollutants as well as acceleration in the rate at which fossil fuels and other natural resources are consumed, the standard of living is high enough and further attempts at economic growth should be stopped.

ZERO POPULATION GROWTH (ZPG). See NET REPRODUCTION RATE.

APPENDIX

MATHEMATICAL REGRESSION

In beginning algebra courses students learn to evaluate a function at several points, make an x-y table, and plot a graph of the function. Regression is just the reverse—from a series of data points the equation is determined. But data points from measurements taken in the real world, especially the world of economics, do not fall right on the locus of any equation. Therefore, mathematical regression generally means to find the equation whose locus is the *best fit* for the data points.

If the points themselves come very close to forming a line, it is easy to draw a reasonable approximation of the best-fit curve by inspection. However, most practical situations result in such a scatter of data points that "best-guess best-fit" curves drawn would vary widely from one individual to another. Therefore it becomes necessary to choose a mathematically precise definition of best fit. Several definitions have been used; one that is widely used is the *least squares* criterion, which will be explained in a moment.

We are going to work here with *linear regression,* meaning we shall find the *straight line* that best fits the data points. While some would want to derive a complex equation that will fit any wild set of data points, doing so would not be practical without a computer, and the value of the results would be questionable. Therefore this appendix is limited to a description of linear regression and calculations that can be worked by hand or with an ordinary calculator.

The equation of a straight line is

$$y = mx + b$$

where

y is the quantity measured along the vertical axis

m is the *slope* of the straight line (the number of units y will change when x is changed by one unit)

x is the quantity measured along the horizontal axis

b is the point where the straight line crosses the y axis

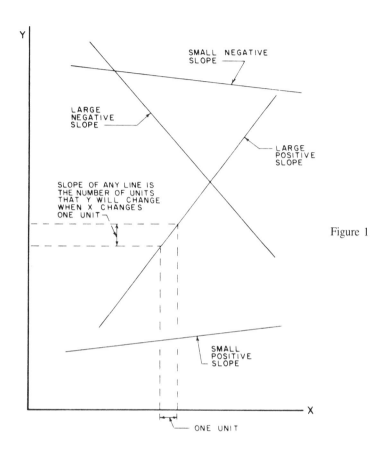

Figure 1

Figure 1 shows that the slope has a positive value when the line runs upper left and lower right, negative for upper left and lower right. The more the line approaches being vertical, the larger the absolute value of its slope.

Now back to the definition of least squares. Figure 2 shows eight data points and a straight line through them; the line is not meant to be necessarily the best fit, but merely one of the lines that could be drawn through the points. The vertical distance between the line and any data point is the error for that point; the error for point 1 is e_1, etc. We want to minimize the total error, not merely cancel positive and negative errors, so we square each error and add the results. Total squared error e_t is then

$$e_t = e_1^2 + e_2^2 + e_3^2 + e_4^2 + e_5^2 + e_6^2 + e_7^2 + e_8^2$$

Of all the straight lines that could be drawn through the data points, the line which has the least total squared error is found when m and b are calculated from

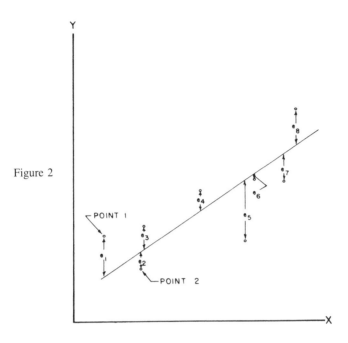

Figure 2

the following equations:

$$m = \frac{\Sigma x_i y_i - (\Sigma x_i \, \Sigma y_i)/n}{\Sigma x_i^2 + (\Sigma x_i)^2/n}$$

$$b = \frac{\Sigma y_i}{n} - \frac{m \, \Sigma x_i}{n}$$

For working on a hand calculator, it is usually more convenient to recognize that the sum of a set of values divided by the number of values is what is generally called the *average* (see AVERAGE). The average of the x values is called x-bar, and written $\bar{x}$; the average of the y values is called y-bar and is written $\bar{y}$. Then, calculations for m and b reduce to fairly simple equations:

$$m = \frac{\Sigma x_i y_i - \bar{x} \, \Sigma y_i}{\Sigma x_1^2 - \bar{x} \, \Sigma x_i}$$

$$b = \bar{y} - m\bar{x}$$

Notice that m is used in calculating b, and therefore m must be calculated first.

Mathematical Regression An Example

Year	45–64 year olds as % of total population	Personal saving rate	$x_i y_i$	x_i^2
1960	20.04	5.6	112.224	401.602
1961	19.99	6.3	125.937	399.600
1962	19.97	6.0	119.820	398.801
1963	19.96	5.4	107.784	398.402
1964	19.98	6.7	133.866	399.200
1965	20.03	7.1	142.213	401.201
1966	20.11	7.0	140.770	404.412
1967	20.23	8.1	163.863	409.253
1968	20.35	7.1	144.485	414.123
1969	20.44	6.4	130.816	417.794
1970	20.49	8.0	163.920	419.840
1971	20.48	8.1	165.888	419.430
1972	20.49	6.5	133.185	419.840
1973	20.47	8.6	176.042	419.021
1974	20.44	8.5	173.740	417.794
1975	20.39	8.6	175.354	415.752
1976	20.31	6.9	140.139	412.496
1977	20.19	5.6	113.064	407.636
1978	20.06	5.2	104.312	402.404
1979	19.91	5.2	103.532	396.408
	404.33	136.9	2770.950	8175.010

Example

Let us derive a formula that will indicate the rate at which residents of the United States can be expected to save (see PERSONAL SAVING RATE) as a function of the percentage of population that is between the ages of 45 and 64 years. The data in columns 2 and 3 of the accompanying table are from the 1982 ECONOMIC REPORT OF THE PRESIDENT, and the columns after them are calculated from that data.

The data in column 2 are plotted along the horizontal axis and are therefore the x values; column 3 gives the y values. Column 4 is the product of x times y in each row, and column 5 is the square of x.

Because there are 20 data points given, $\bar{x}$ is found by summing all the x values (the sum of column 2) and dividing by 20.

$$\bar{x} = 404.33/20$$

$$= 20.22$$

Likewise, $\bar{y}$ is found by summing the numbers in column 3 and dividing by 20.

Putting these numbers, along with the sums of the columns in the table, in appropriate places in the formulas gives

$$m = \frac{2770.95 - 20.22(136.9)}{8175.01 - 20.22(404.33)}$$

$$= 3.81$$

and

$$b = 6.845 - 3.81(20.22)$$

$$= -70.19$$

Therefore the equation for the straight line that is a best fit to the given data, according to the least squares definition of best fit, is

$$y = 3.81x - 70.19$$

This equation is drawn in Figure 3. Since it is a straight line, it can be drawn on a graph after locating only two points. Let us choose points near each end of the x axis. Substituting $x = 20$ in the best fit equation gives

$$y = 3.81(20.00) - 70.19$$

$$= 6.01$$

and then substituting 20.50 for x gives

$$y = 3.81(20.50) - 70.19$$

$$= 7.92$$

Figure 3 shows the 20 data points plus the best-fit line that was just calculated.

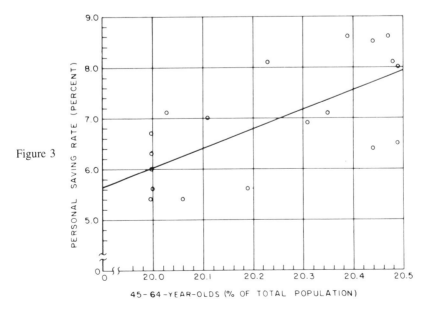

Figure 3

45-64-YEAR-OLDS (% OF TOTAL POPULATION)

When predictions are to be made, the equation can give the expected value. For example, if it is known that the 45 to 64 age group will be 20.3 percent of the population in a certain year, the best estimate is that the personal saving rate in that year will be

$$3.81(20.3) - 70.19 = 7.15$$

Analysts caution that, although good results can be expected when estimating a point within the range of the given data points, there is reason for doubt when making a prediction above or below the points used to arrive at the best-fit equation. For example, professional analysts would be reluctant to use this equation to predict the saving rate if the 45 to 64 age group constituted 21 percent of the population.

LINEAR PROGRAMMING

Linear programming consists of detailed rules for working with matrices to determine optimum performance when several demands are to be satisfied simultaneously by several sources. Optimum performance can be defined for each problem—it may be minimum costs, maximum revenue, maximum profit, minimum capital costs, minimum labor costs, minimum material costs, or any of innumerable criteria. An example will be given to show an arrangement that results in minimum shipping costs when the requirements of five customers are to be supplied by three warehouses.

There are several types of linear programming models; the *transportation model* will be demonstrated here because it is the simplest. Others require more extensive explanation and can be the subject of an entire book.

Linear programming models are generally workable by hand calculations, but many computer programs have been written for them. The calculations involve only simple arithmetic; the main advantage to using a computer is that it does not become bored and miss some of the possible moves or make errors.

For a demonstration of the transportation model, let us assume that five customers, C1 through C5, have ordered cartons of books in the following quantities:

C1 wants 28 cartons.

C2 wants 36 cartons.

C3 wants 18 cartons.

C4 wants 38 cartons.

C5 wants 20 cartons.

They are to be shipped from warehouses W1 through W3, which can supply in the following quantities:

W1 can supply 70 cartons.

W2 can supply 40 cartons.

W3 can supply 30 cartons.

	C_1 28	C_2 36	C_3 18	C_4 38	C_5 20
W_1 70	4	3	1	2	4
W_2 40	2	1	4	3	1
W_3 30	3	3	2	1	2

Figure 1

Shipping costs per carton are as follows:

W1 to C1: $4	W2 to C1: $2	W3 to C1: $3
W1 to C2: $3	W2 to C2: $1	W3 to C2: $3
W1 to C3: $1	W2 to C3: $4	W3 to C3: $2
W1 to C4: $2	W2 to C4: $3	W3 to C4: $1
W1 to C5: $4	W2 to C5: $1	W3 to C5: $2

The first step is to prepare a matrix that displays all the information given, as shown in Figure 1. Then the matrix is to be *loaded*; that is, we insert tentative quantities for shipment from each warehouse to each customer. The initial loading might even be the worst possible arrangement, but the procedure will take us automatically to the optimum arrangement. Of course, if (by experience or some other means) we know of an arrangement that is better than others, we can use that knowledge in our initial loading. We shall then probably arrive at optimum with fewer steps.

Let us start by simply providing all of C1's requirements from W1 and then go down the line to C2, C3, etc. until all of W1's supply is exhausted. We then start on W2, and finally complete W3. When the matrix is loaded properly, the shipments across each row should add up to the amount the warehouse in that row can supply, and the shipments down each column should add up to the amount the customer in that column wanted. The matrix with its initial loading is shown in Figure 2.

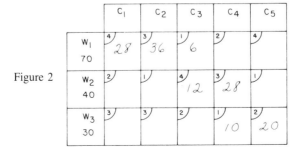

Figure 2

To improve the arrangement, begin by selecting an unoccupied square. Then continue along either the row or the column which contains that square until you find an occupied square (call it the second square) that has another occupied square (call it the third square) at right angles to it. Make the right angle turn at the second square in the direction of the third square and proceed along that row or column until you find an occupied square (call it the fourth square) that has another occupied square at right angles to it. The fourth square may or may not be the same as the third square. Continue in this manner until the path returns to the first unoccupied square.

Now figure shipping costs around this loop, starting with a negative value for the unoccupied square that was selected and alternating negative and positive values around the loop. For example, if we start with the square at the intersection of W2 and C1 and check the following loop, the shipping costs are as follows:

Square	Shipping Cost
W2–C1	− 2
W2–C3	+ 4
W1–C3	− 1
W1–C1	+ 4

Any time we find a loop in which the algebraic sum of shipping costs is a positive number, it will be beneficial to make the changes. Since the algebraic sum of $-2+4-1+4$ is a positive number ($+5$), we should move some quantities around in this loop. If the result had been a negative number, any move would lead to increased shipping costs; a result of zero would mean that a move neither increases nor decreases shipping costs. The quantity to move is the largest quantity which will leave one of the other squares in the loop unoccupied. Moving 12 cartons will give that result.

Take 12 from the W2–C3 square (leaving 0), and add 12 to the W1–C3 square (making 18); take 12 from the W1–C1 square (leaving 16), and add 12 to the W2–C1 square (making 12). This pattern must always be followed—add to squares which were given a positive value in the preceding little table, and subtract from squares where we used a negative shipping cost. The purpose of this alternating

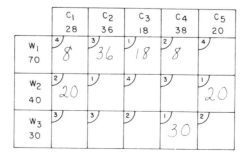

Figure 3

of signs is that we can move quantities without changing the sum of a row (the amount shipped from each warehouse) or the sum of a column (the amount received by each customer). It is a good idea to check the sums after each move to determine if an error has been made in addition or subtraction.

Check each unoccupied square in this manner until no loop can be found that shows a positive sum of alternating positive and negative shipping costs. Squares that are unoccupied because a quantity was moved out of them should also be checked, and it should be noted that sometimes more than one loop can be found from an unoccupied square. Sometimes a quantity in a square will change several times. Figure 3 shows an arrangement such that no loop from an unoccupied square has a positive value. Total shipping costs of the original loading were $408; the changes have reduced that amount to $264. The costs after each iteration are called *shadow prices*.

When we use a transportation model to find optimum profit (or any other desirable quantity) instead of cost, we reverse the rule that tells us whether to move quantities in a loop. For desirable quantities it is beneficial to move items whenever the algebraic sum around a loop is *negative*.